Contributions to Management Science

The series *Contributions to Management Science* contains research publications in all fields of business and management science. These publications are primarily monographs and multiple author works containing new research results, and also feature selected conference-based publications are also considered. The focus of the series lies in presenting the development of latest theoretical and empirical research across different viewpoints.

This book series is indexed in Scopus.

Denis Berberović • Danica Purg
Editors

Hidden Champions in Rising Economies

The Undiscovered Roads to the Future

Springer

Editors
Denis Berberović
School of Economics and Business
University of Sarajevo
Sarajevo, Bosnia and Herzegovina

Danica Purg
IEDC Bled School of Management
and CEEMAN
Bled, Slovenia

ISSN 1431-1941 ISSN 2197-716X (electronic)
Contributions to Management Science
ISBN 978-3-032-08262-6 ISBN 978-3-032-08263-3 (eBook)
https://doi.org/10.1007/978-3-032-08263-3

This Springer imprint is published by the registered company Springer Nature Switzerland AG
The registered company address is: Gewerbestrasse 11, 6330 Cham, Switzerland

Foreword

This remarkable book is the result of a bold and wide-reaching research project, initiated and led by Danica Purg and Denis Berberović. Thanks to their vision, persistence, and coordination skills, over 85 researchers from 30 countries in Europe, Asia, and Africa, from Albania to Zambia, came together. This is probably the most comprehensive explorations of the Hidden Champions concept ever undertaken. Managing such a global initiative - across cultures, time zones, and economic conditions - is a remarkable achievement. Doing so with scientific rigor and editorial consistency makes it even more impressive. I thank all contributors for sharing their insights.

The idea of Hidden Champions has always been based on the insight that small- and medium-sized companies, operating under the radar, can shape global markets. They succeed through ambition, focus, globalization, innovation, and close customer ties. When I first coined the term in the context of the German Mittelstand, I could not have imagined how far the concept would travel. But over the decades, I have witnessed its relevance in many parts of the world. This book provides further proof: the Hidden Champions model flourishes in a wide range of institutional and cultural settings - especially in what we now call rising economies.

Why are Hidden Champions so important for these countries? Because they offer exactly the kind of business model needed to stay competitive in a global, knowledge-driven economy. They show that success is not about size, but about focus - not about public attention, but about excellence. In economies marked by rapid change, limited capital, and political uncertainty, export-oriented niche players are not just valuable - they are essential. These firms create high-value jobs, foster innovation, and set an example for others. They are quiet, but powerful forces of progress.

This volume gives us a broad and deep understanding of how Hidden Champions emerge and succeed under different conditions. It does not propose a fixed formula. Instead, it reveals how the core principles are applied and adapted - from human capital and digital transformation to regulatory hurdles and sustainability. The diversity of perspectives matches the richness of the phenomenon.

My wish is that this book will not only contribute to scholarship, but also inspire. May it encourage entrepreneurs, leaders, and educators in rising economies to pursue the Hidden Champions path - not as a rigid recipe, but as a mindset grounded in performance, persistence, and purpose. I am convinced that the next generation of global business leaders will include many more Hidden Champions from countries that, until recently, were not part of the conversation. This book brings them to light and gives them the recognition they deserve.

Bonn, Germany
Summer 2025

Hermann Simon

Contents

About the Editors

Denis Berberović, PhD is associate professor and member of the Marketing department at the School of Economics and Business in Sarajevo. He lectures modules "Marketing Communications" and "Marketing Research" on undergraduate and "Methodology of Scientific Research" on graduate studies.

Dr. Denis Berberović received the Chevening scholarship granted by the British Government. He got his Master of Science degree with distinction at one of Europe's top management schools, Bradford University School of Management. He extends continuously his horizons by additional education such as attending courses in IEDC Bled, Prague (AIPES) or WU Vienna.

Until today he has published several papers, book chapters, and books, some of them for the leading global publisher Springer. He received an award for his scientific work at his alma mater university, the University of Sarajevo. He was member of project teams for business clients such as UNDP, BH MAC, ACIPS, RAK, Bosch, Bosnalijek, Federal Ministry of Tourism and Environment, SOS Kinderdorf, etc. Currently, he is leading a global network of researchers from South-East Europe, South America, Africa, and Asia, investigating the concept of Hidden Champions.

He is the newly appointed President of the Scientific Council to the Federal Ministry of Education and Science in the Federation of Bosnia and Herzegovina.

Danica Purg is the founder and Dean of IEDC-Bled School of Management, Slovenia, and President of CEEMAN, an association of 200 management schools from 50 countries.

Professor Purg has been an innovator in management education, incorporating arts and artistic processes into management education and bringing ethics into the curriculum of all longer management programs at IEDC since its inception. She authored and co-authored several books and numerous articles on leadership issues. She is a frequent guest speaker at universities around the world and at international conferences.

For her work in international management education, Danica Purg has been recognized worldwide. She received the International Educator of the Year Award from the Academy of International Business in 2010. The President of the Republic of

Slovenia bestowed upon her the Honorary Order of Freedom, and she has received highest awards from the French and Brazilian governments. Recently Prof. Danica Purg has been inducted into the Thinkers50 Hall of Fame, joining a distinguished group of the world's most influential business and management thinkers.

Her influence extends to universities worldwide. She is a member of international advisory boards at management schools around the world, and serves as the Chairlady of the Academic board of the International Research Center for Hidden Champions at Zhejiang University, China. Prof. Danica Purg is very active in PRME (Principles of Responsible Management Education), an initiative started by UN Global Compact, where she held many important roles in the past, and in July 2017, the Global UN PRME Forum awarded Prof. Purg for her pioneering work in establishing the UN PRME initiative.

She has received the titles Doctor Honoris Causa at several universities around the world (the most recent is from the University of Wollongong, Australia), and holds two honorary professorship titles.

Introduction

Danica Purg

It was Hermann Simon who extended his first survey on Hidden Champions from Germany to the German-speaking countries. Inspired by this initiative, we decided to extend the survey beyond Central and Eastern Europe, convinced that the phenomenon of Hidden Champions is a global one, or in different terms, the Hidden Champions paradigm can be universally applied.

In this book, we report on the first step to extend our survey to other continents. We found out that to realise country reports, one needs a capable, dedicated research platform. In Chapter "Hidden Champions: Common Lessons Learned in VUCA Times", Denis Berberović shows how CEEMAN offered and organised such a platform. In my view, only an organisation as CEEMAN is capable of bringing together researchers from so many so-called rising economies.

Although the research is mainly built on the original methodology of Hermann Simon, we noticed again that the concept of Hidden Champions is defined differently in various socio-economic environments. This can also be seen in the slightly different composed and formulated country chapters. Although we started from a common model, we accepted some deviations if the content covered agreed with the formulated conditions.

Having noticed this, we can assure that the report offers a much richer perspective on Hidden Champions than former publications. It also offers actualised inside information about entrepreneurial culture, conditions, and opportunities in a great number of countries, sometimes for the first time participating in the Hidden Champions research.

D. Purg (✉)
IEDC Bled School of Management and CEEMAN, Bled, Slovenia
e-mail: Danica.purg@iedc.si

D. Berberović, D. Purg (eds.), *Hidden Champions in Rising Economies*, Contributions to Management Science,
https://doi.org/10.1007/978-3-032-08263-3_1

The relevance of the book not only lies in the great amount of data in the country reports, but also in the topic-specific section, offering a deeper analysis and insight into this data.

In the chapter entitled "Common lessons learned from Hidden Champions" (Merima Činjarević and Denis Berberović) seven major lessons have been drawn from the meta-analysis of the HC case studies. These are mainly the lessons about leadership, corporate culture, values, and partnerships.

The chapter on leadership deals with leadership of HCs or more precisely with "The strategic focus of Start-ups, Scale-ups and Grown-ups" (Danica Purg and Arnold Walravens). An analysis on the basis of this typology offers a number of remarkable observations concerning six strategic focal leadership issues.

The chapter entitled "Finance and regulatory environment needs of Hidden Champions" (Slavica Singer and Sunčica Oberman Peterka) is, in a very well-founded manner, about the regulatory frameworks in the various countries of Hidden Champions, and the access to different types of financing growth of their business ventures. One of the main conclusions is that institutions across sectors—government, finance, education, and business support—should take into account the experiences of Hidden Champions.

The chapter entitled "Employees Are the Champions: Human Resources Management in Hidden Champion companies" (Amra Kožo) explores a field that is underexplored till today. She analyses the HC cases on different elements of HRM. A striking conclusion is, for example, that the recruitment of qualified employees with specialised knowledge, training, and education is one of the biggest human resource challenges amongst HCs. She shows how HCs find solutions to tackle this problem.

The chapters on technology deal with two very relevant topics:

1. "IT Innovation of Hidden Champions" (Linan Lei and Xiaobo Wu) describes the impact of innovation on the performance of HCs, presents a comparison between Chinese and International Practices, and offers a future outlook of Hidden Champions.
2. "Data-driven Decision Making: The Competitive Edge of Hidden Champions" (Violeta Cvetkoska). She describes the transformation to data-driven decision making and its importance for maintaining competitive advantages and mitigating risks. She also offers insight into the future of HCs in the AI era.

The chapter entitled "Sustainability principles of Hidden Champions": "How Hidden Champions build their success on the application of sustainability principles" (Janka Taborecka and Simona Bartosova) analyses sustainability practices amongst Hidden Champions across countries. They find that the cross-country comparison of Hidden Champions reveals a diversity of priorities, approaches, and strategies. They also offer an interesting explanation for this phenomenon.

In the chapter entitled "Strategic Entrepreneurship in Global Business Environment: A Comparative Framework of Hidden Champions" (Meelis Kitsing and Julian Enrik Schenkenhofer), they are reframing Hidden Champions as a global entrepreneurial phenomenon, shaped by distinct institutional and environmental

contexts. This study advances a more differentiated theory of niche entrepreneurship and global firm resilience.

Probably the rich data of this survey could still be analysed easily on a number of relevant topics. This is, however, what the international group of researchers considered as the most important outcomes of their work.

Danica Purg is the founder and Dean of IEDC-Bled School of Management, Slovenia, and President of CEEMAN, association of 200 management schools from 50 countries.

Professor Purg has been an innovator in management education, incorporating arts and artistic processes into management education and bringing ethics into the curriculum of all longer management programs at IEDC since its inception. She authored and co-authored several books and numerous articles on leadership issues. She is a frequent guest speaker at universities around the world and at international conferences.

For her work in international management education, Danica Purg has been recognized worldwide. She received the International Educator of the Year Award from the Academy of International Business in 2010. The President of the Republic of Slovenia bestowed upon her the Honorary Order of Freedom, and she has received highest awards from the French and Brazilian governments.

Her influence extends to universities worldwide. She is a member of international advisory boards at management schools around the world, and serves as the Chairlady of the Academic board of the International Research Center for Hidden Champions at Zhejiang University, China. Prof. Danica Purg is very active in PRME (Principles of Responsible Management Education), an initiative started by UN Global Compact, where she held many important roles in the past and in July 2017 was awarded for.

She has received the titles Doctor Honoris Causa at several universities around the world (the most recent is from the University of Wollongong, Australia), and holds two honorary professorship titles. In 2025 Prof. Danica Purg has been inducted into the Thinkers50 Hall of Fame 2025.

Research Methodology

Denis Berberović

Abstract The third cycle of research about hidden champions in non-developed economies has been implemented during a period of almost 3 years. More than 85 researchers and supporting staff have been engaged in 30 countries across Europe, Asia and Africa in order to investigate 70 companies identified as hidden champions. The aim was to explore and understand their success stories in order to present them to the wider academic and professional public. The case study approach was applied, and data was collected through secondary research, survey and in-depth interviews. Results show that in spite of different business environments and challenges they face, these companies show high resilience and adaptability. They manage to strive even in crisis situations such as the pandemic or international wars.

1 Introduction

Almost two decades after Hermann Simon started with the research on so-called "*Hidden Champion*" companies in Germany, his home country, and examined their role and implications for Germany's economic development and innovation, CEEMAN launched an elaborate project in 2011, comprising of 15 research teams that worked with over 130 companies across Central and Eastern Europe (CEE) and Turkey with the purpose of studying the Hidden Champions of their respective countries in turn. Published in 2013 and building its work on Simon's methodology from 1996, the book *"Hidden Champions in CEE and Turkey: Carving out a Global Niche"* sought to uncover examples of Hidden Champions. The same project was launched again in 2018, and was finally published by Springer in 2021 titled: *"Hidden Champions in Dynamically Changing Societies: Critical Success Factors*

D. Berberović (✉)
School of Economics and Business, University of Sarajevo, Sarajevo, Bosnia and Herzegovina
e-mail: denis.berberovic@efsa.unsa.ba

D. Berberović, D. Purg (eds.), *Hidden Champions in Rising Economies*, Contributions to Management Science,
https://doi.org/10.1007/978-3-032-08263-3_2

for Market Leadership". Both books aimed to compare and contrast findings with Simon's work, as well as identify what support Hidden Champions need in CEE, as well as some selected Asian countries, given that business environments and historical backgrounds in which these companies sought to succeed had several key differences when compared to more mature and established market economies.

Main findings of the books *"Hidden Champions in CEE and Turkey: Carving out a Global Niche"* (2013) and "*Hidden Champions in Dynamically Societies: Critical Success Factors for Market Leadership" (2021)* are that Hidden Champions mostly operate in the business-to-business market; and as Simon's second book, *"Hidden Champions of the 21st century: Success Strategies of Unknown World Market Leaders"* (2009), revealed, these companies have proven to be more resilient when it comes to volatility and even meltdowns in the market. In all (re)examined countries, the survival rate of Hidden Champions was significantly higher than the average in their respective sector. Hidden Champions also boast the tendency to be very competitive in their respective market, exhibit a consistent growth trajectory over the last decade and as well as an above-average innovation rate.

Companies identified as Hidden Champions have been the target of an increasing amount of research in recent years due to their extraordinary characteristics and the fact that their overall activities still largely elude academia. Due to the recent successes of some of the companies in the mentioned countries, there is a need to gain insights into the way these Hidden Champions operate in said countries, to understand the key factors of their success. Moreover, it would also be interesting to get insights into the progress made by Hidden Champion companies identified by IEDC and CEEMAN in 2011 that were included in the book *"Hidden Champions in CEE and Turkey: Carving out a Global Niche"* (2013), as well as those companies identified and included in the second book: "*Hidden Champions in Dynamically Societies: Critical Success Factors for Market Leadership" (2021)* and to understand what their management and leadership development needs and requirements regarding financial or regulatory environment are.

At the end of 2021, upon the initiative of IEDC and CEEMAN, we decided to delve into the fascinating subject of Hidden Champions yet again in order to explore and contrast the characteristics of innovative companies operating in rising economies worldwide! Africa, Asia, Central and Eastern Europe, are the continents that are to be explored for Hidden Champions, companies which are leaders in their respective niche sectors and the international market. Theoretical basis appears also to exist. Namely, in a recently published article by Yoo and Key (2025), they argued that the concept of hidden champions is a management paradigm different from the American concept of management. It also seems to be different from the management concept that can be found in some Asian countries. They claim that the HC concept has been lifted to a higher level, thus relativizing the American dominance in management.

2 Research Objectives

Objectives that were intended to be met throughout this exploratory study were as following:

1. The first objective of this exploratory study was to understand the progress that has been done by Hidden Champion companies identified by IEDC and CEEMAN in 2011 and 2018 that were included in the books *"Hidden Champions in CEE and Turkey: Carving out a Global Niche"* (2013) and "*Hidden Champions in Dynamically Societies: Critical Success Factors for Market Leadership" (2021)*. Throughout the interviews with CEOs of Hidden Champion companies, research partners collected data about these companies and sought to understand what has happened with these companies since 2011 and 2018, respectively. Particularly considering that since then two global crises have struck and two "*new normals*" have been introduced: (Brinkmann & Kvale, 2015) the first *new normal* resulted in the sharply progressive digitalization of businesses due to the global pandemic COVID-19; (Gummesson, 2000) the second *new normal* resulted in finding swiftly applicable alternatives for resources and energy, a need which emerged due to the global resource crisis induced by the war between Russia and Ukraine. The research partners may identify that these companies have made a significant progress further, some of them may be taken over by other companies and cannot be characterized as Hidden Champion companies anymore, etc.

   Furthermore, besides understanding the progress/changes that have been done in these companies since 2011 and 2018, it would be very valuable to also understand what their management and leadership development needs are and how different stakeholders (governments, financial institutions, management education institutions) could support them in their future success stories.

   The main aim of approaching the Hidden Champion companies identified in 2011 and 2018 was to create a loop through which we would not only learn from these companies and their development characteristics, but also understand their needs. By understanding their needs, the research partners could develop recommendations and promote them among different stakeholders such as, governments, financial institutions, management education institutions with the aim to support and assist these companies in their further expansion.
2. The second objective of this exploratory study was to identify new Hidden Champions in countries of rising economies by following Simon's criteria. Those criteria were defined in his first published book on Hidden Champions in 1996. They were slightly altered and presented in Simon's recent book on hidden champions (2022). These upgraded criteria have been used for this research and are given in Table 1. The research partners were encouraged to arrange interviews with CEOs of these companies. The goal was to understand their characteristics and what their management and leadership development needs were (like it was described for the already identified Hidden Champion companies—within the previous paragraph).

Table 1 Hermann Simon's criteria for hidden champions

Hidden Champions, based on Simon's (1996, 2022) definition, are:
1. Companies that occupy one of the top three positions in the world in their respective market, or No. 1 position on its continent in their respective market
2. A Hidden Champion company must be small- or medium-sized and its sales revenue does not exceed 5 billion Euros
3. A Hidden Champion company must have a low level of awareness among the general public

3. The third objective of this exploratory study was to extend this fascinating project to other countries. In 2011, IEDC and CEEMAN identified 165 companies from 16 CEE countries and Turkey. In 2018, a network of 66 academic researchers identified additional 105 companies in 22 countries. In this exploratory study we aimed to extend this study not only to other countries but also to other continents: Africa, Asia, Central and Eastern Europe. South America was also initially planned, but the response was not satisfactory.

The study also sought to assess the development needs of Hidden Champions in order to determine how their further expansion can be supported in terms of management, financing or the regulatory environment.

Finally, based on the interviews with the CEOs of the Hidden Champion companies, the case study approach will be applied in the data analysis, which will hopefully represent a source of inspiration and encouragement to other companies in the world.

3 Geographical Scope

As already mentioned, the geographical scope of the Hidden Champion research has been widened to several continents: Africa, Asia, Central and Eastern Europe. The research was carried out by a research team in each respective country. Each research team had a national lead researcher who was coordinating the research in his/her country together with IEDC and CEEMAN. A total of 30 countries participated in this research. An overview of countries, as well as number of hidden champions and researchers are given in Table 2.

4 Research Phases

The research process was divided into three phases.

1. The first phase of the exploratory study lasted from September 2022 to May 2024 and was concentrated on data collection about Hidden Champion companies. This phase started with a series of webinars. Purpose of the webinars was to introduce the research protocol to researchers and to explain the qualitative approach to data collection.

Table 2 Geographical scope, number of HCs and researchers

#	Country	Number of HCs	Number of researchers
1	Albania	3	3
2	Armenia	2	3
3	Azerbaijan	1	3
4	Bosnia and Herzegovina	4	3
5	Bulgaria	2	2
6	China	2	2
7	Croatia	4	4
8	Estonia	3	1
9	Georgia	2	3
10	Hungary	4	4
11	India	2	3
12	Kazakhstan	2	2
13	Kosovo	1	2
14	Latvia	2	2
15	Lithuania	2	3
16	Moldova	2	1
17	Mongolia	3	5
18	Montenegro	2	5
19	Morocco	3	3
20	Nigeria	1	2
21	North Macedonia	5	4
22	Poland	1	2
23	Romania	3	1
24	Serbia	4	7
25	Slovakia	2	2
26	Slovenia	3	2
27	Türkiye	2	2
28	Ukraine	1	4
29	Uzbekistan	1	3
30	Zambia	1	2
	Total	**70**	**85**

Since this was an exploratory study, qualitative research methodology was applied (Gummesson, 2000). Secondary data was collected first, in order identify hidden champions and to create an initial understanding about them and their business operations. Secondary data for countries were retrieved from the World Bank. Next step was to collect primary data in two ways. First, a questionnaire was sent to identify hidden champions, in order to collect initial primary data. This data collection step served as a preparation for the upcoming interview (Patton, 2015). The interview was set up with the CEOs of the Hidden Champion companies in order to dive in deeper into identified issues. Questions used in the questionnaire and interviews are presented in Table 3.

Table 3 Questions used in questionnaires and interviews

1. Company information Industry: Year of establishment: Sales revenues in the three latest years (2019, 2020 and 2021): Sales revenues 10 years before (2009 or 2011): Average ROA/ROE in the latest year (2019): Average ROA/ROE 10 years before (2009): Latest debt to equity ratio: Number of employees in the latest years (2019, 2020 and 2021): Brainer(s) behind the company:
2. Description of the nature of market leadership *Support definition used in 2011: We consider your company as a "Hidden Champion" when one of your products or product categories has a dominant market position in the respective continent, or the world. The latter group (world) also includes the number two or three position. Please define the market which refers to the title* *Questions for the researchers:* 2.1. Verify if the nature of market leadership is the same as in 2011/2018 or what has changed since then; if something has changed—what are the reasons? 2.2. If a company is still a market leader, what are the reasons for maintaining the market leadership? 2.3. If a company is no longer a market leader, what are the reasons? 2.4. Estimate your market share and the share of your biggest competitor? 2.5. What has changed in terms of market share from 2011/2018? What are the reasons? 2.6. What has changed with regards to growth, exports since 2011/2018?
3. Description of the nature of competitive advantage. 3.1. Verify if the nature or competitive advantage is the same as in 2011/2018 or what has changed since then; if something has changed—what are the reasons? 3.2. How many relevant competitors you have in Europe (?), (CEE?), (World?)? 3.3. What has changed since 2011/2018? What were the driving factors?
4. Core lessons learned on the path to business success (verify if anything could be added to the core lessons identified in 2011; if so—why and what are the rationales behind):
5. What are the main drivers of your company's success? *Supporting question* 5.1. What are the overall strengths of your company thanks to which you hold strong market position? *Possible factors that would help the researchers in case that the interviewee does not know what to answer: Strong personality of a leader; The long history of customer relationships; Motivation of our employees; Image; Patents; Strength of innovation; Risk management; Financial strength; Intuition of entrepreneur(s); Knowledge of the market; Professional marketing; The atmosphere in the company; Continuity of leadership; Loyalty; Qualification of employees; Flexibility; Being part of the larger cluster*
6. What are the main leadership success factors that have contributed to the company's success?
7. What are the main innovation success factors that have contributed to the company's success?
8. What are the main business challenges for your company? The current ones? The future ones?

(continued)

Table 3 (continued)

9. What are the company's development needs in terms of management and leadership (knowledge, skills and competences of your employees):
(a) What are the most underdeveloped skills within your company? Why?
(b) Who needs to be educated the most in your company? Why?
What are your recommendations for educational institutions?
10. What are the company's development needs in terms of financing or the regulatory environment in order to keep or advance business results:
What are your recommendations for financial institutions, governments, international organizations?
11. What are the company's development needs in terms of marketing?
Several questions in regards to current business environment issues:
12. What were the main obstacles for your business during the Covid-19 pandemic?
(a) What solutions did your company use as response to detected obstacles?
(b) How efficient were the applied solutions?
13. Has the pandemic reshaped your business? How?
14. What were/are the main obstacles for your business during the global resource crisis caused by the war in Ukraine?
(a) What solutions did your company use as response to detected obstacles?
(b) How efficient are/were the applied solutions?
15. Has the resource crisis reshaped your business? How?

Although initially planned shorter, this research phase lasted 20 months. Reason for that is the disruption of 9 months due to the start of the war between Russia and Ukraine. Both researchers and companies in the affected regions of East Europe asked for a delay of research activities since the development of the situation was quite unforeseeable.

2. During the second phase of the exploratory study which lasted from September 2024 to April 2025 all research teams were supposed to analyse the collected data retrieved from questionnaires (Miles & Huberman, 1994) and the interviews (Brinkmann & Kvale, 2015), along with secondary data, and prepare reports in form of case studies (Yin, 2014), which served as country chapters for this book.
3. In the third phase of the exploratory study which lasted from May to July 2025 country chapters were finalized. Final book editing activities have been undertaken in order to prepare the book manuscript to be handed in to the publisher by July 31.

5 Conclusion

Given the fact that the concept of Hidden Champions is novel, extensive exploratory research had to be done (Patton, 2015). More data needed to be gathered about Hidden Champions and why they outmatch their more orthodox competitors in terms of survival rates, and what long-term effects they have on their domestic environment, their respective niche sectors, and the international market. By means of this extensive study, we have gained an improved understanding of how Hidden Champions in different business environments navigate through obstacles when operating and creating value and sustain their levels of success, and how their practices could be beneficial for the development of their respective national economies.

This study explored critical drivers of success of Hidden Champions from Africa, Asia, Central and Eastern Europe, improved the understanding of competitiveness of small- and medium-sized innovative companies which will result in enhancement of business cohesion in countries that participated in this research.

Moreover, the insights into development needs of "Hidden Champions" in terms of management, financing or the regulatory environment and management and leadership development obtained through this exploratory study can be used for developing recommendations for different stakeholders (governments, financial institutions, management education institutions) that would help a broader pool of companies thrive in the near future as well.

Finally, this study will hopefully also encourage collaborative initiatives between companies operating in Africa, Asia, Central and Eastern Europe, on one side and other stakeholders such as governments, financial institutions, management education institutions on the other.

References

Brinkmann, S., & Kvale, S. (2015). *InterViews: Learning the craft of qualitative research interviewing* (3rd ed.). Sage.

Gummesson, E. (2000). *Qualitative methods in management research* (2nd ed.). Sage.

Miles, M. B., & Huberman, A. M. (1994). *Qualitative data analysis: An expanded sourcebook* (2nd ed.). Sage.

Patton, M. Q. (2015). *Qualitative research & evaluation methods* (4th ed.). Sage.

Simon, H. (1996). *Hidden champions–lessons from 500 of the world's best unknown companies*. Harvard Business School Press.

Simon, H. (2022). *Hidden champions in the Chinese century—ascent and transformation*. Springer Nature.

Yin, R. K. (2014). *Case study research design and methods* (5th ed.). Sage.

Yoo, P. H., & Key, S. (2025). Die Fans der stillen Riesen. *Harvard Business Manager*.

Denis Berberović, PhD, is associate professor and member of the Marketing department at the School of Economics and Business in Sarajevo. He lectures modules "Marketing Communications" and "Marketing Research" on undergraduate and "Methodology of Scientific Research" on graduate studies. Dr. Denis Berberović received the Chevening scholarship granted by the British Government. He got his Master of Science degree with distinction at one of Europe's top management schools, Bradford University School of Management. He extends continuously his horizons by additional education such as attending courses in IEDC Bled, Prague (AIPES) or WU Vienna.

Until today he has published several papers, book chapters and books, some of them for the leading global publisher Springer. He received an award for his scientific work at his alma mater university, the University of Sarajevo. He was member of project teams for business clients such as UNDP, BH MAC, ACIPS, RAK, Bosch, Bosnalijek, Federal Ministry of Tourism and Environment, SOS Kinderdorf, etc. Currently he is leading a global network of researchers from South-East Europe, South America, Africa, and Asia, investigating the concept of Hidden Champions. He is the newly appointed President of the Scientific Council to the Federal Ministry of Education and Science in the Federation of Bosnia and Herzegovina.

Hidden Champions: Common Lessons Learned in VUCA Times

Merima Činjarević and Denis Berberović

Abstract Hidden champions have served not only as case studies and examples for successful business undertakings, but also as a pool of important business lessons. Learning from their success and trying to apply it to other small- and medium-sized enterprises is a long-term legacy of hidden champions. Exploring their development trajectories and learning from their business models is the main objective of the research project which is presented through this book. Seven major lessons have been drawn from the meta-analysis of HC (hidden champion) case studies from rising economies. Lesson 1 suggests that strong leadership is the motor of hidden champions' success. Lesson 2 says that employees and a strong corporate culture is the reason hidden champions endure and flourish. Lesson 3 teaches that hidden champions create and deliver values. Lesson 4 further suggests that the value-creation process as well as the value itself need to be innovative. Lesson 5 contains the main message that the value is created through a partnership network that hidden champions construct and rely on. Lesson 6 claims that resilience is engraved at the DNA of hidden champions. Finally, Lesson 7 emphasises the importance of sustainable business practice, which leads to long-term business success. All these lessons are embedded in the business environment which is under strong influence of VUCA times in which hidden champions manage to survive and strive.

M. Činjarević
Department of Microeconomics, University of Sarajevo – School of Economics and Business, Sarajevo, Bosnia and Herzegovina
e-mail: merima.cinjarevic@efsa.unsa.ba

D. Berberović (✉)
School of Economics and Business, University of Sarajevo, Sarajevo, Bosnia and Herzegovina
e-mail: denis.berberovic@efsa.unsa.ba

D. Berberović, D. Purg (eds.), *Hidden Champions in Rising Economies*, Contributions to Management Science,
https://doi.org/10.1007/978-3-032-08263-3_3

1 Introduction

This chapter identifies the key capabilities that drive the business success of hidden champions during the volatile, uncertain, complex, and ambiguous (VUCA) times (e.g. the COVID-19 pandemic, the Russia-Ukraine war). The concept VUCA describes the nature of the modern global environment, in which companies face increasing challenges in managing operations while responding to external changes (Atanassova et al., 2025). Yet hidden champions manage to flourish and grow during these difficult times as well as business environments which are not supportive of innovative businesses (Berberović et al., 2019). To determine what makes hidden champions successful in VUCA times and to derive actionable lessons for other small- and medium-sized enterprises (SMEs), we employed the dynamic capabilities perspective. The dynamic capabilities perspective is a framework that focuses on a company's ability to integrate, reconfigure, and adapt its resources in response to rapidly changing environments (Teece, 2007). Unlike ordinary capabilities that facilitate operational efficiency, dynamic capabilities enable a company to sense opportunities and threats, seize them effectively, and reconfigure internal resources in response to changing environments (Schriber & Löwstedt, 2020). In the context of hidden champions, ordinary capabilities empower them to "make a living" in the short term (Winter, 2003). However, their genuine strength lies in their ability to adapt rapidly to changing circumstances. Based on the meta-analysis of individual case studies, the main dynamic capabilities were derived and categorised into seven lessons. These lessons are the main pillars of the success of hidden champions in VUCA times and beyond.

2 How to Navigate the Business in VUCA Times?

2.1 Lesson 1: It All Begins and Endures with Leaders

Leadership capabilities are one of the major drivers of the success of hidden champions analysed in this study. Leadership capabilities encompass the knowledge, skills, abilities, traits, and behaviours that allow a person to be an effective leader (Dabić et al., 2023; Megheirkouni, 2016). Since the leadership capabilities of hidden champions differ from country to country as well as from one company to another, we selected those that are common for most hidden champions. These are (1) the ability of a leader to inspire followers through a compelling vision and strong commitment to a vision; (2) the ability to build trust with the employees and guide them towards shared goals; (3) the ability to embrace the change through employee empowerment and the development of culture of continuous learning; and (4) the ability to balance the big picture (vision) with the execution of strategies. Identified leadership capabilities align with the primary characteristics of contemporary leadership approaches, including authentic leadership, visionary leadership, transformational leadership, and servant leadership. Regardless of their market niche—being specialised in manufacturing of construction equipment (e.g. Ading—North Macedonia), providing cutting-edge technological solutions for other industries (e.g. Dmiteh—Serbia; Koshi—Kosovo, Parqour—Kazakhstan), creating avatars for digital games (e.g. Ready Player Me—Estonia), crafting a furniture (e.g. Artisan—Bosnia and Herzegovina) or a producing a wine (e.g. Tbilvino—Georgia), they all have a clear and ambitious vision that is important just as their technical know-how.

2.2 *Lesson 2: Enduring Success Also Comes from Capable Employees*

Employee capabilities are another building block of the success of hidden champions. Employee capabilities refer to the "personality attributes or characteristics such as knowledge, skills, attitudes, abilities, motives and self-concept demonstrated by employees that result in effective and superior performances" (Salman et al., 2020, p. 3). The distinctive employee competencies of hidden champions include technical expertise (the ability to execute daily tasks), social skills such as the capacity to work in teams and engage in interdisciplinary collaborations, and personal capabilities (e.g. flexibility, adaptability, and the ability to learn). The hidden champions recognise that employee capabilities are key to the company's success. For instance, Krips, Armenia's leader in noise cancellation and transcription technologies, acknowledges that the talented team has been essential to the company's ability to innovate and deliver cutting-edge solutions. Similar views about the importance of talented employees are shared by other hidden champions such as Santino-Service from Moldova, Emerus from Bosnia and Herzegovina, Uniplast from Serbia, or Mertcontrol from Hungary. Thus, hidden champions place focus on talent acquisition and retention strategies. Regarding their efforts to retain talent, hidden champions combine various employee practices to create an organisational culture that nurtures teamwork, mentoring, and the empowerment of talent. Empowering talented employees is a pivotal employee practice among hidden champions. Besides formal strategies of retention (e.g. training and development; mentoring), hidden champions promote the empowerment of their talents by providing them with a certain level of autonomy and showing them that their ideas and opinions are heard and valued by leaders.

2.3 *Lesson 3: Do Not Just Deliver Value – Co-Create It*

The distinctive characteristic of hidden champions is their ability to engage in the customer value co-creation process. According to Bosisio (2024), customer co-creation value refers to the "collaboration between a company and the customer in the joint creation of value" (p. 340). Existing studies suggest that customers are an important source of innovative ideas and play a pivotal role in enriching a company's products and services (Corsaro, 2019; Eggert et al., 2018). The hidden champions participating in this study are aware of the importance of two complementary perspectives on customer value: value in exchange (i.e. value based on product/service attributes promised by a company and expected by customers) and value in use (i.e. all customer-perceived consequences arising from a solution that facilitate or hinder achievement of the customer's goal). For example, Moldavia's *Noction* integrates direct customer input, particularly regarding product functionality, into its design and development processes. In this way, the company ensures that products are developed based on actual customer needs, supporting a value-in-use orientation.

2.4 Lesson 4: Innovate from Every Angle … Explore, Exploit, Excel

Innovation ambidexterity lies at the core of the innovation process of the studied hidden champions. Innovation ambidexterity enables companies to successfully balance and succeed in two different but related innovation activities: exploration and exploitation (Lubatkin et al., 2006). Exploratory innovation involves experimenting with new alternatives and seeking new knowledge and skills in product development to reach new customers and markets. In contrast, exploitative innovation is the modification, improvement, and extension of existing products for existing customers (Kortmann et al., 2014). Through innovation and ambidexterity, hidden champions are able to sustain a simultaneous focus on optimising current products and services, as well as processes (incremental innovations), while fostering a proactive orientation towards innovative solutions and groundbreaking advancements (radical innovations). The three main building blocks of innovation ambidexterity of hidden champions are: (1) external knowledge breadth, (2) external knowledge depth, and (3) internal information sharing. In terms of external knowledge breadth, hidden champions draw on a diverse range of external knowledge sources, including customers, suppliers, competitors, government agencies, universities, and other relevant organisations. Regarding the depth of external knowledge, hidden champions nurture long-lasting relationships with all partners as sources of knowledge. Finally, hidden champions accept the idea that internal information sharing serves as a mechanism for transferring and disseminating human capital-embedded knowledge across organisational units.

2.5 Lesson 5: The Network Capability Matters More than Ever

Network capability is an additional ingredient in the success of hidden champions. Network capability captures the company's ability to acquire and integrate the knowledge from customers, suppliers, industry associations, and the broader community of experts (Falahat et al., 2018). Network capability is closely related to the innovation capabilities and internalisation path of hidden champions. Although technological innovations of hidden champions are mainly the result of internal knowledge sources, they cooperate with external knowledge sources, such as customers. For hidden champions, customers serve as "idea generators" in identifying unmet market demand. Based on these ideas, hidden champions, equipped with the necessary technological knowledge, engage in the process of developing high-quality and highly innovative solutions. In terms of internationalisation paths, our research revealed that hidden champions do not follow the traditional gradual international pattern—the Uppsala Model. Instead, the researched hidden champions follow the internationalisation path of Born Globals (i.e. rapid internationalisation after inception) and Born-Again-Globals (i.e. rapid internalisation after years of focusing only on the domestic market). The internationalisation process of hidden champions is often supported by a network of partners worldwide.

2.6 Lesson 6: Resilience Isn't Luck – It's Built In

Resilience is embedded in the DNA of hidden champions. When confronted with a crisis, whether it is a "black swan" (a small-probability but high-impact event) or a "grey rhino" (a high-probability and high-impact event), hidden champions demonstrated that they can bounce back and adapt to challenging conditions. Due to its capability to rearrange resources, optimise processes, and change relationships with partners during a crisis, many hidden champions managed to turn adversity into success. According to the Hungarian hidden champion *Pallet Solution Kft.*, the COVID-19 pandemic became a turning point. The COVID-19 pandemic helped the company to reveal the strength of its supplier network, sharpen its strategic focus, and reinforce its path toward organic growth. In a similar vein, Slovenian *Arctur* believes that crises are more than simply setbacks; they are catalysts for innovation. That approach inspired *Arctur* to develop an award-winning AI tourism platform, demonstrating that resilience is not about avoiding disruption, but rather flourishing in it.

Besides the strategic resilience (i.e. staying focused on long-term goals) and relationship resilience (i.e. building strong, two-way relationships with key stakeholders), hidden champions exhibited ability to keep learning and improving (learning resilience), ability to keep running and find the funds (capital resilience) as well as ability to nurture the entrepreneurial spirit of employees and the commitment of the employees (cultural resilience). For example, within Slovenia's *Dewesoft,* resilience is embedded in the organisational culture, indicating that resilience is not just the ability to adapt, but a commitment to continuous learning and personal growth. Through trainings, mentorships, and inspiring experiences, such as visiting SpaceX, *Dewedoft's* employees are empowered to evolve with change, stay motivated, and develop a deep sense of meaning in the work they do. As the owner of *Dawesoft* states, "*Working for Dewesoft is more than just a job; it is a way of living with passion and motivation to make a difference*". Moreover, even in volatile, uncertain, complex, and ambiguous (VUCA) times, hidden champions demonstrate capital resilience—the ability to sustain financial strength. At the same time, hidden champions demonstrated the ability to stay agile in VUCA times by avoiding hasty cost-cutting measures (e.g. layoffs or wage cuts) and continuing to invest in strategic priorities.

2.7 Lesson 7: Being Sustainable for Oneself Is Not Enough; You Need to Be Sustainable to the Planet

The pressure to modify production methods in response to challenges related to biodiversity loss, soil pollution, and depletion of scarce natural resources has led hidden champions to rethink their strategic priorities and encourage them to integrate more sustainable practices and technologies in their business models. Most of the hidden champions, particularly in the manufacturing sector, emphasised that they prioritise conventional green innovation through a range of sustainable technologies, including renewable energy solutions and environmentally friendly production methods. Although previous research suggests that the main drivers of green innovation are external pressures, including regulatory, customer, and competitor pressures (Xie et al., 2024), the green initiatives of hidden champions are primarily driven by internal factors such as organisational culture and lowering the cost associated with the production process. Thus, the sustainability path of a hidden champion is driven by its desire to be recognised as a cost-effective company that tries to be environmentally conscious. Aiming to achieve net-zero carbon emissions, hidden champions are seeking ways to reduce the carbon footprint by integrating low-carbon technologies and renewable energy sources into existing production processes (e.g. Emerus in Bosnia and Herzegovina, Mermer Imperial in North Macedonia).

3 Conclusion

In this chapter we have summarised the lessons learned from the hidden champions research project presented in this book. Compared to the same chapter (Berberović et al., 2021) we have noticed a consistency in implementing the mail lessons amongst hidden champions from rising economies. Although the VUCA environment inevitably poses significant challenges to the striving business operations of hidden champions, these companies once again confirmed that resilience is one of their hallmarks. This has been confirmed through all the previous research cycles so far. Although challenges they faced were different, they still approached these challenges in the same manner—adapt, adopt, and apply. They adapted to new circumstances, adopted new business processes, and applied them throughout the business model. One of the main challenges and changes in this respect is the concept of sustainability, which has become one of the flagship concepts of hidden champions. Not only do these companies implement sustainability concepts in their own businesses, but they promote it within industries and markets, and launch sustainable product solutions. Thereby hidden champions have positioned themselves as trend setters in respective markets, market niches, and industries. That is due to their innovative approach to business. They explore and exploit technological innovations, process innovations or conceptual innovations in order to serve the market niches as efficient as possible. Innovations are drawn not only from internal sources, such as highly professional teams; but they are drawn also from external sources, from networks they created amongst their customers, suppliers, distributors, and other business partners. This implies another important lesson that we can learn from hidden champions—they are not focused only on delivering high value, they are focused on creating it. Although the value creation model rests on the company itself, unavoidable part of it is the customer base which actively participates in vale creation; from generating ideas to implementing and testing solutions. Yet the basis for all of these lessons are two major lessons. Hidden champions have a strong, supportive, and innovation-stimulating corporate culture in which employees strive and excel, resulting in business expansion. Finally, strong leadership of hidden champions is the main reason behind their success.

References

Atanassova, I., Bednar, P., Khan, H., & Khan, Z. (2025). Managing the VUCA environment: The dynamic role of organizational learning and strategic agility in B2B versus B2C firms. *Industrial Marketing Management., 125*, 12–28. https://doi.org/10.1016/j.indmarman.2024.12.008

Berberović, D., Kožo, A., & Činjarević, M. (2021). Hidden champions: Common lessons learned on the path to success. In A. Braček Lalić & D. Purg (Eds.), *Hidden champions in dynamically changing societies*. Springer. https://doi.org/10.1007/978-3-030-65451-1_4

Berberović, D., Činjarević, M., & Kožo, A. (2019). Success despite lack of support: Lessons learned from hidden champions doing business in fragile business environments. *Sarajevo Business and Economics Review., 37*, 192–204.

Bosisio, J. (2024). A research landscape on customer co-creation value: a systematic literature network analysis. *Italian Journal of Marketing, 2024*, 339–368. https://doi.org/10.1007/s43039-024-00092-9

Corsaro, D. (2019). Value co-destruction and its effects on value appropriation. *Journal of Marketing Management, 36*(1/2), 100–127. https://doi.org/10.1080/0267257X.2019.1696876

Dabić, M., Maley, J. F., Črešnar, R., & Nedelko, Z. (2023). Unappreciated channel of manufacturing productivity under industry 4.0: Leadership values and capabilities. *Journal of Business Research, 162*, 113900. https://doi.org/10.1016/j.jbusres.2023.113900

Eggert, A., Ulaga, W., Frow, P., & Payne, A. (2018). Conceptualizing and communicating value in business markets: From value in exchange to value in use. *Industrial Marketing Management, 69*, 80–90. https://doi.org/10.1016/j.indmarman.2018.01.018

Falahat, M., Knight, G., & Alon, I. (2018). Orientations and capabilities of born global firms from emerging markets. *International Marketing Review, 35*(6), 936–957. https://doi.org/10.1108/IMR-01-2017-0021

Kortmann, S., Gelhard, C., Zimmermann, C., & Piller, F. T. (2014). Linking strategic flexibility and operational efficiency: The mediating role of ambidextrous operational capabilities. *Journal of Operations Management, 32*(7/8), 475–490. https://doi.org/10.1016/j.jom.2014.09.007

Lubatkin, M. H., Simsek, Z., Ling, Y., & Veiga, J. F. (2006). Ambidexterity and performance in small- tom medium-sized firms: The pivotal role of top management team behavioral integration. *Journal of Management, 32*(5), 646–672. https://doi.org/10.1177/0149206306290712

Megheirkouni, M. (2016). Leadership behaviours and capabilities in Syria: an exploratory qualitative approach. *Journal of Management Development, 35*(5), 636–662. https://doi.org/10.1108/JMD-02-2015-0022

Salman, M., Ganie, S. A., & Saleem, I. (2020). Employee competencies as predictors of organizational performance: A study of public and private sector banks. *Management and Labour Studies, 45*(4), 416–432. https://doi.org/10.1177/0258042X2093901

Schriber, S., & Löwstedt, J. (2020). Reconsidering ordinary and dynamic capabilities in strategic change. *European Management Journal, 38*(3), 377–387. https://doi.org/10.1016/j.emj.2019.12.006

Teece, D. J. (2007). Explicating dynamic capabilities: The nature and micro foundations of (sustainable) enterprise performance. *Strategic Management Journal, 28*, 1319–1350. https://doi.org/10.1002/smj.640

Winter, S. G. (2003). Understanding dynamic capabilities. *Strategic Management Journal, 24*, 991–995. http://dx.doi.org/10.1002/smj.318

Xie, J., Abbass, K., & Li, D. (2024). Advancing eco-excellence: Integrating stakeholders' pressures, environmental awareness, and ethics for green innovation and performance. *Journal of Environmental Management, 352*, 120027. https://doi.org/10.1016/j.jenvman.2024.120027

Merima Činjarević is an Associate Professor at the Department of Microeconomics at the University of Sarajevo, School of Economics and Business, where she teaches microeconomics, managerial economics, and behavioral economics. She has published over 30 peer-reviewed articles in respected international journals, including the European Journal of Marketing, Journal of Knowledge Management, and the British Food Journal. Her work extends to book chapters with top academic publishers, including Springer and Emerald. She is the co-author of the textbooks Managerial Economics and Behavioural Economics. In recognition of her impactful research, she was twice awarded the prestigious Rector's Award for Excellence in Scientific Research by the University of Sarajevo (2020, 2021). In addition to her academic work, she has participated in numerous international and national projects, including those implemented within transnational cooperation programs. Through her project involvement, she has contributed to the development of strategies, policy papers, feasibility studies, and economic analyses aimed at enhancing the competitiveness and sustainable development of local communities in Bosnia and Herzegovina and the European region.

Denis Berberović, PhD, is associate professor and member of the Marketing department at the School of Economics and Business in Sarajevo. He lectures modules "Marketing Communications" and "Marketing Research" on undergraduate and "Methodology of Scientific Research" on graduate studies. Dr. Denis Berberović received the Chevening scholarship granted by the British

Government. He got his Master of Science degree with distinction at one of Europe's top management schools, Bradford University School of Management. He extends continuously his horizons by additional education such as attending courses in IEDC Bled, Prague (AIPES) or WU Vienna. Until today he has published several papers, book chapters and books, some of them for the leading global publisher Springer. He received an award for his scientific work at his alma mater university, the University of Sarajevo. He was member of project teams for business clients such as UNDP, BH MAC, ACIPS, RAK, Bosch, Bosnalijek, Federal Ministry of Tourism and Environment, SOS Kinderdorf, etc. Currently he is leading a global network of researchers from South-East Europe, South America, Africa, and Asia, investigating the concept of Hidden Champions. He is the newly appointed President of the Scientific Council to the Federal Ministry of Education and Science in the Federation of Bosnia and Herzegovina.

The Leadership of Hidden Champions: The Strategic Focus of Start-Ups, Scale-Ups, and Grown-Ups

Danica Purg and Arnold Walravens

Abstract This chapter analyzes the interviews with founders, entrepreneurs, and leaders of Hidden Champions on focal strategic leadership items. Hidden Champions are differentiated in three types of companies: start-ups, scale-ups, and grown-ups. The found 96 focal items are structured in six sections: governance items, technical items, development items, cultural and mindset items, cooperation items, and diverse relevant issues. The analysis of the detailed description of focal items leads to a number of remarkable observations on the presence and impact they have in the different phases of development of Hidden Champions. One of important conclusions is that the building of leadership platforms, i.e., not to limit to solitary entrepreneurs, is considered as an essential condition for growth of the company.

1 Introduction

Features, styles, and forms of leadership have been important topics in all studies of Hidden Champions. Particularly the bivalent performance factors of Hidden Champions related to family ownership and single entrepreneurship have been analyzed extensively (Walravens & Filipović, 2013). Especially in the small Hidden Champions the leadership shows to be strongly related to the vision and expert knowledge of the founders. These characteristic elements have been always accompanied by passion to perform.

Although the definition of small- and medium-sized companies is generally related to the number of employees, characteristic for HCs (Hidden Champions) however is the reach of their activities beyond regional or national dimensions. This can be observed also in the holistic vision and strategy of the founders/entrepreneurs and management/leaders of the companies (Best, 2011).

D. Purg (✉) · A. Walravens
IEDC Bled School of Management and CEEMAN, Bled, Slovenia
e-mail: Danica.purg@ceeman.org; Arnold.Walravens@iedc.si

D. Berberović, D. Purg (eds.), *Hidden Champions in Rising Economies*, Contributions to Management Science,
https://doi.org/10.1007/978-3-032-08263-3_4

Distinctive for smaller `SMEs is also a high degree of identification amongst employees with the values and goals of the company. This has in former research of HCs also led to the understanding of the underlying factor, how long this attitude of high identification and related motivation can be maintained in a successful and growing company (Fiol, 1991). This has in former research of HCs also led to the interesting question, how long this attitude of high identification and related motivation can be maintained in a successful and growing company (Walravens & Filipović, 2013).

How long the "family" culture can be nurtured without materializing it in greater participation of employees in decision-making and generally sharing the success of the company? This research on HCs and particularly the interviews with the entrepreneurs and leaders may offer more insights in this important issues for the companies in different phases of their development.

2 Analysis of the Interviews with Founders, Entrepreneurs, and Leaders

2.1 The General Picture of Mentioned Focal Items

On the basis of the participating companies in the research we decided to differentiate three types of companies:

- Start-ups (25 companies), established after 2015
- Scale-ups (25 companies), established in the period 2000–2015
- Grown-ups (13 companies), established before 2000

From the reports and interviews we deduced 96 focal strategic issues. We structured them in the following sections (see Scheme 1):

- Governance issues
- Technical issues
- Development issues
- Cultural and mindset issues
- Cooperation issues
- Diverse relevant issues

Type of Issue	**Start-ups**	**Scale-ups**	**Grown-ups**	**Total**
1. Governance Issues	7	14	11	32
2. Technical Issues	5	4	0	15
3. Development Issues	4	14	6	24
5. Cultural and mindset Issues	3	4	7	14
6. Cooperation Issues	4	3	4	11
Total	**23**	**39**	34	**96**

Scheme 1 Selection of strategic focal issues in HCs

2.1.1 A Few Remarkable Observations in Scheme 1

Scheme 1 shows that leaders in HCs in all categories of companies are strongly focused on governance issues, particularly in scale-ups (Jansen et al., 2023) and grown-ups. It suggests that growth asks for special attention for the leadership platform. The development issue becomes a leadership field of attention in the scale-ups. Probably again the same explanation can be found in the growth process and related conditions.

On the next paragraphs, we shall be able to look deeper in the overall results by the description of all underlying items.

2.2 *The Presentation and Analyses of Detailed Descriptions of Focal Items*

2.2.1 The Governance Issues

A Few Remarkable Observations in Scheme 2

The leadership and management platform shows up in various forms:

- Visionary leadership
- Corporate governance
- Senior management
- (Managerial, project-) teams

Start-ups	Scale-ups	Grown-ups
– Strategic leadership – Enhancing corporate governance – Quality of management and leadership – Cultivating the team and team empowerment – Cross-cultural management – Involvement in decision-making by employees	– Building, engaging and promoting teams (including, internationalization and forming project teams) – Communication (two -sides, improving and funding the right system in a wide-spread organisation) – Visionary leadership – International experienced leadership – Innovation leadership and technical management – A sustainable organization, in which knowledge and values smoothly can be transferred to the next generations	– Assistance in developing corporate governance – A system for senior management to retain control over business activities – Professional teams (rather than family members in the management) – Upgrading position of middle management – Engaging the staff fully in business matters – Skilled project-management – Maintaining an expert image – Succession planning / possible listing on the stock exchange

Scheme 2 The governance issues

Especially in scale-ups the formation and development of teams is an important issue in many companies. Growth apparently leads also to increasing communication needs. In grown-ups two phenomena related to governance come up:

- A system for senior management to retain control of the business activities, also impacting the role of family members
- Developing and upgrading middle management and the staff of the company

2.2.2 The Technical Issues

A Few Remarkable Observations in Scheme 3

Start-ups face the importance of technical skills and the expertise of team members. Both elements are usually the basis for start-ups. For scale-ups the need to acquire and develop a qualified workforce is felt as a condition for growth. This counts also for grown-ups, but then digitalization is already a normal process in start-ups and scale-ups, leaders in grown-ups have to make special efforts to digitalize their own "traditional" systems in production and administration.

2.2.3 The Development Issue

A Few Remarkable Observations in Scheme 4

Start-ups, often founded on technical expertise, generally come to feel—early in their growth—the need for managerial, leadership, and especially "soft" skills, such as team management and interpersonal communication.

In scale-ups, this need for management and leadership skills and staff development becomes an absolute strategic issue to make growth possible. It is a real danger otherwise to have promoted people to occupy positions, for which they are not prepared.

Start-ups	Scale-ups	Grown-ups
– technical skills (p riority to attract qualified professionals, challenge to build local experts, priority to develop technical skills) (3x) – expertise of team members – Investing in ERPsystem to manage the growing number of products and customers	– technology management – investment in know-how – requiring and developing a qualified workforce – Investing in leadership and technical skills	– technical knowledge (is essential also for HRM) (2x) – digital leadership and digital transformation, and lean-driven digital empowerment strategy (3x) – recruiting and developing young talents

Scheme 3 The technical issues

Start-ups	Scale-ups	Grown-ups
– developing managerial and leadership skills (2x) – improving leadership of teams skills – development of soft skills – developing employees skills – improving leadership courses for students – develop people for a creative environment	– management and leadership development (also related to HRM) (3x) – training managers to foster critical thinking – developing amongst leaders skills for coaching, mentoring, and constructive feedback to employees – building skills for encouraging innovation and entrepreneurship – develop communication skills – assist leaders to stay informed about global trends in their industry	– management and leadership development (6x) – developing (local) staff (3x) – recruiting and retaining talents and experienced people – improving skills for working in teams – high-quality education for employees (also outside their functional comfort zone) (2x) – preparing promoted people for their new responsibilities

Scheme 4 The development issue

In grown-ups, there is besides continuous manager development a need to develop skills amongst managers and leaders to mentor, coach, and inspire people to be entrepreneurial and innovate.

2.2.4 Cultural and Mindset Issues

A Few Remarkable Observations in Scheme 5

Start-ups need creative people to deal with unexpected and surprising developments.

In scale-ups it becomes an issue for leaders to develop, but particularly to maintain an entrepreneurial mindset and a corporate spirit of working together in a good atmosphere, based on a shared culture and commitment.

Grown-ups need to develop a clear strategy based on a long-term vision. The different ethics of a younger generation in comparison with the passion and ethics of the founders and the older generation causes also problems to be managed.

2.2.5 The Cooperation Issues

A Few Remarkable Observations in Scheme 6

Start-ups are mostly partners. Often they are spin-offs from a research institute and development institutes. Their cooperation will continue. They also need business partners.

Scale-ups have to combine cooperation on an international level with a good relationship with the local community, if they smoothly want to extend their activities and need infrastructural provisions.

Start-ups	Scale-ups	Grown-ups
– to develop people for a creative environment – development of soft skills – maintaining a strong identification with the product	– Developing and maintaining entrepreneurial mindset – Maintaining corporate spirit and friendly and fair relations between all employees – A shared culture and commitment – Building a sustainable organization, where knowledge and skills can be smoothly transferred to the next generation	– Commitment to ethical practices and sustainability – Strategy based on the long-term vision and aims of the founder (2x) – Leadership based on strong personality, intuition, vision, and passion – Focus on a clear strategy – Installing a sense of responsibility of the younger generation

Scheme 5 Cultural and mindset issues

Start-ups	Scale-ups	Grown-ups
– Developing strategic partnerships – Collaboration with external business partners (2x) – Partnership with research and development institutes	– Internationalization and recruiting people for it – Good relations with the local community – Cultivate an ecosystem that fosters the emergence and development of HC	– Strategic partnerships – Focus on international cooperation – Partnerships with educational institutions – Joint educational programs with schools in the field of arts

Scheme 6 The cooperation issues

Leaders of grown-ups focus on international cooperation to extend their markets. For development programs they look for sustainable relations with educational institutions for leadership or professional development programs.

3 Conclusions

As it already often said HCs are special companies letting you wonder, how it is possible that they have such an important position on the market and are not largely "known," on the other hand they are "normal" companies with the usual issues. If one considers for example the leadership focal points of start-ups in this study we see that other research in small SMEs mentions the same strategic issues.

Besides also financial management, topic of another chapter in this study, Eisenmann (2021) mentions the importance of strategy, hiring the right people, and the knowledge and skill gap for succeeding or failing. Wetzel and Eiche (2024) write: "the influence of knowledge, personality traits, and experiences of founding members on the startup should be mentioned." They also stress "the optimal team composition." All these elements come back in the focus of start-ups in this research.

The "rapid growth can be a double-edged sword for SMEs, bringing both new opportunities and challenges" (Harrington, 2023). Harrington (2023) mentions in this context also the limited sources for hiring and retaining of top talents. Also the poor management skills that are needed to be improved results from analysis of the problems in SMEs (UK IT Service, 2020).

The reservations on the leadership focus on securing and integrating talents and new staff, particularly in scale-ups is also confirmed by Kindström et al. (2024) when they talk about the "challenge in the process of growth" or "resource bottlenecks." They also noticed that "challenge related to building and maintaining effective, functioning leadership structures are high on the agenda of SME managers" (Kindström et al., 2024, p. 709).

And where we talk about building and extending leadership platforms they mention "the embracement of a broader portfolio of leadership roles," and including others in the decision-making process. The building of leadership platforms is essential for growth, not to limit the leading to solitary entrepreneurs.

The leadership focus in scale-ups is as we mentioned before also focused on mindset issues as maintaining an entrepreneurial mindset, corporate mindset, a shared culture and commitment. Kindström et al. (2024) noticed a comparative challenge to promote and maintain a healthy firm culture in a growing company, saving "the small firm feeling" and "family atmosphere, emphasizing cooperation, and team mindset approach."

Particularly in grown-ups it will be difficult to keep this feature of a small firm. Then leadership orient itself more on a commitment to several ethical practices and sustainability, and trying to close the gap between generations on commitment and identification with the company. What is in fact characteristic for HCs. They are confronted with the same challenges as other companies, but they still exist, and are even champions. This means that their managers and leaders are succeeding to find the right answers on the challenges. That's what we can learn from them.

References

UK IT Service. (2020). Biggest problems For SMEs & their solutions (IT in 2020). Retrieved from https://www.ukitservice.co.uk/blog/biggest-problems-small-business-smes-solutions/.

Best, K. C. (2011). Holistic leadership. A model for leader–member engagement and development. *The Journal of Values Based Leadership, 4*(1) Retrieved from https://scholar.valpo.edu/jvbl/vol4/iss1/5

Eisenmann, T. R. (2021). Why start-ups fail. *Harvard Business Review.*

Fiol, C. M. (1991). Managing culture as a competitive resource: An identity-based view of sustainable competitive advantage. *Journal of Management, 17*(1), 191–211.

Harrington, S. (2023, 10 12). Understanding the top 10 challenges for SMEs today. Retrieved from https://williambuck.com/news/business/general/understanding-the-top-10-challenges-for-smes-today/.

Jansen, J. J., Heavey, C., Mom, T. J., Simsek, Z., & Zahra, S. A. (2023). Scaling-up: Building, leading and sustaining rapid growth over time. *Journal of Management Studies, 60*(3), 581–604.

Kindström, D., Carlborg, P., & Nord, T. (2024). Challenges for growing SMEs: A managerial perspective. *Journal of Small Business Management, 62*(2), 700–723.
Walravens, A., & Filipović, N. (2013). Three bivalent performance factors of hidden champions: Ownership, organizational culture and organizational governance. In P. McKiernan & D. Purg (Eds.), *Hidden champions in CEE and Turkey. Carving out a global niche* (pp. 37–53). Springer.
Wetzel, T., & Eiche, J. (2024). Challenges of start-ups—an analysis of individually tailored recommendations based on the development phases, branches, business models and founding teams. *Open. Journal of Business and Management*. https://doi.org/10.4236/ojbm.2024.123084

Danica Purg is the founder and Dean of IEDC-Bled School of Management, Slovenia, and President of CEEMAN, association of 200 management schools from 50 countries.

Professor Purg has been an innovator in management education, incorporating arts and artistic processes into management education and bringing ethics into the curriculum of all longer management programs at IEDC since its inception. She authored and co-authored several books and numerous articles on leadership issues. She is a frequent guest speaker at universities around the world and at international conferences.

For her work in international management education, Danica Purg has been recognized worldwide. She received the International Educator of the Year Award from the Academy of International Business in 2010. The President of the Republic of Slovenia bestowed upon her the Honorary Order of Freedom, and she has received highest awards from the French and Brazilian governments.

Her influence extends to universities worldwide. She is a member of international advisory boards at management schools around the world, and serves as the Chairlady of the Academic board of the International Research Center for Hidden Champions at Zhejiang University, China. Prof. Danica Purg is very active in PRME (Principles of Responsible Management Education), an initiative started by UN Global Compact, where she held many important roles in the past and in July 2017 was awarded for.

She has received the titles Doctor Honoris Causa at several universities around the world (the most recent is from the University of Wollongong, Australia), and holds two honorary professorship titles. In 2025 Prof. Danica Purg has been inducted into the Thinkers50 Hall of Fame 2025.

Arnold Walravens is a Professor of Arts & Leadership and Corporate Governance, Chair of the Postgraduate Studies and Quality Commission at IEDC-Bled School of Management. He teaches the courses on Corporate Governance and Arts and Leadership in Executive MBA and General Management Programs at IEDC-Bled School of Management.

He is Professor Emeritus of Economic Sociology at the University of Technology, Delft, The Netherlands, where he also served as the dean of the Faculty of Philosophy and Social Sciences. He received his Ph.D. from the University of Technology, Twente, the Netherlands and served as faculty member at the Free University of Amsterdam.

His academic research focuses on various topics, such as participation and human resources, corporate governance, arts and leadership, executive development, and artificial intelligence. As UNDP/ILO consultant, he was active in Zambia, dealing with workers' participation, privatization issues, and corporate governance. For fifteen years he served as the chairman of the Commission for Entrepreneurship of the Dutch Economic Institute for Small and Medium-sized Companies.

Professor Walravens served as Chairman of the Supervisory Board Achmea Insurances, Connexxion, Tauw Infra Consult, and Sneep bv, and as a member of the board of multinational companies as Bull Netherlands, CSM, Rabobank, and Wolters-Kluwer. He is director-owner of "Aan de Oude Delft," Art and Auction Services.

Finance and Regulatory Environment Needs of Hidden Champions

Slavica Singer and Sunčica Oberman Peterka

Abstract In order to understand how Hidden Champions design their 'swimming' capability to reach 'blue ocean' within given regulatory context and available access to finance, this chapter explores the (non) supportive features of the entrepreneurial context. Its dynamism is determined by different nature of its components (e.g. regulatory framework, access to finance, education, collaboration between research and business sector…), but even more by different intensity of interactions among them. Regulatory Quality Indicator (as part of the Worldwide Governance Indicators, developed by the World Bank Group) provides a very informative baseline for clustering all 30 countries involved in 2022 HC (Hidden Champion) cycle according to the level of quality of their respective regulatory frameworks and intensity of interventions aiming to improve them. Higher Regulatory Quality indicators usually are found in more developed countries, what means that context is supportive for entrepreneurial intentions contributing to new value-adding economic activities. Bringing opinions of interviewed HC owners/managers enriched understanding of rough roads towards 'blue ocean' competitive level in a globalized world (Simon, Hidden Champions in the Chinese Century: Ascent and Transformation, 2022).

Uniqueness of Hidden Champions (HCs) is a synergetic effect of a way how customers' needs are satisfied and how this process is designed in implemented business model. It means, that uniqueness is formed by a 'driving' capability of a HC to swim out of the 'red ocean' to the 'blue ocean', with the supportive features of the entrepreneurial context.

S. Singer (✉)
UNESCO Chair in Entrepreneurship Education, J.J. Strossmayer University, Osijek, Croatia
e-mail: singer@efos.hr

S. O. Peterka
Faculty of Economics and Business in Osijek, J.J. Strossmayer University, Osijek, Croatia
e-mail: suncica.oberman.peterka@efos.hr

D. Berberović, D. Purg (eds.), *Hidden Champions in Rising Economies*, Contributions to Management Science,
https://doi.org/10.1007/978-3-032-08263-3_5

1 Relevancy of Entrepreneurial Context

There are no significant differences in defining entrepreneurial context across academic discussion (e.g. Isenberg, 2011; Stam, 2015; Stam & Spigel, 2016; Spigel, 2017) neither across major international surveys (World Bank, OECD) because all agree that the interactions determine if such context will be supportive or not to strategic visions of business entities. Stam (2015) describes the entrepreneurial ecosystem as dynamic interconnectedness of different elements (framework and systemic conditions) enabling entrepreneurial activity (outputs) which leads to aggregate value creation (outcomes). Conceptual frameworks of clusters (Porter, 1990) and Triple Helix (Etzkowitz & Leidesdorff, 1995) also deal with context.

All those approaches confirm underlying understanding of systems theory in designing successful business models based on interactions between internal resources and external influences. A major difference between definitions is a territorial (socio-economic) dimension of the context, which can be international, national and subnational. This fine-tuning explains how the context is composed—with components relevant for any business entity (national, e.g. regulatory framework) or focusing on components more relevant on subnational level (e.g. professional services for SMEs with growth potential, availability of incubators, accelerators, specific education programmes…). Since this chapter is dealing with two components of context which are mostly defined on national level (access to finance and regulatory framework) when referring to the context, it is the national entrepreneurial context. It is interesting to note that international context is usually neglected, but it becomes increasingly important (e.g. clean production standards, environmental standards…).

In order to understand how Hidden Champions design their 'swimming' capability to reach 'blue ocean' within given regulatory context and available access to finance, Simon's (2022) reflections on globalization are important in answering the question which context is relevant. Globalization is not going to shrink, because it would be against any concept of effectiveness and efficiency, but it will take different modes and Simon (2022:65) labelled it as 'rough roads to Globalia'. For example, the decisions related to supply chains need to take into account how to make them more resilient without compromising their competitiveness (Shih, in Simon, 2022:83), and it will go toward dematerialization of export which will be replaced by exports of services and by direct investments. Simon (2022:85) sees it as a search for locations where business conditions are optimal, and calls this approach a location-competence assimilation. This trend is expected to reshape not only the business models and organizational cultures of Hidden Champions but also the broader contexts in which they operate—a process that is already underway. Hidden Champions should be aware of it and prepare themselves for rough roads to the new competitive features in a new *glocalized* world.

Political conflicts, climate changes, technological novelties, tariff wars, and connected supply chains…all contribute to rising overall uncertainty. It is not anymore enough to know an immediate context in which a company acts, but it is important to know which segments of the supply chain are suffering (Shih, 2020:84) because of not supportive context (low regulatory quality). Broadening the knowledge on regulatory quality along the supply chain is contributing to lowering uncertainty in decision-making process of a Hidden Champion in order to improve the flow of business activities across the supply chains.

2 Where to Find Data on the Regulatory Quality Across the World?

Overall agreement on the definition of entrepreneurial activity as a synergetic effect of an individual and the relevant context (international/national/subnational) opened the door to initiatives of developing indicators to evaluate if regulatory framework is stimulating or limiting entrepreneurial activities in all phases of a business venture (starting, growing, exiting).

Regulatory framework is usually evaluated as a part of interactions among different components of a context in which a business operates. The World Bank Group developed a composite indicator approach using different aspects of the entrepreneurial context, named Worldwide Governance Indicators (WGIs).

Worldwide Governance Indicators (2024) provide insights into six aggregate indicators (Voice and Accountability, Political Stability and Absence of Violence/Terrorism, Government Effectiveness, Regulatory Quality, Rule of Law, Control of Corruption). Two informational perspectives are available: cross-country comparisons of governance for over 200 economies and trends over time (from 1996, updated annually). Regulatory quality *'captures perceptions of the ability of the government to formulate and implement sound policies and regulations that permit and promote private sector development'* (WGI, 2024). Regulatory Quality indicator is based on information from different organizations (mostly think-tanks) and cover different dimensions of the regulatory framework, like burden of government regulations, ease of starting a business or setting up a subsidiary for a foreign firm, share of administered prices, tax inconsistency, discriminatory tariffs, investment freedom, financial freedom, labour regulations, unfair competitive practices, excessive protections, and efficiency of competition regulation in the market sector.

Two features of Regulatory Quality indicator are important for those who are in charge of designing policies relevant to regulatory frameworks:

- High-income countries have higher Regulatory Quality indicators.
- Improving regulatory framework requires consistent policies in longer period, but deterioration is faster.

The first finding that Regulatory Quality indicator is higher in more developed countries confirms that regulatory framework is a component of the context which has a strong positive influence on value-adding processes in economies (Fig. 1).

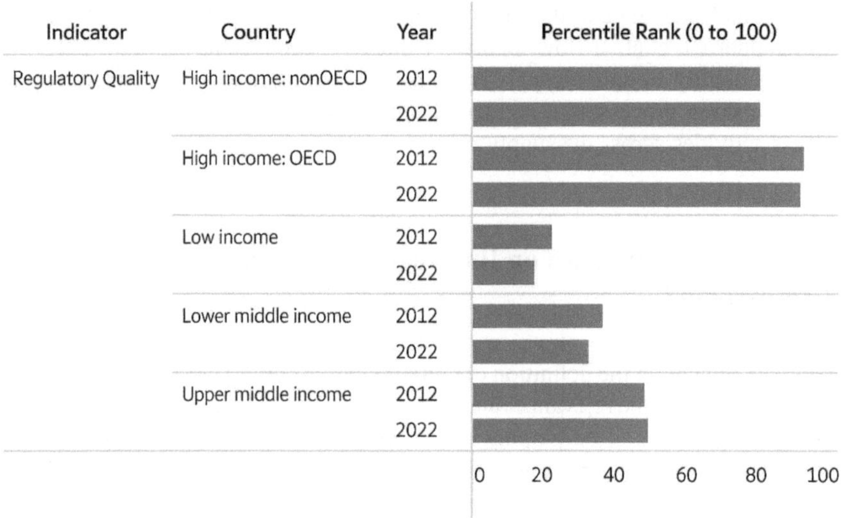

Fig. 1 Regulatory quality indicator, Worldwide Governance Indicators. Source: Worldwide Governance Indicators, 2024 Update, World Bank (www.govindicators.org)

The second finding confirms that a regulatory framework is a live system, which should be carefully designed, built and maintained by all networked actors. It takes time to build a supportive regulatory framework, but if it is not maintained, its deterioration is much faster. Less developed economies show higher vulnerability of their regulatory frameworks—e.g. the Regulatory Quality indicator deteriorated in 10 years period (2012 vs. 2022) in low-income economies (from 20.69 percentile to 16.18 percentile), but improvement of Regulatory Quality indicator in high-income OECD economies is much slower (from 86.87 in 2012 to 87.28 in 2022) (Fig. 1). The differences between values of Regulatory Quality indicators of high income OECD countries and low income countries are enormous: 87.28 percentile rank vs. 16.18 percentile rank, respectively (in 2022). It warns policymakers, responsible for designing and maintaining regulatory frameworks that there are no quick interventions in improving it, and that consistent policies are needed to be implemented in longer period.

Methodology of identifying Hidden Champions includes evaluation of regulatory framework, by business owners/managers of nominated HCs. Therefore it is interesting to check the values of Regulatory Quality indicators for countries in which those HCs are located (Table 1).

Estonia, Lithuania, Latvia and Georgia are leading with highest Regulatory Quality indicators and all those countries showed more intensive improvements in quality of their regulatory frameworks (comparing 2012 and 2022, in percentiles):

- Georgia—from 72.04 to 81.60 (13.3%)
- Latvia—from 79.62 to 84.91(6.6%)
- Lithuania—from 82.94 to 87.74 (5.8%)
- Estonia—from 91 to 92.92 (2.1%)

Table 1 Regulatory quality indicator, Worldwide Governance Indicators, 2022

Economy	Percentile rank (0–100)*
High-income economies—non-OECD	**72.19**
High-income economies—OECD	**87.28**
Bulgaria	61.79
Croatia	68.40
Estonia	92.92
Hungary	64.62
Latvia	84.91
Lithuania	87.74
Poland	74.53
Romania	63.68
Slovakia	76.89
Slovenia	73.58
Upper-middle-income economies	**44.52**
Albania	57.55
Armenia	51.89
Azerbaijan	48.11
Bosnia and Herzegovina	45.75
China	36.79
Georgia	81.60
Kazakhstan	52.83
Kosovo	38.21
Moldova	54.72
Mongolia	42.45
Montenegro	69.34
North Macedonia	66.98
Serbia	56.13
Turkey	43.40
Ukraine	40.57
Lower-middle-income economies	**29.89**
India	50.94
Morocco	49.06
Nigeria	12.26
Uzbekistan	31.60
Zambia	32.08

Source: https://www.worldbank.org/en/publication/worldwide-governance-indicators/interactive-data-access

[a] Indicates rank of country among all countries in the world. 0 corresponds to lowest rank and 100 corresponds to highest rank

Table 2 Intensity of changes of Regulatory Quality indicators, 2012–2022

	'Going ahead' changes of +3% or more	'Falling back' changes of −3% or more	'Not moving' changes between −3% and +3%
High-income economies	Croatia (8.5%) Latvia (6.6%) Lithuania (5.8%)	Bulgaria (−10.7%) Hungary (−17.9%) Poland (−5.8%) Romania (−7.3%) Slovakia (−5.0%)	Estonia (+2.1%) Slovenia (+2.8%)
Upper-middle-income economies	Azerbaijan (45.0%) Georgia (13.3%) Kazakhstan (37.6%) Moldova (11.0%) Montenegro (25.2%) North Macedonia (11.3%) Serbia (10.7%) Ukraine (29.7%)	Armenia (−16.4%) Bosnia and Herzegovina (−11.4%) China (−13.7%) Kosovo (−26.7%) Mongolia (−7.7%) Turkey (−34.6%)	Albania (−2.1%)
Lower-middle-income economies	Uzbekistan (833%) India (51.4%)	Zambia (−9.8%)	Morocco (−1.4%) Nigeria (−47.9%)

Calculated from data https://www.worldbank.org/en/publication/worldwide-governance-indicators/interactive-data-access

The changes in the Regulatory Quality indicators have very high informational value, because they are evaluating interventions (or lack of them) into building a stimulative entrepreneurial context.

In 10 years (2012–2022) using Regulatory Quality indicators, the economies covered by this survey of HCs can be grouped as 'going ahead', 'falling back' or 'not moving' (Table 2).

There are some good and bad news from changes in the period 2012–2022: good news is that 13 economies (out of 30 included in this survey on HCs) are moving ahead by upgrading the quality of their regulatory frameworks. But, the bad news is that five (out of 10 high-income economies involved in this study on HCs) are falling back as well as six out of 15 upper-middle-income economies. It is a very important message to policymakers, which is additionally supported by collected opinions of HC owners/managers regarding the regulatory quality and access to finance in their countries.

3 What HCs Say About the Regulatory Quality and Access to Finance in Their Countries?

All interviewed HCs reported their needs for making regulatory frameworks more simple (Table 3) and have access to different types of financing the growth of their business ventures (Table 4).

Regulatory burden (complicated regulations, slow bureaucratic processes, delayed reactions on changes) directly influence competitiveness and value-adding

Table 3 What is wrong with regulatory frameworks in HCs' countries?—the position on the list represents the frequency of complaints/suggestions

Government bureaucracy
– Simplification of regulatory framework (Slovenia, Mongolia, Serbia, Morocco) —e.g. legal restrictions to establish childcare premises in a company (Slovakia) – Stable and friendly regulatory framework is missing, too bureaucratic, time-consuming, frequently changing laws and regulations (Poland, Romania, Mongolia) – No regular consultation with business regarding regulatory framework (Poland, Kazakhstan, North Macedonia) – Complicated administrative procedures to get government financial support (Poland) – Not clear and often conflicting regulatory recommendations related to AI is leading to regulatory uncertainty (EU vs. national solutions) (Estonia) – Difficult administrative requirements to enter the EU markets—standards (Morocco) – Complicated procedure to employ foreign workers outside of EU (visa, work permits) (Slovakia) – Labour law—to be less restrictive for employing people outside of a country and recognize new employment modalities (like platform employees) (Kazakhstan) – Expensive way to adjust regulatory framework to EU requirements (Montenegro)
Legal framework for supporting innovations and collaboration between business and research sector
– No stimulating programmes for collaboration between business and research sector (Poland, Romania, Bosnia and Herzegovina, Zambia)
The role of education sector in supporting businesses with growth potential
– Too slow process of changing curricula, administrative procedures are complicated and time-consuming (Romania, Bosnia and Herzegovina, Turkey, Zambia)
Tax burden
– Needed tax reliefs (Croatia, Latvia, Kosovo) to support growth and investments in R&D, as well as for exporting – Non-predictable tax regulations (Romania) – Tax policies to stimulate R&D within SMEs (Slovenia, Mongolia) – Tax refunds are slow, government is not paying any interest on not paid obligations: '*It also takes very long for the tax authorities to meet their obligation without an interest on the funds owed*' (Zambia)
General
– Political instability leads to unstable regulatory framework – To design globally competitive environment, e.g. join the World Trade Organization (Bosnia and Herzegovina) – Low level of understanding the regulatory framework among entrepreneurs (Azerbaijan) – Need for more local support (Morocco)

business processes. In this HC survey cycle, next to government bureaucracy, the absence of efficient and intensive collaboration between businesses and research sector was very much emphasized as a missing aspect of a supportive regulatory framework. For the first time, the role of education in providing innovative capabilities of businesses was specifically mentioned and openly requested to introduce programmes for jobs of the future.

Presented comments of interviewed HC owners/managers on regulatory frameworks and access to finance are in the line with World Bank's Regulatory Quality indicators, as well as many other surveys.

Table 4 What is wrong with access to finance in HCs' countries?—the position on the list represents the frequency of complaints/suggestions

Banks
– Limited capacity of local banks (Armenia)
Government support
– Missing financial support for innovations, R&D and export (and expansions in general) (Estonia, Hungary, Latvia, Armenia, Bosnia and Herzegovina, Georgia, Mongolia) – Special financial support for projects in selected industries (e.g. food and garment sectors (Mongolia) – High inflation rate—government support for export-oriented businesses (subsidies) is needed (Romania)
Type of financial sources
– Lack of long-term financial arrangements (through strategic partnerships, debt financing to drive further expansion and innovation (Croatia, Estonia, Hungary, Georgia, Kazakhstan) – Overdependence on banking loans, lack of other financial instruments (Georgia, Moldova, North Macedonia, Turkey) – No adequate financial support for businesses in growing/expansion phase (mostly focused on start-up phase) (Slovenia, Turkey) – Limited availability of venture capital (Bulgaria, Armenia) – EU grants for R&D are very helpful (Hungary)
Low financial literacy
– Financial institutions to invest in the clients' financial literacy (Bulgaria)

For example, Global Entrepreneurship Monitor, the largest worldwide survey on entrepreneurship, developed a composite index on quality of entrepreneurial context on national level and is implementing it from 2018. The composite index NECI (National Entrepreneurship Context Index) is composed of 12 components, among which are: access to entrepreneurial finance, government policy: support and relevance, government policy: taxes and bureaucracy, government entrepreneurship programmes, education for entrepreneurial competences and transfer of research into business ventures.

For years, the weakest scores are for government policy: taxes and bureaucracy, education for entrepreneurial competences and efficiency of collaboration between research and business sector (https://gemconsortium.org/report).

4 Conclusions and Recommendations

Hidden Champions represent invaluable yet often overlooked assets within national economies and act as powerful engines of innovation. Their potential can be significantly amplified through a well-structured entrepreneurial ecosystem—one in which policy, regulatory, financial, and educational components are seamlessly aligned to minimize friction and close structural gaps.

Insights from a 2022 study on Hidden Champions highlighted specific misalignments within the ecosystem that hinder its full potential. To maintain a dynamic and resilient entrepreneurial environment, it is essential to regularly consult international benchmarking tools—such as those measuring entrepreneurship (Global Entrepreneurship Monitor), competitiveness (IMD World Competitiveness Ranking, e.g. IMD 2025), ease of doing business, and transparency (OECD), regulatory and governance framework (World Bank). These assessments help uncover national trends, inform comparative analysis, and guide targeted responses to ecosystem inefficiencies.

Feedback derived from these instruments should inform policy refinement and help identify areas where systemic bottlenecks persist. Institutions across sectors—government, finance, education, and business support—should take into account the experiences of Hidden Champions, as their insights serve as a valuable diagnostic tool for enhancing the entrepreneurial landscape. Findings from 2022 study on Hidden Champions confirmed again that HC operates not as an isolated bubble (Simon, 1996) but in intensive and dynamic interactions with its environment and that HCs are more resilient on bad news (Simon, 2009).

For policymakers and institutions across sectors, listening to the experiences of Hidden Champions offers a valuable source of insight—an additional diagnostic instrument for shaping more effective, inclusive, and forward-looking entrepreneurship ecosystems. A smart, feedback-driven approach to policy, infrastructure, and institutional support not only sustains the momentum of current Hidden Champions but also nurtures the development of future ones.

References

Etzkowitz, H., Leydesdorff, L. (1995). The triple helix—university-industry-government relations: A laboratory for knowledge based economic development. Rochester, NY. SSRN 2480085.

From Government Policy to Business Acumen: Strategizing for Competitiveness in a Fragmented World. (2025). IMD World Competitiveness Center. https://imd.widen.net/s/rzpp6psbnc/from-government-policy-to-business-acumen.

Global Entrepreneurship Monitor—global reports. (n.d.). https://gemconsortium.org/report.

Isenberg, D. J. (2011). Introducing the entrepreneurship ecosystem: Four defining characteristics. *Forbes*..

OECD. (2022). 2022 Updated G20/OECD high-level principles on SME financing. *OECD SME and Entrepreneurship Papers*, No. 38, OECD Publishing, Paris, https://doi.org/10.1787/cd1f7694-en.

Porter, M. E. (1990). *The competitive advantage of nations*. Macmillan.

Shih, W. C. (2020). Global supply chains in a post-pandemic world. *Harvard Business Review*, 84.

Simon, H. (1996). *Hidden Champions: Lessons from 500 of the world's best unknown companies*. Harvard Business School Press.

Simon, H. (2009). *Hidden champions of the 21st century: Success strategies of unknown (World market leaders)*. Springer.

Simon, H. (2022). *Hidden Champions in the Chinese Century: Ascent and Transformation*. Springer Nature Switzerland AG.

Spigel, B. (2017). The Relational Organization of Entrepreneurial Ecosystems. *Entrepreneurship Theory and Practice*.

Stam, E. (2015). Entrepreneurial ecosystems and regional policy: A sympathetic critique. *European Planning Studies, 23*(9), 1759–1769. https://doi.org/10.1080/09654313.2015.1061484

Stam, E., & Spigel, B. (2016). Entrepreneurial ecosystems. In R. Blackburn, D. De Clercq, J. Heinonen, & Z. Wang (Eds.), *Handbook for Entrepreneurship and Small Business*. SAGE.

Worldwide Governance Indicators. (2024). Update, World Bank (www.govindicators.org), Accessed on October 30, 2024.

Slavica Singer is Professor Emerita at the Josip Juraj Strossmayer University of Osijek, Croatia (Faculty of Economics and Business). UNESCO recognized her academic and professional contribution in developing education for entrepreneurial competences, and from 2008 she is a holder of the UNESCO Chair in Entrepreneurship Education. Slavica's research focus is on connecting holistic approach with understanding of entrepreneurship as a mindset, the role of small businesses in the economic development, gender gap in entrepreneurship, entrepreneurship ecosystem and the role of the entrepreneurial university in the Quintuple Helix model (academia, government, business, civil society and environment). From 2010 she leads the interdisciplinary doctoral program ENTREPRENEURSHIP AND INNOVATIVENESS designed by collaborative efforts of five universities (Osijek, Croatia; Turku, Finland; Maribor, Slovenia; Klagenfurt, Austria, and Durham, UK). Next to students from Croatia, there are doctoral students from Bosnia and Herzegovina, Canada, China, Germany, Ghana, Greece, Kosovo, Nigeria, Oman, Pakistan, Spain, and USA. Slavica participates as guest speaker or panelists on numerous international conferences, and she is very active in researching different perspectives of entrepreneurship in international research teams, funded by EU funding schemes. She initiated participation of Croatia in Global Entrepreneurship Monitor (GEM) and from 2002 she leads the Croatian GEM team. Slavica is often engaged by the OECD as a consultant/expert in the field of reviewing national policies on entrepreneurship, inclusivity, and entrepreneurship education. In 2010 she was awarded with the honorary doctorate by the University of Turku, Turku School of Economics. In 2021, she was awarded with the European Entrepreneurship Education Award, by the Lund University (School of Economics and Management), Sweden.

Sunčica Oberman Peterka is a full professor at the Josip Juraj Strossmayer University of Osijek, Faculty of Economics and Business, where she teaches courses in entrepreneurship and strategy at the undergraduate, graduate, and postgraduate levels. She is also a member of the UNESCO Chair in Entrepreneurship Education. Before joining the university, she was a project manager, trainer, and consultant at the Osijek Centre for Entrepreneurship, and she currently serves as a member of its Assembly. She has been a member of the Global Entrepreneurship Monitor (GEM) research team for Croatia since 2002 and is also part of the research team of the CEPOR—policy center for small and medium-sized enterprises and entrepreneurship. She is a member of the European Council for Small Businesses and Entrepreneurship (ECSB), the Croatian Society of Economists and Croatian Corporate Governance and Management Society. Sunčica Oberman Peterka has participated in numerous EU-funded projects related to entrepreneurship and entrepreneurial education, and regularly conducts workshops and lectures on these topics. She has also participated in multiple accreditation processes organized by the Agency for Science and Higher Education of the Republic of Croatia. Her areas of interest include entrepreneurship education, entrepreneurial universities, authentic leadership, new venture creation, small business management, gender and entrepreneurship, and the quality of higher education.

Employees Are the Champions: Human Resource Management in Hidden Champion Companies

Amra Kožo

Abstract This chapter provides insights into the role and significance of human resources in hidden champion companies. Hidden champions (HCs) are typically highly specialized leaders in niche markets, with a strong focus on both internationalization and innovation strategies. The strength, adaptability, and resilience of these companies stem from visionary leadership and highly skilled employees who are educated and trained in specialized business areas served by HCs. HCs foster more personalized relationships with their employees which they achieve through a supportive and inclusive organizational culture. Considering the core activities of human resource management, HCs are primarily focused on attracting, developing, and retaining talented employees. Consequently, the most significant challenges for human resource management in HCs relate to the recruitment of qualified employees, providing education and training relevant and tailored to the particular workplace, and ensuring effective managerial succession. Still, the results of our research illustrate that organizational culture, talent management, education and knowledge sharing, employee empowerment, employee engagement, job satisfaction, motivation and well-being are areas where forward-thinking human resource activities are carried out.

1 Introduction

The business philosophy of hidden champions (HCs) was recognized and presented in the work of Hermann Simon in the 1990s (e.g., Simon, 1992, 1996). These companies are strategically focused on leadership in niche markets and oriented toward internationalization and the development of a strong technological base in their

A. Kožo (✉)
University of Sarajevo – School of Economics and Business,
Sarajevo, Bosnia and Herzegovina
e-mail: amra.kozo@efsa.unsa.ba

D. Berberović, D. Purg (eds.), *Hidden Champions in Rising Economies*, Contributions to Management Science,
https://doi.org/10.1007/978-3-032-08263-3_6

sectors. From the early beginnings, it was noticeable that motivated and qualified employees were among the main contributors to the success and recognition of HCs. Relationship networks built by leaders through the various aspects of organizational behavior, including organizational culture, motivation, and reward systems, form the basic operational framework and predict employee satisfaction.

The constant changes that have influenced the workplace globally over the past several decades have certainly (re)shaped the workplace in HCs. The accelerated changes brought by political, economic, sociodemographic, cultural, environmental, and technological factors have a profound influence on the workplace (Kožo et al., 2022). Global trends, such as the emergence of new communication tools, online shopping, increased competition, rapid technology development, artificial intelligence, increasing pressure for consistency in work-life balance and the ubiquitous idea of lifelong learning, are just some of the factors that actively influence and shape the modern workplace. In addition, migration trends add to workplace changes through the movement of a qualified workforce that seeks better work opportunities and higher living standards. Concurrently, employees are expected to be flexible in their career development, while companies should respond to the growing needs of their employees. Thus, managing employees, attracting and retaining talent, and keeping them motivated and dedicated to their work in a highly dynamic business environment where information is easily accessible and comparable, are becoming some of the leading challenges for all companies, including HCs.

To date, the literature on human resource management in HCs is scarce, and only a limited number of studies directly address the topic of human resources in HCs. To be more precise, although most of the research on HCs implies the importance of employees in HCs, a negligible number of studies are specifically devoted to the area of human resource management in HCs. According to recent literature review on HCs conducted by Schenkenhofer (2022), research on HCs can be divided into four main groups: (1) internationalization strategies, (2) R&D and innovation strategies, (3) worldwide and regional geographic distribution of HCs, and (4) other research that could not be categorized into one of the first three groups. Indeed, works on human resource management in HCs fall into the last group, due to the small number of studies on the topic. Therefore, this chapter aims to: (1) provide new insights into human resource management concepts, activities, and challenges prevalent in HCs and (2) outline the human resource needs that HCs face, particularly emphasizing educational requirements. Hence, this chapter describes human resource management concepts, activities, challenges and educational needs prevailing in the work of HCs, based on interviews with HCs conducted in 30 countries. The current human resource practices of HCs may also serve as a roadmap for other companies that align their business strategies with strategic directions of HCs, helping them shorten their learning curves.

After the introduction, the chapter continues with an overview of human resource management, which ensures a stable yet dynamic and challenging work environment in which HC employees can develop their full potential and thus contribute to the company and the environment in which they operate. The third part of the chapter addresses the educational needs of HC employees and the ways in which HCs gain access to knowledge and generate knowledge independently, often serving as knowledge pioneers. The final section of the chapter draws conclusions based on the research and presents recommendations for future work.

2 Human Resource Management in HCs

Human resource management refers to the design and application of formal systems within an organization that enable the effective and efficient utilization of talent to achieve organizational goals (Daft & Marcic, 2015). It encompasses all activities planned by the company to identify suitable and qualified employee profiles for specific jobs, ensure the best fit between an employee and job requirements, develop employees, retain top talent, and enable them to reach their full potential. Hence, the knowledge, skills, abilities, and experiences of employees are the crucial organizational assets essential for building and maintaining long-term competitive advantages.

In a rapidly changing business environment characterized by technological development, HCs rely on their core activities and internal strengths that enable them to operate successfully and exhibit high resilience in selected markets. According to Simon (1996), an HC is made up of three nested circles: the core, the inner circle, and the outer circle. The core is represented by strong leadership and ambitious goals, and is a pillar of the company's competencies. The inner circle of competencies is based on motivated employees, continuous process and product innovation, and reliance on the company's own strength. The outer circle focuses on external opportunities, including niche markets, global orientation, and competitive advantages. By balancing the three nested circles, HCs develop dynamic capabilities, as they build and adapt their internal and external competencies in response to continuous changes. Constant changes require businesses to rethink their approach and to have motivated employees with a penchant for innovative behavior, as well as to design and implement new ways of doing business (Turulja & Kožo, 2022).

As stated above, knowledge of human resource management in hidden champion companies remains underexplored. A search in the Web of Science and Scopus databases yielded a modest number of works that focus on human resource management in HCs.[1] Specifically, two journal articles were found that address specific aspects of human resource management in HCs, with this topic as the central focus of research. One of them, written by Garaus et al. (2016), employs a qualitative methodology to investigate how an ambidextrous human resource system can function as a high-performance work system, facilitating flexibility, efficiency, and knowledge integration. The other, authored by Mear and Werner (2021), presents a conceptual

[1] The search within article title, abstract, and keywords is conducted by combining the search terms "hidden champions," "human resource management," "human resource practices," and "human resource systems," and only a few results were found within the articles, books, book chapters, and conference papers.

analysis based on case studies and discusses the relationship between human resource management and innovation in HCs by identifying the role of subsidiarity.

Most of the other works found in the two databases observe human resources as one of the key factors of success among HCs, however, these studies do not primarily focus on studying human resource management topics in works on HCs. For example, in their study on HCs, Voudouris et al. (2000) explore factors that contribute to the success of HCs, and among other things, they identify human resource management practices. In their chapter on HCs in Bosnia and Herzegovina, Berberović et al. (2021) present employee loyalty as one of the factors contributing to the success of HCs. In a chapter dedicated to management and leadership development needs in HCs, among other identified needs, Kožo and Braček-Lalić (2021) emphasize human resource management (such as recruiting and talent development) and educational needs (such as in-house training and stronger collaboration with educational institutions). In light of this dearth of literature, the topic of human resource management in HCs requires further research.

This chapter stresses the importance and role of the overall organizational setting for human resource management. Firstly, all observed HCs emphasized that employees are their primary organizational resource and the key to continuous organizational success. They are passionate, fearless, eager to learn and share knowledge, flexible, creative, and curious, which contributes to the innovative business solutions that distinguish HCs from other companies. It is certainly noticeable that companies that attract such a profile of employees already foster an open and supportive culture that enables the personal and professional development of employees.

Secondly, several common concepts pertinent to human resource management and crucial for a prosperous business were identified in HCs, including: organizational culture, talent management, knowledge sharing, employee empowerment, employee engagement, job satisfaction, motivation, and well-being. The application of these organizational variables establishes a comprehensive organizational framework within which motivated, dedicated, and loyal employees can operate. Their main characteristics, as recognized and implemented in the work of HCs, are described below.

Organizational Culture In HCs, organizational culture is closely tied to visionary leadership and the entrepreneurial mindset of the company's founder. In these companies, organizational culture has the power to attract and retain skilled and qualified employees. Generally, it is a caring and supportive culture based on values that promote employee development, mutual support, and respect. In HCs, organizational values are promoted through internal networking, often through casual everyday conversations. Employees' initiative and new ideas are welcome. However, they should be accompanied by responsibility and productivity. Most often, HCs describe their organizational culture as a learning and knowledge-sharing culture, as well as a culture of excellence that fosters innovation, encourages creativity, promotes thinking outside the box, and allows risk-taking. Innovation rooted in such organizational culture is one of the pillars of competitive advantages of HCs. Ultimately, this kind of organizational culture empowers HCs to establish a flexible and adaptable work framework that enables companies to build resilience.

Talent Management HCs recognize that attracting, developing, and retaining top talent is one of the most challenging tasks, especially for companies operating in niche markets, which HCs do. As mentioned earlier, organizational culture is one of the strongest pull factors that HCs rely on to attract talent. Since they are aware that talent loss incurs high costs and is time-consuming in terms of replacing the right people, HCs proactively invest in their existing employees. This practice is particularly relevant for developing employees and preparing them for managerial positions at different levels. Additionally, HCs appeal for stronger cooperation with educational institutions, as they are willing to recruit and invest in the development of young talent from the early stages of their careers. Additional appeals are directed at policymakers to enable better mobility and access to global talent and facilitate remote working conditions for workers located abroad, who are needed due to their industry-specific knowledge and expertise.

Knowledge Sharing Qualified and trained staff provide high-level performance. Intraorganizational knowledge sharing is a crucial aspect of organizational culture, reflecting the commitment of HCs to continuous development and lifelong learning. Indeed, HCs are learning organizations.

Employee Empowerment Delegating duties and responsibilities, transferring authority, and involving employees in everyday decision-making contribute to employee empowerment. Employee empowerment relies on mutual trust between the company and its employees. Additionally, management of HCs is committed to developing employees and identifying future leaders through this mode of employee participation.

Employee Engagement To foster innovation and remain competitive in a niche market, HCs nurture and promote employee engagement. Only engaged employees are fully absorbed and dedicated to challenging work tasks. Some of the HCs achieve a higher level of engagement through supportive organizational culture, supervisor feedback, social cohesion among coworkers, and open communication. Employee engagement and employee empowerment are associated with higher staff retention rates.

Job Satisfaction Human resource strategy in HCs usually relies on a human-centric approach that prioritizes employee growth and development. Investing in employees enables them to develop skills, acquire knowledge, and reach their full potential, ultimately leading to greater job satisfaction. Continuous investment cultivates a competitive and reliable workforce, as satisfied employees are less likely to leave their companies for better job opportunities.

Motivation Motivational packages include both financial and nonfinancial forms of compensation. Bonus policies are among the most preferred forms of rewards. Motivated employees are actively and energetically involved in their work assignments, which contributes to high work productivity and employee performance.

Well-Being In HCs, investment in employee well-being is perceived as investment in professional development. Well-being policies are integrated into the leadership model, meaning that leaders promote and prioritize the work-life balance of their employees. Interestingly, some of the HCs view well-being as an integral part of their commitment to the United Nations Sustainable Development Goals 2030 (Goal 3), which promotes a healthy lifestyle, thereby contributing to the health and well-being not only of the company but also of broader society.

The critical role of employees in HCs is best illustrated by the statements of HCs that, among other things, identify "highly skilled professionals" (Moldova), "employees" (North Macedonia), "high core technical knowledge and experienced professionals" (Slovenia) as the cornerstone of their strategies for building competitive advantages.

Next, the core activities of human resource management in HCs involve attracting, developing, and retaining qualified and skilled employees. Their desire to stay out of the limelight is evident in the way they recruit employees in the global talent competition. Since HCs are not as visible as high-profile global corporations, in attracting top talent they rely on an open, supportive, and challenging organizational culture that encourages employee development and facilitates professional growth and advancement. To retain top performers, HCs ensure competitive compensation, flexible work arrangements, and various development opportunities, including training and education.

At the same time, the most significant challenges faced by human resource management in HCs include finding a qualified workforce, addressing specific educational needs, and managing managerial succession. The shortage of qualified employees in various occupations and the limited pool of industry-specific specialists present some of the greatest challenges for HCs. For instance, HCs are faced with the lack of different types of engineers, IT professionals, marketing specialists, technically qualified workers, blue-collar workers, artisans and similar professions. Many of the HCs develop in-house education for specific needs, which, however, is not in itself enough to meet their needs. Thus, HCs work on developing partnerships with educational institutions, but also try to recruit globally, which is often quite challenging due to the demanding administrative procedures. Although a broader discussion on the educational needs of HCs is presented in the following section of this chapter, it is worth mentioning another challenge faced by HCs related to mid-level managers who need to develop and improve their delegation skills. By learning to transfer responsibility for specific tasks to their subordinates, managers free up time needed for higher-value activities, while at the same time delegation empowers employees.

Furthermore, HCs highlight the importance of effective managerial succession. As the business expands and HCs grow, founders and senior-level managers typically need to select and prepare younger managers to succeed them in managerial positions and take on corresponding responsibilities. Successor managers usually undergo a mentorship and leadership program that fosters behavior aligned with long-term strategic thinking and ensures business continuity. By the time HCs transfer managerial duties and responsibilities to the next generation of managers, some of them decide to move toward the professionalization of management to ensure control and effectiveness. Additionally, knowledge transfer is facilitated among different generations of managers to ensure sustainable business operations and provide certainty for stakeholders.

3 Education and the Educational Needs of Human Resources in HCs

HCs cultivate the learning and development of their human resources, thereby ensuring continuous advancement in business operations. Given their size, work organization, and overall commitment to excellence, HCs are adaptable, resilient, and enthusiastic about embracing new challenges presented by the markets in which they operate. Their readiness to act as first movers or first responders to challenging market demands originates from their business philosophy and strategic commitment to innovation, continuous development, and learning. At the same time, this adaptability is one of the reasons why HCs succeed even in uncertain business conditions.

These companies attain high levels of achievement through ongoing investment in the development and training of their human resources. Employees are likely to acquire, test, and implement new knowledge and skills related to evolving work methods and techniques. Additionally, employees display prosocial behavior, as they are willing to benefit their coworkers and the company. Therefore, HCs recognize that investing in employee education is essential for their success and business continuity.

Nevertheless, as steady leaders in niche markets, HCs require general and industry-specific knowledge. In the interviews, HCs noted a shortage of qualified employees across various occupations and different industry backgrounds. The most commonly identified educational needs of HCs are grouped and described below and presented in Fig. 1.

1. **Leadership and management competencies.** This group of educational needs refers to managerial skills such as delegation, communication, decision-making, motivation, and leadership competencies.
2. **Business-related knowledge.** A wide range of educational initiatives, including finance, marketing, digital marketing, human resource management, quality management, customer relationship management, business-to-business sales,

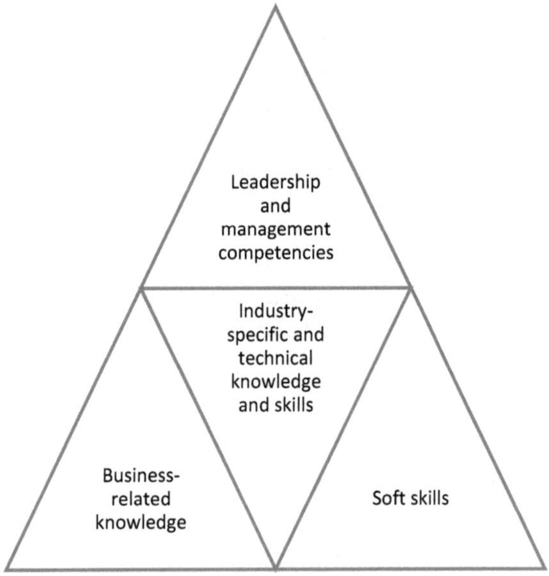

Fig. 1 Educational needs of HCs

international business strategy, innovation management, crisis management, and change management are encompassed in this group.

3. **Industry-specific and technical knowledge and skills.** Educational needs in this group refer to the knowledge and skills required to perform job-specific tasks, including digital skills, skills related to digital transformation, technical skills, and IT skills. Additionally, education in the STEM disciplines is included as well.
4. **Soft skills.** This group of skills encompasses professional communication, both with coworkers within an organization and external stakeholders, as well as teamwork.

Indeed, not all HCs have the same educational needs. Their needs depend on their internal and external environments (i.e., industry, and the education system in the country of origin of a particular HCs). Most of the time, the educational needs of HCs are addressed through the recruitment of qualified employees. The specific education-related needs of HCs often arise rapidly, and HCs cannot afford to wait for educational institutions to provide solutions. Additionally, the number of graduates who complete the formal education annually is often insufficient to meet the needs of HCs that recognize their own specific educational needs and organize various in-house training programs. When seeking new methods to improve business, employees act as change agents, promoting transformational learning, enhancing their professional growth, and facilitating change that has holistic effects within organizations.

However, HCs believe that there is room for fruitful collaboration with educational institutions, especially higher education institutions. Firstly, HCs tend to organize practical training in different disciplines for their employees in cooperation with higher education institutions. Moreover, higher education institutions can establish entrepreneurial incubators and help spread the entrepreneurial spirit, knowledge, and skills among students whom the HCs will recruit. Second, HCs call for higher education institutions to be agile and act proactively, so that they can adjust and align their educational programs and traditional curricula more quickly with the needs of prosperous businesses. Here, higher education institutions should offer a broad spectrum of executive education programs and also develop lifelong learning training and courses that are relevant to the knowledge and skills required by HCs. Therefore, formal education should be aligned with new emerging professions and the actual needs of companies.

Knowledge transfer, learning, and development should take place within a broader ecosystem. This is why cooperation among higher education institutions, industry, relevant government agencies, and appropriate financial institutions can benefit all parties involved, and most importantly, it can help stop brain drain and contribute to societal development. Naturally, to achieve this, governments and decision-makers should prioritize investment in education.

4 Conclusion

In times of unpredictable business challenges, human resources are more than ever a most potent source of a company's strength and resilience, and HCs are no exception. Their employees generate, test, and implement innovative business ideas that enable the organization to respond quickly to market needs. Hence, through well-developed practices, motivated and empowered employees, human resource management can play a crucial role in achieving planned organizational performance. HCs are characterized by an organizational culture oriented toward excellence and high performance. The insights from the interviewed HCs suggest that core human resource activities are related to attracting, developing, and retaining qualified employees. The recruitment of qualified employees with specialized knowledge, training, and education, along with generational transition, is the biggest human resource challenge among HCs. Champions often overcome these challenges by developing internal training and knowledge transfer systems and working on their own, without external support. At the same time, HCs invite educational institutions to cooperate, which can facilitate the fulfillment of the needs for educated, skilled, and trained employees in specific occupations.

Given the limited research on human resources in hidden champion companies, we encourage further investigation into this area. This chapter is based on interviews conducted with experienced professionals and higher-level managers in HCs. To provide a more robust understanding of the activities and needs of human resources in HCs, further studies on human resource management in HCs should incorporate employees' perspectives. Lastly, since a significant portion of research on HCs and human resources among HCs is based on qualitative methodology, we suggest adopting a quantitative methodology for human resources among HCs as well.

As a practical consideration, collaboration between educational institutions and HCs is advised. HCs and educational institutions should cooperate to develop and offer customized educational programs and specialized training for employees, addressing the talent shortage in the market, while also facilitating further development for talented, motivated, and committed employees. There is no doubt that behind every successful company are motivated, dedicated, and loyal employees.

References

Berberović, D., Činjarević, M., Kožo, A., & Brkić, N. (2021). Hidden champions of Bosnia and Herzegovina. In A. Braček-Lalić & D. Purg (Eds.), *Hidden champions in dynamically changing societies: Critical success factors for market leadership* (pp. 107–122). Springer. https://doi.org/10.1007/978-3-030-65451-1_9

Daft, R., & Marcic, D. (2015). *Understanding management*. Cengage Learning.

Garaus, C., Güttel, W. H., Konlechner, S., Koprax, I., Lackner, H., Link, K., & Müller, B. (2016). Bridging knowledge in ambidextrous HRM systems: empirical evidence from hidden champions. *The International Journal of Human Resource Management, 27*(3), 355–381. https://doi.org/10.1080/09585192.2015.1045007

Kožo, A., & Braček-Lalić, A. (2021). Hidden champions: Management and leadership development needs. In A. Braček-Lalić & D. Purg (Eds.), *Hidden champions in dynamically changing societies: Critical success factors for market leadership* (pp. 57–65). Springer. https://doi.org/10.1007/978-3-030-65451-1_6

Kožo, A., Hodžić, I., & Bičo-Ćar, M. (2022). Job insecurity and psychological safety in the workplace: Evidence from Bosnia and Herzegovina. In *International conference "New Technologies, Development and Applications"* (pp. 981–990). Springer. https://doi.org/10.1007/978-3-031-05230-9_115

Mear, F., & Werner, R. A. (2021). Subsidiarity as secret of success: "Hidden Champion" SMEs and subsidiarity as winning HRM configuration in interdisciplinary case studies. *Employee Relations: The International Journal, 43*(2), 524–554. https://doi.org/10.1108/ER-03-2020-0141

Schenkenhofer, J. (2022). Hidden champions: A review of the literature & future research avenues. *Management Review Quarterly, 72*(2), 417–482. https://doi.org/10.1007/s11301-021-00253-6

Simon, H. (1992). Lessons from Germany's midsize giants. *Harvard Business Review*, 115–123.

Simon, H. (1996). You don't have to be German to be a "Hidden Champion". *Business Strategy Review, 7*(2), 1–13. https://doi.org/10.1111/j.1467-8616.1996.tb00118.x

Turulja, L., & Kožo, A. (2022). Modeling employee job performance through organizational communication, organizational commitment and innovative behavior. In *International conference on sustainable development* (pp. 109–128). Springer. https://doi.org/10.1007/978-3-031-17767-5_9

Voudouris, I., Lioukas, S., Makridakis, S., & Spanos, Y. (2000). Greek hidden champions: Lessons from small, little-known firms in Greece. *European Management Journal, 18*(6), 663–674. https://doi.org/10.1016/S0263-2373(00)00057-8

Amra Kožo is an Associate Professor at the University of Sarajevo, School of Economics and Business, Management and Organization Department. She obtained her Ph.D. degree from Marmara University, Institute of Social Sciences (Istanbul, Turkiye). Amra gained teaching and research experience at the University of Sarajevo, School of Economics and Business and participated via Erasmus Mobility programs at Lille Catholic University (Lille, France), Wroclaw University of Economics and Business (Wroclaw, Poland), and Porto Accounting and Business School (ISCAP, Porto, Portugal). During her academic career, she attended various educational programs related to her field of interest and also served as a trainer and educator for the business community. Amra has participated in several domestic and international projects related to sensitive social groups (i.e., women and youth) as a researcher or evaluator (national stakeholder). She is (co)author of more than 25 papers published in indexed journals and conferences, six chapters in books, one book, and one book's editor. Her primary research interests are organizational behavior, human resource management, and cultural studies. For her scientific work, Amra obtained a reward from the University of Sarajevo (2021). Some of her current projects are related to sustainability competencies in higher education and Global Leadership and Organizational Behavior Effectiveness (GLOBE) 2020 research.

IT Innovations of Hidden Champions

Linan Lei, Xiaobo Wu, and Yuan Xiang

Abstract Global digital technology is undergoing a profound transition from information technology (IT) to digital technology (DT). As cloud computing, big data, artificial intelligence, and the Internet of Things become increasingly mature, IT has gradually acquired capabilities in data mining, intelligent analysis, and autonomous decision-making, transforming from passive process tools into proactive value creation engines. The digitalization of global hidden champions exhibits distinct regional characteristics: Germany focuses on technological deepening and process reengineering with Industry 4.0 at its core; the United States leverages software and AI to build open ecosystems, dominating value chains through open source and standard setting; Japan integrates the Industrial Internet with lean production as its foundation to achieve process standardization; China achieves rapid application implementation under policy empowerment, demonstrating unique advantages of high R&D investment intensity and agile application transformation, effectively driving industrial transformation and upgrading through technology integration and scenario innovation. Digital technology is propelling hidden champions to evolve from "irreplaceable technological nodes" to "global ecosystem leaders." The key to future competition lies in transitioning from "single-point technological leadership" to "ecosystem leadership." Firms must deepen fundamental

L. Lei (✉) · Y. Xiang
International Research Center for Hidden Champions, International Campus, Zhejiang University, Jiaxing, China
e-mail: leilinan@zju.edu.cn; yuanxiang@intl.zju.edu.cn

X. Wu
School of Management, Zhejiang University, Hangzhou, China

International Research Center for Hidden Champions, International Campus, Zhejiang University, Jiaxing, China
e-mail: xbwu@zju.edu.cn

D. Berberović, D. Purg (eds.), *Hidden Champions in Rising Economies*, Contributions to Management Science,
https://doi.org/10.1007/978-3-032-08263-3_7

technology breakthroughs and ecosystem collaboration capabilities while maintaining innovation vitality, building diverse innovation teams and open ecosystems to forge sustainable competitive advantages in the digital wave.

1 Digital-Driven Innovation in Hidden Champion Enterprises

In today's era of global digital transformation, hidden champions specializing in niche markets are encountering unprecedented innovation opportunities. While these companies may be modest in size, they command technological leadership in their respective domains, and the deep integration of digital technologies is fundamentally redefining their competitive advantages. As they transition from traditional specialized production to smart manufacturing, these hidden champions leverage IoT (Internet of Things), artificial intelligence, and big data to not only enhance production efficiency and product quality, but more importantly, to construct entirely new business models. More critically, digital transformation enables these hidden champions to transcend geographical and scale limitations, achieving global reach through digital platforms and extending their specialized capabilities to broader market spaces. This innovation not only reinforces their positions in traditional areas of strength, but also establishes a solid foundation for sustainable future development. This phenomenon does not exist in isolation, but represents a significant microcosm of the broader tide of global digital technology evolution. To deeply understand the underlying logic of digital innovation among hidden champions, it is essential to return to the origins of digital technology development and examine this profound transformation from information technology to digital technology.

1.1 The Development of Global Digital Technology

Global digital technology is undergoing a profound transition from IT to DT with the essence of this transformation being enterprises' strategic shift from "process efficiency tools" to "data value engines." Early information technology primarily served data storage, transmission, and basic processing functions, with systems like Enterprise Resource Planning (ERP) and Customer Relationship Management (CRM) focusing on optimizing process efficiency. However, with the maturation and application of emerging technologies such as cloud computing, big data, artificial intelligence, and the Internet of Things, technological systems have gradually acquired advanced capabilities including data mining, intelligent analysis, and autonomous decision-making, evolving from passive process support tools into proactive value creation engines. Information technology (IT) is an important means to address innovation challenges (Andrade-Rojas et al., 2024; Karhade & Dong, 2021;

Kohli & Melville, 2019). The core of this transformation lies in the fundamental restructuring of data's role: data has shifted from being a "by product" of business operations to becoming a core "production factor," while technology has evolved from traditional "supporting means" to the "driving core" of business development. From a theoretical perspective, digital technology serves as the source of digital industrialization, driving traditional industry transformation through industrial digitalization and gradually building a comprehensive digital economy system (Goldfarb & Tucker, 2019). Digital technology not only provides technical support for supply chain flattening and shortening while strengthening intermediate goods market functions, but also effectively reduces enterprise costs and enhances productivity. As a key production factor, digital technology creates favorable conditions for enterprise innovation (Qi & Xu, 2020) and optimizes the overall innovation environment (Li et al., 2022). At the business practice level, this transformation manifests more directly. Traditional information technology primarily focused on cost reduction and efficiency enhancement, while digital technology is fundamentally restructuring business logic through the deep integration of data elements and intelligent algorithms. For instance, cloud computing and AI technologies have made data the core productive force, enabling retail enterprises to leverage real-time data analysis for predicting restocking needs and significantly improving inventory turnover efficiency. Accompanied by the rapid development of computer chip and software technologies, digital technology continues to mature, with platform economy and service-oriented transformation comprehensively disrupting traditional business models. Within the broader global economic landscape, this technological evolution is generating far-reaching impacts. Facing complex and volatile international trade environments, digital technology has become a key factor in enhancing global value chain resilience (Xie & Gao, 2025). Meanwhile, this technological transformation is triggering structural changes in labor markets, with impacts characterized by multi-dimensional penetration and paradigm reconstruction, fundamentally reshaping the global economic development landscape.

1.1.1 Digital Technology Reshapes the Global Competitive Landscape

Digital technologies centered on artificial intelligence, the Internet of Things, and big data are currently driving fundamental transformations in global industrial paradigms. According to data from the China Academy of Information and Communications Technology's Global Digital Economy White Paper (2024), in 2023, the combined digital economy of five countries—the United States, China, Germany, Japan, and South Korea—exceeded $33 trillion, representing year-over-year growth of over 8%. The digital economy's share of GDP reached 60%, an increase of approximately 8 percentage points compared to 2019. Industrial digitalization contributed 86.8% of this growth momentum. Throughout this process, enterprises face dual challenges: they must enhance the efficiency of existing operations through digital transformation while simultaneously pioneering new growth engines through innovation. Although these two concepts are often conflated, they differ fundamentally in nature. Digital transformation represents systematic business restructuring. The China Academy of Information and Communications Technology, in its "Enterprise Digital Transformation White Paper (2021 Edition)," defines enterprise digital transformation as "a comprehensive integration process between traditional production factors and digital technologies. Through the fusion of information, computing, communication, and connectivity technologies, it triggers major changes in enterprise productivity and production relationships, thereby achieving full-chain resource optimization and integration to better realize enterprise development performance." For instance, Schaeffler, a German automotive parts hidden champion, partnered with Ansys, a leading global engineering simulation software company, to embed simulation technology throughout the entire product development process. This enabled a leap from physical prototypes to digital twins, effectively shortening development cycles and reducing material waste. Such transformation does not alter the enterprise's core business logic but achieves "incremental evolution" through technological empowerment. Innovation, by contrast, represents disruptive value creation. Schumpeter (1912) defined it as the "recombination of production factors," encompassing five forms including new product development and new market creation (Li & Zhao, 2024). Ko et al. (2020) proposed an (IT)-based product innovation strategy, contending that the key for enterprises (especially small businesses) lies in "matching strategic orientation with IT core capabilities," making IT serve as a bridge connecting "strategic intent" and "innovation outcomes." Nambisan (2013) defined different roles that IT plays to trigger innovation processes or enable innovation outcomes. For example, Xiamen Liju, a Chinese automation hidden champion, combined traditional equipment manufacturing with digital technologies to develop modular intelligent production lines. This dramatically compressed customer customization cycles while expanding product applications from consumer electronics to new energy vehicles. Such innovation often breaks existing industry rules, achieving "leapfrog development."

1.1.2 Digital Transformation and Digital Innovation Practices of Hidden Champions

Digital Transformation As a global hidden champion in semiconductor dicing equipment, Japan's DISCO Corporation clearly demonstrates the core logic of digital transformation. Through ultra-precision technology penetration and comprehensive intelligent process transformation, the company has established an unshakeable competitive advantage in the semiconductor back-end process equipment market. At the technology penetration level, DISCO's self-developed laser dual-blade dicing saw (such as the DFL7361 model) achieves cutting precision of ±1 μm, serving top-tier global foundries including TSMC, Samsung, and Intel. In terms of process transformation, the company integrates equipment data from multiple global production bases through an Industrial Internet platform, establishing a real-time process optimization system.

Digital Innovation The innovation practices of KLA-Tencor, America's hidden champion in semiconductor inspection equipment, are manifested at two levels: At the technological paradigm shift level, traditional inspection relies on manually configured rule-based template matching, while KLA-Tencor's electron beam inspection system introduces AI-driven Automatic Defect Classification (ADC) technology. At the data asset reconstruction level, KLA-Tencor has built a semiconductor defect database containing over 1 billion defect images, covering comprehensive data from wafer to packaging processes. By sharing anonymized data with customers, its AI models can dynamically optimize inspection parameters. Additionally, its real-time temperature measurement system can capture data from over 2000 temperature points on wafer surfaces in real-time. Combined with machine learning models to predict process variations, it helps customers effectively reduce the standard deviation of etching uniformity. Through data-defined processes and AI-reconstructed inspection logic, KLA-Tencor accomplishes quality control and optimization of the physical world within virtual space. Its practices demonstrate that competition in the digital era essentially represents "data capabilities" delivering a dimensional reduction attack against "experience-based capabilities." The true moat for hidden champions lies in constructing irreparable closed-loop systems of inspection-data-optimization.

1.1.3 The Relationship Between Transformation and Innovation: Dual-Wheel Drive

In enterprise practice, transformation and innovation are not disconnected or antagonistic, but rather constitute a dynamic symbiotic system of "efficiency foundation-building → innovation breakthrough → renewed transformation and upgrading." Like dual wheels driving enterprise development, both are indispensable. Transformation serves as the "stable foundation" for innovation, constructing a support system for innovation through systematic optimization. The digital infrastructure, process capabilities, and organizational resilience accumulated during transformation become fertile ground for innovation incubation. DISCO achieved stable wafer yield through its Industrial Internet platform. This digital reconstruction of traditional processes not only consolidated the competitiveness of existing products but also provided high-quality training datasets for subsequent laser stealth dicing technology development through standardized real-time production data collection, making innovative breakthroughs engineering-feasible for implementation. Innovation serves as the "boundary-breaking engine" for transformation, injecting new momentum into transformation through disruptive breakthroughs. When market demands or technological paradigms shift, innovation can break through the "optimization boundaries" of existing transformation, propelling enterprises into higher-dimensional competitive spaces. For instance, Ansys, America's hidden champion in industrial software, built upon its deep expertise in engineering simulation software by integrating AI algorithms with digital twin technology to develop real-time predictive simulation tools, significantly enhancing computational efficiency for complex fluid dynamics. This innovation not only pioneered new tracks in intelligent design but also compelled the enterprise to reconstruct its R&D processes and talent systems—transitioning from the traditional "code development + physical validation" model toward an "AI-driven + virtual iteration" agile development paradigm, driving overall digital transformation into a new phase of "technology-defined processes." Innovation's value lies in "exploring incremental space," forcing transformation to break beyond the linear path of efficiency optimization and achieve reconstruction of business models and competitive rules. Transformation provides resources and risk mitigation for innovation, while innovation points the direction for transformation. The technological, data, and organizational capabilities accumulated through transformation support innovative breakthroughs, while the scaling of innovation outcomes drives enterprises from local optimization toward systematic reconstruction. Global hidden champions neither purely pursue efficiency nor blindly venture into innovation, but rather construct a balance of "transformation for foundation-building, innovation for breakthrough" within their specialized sectors, thereby establishing irreplaceable competitive advantages in the digital era.

1.2 Global Overview of Hidden Champions Digitalization

Globally, hidden champions are embracing digital transformation at an accelerating pace. These firms leverage digital technologies to enhance operational efficiency, expand market reach, and strengthen competitive advantages.

1.2.1 National Perspective: Digitalization Overview and Differentiation Among Hidden Champions

The digitalization processes of global hidden champion enterprises exhibit significant regional differences, stemming from variations in industrial foundations, industrial policies, technological pathways, and market demands across countries.

German hidden champions digitalization centers on the Industry 4.0 strategy, emphasizing technological depth and system integration. Their digitalization journey began with Programmable Logic Controller (PLC) and ERP technology applications during the Industry 3.0 era, subsequently deepening into "technology-defined processes" intelligent transformation during the Industry 4.0 phase. German enterprises maintain long-term stability in digital investments, with R&D and digitalization expenditures growing counter-cyclically during the pandemic. For instance, Harting, a hidden champion in industrial connectors, continuously improves plug-in industrial connector technology, while Linde Hydraulics, a hidden champion in hydraulic systems, has established "lights-out" inspection workshops. This "deep technology cultivation + process reengineering" model enables German hidden champions to maintain global leadership in precision manufacturing and industrial software.

American hidden champions digitalization centers on software and AI technologies, achieving value chain reconstruction through open ecosystem development. U.S. enterprises excel at dominating industry ecosystems through technological open-sourcing and standard-setting. For example, Upstart, a fin-tech hidden champion, leverages AI models to reconstruct credit assessment systems, effectively improving loan approval efficiency while providing technical capabilities to traditional banks through a SaaS model. This "software-defined hardware + ecosystem expansion" strategy enables them to create barriers in sectors like semiconductor design and fin-tech.

Japanese hidden champions digitalization features lean production and process optimization, emphasizing incremental improvement and scenario adaptation. Avex, a hidden champion in automotive high-precision valve cores, constructs an extremely standardized production system by integrating 5S management with Industrial Internet technologies. Its dynamic vision system monitors materials in real-time with tool positioning accurate to the millimeter level, incorporating all operations into digital traceability. In equipment intelligence, the hub bearing assembly line can make autonomous decisions: automatically switching to backup solutions when detecting anomalies and synchronizing data to engineer terminals, minimizing production interruption time. This "hardware intelligence + process standardization" model has created irreplicable precision manufacturing barriers in the automotive bearing sector, inheriting craftsmanship spirit while achieving dual improvements in efficiency and quality through digitalization, becoming an exemplar of "small but advanced hidden champions."

Chinese hidden champions (represented by "Specialized, Advancement, Differentiation and Innovation" enterprises) exhibit dual characteristics of policy enablement and application innovation in their digitalization. The state promotes enterprise "cloud and platform adoption" through policies such as the "SME Digital Transformation Guidelines," with Chinese hidden champions like Kingdee helping enterprises reconstruct product capabilities and delivery capabilities. Meanwhile, Chinese enterprises' digitalization emphasizes market response speed and scenario implementation. However, compared to German hidden champions, Chinese enterprises still face gaps in global expansion and fundamental technological innovation. For instance, Tripod Technology, a global hidden champion in printed circuit boards, reported in its 2024 annual report that overseas revenue accounts for less than 25%, with core equipment still relying on some imported components. This characteristic of "leading application innovation, catching up in foundational technology" highlights the developmental features of Chinese hidden champions in their digitalization journey—rapidly implementing applications leveraging policy enablement and market scenarios while launching efforts to transition "from catching up to running alongside" in deep technological waters.

1.2.2 Information Technology Innovation Models

Hidden champions IT innovation exhibits multidimensional characteristics that can be analyzed across four perspectives: products, industrial processes, industrial services, and ecosystems.

Product Perspective Digital products are those that can be transmitted through digital networks such as the Internet (Kalyanam & McIntyre, 2002). Today, digital technologies are deeply embedded in the core of many organizations' products, services, and operations. For instance, when drivers are troubled by bumpy roads and unpredictable suspension failures, German hidden champion Kern-Liebers developed intelligent suspension springs with embedded sensors that collect load data in real-time, predict service life through edge computing, and dynamically optimize suspension stiffness, successfully transforming from a component supplier to a "driving dynamics solution provider." American pharmaceutical delivery packaging hidden champion Aptar launched OSD antimicrobial droplet technology, achieving microbial barrier protection through pure physical sealing without preservatives while developing recyclable single-material pump heads. Its clients span globally, including renowned brands such as L'Oréal, Procter & Gamble, and Unilever, driving green transformation across the packaging industry chain.

Industrial Process Perspective Currently, based on widespread understanding of digital transformation, digitalized industrial processes involve deep integration of digital technologies with traditional industrial processes to achieve intelligent, automated, and efficient industrial production throughout the entire process. For example, Belgium's Bekaert, a hidden champion in steel cord, utilizes MES (Manufacturing Execution Systems) for real-time production data traceability, effectively monitoring production processes and product quality information to achieve intelligent manufacturing. From China, PCB cutting tool hidden champion Tripod Technology's smart factory deploys self-developed grinding machines, achieving equipment self-networking through 5G + MEC (Multi-access Edge Computing) to support communication and collaborative work between devices. Additionally, the production line achieves 89% OEE (Overall Equipment Effectiveness: an important indicator measuring manufacturing equipment efficiency, comprehensively considering multiple factors including equipment availability, performance, and quality), with unmanned night shift production exceeding 70%, significantly improving per capita output value.

Industrial Service Perspective The German Electrical and Electronic Manufacturers' Association (ZVEI) Digital Industry Services report indicates that digital industrial services can support enterprise digital transformation, including consulting, training, and integration, implementation, and operation of digital technologies, helping enterprises find suitable solutions for specific industries, plants, or processes to address challenges brought by digitalization. For instance, ServiceNow from the United States is a SaaS hidden champion focusing on IT Service Management (ITSM). Its core functions include IT service management and IT operations management. Using cloud platform architecture, it can easily scale and support different operating systems, databases, and browsers while providing a series of APIs and script libraries for developers to customize according to needs. After using the ServiceNow platform, users experience effectively shortened IT incident response times and significantly improved procurement approval efficiency. For example, Mitsubishi UFJ Bank in Tokyo reduced its procurement approval process from an average of 3.2 days to 11 min, with accuracy improving to 99.7%. Siemens Energy is Germany's energy hidden champion with deep technical expertise and rich experience in energy equipment R&D, manufacturing, and operations. Its remote operations platform connects over 2000 gas turbines globally, utilizing advanced AI technology and big data analytics for real-time monitoring and analysis of equipment operating conditions. The company launched an innovative "pay-per-generation" model, transforming from traditional equipment sales or fixed service fee models to one linked to customer power generation and revenue, achieving risk sharing and benefit sharing, enhancing customer stickiness, and improving the company's differentiated advantages in market competition.

Ecosystem Perspective A digital ecosystem is a network of loosely coupled contributors who interact closely to create shared value, with interdependent relationships among ecosystem partners—individual partners can only succeed when the ecosystem succeeds (Omar Valdez-De-Leon, 2019). For example, EBM Papst, the global hidden champion in ventilation fan markets from Germany, has established its own startup company called EBM Papst Neo in Dortmund. EBM Papst Neo works with local universities, two Fraunhofer institutes, and two other startups focusing on indoor ventilation. Japanese semiconductor hidden champion Shin-Etsu Chemical has built a global ecosystem centered on semiconductor materials, covering wafer manufacturing, equipment collaboration, hydrogen energy, and new energy sectors. Its partners include giants like TSMC, Samsung, Tokyo Electron, and Toyota, forming deep dependencies through technical standard control, vertical integration from polysilicon to wafer full-chain, and cross-industry collaboration. Together with the University of Tokyo and RIKEN (Japan's Institute of Physical and Chemical Research), they jointly develop new semiconductor materials (such as gallium nitride epitaxial layers) and photoresist formulations, accelerating technology commercialization ecosystems. Additionally, through data sharing and sustainable deployment, they achieve closed-loop integration from materials to applications, supporting global semiconductor industry and new energy development.

The essence of hidden champions digital innovation lies in transforming technological advantages into scenario-based capabilities. German enterprises excel in industrial interconnection and ecosystem collaboration, exemplified by Kern-Liebers' intelligent suspension spring "hardware + data" transformation and EBM Papst's collaboration with research institutions to build ventilation ecosystems, upgrading mechanical manufacturing to "dynamics solutions" through sensor embedding and industry-academia-research cooperation. American enterprises specialize in software definition and service reconstruction, such as Aptar driving packaging green revolution with OSD antimicrobial technology and ServiceNow reshaping IT service processes with SaaS platforms, excelling at creating new value through digital product design and subscription models. Chinese enterprises focus on manufacturing efficiency and scenario implementation, with Tripod Technology achieving unmanned cutting tool production lines through 5G + MEC, entering global supply chains through efficiency improvement and localized innovation. Japanese enterprises persist in material technology and standard barriers, with Shin-Etsu Chemical building semiconductor material ecosystems through photoresist patents and polysilicon full-chain control, forming "technology-standard-application" closed loops in collaboration with TSMC and the University of Tokyo. The core of digital innovation lies not in technology itself, but in the deep integration and collaborative resonance between technology and corporate DNA, industrial scenarios, and national resources.

2 Digital Transformation Practices of China's "Specialized, Advancement, Differentiation and Innovation" Enterprises

2.1 Current Development Status

On June 1, 2022, the Ministry of Industry and Information Technology (MIIT) issued the "Interim Measures for the Tiered Cultivation and Management of High-Quality Small and Medium-sized Enterprises," proposing a three-tier cultivation system for high-quality SMEs: innovative SMEs, "Specialized, Advancement, Differentiation and Innovation" (SADI) enterprises, and "little giant" enterprises. Today, China's "SADI" enterprises are drawing global attention for their digital transformation practices. According to our team's research, the "Report on the Innovation and Development of 'little giant' Listed Enterprises (2024)" shows that these companies are increasingly focused on digital transformation. In 2023, the 1935 listed companies included in the report mentioned digital transformation keywords 17,967 times in their annual reports—averaging 9.27 mentions per company, an increase of 0.51 mentions compared to the previous year. Notably, these enterprises remain technology-centric in their digital transformation efforts, with eight of the top ten most frequently mentioned keywords being technology-oriented rather than application-oriented. The three most referenced technologies were the Internet of Things (4297 mentions), big data (3758 mentions), and artificial intelligence (2883 mentions), followed by cloud computing and industrial Internet (Fig. 1).

From an industry perspective, the top five sectors focusing on digital transformation are: Computer, Communication and Other Electronic Equipment Manufacturing (5817 mentions), Software and Information Technology Services (5633 mentions), Instrument and Meter Manufacturing, Special Equipment Manufacturing, and General Equipment Manufacturing. Additionally, Ecological Protection and

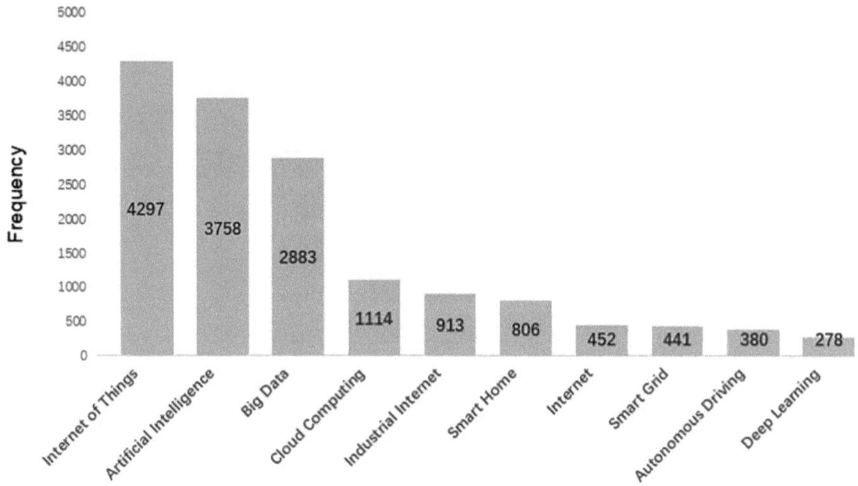

Fig. 1 Top ten digital transformation keywords by frequency among listed SADI firms. (Source: Report on the Innovation and Development of "little giant" Listed Enterprises (2024))

Environmental Governance, and Automobile Manufacturing have surpassed Rubber and Plastic Products and Chemical Raw Materials and Chemical Products Manufacturing, ranking ninth and tenth respectively. Technology-iterative industries (such as computer and software sectors) require companies to develop balanced capabilities across all four dimensions of "Specialization, Advancement, Differentiation, and Innovation." Highly standardized industries (such as chemical raw materials) rely more heavily on refined management and efficiency improvements (Fig. 2).

Furthermore, we analyzes ten industries with digital transformation keyword frequencies exceeding 100 mentions, revealing both common patterns and industry-specific characteristics in their focus areas. At the foundational technology level, all ten industries show significant interest in five core digital transformation technologies: big data, artificial intelligence, Internet of Things, cloud computing, and industrial Internet. Special equipment manufacturing demonstrates increased attention to deep learning, while Internet-related services and ecological protection and environmental management sectors place greater emphasis on machine learning. Railway, shipping, aerospace and other transportation equipment manufacturing, along with automobile manufacturing, focus more on connected networks. Regarding application scenarios, smart homes receive the most attention, followed by smart grids—indicating substantial market demand and technological maturity in these areas, which provides cross-industry collaboration opportunities for enterprises (Fig. 3).

Currently, China has 1118 national-level little giants in the AI industry, primarily distributed in Guangdong (184), Beijing (151), Zhejiang (117), and Jiangsu (102). Industry-wise, software and information technology services (259), research and

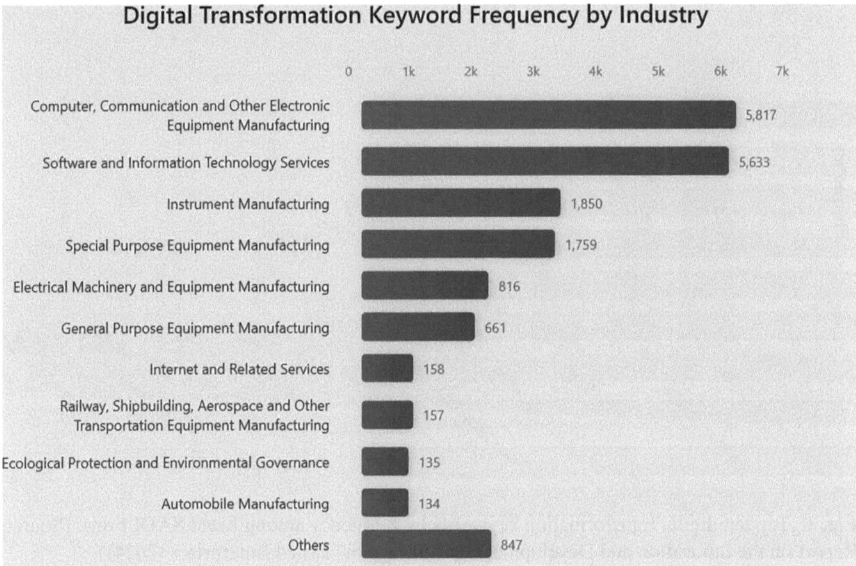

Fig. 2 Digital transformation focus by industry among SADI enterprises. (Source: Report on the Innovation and Development of "little giant" Listed Enterprises (2024))

Industry	Top6 Words					
Computer, communications and other electronic equipment manufacturing	Internet of Things (IoT)	artificial intelligence (AI)	big data	intelligent home	cloud computing	industrial internet
Software and information technology services	artificial intelligence (AI)	big data	Internet of Things (IoT)	cloud computing	industrial internet	intelligent home
Instrument Manufacturing	Internet of Things (IoT)	big data	artificial intelligence (AI)	cloud computing	industrial internet	smart Agriculture
Specialized equipment manufacturing	artificial intelligence (AI)	big data	Internet of Things (IoT)	cloud computing	industrial internet	deep learning
Electrical machinery and equipment manufacturing	smart grid	Internet of Things (IoT)	artificial intelligence (AI)	big data	intelligent home	industrial internet
General equipment manufacturing	artificial intelligence (AI)	Internet of Things (IoT)	big data	intelligent robot	industrial internet	e-commerce

Fig. 3 Digital focus for listed little giants (2023). (Source: Report on the Innovation and Development of "little giant" Listed Enterprises (2024))

experimental development (195), and professional technical services (134) rank top three, indicating high concentration of Chinese AI companies in software services and R&D (Fig. 4).

Regarding financing, the New Third Board has become the primary IPO channel for AI little giants with 92 companies, followed by the STAR Market (30) and

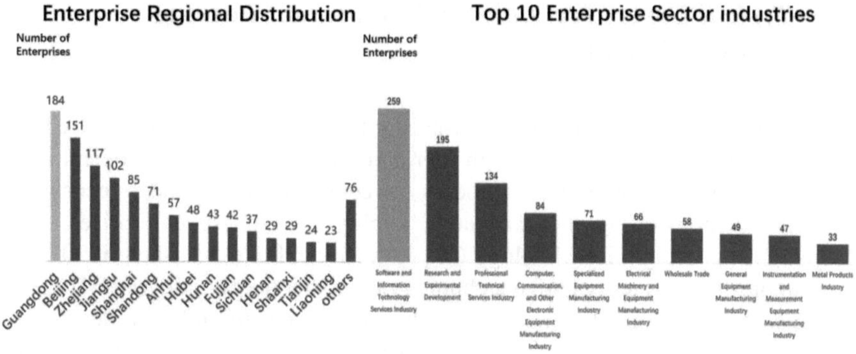

Fig. 4 Overview of national-level little giants in China's AI industry. (Source: Zhejiang Youshu Digital Technology Co., Ltd)

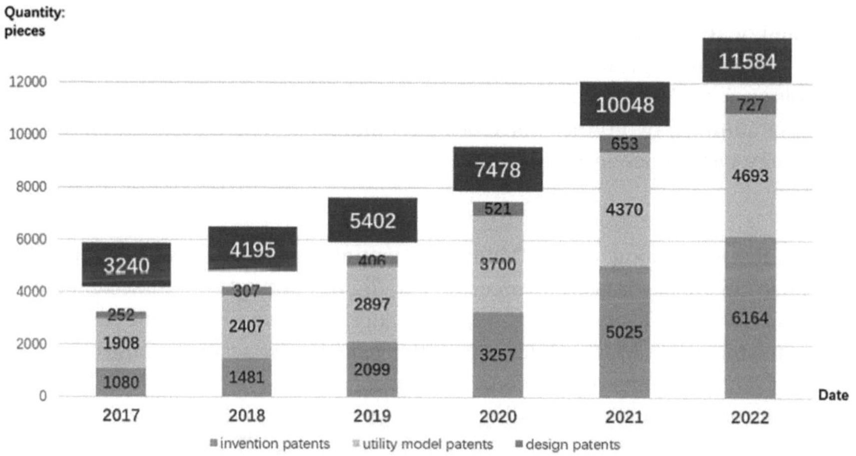

Fig. 5 Changes in the number of authorized patents for enterprises from 2017 to 2022. (Source: Shangqi Industrial Information Platform)

ChiNext (21). Between 2017 and 2022, Beijing (180) and Guangdong (111) saw the most active financing events, fully demonstrating these regions' leading positions in AI innovation and entrepreneurship. In terms of innovation capability, as of July 31, 2022, China's AI little giants held 11,584 authorized patents, including 6164 invention patents (53.21%), 4693 utility model patents (40.51%), and 727 design patents (6.28%). Patent numbers rapidly increased from 3240 in 2017 to 11,584 in 2022, with invention patents growing significantly from 1080 to 6164, demonstrating these enterprises' continuous investment in key technology R&D (Fig. 5).

2.2 Typical Cases: Technological Innovation Leading Industrial Change

Among the numerous "SADI" enterprises, digital technology companies are leading industrial transformation through four core dimensions—technological innovation, service upgrade, process reengineering, and ecosystem building—demonstrating the innovative vitality of Chinese enterprises. Take Zhejiang Lingdi Digital Technology Co., Ltd. (Style3D), established in 2015, as an example. This digitally native technology company deeply integrates 3D technology and artificial intelligence into the traditional apparel industry, developing professional-grade 3D fashion design software that addresses three major industry pain points: "lengthy design cycles, severe resource waste, and inefficient ecosystem collaboration," driving industrial transformation toward precision, flexibility, and sustainability.

Technological Innovation 3D + AI Reconstructs Design Productivity. Style3D centers on technological convergence innovation, deeply coupling 3D modeling technology with AI algorithms. Its developed 3D fashion design software breaks through traditional two-dimensional design limitations: AI-driven fabric simulation technology can render in real-time the drape, luster, and breathability of diverse fabrics.

Process Reengineering From "Months of Waiting" to "Hour-Level Delivery." The enterprise disrupts industrial process paradigms through digital technology: Traditional model: Design draft → Manual pattern-making → Multiple sample garment adjustments → Mass production, with cycles lasting several months and high costs per modification; Digital model: Designers utilize software to complete comprehensive digital creation including fabrics, structure, and dynamic effects within short time frames, directly outputting production-ready 3D pattern data that connects with intelligent cutting equipment on production lines, achieving a "design-production" full-cycle closed loop.

Service Upgrade From "Tool Supplier" to "Full-Chain Enabler." Style3D transcends traditional technology enterprises "tool mindset," constructing an integrated "design-collaboration-verification" digital service system. Through virtual model dynamic display systems, designers can verify realistic garment effects without creating physical samples, dramatically reducing sampling costs. Meanwhile, it supports online sharing of design data among brands, designers, fabric suppliers, and manufacturers, breaking down cross-departmental "information silos" and significantly improving project communication efficiency.

Ecosystem Building Creating "Digital Twin" New Infrastructure for the Fashion Industry. The enterprise constructs a cross-industry-chain digital ecosystem with digital assets as the connecting link. For example, the fabric digital asset library: designers can scan real fabric QR codes to high-precision reproduce fabric texture, drape, and other detailed characteristics in virtual scenarios. The system contains massive fabric data, providing diverse choices for design. The Style3D case demonstrates that digital transformation is not simply technological stacking, but rather reconstructing industrial value chains through comprehensive innovation, enabling "manufacturing" to evolve toward "intelligent manufacturing" and allowing "tradition" to embrace "renewal."

2.3 *Comparison Between Chinese and International Practices: Advantages and Challenges*

Compared to international hidden champions, China's "SADI" enterprises display distinctive advantages and challenges in digital transformation. These advantages are evident across several key dimensions: First, Chinese companies excel at rapid application scenario adaptation, transforming technological innovations into market applications with significantly shortened time frames from proof of concept to commercialization. This agility enables them to respond quickly to market changes and emerging opportunities. Second, these enterprises operate within a more vibrant open innovation ecosystem. For example, Shenzhen's open-source strategy contrasts sharply with the traditional patent protection models of European hidden champions, reflecting different approaches to knowledge sharing and collaborative development. Third, Chinese companies demonstrate exceptional cross-domain integration capabilities, skillfully combining technologies from different fields to create novel value propositions that transcend traditional industry boundaries. Our research provides quantitative analysis of 1935 listed companies from the first five batches, confirming these advantages. These enterprises show substantial R&D investment, with an average intensity of 9.9%—significantly exceeding the 6% of German hidden champions. This substantial R&D investment translates into concrete innovation outputs. From a patent perspective, these specialized enterprises represent a significant force in digital technology development, with over half of valid patents between 2021 and 2023 related to the digital economy. Each company holds an average of 22 relevant patents. Industries are highly concentrated in digital technology research (11,903 patents), display device manufacturing (11,326 patents), and IoT services and electronic component manufacturing (Fig. 6).

Digital transformation and data assets have become core drivers of high-quality development for "Specialization, Advancement, Differentiation, and Innovation" enterprises, demonstrating strong innovation capabilities and competitive market advantages. However, challenges remain equally evident. Compared to the deep industrial foundation of German hidden champions, Chinese enterprises still face shortcomings in core technology development. Their degree of internationalization is limited, with only about one-fifth of these specialized enterprises reporting overseas revenue. Simultaneously, gaps exist between these firms and international leaders in data asset valuation and governance system construction. Currently, these specialized enterprises are at a critical window period of technological paradigm

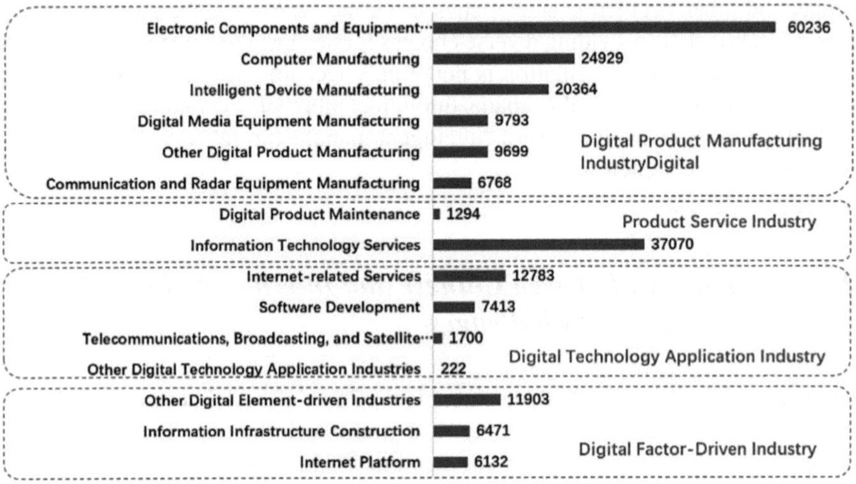

Fig. 6 Category distribution of patents in core industries of digital economy among listed SADI firms. (Source: Report on the Innovation and Development of "little giant" Listed Enterprises (2024))

shift. During this stage, companies need to leverage China's first-mover market advantages to explore new artificial intelligence application domains, adapt to technological paradigm changes, and drive business model innovation through digital technologies. This process requires companies to continuously learn and "unlearn," creating strategic opportunities for well-prepared enterprises. These specialized enterprises face management paradoxes in the digital era. Traditional hidden champion competitive advantages typically derived from exclusivity and uniqueness, while the digital age emphasizes inclusivity and complementarity. Companies need to strategically manage nonlinear changes, especially in an interconnected world supported by ABCDE technologies (Artificial Intelligence, Blockchain, Cloud Computing, Data, Edge Computing), reshaping competitive advantages through organized abandonment, nonlinear dynamics in value networks, and process innovation. This requires enterprises to build new organizational capabilities adapted to boundaryless ecosystems.

3 Future Outlook of Hidden Champions (Digital Area)

The core competitiveness of hidden champions in the information technology sector stems from their deep control over technological nodes and precise penetration of industrial chain ecosystems. Digital technology is reshaping the global hidden champion ecosystem across multiple dimensions: first, it breaks down geographical and scale limitations, enabling enterprises to serve global customer bases; second, open-source models and digital collaboration tools accelerate innovation and knowledge dissemination; third, the source of enterprise competitive advantage is shifting from pure technological superiority to comprehensive competitiveness in "technology, data, and services"; fourth, hybrid business models integrating hardware, software, and services are emerging. Under the global digitalization wave, these enterprises are experiencing a strategic transition from "single-point technological leadership" to "systemic ecosystem dominance." The core opportunity in the digital era lies in AI technology driving industrial transition from "experience-driven" to "data-defined" paradigms. American semiconductor inspection hidden champion KLA-Tencor, through building massive defect image databases and combining AI-driven automatic defect classification technology, has effectively compressed etching uniformity standard deviation, achieving an upgrade from equipment supplier to "process optimization decision-maker." German industrial software enterprise Ansys integrates AI with digital twin technology, developing real-time predictive simulation tools that reconstruct "physical verification"-dominated R&D processes into "AI-driven + virtual iteration" agile models. The combination of data and algorithms enables hidden champions to establish "data-algorithm-standard" trinity barriers, achieving the leap from "technology following" to "rule-making." The key to future competition lies in transitioning from "single-point breakthroughs" to "ecosystem construction": at the technological level, focus is needed on choke-point areas such as AI computing networks and industrial software open-sourcing, learning from Ansys's model of continuous investment in fundamental algorithm research and embedding AI into simulation tool foundations; at the ecosystem level, a "scenario-defined technology" strategy should be adopted to penetrate global industrial chains. China's Style3D "cloud tailor shop" model, through fabric digital asset libraries and virtual design ecosystems, promotes sustainable development in the fashion industry with "zero inventory, zero samples" concepts, demonstrating a new paradigm of global expansion combining "technology + scenarios + values." The ultimate competitiveness of hidden champions lies in becoming "irreplaceable nodes" in industrial chains, establishing "implicit technological barriers + explicit ecosystem dominance" composite advantages through three-dimensional coordination of "data-defined processes, software-defined products, standard-defined ecosystems," ultimately achieving value transition from hidden champions to "global ecosystem leaders."

The development of technological ecosystems and globalized trade present enterprises with the following core challenges: first, layout restructuring under tariff barriers—trade protectionism forces enterprises to adjust supply chains and shift toward regionalized deployment, but faces dual pressures of insufficient supporting systems and increased compliance costs; second, additional tariff requirements such as environmental standards and technical barriers further raise market entry thresholds, squeezing enterprise innovation investment space; additionally, data sovereignty requirements lead to fragmentation of global digital ecosystems, with localized storage restrictions limiting cross-regional collaboration efficiency, while privacy computing technology bottlenecks cause significant delays in cross-enterprise data sharing, making the contradiction between data compliance and commercial efficiency a long-term proposition; finally, core technological ecosystem dependency issues are prominent: bottom-layer technology dependence on open-source frameworks, patent barriers, and standard monopolies limit innovation freedom, causing enterprises to remain in passive following positions within industrial chains, making it difficult to participate in rule-making.

For hidden champion enterprises, we proposed following the principle of "global technological vision, localized implementation" in the digital era: maintaining close tracking of global technological frontiers while flexibly adjusting solutions according to local market demands. At the organizational level, diverse innovation teams need to be constructed, integrating talent from different cultural backgrounds and professional disciplines to promote cross-boundary innovation; utilizing data analysis to identify unique demands in different markets while establishing open innovation ecosystems through deep cooperation with global top research institutions and local universities. Currently, digital technology has become a key force driving global hidden champion transformation, with China's "little giant" enterprises demonstrating strong development momentum, with continuously growing patent portfolios and steadily improving innovation capabilities. Looking ahead, as emerging technologies such as artificial intelligence and robotics deepen their applications, enterprise digital transformation will enter more profound stages, creating new opportunities and challenges for specialized market leaders.

References

Andrade-Rojas, M. G., Kathuria, A., & Lee, H. H. (2024). Multilevel synergy of IT for operational integration: Competition networks and operating performance. *Production and Operations Management*. Forthcoming.

Goldfarb, A., & Tucker, C. (2019). Digital economics [J]. *Journal of Economic Literature, 57*(1), 3–43.

Kalyanam, K., & Mcintyre, S. (2002). The e-marketing mix. A contribution of the e-tailing wars[J]. *Journal of the Academy of Marketing Science, 30*(4), 487–499.

Karhade, P. P., & Dong, J. Q. (2021). Information technology investment and commercialized innovation performance: Dynamic adjustment costs and curvilinear impacts. *MIS Quarterly, 45*(3), 1007–1024.

Ko, W. W., Chen, C. H., Liu, G., Nguyen, B., & Takeda, S. (2020). IT-based product innovation strategies for small firms. *Information Technology and People, 33*(6), 1489–1514.

Kohli, R., & Melville, N. P. (2019). Digital innovation: A review and synthesis.[J]. *Inform Systems, 29*(1), 200–223.

Li, J., Zhang, J. L., & Dong, X. F. (2022). How does digital economy affect Enterprise innovation capability: Underlying mechanisms and empirical evidence [J]. *Economic Management, 8*, 5–22.

Li, L. Z., & Zhao, N. N. (2024). Schumpeter's legacy—tracing the intellectual origins of disruptive and combinative innovation in innovation studies[J]. *Sociological Research, 39*(6) 154–175+229–230.

Nambisan, S. (2013). Information technology and product/service innovation: A brief assessment and some suggestions for future research. *Journal of the Association for Information Systems, 14*(215–226), 1536–9323.

Qi, Y. D., & Xu, X. (2020). Enterprise management transformation in the digital economy era[J]. *Management World, 6*. 135–152+250.

Valdez De-Leon, O. (2019). How to develop a digital ecosystem: a practical framework[J]. *Technology Innovation Management Review, 9*(8): 43–54.
Xie, S. X., & Gao, X. R. (2025). Enterprise digital technology and global value chain resilience[J]. *International Economics and Trade Research, 41*(5), 21–36.

Linan Lei is an Assistant Professor of Innovation and Strategy at International Business School, Zhejiang University, and Deputy Director of the International Research Center for Hidden Champions.

Xiaobo Wu is Professor of Innovation and Strategic Management, School of Management, Zhejiang University. He is honored as Chang Jiang Scholar Professor by Ministry of Education, China, for his outstanding achievements in innovation and entrepreneurship research and education. He is director of National Institute for Innovation Management, and also director of the International Research Center for Hidden Champions at Zhejiang University. He also serves as the vice-president of The International Association for Management Development in Dynamic Societies (CEEMAN).

Yuan Xiang is a Researcher at the International Research Center for Hidden Champions, International, Campus, Zhejiang University.

Data-Driven Decision-Making: The Competitive Edge of Hidden Champions

Violeta Cvetkoska

Abstract Hidden champions, specialized, market-leading firms that dominate global niches are entering a decisive stage in their evolution where data-driven decision-making and artificial intelligence (AI) define sustainable competitiveness. Unlike corporate giants that scale through size, hidden champions leverage deep expertise, agility, and customer intimacy. Today, these advantages must be reinforced with analytics, big data, and AI to maintain leadership in volatile markets. This study examines how hidden champions can transform vast datasets into actionable intelligence, moving beyond intuition to precision-driven strategies. Through the integration of the five pillars of analytics: descriptive, diagnostic, predictive, prescriptive, and cognitive, combined with AI capabilities such as machine learning, NLP (natural language processing), computer vision, and agentic AI, hidden champions can anticipate demand shifts, optimize supply chains, personalize customer experiences, and foster resilience against disruption. The analysis highlights both opportunities and challenges of embedding data into organizational DNA, emphasizing the need for cultural transformation, ethical governance, and continuous learning. The success in the AI era will not belong to those with the most data, but to those who can harness it best. Hidden champions that master this transformation will redefine industry benchmarks, proving that the future of competition lies in the intelligent fusion of human expertise and digital intelligence.

> *The businesses and organizations that succeed with AI will be those that invest steadily, rise above the hype, make a good match between their business problems and the capabilities of AI, and take the long view.*
>
> – Thomas H. Davenport

V. Cvetkoska (✉)
Faculty of Economics-Skopje, Ss. Cyril and Methodius University in Skopje, Skopje, North Macedonia
e-mail: vcvetkoska@eccf.ukim.edu.mk

D. Berberović, D. Purg (eds.), *Hidden Champions in Rising Economies*, Contributions to Management Science,
https://doi.org/10.1007/978-3-032-08263-3_8

1 The Data-Driven Revolution for Hidden Champions

We live in an era where data is the most valuable asset a business can possess. It is the new currency of competition, the lifeblood of decision-making, and the foundation of innovation. Every click, transaction, and interaction generate a stream of information that, when harnessed effectively, unveils patterns, anticipates trends, and fuels smarter strategies. In this data-saturated world, companies that fail to embrace analytics and artificial intelligence (AI) risk irrelevance, while those that master these tools gain an unparalleled edge. The future belongs to those who can transform raw data into actionable intelligence, making precision-driven choices that propel them ahead of their competitors.

Hidden champions thrive in the shadows, quietly dominating niche markets while larger competitors battle for visibility. Their success is no accident, it is a product of relentless innovation, strategic agility, and an uncompromising focus on excellence. In the digital age, these companies must harness the transformative power of big data, advanced analytics, and artificial intelligence to sustain their competitive advantage. Data-driven decision-making is not just an enhancement to their strategy; it is a fundamental shift that redefines how they operate, innovate, and outperform rivals.

The shift from intuition to data-backed insights enables hidden champions to refine their strategies, optimize operations, and enhance customer experiences. Data no longer serves as a passive resource but as a dynamic driver of growth and differentiation. Companies that fail to recognize this shift risk falling behind as competitors leverage data to anticipate market trends, optimize resources, and create personalized experiences.

For hidden champions, the challenge lies not only in collecting data but in converting it into actionable insights. Information overload can be overwhelming, making it imperative to deploy the right analytical tools. This transformation demands an organizational commitment to integrating data-driven decision-making into every facet of business, from marketing to product development and supply chain management. Decisions driven by data are more precise, accurate, and yield superior outcomes compared to other decision-making approaches in nearly all situations (Davenport, 2023, March 17).

Understanding this transformation requires a deep dive into how big data, analytics, and artificial intelligence intersect the future of these market leaders. By adopting a systematic approach to data utilization, hidden champions can ensure sustainable competitive advantages while maintaining the agility that defines their success.

Unlike corporate giants that often rely on economies of scale, hidden champions achieve dominance through specialization, deep customer relationships, and an unwavering commitment to quality. However, in a world where agility is crucial, data serves as a force multiplier, allowing them to anticipate shifts in demand, fine-tune production, and respond dynamically to evolving market conditions. The ability to act on real-time insights ensures that these companies maintain their competitive edge while continuously refining their business models.

Data-driven decision-making also enhances the ability of hidden champions to mitigate risks. Whether it is identifying vulnerabilities in their supply chains, predicting fluctuations in raw material costs, or preempting shifts in regulatory policies, access to predictive analytics allows these companies to remain resilient in uncertain environments. By leveraging AI-powered forecasting, hidden champions can pivot swiftly, turning potential disruptions into strategic opportunities.

Beyond operational efficiency, the integration of data and AI fosters a culture of continuous learning. Hidden champions that embrace this transformation empower their workforce to make more informed decisions, enabling teams to experiment, iterate, and optimize processes without relying on trial-and-error approaches. This culture of adaptability strengthens the company's ability to innovate, helping them to craft new solutions that cater to the specific needs of their customers.

Moreover, personalization powered by AI and analytics has become a cornerstone of differentiation. Hidden champions that harness customer data effectively can tailor their products, services, and experiences in ways that large competitors struggle to replicate. By analyzing buying behaviors, preferences, and pain points, they can craft hyper-personalized solutions, strengthening customer loyalty and deepening their market positioning.

The real power of data-driven strategies for hidden champions lies in their ability to combine digital intelligence with their existing strengths, industry expertise, craftsmanship, and customer trust. Integrating AI with process management is a strategic imperative that transforms businesses by seamlessly aligning people, technology, data, and analytics to drive scalable efficiency and informed decision-making, though it requires structured change management to unlock its full potential (Davenport & Redman, 2025).

2 Big Data: Fueling Smart Decisions for Hidden Champions

Big data encompasses vast and intricate datasets that surpass the capacity of conventional storage and analytical tools. Traditional databases and legacy systems are incapable of processing such immense volumes of information, necessitating advanced computational methods. The defining characteristics of big data are encapsulated in the seven V's (Cvetkoska & Peovski, 2025): Velocity, Volume, Variety, Veracity, Variability, Visualization, and Value. Each of these characteristics plays a crucial role in transforming raw data into actionable insights.

Velocity signifies the rapid pace at which data is generated and transmitted. Every second, an overwhelming amount of digital activity takes place, millions of emails are exchanged, search queries are executed, social media posts are shared, and vast amounts of content are uploaded. This real-time influx of information offers businesses an unprecedented opportunity to analyze consumer behaviors, detect emerging trends, and adjust their strategies instantaneously.

Volume pertains to the sheer magnitude of data being generated daily. With the explosion of digital interactions, businesses are dealing with unprecedented amounts of structured and unstructured data. From customer transactions to social media engagements and Internet of Things (IoT) sensor readings, the exponential growth of data presents both challenges and opportunities. Organizations that develop the capability to efficiently process and store such vast datasets can unlock hidden insights that drive strategic advantages.

Variety represents the diverse forms of data that organizations must manage. Unlike traditional structured data confined to tables and spreadsheets, modern businesses must interpret unstructured data such as multimedia files, sensor outputs, social media activity, and textual information. By integrating these various data streams, companies can construct a more comprehensive understanding of their markets and operations.

Veracity underscores the importance of data accuracy and reliability. As the saying goes, "garbage in, garbage out," poor-quality data can lead to flawed insights and misguided decisions. Ensuring data integrity through proper validation, cleaning, and governance mechanisms is essential for businesses aiming to derive meaningful conclusions from their analytics efforts.

Variability is associated with the complexity of data interpretation. The same data point may carry different meanings depending on its context, industry, or user intent. Advanced analytics tools, powered by AI, help businesses extract insights from complex datasets, reducing ambiguity and enhancing decision-making accuracy.

Visualization plays a critical role in making big data comprehensible and actionable. By presenting complex datasets in visually intuitive formats such as heat maps, trend graphs, and interactive dashboards, decision-makers can quickly grasp key insights without needing technical expertise in data science.

Finally, Value is the ultimate goal of big data utilization. The ability to convert raw data into meaningful business insights is what sets successful companies apart. Whether it is optimizing supply chains, enhancing customer experiences, improving operational efficiency, or driving revenue growth, the strategic application of data analytics creates tangible competitive advantages.

In today's digital landscape, businesses that fail to leverage big data risk being outpaced by competitors who harness their potential to refine strategies, anticipate market changes, and enhance overall performance. Hidden champions can significantly benefit from embracing big data analytics, ensuring they remain leaders in their specialized industries while adapting to future technological advancements.

This analytical foresight allows hidden champions to stay ahead of competitors, adjusting their strategies in real time rather than reacting after the fact. Big data enables firms to segment their customer base with high granularity, ensuring hyper-personalized services and precise targeting. Furthermore, hidden champions can use real-time analytics to assess external market conditions, optimizing supply chain decisions and risk management strategies with unparalleled accuracy.

Hidden champions can use big data to refine their pricing strategies dynamically. By analyzing customer demand patterns, competitors' pricing models, and supply chain fluctuations, companies can adjust prices in real time to maximize profitability while maintaining customer satisfaction. Additionally, predictive analytics can inform product development by identifying gaps in the market, ensuring that new offerings align with customer expectations and emerging trends.

Big data also plays a crucial role in supplier and risk management. By integrating data from multiple sources, hidden champions can assess the financial health, reliability, and efficiency of suppliers, reducing the risk of supply chain disruptions. This proactive approach allows companies to identify alternative suppliers before bottlenecks occur, ensuring operational continuity.

Beyond market intelligence and operational efficiencies, big data enhances customer engagement strategies. Hidden champions can use sentiment analysis to gauge consumer preferences, analyzing reviews, social media activity, and direct customer feedback. By understanding what customers truly value, businesses can refine their messaging, improve service delivery, and create products that resonate more effectively with target audiences.

Furthermore, predictive analytics help hidden champions navigate economic volatility. By leveraging data from multiple sources, including financial markets, geopolitical trends, and industry-specific indicators, businesses can anticipate downturns or surges in demand. This level of preparedness allows them to allocate resources efficiently, mitigate risks, and seize opportunities before their competitors recognize them.

Another critical advantage of big data is its role in workforce optimization. By analyzing employee performance metrics, HR analytics, and training effectiveness, hidden champions can cultivate high-performing teams. Data-driven talent management strategies help companies identify skill gaps, optimize training programs, and enhance overall workforce productivity, ensuring that they maintain a competitive edge through human capital development.

Additionally, big data strengthens digital transformation efforts by integrating IoT technologies into manufacturing and logistics. Hidden champions can leverage IoT-enabled devices to monitor equipment performance, track shipments in real-time, and enhance production efficiency. By harnessing machine-generated data, companies can achieve predictive maintenance, reducing downtime and operational costs while improving overall efficiency.

The ethical and security implications of big data also require careful attention. Hidden champions must ensure data governance, regulatory compliance, and cybersecurity measures to maintain trust with customers, suppliers, and stakeholders. Companies that prioritize transparency in data collection and usage will not only avoid legal risks but also strengthen their brand reputation as responsible and ethical market leaders.

By embedding big data into their core strategies, hidden champions transform information into actionable intelligence. The ability to analyze trends, anticipate challenges, and seize new opportunities empowers them to make better decisions at every level. Companies that embrace this data-driven evolution will continue to push boundaries, proving that success in niche markets is not just about expertise but about leveraging knowledge faster and smarter than competition.

3 The Five Pillars of Analytics: Unlocking Competitive Strength for Hidden Champions

In the fast-evolving digital landscape, hidden champions must harness the power of business analytics to maintain their leadership in niche markets. Analytics transforms raw data into actionable insights, allowing these companies to optimize operations, enhance decision-making, and drive innovation. The five pillars of analytics (Cvetkoska & Peovski, 2025): descriptive, diagnostic, predictive, prescriptive, and cognitive analytics, form the foundation of data-driven strategy, enabling hidden champions to sharpen their competitive edge and sustain long-term success.

Descriptive analytics serves as the starting point of data exploration, answering the fundamental question: What happened? By analyzing historical data, hidden champions gain a comprehensive overview of key performance indicators such as total revenue, operating costs, profit margins, and customer segmentation. This approach utilizes data aggregation, visualization techniques, and statistical summaries to highlight trends and patterns in business performance. For hidden champions, descriptive analytics provide clarity on their market position. It enables them to track changes in customer demand, measure operational efficiency, and assess financial stability. However, while it paints a clear picture of past events, it does not explain the underlying causes behind the results. This limitation leads to the next stage, diagnostic analytics.

Once descriptive analytics establishes the "what," diagnostic analytics delves into the "why." Hidden champions need to identify the reasons behind fluctuations in performance, allowing them to make informed strategic adjustments. This pillar employs correlation analysis, anomaly detection, drill-down techniques, and comparative analysis to uncover root causes. For example, if a hidden champion in the precision manufacturing industry experiences a decline in sales, diagnostic analytics can reveal whether the issue stems from supply chain disruptions, pricing inefficiencies, customer attrition, or increased competition. By segmenting the problem at multiple levels, geographically, customer-specific, or operational, companies can pinpoint the factors influencing performance and take targeted corrective action. This leads to better resource allocation and proactive business improvements.

Predictive analytics shifts the focus from understanding past and present data to forecasting the future. By leveraging machine learning algorithms, statistical modeling, and data mining techniques, hidden champions can predict customer demand, market fluctuations, and potential risks before they materialize. For instance, a hidden champion in the renewable energy sector can use predictive analytics to estimate energy consumption trends based on weather patterns, economic conditions, and customer behavior. This foresight allows companies to optimize production schedules, streamline inventory management, and anticipate shifts in market dynamics. Predictive analytics help hidden champions stay ahead of uncertainties and make data-driven decisions that minimize risks and maximize opportunities.

While predictive analytics provides a roadmap for potential future scenarios, prescriptive analytics takes it a step further by offering specific recommendations on what should be done. This advanced form of analytics integrates decision analysis, optimization models, and multi-criteria decision-making techniques to enhance strategic planning. Hidden champions can use prescriptive analytics to optimize supply chain logistics, determine the most profitable product mix, or identify the best market entry strategy. For example, in pharmaceuticals, companies can use prescriptive models to streamline drug development by selecting the optimal combination of ingredients and testing methods, reducing both cost and time to market. By applying optimization techniques, hidden champions can allocate resources more efficiently, improve productivity, and enhance overall performance.

The newest addition to the analytics spectrum, cognitive analytics, goes beyond traditional data processing by incorporating artificial intelligence, natural language processing (NLP), and machine learning to simulate human-like decision-making. It provides context-aware insights by analyzing vast amounts of unstructured data, such as customer feedback, emails, and social media interactions, in real time. For hidden champions, cognitive analytics offers a game-changing advantage. AI-powered systems can continuously learn from data, refining predictions and recommendations over time. In industries like high-tech manufacturing, cognitive analytics can detect inefficiencies in production lines by analyzing sensor data and making autonomous adjustments to improve quality and efficiency. In customer service, chatbots and AI-driven assistants provide personalized support, enhancing user experience and customer retention. Cognitive analytics allows hidden champions to operate in a more agile and responsive manner, ensuring that business strategies evolve dynamically based on continuously updated insights. It bridges the gap between human expertise and machine intelligence, allowing companies to scale their decision-making capabilities without losing the precision that defines their success.

Each pillar of analytics plays a critical role in empowering hidden champions. Descriptive and diagnostic analytics provide clarity on past and present performance, while predictive and prescriptive analytics offer a proactive approach to future challenges. The addition of cognitive analytics ensures continuous learning and automation, enabling hidden champions to make faster, smarter, and more adaptive decisions.

By fully integrating these analytics capabilities, hidden champions can reinforce their competitive advantage in niche markets. Companies that embrace a data-driven culture will not only improve operational efficiency but also uncover new opportunities for innovation and expansion. In an era where data dictates success, those who harness its power effectively will remain ahead of the curve, setting new benchmarks for excellence in their industries.

4 Artificial Intelligence: A Game-Changer for Hidden Champions

Artificial intelligence is the science of creating systems that can learn, reason, and make decisions, mimicking human intelligence while operating at speeds and scales far beyond human capability. Unlike traditional software that follows predefined rules, AI continuously adapts based on patterns, feedback, and evolving datasets. AI-powered systems can recognize speech, analyze images, process natural language, and make predictions, offering businesses unprecedented opportunities to optimize operations and enhance decision-making. In a world driven by data, AI is becoming the backbone of digital transformation, revolutionizing industries, and reshaping competitive dynamics.

For hidden champions, AI serves as a force multiplier, enabling them to maintain their niche market leadership while accelerating innovation and efficiency. AI-driven solutions allow these companies to analyze massive datasets, detect trends before they become mainstream, and automate complex processes that once required significant human intervention. Whether optimizing production workflows, personalizing customer experiences, or fortifying cybersecurity defenses, AI empowers hidden champions to operate smarter, more agile, and with a level of precision that outpaces traditional business models.

AI encompasses several subfields, each contributing uniquely to how businesses harness its power. These subfields allow hidden champions to automate tasks, generate insights, and make strategic decisions with unprecedented precision.

Machine Learning (ML) Machine learning is the backbone of AI, enabling systems to learn from data without explicit programming. It can be categorized into three main types:

- **Supervised Learning:** In this approach, models are trained using labeled data, meaning the system is provided with input-output pairs to learn patterns. This is widely used for fraud detection, demand forecasting, and customer segmentation, helping hidden champions predict outcomes based on historical trends.
- **Unsupervised Learning:** Here, AI models identify patterns and relationships in data without predefined labels. This technique is valuable for market segmentation, anomaly detection, and discovering hidden trends in customer behavior, allowing businesses to uncover insights that might not be immediately obvious.
- **Reinforcement Learning:** This method involves training AI through trial and error, rewarding optimal decisions and penalizing poor ones. It is often applied in robotics, process optimization, and dynamic pricing models, enabling hidden champions to develop self-improving systems that adapt to changing conditions.

Natural Language Processing NLP allows AI to interpret and generate human language, facilitating chatbots, automated customer support, and sentiment analysis. Hidden champions can use NLP to analyze customer feedback, extract insights from reports, and enhance communication efficiency, leading to improved customer engagement.

Computer Vision This subfield enables AI to process and interpret visual data, making it useful in quality control, defect detection, and facial recognition. Manufacturers can integrate computer vision into their production lines to automate inspections, ensuring consistent product quality and reducing errors.

Robotics and Automation AI-driven robots and automation systems enhance productivity by streamlining repetitive tasks. Hidden champions in logistics, manufacturing, and healthcare can deploy robotics to improve efficiency, reduce operational costs, and maintain precision in high-stakes environments.

Cognitive Computing Combining AI with human-like reasoning, cognitive computing systems analyze unstructured data, recognize emotions, and make complex decisions. Hidden champions can leverage cognitive AI to improve decision-making processes, such as risk assessment and personalized recommendations for customers.

5 AI-Driven Transformation in Hidden Champions

Hidden champions are specialized, market-leading companies that have long thrived on innovation, agility, and deep customer relationships. Today, AI is not just an enabler but a game-changer, reshaping how these companies operate, compete, and innovate. From predictive intelligence to generative AI-driven solutions, the adoption of artificial intelligence is no longer a choice but a necessity for sustaining leadership in niche markets.

AI amplifies the transformative potential of hidden champions by unlocking automation, hyper-personalization, and strategic foresight at an unprecedented scale. AI-driven algorithms process vast datasets beyond human capability, revealing patterns and correlations that drive smarter decision-making. Hidden champions can leverage AI to enhance customer experiences, streamline production, optimize pricing, and pioneer new business models with precision and agility.

Generative AI is revolutionizing knowledge work by automating content creation, generating synthetic data for model training, and accelerating product design cycles. AI-powered simulations allow hidden champions to experiment with multiple market scenarios, test pricing strategies, and refine value propositions in risk-free environments before execution. This capability significantly reduces trial-and-error costs while enhancing decision-making accuracy.

Machine learning models take predictive analytics to new heights, enabling hidden champions to anticipate customer needs before they arise. AI-driven recommendation engines dynamically adapt product and service offerings based on evolving consumer behavior, strengthening brand loyalty and customer retention. By harnessing generative AI, companies can create customized marketing campaigns, automate customer support interactions, and refine sales approaches with contextual intelligence.

In manufacturing and supply chain management, AI-driven demand forecasting minimizes overstocking and stockouts, optimizing inventory flows and reducing operational inefficiencies. Predictive maintenance powered by AI ensures machinery operates at peak efficiency by analyzing sensor data and preemptively scheduling repairs, reducing downtime, and extending asset lifecycles. AI-driven quality control systems enhance product consistency, ensuring hidden champions maintain their reputation for excellence.

Agentic AI represents a transformative shift in artificial intelligence, enabling systems to move beyond passive data processing and actively plan, adapt, and execute complex tasks autonomously. Unlike traditional AI models that require predefined workflows, agentic AI leverages the reasoning capabilities of generative AI to make strategic decisions, dynamically optimize actions, and manage intricate sequences of tasks with minimal human intervention. This technology is particularly valuable in areas such as supply chain management, where it can autonomously monitor inventory levels, predict demand fluctuations, and trigger replenishment at optimal times based on real-time data. By integrating agentic AI with predictive and generative AI, businesses can create intelligent systems that not only react to past patterns but also proactively reshape operations to improve efficiency and responsiveness (Persona, 2025).

The synergy between AI and robotic process automation (RPA) is another game-changer. By integrating AI with RPA, hidden champions can eliminate repetitive tasks such as order processing, compliance reporting, and financial reconciliations. This frees employees to focus on strategic initiatives, fostering a culture of continuous innovation. AI-powered knowledge management systems further enhance decision-making by dynamically curating and contextualizing insights, accelerating problem-solving and strategic execution.

Security is another critical area where AI is transforming hidden champions. AI-driven cybersecurity systems proactively detect and neutralize threats by analyzing network behavior, identifying anomalies, and mitigating risks in real time. This is particularly vital for companies managing sensitive intellectual property or operating within highly regulated environments.

For hidden champions to sustain their leadership, embracing AI is not enough, they must cultivate an AI-first mindset. This means investing in AI talent, upskilling employees, and fostering a culture of experimentation and continuous learning. Organizations that integrate AI into their core strategy will not only optimize operations but redefine industry benchmarks, pioneering new paradigms of efficiency, innovation, and customer engagement.

By embedding AI-driven intelligence into their decision-making frameworks, hidden champions unlock unprecedented levels of agility and foresight. In an increasingly complex and competitive global landscape, those who master AI will not only withstand disruption but turn it into a competitive advantage, transforming challenges into opportunities and securing their dominance in specialized markets.

6 Overcoming Challenges in Data Transformation

The path to a fully data-driven organization is not without challenges. Many hidden champions, despite their industry leadership, struggle with the cultural and technological shifts required for true data transformation. Legacy systems, resistance to change, and a lack of in-house expertise can hinder progress.

The key to overcoming these barriers lies in fostering a data-centric culture, one that prioritizes evidence-based decision-making across all levels of the organization. Leadership must champion this transformation, investing in talent, training, and infrastructure to embed data-driven processes into everyday operations.

Ensuring company-wide data literacy, implementing cross-functional analytics teams, and establishing clear governance frameworks are crucial steps in this transition. Moreover, effective change management strategies are essential to overcoming skepticism and building an innovation-first mindset within the organization.

One of the biggest challenges for hidden champions is the integration of modern analytics tools with outdated legacy systems. Many of these companies have built their success on well-established processes that, while efficient in the past, may not align with today's data-driven environment. Migrating from traditional databases to cloud-based or AI-powered analytics platforms requires careful planning and phased implementation to avoid operational disruptions.

Another critical hurdle is resistance to change among employees. Data transformation is not solely a technological shift, it is a cultural one. Employees accustomed to intuition-based decision-making may initially resist the adoption of analytics-driven approaches. Providing continuous education, highlighting real-world successes, and creating incentives for data-driven performance can help ease this transition.

Security and compliance concerns also present significant obstacles. Hidden champions operating in specialized industries often manage sensitive customer data, proprietary research, and intellectual property. Implementing robust cybersecurity measures, ensuring compliance with global data protection regulations, and adopting ethical AI practices are essential to maintaining trust while embracing digital transformation.

Data silos further complicate the transition. In many organizations, different departments operate independently, leading to fragmented data storage and analysis. Breaking down these silos by creating unified data ecosystems enables companies to gain a holistic view of their operations. Establishing a centralized data governance strategy ensures consistency, accuracy, and accessibility across all business functions.

Finally, the financial investment required for data transformation can be daunting. While advanced analytics, AI-driven insights, and cloud computing offer long-term benefits, the initial costs of implementation, training, and system upgrades may deter some companies from taking the leap. A strategic, phased approach, starting with smaller pilot projects that demonstrate tangible benefits, can help justify larger investments and build confidence in the process.

By addressing these challenges head-on, hidden champions can unlock the full potential of data transformation. Those that successfully integrate analytics, AI, and data-driven decision-making will not only enhance efficiency but also future-proof their businesses, ensuring sustained growth and industry leadership in an increasingly digital world.

7 The Future of Hidden Champions in the AI Era

The future of hidden champions will be defined by their ability to harness AI-driven technologies and advanced analytics to maintain a competitive edge. The convergence of AI, quantum computing, and real-time analytics will create new opportunities for these companies to further dominate their respective niches. Autonomous decision-making systems will enable businesses to make instantaneous, data-backed choices, eliminating inefficiencies and maximizing productivity.

Furthermore, hyper-automation, where AI and robotic process automation handle vast amounts of repetitive tasks, will become a key driver of operational excellence. AI will optimize not only supply chains but also research and development, enabling companies to innovate at an accelerated pace. Businesses that leverage AI-powered simulations can test new products and strategies in virtual environments before launching them, reducing risks, and increasing efficiency.

AI-driven collaboration tools will facilitate knowledge sharing among global teams, ensuring that insights and best practices are rapidly disseminated across the organization. AI-powered personalization engines will also allow hidden champions to offer highly customized products and services, increasing customer engagement and revenue.

As AI continues to evolve, hidden champions will need to embrace adaptive intelligence, systems that not only analyze data but also adjust strategies in real time based on changing market dynamics. AI-powered predictive models will allow companies to foresee disruptions, shifts in consumer behavior, and emerging competitive threats, enabling them to pivot swiftly and maintain their market leadership.

Sustainability will also play a crucial role in the future of AI-driven hidden champions. With growing regulatory pressures and customer expectations for eco-conscious business practices, AI can optimize resource efficiency, reduce waste, and minimize carbon footprints. Smart AI-driven energy management systems, predictive maintenance for equipment longevity, and AI-optimized logistics will help hidden champions align profitability with sustainability goals, ensuring long-term resilience.

Human-AI collaboration will redefine the way hidden champions operate. Rather than replacing human expertise, AI will augment decision-making by providing deeper insights, automating repetitive tasks, and enhancing creativity. Companies that successfully integrate AI into their workforce, equipping employees with

AI-driven tools and fostering a culture of digital fluency, will achieve unparalleled innovation and agility.

The integration of AI with edge computing and 5G connectivity will further revolutionize hidden champions' operations. AI-driven devices will process data at the source, reducing latency and enabling real-time decision-making in industries such as manufacturing, healthcare, and logistics. This decentralized intelligence will empower hidden champions to enhance efficiency, improve service delivery, and accelerate response times in critical business functions.

Companies that embrace these advancements will sustain their leadership and redefine industry standards. The future belongs to those who adapt, innovate, and fully integrate AI into their long-term vision, ensuring that hidden champions remain at the forefront of technological progress. The next era of business dominance will be shaped by those who see AI not just as a tool but as an integral part of their strategic DNA, leveraging it to outthink, and outperform the competition.

8 Conclusion

The ability to make data-driven decisions has become the defining factor in the success of hidden champions. These companies thrive in specialized markets where precision, agility, and strategic foresight are crucial. By embedding analytics, AI, and real-time insights into their core operations, hidden champions are not just optimizing their processes, they are reshaping industries. The transition to data-driven decision-making allows them to unlock new growth avenues, anticipate risks before they arise, and develop products that align perfectly with market needs.

A key advantage of hidden champions lies in their ability to combine deep industry expertise with cutting-edge data intelligence. Unlike larger corporations that often struggle with rigid structures, hidden champions have the flexibility to implement AI and analytics solutions quickly and efficiently. This agility enables them to stay ahead of competitors, rapidly adjust to market disruptions, and turn insights into action at an unmatched pace. The future of business competition will not be determined by size alone but by the ability to harness data in meaningful and innovative ways.

As industries become increasingly complex and unpredictable, hidden champions must continue evolving. The next wave of competitive advantage will belong to those who integrate AI-driven decision-making as a fundamental part of their business model. Companies that master this transformation will not only solidify their dominance in niche markets but also set new benchmarks for excellence in the AI era. The future is not about who has the most data, but who can use it best, hidden champions that embrace this philosophy will define the next generation of industry leaders.

References

Cvetkoska, V., & Peovski, F. (2025). *Business analytics* (2nd ed.). Stobi Trejd Dooel.

Davenport, T. H. (2023, March 17). How to use data to make better decisions [video]. Harvard Business. Available at: https://video.search.yahoo.com/search/video?fr=mcafee&p=big+data%2C+hbr%2C+thomas+davenport&type=E210US714G0#id=2&vid=cc118b760b214bf9a3eeb4c4c9f3e6c1&action=click.

Davenport, T. H., & Redman, T. C. (2025). How to marry process management and AI. *Harvard Business Review, January–February 2025*. Available at: https://hbr.org/2025/01/how-to-marry-process-management-and-ai.

Persona, L. (2025, March 10). Agentic, generative, and predictive: How the AI orchestra works in harmony. Forbes Technology Council. Available at: https://www.forbes.com/councils/forbestechcouncil/2025/03/10/agentic-generative-and-predictive-how-the-ai-orchestra-works-in-harmony/.

Violeta Cvetkoska, PhD, is a Professor of Operational Research and Machine Learning for Management, Coordinator of the Fundamentals of Business Analytics course, and Head of the EUi at Ss. Cyril and Methodius University in Skopje, Faculty of Economics-Skopje. She holds a master's degree in Operational Research and Quantitative Methods from the University of Belgrade, alongside a PhD in Economics from Ss. Cyril and Methodius University in Skopje. A passionate educator and mentor, Prof. Cvetkoska translates her extensive knowledge into real-world impact, empowering students and managers to become data-driven professionals. Her work in operational research, business analytics, and AI strategically supports companies in gaining a competitive edge. Prof. Cvetkoska's international perspective is shaped by academic visits and active participation in conferences, symposia, and workshops across Europe, the Americas, and Asia. An advocate of experiential learning, she is a certified MonsoonSIM trainer, leveraging its AI-driven platform to equip future leaders with analytical skills. She has published numerous scientific papers in respected international journals and conference proceedings. Beyond her research, Prof. Cvetkoska contributes to the scholarly community by serving on editorial boards of international journals, on scientific boards of major conferences, and as an active member of professional societies like the Croatian Operational Research Society (CRORR), the Society for Economic Measurement (SEM), the EURO Working Groups on Multicriteria Decision Aiding and Behavioural Operational Research (BOR). Her current research interests span digital transformation, performance measurement, labor market, education, banking, and finance, driving innovation and excellence in the dynamic field of business analytics.

Sustainability Principles of Hidden Champions: "How Hidden Champions Build Their Success on the Application of Sustainability Principles"

Janka Taborecka and Simona Bartosova

Abstract This chapter provides insight into how highly successful mid-sized companies with global market leadership in niche segments—so-called hidden champions—integrate sustainability principles into their strategic decision-making. Based on comparative case studies from a diverse range of countries across Central and Eastern Europe, Asia, and Africa, the analysis provides similar patterns, differences and peculiarities in the depth and form of sustainability implementation. While many hidden champions demonstrate strong alignment between environmental, social, and innovation strategies, others remain at an early stage of integration. Key drivers include regulatory pressures (e.g. Environmental, Social, Governance (ESG) and The Corporate Sustainability Reporting Directive (CSRD) frameworks), innovation capacity, family ownership values, industrial factors, and geopolitical developments. The chapter highlights that sustainability is evolving from a peripheral concern into a core source of competitive advantage and it is becoming an integral part of hidden champion strategic framework. By identifying three distinct clusters of integration (high, medium, low), the study offers original empirical evidence from under-researched regions and provides inspirational practices how to support sustainable transformation among mid-sized companies globally.

1 Introduction

Sustainability has become a key concept in business, politics, science, and everyday life. We are faced with worsening environmental problems, climate change, social inequalities, and growing pressure for responsible economic management. Traditionally, sustainability has been closely associated with environmental protection, but the concept encompasses different perspectives. It can be understood

J. Taborecka (✉) · S. Bartosova
Faculty of Economics, University of Matej Bel, Banska Bystrica, Slovakia
e-mail: janka.taborecka@umb.sk; simona.bartosova@umb.sk

D. Berberović, D. Purg (eds.), *Hidden Champions in Rising Economies*, Contributions to Management Science,
https://doi.org/10.1007/978-3-032-08263-3_9

in a general societal or global context, or more specifically as corporate sustainability, which focuses on companies' long-term viability and impact on the environment. Companies, public institutions, and consumers are under increasing pressure to adopt sustainable practices. CSR (Corporate Social Responsibility), ESG, and SDG (Sustainable Development Goal) concepts are often associated with sustainability. Still, they are not synonyms, as each has a different origin, focus, and implementation method in business practice. The report "Hidden Champions, Missed Opportunities" (2024) by the European Investment Bank and the European Policy Centre highlights their importance in innovation, job creation, and investment in sustainability. It also emphasises that mid-caps have the potential to become leaders in implementing CSR and ESG standards, which are essential for sustainable economic growth in the EU.

The Sustainable Development Goals (SDGs) are 17 global objectives adopted by the United Nations as part of the 2030 Agenda for Sustainable Development. They represent a universal commitment to eradicating poverty, protecting the environment, and promoting prosperity and peace for all (Sdgs.un, 2025). Corporate Social Responsibility (CSR) is defined as business activities and policies that govern a company's responsibility towards society and the environment (Christensen et al., 2021). CSR is based on three pillars: economic (profit), environmental (planet), and social (people) (Księżaka & Fischbach, 2017) and represents a broad view of doing business by emphasising the company's responsibility in those pillars (Ubrežiová & Sokil, 2018). Moreover, this framework highlights the essence of sustainability in business and emphasises the need for a balance between economic growth, environmental management, and social justice (Kalra, 2024). CSR activities should be aligned with the interests of shareholders and the expectations of other individuals, and aim to improve the well-being of society, even at the cost of sacrificing profits in favour of more sustainable corporate behaviour (Christensen et al. (2021), Adomako and Tran (2022)). Proponents of CSR view it as a strategic opportunity for companies to differentiate themselves from competitors and to better meet the needs of direct and indirect stakeholders (Fatima & Elbanna, 2023). Since CSR is a comprehensive management approach that aims to create value for the company and society, it should not be reduced to charity or sponsorship (Blagoycheva, 2016).

Within the European Union, legislation on Environmental, Social, Governance (ESG), non-financial reporting (e.g. the CSRD Directive), and climate change commitments are tightening. At the same time, consumer behaviour is changing, with growing demand for ethical, environmentally friendly and locally produced products. Sustainability is becoming an important investment criterion, and ESG factors are playing an increasingly important role in the decision-making of investors and financial institutions. ESG is a set of quantifiable criteria used by investors to assess the risks and impacts of companies in areas such as environmental sustainability, social issues, and governance. It is a key tool in investment decision-making, particularly for listed companies. ESG scores affect companies' access to capital, investors and banks, affecting their competitiveness and long-term performance. Medium-sized companies (mid-caps), often called "hidden champions", play a key role in Europe's transition to a green and digital economy.

Jungwirth and König (2019) examined the approach of Austrian mid-cap hidden champions to Corporate Social Responsibility (CSR). They found that these companies often integrate CSR into their business strategies, which provides them with competitive advantages and strengthens their reputation (Coppa and Sriramesh (2013); Zhexembayeva (2013)). The study also highlighted differences in CSR approaches between family and non-family businesses. Family businesses often see CSR as an integral part of their identity and long-term vision, while non-family businesses may approach CSR more formally and strategically. Hidden champions rely on a highly qualified workforce, continuously investing in their education and development (Lehmann et al., 2019; Voudouris et al., 2000).

Sustainability has been closely linked to environmental protection. However, this view is increasingly being replaced by a broader perspective: sustainability resulting in a long-term strategy rather than short-term measures. Thus, sustainability and long-term orientation are closely related. Simon (2022) noted that hidden champions are characterised by long-term leadership. Several surveys have repeatedly found that the average tenure of chief executives is over 20 years, whereas the average tenure of CEOs in large companies is only about 6 years. While this cannot be statistically proven, the considerably longer tenure of hidden champion CEOs likely leads to more sustainable conduct.

Hidden champions represent a specific type of small- and medium-sized enterprises that have been able to establish themselves in global markets thanks to their high level of innovation, close specialisation, and strong customer relationships. According to Voudouris et al. (2000), the main factors behind their success are specialisation in niche markets, a strong customer service orientation and an emphasis on innovation and technology. These characteristics are also reflected in regional contexts. For example, hidden champions in Croatia are characterised by excellent customer service, professionally managed finances and high investments in research and development (Omazić & Vlahov, 2013). According to Schenkenhofer (2021), hidden champions are also often characterised by a close relationship with customers, even if of a different nature. Hidden champions and their customers are highly interdependent due to the narrow market and few substitutes, and therefore work closely together, even though the customers are spread around the world. This suggests that customer loyalty is based less on emotional and local proximity than on technological dependence. In Slovenia, close relationships with customers play a crucial role and significantly influence the innovation process. The management of these companies often has in-depth product knowledge (Rant, 2013). In many cases, their success is linked to family ownership, which creates a specific corporate culture conducive to innovation (Venohr & Meyer, 2007). Petraite & Dlugoborskyte (2017) found that Lithuanian hidden champions are characterised by high entrepreneurial orientation, technological advantage, and intensive use of partnerships. Similarly, in the case of South Korean firms, a link can be identified between innovation capabilities, transformational leadership and talent management, which have a direct impact on organisational performance (Kim & Sung, 2019). From the point of view of regional development, these hidden champions are also important. According to Vonnahme et al. (2018), hidden champions are an important factor of economic growth in small towns, while also contributing to the development of cultural, educational, and social life. Their connection to communities, job creation, and sustainable business practices shows that these businesses can be considered sustainable in this regard.

Subsequently, Simon (2022) examined social sustainability, focusing on how hidden champions contribute to societal well-being through employee engagement, fair working conditions, commitment to the local area, and long-term stakeholder relationships. Notable examples include Uzin Utz, a flooring systems provider that emphasises sustainable, low-emission products and transparent Environmental, Social and Governance (ESG) reporting; Voss Group, an automotive fluid line systems specialist known for its comprehensive sustainability reporting and strong employee-centred practices; and Visiconsult X-Ray Systems & Solutions, the global leader in non-destructive material testing technologies for sectors such as rail and aerospace, which contributes indirectly to safety and societal benefit.

The Financial Times, in partnership with Statista (2025), has published an interactive list, "Europe's Climate Leaders, 2025", which identifies companies with significant reductions in greenhouse gas emissions. Although the list does not specifically identify "hidden champions", several medium-sized companies appear on it (such as Tele2, Trane Technologies, Sekab, Amplifon, and British American Tobacco (BAT)), demonstrating their commitment to sustainability and environmental responsibility.

As Tilt (2016) noted, companies are engaging in responsibility-related activities, resulting in the availability of more information on social and environmental issues. Moreover, companies that have integrated sustainability into their core operations, from supply chains to product design, often achieve better reputations, increased customer loyalty and better access to capital. Sustainability is no longer just about image; it is becoming a competitive advantage and a key component of business resilience. Many hidden champions have long been active in this field (Simon, 2022).

Technological innovation also plays an important role, helping to increase efficiency and reduce the environmental impact of business through green technologies, circular economy principles, and digitalisation. Zhang et al. (2024) explored the potential of blockchain technology in economic management, focusing on its role in promoting sustainable development among emerging companies, often referred to as hidden champions. The authors highlight that blockchain enables the creation of transparent and traceable supply chains, allowing stakeholders to monitor the origin, movement, and environmental and social impacts of products and raw materials. Such transparency helps to identify inefficiencies, reduce waste and promote responsible sourcing practices. Furthermore, blockchain technology empowers consumers to make informed purchasing decisions based on verified data, encouraging more sustainable consumption patterns. In addition to improving the flow of information, blockchain also facilitates the active engagement of stakeholders in sustainability initiatives. By leveraging a decentralised platform, various actors, including suppliers, consumers, non-governmental organisations and government agencies, can directly participate and collaborate, thereby increasing the overall effectiveness of sustainability strategies (Hayton et al., 2002; Shavarani et al., 2018; Ghasemi et al., 2021).

Zhexembayeva (2013) points out that the innovation potential of these firms allows them to develop resource-saving processes, making them more sustainable. Hidden champions thus use the eco-efficiency approach to drive new product development. Muñoz et al. (2017) highlight that their competitive advantage combines innovation strategy, internationalisation, close customer relationships and product specialisation. Such a focus on innovation, quality, and a B2B service model is also highlighted by Táborecká-Petrovičová et al. (2013).

According to Schenkenhofer (2021), what distinguishes Hidden champions from other Mittelstand (including both SMEs (IfM Bonn, 2016) and midcaps (Röhl, 2018)) and family-owned companies is that they are technology leaders in their product niche. They often carry out continuous technological development in close cooperation with their customers' needs and suggestions. Born hidden champions emphasised technological innovation. Since the companies target the global markets with highly developed technology and potential market opportunities, they naturally must possess high technological competence (Yoon, 2013). Simon (2022) explored sustainability among German and Austrian hidden champions, classifying them by their product- and process-oriented sustainability approaches. Product-focused examples include Lenzing (cellulose fibres), Golden Compound (biodegradable coffee capsules), and Golden Mill (sustainable hulling technologies). Process-oriented sustainability is represented by companies such as Huttenes-Albertus (eco-friendly chemical production), Taifun-Tofu (environmentally responsible tofu manufacturing), Werner & Mertz (packaging collection and reuse), Der Grüne Punkt (recycling systems), and Alpla (sustainable packaging solutions). Other examples are Momox (recommerce and second-hand clothing), KWS (agricultural seeds), Steico (wood fibre insulation), and Sonnen GmbH (battery storage and energy management). Traditional fashion brands like Tommy Hilfiger, Boss, and Polo Ralph Lauren were also included due to their growing commitment to sustainability.

Hidden champions tend to be particularly cautious about relinquishing control and independence (De Massis et al., 2018). As niche specialists focused on high-quality products, they strive to maintain control over key activities at every stage of value creation and along the entire value chain (Rammer & Spielkamp, 2015; Schenkenhofer, 2022; Simon, 2022; Lampe et al., 2025). Most hidden champions are constantly searching for new designs and materials and optimising work processes for highly efficient and flexible production to secure their competitive advantage over competitors in the niche market (Cai et al., 2024).

2 Sustainability Practices Among Hidden Champions

Analysis of hidden champion case studies in this research project revealed that hidden champions across regions are increasingly acknowledging that sustainability is becoming an integral part of their strategies. Companies show their growing commitment to environmental and social responsibility through innovations, cutting-edge technology, ESG frameworks, or local and community engagement. The future success of hidden champions may depend on their ability to successfully implement, deepen, enlarge, and communicate their sustainability strategies.

2.1 *Patterns of Sustainability Integration Among Hidden Champions Across Countries*

The comparative analysis of hidden champions across studied countries reveals how sustainability principles are understood, prioritised, and implemented. While the level of integration varies widely, several unifying trends and regionally specific approaches can be observed:

- A strong connection between innovation and sustainability
- Integration of CSR and ESG
- Sustainability derived from the industry or sector
- Sustainability emphasising social factor and community engagement
- External conditions resulting in adoption of sustainability principles
- Varying level of sustainability integration among hidden champions from different countries

Analysis revealed the ability of hidden champions to link innovation with environmental and social sustainability. Companies in countries like Lithuania, Mongolia, and Poland integrate and develop advanced technologies, such as green manufacturing, circular economy models, or blockchain, contributing to reduction of coal power emissions. They focus on eco-conscious consumers, support eco-friendly production and zero waste initiatives. These companies develop cutting-edge products by combining innovation, inclusivity and functionality that address industry needs and align with social sustainability trends. A growing number of hidden champions, particularly in EU countries, are formalising their sustainability strategies having them in line with increasing regulation (ESG requirements). Companies in Croatia, Bosnia and Herzegovina, Slovakia, and Serbia demonstrate progress in aligning with ESG frameworks. Some family-owned companies introduce CSR more implicitly through long-term cooperations and relationships with partners and through ethical leadership. In several countries, sustainability is directly connected to the nature and peculiarities of the industry they operate in. For example, Georgia's wine industry, Latvia's concrete sector, India's home appliances, and Zambia's agricultural machinery show fulfilment of environmental and social goals that are relevant for specific markets. This approach often interconnects local traditions with global trends. Some of the hidden champions, especially in Lithuania, Mongolia, Poland, and the Western Balkans emphasised their commitment in the field of social sustainability. These companies showed how to include inclusivity, diversity, well-being of employees, regional development, and educational impact into their strategies. This was often connected with family business values. Also, geopolitical events (like the war in Ukraine or energy crises) and climate challenges led to adoption of sustainability principles in countries like North

Macedonia, Ukraine, and Hungary. Due to these pressures, companies were motivated to adopt renewable energy, digitalise operations, or ensure energy independence, leading to changes in their strategies. While many firms actively implement sustainable practices, others—especially in Armenia, Azerbaijan, Kosovo, Moldova, and some Central Asian countries—are still at early stages. Sustainability is not a core part of their strategies; they focus more on different aspects and sustainability practices are rather fragmented or limited rather than integral part of their strategies.

2.2 Level of Sustainability Integration into the Strategies Among Hidden Champions Across Countries

The cross-country comparison of sustainability practices that were mentioned to various extend in case studies of hidden champions reveals differences among countries. The Table 1 shows from high through medium to low level of integration based on the depth of sustainability integration, presence of ESG/CSR strategies, innovation in sustainable practices, and impact on social or environmental aspects.

Table 1 Integration of sustainability principles into the strategies of hidden champions from studied countries

Country	Sustainability integration	Key focus	Notable practices/companies
Albania	Medium	Environmental, customer relationships	Bio-organic products; emphasis on quality and long-term customer ties
Armenia	Low	Economic growth	Only mentions sustainable growth conceptually
Azerbaijan	Low	Quality	No reference to sustainability practices
Bosnia & Herzegovina	High	Environmental, social, innovation	Solar energy, zero waste, CSR, green manufacturing (Emerus, Mladegs Pak)
Bulgaria	Medium	Environmental (transport)	Electric go-karts, green mobility (Kinetik E-Karts)
Croatia	High	Digital agriculture, ESG compliance	Digital agriculture, sustainability reporting support (Agrivi)
Estonia	Low	Innovative technologies	No notable sustainability information provided
Georgia	High	Environmental, community engagement	Wine and eco-automotive firms; sustainable land use; community-based development (Tbilvino, Tegeta Motors)
Hungary	Medium	Circular economy	Used pallets; emphasis on reuse and efficiency (pallet solution)
China	Medium	Innovations, sustainable development	Ecological construction of a platform-type supply chain (Shuanghuan)
India	High	Environmental, innovation	Energy-efficient products, recyclable materials, green manufacturing (VL appliances)

(continued)

Table 1 (continued)

Country	Sustainability integration	Key focus	Notable practices/companies
Kazakhstan	Medium	Urban sustainability	Smart parking systems to reduce emissions (Parqour)
Kosovo	Low	Innovations, strategic partnerships	No reference to sustainability
Latvia	High	Green construction solutions	CO_2-reducing concrete technology, efficiency, green construction (Primekss)
Lithuania	High	Social inclusion, innovation	Accessible design, inclusivity, R&D cooperation (Jump Seat Duo project)
Moldova	Low	Environmental awareness	General awareness; limited detail on sustainability initiatives
Mongolia	High	Environmental, social, innovation	Zero waste, carbon credits, renewable energy, organic cosmetics (Lhamour, Coal to Solar project)
Montenegro	Medium	ESG strategy, education	CSR aligned with ESG practices (Marina Porto Montenegro)
Morocco	Medium	CSR, eco-packaging	HSE standards, use of recycled materials (Seprob, PlastikPack)
Nigeria	Medium	Local sourcing, economic sustainability	Agro-processing using local inputs, sustainable value creation (WASIL)
North Macedonia	High	Energy, production efficiency	Green energy, digital tools, sustainable transformation (Ading, Korab Trnica)
Poland	High	Ethical leadership, renewable energy	Social impact, energy transition, employee-centred (MB Pneumatyka)
Romania	Medium	Eco-products	Natural, sustainable wool bedding (Sanodor)
Serbia	High	Renewable energy, product sustainability	Solar power, recyclable products, certified ESG practices (BG Reklam, Uniplast)
Slovakia	Medium	Social impact, green technologies	LED tech, education/community cooperation, family-business sustainability (FOSALI, Gevorkyan)
Slovenia	High	Diversity, digital sustainability	HPC, creative technologies, gender diversity, sustainability in tourism (Arctur)
Turkey	Medium	Renewable energy, innovation	Solar technologies, insulation materials, focus on green production (Smart Solar, Berkosan)
Ukraine	Medium	Digital green economy	Electronic document systems, resource efficiency
Uzbekistan	High	Waste-free production	Oil extraction from waste, recyclable packaging, ethical and certified practices (ERMAK)
Zambia	Medium	Renewable energy access	Solar-powered agricultural tools, energy-efficient adaptation

Source: Elaborated on the basis of data from case studies of hidden champions in studied countries

Hidden champions from countries such as Bosnia and Herzegovina, Croatia, Georgia, India, Lithuania, Latvia, Mongolia, North Macedonia, Poland, Serbia, Slovenia, and Uzbekistan can be characterised as the ones with a high level of sustainability integration. We could see a deep alignment of environmental, social, and innovation strategies within their core business operations. These firms do not only meet regulatory demands but also often exceed them through advanced green technologies, social innovation, or circular economy models.

Then we identified the second group of countries including Albania, Bulgaria, Hungary, China, Kazakhstan, Montenegro, Morocco, Nigeria, Romania, Slovakia Turkey, Ukraine, and Zambia, that can be classified as medium-integration cluster, where sustainability practices were frequently mentioned, evident but not fully systematic or as a core element of their strategy. These often appeared as a pragmatic response to the requirements of the industry or market (e.g. renewable energy, packaging, digital agriculture), caused by external influences (like energy crises or war), or leadership values rather than by corporate strategies. Finally, we grouped into the third cluster countries such as Armenia, Azerbaijan, Estonia, Kosovo, and Moldova displaying low levels of sustainability integration. In hidden champions from these countries, we did not find any significant information about sustainability, information about it were rather fragmented or it was not mentioned as a primary focus in the reviewed case studies. These companies are only beginning to engage with environmental or social responsibility. However, these hidden champions often demonstrated strengths in innovation, adaptability, or leadership.

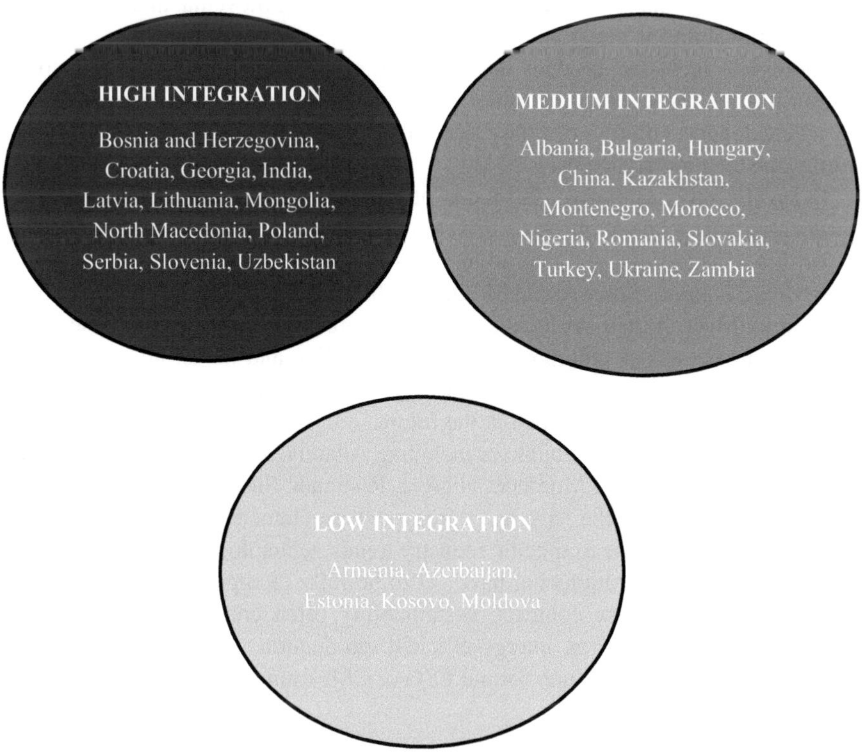

To conclude, analysis of hidden champions case studies from studied countries revealed the increasing role of innovation linked to sustainability, the influence of family ownership and long-term orientation in adopting responsible practices, and the growing importance of social sustainability and community engagement. Additionally, regulations like ESG and CSRD compliance is becoming mandatory particularly from the European Union can serve as a key catalyst to implementation of sustainability principles.

Overall, the table confirms that hidden champions are not a homogenous but diverse group of companies that demonstrate various levels of sustainability implementation. Their common traits involved especially niche specialisation, innovation, close relationships with customers, adaptability and great leadership with the possibility to further advance sustainability as a strategic pillar of their business success.

3 Conclusions

The cross-country comparison of sustainability practices among hidden champions reveals a diversity in priorities, approaches, and strategies. In many cases, companies demonstrate a clear and often strategic commitment to sustainability, particularly in countries such as Bosnia and Herzegovina, Croatia, Georgia, India, Latvia, Lithuania, Mongolia, North Macedonia, Poland, Serbia, Slovenia, and Uzbekistan. Here, sustainability is integrated into business models through innovations in clean technologies, inclusive product design, circular economy practices, and social responsibility. These firms are often proactive in addressing environmental and social challenges, either in response to regulatory demands or as part of their long-term value creation strategies.

In several other countries, the focus of the case studies was not primarily on sustainability but rather on other drivers of success, such as innovation, market expansion, leadership, or operational resilience. For instance, in Armenia, Azerbaijan, Estonia, Kosovo, and Moldova, while sustainability may not have been the central driver of their strategic decision-making processes, the companies were strong in areas such as entrepreneurship, adaptability, and industrial competitiveness. These qualities are essential foundations upon which more structured sustainability practices can be developed in the future.

A significant number of countries including Albania, Bulgaria, Hungary, China, Kazakhstan, Montenegro, Morocco, Nigeria, Romania, Slovakia, Turkey, Ukraine, and Zambia, belong to the "average" group, where elements of sustainability are present often in response to specific industry trends, technological opportunities, or environmental considerations but have yet to be fully incorporated into company-wide strategies. In these contexts, sustainability often emerges through sector-specific solutions, such as energy-efficient production, digital agriculture, or eco-design, rather than through formal ESG or CSR frameworks.

These empirical insights are broadly consistent with the literature reviewed in the Introduction, which highlighted the growing relevance of corporate sustainability, CSR, and ESG frameworks as strategic tools for long-term competitiveness and stakeholder engagement (e.g. Christensen, Hail & Leuz, 2021; Fatima & Elbanna, 2023). The cases are in line with findings by Simon (2022), who emphasised the long-term orientation and social responsibility of hidden champions, and by Coppa and Sriramesh (2019), who noted that CSR in mid-caps is often culturally embedded especially in family-owned businesses. Furthermore, the link between innovation and sustainability observed in countries like Lithuania and Mongolia aligns with research by Zhexembayeva (2013) and Zhang et al. (2024), who highlight the role of eco-efficiency, blockchain, and circular design in sustainable business models.

At the same time, the case studies also extend the literature by highlighting regional peculiarities and differences in patterns of sustainability integration, which are often underrepresented in the academic literature. For example, while much research has focused on Western European contexts, this chapter provides insights into less-studied countries in Central and Eastern Europe, Asia, and Africa, contributing and offering new evidence of how sustainability is interpreted and implemented in diverse institutional, cultural, and economic backgrounds.

Overall, the diversity of sustainability engagement reflects not only varying levels of regulatory pressure and market expectations, but also the specific development paths, priorities, and contextual environments in which hidden champions operate. Their shared characteristics, such as strong customer focus, innovation, and long-term orientation provide a solid basis for deepening sustainability integration as a strategic differentiator in the future.

References

Adomako, S., & Tran, D. M. (2022). Stakeholder management, CSR commitment, corporate social performance: The moderating role of uncertainty in CSR regulation. *Corporate Social Responsibility and Environmental Management, 29*(5), 1414–1423.

Blagoycheva, H. (2016). The social responsibility of business regarding education. *Izvestia Journal of the Union of Scientists – Varna.* https://doi.org/10.36997/IJUSV-ESS/2020.9.2.60

Cai, Q., Wu, J., Wu, T., Chang, P.-C., & Mardani, A. (2024). The impact of digital leadership on hidden champions' competitive advantage: A moderated mediation model of ambidextrous innovation and value co-creation. *Journal of Business Research, 182*. https://doi.org/10.1016/j.jbusres.2024.114819

Coppa, M., & Sriramesh, K. (2013). Corporate social responsibility among SMEs in Italy. *Public Relations Review, 39*(1), 30–39.

De Massis, A., Audretsch, D., Uhlaner, L., & Kammerlander, N. (2018). Innovation with limited resources: management lessons from the German Mittelstand. *Journal of Product Innovation Management, 35*(1), 125–146.

Europe's Climate Leaders. (2025). Interactive listing. Available at: https://www.ft.com/content/44f56758-9158-4b40-b59a-b2ffe6fc74ba?utm_source=chatgpt.com.

European Investment Bank. (2024). Hidden champions, missed opportunities Mid-caps' crucial roles in Europe's economic transition from https://www.eib.org/attachments/lucalli/20230277_hidden_champions_missed_opportunities_en.pdf. Accessed May 10, 2025.

Fatima, T., & Elbanna, S. (2023). Corporate social responsibility (CSR) implementation: A review and a research agenda towards an integrative framework. *Journal of Business Ethics, 183*(1), 105–121.

Ghasemi, M., Nejad, M. G., & Aghaei, I. (2021). Knowledge management orientation and operational performance relationship in medical tourism (overview of the model performance in the COVID-19 pandemic and post-pandemic era). *Health Services Management Research, 34*(4), 208–222.

Hayton, J. C., George, G., & Zahra, S. A. (2002). National culture and entrepreneurship: A review of behavioral view of behavioral. *Entrepreneurship Theory and Practice, 26*(4), 33–52.

Hidden Champions, Missed Opportunities. *Mid-caps' crucial roles in Europe's economic transition from* https://www.eib.org/attachments/lucalli/20230277_hidden_champions_missed_opportunities_en.pdf. Accessed May 10, 2025.

Christensen, H. B., Hail, L., & Leuz, C. (2021). Mandatory CSR and sustainability reporting: Economic analysis and literature review. *Review of Accounting Studies, 26*, 1176–1248. https://doi.org/10.1007/s11142-021-09609-5

IfM Bonn. (2016). Arbeitsbericht 2016 from https://www.ifm-bonn.org/fileadmin/data/redaktion/ueber_uns/dokumente/Arbeitsbericht-2016.pdf. Accessed May 12, 2025.

Jungwirth, G., & König, D. (2019). Corporate social responsibility in medium-sized hidden champions from Austria. *Ekonomiaz, 95*(01), 203–227.

Kalra, P. (2024). Corporate social responsibility and stakeholder theory: An integrated review. *Journal of Management & Entrepreneurship, 18*(1), 30–45. https://doi.org/10.13140/RG.2.2.32886.82243

Kim, D., & Sung, S. H. (2019). An analysis on the growth factors and organizational performance of small giant enterprises in South Korea. *Productivity Review, 33*(3), 69–95.

Księżaka, P., & Fischbach, B. (2017). Triple bottom line: The pillars of CSR. *Journal of Corporate Responsibility and Leadership, 4*(3), 95–110.

Lampe, H. W., Block, J., Willeke, T., Clauss, T., & Steinmetz, H. (2025). Technological innovations of hidden champions: Evidence from patent data. *Journal of Product Innovation Management, 42*(3), 502–527. https://doi.org/10.1111/jpim.12766

Lehmann, E. E., Schenkenhofer, J., & Wirsching, K. (2019). Hidden champions and unicorns: A question of the context of human capital investment. *Small Business Economics, 52*(2), 359–374.

Muñoz, E. P., Ripoll-i-Alcon, J., & Silvente, V. B. (2017). Hidden champions in Spain: The path to successful business decisions. *Revista De Métodos Cuantitativos Para La Economía y La Empresa, 24*, 190–208.

Omazić, M. A., & Vlahov, R. D. (2013). Hidden champions of Croatia. In *Hidden champions in CEE and Turkey: Carving out a global niche* (pp. 163–181). Springer.

Petraite, M., & Dlugoborskyte, V. (2017). Hidden champions from small catching-up country: Leveraging Entrepreneurial Orientation, Organizational Capabilities and Global Networks. In *Global opportunities for entrepreneurial growth* (pp. 91–122). Emerald Publishing.

Rammer, C., & Spielkamp, A. (2015). Hidden champions—driven by innovation... ZEW—Leibniz-Zentrum für Europäische Wirtschaftsforschung, Mannheim.

Rant, M. B. (2013). *Hidden champions of Slovenia. Hidden champions in CEE and Turkey: Carving out a global niche* (pp. 357–381). Springer.

Röhl, H. K. (2018). Mid Caps: der große Mittelstand. Die Wirtschaftspolitik berücksichtigt die Relevanz der Mid Caps nicht ausreichend, IW policy papers n 4.

SDGS.UN. (2025). Eurofins United Nations, 17 Sustainable Development Goals (SDGs) from https://sdgs.un.org/goals. Accessed May 10, 2025.

Schenkenhofer, J. (2021). Hidden champions: A review of the literature & future research avenues. *Management Review Quarterly, 72*, 417–482. https://doi.org/10.1007/s11301-021-00253-6

Shavarani, M. S., Nejad, G. M., Rismanchian, F., & Izbirak, G. (2018). Application of hierarchical facility location problem for optimization of a drone delivery system: a case study of Amazon

prime air in the city of San Francisco. *International Journal of Advanced Manufacturing Technology, 95*, 3141–3153.
Simon, H. (2021). Hidden champions. The new rules of the game in the Chinese century. Campus, Frankfurt. 280 p. https://doi.org/10.22363/2313-0660-2022-22-2-429-432.
Simon, H. (2022). Hidden champions and the development of regions. *IAR Journal of Business Management, 3*(2), 1–5. https://doi.org/10.47310/iarjbm.2022.v03i02.001
Táborecká-Petrovičová, J., Ďado, J., & Bobáková, T. (2013). Hidden champions of Slovakia. In *Hidden champions in CEE and Turkey* (pp. 331–355). Springer.
Tilt, C. A. (2016). *Corporate social responsibility research: The importance of context, international journal of corporate social responsibility (JCSR), ISSN 2366-0074* (Vol. 1, pp. 1–9). Springer. https://doi.org/10.1186/s40991-016-0003-7
Ubrežiová, I., & Sokil, O. (2018). The evaluation of three pillars of corporate social responsibility in practise. International scientific days 2018: Towards productive, sustainable and resilient global agriculture and food systems—proceedings. (pp. 1331–1343). Wolters Kluwer ČR. https://doi.org/10.15414/isd2018.s5.15.
Venohr, B., & Meyer, K. (2007). The German miracle keeps running: How Germany's hidden champions stay ahead in the global economy Berlin. Working paper no 30, Institute of Management Berlin, Berlin School of Economics.
Vonnahme, L., Graffenberger, M., Görmar, F., & Lang, T. (2018). *Kaum beachtet, gemeinsam stark-* Versteckte Potenziale von Kleinstädten mit Hidden Champions. *Informationen Zur Raumentwicklung, 6*, 38–49.
Voudouris, I., Lioukas, S., Makridakis, S., & Spanos, Y. (2000). Greek hidden champions: lessons from small, little-known firms in Greece. *European Management Journal, 18*(6), 663–674.
Yoon, B. (2013). How do hidden champions differ from normal small and medium enterprises (SMEs) in innovation activities. *Journal of Applied Sciences Research, 9*(13), 6257–6263.
Zhang, X., Sheng, Y., & Liu, Z. M. (2024). Using expertise as an intermediary: Unleashing the power of blockchain technology to drive future sustainable management using hidden champions. *Heliyon, 10*.
Zhexembayeva, N. (2013). *In search of sustainable business in central and Eastern Europe. Hidden champions in CEE and Turkey* (pp. 81–93). Springer.

Janka Táborecká, PhD. works at the Faculty of Economics, Matej Bel University in Banská Bystrica, Slovakia, where she serves as the guarantor of the Bachelor's program and co-guarantor of the Master's and PhD programs in Business Economics and Management. She is also a member of the coordination team of the European University Alliance EMERGE, where she leads the work package focused on community engagement. In addition, she serves as Head of the Marketing Research Centre at the European Marketing and Management Association (EUMMAS) and holds the position of Vice President of the Honorary Board of the association. She is also an assessor for the Slovak Accreditation Agency for Higher Education. Her long-term pedagogical, project-based, and research focus lies in the fields of marketing and consumer behavior, currently with an emphasis on sustainability and digital transformation. Over the years, she has demonstrated extensive experience in the coordination and implementation of 20 scientific and applied research projects, including national grants (VEGA), practice-oriented collaborations (NFP—Operational Programme Integrated Infrastructure), and international initiatives (CEEMAN & EBRD). Dr. Táborecká has authored or co-authored over 100 scholarly publications, including 27 indexed in Web of Science (WoS) and Scopus, with over 300 citations.

Simona Bartošová, PhD., works at the Faculty of Economics of the Matej Bel University in Banská Bystrica, where she holds the position of assistant professor at the Department of Economics and Business Management. In her teaching and scientific activities, she focuses on the field of marketing and international trade. She earned her doctorate (2021–2024) in Business

Economics and Management with a marketing specialization. Her dissertation, titled "Current Approaches to Market Segmentation in the Context of Environmental Trends and Consumer Behaviour," addresses responsible consumer behavior and CSR aligned with evolving sustainability trends. Her co-authored research includes a 2025 publication, Consumers' Preferences for Clothing Purchases in the Context of Circular Economy Principles. Her academic interests revolve around sustainable marketing, green branding, and how global environmental trends influence consumer segmentation. She supervises student theses on topics such as slow fashion, second-hand markets, and CSR within various sectors (e.g., textiles, banking). Committed to bridging theory and practice, Dr. Bartošová regularly incorporates case studies and empirical findings into her teaching to help students understand real-world applications. She also collaborates on interdisciplinary projects within the university's Research and Innovation Centre, contributing to debates on ethical marketing and environmental sustainability in business.

Strategic Entrepreneurship in Global Business Environments: A Comparative Framework of Hidden Champions

Julian Enrik Schenkenhofer and Meelis Kitsing

Abstract Hidden champions are increasingly recognized as pivotal players in global markets, far beyond their traditional German roots. This paper reframes hidden champions as a global entrepreneurial phenomenon shaped by distinct institutional and environmental contexts. Through a novel typology encompassing four business environments, emerging economies, post-socialist transitions, innovation-oriented EU states, and geopolitically fragile regions, we explore how firms navigate structural challenges in human capital, institutional trust, and financial infrastructure. Our comparative analysis reveals how hidden champions strategically adapt through lean innovation, selective internationalization, vertical integration, and embedded workforce development. These firms demonstrate that global competitiveness can emerge from local constraints through contextually embedded strategies. By extending the conceptual foundations of hidden champions to diverse ecosystems, this study advances a more differentiated theory of niche entrepreneurship and global firm resilience. We conclude by outlining present and future-oriented policy and research implications aimed at fostering the growth of hidden champions across varied economic landscapes.

J. E. Schenkenhofer (✉)
Center of Excellence for Entrepreneurial Families, WHU Otto Beisheim School of Management, Vallendar, Germany
e-mail: julian.schenkenhofer@whu.edu

M. Kitsing
Estonian Business School, Tallinn, Estonia
e-mail: Meelis.Kitsing@ebs.ee

D. Berberović, D. Purg (eds.), *Hidden Champions in Rising Economies*, Contributions to Management Science,
https://doi.org/10.1007/978-3-032-08263-3_10

1 Introduction

Hidden champions have increasingly captured the attention of scholars and policymakers alike. Originating from Simon's (2009, 2012) foundational work, these firms are defined by three core attributes: top-three market leadership in a global or continental niche, annual revenues typically below $5 billion, and an intentional avoidance of visibility in mainstream discourse. Despite their relative obscurity, hidden champions occupy pivotal roles in international value chains, often delivering technologically advanced, mission-critical components within B2B (business-to-business) contexts.

While initial research emphasized their concentration in German-speaking economies, especially within the Mittelstand,[1] contemporary studies reveal that hidden champions now operate across a wide range of institutional landscapes. Recent empirical work (e.g., Audretsch et al., 2021; Lehmann et al., 2024; Schenkenhofer et al., 2024) demonstrates their emergence in versatile settings. This global diffusion raises important questions about how context conditions the strategic behavior and competitive resilience of hidden champions.

This chapter aims to reframe the hidden champion phenomenon through the lens of comparative institutional analysis. We therefore collect data on the global distribution of hidden champions, combining existing sources with information derived from other chapters in this book. In doing so, we extend prior efforts by Simon (2021) and Audretsch et al. (2021), offering an updated and more comprehensive picture of hidden champion distributions worldwide. This chapter introduces a typology of four global business environments and examine how hidden champions navigate them. Across these varied settings, we analyze the interplay between human capital, institutional trust, and financial infrastructure in shaping firms' adaptive capabilities (Lehmann et al., 2019; Schenkenhofer, 2022). Our findings illustrate that hidden champions do not follow a single model of success; rather, they engage in context-contingent strategies, such as vertical integration, lean innovation, and capability-building, to overcome local constraints and leverage niche global opportunities.

By situating hidden champions within their institutional and geographic environments, this study contributes to a deeper understanding of niche entrepreneurship under varied systemic conditions (Audretsch et al., 2021). The chapter also paves the way for targeted policy discourse by highlighting the institutional mechanisms that enable, or hinder, the emergence of globally competitive firms beyond conventional innovation hubs (Audretsch & Lehmann, 2016; Audretsch et al., 2021). In doing so, we argue for a more differentiated and globally attuned research agenda on hidden champions, one that recognizes their strategic heterogeneity and

[1] Mittelstand firms are generally small- to medium-sized enterprises, often family-owned and managed. They are characterized by long-term strategic thinking, deep local embeddedness, and strong employee loyalty, among other characteristics. Please refer to Audretsch and Lehmann (2016), Pahnke and Welter (2019), Schenkenhofer (2022) or Pahnke et al. (2023) for reviews of the concept.

relevance to entrepreneurship scholarship in both developed and developing contexts. The final section outlines key policy implications, offering practical guidance for fostering hidden champion ecosystems across diverse economic geographies.

2 Hidden Champions: Conceptual Foundations and Research Trajectories

Hidden champions are firms that exemplify an unusual combination of global competitiveness and low public visibility. First conceptualized by Hermann Simon in the 1990s, HCs (hidden champions) are typically defined as firms that (1) rank among the top three in their global niche market, or hold a continental leadership position, (2) generate annual revenues under $5 billion, and (3) maintain a deliberately low media and public profile (Simon, 2009, 2012). Despite their relatively modest size and obscurity, these firms occupy critical positions in global value chains, often supplying highly specialized, technology-intensive products within narrowly defined business-to-business (B2B) segments. Their success is frequently attributed to a focused differentiation strategy, a strong commitment to innovation, and enduring customer relationships rooted in trust and co-creation.

Over the past decade, scholarly interest in hidden champions has accelerated (Lehmann et al., 2024; Schenkenhofer et al., 2024; Lampe et al., 2025). Once regarded as a predominantly German phenomenon, HCs are now recognized as a global class of firms emerging in a wide array of institutional and geographic contexts (Audretsch et al., 2021; Schenkenhofer, 2022). This expanding recognition has sparked a growing body of academic work that clusters into four main research domains.

First, a substantial literature explores HCs' internationalization trajectories (Audretsch et al., 2018), often framing them as "born globals" due to their rapid and early engagement with foreign markets (Witt, 2015). Unlike traditional SMEs, their international expansion is not incremental but strategically driven by the constraints of narrow domestic demand and the necessity to reach dispersed global buyers (Audretsch & Lehmann, 2016). Their modes of entry, typically direct exports or wholly owned subsidiaries, reflect a preference for tight control and safeguarding proprietary knowledge (Audretsch et al., 2018).

Second, HCs' innovation strategies have received significant scholarly attention. Studies consistently find that while their absolute R&D expenditure may not surpass industry averages, their innovation productivity and efficiency are markedly superior (Rammer & Spielkamp, 2015, 2019). Their success stems from a synthesis of focused in-house R&D, open innovation with customers and academia, and an astute intellectual property management system. A culture of incremental, customer-oriented innovation allows them to deliver highly customized, often mission-critical solutions with high value-add.

Third, recent research has turned to the institutional and geographic embeddedness of HCs. They are disproportionately concentrated in certain institutional environments, particularly those characterized by strong vocational education systems, civil law traditions, dual board governance, and moderate levels of financial market liberalization (Lehmann et al., 2019; Audretsch et al., 2021). These institutional complementarities create favorable conditions for the development of firm-specific human capital, long-term planning, and incremental innovation strategies. At the regional level, HCs play a transformative role, acting as growth anchors in rural and peripheral economies (Benz et al., 2021; Vonnahme & Lang, 2021).

Finally, an emergent body of literature examines the organizational dynamics and absorptive capacities of HCs. Their governance structures often reflect family ownership with centralized strategic control and decentralized operational autonomy, enabling agility without sacrificing coherence (Lehmann et al., 2019; Audretsch et al., 2021). Their human capital practices emphasize long-term skill development and firm-specific training, fostering deep product expertise and strong organizational loyalty.

Together, these insights depict hidden champions as a unique and understudied form of niche entrepreneurship. They offer fertile ground for theoretical development at the intersection of strategic management, innovation studies, and comparative institutional analysis. As global data coverage and methodological rigor continue to grow, the HC literature stands poised to contribute more decisively to core debates in entrepreneurship research.

3 Hidden Champions in Global Business Environments

Hidden champions are no longer confined to the industrial heartlands of Western Europe, during the last decades they have been detected on worldwide scale, as documented, e.g., in both compendiums "Hidden Champions in CEE and Turkey" (McKiernan & Purg, 2013) and "Hidden Champions in Dynamically Changing Societies" (Lalić & Purg, 2021). These firms, often leaders in narrow global niches while remaining relatively unknown to the public, emerge from diverse institutional and economic settings. In recent years, scholarly attention to hidden champions has intensified, driven by their sustained performance and their outsized impact on innovation and export competitiveness. Some years ago, Audretsch et al. (2021) analyzed the global distribution of hidden champions investigating numerous determinants of the institutional context. Building on that foundation, Table 1 presents an updated overview of the global distribution of hidden champions based on the most recent data,[2] illustrating their presence not only in developed economies but increasingly in emerging and transitional markets as well. Additionally, Fig. 1 provides a world map of hidden champions. This empirical mapping underscores the

[2] We source data for this overview from prior literature on hidden champions, the accounts of Hermann Simon and the individual country chapters of this book.

Table 1 The top 50 worldwide distribution of hidden champions

Country	Number of hidden champions
Germany	1573
USA	350
Japan	283
Austria	171
Switzerland	171
France	135
Italy	124
China	97
United Kingdom (UK)	74
Sweden	49
Netherlands	38
Poland	37
Russia	29
Finland	28
Canada	23
South Korea	22
Belgium	20
Spain	20
Denmark	19
Liechtenstein	17
Slovenia	15
Norway	13
Brazil	11
Azerbaijan	10
Australia	10
Portugal	10
Bosnia	9
Croatia	8
Lithuania	7
Luxembourg	7
Israel	7
Slovakia	6
Moldova	5
North Macedonia	5
Ireland	4
Serbia	4
Hungary	4
Albania	3
Morocco	3
Romania	3
Mongolia	3
Estonia	3

(continued)

Table 1 (continued)

Country	Number of hidden champions
Georgia	3
Armenia	2
Turkey	2
Latvia	2
Montenegro	2
Nigeria	2
India	2
Bulgaria	2
Kazakhstan	2
Kosovo	2
Ukraine	1
Uzbekistan	1
Zambia	1

Source: own depiction

Fig. 1 The world map of hidden champions. Source: own depiction

importance of context in shaping hidden champion strategies. The remainder of this section develops a typology of four distinct business environments (Table 2), emerging markets with structural constraints, post-socialist transitional economies, EU-based innovation-driven economies, and geopolitically fragile settings. Each context is defined along dimensions such as human capital, institutional trust, and

Table 2 Strategic responses of hidden champions across business environments

Business context	Countries	Human capital	Institutional trust	Financial capital	Hidden champion strategies
Emerging markets with structural constraints	e.g., Morocco, Turkey	High in volume but often informally acquired; misaligned with formal sector requirements due to weak vocational and tertiary systems	Low institutional credibility; businesses rely on informal networks to mitigate systemic corruption and enforcement gaps	Access to capital remains severely restricted; high borrowing costs and minimal formal financing options prevail	Capitalize on cost advantages and local inputs; adopt export-oriented, resource-leveraging models with minimal reliance on formal finance
Post-socialist transitional economies	e.g., Serbia, Bosnia and Herzegovina	Strong foundational skills in technical fields; insufficient alignment with managerial and entrepreneurial competencies	Moderate trust with improved legal frameworks; enforcement remains inconsistent and bureaucratic hurdles persist	Limited access to risk-tolerant financing; conservative lending practices dominate, venture capital is scarce	Revive traditional sectors through modernization; prioritize in-house talent development and regionally adaptive organizational structures
EU-based innovation-driven economies	e.g., Estonia, Slovenia	Highly educated, particularly in STEM disciplines; facing outmigration of young, skilled professionals	Comparatively high trust due to EU-aligned legal norms, transparency, and regulatory predictability	Significant access to public and private funding, including EU structural and innovation funds	Lead in R&D-intensive domains; integrate sustainability and compliance into innovation, with talent strategies focused on retention and advancement
Geopolitically and politically unstable economies	e.g., Ukraine, Nigeria	Legacy education systems provide technical grounding, but instability drives talent loss and underinvestment in human capital	Deeply fragmented trust in institutions; governance perceived as politicized and often unreliable	Characterized by volatile currencies and constrained credit access; often further hampered by sanctions or political risk	Design for operational resilience and international agility; invest in autonomous infrastructure and embed scenario-based strategic planning

financial capital availability. We then analyze how hidden champions operating within these contexts adapt strategically to their environments, providing a comparative lens for understanding their success across a range of global ecosystems.

3.1 Emerging and Developing Markets: (e.g., Morocco, Turkey)

In emerging and developing markets, the business environment is defined by a combination of systemic institutional constraints, infrastructure gaps, and evolving economic structures. Human capital, while abundant in absolute terms due to young and growing populations, remains underutilized due to weaknesses in formal education systems and limited alignment with the needs of globally competitive industries. Vocational and tertiary education programs often lack responsiveness to labor market demands, and informally acquired skills remain widespread, reflecting the significant role of the informal economy in shaping employment. These settings are further marked by low institutional trust. Corruption, rent-seeking behavior, and opaque regulatory environments reduce confidence in state institutions, compelling entrepreneurs to rely on informal norms and personal networks for business transactions and contract enforcement. Financial systems are typically shallow and risk-averse, characterized by high collateral requirements, underdeveloped capital markets, and minimal venture capital presence. Firms are often forced to self-finance or depend on informal lending. Infrastructure, including transportation, energy, and digital connectivity, is often uneven, with chronic energy shortages, unreliable Internet access, and underdeveloped logistics limiting operational efficiency. Market demand is constrained by low purchasing power, making price sensitivity a dominant feature of domestic consumption.

Amid these constraints, hidden champions succeed by embracing strategic pragmatism, deep contextual knowledge, and a culture of lean innovation. These firms often emerge from local ecosystems but rapidly orient themselves toward international markets to bypass the limitations of their domestic demand base. Leveraging cost-efficiency and adaptability, they design operations that are financially sustainable even in resource-constrained environments. Vertical integration is a common strategy, reducing reliance on unreliable suppliers and enabling greater control over quality and timelines. Without access to sophisticated financial products, these companies grow incrementally, often reinvesting profits and leveraging social capital to secure trust-based financing. Many draw on indigenous resources, such as agricultural inputs, raw materials, or artisanal skills, to create niche products with export potential. They utilize informal diaspora networks and regional markets as initial launch pads for internationalization. Trust-based client relationships, personal service, and localized branding strategies replace formal reputational mechanisms. Ultimately, these hidden champions exhibit an exceptional ability to navigate volatility, build resilience, and create globally competitive offerings from locally constrained environments.

3.2 *Transition and Post-Socialist Economies (e.g., Serbia, Bosnia and Herzegovina)*

In post-socialist transition economies, the entrepreneurial environment reflects the legacies of centrally planned governance, combined with the challenges of economic liberalization and market development. Human capital in these countries is often rooted in a strong foundation of technical and scientific education, a vestige of past state investments in industrial development. However, the transition to a market economy has exposed a misalignment between existing skillsets and the competencies required for agile, innovation-driven firms. Managerial talent, soft skills, and customer-centric thinking are frequently underdeveloped. Institutional trust, while improved compared to earlier decades, remains fragile. Regulatory frameworks exist, but implementation is inconsistent, and bureaucratic inefficiencies, corruption, and overlapping jurisdictions continue to hamper business operations. The financial ecosystem has matured significantly since the 1990s, yet small- and medium-sized enterprises (SMEs) still struggle with limited access to growth-oriented financing. Banks are risk-averse and often reliant on collateralized lending, while venture capital remains nascent. Infrastructure ranges from functional to obsolete. Industrial facilities are often remnants of the socialist era and require modernization, while digital infrastructure and transport logistics vary widely in quality. Domestic markets are fragmented and limited in scale, with significant urban-rural divides in purchasing behavior and access (Berberović et al., 2019).

In this complex environment, hidden champions rise by leveraging deep knowledge of legacy industries and introducing modern practices to rejuvenate them. Rather than abandoning traditional sectors, many firms specialize in upgrading them, bringing new technologies, product designs, and business models to agriculture, manufacturing, and industrial services. Given the mismatch between labor market output and business needs, workforce development becomes a strategic priority. Leading firms often establish in-house training centers, engage in dual-education partnerships, or offer extensive on-the-job learning to build internal capabilities. Organizational structures are designed to be flexible and responsive, avoiding the hierarchical rigidity that characterizes much of the public sector. Family ownership or founder-led governance provides long-term strategic stability and insulates firms from short-term market pressures. Strategically, these hidden champions pursue gradual but focused internationalization, often starting with culturally or geographically proximate markets. They cultivate adaptive capabilities to navigate shifting policy regimes and economic uncertainties, making them uniquely resilient and effective in transitional settings.

3.3 Innovation-Oriented EU Economies: (e.g., Estonia, Slovenia)

The innovation-driven economies of Eastern and Central Europe represent a dynamic intersection of advanced institutional frameworks and competitive market conditions. These countries benefit from access to the European market, strong legal institutions, and integration into the European Union's regulatory and funding infrastructure. Human capital is one of their greatest assets, with a highly educated workforce, especially in STEM disciplines, and increasing entrepreneurial orientation among younger generations (Lehmann et al., 2019). Like many transition and post-socialist economies, these countries face demographic headwinds, including population aging and persistent brain drain, as skilled professionals migrate to Western Europe in search of better opportunities. Institutional trust is high by regional standards, underpinned by transparent governance, EU-aligned regulation, and effective bureaucratic systems. Financial capital is relatively abundant, with access to EU funds, innovation grants, and a growing ecosystem of angel investors and early-stage venture capitalists. Infrastructure is robust, with widespread broadband Internet, advanced logistics networks, and integration into European energy grids. However, domestic markets are relatively small and highly competitive, necessitating early and sustained international engagement for firms aiming to scale.

Hidden champions in this environment distinguish themselves through technological sophistication, strategic internationalization, and institutional embeddedness. These firms operate at the forefront of R&D, often in partnership with local universities, EU-funded research consortia, and regional innovation clusters. They specialize in high-tech manufacturing, IT services, green technologies, and other IP-intensive sectors, allowing them to carve out defensible niches in global value chains. Compliance with stringent EU regulations, whether environmental, digital, or labor-related, is not viewed as a constraint but rather as a catalyst for innovation and differentiation. These firms invest in sustainable production methods, digital transformation, and advanced automation to meet evolving compliance demands while boosting efficiency. Given the tight labor market, they place strong emphasis on talent retention through employee empowerment, competitive compensation, and exposure to global best practices. Their branding strategies emphasize not only product quality but also transparency, customer experience, and social responsibility. Agile, digitally enabled, and globally minded, these hidden champions are emblematic of a new generation of firms leveraging European integration for global impact.

3.4 *Politically and Geopolitically Fragile Contexts: (e.g., Ukraine, Nigeria)*

Fragile and geopolitically exposed economies are marked by persistent volatility, stemming from internal political unrest, external conflict, or systemic governance challenges. In these environments, business continuity itself is a central concern. Human capital may be well-developed in absolute terms, particularly in post-Soviet contexts where education systems once emphasized engineering, science, and mathematics. However, political instability, limited state investment, and widespread emigration of skilled workers erode this advantage. Institutional trust is severely compromised. State institutions are often seen as politicized or ineffective, and formal rule of law is undermined by patronage networks and corruption. Financial capital is both scarce and volatile. Currency fluctuations, inflationary pressures, and limited integration with international capital markets constrain firms' access to credit. In extreme cases, international sanctions or banking restrictions further impede financing. Infrastructure, including energy grids, transportation systems, and digital networks, is vulnerable to disruption from conflict, political neglect, or natural shocks. Domestic markets are fragmented and unpredictable, shaped by high inflation, uncertain regulation, and rapidly shifting consumer behavior.

In such high-risk environments, hidden champions develop extraordinary adaptive capacities and prioritize strategic resilience. They design business models that can withstand systemic shocks, often incorporating geographic and operational diversification to reduce overexposure to any single market or supply chain. Export-oriented strategies dominate, as firms seek more stable demand and currency environments beyond national borders. Many cultivate diaspora links or regional partnerships to facilitate internationalization and hedge against local instability. Operationally, they invest in autonomy and redundancy, generating their own energy, establishing internal logistics capabilities, and digitizing operations to enable remote management and rapid reconfiguration. These firms are often deeply embedded in informal or semi-formal institutional networks, enabling them to access local intelligence, secure permissions, and mitigate political risk. Strategic scenario planning, risk mapping, and contingency design become routine management practices. Their ability to navigate fluid, high-stakes environments with agility and resolve makes them some of the most innovative and crisis-hardened firms in the global hidden champion landscape.

4 Policy Implications

Since this volume highlights the importance of hidden champions and this chapter addresses the global context, it would be incomplete without a discussion of the policy implications. As the earlier sections of the chapter have outlined, the contexts in which hidden champions operate are institutionally complex and diverse.

Therefore, it is crucial to present nuanced policy implications rather than adopt a one-size-fits-all approach. This section offers general policy implications that are broadly applicable across different institutional environments. More context-specific recommendations, which reflect the unique characteristics of the home markets of hidden champions, are briefly illustrated through the scenario narratives. Perhaps the most immediate implication is the need to enhance understanding of hidden champions, particularly their role in domestic economies and global value chains. As the term "*hidden*" suggests, many aspects of these firms remain obscure, making them difficult to identify and their contributions easy to overlook. Hidden champions often operate in complex global value chains involving trade, finance, innovation, and other interconnected domains. Yet these value chains are poorly mapped and inadequately understood, as government agencies tend to focus on traditional trade and financial statistics.

Moreover, the innovation models of hidden champions are often multifaceted. They involve not only formal research and development (R&D)-driven innovation, but also significant non-R&D innovation, such as process improvements, design, and organizational capabilities. Policymakers frequently emphasize the former while neglecting the latter. At the same time, many hidden champions have emerged specifically because of their ability to organize and manage innovation processes in ways that make them globally competitive. Developing analytical capabilities to better understand these firms is a natural and necessary first step. This will likely require more qualitative approaches to capture the subtleties of how hidden champions operate, innovate, and grow. Deeper understanding can, in turn, support more effective institutional design, strengthening the "*rules of the game*" to better facilitate the growth and internationalization of these firms.

It is also important to recognize that the agency of hidden champions is context-dependent. While they have some capacity to shape their own futures, their operations are constrained and enabled by institutional environments. Institutions are not only barriers; they can be powerful enablers of growth (Campbell, 2010, 99). Even in a potential scenario of deglobalization, domestic institutions can offer the necessary support for international operations. By doing so, hidden champions can enhance a country's financial, human, and social capital. Successful global businesses bring in revenue that can spill over into non-tradable sectors, increasing overall prosperity. They foster the development of globally competitive skills and know-how, with positive externalities for broader economic development. They can also serve as inspirational narratives, motivating the emergence of new hidden champions and other high-performing businesses.

However, this seemingly straightforward idea that success stories inspire others can play out quite differently depending on the institutional context. In environments where public exposure involves risks, such as arbitrary or poorly designed policy interventions, hidden champions may deliberately choose to stay under the radar and avoid engagement with public institutions. Ultimately, the most crucial policy implication is the importance of looking beyond the present and developing future-oriented approaches to explore potential, possible, and plausible trajectories for hidden champions. Given the global uncertainty and institutional complexity

Table 3 Illustrative four scenarios for hidden champions until 2040

	High global openness	Low global openness
High institutional support	S1: Champions without borders	S2: Fortress flourishers
Low institutional support	S3: Global guerillas	S4: Stuck in the silo

that surround these firms, it is more useful to approach the future through alternative scenarios than to rely on forecasts or linear planning.

One of the simplest and most effective tools for this is the 2x2 scenario matrix, which is based on two critical driving forces that are both highly significant and uncertain in how they will evolve (Kitsing, 2021). A stylized scenario framework for hidden champions uses this method to explore how institutional support and global openness may shape the futures of these firms (Table 3).

X-Axis (Degree of Institutional Support)

- Strong Institutional Support: Strong rule of law, access to capital, stable regulations, support for SMEs and innovation.
- Weak Institutional Support: Weak governance, corruption, poor infrastructure, unstable policies.

Y-Axis (Global Market Openness)

- High Global Openness: Integrated trade, tech transfer, foreign partnerships, stable globalization.
- Low Global Openness: Rising protectionism, regionalism, fragmented digital ecosystems.

4.1 *Scenario 1: Champions Without Borders (Strong Institutional Support + High Global Openness)*

By 2040, a new generation of Hidden Champions will have transformed the economic landscape across Eastern Europe and Central Asia.. A generation of pragmatic, globally minded reformers invested in digital infrastructure, education, and rule of law. Public-private partnerships flourished, and stable institutions laid a foundation for long-term growth. From Vilnius to Tbilisi, small- and mid-sized firms, once underdogs, have become quietly dominant players in global niches. A Lithuanian photonics company powers satellite optics. A Kazakh firm designs precision components for electric vehicles. A Bulgarian biotech startup supplies diagnostic kits worldwide. These companies are small in headcount but vast in impact. Their leaders speak four languages, travel across continents, and participate in EU, NATO, or other trade-friendly ecosystems. Thanks to generous R&D tax credits, well-functioning IP systems, and state-backed innovation hubs, they were able to scale rapidly without leaving their home countries. The global economy remains open and dynamic. Trade flows are complex but fluid. Cloud platforms, AI services, and logistics networks are interoperable across borders. Hidden champions now see the world not as a battleground, but as a network of opportunity.

4.2 *Scenario 2: Fortress Flourishers (Strong Institutional Support + Low Global Openness)*

By 2040, the world will have become more fragmented. Trade blocs and digital ecosystems have hardened into spheres of influence. While globalization hasn't reversed entirely, the era of seamless international exchange is long gone. Supply chains are regional. Standards diverge. Yet in the heart of the former Eastern Bloc, a new model has emerged. Governments having invested steadily in education, legal stability, and SME support turned inward, building economic resilience through self-reliance. Hidden champions adapted, not by conquering the world, but by dominating local and regional markets. Take Slovakia's industrial robotics sector. Once a junior player, it now leads the Central European market thanks to deep integration with regional suppliers and public R&D co-investment. In Serbia, a family-run agritech firm builds sensors tailored for Balkan microclimates. These firms flourish behind high walls, not by isolation, but by developing sophisticated capabilities within protected or semi-protected zones. Local innovation ecosystems thrive. Universities and startups work hand-in-hand. Regional supply chains shorten but deepen. While their brands may be unknown in Tokyo or San Francisco, these champions are household names in their blocs. They've proven that scale doesn't require sprawl and resilience, not reach, is their key advantage.

4.3 *Scenario 3: Global Guerrillas (Weak Institutional Support + High Global Openness)*

By 2040, firms will face fewer barriers abroad but too many in the domestic market. In much of the post-communist world, structural reform stalled or reversed. Corruption persists. Legal protections are uneven. Education systems lag. Yet out of this uneven terrain, guerrilla entrepreneurs have emerged. These hidden champions operate more like insurgents than institutions. They leapfrog domestic dysfunction by plugging into the digital global economy, often bypassing the state entirely.

A software firm in Moldova sells cybersecurity services to Nordic banks while operating out of a co-working space with solar panels and satellite Internet. An Uzbek design studio builds immersive AR experiences for U.S. museums. These firms scale fast but live on the edge. They rely on remote clients, diaspora investors, and cloud-based tools. They keep a low profile locally to avoid rent-seeking officials. Many officially register in Estonia or Singapore to avoid legal chaos at home. They are globally connected but locally fragile. Their success is built on talent, not institutions. And while some become legends in startup lore, many burn out or flee. Still, they persist, adaptable, invisible, and essential in an age where agility often beats structure.

4.4 Scenario 4: Stuck in the Silo (Weak Institutional Support + Low Global Openness)

By 2040, the optimism of the early 2000s will have faded across many transition economies. The world has fractured into competing blocks. Trade is politicized. Information flows are censored or fragmented. Meanwhile, domestic reforms have stalled or backslid.

In this environment, hidden champions barely survive. In places like parts of the Western Balkans or Central Asia, SMEs face red tape, clientelism, and limited access to finance. Cross-border expansion is impossible; even domestic markets are fraught. A promising Albanian agritech firm is stuck navigating unpredictable tariffs and unstable Internet. A once-ambitious Ukrainian logistics startup is confined to provincial operations. Talent drains away. Innovation shrinks to imitation. Many firms retreat into niches, small, stagnant, protected. Others become subcontractors to politically connected conglomerates or state-owned enterprises. Informal economies flourish, but sustainable growth does not. In this siloed world, hope lies mostly in local resilience community networks, individual heroism, and underground innovation. But the systemic challenges are too high. Without open markets or open governance, hidden champions remain hidden, not by strategy, but by suppression.

Key Message: It is important to emphasize that hidden champions from different countries will not necessarily fall into the same scenario. Even in a context of low global openness, the level of institutional support for hidden champions can vary significantly depending on each country's domestic institutional environment. The scenarios presented above are illustrative, they are intended to demonstrate a range of possible futures. The most effective way to develop meaningful scenarios is from the perspective of a specific hidden champion, involving key stakeholders of the company through workshops and other participatory methods. This is because the true value lies more in the process of scenario creation than in the specific content of any single scenario.

5 Conclusion

Hidden champions are crucial players in global and domestic economies. They operate in many domestic and international markets, extending far beyond their traditional affiliation with the global value chains of German business-to-business Mittelstand companies. They must therefore be reframed as a global entrepreneurial phenomenon shaped by diverse institutional contexts. This chapter introduces a novel typology of hidden champions, developed from the country case studies presented in this volume, encompassing four distinct institutional settings.

First, there are emerging economies such as Morocco and Turkey, where hidden champions demonstrate the ability to navigate constraining institutional environments while capitalizing on global business opportunities, often through informal networks. Second, in post-socialist transition countries like Bosnia and Herzegovina or Serbia, hidden champions play a key role in rejuvenating legacy industries within complex institutional landscapes. Third, innovation-oriented EU member states such as Estonia and Slovenia foster hidden champions that thrive on technological sophistication and strategic internationalization, supported by robust domestic institutions and EU integration. Fourth, in geopolitically fragile regions such as Nigeria and Ukraine, agile and highly innovative hidden champions operate under persistent uncertainty, managing the negative externalities of conflict and instability.

The chapter explored how these firms navigate structural challenges, including deficits in human capital, institutional trust, and financial infrastructure. The comparative institutional analysis reveals that hidden champions strategically adapt through lean innovation, selective internationalization, vertical integration, and embedded workforce development. These firms show that global competitiveness can emerge from local constraints through contextually embedded strategies. By extending the conceptual foundations of hidden champions to diverse ecosystems, this study advances a more differentiated theory of niche entrepreneurship and global firm resilience.

The chapter outlines both present and future-oriented policy and research implications by recognizing that hidden champions are vital drivers of innovation, competitiveness, and economic resilience across a range of institutional environments. Their development paths are highly sensitive to both domestic institutional conditions and global market dynamics. The four scenarios: *Champions Without Borders*, *Fortress Flourishers*, *Global Guerrillas*, and *Stuck in the Silo* illustrate the diverse futures these firms may face by 2040. These futures are not predetermined; they will depend on how countries shape institutional support and engage with an evolving global economy.

A central insight is that hidden champions should not be viewed in isolation but as products of broader institutional structures that either enable or constrain their potential. Consequently, policy responses must move beyond generic SME support strategies toward more tailored, context-aware approaches. Strengthening institutional capacity, fostering innovation (including non-R&D forms), and improving the understanding of global value chains are essential first steps. Scenario planning offers a valuable framework, not for predicting the future, but for enabling strategic thinking amid uncertainty. When used inclusively, it fosters shared understanding and informed action among key stakeholders. In doing so, hidden champions can not only adapt to shifting global landscapes but also actively shape them.

References

Audretsch, D. B., & Lehmann, E. (2016). *The seven secrets of Germany: Economic resilience in an era of global turbulence*. Oxford University Press.

Audretsch, D. B., Lehmann, E. E., & Schenkenhofer, J. (2018). Internationalization strategies of hidden champions: Lessons from Germany. *Multinational Business Review, 26*(1), 2–24. https://doi.org/10.1108/MBR-06-2017-0035

Audretsch, D. B., Lehmann, E. E., & Schenkenhofer, J. (2021). A context-choice model of niche entrepreneurship. *Entrepreneurship Theory and Practice, 45*(5), 1276–1303. https://doi.org/10.1177/1042258719895345

Benz, L., Block, J. H., & Johann, M. (2021). Hidden champions as a determinant of regional development: An analysis of German districts. *Zeitschrift für Wirtschaftsgeographie*. https://doi.org/10.1515/zfw-2020-0043

Berberović, D., Činjarević, M., & Kožo, A. (2019). Success despite lack of support: lessons learned from hidden champions doing business in fragile business environments. *Sarajevo Business and Economics Review, 37*, 192–204.

Campbell, J. L. (2010). Institutional reproduction and change. In G. Morgan et al. (Eds.), *The oxford handbook of comparative institutional analysis* (pp. 87–115). Oxford University Press.

Kitsing, M. (2021). *The political economy of digital ecosystems. Scenario planning for alternative futures*. Routledge.

Lalić, A. B., & Purg, D. (2021). *Hidden champions in dynamically changing societies: Critical success factors for market leadership*. Springer Nature.

Lampe, H. W., Block, J., Willeke, T., Clauss, T., & Steinmetz, H. (2025). Technological innovations of hidden champions: Evidence from patent data. *Journal of Product Innovation Management, 42*(3), 502–527. https://doi.org/10.1111/jpim.12689

Lehmann, E. E., Schenkenhofer, J., & Vismara, S. (2024). Hidden champions and knowledge spillovers: Innovation-enhancing agglomeration effects and niche technology specificity. *Small Business Economics*, 1–21. https://doi.org/10.1007/s11187-024-00839-9

Lehmann, E. E., Schenkenhofer, J., & Wirsching, K. (2019). Hidden champions and unicorns: A question of the context of human capital investment. *Small Business Economics, 52*(2), 359–374. https://doi.org/10.1007/s11187-018-0096-0

McKiernan, P., & Purg, D. (2013). *Hidden champions in CEE and Turkey*. Springer.

Pahnke, A., & Welter, F. (2019). The German Mittelstand: Antithesis to Silicon Valley entrepreneurship? *Small Business Economics, 52*, 345–358.

Pahnke, A., Welter, F., & Audretsch, D. B. (2023). In the eye of the beholder? Differentiating between SMEs and Mittelstand. *Small Business Economics, 60*(2), 729–743.

Rammer, C., & Spielkamp, A. (2015). Hidden champions—driven by innovation: Empirische Befunde auf Basis des Mannheimer Innovationspanels. ZEW—Leibniz-Zentrum für Europäische Wirtschaftsforschung. Retrieved from https://www.zew.de

Rammer, C., & Spielkamp, A. (2019). German hidden champions: Competitive strategies, knowledge management and innovation in globally leading niche players. *Ekonomiaz, 95*(1), 65–87.

Schenkenhofer, J. (2022). Hidden champions: A review of the literature & future research avenues. *Management Review Quarterly, 72*(2), 417–482. https://doi.org/10.1007/s11301-021-00237-3

Schenkenhofer, J., Block, J., & Vismara, S. (2024). University knowledge spillovers and innovation of hidden champions: Evidence from Italy. *R&D Management, 55*(2), 598–613. https://doi.org/10.1111/radm.12552

Simon, H. (2009). *Hidden champions of the 21st century: Success strategies of unknown world market leaders*. Springer.

Simon, H. (2012). *Hidden champions—Aufbruch nach Globalia: Die Erfolgsstrategien unbekannter Weltmarktführer*. Campus Verlag.

Simon, H. (2021). *Hidden champions–Die neuen Spielregeln im chinesischen Jahrhundert*. Campus Verlag.

Vonnahme, L., & Lang, T. (2021). Hidden champions in rural Germany: Innovation strategies to compete in global markets. In B. Leick, S. Gretzinger, & T. Makkonen (Eds.), *The rural enterprise economy* (pp. 35–52). Routledge.

Witt, A. (2015). Global hidden champions: The internationalisation paths, entry modes and underlying competitive advantages of Germany's and Britain's global 'top three' niche players (Doctoral dissertation). University of Edinburgh.

Julian Enrik Schenkenhofer is a Junior Professor of Entrepreneurial Families at WHU – Otto Beisheim School of Management and an Adjunct Research Fellow at Indiana University Bloomington (USA). His research focuses on entrepreneurial families, family firm innovation, and hidden champions, with particular emphasis on socioemotional wealth, artificial intelligence, and green innovation. His work has been published in leading international journals such as Entrepreneurship Theory and Practice, Small Business Economics, and R&D Management, and presented at major conferences including AoM and EURAM. He serves as a reviewer for top-tier journals in entrepreneurship, innovation, and family business and is among the leading international scholars on hidden champions. Schenkenhofer was recognized among Germany's 'Top 40 under 40' by Capital Magazine and contributes as an expert to initiatives on the Mittelstand and SMEs at the European Commission and the RKW Competence Center, which is supported by the German Federal Ministry for Economic Affairs and Climate Action (BMWK).

Meelis Kitsing is the Rector at the Estonian Business School (EBS), where he also serves as a Professor of Political Economy. He is a member of the boards of the Estonian Council on Foreign Relations, the Estonian Service Industry Association, and Eurofound, a European Union research agency based in Dublin, Ireland.

Kitsing has been Head of Research and Acting Director at the Foresight Center, a think tank within the Estonian Parliament; Adviser at the Strategy Unit of the Estonian Government Office; and Head of Economic Analysis at the Estonian Ministry of Economic Affairs and Communications. Additionally, he has served as President of the Estonian Economic Association and chaired the supervisory boards of the public-sector companies.

Kitsing is the author of The Political Economy of Digital Ecosystems (Routledge, 2021 & 2023). His research has been published by Springer, IEEE, ACM, Leuven University Press, and MIT Press. He has conducted research and taught at universities across Asia, Europe, and North America, such as the University of Massachusetts, Central European University, Harvard University, the University of Connecticut, the Stockholm School of Economics, and the Institute of Management Technology (Dubai and Ghaziabad campuses).

Meelis Kitsing earned his PhD from the University of Massachusetts, Amherst (USA), and his MALD degree from the Fletcher School at Tufts University (USA) as a Fulbright scholar. He also holds an MSc from the London School of Economics (UK), where he studied as a Peacock scholar. Before transitioning to academia, Kitsing worked for multinational corporations and founded an e-commerce startup.

Hidden Champions of Albania

Anisa Kume, Elona Garo, and Vasilika Kume

Abstract This nation case study outlines Albania's economic, business, and past development trajectory, emphasizing the emergence of "hidden champions" as regional competitiveness forces. Having spent decades isolated and weathering the turbulent transition from a market to a centrally planned economy, Albania has progressively achieved macroeconomic stability, EU integration progress, and diversification by sector. Agriculture, natural resources, and tourism remain fundamental pillars, with small- and medium-sized enterprises (SMEs) key to employment and growth.

Three case studies—Mare Adriatik, Alb Kalustyan, and Venice Art Masks Factory—are shown as representative hidden champions who turn out to be robust, creative, and market leaders on the international scene despite challenges such as limited access to finance, trade barriers, the COVID-19 pandemic, and the Ukrainian war. They are successful due to quality orientation, adaptability in responding to shifting markets, quality entrepreneurial leadership, and the combination of tradition and innovation.

Major evidence shows that Albania's hidden champions are founded on focused strategies, long-term ownership, and significant investments in human capital but are limited by infrastructure, managerial competences, and institutions. The research points out that Albanian SMEs should ground themselves on uniqueness, bioproducts, and design competitiveness to improve global positioning. Governance, innovation abilities, and sustainable business models should be strengthened to support Albania's vision towards 2030 as an inclusive, dynamic, and EU-connected economy.

A. Kume (✉)
Faculty of Economics, Tirana University, Management and Communication, Tirana, Albania
e-mail: anisa.kume@unitir.edu.al

E. Garo
Faculty of Economics, Tirana University, Strategic Management, Tirana, Albania
e-mail: elona.garo@unitir.edu.al

V. Kume
Tirana Business University College, Strategic Management, Tirana, Albania
e-mail: vasilika.kume@tbu.edu.al

D. Berberović, D. Purg (eds.), *Hidden Champions in Rising Economies*, Contributions to Management Science,
https://doi.org/10.1007/978-3-032-08263-3_11

Overview
Official name: Republic of Albania
Type of government: Parliamentary democratic republic
Population in 2022: 2846 million[1]
Land area: 28,748 km^2

GNI (U.S.$ '000,000)	(2022) 18,801
GNI per capita (U.S.$)	(2022) 6770

Key Dates in Albania's History[2]

1190–1257	Principality of Arbanon. First recorded Albanian state.
1385	Ottoman forces defeat local rulers at the Battle of Savra. Most local leaders become Ottoman vassals.
1415–1431	Albania is gradually incorporated into the Ottoman Empire.
1444–1468	After Ottoman defeat in the Battle of Nis, Gjergj Kastrioti Skanderbeg unites Albania rulers in the League of Lezhë and leads a 25-year struggle against Turkish rule.
Eighteenth to nineteenth century	Albanian Renaissance: flourishing of Albanian culture and society, coupled with rising nationalism and moves for independence.
1912	Albania declares independence from the Ottoman Empire.
1913	Treaty of London of May 1913 recognizes Albania as an independent state.
1928	Albania becomes a monarchy under Zog I.
1941	Albania is occupied by Nazi Germany and Italy during World War II.
1944	At the end of the war, Albania becomes a socialist republic and Enver Hoxha is installed as Albania's new leader.
1961	Albania allies itself with China, after the Soviet Union breaks diplomatic relations over ideological rift.
1967	Violent clampdown on religious activity. Albania was declared the world's first atheist state.

[1] INSTAT 2024.
[2] BBC News. (2023). Albania country profile. https://www.bbc.com/news/world-europe-17679574.

1990	Demise of communism and first steps on the road to a market economy. Albanians were granted the right to travel abroad. Thousands try to flee through Western embassies.
1997	The fall of pyramidal financial schemes causes a political and economic crisis.
2006	The Stabilization and Association Agreement (SAA) signed with the EU in June.
2006	Free Trade Agreement (CEFTA).
2009	Albania becomes a NATO member country and applies for EU membership.
2014	The European Commission recommends Albania as a candidate for European Union membership.

See Exhibit 1.

Exhibit 1 Core economic indicators for Albania

Indicator	2019	2020	2021	2022	2023	2024
GDP per capita (current US$)	5460.43	5370.78	6413.28	6846.43	8575.17	..
GDP per capita growth (annual %)	2.5	−2.76	9.98	6.11	5.14	..
Unemployment, total (% of total labor force) (modeled ILO estimate)	11.47	11.69	11.47	10.14	10.11	10.25
Foreign direct investment, net inflows (% of GDP)	7.71	7.02	6.76	7.58	6.88	..
GDP (current US$, mio)	15585.11	15241.46	18032.01	19017.24	23547.18	..
Exports of goods and ser- vices (current US$, mio)	4821.43	3435.54	5613.91	7073.86	9104.54	..
Exports of goods and services (% of GDP)	30.94	22.54	31.13	37.2	38.67	..
Merchandise exports (current US$, mio)	2716	2506	3559	4309	4374	..
Merchandise exports to high-income economies (% of total merchandise exports)	79.31	77.84	76.33	78.9	77.71	..
Merchandise exports to low- and middle-income economies in Europe & Central Asia (% of total merchandise exports)	17.96	19.09	20.38	18.37	19.52	..
Ores and metals exports (% of merchandise exports)	3.1	4.09	2.47	0.06	5.35	..
Agricultural raw materials exports (% of merchandise exports)	0.49	0.57	0.47	0.23	0.41	..

(continued)

Indicator	2019	2020	2021	2022	2023	2024
Food exports (% of merchandise exports)	10.38	13.6	10.85	8.77	11.96	..
Fuel exports (% of merchandise exports)	0.6	0.91	0.02	0.41	6.35	..
Manufactures exports (% of merchandise exports)	50.2	55.18	42.72	34.51	56.61	..
High-technology exports (% of manufactured exports)	0.13	0.29	0.42	0.06	0.68	..

Source: World Bank, 2025 https://data.worldbank.org/indicator/TX.VAL.TECH.MF.ZS?locations=AL

[a] https://www.seejobsgateway.net/sites/job_gateway/files/Western%20Balkans%20Labor%20Market%20Trends%2019; https://data.worldbank.org/indicator/TX.VAL.MRCH.R2.ZS?end 2017& locations AL&start 1981

[b] These data are from World Bank, Eurostat and International Labour Organization

[d] Merchandise exports to developing economies in Europe & Central Asia (% of total merchandise exports)

1 Introduction: Context and History

1.1 History

Albania is a small, mountainous country in the Balkan peninsula, with a long Adriatic and Ionian coastline.

Along with neighboring and mainly Albanian-inhabited Kosovo, it has a Muslim majority—a legacy of its centuries of Ottoman rule. As a legacy of nearly five centuries of Ottoman rule, Albania is a predominantly Muslim country (Encyclopædia Britannica, 2024).

However, as a result of the rigid enforcement of atheism during the communist regime, today most Albanians are adherents of religious groups in name only and practice largely secular lifestyles.

After World War Two, Albania became a Stalinist state under Enver Hoxha, and remained staunchly isolationist until it transitioned to democracy after 1990.

The 1992 elections ended 47 years of communist rule, but the latter half of the decade saw a quick turnover of presidents and prime ministers.

In 1992, the new Democratic Government announced a "shock therapy" program to establish a market economy. Such an absolute rejection of the past left its imprint on the growth model adopted in Albania. The economic theory of shock therapy was misinterpreted and, in several cases, yielded the destruction of fixed assets accumulated and inherited from the socialist economy in the past. The prevailing attitude that state property did not belong to anyone and total ignorance concerning market economics and the market value of physical capital, presented the factors for releasing destructive forces into action.

There were these trends of developments, which triggered massive internal migration, emigration, and "brain drain." Traditional markets and potential industries became dysfunctional and lost relevance and the traditional trades were lost with them.

Thirty-four years after the demise of communism, Albania is finally on a stable path to economic development and economic integration. Slowly but surely the country is beginning to emerge as a land of opportunities, opening its doors to foreign investment. In 2023, growth reached 3.3% as private consumption, exports, and investment increased despite rising energy and food prices. Despite another year of exceptional growth in tourism, growth is likely to remain at similar levels in 2024. Poverty is expected to continue to decline as employment and wages rise. The country's medium-term prospects hinge on global recovery, structural reforms, and fiscal consolidation (The World Bank, 2024).

However, despite the full range of institutional reforms, Albanian export remains small and narrow and is not diversified. The country is rich in natural resources, and the economy relies mainly on agriculture, food processing, lumber, oil, cement, chemicals, mining, basic metals, hydropower, tourism, the textile industry, and petroleum extraction. The Albanian economy still suffers from a trade deficit, albeit declining. The country's main trading partners are Italy, Greece, Turkey, China, and Russia.

Emerging from decades of isolation during communism, Albania has adopted a foreign policy orientation centered on active cooperation and engagement in international affairs. At the core of Albania's foreign policies lie a set of objectives, which encompass the commitment to protect its sovereignty and territorial integrity, the cultivation of diplomatic ties with other countries, advocating for international recognition of Kosovo, addressing the concerns related to the expulsion of Cham Albanians, pursuing Euro-Atlantic integration and protecting the rights of the Albanians in Kosovo, Greece, Italy, Montenegro, North Macedonia, Serbia and the diaspora (Wikipedia Contributors, 2024).

The transformation of Albanian economy into a market one is a long and difficult process. The first years twenty-first century witnessed numerous successes, but at the same time, failures were not rare. The struggle for progress showed, among others, the lack of expertise. This holds also true in the management field. Some may contradict it since our macroeconomic performance is good and it continued improving further during the last years. But the history of macroeconomic performance and especially its stabilization tells us that even in Hoxha's time we had a stabilized macroeconomic situation, though the result was a poor economy and an even worse management. The national economy is also suffering from a lack of managerial expertise. The main concern, at least among the specialists in this area, is the answer to the question: When it will be achieved a reasonable level of required managerial skills?

Leaving aside other problems, the transformation process of Albanian economy was accompanied by some special features of the new emerging businesses, which have to face various difficulties and problems. Nowadays, as the severity of the market competition is expected to be more emphasized and the environment is changing rapidly, the need for increased effectiveness in the businesses' management is becoming more evident. To understand and explain the various managerial aspects of Albanian businesses, as well as the problems they are facing, a survey was undertaken. It sees the management process as a set of four main managerial functions such as planning, organizing, leading, and controlling. It also makes a classification according to areas of management (marketing, finance, operation, human resources, etc.).

Agriculture in the country is based on small- to medium-sized family-owned dispersed units. It remains a significant sector of the economy of Albania. It employs 41% of the population, and about 24.31% of the land is used for agricultural purposes. Albania produces significant amounts of fruits, vegetables, sugar beets, tobacco, meat, honey, dairy products, traditional medicine, and aromatic plants. Further, the country is a worldwide significant producer of salvia, rosemary, and yellow gentian (OECD, 2023).

The country's proximity to the Ionian Sea and the Adriatic Sea gives the underdeveloped fishing industry great potential. Albania's fishing industry has good potential to generate export earnings because prices in the nearby Greek and Italian markets are many times higher than those in the Albanian market.

Albania's secondary sector has undergone many changes and diversification since the communist regime collapsed. It is very diversified, from electronics, manufacturing, textiles, food, cement, mining, and energy. Albanian oil and gas are one of the most promising, albeit strictly regulated, sectors of its economy. Albania has the second-largest oil deposits in the Balkan peninsula after Romania, and the largest oil reserves in Europe. The textile industry has seen an extensive expansion.

Albania is a significant mineral producer and ranks among the world's leading chromium producers and exporters. The nation is also a notable producer of copper, nickel, and coal.

The tertiary sector represents the fastest-growing sector of the country's economy. A total of 36% of the population work in the service sector which contributes to 65% of the country's GDP. Tourism is recognized as an industry of national importance and has been steadily increasing since the beginning of the twenty-first century. It directly accounted for 8.4% of GDP in 2016 though including indirect contributions pushes the proportion to 26% In the same year, the country received approximately 4.74 million visitors mostly from across Europe and the United States as well (OECD, 2020).

The bulk of the tourist industry is concentrated along the Adriatic and Ionian Seas in the west of the country. But the Albanian Riviera in the southwest has the most scenic and pristine beaches; its coastline has a considerable length of 446 kilometers (277 miles). The coast has a distinctive character, rich in varieties of virgin beaches, capes, coves, covered bays, lagoons, small gravel beaches, sea caves, and many landforms. Some parts of this seaside are very clean ecologically, including unexplored areas, which are very rare within the Mediterranean.

1.2 *Identifying Strategic Opportunities for Albania*

When Dustin Hoffman, playing the part of Hollywood producer Stanley Moss, was asked in David Mamet's satirical movie "Wag the Dog" to create e media diversion for U.S. international problems, his first choice was to fabricate a fictional war in a country where nobody knew anything about: Albania. When the film came out in 1997, the choice was effective for the plot, as indeed 40 years of dictatorial isolation under Enver Hoxha had made the southwest Balkan nation the most mysterious piece of land on the earth.

Over the last 30 years, Albania has made remarkable progress in becoming a democratic society with a functional open market economy. Productivity growth across all sectors has improved employment, incomes and standards of living. While deprivations remain, extreme poverty is very low and life expectancy is increasing. Institutional development and global integration also progressed. Albania's accession to the European Union is a cornerstone of Albania's foreign policy and a key driver of reforms (OECD, 2020).

Building on its success, Albania must now create the capabilities for continued strong development. Gross domestic product (GDP) and productivity growth rates have declined since the global crisis of 2008 and have not recovered, indicating that the early gains from the post-communist transition have been achieved, and new engines for a sustainable model of development must be built. Stronger institutions, with the capacity to implement and deliver quality public services to all citizens, will be key, as will be the process toward further integration with the European Union.

To succeed, Albania prepared a new Strategy for Development and Integration 2021–2030 (Government of Albania, 2021). This strategy comes at a crucial time, as the accession process with the EU has moved to a new level, while Albania, Europe and the world grapple with the COVID-19 pandemic and its aftermath. Building on the previous National Strategy for Development and Integration 2014–2020, the new strategy will have to lay out a vision for Albania in 2030, chart the path and key objectives for achieving this vision and tackle the most important constraints that can hold Albania back.

Vision for Albania in 2030: an attractive society with a high quality of life and strong human capital, built on reliable, resilient, and efficient institutions, a dynamic economy, and integration into Europe and the region.

Anchored in the European Union, Albania of 2030 is envisioned as an economy with stable, reliable, and accountable institutions and a functioning system of checks and balances. It has a competitive economy with an attractive framework for business and growth thanks to higher productivity, a skilled labor force, and better use of natural resources. Last, Albania of 2030 is a knowledgeable and inclusive society that benefits fully from improved health and education systems and quality jobs and where human capital and well-being are at the heart of the country's development. In terms of the individual dimensions of this vision, education, good governance, strong institutions, and public services are considered the most important, as identified through a voting exercise.

1.3 Main Distinguished Characteristics of Business in Albania

- *First,* the geographical distribution of Albanian business is disproportional. There would be no "harmonious development," but it is necessary for a larger development of business in smaller districts of the country. The experience has shown that the state intervenes with appropriate mechanisms in the encouragement of private entrepreneurs to invest in the less developed zones, as well as in putting barriers to hinder the industrial super development of other zones.
- *Second*, the number of businesses in the production sector is still behind the possibilities and the demands set before, from the actual and future development. At the early stage of business birth, it was a natural phenomenon for them to be oriented in the trade sector for many reasons, and above all they were attracted by the high profits generated from a small capital with a high rate of return in a market which was in need for almost everything. There are a lot of entrepreneurs who wish to invest in production, but they still notice a kind of withdrawal, which more than anything else is based on the small capital they possess, the relatively long period of return of capital, and high risk as a result of foreign firm competition.
- *Third,* the danger of bankrupt is a normal phenomenon for those who do not obey the rules of the game. Being in the position of the referee, the state must take care that all the businesses respect the rules. The state control and the penalties for those who do not obey the laws of the market economy must be tougher than up to now.
- *Fourth*, about half of the economically active population is employed in agriculture, which contributes about one-fifth of Albania's GDP. In itself, the division of the land into small parcels is difficulty for growth. Besides, the modernization of the country requires a shift of this percentage from the countryside to the cities.
- *Fifth,* another important business area where Albania can rely for its development is tourism. However, it is well known that tourism requires a developed infrastructure. So, under the actual conditions is present the danger of the development of spontaneous tourism, which might deepen the urban crises as a result of agriculture destruction.
- *Sixth,* taking into consideration that Albania is predominating the micro-enterprises, their organizational structure is generally simple. Usually, they have linear structures with one (rarely two) levels of management. There is a tendency for the authority to be centralized in the hands of the owner-manager. The process of decision-making is relatively fast, but this does not mean that in every case they make effective decisions. The quality of management is far from the demands of the present situation. A basic condition for success requires intensifying the qualifications of new Albanian managers.

1.4 The Impact of Pandemic on Albanian Businesses

The COVID-19 pandemic has had a major impact on small businesses in Albania, as in many other countries. Some of the main effects include:

1. Decreased income: Many small businesses have experienced a significant decrease in income due to restrictions on economic activity and social distancing measures. This has particularly affected sectors that depend on the circulation of people, such as restaurants, hotels and other similar services.
2. Facing financial difficulties: Lack of liquidity and low income have caused many businesses to struggle to pay rent, wages and suppliers. Some businesses have been forced to close temporarily or even permanently.
3. Adapting to technology: The pandemic has prompted many small businesses to adapt to technology, switching to online sales and using digital platforms to keep in touch with their customers.
4. Government aid: The Albanian government has taken several measures to help small businesses, including subsidies, soft loans and tax deferrals. However, many businesses have reported that the aid has not been enough to cope with the difficulties.
5. Reorganization and innovation: Some businesses have found new ways to operate, diversifying their products or services and exploring new markets.

Overall, the pandemic has created major challenges for Albanian small businesses, but it has also spurred a rapid process of adaptation and innovation in ways of operating.

1.5 The Impact of the War in Ukraine on Albanian Businesses

The war in Ukraine has had a significant impact on the global economy, and small businesses in Albania have not been exempt from these effects. Some of the main impacts include:

1. Rising prices of energy and raw materials: The war has led to significant increases in the prices of energy, such as oil and gas, as well as some raw materials, due to disruptions in global supply chains and the sanctions imposed on Russia. This has increased operating costs for small businesses, which are more vulnerable to sudden changes in costs.
2. Inflation: The increase in the prices of energy and raw materials has contributed to high inflation in Albania, reducing the purchasing power of consumers. This has affected the demand for products and services of small businesses, causing many of them to face financial difficulties.
3. Difficulty in supply: The war has caused disruptions in the supply of several essential products, including wheat and other grains, which have particularly affected the food and beverage sector. This has caused some small businesses to

face difficulties in securing raw materials or to cope with the increase in their prices.
4. Economic uncertainty and investment: The uncertainty created by the war has had the effect of reducing investment and making many entrepreneurs reluctant to expand or invest in new businesses. This negatively affects the growth and development of the small business sector.
5. Impact on the tourism sector: Albania, as a growing tourist destination, has seen an indirect impact from the war due to the general insecurity in the region and the decline in the number of tourists from Eastern European countries. This has affected small businesses that depend on tourism, such as hotels, restaurants, and tourist services.

In summary, the war in Ukraine has created several challenges for small businesses in Albania, affecting operating costs, demand for products and services, and overall, the country's economic stability.

2 Case Studies of Selected Hidden Champions

2.1 Mare Adriatik Ltd

Overview
Collection, processing, and packaging of anchovies and sardines

Contact: CEO Mark Babani
Address: Shelqet—Vau i Dejes, Lezhe, Albania
Tel: 00355 266 22146 Fax: 00355 266 22146
Email: mare.adriatik@yahoo.it www.mareadriatik.com

Company Information

Industry	Fish processing
Year of establishment	1995
Sales revenue in 2021	€9. 000,000
Sales revenues in 2010	€1,080,000
Sales revenues in 2000	€261,135
Average number of employees in 2021	600
Average number of employees in 2017	400
Average number of employees in 2010	150
Brainer(s) behind the company	CEO and founder Mark Babani

2.1.1 Nature of Market Leadership

Mare Adriatik, one of Albania's leading seafood processors and exporters, whose customers include some of Europe's leading supermarkets. Mare Adriatik is one of the largest Albanian processors and exporters to the European market of anchovies and sardines from the Adriatic Sea and is first in the Southwestern Balkan region, in terms of market share.

The company operates in cooperation with Spain, Croatia, and Greece. Adriatic anchovies are very rich in omega-6 oils. The company guarantees high-quality products, processed with craft methods, enabling clients to enjoy authentic bluefish. In 2021, the market share of the company in the Southwestern Balkans increased from to 80%.

2.1.2 Nature of Competitive Advantage

Mare Adriatik has the largest market share in Albania. The company processes about 5000 tons of fish per year equal to 1000 tons of fish fillet (equal to the production of all European companies taken together). Mare Adriatik carries out the full chain of processing activities, preparing the product for the end consumer. The main competitors of anchovy fillets are companies in Italy, mainly in Sicily. Also, Morocco is a serious competitor in the European market.

Competitive advantages mentioned by the founder are:

- Leveraging cutting-edge technology to improve products or processes
- Experience in the field
- Geographic position of Albania
- Implementing best practices and optimizing supply chains
- Very long experience
- Achieving the lowest production and operation costs
- Potential international clients for salt anchovy fillets
- Adriatic Sea fish is rich in omega-3 and there is a high demand for it

2.1.3 Core Lessons Learned on the Path to Business Success

- Be prepared to pivot your strategy based on market feedback and changing conditions.
- Maintain strict control over finances and ensure healthy cash flow. Listen to your team, customers, and peers. The different perspective is valuable.
- Continuously investing in new products, mainly focusing on introducing high-quality products in the market; and improving technology, always aiming to add value to the product.

2.1.4 Management and Leadership

In 1991 Mark, as many other Albanians, emigrated to Italy, Sicily. There he worked in a processing plant of anchovies. Since the first years of work he began to think about opening up such a factory in his village, in Albania. One of the Italian owners proved willing to cooperate. They first opened a small workshop and bought a fishing boat in 1994. After 2 years of collaboration, co-Italian died. Mark was left alone. What to do? "I fell in the sea and I had to swim"—he says.

Mark Babani (age 43) is the sole shareholder and administrator of the company. He is the one who takes care in the decision-making of the company, in all the company's legal acts, in maintaining the relationship with his clients and his suppliers.

Mr. Mark is a democratic leader. He is aware that employees are at the same time his clients. Taking care to increase the satisfaction of employees at work, on the other hand it provides the guarantee for quality products. Most important values protected in the company are working together, communication and execution of tasks in time and quality.

2.1.5 Financing, and Regulatory Environment Development Needs

The expansion of the company was achieved by cooperating with the banking sector. Currently, the company works with its income.

The problem that arises is that not being a country of the European community, Albania has low fishing quotas. If you add to this the fact that these quotas are distributed by the government among businesses, this increases dissatisfaction both in terms of bureaucratic procedures and how these quotas are distributed.

On the other hand, if companies exceed the limit of exports set by the EU, they pay higher customs tariffs. The customs tariffs hinder company growth, as they involve a 25% extra tax.

2.1.6 The Impact of Strategy Based on Market Feedback and Changing Conditions

Fishing in Albania is primarily marine fisheries, although lagoon and inland fishing does take place on a limited scale. During recent years aquaculture is being increasingly promoted. Albania has a well-established fishing industry with capacities to process fresh and frozen fish and seafood as well as to trans-form them into delicious ready to eat products as marinated salads or canned food, or skewers.

Albanian seafood industry delivers as well the domestic market as well many export destinations mainly in southern Europe.

Fishery and Aquaculture Country Profile for Albania—aquatic species caught by country or area, by species items, by FAO major fishing areas, and year, for all commercial, industrial, recreational and subsistence purposes. The harvest from mariculture, aquaculture, and other kinds of fish farming is also included.

An international bottom trawl survey in the Mediterranean—in the Mediterranean, the main demersal fisheries are localized on narrow continental shelves along the coasts. Experiences during the last decades in this area have shown that it was difficult to obtain a global estimate of the demersal resources from fishing activity, especially due to the very large dispersion of the landing places, the important diversity of the species caught and the scarceness of reliable statistics.

Fish processing business in particular and that of anchovies in particular is a business in which employees work covers a high specific weight. However, Mr. Mark has attached particular importance to the improvement of technology, always aiming to modern technology. He is aware that the processing of the product has an increased added value about 4 times, compared with raw materials. Another factor that fuels the innovation process is market need. For this the company operates very close with suppliers and customers.

A strategy based on market needs and changes that occur in it offers several key benefits for businesses and organizations Mare Adriatica has always emphasized adaptation to the market and flexibility. This has led to being resilient to new challenges and trends. And modifying their offer based on customer demands.

By understanding the needs of the market, the company has offered products or services that differentiate it from competitors, which has helped create a stronger image in the market as well as creating a competitive advantage.

As a result of a strategy in line with current customer demands, Mare Adriatica has enabled increased sales and avoided unnecessary investments, helping to increase efficiency and profit. On the other hand, this has helped in greater customer loyalty and the creation of long-term relationships with them. Following trends and analyzing customer behavior has helped the company develop new and innovative ideas.

A successful strategy requires continuous market research and a dynamic approach to change. Adaptation and innovation are key factors for success in any industry.

2.1.7 COVID-19 Pandemic and Ukraine War in Fish Sector

The fish sector, like the entire food industry, has been significantly impacted both from the pandemic and the war in Ukraine

Regarding COVID-19, the fish processing sector faced several challenges:

1. As a result of the decline in consumption, this sector faced a decline in demand and exports.
2. Difficulties arose in the supply of raw materials (fresh fish, due to movement restrictions).

3. Anti-Covid measures such as disinfection and social distancing increased operating costs for both fishing and processing companies.
4. Due to restrictive measures and quarantine, companies faced a shortage of labor force.

On the other hand, the crisis in Ukraine was accompanied by an increase in fuel prices, an increase in the prices of raw materials (plastic, and fish feed) and increased competition in markets, especially in exports.

To overcome these challenges and adapt to the new environment, fish processing companies have undertaken several long-term strategies such as market diversification and investment in aquaculture (fish farms). On the other hand, the government has supported this sector through subsidizing oil costs.

2.2 *Alb Kalustyan*

Overview
Collecting and marketing bio-medicinal herbs
Contact: CEO Xhevit Hysenaj
Address: Vlashaj Nr. 101, Maminas, Durres, Albania
Tel: +355 69 20 60915
Fax: +355575 80645
Email: xhevit@albkalustyan.com
Web: www.albkalustyan.com

Industry	Agriculture, forestry and fishing
Year of establishment:	1991; 1995 (registered as Xherdo shpk); 2014 (joint venture, renamed Alb Kalustyan shpk)
Sales revenue in 2021	€18,191,000
Sales revenues in 2010:	€3,058,196
Revenues in 2000:	€935.000
Average number of employees in 2021	200
Average number of employees in 2017	150
Average number of employees in 2010	120 employees
Brainer(s) behind the company	CEO and founder Xhevit Hysenaj

2.2.1 Nature of Market Leadership

Alb Kalustyan is a leader in the Southwestern Balkans in the niche of collecting and marketing medicinal herbs, meeting the quality standards of the prestigious USA and EU markets. The company exports mostly to the USA, but also to Canada, Germany, France, Italy, Spain, Austria, Belgium, Switzerland, the United Kingdom, Netherlands, Morocco, and Malaysia.

It is the leading provider of essential oils and processed medicinal plants in Albania and the largest exporter of herbal essences in terms of experience, technology, and marketing. The company is mainly focused on bio-products. Its market share increased to 75%.

2.2.2 Nature of Competitive Advantage

AlbKalustyan began in 2014 as a collaboration between Xherdo of Albania and Kalustyan of USA. Target supplies products worldwide to their customers with the highest quality, latest technology, and excellent customer service. They are manufacturer and exporters of more than 26 Bio Organic Medicinal Aromatic plants & Essential oils.

Competitive Advantages mentioned by the founder are:

- Full production line
- High quality
- Modern technology
- Keeping the tradition
- Exclusive focus on organic products
- Highest possible standards of food safety
- Processing activities.
- Building strong relationships with customers.
- Expanding market reach and resources through joint ventures.

2.2.3 Core Lessons Learned on the Path to Business Success

Follow your vision. Mr. Hysenaj is a risk-taker, but firm in his vision. Although this is a simple business, they couldn't possibly have grown this quickly without technology.

Build relationships with your customers. In general, customers are loyal, but it is conditioned by the quality of production. If you neglect quality, customers will immediately leave. Mr. Hysenaj states: "*Our foreign partners are in the business of 150–200 years and inherited generations. Fifty percent of the product is purchased from the 3 most important customers of the company. Relations with clients are cooperative, and very correct, while we are dealing with very loyal customers.*

Challenge difficulties. *Threats to wild plants (MAP).* MAP plant sources within Albania are affected by many activities, including development of the territory, and unregulated collection, especially during the last 15 years. Other risks for actual habitat, or that can increase the risk for the future, are gathering and cultivating techniques, as well as grazing and fires; on the other hand, overexploitation of some medicinal plants, lack of inventory and possible risks of irregular collection can lead to damage of the habitat;

Best combine new technology and old methods of work. Sustainability, efficiency, and economic sense made it clear to Hysenaj that the best thing to do was to adapt the technology himself in a way that would fit his company's needs and further empower Albania's agro-processing industry. Hysenaj believed members of a small organization must have a sense of identity, ownership, and purpose. In turn, these feelings fostered commitment, conviction, innovation, and interest in long-term success. Despite the authoritarian style, which according to Hysenaj is necessary and dictated by the geographical distribution of the company, he emphasizes teamwork. Employees, are carefully approached and educated in the workplace, but also tested after a short time of working. The workers are motivated with support, and reward for the good work they do.

Build relationships with your customers. In general, customers are loyal, but it is conditioned by the quality of production. If you neglect quality, customers will immediately leave. Mr. Hysenaj states: "*Our foreign partners are in the business of 150–200 years and inherited generations. Fifty percent of the product is purchased from the 3 most important customers of the company. Relations with clients are cooperative, very correct, while we are dealing with very loyal customers.*

Adapt quickly. Hysenaj, acts quickly in his day-to-day management and decision-making. He typically responds very fast to new items and requests because, as he said, "I know something else will happen and will ask for response."

2.2.4 The Company Management and Leadership

In this phase of business development strategic thinking is important. First of all, it is important that companies have a clear vision, real objectives, problem-solving and decision-making skills. Growing with the customer is a must nowadays, as the business, customers, distributors, and markets are becoming more sophisticated.

Investment in people as the main asset in business should be considered seriously and incorporated into the larger picture. Continuously developing the skills and abilities of the staff should be a matter of high priority.

Management needs to engage the company's staff in business matters fully. Without their cooperation, success is impossible.

2.2.5 Financing, and Regulatory Environment Development Needs

The company cooperates successfully with banks. Regardless of this, due to strict bank policies, especially after COVID-19 pandemia, the business have had difficulties in securing loans.

On the other hand, irregular income and late payments from customers sometimes create liquidity problems.

2.2.6 Impact of Following Your Vision and Building Sustainable Relationships with Customers

The production of essences from wild plants began during the communist era. Secondary products such as sage and thyme were extracted from the remains of these plants. Historically, over 98% of medicinal plants were exported and accounted for the main share of exports. After the 1990s, the processing of medicinal plants and their essences decreased by 4 times. This was mainly due to the population moving to cities. After 1995, there was a renaissance of the market. Many traders and plant processors turned their attention from the process of collecting plants and later on the production of essences. Since Albania has a tradition in exporting medicinal plants, USAID helped producers add value to their products, emphasizing quality in order to meet market demands.

The company's success is based on:

- Serious investments in production lines and laboratories.
- Good, reciprocal relationships with customers, punctuality, responsibility and maximum speed in customer service.
- A clear vision for the future development and modern spirit of cooperation.

Following a clear vision has a great impact on the success of a company. A clear vision helps the company set clear objectives and priorities, motivates and engages employees, serves as a compass in decision-making, and creates a clear identity in the market. The new requirement is that the vision be clearly communicated to employees and become a motto for action for everyone.

On the other hand, stable relationships with customers directly affect its growth and stability. Satisfied customers will return again. This leads to lower marketing and sales costs, differentiation from the competition, the opportunity to develop new products as a result of recognizing customer needs, as well as minimizing uncertainty.

2.2.7 COVID-19 Pandemic and Ukraine War in Agriculture and Forestry

The COVID-19 pandemic had significant impacts on agriculture and forestry worldwide, including disruptions in production, supply chains, and labor availability. In Albania it is characterized by: slowing the movement of goods because of lockdowns and border restrictions; some countries posed trade restrictions; due to restaurant and hotel closures, demand for some products dropped, causing financial losses for company. Smallholder farmers, in particular (suppliers of the company), faced income losses as they struggled to survive.

The war in Ukraine has had a significant impact on the agricultural and forestry sector in Albania, causing major changes in supply markets and prices of agricultural products.

Among the main factors has been the increase in the prices of agricultural inputs, because a good part of the fertilizers come from Ukraine. The war also led to the increase in the price of oil and the lack of labor force (some of the seasonal workers came from Ukraine).

However, the sector has diversified its sources of supply and increased local production as a way to address some of these challenges. Also, the government and relevant institutions have forgotten the policy to support the agricultural industry with appropriate measures to cope with these shocks.

2.3 *Venice Art Masks Factory*

Overview

Production of masks
Contact: CEO Edmond Angoni
Address: Rr. Vasil Shanto, No.783, Shkoder, Albania.
Mob.: +355 67 20 47291
E-mail: edmondangoni@gmail.com
https://www.instagram.com/explore/locations/171665940044825/venice-art-mask-factory

Company Information

Industry	Carnival masks
Year of establishment	1998
Sales revenues in 2021	€2,431,830
Sales revenues in 2010	€1,545,725
Sales revenues in 2000	€86,835
Average number of employees in 2021	90
Average number of employees in 2017	90
Average number of employees in 2010	70
Brainer(s) behind the company	CEO and founder Edmond Angoni

2.3.1 Nature of Market Leadership

Venice Art's main market is Venice, from which it receives large orders for the day of carnivals. The company also exports carnival masks to Las Vegas and Australia. It is one of the biggest and finest mask-making workshops in the world. The company is known for one reason: its respect for tradition. However, the company has been able to interpret tradition in innovative ways, creating new and unique decorative styles and shapes. Venice Art crafts hand-made masks in the same way as Venetian artisans 800 years ago.

The company never repeats a decoration, so each mask is unique. The products are hand-made, characterized by high quality, and dedicated to a selected clientele. The advantages of Venice Art include expertise, a relatively long experience in the market, and a rich catalog of models. The company's market share achieved 80% of European market.

The company has opened a showroom in Shkoder, which will be a museum, production area, and teaching center for future generations.

2.3.2 Nature of Competitive Advantage

Venice Art builds its reputation on quality products and efficient response to client needs. It has adopted the mission statement "Quality is our standard."

Since 2011, many improvements have been made in the process of mask production. As a result of experience and improvement of equipment, production times have been reduced.

Competitive advantages mentioned by the founder are:

- Offering unique products or services that are valued by customers.
- Innovation, quality, branding, and superior customer service.
- Continuous development of new products.
- Prioritize customer satisfaction and build strong relationships.
- The quality and originality of the products, the handling of every mask as if it were an artwork. This has resulted in the reputation of masks spreading almost at the same speed as globalization.
- The know-how was created through years of experience. As a result, it is difficult for new entrants to be competitive in the market.
- Flexibility and continuous innovation: Eight hundred new models have been designed and crafted in the last 20 years.
- A rich catalog of models that is very difficult to be created by a new entrant in the market.

2.3.3 The Core Lessons Learned on the Path to the Business Success

Love the job and treat it as a child. His uniqueness lied in the way he had brought his personal beliefs and philosophy into his management. Edmond's experiences of overcoming various difficulties first as a refugee and later as an entrepreneur formed the basis of some of the tenets of his personal philosophy.

Consider your business a big family. Edmond sees leadership as unique for each company. He says: "We just have to keep up the practical magic. I just want to be part of a group of people that work hard to make reality my ideas. In the same time, they must be creative. If you don't, then you get neither art nor commerce." Treating people with kindness and learning from them humbly are the most valuable human qualities

- Surround yourself with creative people who challenge, inspire, and propel forward the company vision.
- Understand Your Market: Conduct thorough market research to understand customer needs, preferences, and trends. Since 1998, a lot of improvements are done on the process of masks production. As a result of experience and improvement of equipment, time of production of a mask is cut.

Since uniqueness stems from the work of the hand, we cannot talk about research-development costs.

However, we can say that the mask patterns always change. Each model differs from predecessors. This is also depending on customer requirements.

- Invest in employee skills and knowledge. The fact that Edmondi attributes the success of the company to the people that work for him, he put his emphasis on training, trust, and respect.
- Create a culture that attracts and retains top talent. Mr. Angoni says: "We consider each other as a family. Employees of the company are one of the basic factors of success. It is their professionalism that makes my product unique," says Edmond. Further, he continues: "In 15 years there is no worker left the workplace. They have grown together with the business."

2.3.4 Management and Leadership

The company is known for one reason: its respect for tradition. However, the company has been able to interpret tradition in innovative ways: creating new and unique decorative styles and shapes, understanding one's strengths and weaknesses, fostering teamwork and collaboration and conflict resolution and negotiation.

Finding a workforce with a working culture is a challenge for the company. New employees need time to learn the work culture and adjust to company values. They lack creativity and have few practical skills. For this reason, employees undergo periodic training. As a result, the company needs to develop joint training programs with schools in the field of art.

2.3.5 Financing and Regulatory Environment Development Needs

Relationships with financial institutions are improving due to the strengthening of the business. The company is satisfied with the financing and regulatory environment.

2.3.6 Impact of Considering Your Business as a Big Family and Investing in Employee Skills and Knowledge

Mr. Edmond attributes the company's success to the people who work for him, emphasizing training, trust, and respect. "We consider each other as family. The company's employees are one of the key factors in our success. It is their professionalism that makes our product unique," says Mr. Angoni.

"We have been advised to increase market share and introduce masks at low prices. But we want to serve our customers exclusively. We seek to differentiate ourselves with products focused on a market segment. Arti Venecian insists on serving exclusively a selected market segment."

Venice Arts builds its reputation in quality products and efficient response to client needs. It had adopted the mission statement "Quality is our Standard."

As a result of this culture, employees are motivated and collaborate better, conflicts are avoided, productivity increases, emotional well-being increases, more talent is attracted, and creativity and innovation increase.

2.3.7 Impact of the Pandemic and the War in Ukraine on Craftsmanship and Carnival Mask Production

The pandemic and the war in Ukraine have had an indirect impact on Albanian crafts and carnival mask production. Among the most important impacts are:

1. Increase in material prices and production costs: Especially paints and metals used in the creation of masks.
2. Disruption in supply chains: Ukraine and Russia are important producers of some materials, such as paper pulp, pigments, synthetic resins, metallic foils, and certain types of decorative fabrics, which are often used in the crafting and ornamentation of carnival masks.
3. Decline in exports and international demand: Several important markets for handicraft products, including European ones and those related to tourism, have been affected by the war. Demand has fallen due to economic uncertainty and the slowdown in global tourism.

The pandemic and the war in Ukraine have created major challenges for the crafts sector and carnival mask production in Albania. The above factors have forced many producers to adapt or diversify their activity.

3 Conclusions and Recommendations

There is a qualitative change in how businesses operate now, easily identified in the profile of the hidden champions. Still, they remain small, young, and focused mostly on the region. The median age of the companies identified in this study is 28 years.

They have successfully survived, grown, and expanded globally. For instance, Xherdo has formed a joint venture with Kalustyan, an American world leader in sage manufacturing and sales. Some companies are focused mainly on small customer groups and can create superior customer value (Mare Adriatik, Venice Art Masks) than their competitors.

Strong entrepreneurial founders lead the majority of companies that were studied but, in a few cases (Venice Art Masks), founders are sharing power with managers from the younger generation.

The nature of the competitive advantage of Albania's hidden champions shows diversity in the quality of products, partnerships, qualified staff, labor costs, market knowledge, customer orientation, expert knowledge, barriers to new entries, design, and more. Hidden champions in Albania have the following characteristics:

They follow a focused strategy. They are deep instead of broad. Meanwhile they apply a wide range of innovative solutions to meet client expectations, particularly when it comes to design features, an extremely important factor in their competitive advantage.

On the other side, one important thing for hidden champions is to realize that employees are the main assets. They attribute the success of the company to the people who work for them and emphasize training, trust, and respect.

The ownership is long-term oriented and capital markets do not play a big role. Rather the hidden champions in Albania rely on self-financing. They are conservative in financial matters. They are integrating forward along the industry value chain and are trying to appropriate more value from the industry value chain.

Hidden champions in Albania adapt to changes. They always look on the bright side and turn problems into motives to achieve goals. They think that leadership must be authoritarian in the principles, but flexible in the details.

The businesses are aware that it is important to create better conditions of life for our fellow citizens, especially in disadvantaged areas. This will help to create a climate of peace and security and will discourage emigration of the population.

In a country like Albania, which is not so much developed in terms of service and quality, there are a lot of opportunities for SMEs, but you have to be different, to offer something unique. Hidden champions must have a clear vision and ambitious goals for the future. They find opportunities where others find difficulties.

In Albania's business environment, tradition is an important factor. Hidden champions in Albania look for the advantage in bioproducts. To cope with global market requirements, they emphasize quality products.

At the same time, they have a great need for control. This is a significant theme in the life and personality of many Albanian entrepreneurs. They often display a sense of distrust as they typically live in fear of being victimized, and they want to be ready should disaster strike. They have a desire for applause when success is knocking on their door. In their portfolio of skills, they have a good set of survival instincts. They tend to throw their life, family, and business partners into turmoil by getting into battles where they dodge bullets. This gives them the energy to start afresh.

References

Encyclopædia Britannica. (2024). People of Albania. https://www.britannica.com/place/Albania/People.

Government of Albania. (2021). National Strategy on development and integration. One Planet Network. https://www.oneplanetnetwork.org/knowledge-centre/policies/national-strategy-development-and-integration-albania.

OECD. (2023). *Overview: Identifying strategic opportunities for Albania.* https://www.oecd-ilibrary.org/sites/7c2fa8bd-en/index.html?itemId=/content/component/7c2fa8bd-en.

OECD. (2020). Competitiveness in south East Europe: A policy outlook 2018. OECD Publishing. https://doi.org/10.1787/9789264298576-en.

The World Bank. (2024). Albania overview. https://www.worldbank.org/en/country/albania/overview.

Wikipedia Contributors. (2024). Albania—politics. In *Wikipedia,* The Free Encyclopedia. https://en.wikipedia.org/wiki/Albania#Politics.

Anisa Kume graduated in Business Administration, Management, at the Faculty of Economy, University of Tirana (2008). Immediately after graduation, she applied for and in 2010 completed the Second Level Master "Master in European Economics and Financial Institutions," at Tor Vergata University, Rome. In 2011, she completed the Second Level Master "Master in European Economic Studies," a cooperation between Faculty of Economy and Bamberg University. She holds the title Doctor of Science since 2015.

During the March 2011–July 2016, she worked as an Expert for Budget Monitoring and Management, at the Budget Directorate, Ministry of Finance. From 2016–April 2024, she was responsible for the analysis and monitoring of the local budget, and the management of fiscal risks, Budget Directorate, Ministry of Finance and Economy.

Anisa has taught as a guest lecturer at the Faculty of Economy and private universities in Albania from 2008 until now. She is currently engaged full-time at the Faculty of Economy, in the subjects of Management and Business Communication for undergraduate and graduate levels of study.

Anisa Kume has had successful experiences with technical assistance and national and international projects. For about 9 years she has worked with the IMF and World Bank on reforms implementation in local governance, fiscal risks from PPPs and other contingent liabilities or the state-owned enterprise sector.

During her academic journey, she has participated in many international conferences and has published a number of scientific articles. She is a trainer employed by public and private institutions for budget management and monitoring of fiscal risks and has attended a series of training programs and held conferences abroad in Germany, Austria, Netherlands, Slovenia, China, etc.

Elona Garo has expertise in Public Administration and Management, with advanced training from Harvard University's Kennedy School of Government and Syracuse University's Maxwell School of Citizenship, where she studied as a Fulbright Scholar. She earned her Doctorate from the University of Tirana in 2016 and currently teaches at the university level while training public officials in Project Management, Strategic Management, and Organizational Behavior. She also advises individuals, companies, and organizations on strategic planning, capacity development, and human resource management.

Dr. Garo has contributed extensively to the academic and professional field through publications including peer-reviewed articles, case studies, and book chapters. Her career includes serving as Dean of Students at the University of New York Tirana, where she led student service policy and program design. She collaborated with UNDP to support institutional development and strengthen citizen-centered service delivery in local governance.

In her work with Albania's Department of Public Administration, she played a key role in assessing organizational structures, developing functional analyses and job descriptions, and aligning ministry operations with Civil Service Law. She also served as a liaison between the Prime Minister's Office and Line Ministries, facilitating institutional coordination and policy implementation.

Vasilika Kume is an expert in Management and Strategic Planning, with extensive competencies in analytical decision-making, SME development, project cycle management, negotiations, clusters, and leadership.

She graduated in Industrial Economics from the Faculty of Economics at Tirana University in 1979 and completed her postgraduate studies in Management (1986–1991), and became a Full Professor in 2001.

From 1998 to 2012, she served as Executive Director of the Master's Program at the Faculty of Economics, UT. Currently, she is the Rector of Tirana Business University College, while also lecturing on Strategic Management and Decision-Making at graduate and postgraduate levels. Prof. Kume has taught, for several semesters, as a visiting professor at Worms University in Germany, where she delivered the entire "International Strategic Management" course for IMBA students, and as a part-time lecturer at universities in Kosovo and North Macedonia.

She has trained executives and staff in Customer Care, Problem Solving, Leadership, and Change Management, and has supervised numerous PhD candidates domestically and abroad. Her international experience includes academic and professional engagements in the USA, UK, Greece, Germany, Italy, China, etc.

Prof. Kume has been a member of the Scientific Council of the Faculty of Economics, UT since 1996 and serves on scientific boards of journals abroad. Author of over 40 papers, textbooks, and scientific works, she has contributed to major national projects such as the Poverty Monitoring Indicators, Regional Development Strategy, Urban Waste Management, the National Environmental Management Plan, etc.

Hidden Champions of Armenia

Vanine Yeranosyan, Astghik Sargsyan, and Tigran Mnatsakanyan

Abstract The phenomenon of hidden champions deserves special observation in economies like Armenia, as such companies may play a crucial role in the development and even survival of countries with a number of economic disadvantages. This chapter of the study explores the social, economic, historical, political, and cultural background of the local business environment, which makes the formation of future hidden champions realistic and specific. Two typical cases are studied in detail: The Crowdfunding Formula, a very specific niche service provider with huge market expansion opportunities, and Krisp, one of the most prospective companies in Armenia with lots of new market possibilities. It is worth mentioning that the scale of the Armenian economy limits the potential number of hidden champions, as do the limitations of economic activities in many industries. Hence, given the contemporary difficulties, competition, and scaling possibilities, companies that may to some extent be described as "blue ocean" strategy followers or pioneers have better chances of success.

Overview

Official name: Republic of Armenia
Type of government: Unitary parliamentary republic
Population in 2023: 2,977,100
Land area: 29,743 km^2

History

782 BCE	The fortress of Erebuni was founded (modern capital city Yerevan).
301 CE	Christianity is adopted as a state religion of the Kingdom of Armenia.

V. Yeranosyan
InTagma, Yerevan, Armenia
e-mail: vanine@intagma.org

A. Sargsyan · T. Mnatsakanyan (✉)
Matena International School of Leadership and Professional Development, Yerevan, Armenia
e-mail: Astghik.Sargsyan@matena.am; Tigran.Mnatsakanyan@matena.am

D. Berberović, D. Purg (eds.), *Hidden Champions in Rising Economies*, Contributions to Management Science,
https://doi.org/10.1007/978-3-032-08263-3_12

1915	The Armenian genocide in the Ottoman Empire peaked forcing hundreds of thousands of Armenians to escape from their homeland and line up the Armenian diaspora.
1918	After the collapse of the Ottoman and Russian empires, the First Republic of Armenia is established.
1920	Sovietization of Armenia started a near 70-year period of communism.
1988	A severe earthquake hit northern Armenia killing tens of thousands of people and destroying several towns.
1991	The referendum confirmed the independence from the Soviet Union and the formation of the Republic of Armenia.
1993	The Central Bank of Armenia introduced the Armenian dram as the currency of the Republic of Armenia.
1994	The First Artsakh War ended after more than 6 years of active phase.
2001	Armenia joined the Council of Europe.
2001–2007	Armenia became one of the world leaders by the annual growth of GDP (up to 14%).
2003	Armenia became a member of the World Trade Organization.
2009	Along with five other non-EU countries, Armenia joined the Eastern Partnership.
2015	Armenia became a member of the Eurasian Economic Union.
2018	A series of anti-government protests led to the 2018 Armenian Revolution.
2019	Several tax benefits for IT businesses were introduced to stimulate the growth of the industry. Those benefits were extended until the end of 2024.
2020	The Second Artsakh War escalated.
2022–2023	Following the military actions and sanctions in Russia, tens of thousands emigrated to Armenia. Many companies moved their offices to Armenia.
2022	With 12.60% of annual growth of GDP, Armenia approached its historical record and once again became one of the fastest-growing economies.

1 Introduction: Context and History

The business environment in Armenia, as well as the business mindset, are affected by a number of factors, some of which come from centuries, and some are relatively modern. The Armenian "meme pool" is diverse and sometimes even contradictory, as it was influenced by neighbors and invaders with completely different cultures; Assyrian, Persian, Roman, Byzantine, Arab, Turkic, and Russian states (Bournoutian, 2002; Vardanyan, 2021). While each of the periods had its unique footprint given the diverse aspects and timeframe, there was a cumulative and persistent impact of the creation of times of uncertainty and turbulence, which formed specific attitudes in setting a planning horizon and risk tolerance.

The huge footprint of the 70-year soviet period changed the people's expectations of the state authorities and their understanding of the economy, business, and private property. Like other Soviet republics, Armenia operated under a centralized economy where private property and entrepreneurship were largely restricted, which shaped people's mindset, making them rely on state authorities for economic security, jobs, and social benefits, while also fostering skepticism toward private business and market-driven competition. Those deeply ingrained attitudes influenced the way people perceived the role of the government in economic affairs and the legitimacy of private enterprise. Additionally, the loss of savings after the collapse of the Soviet Union affected spend-save-invest ratio intentions (Denizer & Wolf, 2000). Since independence and switching to the free market and until the rise of digital businesses, the common approach was to do some safe, already explored, or easy-to-explore business. However, growth in such "red oceans" was limited because of bigger competing companies in the region. Hence, in the 1990s, microbusinesses weren't sustainable and successful across the country, and neither were the big factories because of the total failure of privatization processes (Scannell & Newton, 2004). Moreover, being a landlocked country with closed borders (having only the borders with Georgia and Iran open), Armenia had limited access to global markets and global supply chains.

In the 2000s, partially as a result of the centralization of capital and partially as a result of several foreign investments and other factors, commercial banks and telecommunication companies joined the "premier league" of companies operating in Armenia along with some traditional manufacturing (copper and other raw materials, brandy, tobacco, etc.). Such a drift in the economy significantly impacted the labor market and attitudes toward professional education, as well as fostered internal migration into the capital city of Yerevan. The regional development disparity is still a major issue in the country (Mnatsakanyan et al., 2021; Hayrapetyan & Mnatsakanyan, 2022).

However, the development of the banking system did not result in the formation of stock markets. It was still hard for local companies to attract investors, and it was hard to become a small individual investor.

Besides the internal migration, emigration (including labor migration) flows to the USA, Russia, and European countries increased the number of Armenians living outside Armenia (by 2000, approx. 7.5 mil in contrast to approx. 3 mil living in Armenia) (Cohen, 2008). Personal remittances sent by labor migrants in particular and the Armenian diaspora in general have made the Armenian economy one of the most remittance-dependent in the world. Received personal remittances peaked in 2004, being estimated as 22% of GDP (in recent years it was around 11%) (The World Bank, n.d.-a).

In the 2010s, Armenia gradually improved its overall business environment and the "Doing Business" ranks, especially becoming one of the highest-ranked countries for starting a business (lately ranked 10th) (The World Bank, n.d.-b). However, despite achievements by various indicators, Armenia wasn't widely enjoying economic development because of the existing corruption and social injustice. These tensions led to many protests and, remarkably, the revolution in 2018.

In the late 2010s, the boom of the IT industry occurred. The number of IT companies and their employees increased drastically (PwC, 2021). IT companies became the most common "first choice" for investors and young specialists. Digital technologies influenced business attitudes, and "blue ocean" explorers started appearing more and more frequently, with a higher risk appetite. The knowledge of the leading specialists from the Armenian diaspora became more relevant to the Armenian economy.

Regarding foreign trade, two main export directions are the EU countries, which also reflect Armenia's endeavor to join the EU, and the CIS countries, which are driven by former economic ties and a better understanding of the market (Fig. 1).

Recently, China, India, and the UAE have also become major export partners (Exhibit 1).

The observation of the cultural dimensions suggested by Geert Hofstede would complement the overview of the Armenian business environment and culture by making the differentiation from the other countries more distinguished and its corresponding impact on the aspects shaping the overall mindset, which in its turn influences organizational behavior, business settings, obstacles of conducting business and many other consequences, more apparent (The Culture Factor Group, n.d.).

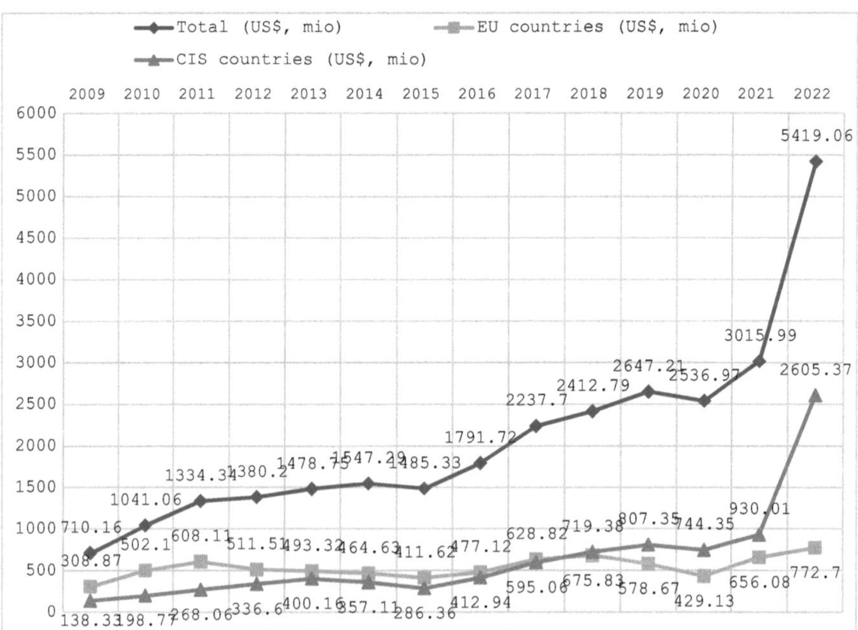

Fig. 1 Exports of the Republic of Armenia. Source: Statistical Committee of the Republic of Armenia (n.d.)

Exhibit 1 The biggest foreign trade partners cf Armenia by exports (USS, mio)

Country	Year									
	2013	2014	2015	2016	2017	2018	2019	2020	2021	2022
Russian Federation	334.13	308.25	244.89	374.47	557.26	666.13	741.44	680.34	840.68	2462.78
United Arab Emirates	9.44	12.06	9.1	63.84	102.21	73.83	57.27	95.92	74.39	534.15
China	106.06	171.03	165.36	96.45	118.53	107.22	193.71	289.83	393.18	369.5
Switzerland	24.55	13.97	38.95	74.64	261.39	337.46	457.86	453.95	359.49	254.5
Netherlands	66.44	74.43	47.31	50.84	88.61	132.36	153.85	97.77	191.25	214.86
Bulgaria	152.21	85.61	78.93	152.42	282.33	214.89	207.41	150.8	198.44	208.37
Georgia	85.17	84.33	125.32	146.94	152.89	68.69	69.27	57.45	68.31	162.41
Iran, Islamic Republic of	94.96	84.98	81.73	75.25	84.12	94.2	83.86	84.56	65.52	110.37
Germany	85.57	158.57	140.25	138.95	133.13	136.07	69.62	56.47	77.58	106.03
India	0.2	0.23	0.43	1.77	3.3	0.57	3.49	73.45	126.7	99.42
Belgium	131.14	62.41	42.45	41.6	45.79	49.2	44.47	36.56	51.92	85.73
United States	89.03	91.41	52.93	38.79	66.19	47.68	53.91	67.87	81.8	78.26
Belarus	8.56	9.04	6.81	13.41	7.05	11.94	17.82	21.32	28.32	76.96
Italy	23.19	34.58	32.54	31.88	43.28	49.88	59.69	40.97	63.51	65.1
Turkey	1.6	1.49	1.5	0.5	0.91	2.53	2.22	0.5	0.44	61.2
Rest of countries	266.51	354.84	416.83	489.95	290.71	420.16	431.32	329.22	394.46	529.42
Total exports	1478.75	1547.29	1485.33	1791.72	2237.7	2412.79	2647.21	2536.97	3015.99	5419.06

Sources: Statistical Committee of the Republic of Armenia (n.d.)

Power Distance: With a very high score of 85, Armenia is a nation where power holders are very distant in society. People in this society accept a hierarchical order in which everybody has a place, and which needs no further justification. Hierarchy is seen as reflecting inherent inequalities, and the different distribution of power justifies the fact that power holders have more benefits than the less powerful in society. The discrepancy between the less and the more powerful people leads to the great importance of status symbols.

Individualism: At a very low score of 17, Armenia is clearly a collectivist culture. This is evident in the early integration and close, long-term commitment to a strong, cohesive "in-group." These societies foster strong relationships where everyone takes responsibility for and protects fellow members of their group. Loyalty is paramount and overrides most other societal rules. In these societies, offense leads to shame and loss of face.

Motivation Towards Achievement and Success: With an intermediate score of 50, Armenia has a bit of both worlds—high Motivation towards Achievement and Success for certain parts and low Motivation towards Achievement and Success for others, but no distinctly dominant cultural value.

Uncertainty Avoidance: At 88, Armenia scores very high on Uncertainty Avoidance, demonstrating that as a nation they see mechanisms to avoid ambiguity. People do not readily accept change and are very risk-averse. They maintain rigid codes of belief and behavior and are intolerant of unorthodox behavior and ideas. To minimize the level of uncertainty, there is an emotional need for strict rules, laws, policies, and regulations.

Long-Term Orientation: At a score of 38, Armenia exhibits a normative culture. In societies like this, people have a strong concern with establishing the absolute Truth; they are normative in their thinking. They exhibit great respect for traditions, a relatively small propensity to save for the future, and a focus on achieving quick results.

Indulgence: The low score of 25 in this dimension shows that Armenia has a culture of restraint. Restrained societies have a tendency toward cynicism and pessimism. Also, they do not put much emphasis on leisure time and control the gratification of their desires. People have the perception that their actions are restrained by social norms and feel that indulging themselves is somewhat wrong.

It would be of obvious scientific interest to study any causation between specific cultural dimensions and the number or success of hidden champions in a country. For now, it's just our hypothesis that correlation exists, most visibly a negative correlation with the power distance, and a positive correlation with individualism and motivation scores (Exhibit 2). Certainly, many side factors may have affected here, e.g., the extent of hidden champion explorations in different countries.

To summarize with a focus on the hidden champions' phenomenon and its potential embodiments in the cultural and economic context (Exhibit 3) of Armenia, the most successful Armenian companies typically are based on an original idea, have only a few investors, are at least partially digitalized or connected to digital technologies, and most importantly with leaders who are out-of-the-frame thinkers (Exhibit 3).

Exhibit 2 Hidden champions per 1 mio inhabitants and cultural dimension scores for countries with more than 20 hidden champions

Country	Hidden champions per 1 mio inhabitants	Power distance	Individualism	Motivation towards achievement and success	Uncertainty avoidance	Long-term orientation	Indulgence
Switzerland	19.84	34	79	70	58	42	66
Austria	19.19	11	77	79	70	47	63
Germany	18.91	35	79	66	65	57	40
Finland	5.09	33	75	26	59	63	57
Denmark	3.43	18	89	16	23	59	70
Sweden	2.32	31	87	5	29	52	78
Japan	2.25	54	62	95	92	100	42
Netherlands	2.17	38	100	14	53	67	68
Belgium	1.73	65	81	54	94	61	57
Italy	1.69	50	53	70	75	39	30
France	1.65	68	74	43	86	60	48
United Kingdom	1.11	35	76	66	35	60	69
USA	1.06	40	60	62	46	50	68
Poland	0.96	68	47	64	93	49	29
Canada	0.6	39	72	52	48	54	68
Korea	0.42	60	58	39	85	86	29
Spain	0.42	57	67	42	86	47	44
Russia	0.2	93	46	36	95	58	20
China	0.07	80	43	66	30	77	24
Correlation with hidden champions per 1 mio inhabitants	n/a	−0.536	0.337	0.322	−0.042	−0.309	0.209

Sources: Simon (2022), The Culture Factor Group (n.d.)

Exhibit 3 Core economic indicators for Armenia

Indicator	2019	2020	2021	2022	2023	2024
GDP per capita (current US$)	4597.23	4268.68	4685.18	6571.97	8053.01	..
GDP per capita growth (annual %)	7.84	−7.17	5.77	12.34	7.51	..
Unemployment, total (% of total labor force) (modeled ILO estimate)	18.3	18.18	15.47	13.38	13.25	13.33
Foreign direct investment, net inflows (% of GDP)	0.74	0.46	2.64	5	2.41	..
GDP (current US$, mio)	13,619.29	12,641.70	13,878.91	19,513.51	24,085.75	..
Exports of goods and services (current US$, mio)	5631.69	3762.80	4983.42	9800.65	14,319.48	..
Exports of goods and services (% of GDP)	41.35	29.76	35.91	50.22	59.45	..
Merchandise exports (current US$, mio)	2640	2544	3023	5360	8415	..
Merchandise exports to high-income economies (% of total merchandise exports)	75.08	69.45	68.81	77.43	86.13	..
Merchandise exports to low- and middle-income economies in Europe & Central Asia (% of total merchandise exports)	5.1	4.76	5.06	6.69	4.72	..
Ores and metals exports (% of merchandise exports)	36.14	36.82	39.65	21.86	14.97	15.83
Agricultural raw materials exports (% of merchandise exports)	0.34	0.33	0.31	0.37	0.36	0.32
Food exports (% of merchandise exports)	31.68	31.75	30.84	23.42	13.16	9.58
Fuel exports (% of merchandise exports)	2.85	3	1.84	1.9	0.91	0.67
Manufactures exports (% of merchandise exports)	19.36	16.99	22.69	44.37	48.17	30.56
High-technology exports (% of manufactured exports)	9.79	7.14	5.96	21.85	21.11	22.03

Source: World Bank, 2025, https://databank.worldbank.org/source/world-development-indicators#

2 Characteristics of Hidden Champions from Armenia

The research process to identify hidden champions from Armenia commenced with a thorough desk review to pinpoint companies meeting specific criteria. Initially, 25 companies were shortlisted based on their potential as market leaders, status as SMEs, low visibility, accessibility, and industry influence.

Following a meticulous evaluation, the research team prioritized companies for in-depth interviews, beginning with those best fitting the criteria.

Ultimately, four companies underwent detailed interviews, resulting in the qualification of two as hidden champions due to their clear market dominance and strategic positioning.

However, despite conducting comprehensive interviews, companies like Nairian and Primusmed, known for organic beauty products and food supplements respectively, did not qualify due to insufficient evidence of market leadership.

Based on the analysis conducted, hidden champions from Armenia exhibit clear market leadership within their respective industries, often surpassing competitors through innovation, capturing significant market share, or offering specialized services. These companies strategically position themselves within niche markets or specific segments of broader industries, consolidating their market presence and maintaining a competitive advantage.

Their strong commitment to innovation and adaptability allows them to continuously evolve their products or services in response to shifting customer needs and market demands.

Operational excellence is a hallmark, with hidden champions excelling in efficiency and effectiveness, leveraging technology and strategic partnerships to optimize processes and enhance productivity.

Despite being headquartered in Armenia, these companies demonstrate a global orientation, expanding internationally and navigating diverse regulatory landscapes with agility.

Operating with modest public visibility, hidden champions wield substantial influence within their industries, establishing leadership positions through exceptional performance and high customer satisfaction. Resilience is another key characteristic, as these companies navigate challenges such as economic volatility or geopolitical tensions, ensuring sustained growth and profitability over the long term.

Talent development is a priority among hidden champions from Armenia, focusing on acquiring and nurturing a skilled workforce capable of driving innovation and maintaining a competitive edge. In essence, these companies embody strategic foresight, operational excellence, and an unwavering commitment to innovation, enabling them to thrive in competitive global markets while maintaining a strong foothold in their respective industries.

3 Case Studies of Selected Hidden Champions

3.1 Case Study 1

3.1.1 The Crowdfunding Formula (TCF)

Overview
Address: Halabyan Street, 65/5, Yerevan, Armenia
Tell: +374 44 441050
Email: tcf@tcf.team
Web: https://thecrowdfundingformula.com/

Company Information
Industry: Marketing and PR (M—Professional, scientific and technical activities)
Year of establishment: 2017
Sales revenues in 2023: Undisclosed
Sales revenues in 2022: Undisclosed
Average number of employees in 2023: 100
Brain(s) behind the company: CEO and cofounder Narek Vardanyan

Company Overview
Founded in 2015 and officially established in 2017, TCF has emerged as a dominant player in the crowdfunding marketing industry. Specializing in helping innovators introduce their products via scale platforms like Kickstarter and Indiegogo, TCF has carved out a significant niche in the market, particularly in handling major projects. Their unique approach and dedicated team have propelled them to the forefront, setting a global benchmark with average project collections of approximately $1.1 million, far surpassing the typical $20,000 gathered by most crowdfunding campaigns.

3.1.2 Nature of Market Leadership

The Crowdfunding Formula (TCF) has established itself as a global market leader in the crowdfunding marketing agency sector, specializing in helping innovators launch products via platforms like Kickstarter and Indiegogo. Founded officially in 2017 (operating since 2015), TCF has rapidly ascended to become one of the top companies globally in its niche. Notably, TCF has achieved unprecedented success, with several projects surpassing $1 million in funding, positioning it among the top three firms in its industry.

3.1.3 Nature of the Competitive Advantage

TCF's competitive advantage lies in its dedicated and customized approach to each project. Unlike competitors with standardized methods, TCF assigns specialized teams of up to 15 experts per project, each deeply invested in its success. This approach, coupled with a unique financial model where TCF shares project risks and rewards, has differentiated it significantly. Moreover, TCF's location in Armenia has enabled it to build a large, specialized team capable of agile strategy adjustments and detailed project management, setting it apart from smaller, less flexible competitors. These methods and approaches adopted by TCF ensure its efficiency in terms of the speed of implementation, flexibility and scale of the campaigns formulating a distinctive competitive advantage over the other marketing crowdfunding companies worldwide.

3.1.4 Core Lessons Learned on the Path to Success

1. Customer-Centric Expansion: Initially focused narrowly on crowdfunding, TCF expanded into full-cycle e-commerce marketing, responding to client feedback for extended service needs.
2. Team Empowerment: TCF nurtures a "champion mindset" among its team, encouraging continuous learning and ownership of projects, fostering creativity and adaptability crucial for success.
3. Agility and Innovation: The ability to swiftly adapt strategies and embrace new ideas has been critical, especially evident during crises like COVID-19 and global resource shortages.

3.1.5 Management and Leadership Development Needs

TCF recognizes the importance of enhancing managerial and leadership skills within its organization, particularly as it expands globally. Key development needs include:

- Managerial Skills: Due to limited experience with large teams in Armenia, there is a significant need to develop robust managerial capabilities to effectively lead and coordinate international operations. Investing in leadership training programs tailored to cross-cultural management and strategic leadership could bolster TCF's managerial effectiveness.
- Digital Marketing Expertise: As digital marketing remains underdeveloped in Armenia, TCF faces challenges in recruiting specialized professionals. Collaborating with educational institutions to offer practical training in digital marketing could help bridge this skill gap and strengthen TCF's competitive edge in the global market.

- Innovation in Leadership: TCF should continue fostering a culture of innovation in leadership by encouraging creativity, risk-taking, and adaptive leadership styles. Implementing mentorship programs and leadership workshops can nurture the next generation of leaders within TCF, ensuring continuity and resilience in leadership.

TCF's success is driven by its commitment to team empowerment, a culture of learning, and a fearless approach to innovation and adaptability. These values have enabled TCF to survive and thrive in dynamic and challenging markets.

3.1.6 Financing and Regulatory Environment Development Needs

- Financial Accessibility: TCF faces challenges accessing local financing in Armenia, relying on international resources due to limited local banking support for innovative sectors.
- Regulatory Support: While Armenia offers a supportive legal framework, more initiatives are needed to facilitate financing for high-growth, technology-driven businesses.

3.1.7 Pandemic's Impact on TCF's Business Approach

During the COVID-19 pandemic, TCF demonstrated resilience and agility by anticipating shifts in consumer behavior. Recognizing increased demand for home-related products, TCF pivoted its strategies to support clients in launching successful campaigns for products like house plants, which saw heightened popularity during lockdowns.

3.1.8 Effect of the Ukraine War on TCF's Business Operations

The conflict in Ukraine disrupted TCF's supply chain and partnerships with Russian and Ukrainian partners, impacting logistics and increasing operational costs. However, TCF responded by diversifying its supplier base and exploring new partnerships, mitigating the immediate impacts and positioning itself for sustained growth amidst geopolitical challenges.

3.1.9 Mastering Niche Markets in Crowdfunding Marketing

In the dynamic landscape of digital marketing, where innovation and adaptability are paramount, The Crowdfunding Formula (TCF) has emerged as a silent force, reshaping the crowdfunding marketing industry. Founded officially in 2017 (with operations commencing in 2015), TCF has swiftly risen to prominence, specializing in helping innovators launch their products through renowned platforms like Kickstarter and Indiegogo. This chapter delves into TCF's journey, exploring the factors that have propelled it to leadership in its niche market.

TCF's journey to becoming a market leader in crowdfunding marketing is underscored by its unparalleled success in managing high-impact crowdfunding campaigns. With an average project collection surpassing $1.1 million—exceeding the typical $20,000 benchmark—TCF has set a global standard. This success rate is reflected in their handling of major projects, with notable achievements such as managing five out of eight projects that exceeded the $1 million mark in the past year alone.

The company's growth trajectory has been robust, with revenues experiencing a consistent annual growth rate of 15–20%. From modest beginnings, TCF has tripled its earnings since inception, showcasing resilience and strategic foresight in a competitive market environment.

At the heart of TCF's success lies its strategic leadership and innovative approach. The company's operational model prioritizes a customized and dedicated team approach, assigning up to 15 specialists per project. This unique strategy not only enhances project management efficiency but also ensures a high success rate for their clients.

Moreover, TCF's agility in adapting strategies has been pivotal. Unlike competitors with standardized methodologies, TCF empowers its teams to swiftly pivot strategies in response to market feedback. This flexibility has proven crucial during crises such as the COVID-19 pandemic and global resource shortages, where TCF not only survived but thrived by anticipating and meeting new consumer demands.

Despite its success, TCF has faced its share of challenges, particularly in navigating the Asian market and overcoming cultural differences. The company's expansion into China, while strategically sound, required a deep understanding of local dynamics and consumer behaviors. Additionally, global economic uncertainties and geopolitical tensions have necessitated ongoing adjustments in TCF's operational strategies to mitigate risks and capitalize on emerging opportunities.

Looking ahead, TCF remains focused on expanding its international footprint and enhancing service offerings across the entire business lifecycle. Continued investment in talent development, particularly in managerial and digital marketing skills, will be critical to sustaining growth and competitive advantage. Moreover, forging strategic partnerships and exploring diverse funding sources will enable TCF to navigate evolving market dynamics effectively.

In conclusion, TCF's journey from a nascent startup to a global leader in crowdfunding marketing exemplifies the principles of a hidden champion—low public visibility coupled with exceptional market leadership, innovation, and international orientation. As TCF continues to innovate and adapt, its impact on the crowdfunding marketing landscape is poised to grow, solidifying its position as a beacon of success in niche markets worldwide.

Conclusions and Recommendations

TCF's journey exemplifies how a focused strategy, team-centric culture, and adaptive leadership can propel a company to international prominence. To sustain growth, TCF should consider:

- -Talent Development: Continuously invest in managerial and digital marketing skills locally and internationally.
- Market Expansion: Further penetrate underrepresented markets like Central and Eastern Europe while consolidating its foothold in Asia.
- Partnerships and Funding: Forge strategic partnerships and explore diverse funding sources to fuel expansion and mitigate financial risks associated with global market dynamics.

TCF's success story underscores the importance of innovation, resilience, and strategic foresight in achieving and maintaining market leadership in the competitive crowdfunding sector.

3.2 Case Study 2

3.2.1 Krisp

Overview

Address: 4/1 Marshal Baghramyan Ave, Yerevan
Tell: + +374 11 900901
Email: support@krisp.ai
Web: https://krisp.ai/

Company Information

Industry: Technology and AI (J—Information and communication)
Year of establishment: 2017
Sales revenues in 2023: Undisclosed
Sales revenues in 2022: Undisclosed
Average number of employees in 2023: 120
Brain(s) behind the company: Cofounder Artavazd Minasyan, CEO and cofounder Davit Baghdasaryan

Company Overview

Krisp, an Armenian tech company founded in 2017, has emerged as a leader in AI-driven audio solutions aimed at enhancing productivity through noise cancellation, transcription, and meeting note automation. With a strong focus on professional users and small teams, Krisp has carved a niche for itself in a competitive global market.

3.2.2 Nature of Market Leadership

Krisp, founded in 2017, has rapidly emerged as a market leader in noise cancellation and transcription technologies. The company's flagship "pro product" caters specifically to professionals and small teams, offering advanced features such as automated meeting note-taking and high-quality audio-video transcription. Over the past 3 years, Krisp has expanded its product significantly, evolving from basic noise cancellation to a comprehensive platform offering audio-video transcription, collaborative tools, and integrations with various productivity software. This growth has solidified Krisp's position in the market, supported by a strategic focus on enhancing user experience and functionality.

Krisp's leadership in its niche is characterized by its innovative approach to solving common productivity challenges faced by remote workers and teams worldwide.

3.2.3 Nature of the Competitive Advantage

Krisp maintains a robust competitive advantage through several key factors:

- Desktop Application: Unlike competitors reliant on web-based platforms, Krisp's desktop application allows for on-device transcription, ensuring enhanced privacy and performance.
- Proprietary AI Technologies: Krisp distinguishes itself with in-house AI expertise, enabling the development of proprietary technologies that surpass competitor offerings in both efficiency and effectiveness.
- Technical Expertise: Founded by individuals with deep technical backgrounds and a strong grasp of AI and machine learning, Krisp maintains a leadership position in leveraging technology for audio enhancement and transcription.
- Superior Cost-Efficiency: Krisp's competitive advantage of cost-efficiency ensures their market leadership position and profitability with a gross margin of 97%, which is significantly higher than industry averages.

3.2.4 Core Lessons Learned on the Path to Success

Krisp's journey to success has been shaped by valuable lessons:

- Focus on Innovation: Continuous innovation is critical to maintaining leadership in a competitive market where technological advancements and customer expectations evolve rapidly, and where competitors rapidly emulate features.
- Strategic Adaptability: Krisp's ability to adapt its product offerings to meet changing market needs, such as the shift to hybrid work environments accelerated by the COVID-19 pandemic, underscores its strategic foresight.
- Importance of Talent: Building and retaining a talented team, particularly in AI and machine learning, has been essential to Krisp's ability to innovate and deliver cutting-edge solutions.

3.2.5 Management and Leadership Development Needs

Main development needs for the leadership and management of Krisp are:

- People Management Skills Development: Krisp experienced rapid growth, leading to promotions into management roles for individuals who were not adequately prepared for their new responsibilities. Similar to other rapidly growing companies, Krisp experienced a critical need to enhance people management skills among its middle management team to improve team cohesion and operational effectiveness.
- Short and Comprehensive Courses: Educational initiatives focusing on comprehensive business knowledge, including finance, marketing, and people management, are essential to bridge existing skill gaps.
- Customized Leadership Programs: Challenges include varying levels of readiness among managers and the need for customized leadership development programs tailored to Krisp's unique organizational dynamics.
- Perception of Success Within Companies: The company learned the importance of understanding how individuals perceive success within an organization, contrasting traditional business models, where the success of the manager is mainly measured by the number of people managed. Unlike traditional business paradigms, Krisp emphasizes that success isn't solely about individual contributions but rather about fostering collaborative environments where even small teams can catalyze significant company growth.

3.2.6 Financing and Regulatory Environment Development Needs

Looking forward, Krisp identifies several needs for further growth:

- Enhanced Regulatory Clarity: Clearer regulatory frameworks, particularly in international markets, would facilitate smoother expansion and compliance, reducing operational uncertainties.
- Access to Venture Financing: Increased access to venture capital and funding support for deep tech initiatives would enable Krisp to accelerate its R&D efforts and scale operations more effectively.

3.2.7 Pandemic's Impact on Krisp's Business Approach

The COVID-19 period underscored Krisp's resilience in adapting to changing circumstances and leveraging new opportunities to strengthen its market position and operational strategies.

- Challenges and Rewards of Switching to Remote: Krisp adapted swiftly during the COVID-19 pandemic, transitioning to a fully remote operational model to

maintain business continuity. This shift initially posed challenges, especially concerning Internet reliability and communication tools.
- Embracing Hybrid Work: Over time, Krisp embraced a hybrid work model as the pandemic situation improved, integrating the best aspects of remote work with on-site collaboration.
- Seizing Market Opportunities: The pandemic brought significant opportunities as well. Krisp saw increased industry engagement and collaboration with major companies, enhancing its market visibility and earning accolades like recognition from Forbes as one of the top organizations.
- Enhanced Sales Approach: The experience prompted Krisp to explore outbound sales strategies more aggressively, aiming to improve client engagement through initiatives like cold outreach.

3.2.8 Effect of the Ukraine War on Krisp's Business Operations

Ukraine war's effect on Krisp's business operations:

- Navigating Currency Fluctuations: The global resource crisis stemming from the Russian-Ukrainian war did impact Krisp, primarily through currency fluctuations. The change in the dram-dollar exchange rate in Armenia led to a 15% increase in expenses for the company.
- Workforce Diversity: Additionally, Krisp benefited from positive outcomes related to employee migration. The influx of new employees from Ukraine had a favorable impact on the organization, contributing to its workforce diversity and expertise.

3.2.9 Mastering Niche Markets in AI-Driven Productivity Solutions

The Spirit Behind the Krisp

The entrepreneurial spirit behind Krisp reflects a blend of technical expertise and strategic vision:

- Technical Prowess: Founded by individuals with backgrounds in mathematics and deep tech, Krisp embodies a culture of technical excellence and innovation.
- Strategic Vision: Krisp's leadership demonstrates a forward-thinking approach to product development and market expansion, leveraging insights into emerging trends and customer demands.

In the rapidly evolving landscape of AI and productivity tools, Krisp has established itself as a pioneer and leader in niche markets, particularly focusing on AI-driven audio solutions tailored for professionals and small teams. Since its inception in 2017, Krisp has not only introduced groundbreaking technologies but also mastered the art of penetrating and dominating specific segments within the broader AI and technology market.

Krisp's journey into niche markets has been marked by strategic foresight and innovation, leveraging proprietary AI technologies to address specific pain points and enhance productivity across diverse industries. Key elements of Krisp's success in mastering niche markets include:

1. Targeted Product Development: Krisp began by specializing in noise cancellation and expanded its offerings to include comprehensive audio-video transcription and meeting note automation. This targeted approach has allowed Krisp to differentiate itself from generic solutions and gain deep market penetration.
2. Customized User Experience: Krisp's desktop application features on-device processing for enhanced privacy and performance, reflecting its commitment to providing a tailored user experience. By prioritizing user-centric design and functionality, Krisp has cultivated a loyal customer base that values both innovation and practicality in their daily workflows.
3. Strategic Market Positioning: Krisp's strategic positioning revolves around rapid innovation and anticipation of industry trends. Through continuous R&D and technological advancements, Krisp not only meets but exceeds customer expectations, solidifying its leadership in niche segments such as remote work facilitation and professional audio enhancement.
4. Scalable Growth Strategies: Beyond technological innovation, Krisp pursues scalable growth through strategic partnerships and integrations with leading productivity tools. This approach extends its market reach while enhancing the value proposition for users seeking streamlined and efficient solutions.

Krisp's success in mastering niche markets is exemplified by its impressive growth trajectory and market influence. Krisp has captured a significant market share in noise cancellation and transcription technologies, leveraging a deep understanding of user needs and market dynamics. By focusing on delivering tangible benefits such as improved audio quality and productivity gains, Krisp has successfully attracted a diverse clientele ranging from individual professionals to multinational corporations.

Krisp's innovative solutions have garnered industry recognition, including accolades from tech publications and endorsements from renowned professionals, reinforcing its status as a trusted leader in AI-driven productivity tools.

Conclusions and Recommendations

In conclusion, Krisp's rapid ascent to market leadership in noise cancellation and transcription technologies highlights the power of leveraging proprietary technology, strategic foresight, and a customer-centric approach. To sustain and enhance its position, Krisp should consider:

- Continued Innovation: Invest in R&D to maintain technological superiority and introduce new features that anticipate market needs. Further, develop integrations with HR and marketing tools to solidify its position as a core productivity tool.
- Global Expansion: Strategically expand into new markets while navigating regulatory landscapes effectively.
- Talent Development: Strengthen talent acquisition and development efforts to foster innovation and maintain a competitive edge.

By focusing on these areas, Krisp can further solidify its leadership in the global tech market while meeting the evolving needs of its diverse customer base.

Krisp's journey in mastering niche markets within AI-driven productivity solutions highlights its unwavering commitment to innovation, customer-centricity, and strategic agility. By staying true to its core values and leveraging advanced AI technologies, Krisp continues to redefine industry standards and empower users worldwide with transformative tools for enhanced productivity and collaboration. As Krisp expands its footprint and explores new frontiers, its impact on niche markets serves as a testament to the power of focused innovation and strategic market mastery in driving sustainable growth and leadership in the competitive technology landscape.

References

Bournoutian, G. A. (2002). *A concise history of the Armenian people: From ancient times to the present* (2nd ed.). Mazda Publishers.

Cohen, R. (2008). *Global diasporas: An introduction* (2nd ed.). Routledge.

The Culture Factor Group. (n.d.). Country comparison tool. What about Armenia? Retrieved May 23, 2024, from https://www.hofstede-insights.com/country-comparison-tool?countries=armenia.

Denizer, C., & Wolf, H. C. (2000). The saving collapse during the transition in Eastern Europe. *World Bank Economic Review, 14*(3), 445–455. https://doi.org/10.1093/wber/14.3.445

Hayrapetyan, R., & Mnatsakanyan, T. (2022). Effective local governance: Large or small units (the Armenian case). *Public Administration Issues, 5*, 134–151. https://doi.org/10.17323/1999-5431-2022-0-5-134-151

Mnatsakanyan, T., Hayrapetyan, R., & Molnar, D. (2021). Measuring regional development disparities: Some methodological contributions and evidence from Armenia and Serbia. *Regional Science Inquiry, XIII*(2), 327–348. https://www.rsijournal.eu/ARTICLES/December_2021/RSI_Dec_2021_XIII_(2).pdf

PwC. (2021). Armenia IT industry overview. https://www.pwc.com/am/en/assets/pdf/PwC_Armenia_IT_Industry_Overview.pdf.

Scannell, N. J., & Newton, J. (2004). Voucher-financed privatisation: Lessons from the Armenian experience. *Global Business and Economics Review, 6*(2), 280–302. https://doi.org/10.1504/GBER.2004.006231

Simon, H. (2022). Hidden champions and the development of regions. *IAR Journal of Business Management, 3*(2). https://doi.org/10.47310/iarjbm.2022.v03i02.001

Statistical Committee of the Republic of Armenia. (n.d.). *Foreign Trade of the Republic of Armenia by countries, years and indicators*. Retrieved May 23, 2024, from https://statbank.armstat.am/

pxweb/en/ArmStatBank/ArmStatBank__5%20Foreign%20trade/FT-5-2022.px/table/tableViewLayout2/?rxid=9ba7b0d1-2ff8-40fa-a309-fae01ea885bb.
Vardanyan, V. (2021). *National Identity, Diaspora, and Space of Belonging: An Armenian Perspective*. Gomitas Institute.
The World Bank. (n.d.-a). *Doing business archive. Ease of doing business in Armenia*. Retrieved May 23, 2024, from https://archive.doingbusiness.org/en/data/exploreeconomies/armenia#
The World Bank. (n.d.-b). *Personal remittances received (% of GDP)—Armenia*. Retrieved May 23, 2024, from https://data.worldbank.org/indicator/BX.TRF.PWKR.DT.GD.ZS?locations=AM.

Vanine Yeranosyan holds a position as a Consultant at OPK Executive Consulting, primarily consulting for Coca Cola BIG and Coca Cola Swire. Additionally, she is the founder of InTagma, a company specializing in data processing. With a vast portfolio spanning over 250 projects across Europe, Asia, and North America, she brings extensive experience, particularly in managing large-scale data processing projects. Vanine Yeranosyan is engaged in research activities at Matena International School of Leadership and Professional Development. Concurrently, she serves as an Associate Professor at the Armenian State University of Economics, actively contributing to teaching, research, and projects focused on reforming finance education and curriculum development. Invited as a guest lecturer at various European universities, Vanine holds a Ph.D. in Economics and has published extensively.

Astghik Sargsyan works at Matena International School of Leadership and Professional Development as a Program Manager. She is engaged in environmental scanning, assisting with the development of various academic programs, their implementation, monitoring, and organization. Astghik received her MSc degree in Management from the American University of Armenia. Her previous research activities lie in the areas of the application of behavioral science to environmental sustainability, marketing, and business development.

Tigran Mnatsakanyan works at Matena International School of Leadership and Professional Development as Academic Director and has been engaged in the design and implementation of a number of international academic programs since 2021. He has been involved in research and teaching since 2009, which includes strategic management, decision-making, risk management, and public administration topics. Formerly Dr. Tigran Mnatsakanyan has worked as a consultant on management and strategic development and also as an expert in professional education quality assurance. He delivered lectures and received training at several European universities, has a Ph.D. in Economics and more than 10 publications.

Hidden Champions of Azerbaijan

Leyla Hajiyeva, Mansur Barkhudarov, and Afet Alakbarova

Abstract Following the restoration of state independence, Azerbaijan set out on a path towards a market economy. The adoption of a law on entrepreneurship led to the emergence of numerous small- and medium-sized enterprises. By the late 1990s and early 2000s, several "hidden champion" companies began to thrive in the country's economy. Today, dozens of these "hidden champions" operate across various industries in the republic.

This research focuses on the production, processing, and export of hazelnuts. According to the International Nut and Dried Fruit Council (INC), Azerbaijan ranks third globally in hazelnut exports, both in kernels and in shells. Over the past five years, the country has consistently remained among the top three exporters, maintaining a 5% share in both kernel and in shell hazelnut exports. Within this industry, several companies can be classified as "hidden champions." Our specific focus is on Azerstar LLC, a company that has been operating since 2006 and supplies its products to European markets.

Overview[1]

Official name: Republic of *Azerbaijan*
Type of government: A presidential system
Population in 2023: 10,412,651
Land area: 86.600 square kilometers

[1] *Please provide World Bank data and a history overview of your country.*

L. Hajiyeva (✉) · M. Barkhudarov
Department of Applied Economics, State University of Economics (UNEC), Baku, Azerbaijan
e-mail: Leyla_hajiyeva@unec.edu.az; Mansur_Barkhudarov@unec.edu.az

A. Alakbarova
Department of International Cooperation, Azerbaijan State University of Economics (UNEC), Baku, Azerbaijan
e-mail: Afet.alakbarova@unec.edu.az

D. Berberović, D. Purg (eds.), *Hidden Champions in Rising Economies*, Contributions to Management Science,
https://doi.org/10.1007/978-3-032-08263-3_13

History

1918	Adoption of the "Declaration of Independence." Azerbaijan declared its independence.
1919	The Azerbaijan Parliament passed a law establishing a university in Baku.
1920	The XI Red Army invaded Baku.
1920	The Azerbaijan Soviet Socialist Republic was proclaimed in Baku.
1920	Nationalization of the oil industry. By decree, 272 private oil companies were dissolved. The Azerbaijan Oil Committee, later known as "Azneft," was organized to manage the nationalized enterprises.
1922	The Federative Union of Transcaucasian Soviet Republics was established.
1926	The first electric railway line in the USSR was commissioned.
1942	Martial law was declared in the Azerbaijan SSR due to World War II.
1945	The Academy of Sciences of the Azerbaijan SSR was established.
1947	The USSR Council of Ministers decided to deport Azerbaijanis from the Armenian SSR.
1948-1953	150,000 Azerbaijanis living in the Armenian SSR were forcibly removed from their homeland.
1948	The world's first offshore oil platform was constructed in the Caspian Sea.
1967	Six stations of the Baku Metro were commissioned.
1978	A new Constitution of the Azerbaijan SSR was adopted.
1988	Deportation of Azerbaijanis from the Gafan and Mehri regions of Armenia.
1988	The beginning of the national liberation movement in Azerbaijan.
1988	Completion of the mass deportation of Azerbaijanis from Western Azerbaijan (modern-day Armenia). As a result, 230,000 Azerbaijanis from 185 villages were expelled from their ancestral homes.
1990	The bloody massacre of the Soviet army in Baku. In Baku and other regions, 131 people were killed, 744 were injured, 400 were arrested, and four went missing.
1991	The Supreme Soviet of the Republic of Azerbaijan adopted the "Constitutional Act on the State Independence of the Republic of Azerbaijan," restoring Azerbaijan's state independence.
1991	The USSR ceased to exist as a subject of international law, and the CIS was created according to the Brest-Litovsk Treaty.
1991	A referendum was held to express an opinion on the Constitutional Act "On the State Independence of the Republic of Azerbaijan."
1992	The Khojaly tragedy occurred. At 9 p.m., Armenian armed forces, along with the 366th Russian regiment and mercenary bandits, attacked Khojaly, resulting in the massacre of the century. As a result, 613 people were killed, 487 were injured, and 1275 were taken hostage. Six families were completely wiped out, and the city was burned.

1992	The Republic of Azerbaijan was admitted to the UN at its 46th session.
1992	Abulfaz Elchibey was elected President of Azerbaijan.
1992	The Republic of Azerbaijan was admitted to UNESCO.
1992	The national currency (manat) was put into circulation.
1993	"National Liberation Day." H. Aliyev was elected Chairman of the Supreme Soviet, preventing civil war and separatism.
1993	Azerbaijan joined the CIS.
1993	H. Aliyev was elected President of the Republic of Azerbaijan.
1980–1994	The First Karabakh War, an ethnic and territorial conflict between the Republic of Armenia and the Republic of Azerbaijan in the Karabakh region. As a result, 20% of Azerbaijan's territory was occupied by Armenia.
1994	The signing of the "Contract of the Century." The State Oil Company of Azerbaijan signed agreements with foreign oil companies for the joint exploitation of the Caspian Sea's hydrocarbon resources.
1995	Approval of the "State Program of Privatization of State Property in the Republic of Azerbaijan in 1995–1998."
1995	Adoption of the "Constitution of the Republic of Azerbaijan."
1996	At the Lisbon Summit, 53 out of 54 OSCE member countries supported the principle of Azerbaijan's territorial integrity in the accepted statement on the resolution of the Nagorno-Karabakh conflict.
2001	Azerbaijan was accepted as a full member at the meeting of the Committee of Ministers of the Council of Europe.
2001	Signing of the agreement with Turkey on the transit, transportation, and sale of Azerbaijani gas through the Baku-Tbilisi-Erzurum gas pipeline.
2001	PACE adopted a document confirming the territorial integrity of Azerbaijan.
2001	An agreement on the legal status of the Caspian Sea was concluded between Azerbaijan and Kazakhstan.
2003	Ilham Aliyev was elected President of the Republic of Azerbaijan.
2006	The Baku-Tbilisi-Ceyhan pipeline was commissioned.
2012	The "Azerbaijan 2020: Looking to the Future" development concept was approved.
2013	Azerbaijan's first artificial space satellite "Azerspace-1A" was launched into space.
2016	Strategic roadmaps for the national economy and key sectors were approved.
2020	The beginning of the Second Karabakh War.
2020	Signing of the ceasefire declaration. According to the agreement, Azerbaijan retained control over the territories it liberated during the war and restored its territorial integrity.
2024	The 29th annual UN climate conference will be held in Baku.

1 Introduction: Context and History

The problems faced by Azerbaijan's economy since independence are similar to those encountered by other post-Soviet countries. All these countries needed to establish the foundations of a new economic system and rebuild economic relations, considering the disruption of previous connections. Economic recovery in Azerbaijan was faster compared to other post-Soviet countries. In subsequent years, the Azerbaijani economy experienced a sharp acceleration in growth, and by 2008, it had become a leader in GDP growth. Today, Azerbaijan is known as one of the main exporters of oil and gas and participates in several international projects. At the same time, the government's economic policy aims to diversify the economy and develop the non-oil sector. Azerbaijan's main trading partners include Russia, Turkey, China, Italy, Georgia, the United Kingdom, Belarus, Israel, and the Central Asian republics.

In general, we can distinguish five main stages in the development of the country's economy since it gained independence (Ibadoghlu and Niftiyev, 2022):

1. Transformational recession (1992–1995).
2. Stabilization and recovery growth (1996–2000).
3. Investment spurt (2001–2004).
4. Economic boom (2005–2008).
5. Stagnation (2009–2014).
6. Post-boom (2015–2020).

1.1 Transformational Decline

The initial period of market reforms in Azerbaijan, like in other transitioning economies, was marked by a significant transformational decline. Common reasons included structural changes associated with shifts in price proportions, a sharp reduction in government demand, the collapse of previous economic ties, and the shift of some demand to imported goods. However, in Azerbaijan, these problems were exacerbated by a prolonged military conflict over Nagorno-Karabakh. From 1992 to 1995, the average annual GDP decline rate was 19.4%, with a total economic decline reaching nearly 58%. In contrast, the CIS as a whole (excluding Azerbaijan) saw less severe negative dynamics, with average declines of 13% and 43%, respectively. During this period, production in Azerbaijan fell by more than half, with manufacturing industries experiencing the greatest decline, averaging over 20% annually. Oil production and construction suffered somewhat less but still faced significant declines. Investment also dropped sharply, with a 43% decrease by 1995 compared to 1991. The population's income plummeted, and inflation at the initial stage of transformation (1992–1995) was extremely high, bordering on hyperinflation, with consumer prices increasing on average 9.3 times per year. Monetary policy was accommodative, following price increases.

1.2 Stabilization and Recovery Growth

An important milestone that changed both the political and economic landscape was Heydar Aliyev's accession to leadership in mid-1994. Soon after, the military conflict over Nagorno-Karabakh ceased, political stability increased significantly, and Azerbaijan's international position was strengthened. This allowed for vigorous efforts to establish market institutions and restore the economy, which had been undermined in previous years. At the second stage of the country's development (1996–2000), the authorities focused on both macroeconomic stabilization and structural reforms.

According to the European Bank for Reconstruction and Development (EBRD), in 1994, state-regulated prices accounted for 77% of the consumer basket, and the index of exchange rate and trade liberalization had an initial value of 1, indicating minimal differences from the planned economy or their complete absence. The non-state sector's share of GDP was estimated at only 30%, compared with 43% on average for CIS and CEE countries.

In Azerbaijan, market reforms were implemented swiftly, prioritizing private initiative as the main economic driver and integrating the country into the global economic system. Government orders were abolished, foreign trade was fully liberalized, and export/import quotas and licensing of foreign economic activity were abandoned. A legislative framework for a market economy was rapidly created, including the Civil and Land Codes, the Bankruptcy Law, and the Securities Law. Financial system reforms were prioritized, focusing on reorganizing state banks, rehabilitating them, and preparing them for privatization. Despite progress, Azerbaijan still had relatively low scores in some areas (e.g., privatization of large enterprises, enterprise reform, infrastructure reform) according to the EBRD classification.

The policy of macroeconomic stabilization was highly successful at this stage. Coordinated actions in several areas slowed inflation. The Azerbaijani economy's resilience to external shocks was primarily due to responsible macroeconomic policies.

This stage of economic development was favorable for "hidden champion" companies. For instance, in 1998, Asico was founded, supplying berries and fruits to European markets. Delta Telecom, a leader in telecommunications and information services in the Caucasus region, began operations in 2000. Aqrovest became a leading supplier of natural and processed hazelnuts in Azerbaijan. Founded in 2000, Aqrovest was one of the first companies in Azerbaijan involved in hazelnut production. Following restructuring in 2017, it became a subsidiary of Agrarco LLC.

1.3 Investment Rush

The rapid growth of capital investments in Azerbaijan from 2001 to 2004 accelerated sharply, achieving an extraordinary 51% annual growth rate in fixed capital investment. Azerbaijan managed this by attracting significant foreign investment, particularly foreign direct investment (FDI), which brought essential financial resources, advanced technologies, and management expertise, while opening access to foreign markets. FDI is also less likely to cause macroeconomic instability due to its stable nature. This strategy proved effective during the global financial crisis of 2008, as Azerbaijan's economy showed more resilience compared to other former USSR countries. Azerbaijan's attractiveness for FDI was driven by strong institutional factors: proper infrastructure, a sound regulatory framework, and few obstacles to investment and foreign trade. The 1992 law on the protection of foreign investments guaranteed foreign investors' rights and the free repatriation of profits post-taxation, with preferential customs treatment in some cases. During this period, OASIS FLOWER, part of the international organization "INTERFLORA," opened in 2003, highlighting the increasing presence of "hidden champion" companies.

1.4 Economic Boom

In 2005, Azerbaijan entered a period of economic boom, spurred by large-scale investments in the oil sector. The construction of three oil pipelines significantly increased oil exports, reaching $29 billion in 2008. This boom led to a ninefold increase in oil export value, making Azerbaijan a world leader in economic growth rate. Government revenues increased more than sevenfold, primarily due to the sharp rise in oil sector income. However, this posed challenges related to macroeconomic management and the potential development of "Dutch disease." Azerbaijan's strategy included medium-term state programs for poverty reduction and economic development, focusing on improving citizens' well-being, ensuring macroeconomic stability, and developing non-resource sectors of the economy. Key initiatives included improving the investment climate, enhancing public infrastructure, and strengthening the financial sector.

During this period, the number of active "hidden champions" in Azerbaijan increased. In 2007, ASER LLC was founded, supplying equipment and materials to enterprises in Azerbaijan, Turkmenistan, and Georgia, and establishing partnerships with enterprises in Russia, Ukraine, France, Germany, and Italy. Since 2006, AZERSTAR has been a major national operator in hazelnut processing and export. Under the leadership of Ilham Isaev, AZERSTAR grew from a small workshop to a large factory, exporting over 5000 tons of hazelnuts annually to the CIS and Europe. By 2015, annual sales exceeded $20 million, producing and exporting 25% of Azerbaijan's hazelnuts.

1.5 Stagnation

The slowdown in oil production growth in 2008 led to a decrease in GDP growth rate to 10.6%. The subsequent collapse in oil prices and reduction in export volumes caused a threefold decrease in oil and gas export value. By 2011, Azerbaijan experienced low growth rates due to maintenance issues and delays in commissioning new wells, leading to negative GDP dynamics.

The stagnation period hindered business development, though companies like Bakinar Consulting emerged, providing financial and legal services to Central Asia.

1.6 Post-Boom

Azerbaijan's economic strategy shifted towards sustainable regional development, focusing on investments in the non-oil sector funded by oil revenues. To implement the country's economic development strategy, Strategic Maps for the Development of the National Economy were adopted. The strategic maps indicated the main priorities and goals for economic development until 2025.

The "State Program for the Social and Economic Development of the Regions" aimed to diversify the economy. Despite the pandemic's impact, the non-oil economy showed growth, with the "National Priorities for Socio-Economic Development of Azerbaijan-2030" targeting industrial-innovative development and technological advancement.

According to https://oec.world/ in 2022, Azerbaijan exported $38.9 billion, with crude petroleum and petroleum gas as top exports, mainly to Italy, Turkey, Israel, India, and Greece. In 2023, non-oil and gas product exports increased by 9.8%, reaching $3.348 billion. According to IMF projections, non-oil GDP growth in 2023 was 4.2%, expected to average 3.5% annually from 2025 to 2028. The oil sector decline was 1.5% in 2023, with a projected average decline of 0.5% annually from 2024 to 2028. GDP is expected to grow from $76.8 billion in 2023 to $93.8 billion by 2028.

At the end of 2023, the main trading partners of Azerbaijan among the EU countries were: Italy—12.3 billion euros (a decline of 40.3%), the Czech Republic—1.4 billion euros (a decline of 4.3%), Germany—1.36 billion euros (down 37.8%), Greece—1.32 billion euros (down 45.1%), and Spain—0.9 billion euros (down 36.2%).

Trade turnover between Azerbaijan and the countries of the European Union (EU) at the end of 2023 amounted to 21.4 billion euros, which is 35.3% less than the figure for the same period in 2022, follows from calculations of the Interfax-Azerbaijan agency, based on data from the statistical department European Union (Eurostat).

The decline in trade turnover in 2023 is associated with lower prices for oil and gas than in 2022, which form the basis of trade turnover.

Table 1 The number of active micro, small, and medium enterprises

Indicators	2020			2021		
	Total	of which Legal persons	of which Individual enterprises	Total	of which Legal persons	of which Individual enterprises
Total number of enterprises	316370	33450	282920	355906	37585	318321
The number of micro enterprises	307717	24797	282920	346171	27850	318321
The number of small businesses	5943	5943	–	6856	6856	–
The number of medium businesses	2710	2710	–	2879	2879	–

Source: https://www.stat.gov.az/source/entrepreneurship/?lang=en

According to statistical data, in the first quarter of last year the volume of foreign trade amounted to 5.9 billion euros (a decline of 3.4% year-on-year), in the second quarter—5.5 billion euros (28.3% decline), in the third quarter—5 billion euros (2.1 times decline), in the fourth quarter—5 billion euros (43.7% decline).

The number of small- and medium-sized enterprises in Azerbaijan has increased, contributing to economic diversification and growth, data on their number can be found in the table below (Table 1).

The flexible economic policy pursued in the Republic of Azerbaijan, which provides for changing approaches at various stages of development, has provided unprecedentedly high results. Over the past years, the well-being of the population has increased significantly and living conditions have improved. Large investments in infrastructure laid the foundation for future development; the conditions for doing business are being consistently simplified. All this indicates that Azerbaijan is firmly committed to the development and modernization of the country.

According to Suleymanov et al. (2021), the republic is undergoing a transition from a "raw materials" to an innovative model of economic development with modern infrastructure, developed science and a strong education system. The formation and rational use of human capital is moving to a leading role in the economy of the republic. Azerbaijan, successfully solving economic problems, confidently continues to build a legal, secular state and the formation of a civil society (Exhibit 1).

2 Characteristics of Hidden Champions from Azerbaijan

During our research on the Azerbaijani market, we identified about ten companies that can be classified as "hidden champions." Unfortunately, it is difficult to obtain detailed information about the activities of these companies, so in our research we

Exhibit 1 Core economic indicators for (Azerbaijan)

	2017	2018	2019	2020	2021	2022	2023
GDP per capita (current US$)	14315.9	15283	16675.3	15163.6	20111.4	22512.3	n/e
GDP per capita growth (annual %)	−0.8	0.6	1.6	−5	5.2	4.6	n/e
Long-term unemployment (% of total unemployment)	No data	No data	No data	No data	No data	No data	No data
Foreign direct investment, net inflows (% of GDP)	2.7	1.0	2.1	1.4	2.3	1.7	n/e
GDP (current US$, mio)	643628.3	524819.9	447754. 7	385740.5	487902.6	631133.4	n/e
Exports of goods and services (current US$, mio)	19840	25480	23630	15210	25490	47270	n/e
Exports of goods and services (% of GDP)	11.32	14.44	17.92	16.61	18.00	16.30	n/e
Merchandise exports (current US$)	15.48	20.32	19.64	13.73	22.21	38.15	n/e
Merchandise exports to high-income economies (% of total merchandise exports)	68.6	71.4	64	56	n/e	n/e	n/e
Merchandise exports to developing economies in Europe & Central Asia (% of total merchandise exports)	19.6	17.9	24	31.8	n/e	n/e	n/e
Ores and metals exports (% of merchandise exports)	1.2	0.9	1	1.3	1.2	0.8	n/e
Agricultural raw materials exports (% of merchandise exports)	0	0	1	1	1	0	n/e
Food exports (% of merchandise exports)	4	4	4	5	4	2	n/e
Fuel exports (% of merchandise exports)	91	92	91	87	88	93	n/e
Manufactures exports (% of merchandise exports)	3	3	3	3	5	3	n/e
High-technology exports (% of manufactured exports)	9.21	5.40	5.21	6.90	4.42	4.75	n/e

Source: World Bank, June, 2024

examined in detail the activities of the Azerstar LLC company, which exports shelled hazelnuts to foreign markets.

2.1 *Case Study 1*

2.1.1 "Azerstar" LLC

Overview
Address: Azerbaijan Avenue 100, Zaqatala, Azerbaijan
Tel: +994242254151
Fax: +994242254151
Email: azerstar@mail.ru
Web: https://www.facebook.com/azerstarllc

Company Information
Industry[2]: Hazelnuts processing and exporting
Year of Establishment: 10.05.2006
Sales Revenues in 2017: 1.8 mio US$
Sales Revenues in 2023: 1.4 mio US$
Average number of employees in 2023: 106
Brainer(s) behind the company: CEO and founder İlham İsayev

2.1.2 Nature of Market Leadership

The company is one of the leaders in the production and supply of high-quality hazelnuts that meet the standards of the European market. The main supply markets are Italy, Germany and Russia. The company's products are of high quality and are in great demand among purchasing companies. The company seeks to enter new European markets. The main competitors in this area are companies from Turkey, Italy, and the USA.

2.1.3 Nature of Competitive Advantage

We can highlight a number of competitive advantage indicators that provide the company with a leading position in the market. First of all, this is a limited number of hazelnut producers in the world market, with Turkish companies being the leaders here. The presence of a relatively small number of hazelnut producing companies provides Azerbaijani companies with a competitive advantage in their segment.

[2]*According to NACE Rev. 2—please check the tecnical instructions included in this document (pg. 9).*

The next competitive advantage indicator is the high quality of Azerbaijani hazelnuts, which meets the needs of purchasing companies. The quality of hazelnuts grown in the Zagatala region of Azerbaijan is distinguished by the best taste and high yield. These varieties of hazelnuts are characterized by the presence of a "marketable appearance" that meets European standards, which also provides them with an advantage in the market. We can also note the use of modern technology in the production process, which reduces the cost of hazelnut production.

2.1.4 Core Lessons Learned on the Path to Success

1. The company purchases hazelnuts from small and individual entrepreneurs, and therefore it is very important to establish mutually beneficial relationships with suppliers.
2. During seasonal peaks, the number of company employees increases several times, and therefore the company is an important employer in the region. Establishing relations with the public and officials will help the company build a positive image and receive certain benefits from the state
3. The company's activities are affected by a number of force majeure factors, such as natural disasters, pandemics, and military-political events between countries. All these factors must be taken into account when building an effective strategy for entering foreign markets

2.1.5 Management and Leadership Development Needs

Improving technologies and the production process for processing hazelnuts leads to an increase in labor productivity. It is necessary to constantly conduct training to improve the professional skills of workers and managers. Marketing training will help increase the level of staff involvement in company management.

It is also necessary to take into account that the suppliers of hazelnuts to the company may be entrepreneurs who have tactical goals in the market, such as making short-term profits. Often these entrepreneurs lack the management skills to build an effective market strategy. Therefore, improvement of management knowledge and marketing skills is required.

2.1.6 Financing and Regulatory Environment Development Needs

The industry has problems with legislative regulation and tax authorities. The Ministry of Agriculture needs to strengthen control over the condition of hazelnut orchards in order to reduce possible damage from natural factors.

The company is facing financial difficulties such as delays in payment procedures. To overcome these difficulties, it is necessary to improve relations with banks.

Another problem for the company is the low level of awareness among entrepreneurs about the legislative regulation of the industry. It is necessary to strengthen propaganda among entrepreneurs in order to increase their level of awareness and knowledge.

2.1.7 Pandemic's Impact on "Hidden Champions" Business Approach

2020 has become a serious test for Azerbaijan. The fall in oil prices, restrictions caused by the COVID pandemic, and the 44-day military conflict with Armenia have created real threats to the country's economic development. As a result, according to the State Statistics Committee of the Republic, the decline in GDP in Azerbaijan in 2020 was 4.3%, and the decline in GDP per capita (data for 11 months) was 5%. Significant problems have arisen in the foreign economic sphere. In particular, the foreign trade turnover of Azerbaijan, according to the State Customs Committee, in 2020 compared to 2019 decreased by 26.5%, while the fall in exports was 30%, imports—21.5%. The foreign trade balance remained positive ($4 billion), but its volume decreased by half compared to the previous year.

As a result, many industrial production and service sectors were under attack. Tourism-related industries were hit the hardest. Here, in January–November 2020, the largest decline was recorded compared to the same period in 2019—56.9%; the volume of passenger (40.5%) and cargo transportation (19.6%), paid services to the population (25, 8%), construction (11.3%). In general, industrial production in Azerbaijan fell by 4.7% over the 11 months of 2020. The only industries that showed at least slight growth in 2020 were agriculture (2%) and information and communication services (1.6%).

The pandemic has had a serious impact on the production and processing of hazelnuts. Restrictive measures were taken in the country, which negatively affected the activities of Azerstar LLC. The company lost its customers due to the complete closure or restrictions on the activities of many companies—chocolate manufacturers, cafes and restaurants. The labor activity of entrepreneurs was limited, which affected the volume of hazelnut production. The volume of hazelnut production of Azerstar LLC decreased, the export of products decreased, and sales profit decreased in 2020. If in 2019 the hazelnut production in the company was 2962 tons of hazelnuts, then in 2020 this figure decreased by half and amounted to 1426 tons. The company's profit from the sale of hazelnuts in 2019 was 2.01 million US dollars, in 2020 this figure decreased almost 3 times and amounted to 0.70 million US dollars. These figures allow us to conclude that the pandemic has had a negative impact on the Azerstar LLC operations.

2.1.8 Effects of the Ukraine War on "Hidden Champions" Business Operations

According to officials of Azerstar LLC, the company suffered significant losses from this war, since its export activities were closely linked to the Russian market. The collapse of economic ties between partners, economic sanctions against the aggressor, difficulties with banking operations, late payment for delivered goods and other facts led to a decrease in hazelnut exports to Russia. Considering that economic sanctions against Russian companies continue, Azerstar LLC is looking for new strategic partners among European consumers. In particular, the company intends to expand trade relations with Italian and Swiss chocolate manufacturers. At the same time, the company is looking for new partners to expand its activities in the European market.

2.1.9 "Azerstar LLC Leadership History"

Let's take a closer look at the success story of Azerstar LLC. Back in 1998, two founders, Ilham Isaev and Ramazan Garadjaev, established a small enterprise focused on purchasing and reselling hazelnuts in the domestic market. Over time, the company's activities expanded, the number of founders increased to three, and the company ARI was registered. Under this name, the company operated until 2006, processing and supplying hazelnuts mainly to major cities in Azerbaijan, such as Baku, Ganja, and others. The company's production volumes were small, reaching a maximum of 5–10 tons of processed hazelnuts per year.

The market situation began to change as Azerbaijani hazelnuts gained recognition in the global market, leading to increased demand. The external market is more attractive for national companies as it offers favorable conditions for expanding their production capabilities and achieving higher profits. In 2001–2002, the company started supplying cleaned hazelnuts to Poland and Russia. Later, the company established broader connections with buyer companies and expanded its supplies to the Russian market.

The increase in demand in the external market necessitated an expansion of hazelnut plantations and the company's production capabilities. It should be noted that the main producers and sellers of hazelnuts are located in the Zagatala, Balakan, Gabala, and Khachmaz regions of Azerbaijan. Zagatala, Balakan, and Gabala belong to the same economic region, and similar varieties of hazelnuts are grown here, which are of high quality and are in high demand in the foreign market.

The hazelnut varieties grown in the Khachmaz region differ in their taste and "marketable appearance": although the "marketable appearance" of this variety is very attractive, the taste properties are inferior to the varieties grown in the Zagatala-Balakan region. Hazelnuts from the Khachmaz region are mainly supplied to the domestic and Russian markets, with a small quantity reaching the European market.

In 2006, the founders decided to end their joint activities and pursue entrepreneurial endeavors independently. As a result, ARI ceased operations, and a new enterprise, Azerstar LLC, was established by Ilham Isaev. The company does not own any plantations; instead, it purchases all its products from small and individual entrepreneurs and then cleans and processes the hazelnuts. A portion of the shells obtained during the cleaning process (approximately one-third) is used for artificial drying, while the remaining shells are sold to rural residents for heating purposes during the winter season.

According to http://www.azerstar.com, the number of employees at the company fluctuates throughout the year due to the seasonality of production. In 2020–2021, the number of permanent staff reached 15–20 people, while during the peak season starting around August, it increased to 110–120 people. In subsequent years, as the company's activities expanded, the staff grew to 30–35 permanent employees and 140–150 seasonal workers.

Azerstar LLC's future activities are primarily focused on supplying foreign markets. The company has expanded its exports to Italy, Germany, the Baltic countries, and Russia, while also seeking new markets and striving to establish new connections with hazelnut buyer companies.

Let's examine the data on physical sales volumes for recent years (Table 2) and sales profits (Table 3) for 2017–2023.

The analysis of the presented data shows that the company's decrease in sales volume in 2018 was due to problems that arose in the Italian market with a logistics company responsible for transporting and delivering products to Italian purchasing companies. Azerstar LLC overestimated its trust relations with the intermediary, did not control the activities of the logistics company, which led to delays in the delivery of its products, and the company lost a significant part of its profit. In 2019, the company's sales volume and profit from sales of its products reached their maximum values. The indicators for 2020 were significantly influenced by the global pandemic of coronavirus, as a result of which the sales volume and profit from sales decreased by more than 2 times.

The situation began to improve in 2021, when the physical sales volume of hazelnuts increased by 1.1 times, and the profit from sales increased by 2 times compared to similar indicators in 2020. The Russian market is one of the main sales markets for the company, and for this reason, the aggression of Russia against Ukraine, the beginning of hostilities, the introduction of a number of sanctions

Table 2 Physical sales volume of hazelnuts for 2017–2023

Years	2017	2018	2019	2020	2021	2022	2023
Sales volume, tons	2884	1882	2962	1426	1555	1514	1654.3

Source: obtained by the author during an interview with a representative of Azerstar LLC

Table 3 Profit from hazelnut sales for 2017–2023

Years	2017	2018	2019	2020	2021	2022	2023
Profit from sales, million US dollars	1.78	- 0.06	2.01	0.70	1.43	0.77	1.4

Source: obtained by the author during an interview with a representative of Azerstar LLC

against Russian companies, problems with banking transfers related to the disconnection of Russian banks from SWIFT led to a decrease in the company's performance indicators: the physical sales volume of hazelnuts decreased by 0.97 times, the profit from sales—by 0.5 times.

The situation began to recover by 2023, when the physical sales volume of hazelnuts increased by 1.1 times, and the profit from sales increased by 1.8 times, which is explained by successful management decisions and the establishment of mutually beneficial relations with its partners.

Today, Azerstar LLC is one of the main companies engaged in the export of cleaned hazelnuts to foreign markets. The company's products are characterized by high quality, attractive "commodity appearance," and full compliance with European market standards.

3 Conclusion

About 1 million tons of hazelnuts are grown worldwide every year. There are five leaders in this area: Turkey, Italy, Azerbaijan, Chile, and the United States. In 2021, Turkey's profit from hazelnut exports alone amounted to $2 billion. European countries purchase 91% of the world's hazelnuts, two-thirds of which are used in the confectionery industry. The demand for hazelnuts in the world is growing every day. In Germany, Holland, Belgium, Luxembourg, Austria, Great Britain, Ireland, Switzerland, Denmark, and Hungary, you will not see a single hazelnut bush. However, these countries are actively involved in the hazelnut trade. The European Union creates all possible conditions for member countries to profit from this area through lobbying.

The hazelnut market is unstable and full of contradictions. The state of this market is influenced by a large number of external and internal factors. External factors are mainly related to natural conditions, climate or political and legal conditions, such as European market standards, sanctions and restrictive measures. In Azerbaijan, the main external factors affecting the production and sale of hazelnuts are climate, fungal bacteria, pandemic and sanctions applied to Russian companies.

Currently, there are about ten companies operating in the Azerbaijani market for the production, processing and sale of hazelnuts. Some of these companies are considered hidden champions. For example, hidden champions among hazelnut producers are Aqrovest, Azerbaijan Hazelnut Exporters Consortium (AHEC), Azerstar LLC. These companies compete with each other in taste, appearance and compliance with European standards. Azerstar LLC products have proven themselves on the positive side in the European market. The company cooperates with leading companies in the production of chocolate and sweets. The main strategic tasks facing the company are to enter new European markets, establish mutually beneficial relations with buyer companies, improve management and marketing.

Summarizing the conducted research, we note that in recent years the number of hidden champion companies in Azerbaijan has been increasing. These companies mainly operate in the market of fruits, dried fruits, hazelnuts, nuts, and saffron. If earlier there were only a few such companies, now we can single out dozens of companies—hidden champions, focusing their activities on export markets. These companies do not advertise their activities, it is quite difficult to find detailed information about their activities, for this reason our study was focused only on the activities of Azerstar LLC. In our future studies, we will continue to study the market of hidden champions and consider a wider scope of companies' activities.

References

Ahmadova, E., Hamidova, L., & Hajiyeva, L. (2021). Diversification of the economy in the context of globalization (case of Azerbaijan). *SHS Web of Conferences, 92*(2). https://doi.org/10.1051/shsconf/20219207002

Ibadoghlu, G., & Niftiyev, I. (2022). A retrospective analysis of the Azerbaijani economy during 30 years of independence. *Post-Soviet Issues, 9*(1), 58–76.

Imrani, Z. T., & Musayeva, M. R. (2016). Socio-economic aspects of the concept of sustainable development in Azerbaijan Republic. *South of Russia: ecology, development., 11*(2), 42–49. In Russian. https://doi.org/10.18470/1992-1098-2016-2-42-49

Suleymanov, E., Rahmanov, F., & Qojayeva, E. (2021). Azerbaijan Economy, University Publishing House named after Saints Cyril and Methodius, 413 p. in Russian.

Further Reading

http://www.azerstar.com/.

https://oec.world/en/profile/country/aze.

https://www.imf.org/en/News/Articles/2023/12/11/mcs121123-azerbaijan-staff-concluding-statement-of-the-2023-article-iv-mission.

The State Statistical Committee of the Republic of Azerbaijan. https://www.stat.gov.az/source/entrepreneurship/?lang=en.

The World Bank. https://data.worldbank.org/

Leyla Hajiyeva holds the position of Deputy Director of the Faculty of the Azerbaijan State University of Economics, is an Associate Professor of the Department of Applied Economics. She has about 30 years of experience in academic activities, teaches the disciplines of Marketing, Digital Marketing, Marketing Research, Marketing in Tourism in Russian, Azerbaijani, and English. She lectures at the bachelor's and master's levels. In addition to her teaching responsibilities, she is actively engaged in research activities, studies the state of the consumer market in Azerbaijan, and conducts research in the field of tourism and marketing. She is the author of two books, "Industrial Marketing" and "Marketing of the Service Sector," has about 100 publications, including articles indexed in Scopus, Web of Science, Elsevier database. Leyla Hajiyeva is a participant of national and international grants, within the framework of academic exchange programs (Erasmus +, Mevlana, Orkhun) she lectured at Hacettepe University (Turkey), Anadolu University (Turkey), Dunaújváros University (Hungary), Transylvania University (Romania), Amanzholov University (Kazakhstan).

She actively participates in international conferences and is also one of the organizers of national and international conferences for students, young researchers, and scientists at the faculty.

Furthermore, Leyla Hajiyeva is committed to establishing partnerships between UNEC and foreign universities. She is fluent in Azerbaijani, English, Turkish, and Russian and pays special attention to the internationalization of higher education and strategic academic partnerships.

Mansur Isa Barkhudarov is the Director of the Russian School of Economics at the Azerbaijan State University of Economics (UNEC). He has over 30 years of professional academic experience.

Mansur Barkhudarov has held senior positions at the Azerbaijan State University of Economics since 2014, including as the Dean of the Faculty of International Cooperation and Economic Relations. He is also the Head of the Center for Cognitive Economics. Throughout his career, he has coordinated numerous international projects and facilitated the establishment of dual degree relationships with foreign universities.

In 2003, after defending his dissertation, he earned a PhD in Economics. Currently, he teaches courses in economics, behavioral behavior, and transnational corporations.

Barkhudarov is fluent in Azerbaijani and Russian and pays special attention to the internationalization of higher education and educational management. He has participated in dozens of international forums and conferences held in Russia, Ukraine, Germany, Greece, Turkey, Georgia, Kazakhstan, Uzbekistan, Kyrgyzstan, and other countries. The problems of foreign economic development of the countries of the South Caucasus and Central Asia in the context of globalization are his main scientific and research topic. He regularly appears as an expert in the Azerbaijani media. Currently, he is working on his doctoral dissertation on the topic of "Problems of Foreign Economic Cooperation of the Countries of the South Caucasus and Central Asia in the Context of Globalization."

Afet Alakbarova is a senior advisor in international higher education and policy development, currently serving as Leading Advisor for international projects and cooperation within a central governmental structure in Azerbaijan. She has over 20 years of professional experience in international academic cooperation, institutional development, and educational project management.

From 2002 to 2025, Alakbarova held progressive leadership positions at the Azerbaijan State University of Economics, including Director of the International Cooperation Department and Head of the Foreign Relations Office. She coordinated a wide range of international projects and managed institutional partnerships, student and staff mobility schemes, and the admission of international students.

Her academic background includes a Master of Finance (MBA) from the Azerbaijan State University of Economics and a Master's degree in Education Policy and Management from a joint program between the University of Manchester and the Moscow School of Social and Economic Sciences. She has also served as a lecturer at the Azerbaijan State University of Economics, teaching courses in international business ethics, management, and career development in Azerbaijani, English, and Russian.

Alakbarova has contributed to several international research and capacity-building initiatives supported by multilateral organizations and global education networks. She is fluent in Azerbaijani, English, and Russian, and is particularly interested in the internationalization of higher education, education governance, and strategic academic partnerships.

Hidden Champions of Bosnia and Herzegovina

Amra Kožo, Merima Činjarević, and Adi Alić

Abstract This chapter brings together the story of four companies identified as hidden champions within the hidden champions research wave conducted during 2022 and 2023 in Bosnia and Herzegovina (BIH). Even though the companies presented in this research come from different business sectors, they all exhibited several common features related to their business processes and management: authentic leadership, resilience in turbulent times, focus on innovation and sustainability, high-quality products and services, and supportive organizational culture. In addition, a common characteristic of all companies is an open, sincere, and developmental approach to employees. Companies encourage employees to play a vital role in various activities and develop creative ideas and solutions to challenges. Finally, due to their flexibility, persistence, and vision, hidden champions successfully overcame high-scale changes and challenges, transforming them into opportunities.

Overview

Official name: Bosnia and Herzegovina
Type of government: Parliamentary democracy
Population in 2022: 3,233,526
Land area: 51,209.2 square km

History

1189 First documented mention of Bosnia
1377 Bosnia becomes a kingdom after the coronation of its first king, Tvrtko I Kotromanić
1463 Kingdom of Bosnia is raided and annexed by the Ottoman Empire
1878 Bosnia and Herzegovina annexed by the Austro-Hungarian Empire
1918 Bosnia and Herzegovina joins the Kingdom of Serbs, Croats, and Slovenes

A. Kožo (✉) · M. Činjarević · A. Alić
University of Sarajevo – School of Economics and Business,
Sarajevo, Bosnia and Herzegovina
e-mail: amra.kozo@efsa.unsa.ba; merima.cinjarevic@efsa.unsa.ba; adi.alic@efsa.unsa.ba

D. Berberović, D. Purg (eds.), *Hidden Champions in Rising Economies*, Contributions to Management Science,
https://doi.org/10.1007/978-3-032-08263-3_14

1929	The Kingdom of Serbs, Croats, and Slovenes becomes the Kingdom of Yugoslavia
1945	Bosnia and Herzegovina becomes one of the six constituent republics of the Socialist Federative Republic of Yugoslavia
1992	Bosnia and Herzegovina declares independence from Yugoslavia
1995	Aggression on Bosnia and Herzegovina ends with the Dayton Peace Agreement
2002	Bosnia and Herzegovina becomes a member of the Council of Europe
2008	Bosnia and Herzegovina signs the Stability and Accession Agreement with the European Union
2022	European Union grants candidate status to Bosnia and Herzegovina

1 Introduction: Context and History

According to the OECD (2022), Bosnia and Herzegovina (BIH)[1] represents a small, upper-middle-income Western Balkans economy. The business context in BIH has been significantly influenced by the country's predominant historical and political factors over the past several decades. A transition process brought changes from command-planned economies and their associated managerial practices towards economic liberalization and more participative leadership styles. Generally, the business environment in BIH is considered transitional, post-conflict, with a noticeable amount of risk and uncertainty (Berberović et al., 2019). However, Petričević and Danis (2007) note that, despite the perplexing issues that make BIH a unique case among transition economies, the country has the potential to provide great opportunities for those who decide to do business there.

The literature discusses the political environment in BiH as turbulent (Berberović et al., 2021) and complex with ineffective political structures (Ortlieb et al., 2019). Decentralized, complicated, and bureaucratic political governance impedes the transition processes and hinders business development and the creation of a stable economy. Indeed, the political environment exposes hidden champions to uncertainty and bureaucratic difficulties.

A legal framework also reflects the complexity of a country's political system. Even though the legal environment is relatively stable, business regulations might differ among distinct levels of governance between entities. However, following its application for European Union (EU) membership in 2016 and candidate status obtained in 2022, BIH must make significant efforts to align its laws and judiciary with the standards of the EU.

The economic environment in the country is characterized by complex regulatory procedures, a tense political environment, and limited progress in

[1] Country abbraviation used in chapter is based on ISO (International Standardization Organisation) Country Code Collection (alpha-3 code) (https://www.iso.org/obp/ui/#search last accessed June 2024).

anti-corruption efforts (OECD, 2022). The country relies on foreign direct investments (Ortlieb et al., 2019) but also records the influx of remittances from the diaspora. The majority of companies (over 70%) are located in the entity of the Federation of BIH (OECD, 2022; p. 455). Moreover, the country faces a high unemployment rate despite the growth of the vital national economic indicators (refer to Table 1 for the country's core economic indicators according to the World Bank Data). Due to the small economy in scope and scale, companies focus not only on the narrow domestic market but also on international markets, both in the EU and globally.

Regarding the social environment, BIH has a population of roughly 3.23 million as of 2022, followed by a negative population growth rate of −1.2% annually (World Bank Open Data, 2024). The country records a brain drain since young and educated citizens have been emigrating mainly to the EU countries for better work opportunities and higher life standards. Consequently, the country is confronted with an aging population and a shortage of skilled workforce.

In terms of technological environment, according to the European Innovation Scoreboard Country Profile, BIH is considered an emerging innovator country, performing at 36.2% of the EU average (European Commission, 2023; p. 83), where environment-related technologies, employment in innovative enterprises, and sales of innovative products are identified as some of the relative strengths of the country, while innovative expenditures per employee, lifelong learning, research, and development in the public sectors are recognized as some of the relative weaknesses.

Regarding environmental context, the OECD (2022) reports that green measures related to small and medium enterprises (SMEs) to which, based on the size, hidden champions belong, are included in environmental policies and developmental strategies in both entities (e.g., the Development Strategy of the Federation of BIH (2021–2027) and in Republika Srpska's Strategy for Development of SMEs (2021–2027)). Although this resulted in an increasing number of green infrastructure projects, primarily due to the transition from coal, concerns related to environmental sustainability are present. On the other hand, hidden champions align their policies and practices with the country's 2030 sustainable development goals framework.

1.1 Characteristics of Hidden Champions from BIH

In the current wave of research (2022–2023), four hidden champions have been identified in BIH. The selection process was conducted based on the criteria established by Herman Simon (Braček Lalić & Berberović, 2021) and following the prescribed research protocol. The analyses revealed several common features of identified hidden champions: authentic leadership, resilience, innovation, sustainability, high quality and uniqueness, and supportive culture and talent management.

Authentic leadership: The hidden champions are led by example. Their leaders inspire by communicating purpose and values for the broader community. Empathy

Table 1 Core economic indicators for BIH

Indicator	2019	2020	2021	2022	2023	2024
GDP per capita (current US$)	6122.38	6130.31	7295.34	7655.59	8638.67	n/a
GDP per capita growth (annual %)	4.16	−1.66	9.19	5.53	2.84	n/a
Unemployment, total (% of total labor force) (modeled ILO estimate)	15.69	15.87	14.9	12.66	10.67	10.72
Foreign direct investment, net inflows (% of GDP)	2.19	2.39	3.24	3.47	3.76	n/a
GDP (current US$, mio)	20482.61	20226.04	23672.71	24534.66	27514.78	n/a
Exports of goods and services (current US$, mio)	8201.25	6913.56	10078.26	11851.99	12121.81	n/a
Exports of goods and services (% of GDP)	40.04	34.18	42.57	48.31	44.06	n/a
Merchandise exports (current US$, mio)	6578	6155	8614	9674	9232	n/a
Merchandise exports to high-income economies (% of total merchandise exports)	78.27	78.92	78.88	78.39	78.06	n/a
Merchandise exports to low- and middle-income economies in Europe & Central Asia (% of total merchandise exports)	19.3	19.19	19.48	20.33	20.44	n/a
Ores and metals exports (% of merchandise exports)	6.95	5.51	9.56	11.07	7.02	n/a
Agricultural raw materials exports (% of merchandise exports)	4.86	4.95	4.92	4.65	4.13	n/a
Food exports (% of merchandise exports)	6.9	8.1	6.36	5.85	6.23	n/a
Fuel exports (% of merchandise exports)	8.09	6.74	8.54	9.98	9.51	n/a
Manufactures exports (% of merchandise exports)	73.16	74.69	70.61	68.44	73.09	n/a
High-technology exports (% of manufactured exports)	5.27	4.61	5.32	5.22	4.97	n/a

Source: World Bank, 2025
https://databank.worldbank.org/source/world-development-indicators#

and sincere relationships are at the heart of communication with employees and key stakeholders. Moreover, self-awareness, integrity, and expertise allow them to assess business circumstances objectively. For instance, one of the owners of the Artisan company discusses how their business originates from their great passion and love for wood and art.

Resilience: The flexibility of hidden champions comes from strategic orientation. Usually, resilience is related to diversified business portfolios and the ability to learn from past experience. Moreover, the ability to transform crises into opportunities is one of the critical success factors of hidden champions.

Innovation. Passion for innovation is the main leverage of hidden champion businesses, representing one of the central pillars of the companies' competitive advantage. Innovations and sustainable practices are highly correlated and create value for a broader society.

Sustainability: Sustainable business practices are integrated into strategic and operational activities (e.g., reduced carbon emissions, zero waste, recycling, rational energy consumption).

High quality: Hidden champions never compromise on quality. Quality is embedded in every manufacturing stage, starting with high-quality materials from reliable suppliers, modern production processes, and the final unique and high-quality products or services.

Supportive organizational culture and talent management: This feature of hidden champions encompasses numerous business practices, from employee empowerment, building trust, education and continuous learning, equal opportunities for all employees, and fostering creativity and new ideas.

2 Case Studies of Selected Hidden Champions

2.1 Case Study 1

2.1.1 Artisan Ltd

Overview
Address: Medakovo bb, 74260 Tešanj, Bosnia and Herzegovina
Tel: +387 32 667 910, +387 32 667 911
Fax: +387 32 658 820
Email: info@artisan.ba
Web: www.artisan.ba

Company Information
Industry: Manufacture of other furniture
Year of establishment: 2007
Sales revenues in 2017: € 6.1 MIO
Sales revenues in 2023: € 17.4 MIO

Average number of employees in 2023: 263
Brainer(s) behind the company: Fadil Ćostović and Dražen Poznanović

2.1.2 Nature of Market Leadership

Artisan's market leadership is deeply rooted in its dedication to furniture craftsmanship and design. This commitment to craftsmanship in furniture-making gives the company a distinctive edge in the market, appealing particularly to customers who value uniqueness and authenticity. The Benelux countries and South Korea are major export markets for Artisan furniture. The domestic market only accounts for about 4% of production, with the rest intended for export.

2.1.3 Nature of Competitive Advantage

The competitive advantage of Artisan rests on four pillars: (1) product quality, (2) innovative furniture design that blends modern design lines with retro elements, (3) strong brand equity, and (4) long-lasting relationships with customers.

2.1.4 Core Lessons Learned on the Path to Success

1. Persistence pays off: The company's success may be primarily attributed to its founders' persistence. Even in the face of challenges, the founders' unwavering determination and refusal to give up have been instrumental in the company's success.
2. Reinvestment for growth: Artisan's ongoing reinvestment strategy highlights the benefits of prioritizing long-term growth over short-term gains.
3. Capitalizing on bestsellers: The initial success of Artisan's bestsellers provided leverage for business expansion and the introduction of other Artisan furniture lines.
4. Do not undervalue good luck: While perseverance and hard work are necessary, being in the right place at the right time can significantly impact business success.

2.1.5 Management and Leadership Development Needs

The company strongly emphasizes the urgent need for workers, particularly experienced carpenters, and hopes that the community will take steps to generate professionals with such skills. Training is something that the company offers to new workers, and the learning is perceived as a lifelong process. Artisan stresses the importance of partnerships with top brands to acquire highly specialized knowledge that is otherwise unattainable.

2.1.6 Financing and Regulatory Environment Development Needs

Financially, Artisan is self-sufficient. However, they emphasize that BIH's accession to the World Trade Organization (WTO) would greatly benefit the company. This accession would facilitate the removal of tariffs, particularly the tariff in South Korea, which is one of the most important markets for Artisan's products.

2.1.7 Pandemic's Impact on "Hidden Champions" Business Approach

Artisan experienced minimal COVID-19 disruptions. While demand for cheaper furniture declined, Artisan's high-end luxury category remained resilient. However, the company encountered higher transportation costs, particularly for container shipments to distant markets such as South Korea, Australia, and America. Despite these challenges, Artisan remains steadfast, recognizing that these factors are beyond its control.

2.1.8 Effects of the Ukraine War on "Hidden Champions" Business Operations

The Russia-Ukraine war has not disrupted the continuity of Artisan's production process or its business model. With years of experience, Artisan developed business resilience, characterized by positive adaptation to difficulties and effective crisis management. Their guiding maxim during crises is to view challenges as opportunities.

2.1.9 "Artisan: Tradition Meets Modernity in Woodworking Excellence"

Artisan emerged from the traditional woodwork shop "Ćostović," which boasts over 50 years of experience in wood processing. Specializing in high-quality, hand-made furniture from solid wood, Artisan's commitment to an artisanal work style gives it a competitive edge in the market. The company is export-oriented and is currently the fastest-growing brand under the label "Made in BIH" in the wood sector. The Neva and Latus collections, Artisan's top sellers, consistently attract premium customers, securing the leading market position in the niche market of hand-made furniture from solid wood.

Artisan is dedicated to its vision, operating under the philosophy that every collection and piece of wood tells a unique story. The company's vision has positioned them in the niche market, creating solid wood furniture that combines modern design lines with a touch of retro style, offering a distinctive blend of contemporary and classic aesthetics. Artisan employs a vertical integration strategy by housing all aspects of the development-to-delivery process under one roof (design, milling, wood processing, and furniture production).

In a consumption-driven era, the company focuses on creating furniture with emotional value, ensuring each piece elicits positive emotions and serves as a cherished memory for future generations. The emotional value of Artisan's products is reflected in the words of Mr. Poznanović, one of the company's founders: "The emotional connection with furniture is most evident at trade fairs when people encounter furniture for the first time and start 'touching' it, showing their deep bond with it."

The company's success relies on visionary leadership, dedicated and capable management, and a team of passionate, creative employees, including designers and production workers. Although some companies have attempted to imitate Artisan's approach, they struggle to replicate what truly sets Artisan apart: the genuine passion that fuels every endeavor, the unwavering dedication of Artisan's team, and the creative spark that infuses the workplace.

Visionary leadership paved Artisan's path to success, recognizing the untapped potential in the luxury designer furniture market. As stated by Mr. Poznanović: "In an environment where doubt prevailed, we persevered, investing considerable effort to reach our current market position."

Cooperation with world-renowned designers also contributed to Artisan's success. The company has gained significant know-how from its customers, including owners of high-end luxury fashion brands, hotels, and restaurants worldwide. However, good fortune was one crucial ingredient in Artisan's success. While dedication and hard work are essential, being in the right place at the right moment greatly impacts the company's success.

2.2 Case Study 2

2.2.1 Emerus Ltd

Overview
Address: Knešpolje b.b., 88220 Široki Brijeg, Bosnia and Herzegovina
Tel: +387 39 701 240
Fax: +387 39 701 241
Email: info@emerus.eu
Web: https://emerus.eu/

Company Information
Industry: Manufacture of metal structures and parts of structures
Year of establishment: 2015
Sales revenues in 2017: € 22 MIO
Sales revenues in 2023: € 48 MIO
Average number of employees in 2023: 224
Brainer(s) behind the company: CEO Hrvoje Soldo

2.2.2 Nature of Market Leadership

Emerus is a well-established European manufacturer specializing in producing mechanically processed aluminum products and sophisticated extruded profiles for various industrial sectors. By utilizing premium materials and state-of-the-art machinery to adhere to rigorous European standards, the company demonstrates its commitment to product quality and sustainability. Due to the use of solar energy, the company's carbon footprint is below the European average. Moreover, the company's in-house toolmaking department ensures consistent, on-time deliveries to meet customer needs with outstanding flexibility. Continuous investment in cutting-edge facilities and equipment helps Emerus maintain its position as a market leader.

2.2.3 Nature of Competitive Advantage

The competitive advantage of Emerus rests on four pillars: (1) effective product portfolio strategy, (2) the adoption of flexible manufacturing systems, (3) the integration of sustainable practices in the manufacturing process, and (4) the adoption of lean manufacturing philosophy.

2.2.4 Core Lessons Learned on the Path to Success

1. Visionary leadership: Leaders inspire and mobilize employees toward shared objectives by articulating a compelling vision and demonstrating persistence and enthusiasm.
2. Effective technology management: Adopting new technology and advancements in production techniques are primary drivers of product development.
3. Customer segment diversification: The saying "Do not put all your eggs in one basket" emphasizes the importance of diversifying customer segments, i.e., expanding the range of customer segments a company serves rather than relying solely on a narrow target segment.
4. Green commitment, golden future: Investing in renewable energy sources is both a moral imperative and strategic business decision that leads to greater success and resilience in the future.

2.2.5 Management and Leadership Development Needs

Talent management is essential for Emerus to build a skilled, engaged, and adaptable workforce that drives innovation and ensures long-term company success. Internships and collaboration with higher education institutions are the main pillars of Emerus' talent management strategy. Internships serve as a valuable source for identifying and nurturing potential talent. At the same time, partnering with higher educational institutions allows Emerus to access a pool of motivated and skilled students who bring fresh perspectives, ideas, and energy to the company.

2.2.6 Financing and Regulatory Environment Development Needs

Aluminum extrusion innovation demands costly, cutting-edge equipment and tools, placing a significant financial burden on the company. Thus, government subsidies need to provide public financial resources and reduce the private cost of innovation. Government funding aimed at acquiring cutting-edge technology and tools may help companies looking to pioneer breakthroughs in aluminum extrusion. Furthermore, government subsidies may boost companies' confidence in pursuing innovative ventures by mitigating risks associated with innovation (e.g., uncertainty about return on investment—ROI).

2.2.7 Pandemic's Impact on "Hidden Champions" Business Approach

The COVID-19 pandemic has had a minimal effect on the company's business approach. Key challenges during the COVID-19 pandemic were related to logistics and supply chain management. In addition, Emerus was confronted with transportation challenges caused by international border control measures and insufficient warehouse storage capacity. Moreover, Emerus, as a consumer of semiconductor chips, had been impacted by the global semiconductor shortage during the COVID-19 pandemic.

2.2.8 Effects of the Ukraine War on "Hidden Champions" Business Operations

Emerus is dedicated to achieving sustainability objectives, including reducing carbon emissions and adopting renewable energy sources, like solar power. Solar energy provides Emerus with a reliable and consistent electricity supply, shielding the company from fossil fuel price fluctuations, which are particularly pronounced during geopolitical unrest.

2.2.9 "Emerus: Building a Sustainable Legacy Through Innovation"

Emerus was founded in 2015 by visionary entrepreneur Mr. Hrvoje Soldo. The company is a leading provider of aluminum extruded profiles and mechanically processed aluminum products to industrial sectors. Emerus uses high-quality materials and renewable energy to reduce its carbon footprint and ensure eco-friendly production. The company's founder is a visionary leader who values innovation and sustainability. Since founding the company, Mr. Soldo has guided Emerus to great success with a sharp eye for possibilities and dedication to quality. He believes the company's biggest asset is its employees and is committed to creating an innovative culture, nurturing talent, and helping people reach their full potential. Diversifying customer segments allows Emerus to adapt to evolving market dynamics, enhance resilience to industry shifts, and seize emerging market opportunities. In navigating the complexities of a rapidly evolving business landscape, by prioritizing innovation, sustainability, and operational excellence, Emerus is maintaining its market position and achieving long-term success in the competitive realm of aluminum manufacturing.

Finally, Mr. Soldo emphasized the importance of social responsibility through supporting local initiatives that make a positive impact beyond the company's operations. "The development of this company is also the development of our environment and community," says Mr. Soldo.

Emerus is one of the leading European providers of extruded aluminum profiles, meeting diverse customer needs across industries (e.g., construction, automotive, transportation). Dedicated to engineering excellence and customer satisfaction, Emerus continues to set new standards in the aluminum extrusion industry, driving progress and delivering superior solutions across multiple sectors.

2.3 Case Study 3

2.3.1 Mladegs Pak Ltd

Overview
Address: Vijaka bb, 78430 Prnjavor, Bosnia and Herzegovina
Tel: +387 51 647 620
Fax: +387 51 647 652
Email: info@mladegspak.com
Web: https://www.mladegspak.com/index-en.html

Company Information
Industry: Food industry
Year of establishment: 1996
Sales revenues in 2017: € 10.5 MIO
Sales revenues in 2023: € 19.4 MIO
Average number of employees in 2023: 172
Brainer(s) behind the company: Goran Vrhovac

2.3.2 Nature of Market Leadership

Mladegs Pak has a long-standing tradition of producing delicious, high-quality, safe food products. The company offers a product assortment of over 400 items under its two domestic brands, Bonito and Dominus. A strong focus on consumers' needs, specific demands, and preferences is essential to the company's market leadership. This is achieved through ongoing consumer research, product testing, and their complete adaptation to specific preferences in the markets of different countries. At the same time, the company ensures good value for consumers, characterized by an optimal balance between benefits and price.

2.3.3 Nature of Competitive Advantage

The company's flexibility and capability to quickly and thoroughly adapt to specific customer requirements (e.g., utilizing over 100 different recipes for producing ketchup) is one of the major sources of its competitive advantage. The company focuses on product quality, holds the world's highest food certificates (e.g., HACCP, ISO, and IFS), and continuously invests in the best equipment, technology, and knowledge. A significant portion of its production is dedicated to manufacturing for private brands of European retail chains such as Lidl, Aldi, Rewe, Penny, SPAR, and others. This enhances capacity utilization and the company's profitability and fosters long-term relationships with these chains, which are key distributors of their products.

2.3.4 Core Lessons Learned on the Path to Success

1. Product quality is never questioned and is followed by product availability and a fair price.
2. The approach to consumers must always be carefully carried out to provide sufficient information to successfully satisfy consumers' needs and desires. A higher level of customization provides opportunities for tremendous success.
3. In the consumer industry, such as the food industry, building and nurturing good relations with retail chains can be crucial since the availability of products on the market largely depends on them.
4. The corporate spirit, equal opportunities for all employees, and taking care of their needs are fundamental factors in the development and growth of the company.

2.3.5 Management and Leadership Development Needs

Bearing in mind the dominant market orientation of the company, marketing managers need to have the appropriate knowledge and skills. Since the company operates on the international market and employs various branding strategies (both for its own brands and products under private labels for specific distribution chains), managers with expertise in international marketing and brand management are needed.

2.3.6 Financing and Regulatory Environment Development Needs

The state must recognize the needs of companies and co-finance investment in modern equipment to create new and better jobs. Educational institutions should align with the economy's needs by revising curricula and programs to reflect current business conditions, particularly in marketing management.

2.3.7 Pandemic's Impact on "Hidden Champions" Business Approach

The primary obstacle to business during the pandemic was the reduced availability of certain raw materials. This necessitated a shift in the company's strategy towards diversifying suppliers and maintaining a larger stock of raw materials in the warehouse.

2.3.8 Effects of the Ukraine War on "Hidden Champions" Business Operations

The war in Ukraine led to challenges in procuring certain raw materials and substantial price increases that significantly affected the company's operations. Overcoming these issues required adaptation to the current situation, primarily by enhancing mobility, flexibility, and attentiveness to the needs of customers, suppliers, and employees.

2.3.9 "Mladegs Pak: Global Adaptation to Local Tastes"

In its current form, Mladegs Pak was established in a small town in northern BIH. The company's mission is stated: "Every day, we strive to deliver products of proven quality to our homes, made from naturally grown raw materials, sourced from people who have been growing them all their lives." With this, the company wants to connect households, provide employment opportunities for our neighbors and friends, and create a prosperous future.

One of Mladegs Pak's key advantages lies in its clear marketing orientation, starting with consumers' preferences and creating products accordingly. Hence, the company focuses on continuous consumer research, product testing, and adapting products to meet specific consumer needs. Recognizing the importance of addressing consumer needs and preferences across different countries (over 15 countries worldwide), the company is very clear about applying the glocalization strategy, i.e., adapting products to local needs while operating in the international market. The glocalization strategy is achieved thanks to the company's high flexibility and the ability to quickly and thoroughly adapt to specific customer requirements.

The company has two strong domestic brands, Bonito and Dominus. Brand Bonito, established in 1989, offers high-quality products designed to be a part of local cuisine and food preparation in every household. Dominus, introduced in 2006, aims to fulfill the needs of consumers seeking quality, practicality, and safety, primarily in the business consumption market (HORECA market).

Finally, Mladegs Pak is committed to upholding responsibility and positively impacting the communities where it operates. It is a socially responsible company that invests in sports and culture to support the development of adolescents and children. Mladegs Pak also promotes environmental sustainability through practices such as waste separation, paper recycling, wastewater treatment, and rational energy and waste consumption. Mladegs Pak aims to raise customers' awareness and promote positive ideals through socially conscious actions. As Mr. Vrhovac emphasized, the company's primary goal is "to build a bright future for every one of our neighbors."

2.4 Case Study 4

2.4.1 Wagner Automotiv

Overview
Address: Sarajevska 62, 76250 Gradačac, Bosnia and Herzegovina
Tel: +387 35 816 737
Fax: +387 35 816 737
Email: info@wagner-automotiv.ba
Web: https://wagner-automotiv.ba/?lang=en

Company Information
Industry: Casting of light metals
Year of establishment: 2012
Sales revenues in 2017: € 11.8 MIO
Sales revenues in 2023: € 17.5 MIO
Average number of employees in 2023: 332
Brainer(s) behind the company: CEO Ensar Omeragić, MBA

2.4.2 Nature of Market Leadership

Wagner Automotiv was established in 2012 as a joint venture between TMD AGS Ltd (BIH) and Wagner Waldstatt AG (Switzerland). The company delivers 90% of its products to the EU-based automotive industry, and its customers are reputable Tier 1 suppliers. Producing specific car parts from processed aluminum requires specific technology and knowledge in metal processing, primarily aluminum (high-pressure die casting), which represents the core element of the company's market leadership. In addition, the company can rapidly find necessary solutions and has a highly favorable location.

2.4.3 Nature of Competitive Advantage

The nature of Wagner Automotiv's competitive advantage lies in high productivity, product quality, technological know-how, and vertical integration. The company has a tool shop, an indispensable working component in production, owned by a domestic co-owner. The company creates and sustains long-term relationships with all actors throughout the value chain, particularly with suppliers and customers.

2.4.4 Core Lessons Learned on the Path to Success

1. Investing and maintaining know-how through employees is key to success.
2. In a technology-intensive industry such as aluminum processing, one must be willing to continuously find innovative solutions, experiment, take risks, and learn from mistakes.
3. Building and maintaining long-term relationships with customers is critical. It is essential to try to focus on the product portfolio, which is crucial for the business, while also focusing on the diversification of the customer portfolio to mitigate the business risk.
4. Vertical integration enhances agility and competitive advantage. By controlling multiple stages of production, companies optimize processes and meet market demands, enabling long-term success and resilience.

2.4.5 Management and Leadership Development Needs

In BIH, education catering to the needs of this business sector is very limited and scant. Engineers require training in advanced manufacturing techniques and industry-specific procedures to keep up with technological breakthroughs and enhance production efficiency. Also, proficiency in precise tool and die manufacture is crucial. Since the current education system provides limited training in these essential skills, to bridge this gap, specific knowledge and experiences are provided, on a small scale, through specialized fairs and business events.

2.4.6 Financing and Regulatory Environment Development Needs

Since this sector has solid growth potential in BIH, financial and other regulatory institutions might support companies by providing better access to funding sources.

2.4.7 Pandemic's Impact on "Hidden Champions" Business Approach

The general decline in the automotive industry led to lower demand for Wagner Automotiv products. However, the broad product portfolio and the stability of the company's customers were the basis for its stability during COVID-19.

2.4.8 Effects of the Ukraine War on "Hidden Champions" Business Operations

The crisis in Ukraine turned out to be an opportunity for the company. Namely, the problems in the supply chain resulted in the geographical reallocation of production, shifting it to European countries. Thus, thanks to its location, Wagner Automotiv used this crisis and turned the threat into an opportunity.

2.4.9 "Wagner Automotiv: The Hidden Story Behind the Lord of the Aluminium"

Wagner Automotiv is a relatively young company, founded in 2012 in a small town in the northeastern part of BIH. The company supports a dynamic work environment where passion for work is valued, and diversity is celebrated without room for discrimination. The company specializes in producing specific parts from processed aluminum, primarily for the needs of leading global companies in the automotive industry. As director, Mr. Ensar Omeragić, states, the company is guided by the mission of "being a reliable supplier of aluminum castings and becoming a recognizable brand in this branch of the metal industry."

The company's products, such as aluminum housings for board computers, entertainment systems, and e-mobility, require a specific manufacturing process and distinct technology: high-pressure die casting, which involves casting aluminum under high pressure. Knowledge, experience, and know-how in producing such complex products are critical factors behind the company's success. Wagner Automotiv primarily operates internationally, serving customers such as Mercedes, Audi, BMW, Land Rover, VW, and Ferrari. By leading the industry, Wagner Automotiv places itself at the top of the list of aluminum processing companies.

Market leadership is based on the company's agile work and ability to achieve competitive pricing swiftly through innovative solutions and streamlining. This is highly related to a vertical integration of essential technological components, which refers to the possession of a tool shop that enables the production of specific parts (tailored for each product). In case some issues arise, corrections can be made very quickly. Also, new and/or replacement components for existing tools are produced within a short period. In addition, the location of the Wagner Automotiv also represents an essential element of market leadership. The company is available 24 hours a day for its customers from different countries, which enhances its reliability and competitive advantage.

3 Conclusions and Recommendations

Hidden champions have successfully navigated international markets despite the challenging domestic political environment. International orientation, high quality and unique, innovative products, dedicated employees, vision, and leadership with integrity keep them thriving even in turbulent times. Moreover, hidden champions emphasize sustainability, responsible resource management, corporate social responsibility, and community engagement. More substantial support from the state level is undoubtedly lacking for the further development of businesses, and the majority of recommendations for improvement focus on enhancing government policies, particularly those that can strengthen the growth of private enterprises engaged in innovative processes within the country. Indeed, all market participants should play a role in advancing the state economy, and a robust political and legal framework is essential for establishing a stable knowledge-based economy.

Although the companies from the 2018 research have expanded into new markets and diligently developed new products and services, they still met the hidden champions criteria. However, the current research has identified more hidden champions geographically dispersed across the country, spanning various industries. Our study confirms that hidden champions identified in both past and present research waves demonstrate resilience and flexibility in times of turbulent change. This research underscores the great potential of knowledge, skills, and abilities within the BIH business sector, whose innovative work significantly contributes to the country's economy. Concurrently, the business sector recognizes the need for additional training, education, and employee development directed towards current business needs in contemporary markets. Interestingly, the recommendations provided in the present research align closely with those from the 2018 research. This suggests that hidden champions, owing to their orientation towards global markets, are ahead of formal policies and procedures mandated by official state institutions.

3.1 Recommendations for Governments

1. Provide comprehensive support for businesses whose operations are highly coordinated, directed, and aligned to sustainability.
2. Establish state funds and allocate resources for businesses focused on innovation and high technology.
3. Pursue membership in the World Trade Organization.

3.2 Recommendations for Financial Institutions

1. Provide financial resources and loans under more favorable conditions.
2. Ease and digitalize procedures for accessing financial resources.

3.3 Recommendations for Business Schools and Higher Education Institutions

1. Communicate and cooperate with the business sector to address emerging challenges.
2. The labor market is changing. Adapt curricula accordingly.
3. Foster, promote, and support the development of diverse knowledge and skills tailored to meet the needs of the contemporary labor market across various professions.

The recommendations are summarized from the interviews conducted with experienced business owners and managers possessing substantial expertise in the field. Therefore, they should serve as directions for key decision-makers in the country. Hidden champions are companies that lead by example and implement positive solutions even in challenging circumstances. However, more is yet to come—great hopes and expectations are ahead, especially with recent developments such as BIH being granted the EU candidate status.

References

Berberović, D., Činjarević, M., & Kožo, A. (2019). Success despite lack of support: Lessons learned from hidden champions doing business in fragile business environments. *Sarajevo Business and Economics Review, 37*, 192–204.

Berberović, D., Činjarević, M., Kožo, A., & Brkić, N. (2021). Hidden champions of Bosnia and Herzegovina. In A. Braček Lalić & D. Purg (Eds.), *Hidden champions in dynamically changing societies: Critical success factors for market leadership* (pp. 107–122). Springer. https://doi.org/10.1007/978-3-030-65451-1_9

Braček Lalić, A., & Berberović, D. (2021). Research methodology. In A. Braček Lalić & D. Purg (Eds.), *Hidden champions in dynamically changing societies: Critical success factors for market leadership* (pp. 5–15). Springer. https://doi.org/10.1007/978-3-030-65451-1_2

European Commission, Directorate-General for Research and Innovation, Hollanders, H. (2023). European Innovation Scoreboard 2023, Publications Office of the European Union. https://data.europa.eu/doi/10.2777/119961.

OECD. (2022). SME Policy Index: Western Balkans and Turkey 2022: Assessing the Implementation of the Small Business Act for Europe, SME Policy Index, OECD Publishing, Paris, https://doi.org/10.1787/b47d15f0-en.

Ortlieb, R., Rahimić, Z., Hirt, C., Bešić, A., & Bieber, F. (2019). Diversity and equality in Bosnia and Herzegovina: Limits to legislation, public debate and workplace practices. *Equality, Diversity and Inclusion: An International Journal, 38*(7), 763–778. https://doi.org/10.1108/EDI-10-2017-0231

Petričević, O., & Danis, W. M. (2007). Bosnia and Herzegovina: Navigating a turbulent business environment. *Thunderbird International Business Review, 49*(4), 417–443. https://doi.org/10.1002/tie.20152

World Bank Open Data. (2024, May). The World Bank. https://data.worldbank.org/country/bosnia-and-herzegovina?view=chart https://databank.worldbank.org/source/world-development-indicators#, May 6, 2025.

Amra Kožo is an Associate Professor at the University of Sarajevo, School of Economics and Business, Management and Organization Department. She obtained her Ph.D. degree from Marmara University, Institute of Social Sciences (Istanbul, Turkiye). Amra gained teaching and research experience at the University of Sarajevo, School of Economics and Business and participated via Erasmus Mobility programs at Lille Catholic University (Lille, France), Wroclaw University of Economics and Business (Wroclaw, Poland), and Porto Accounting and Business School (ISCAP, Porto, Portugal). During her academic career, she attended various educational programs related to her field of interest and also served as a trainer and educator for the business community. Amra has participated in several domestic and international projects related to sensitive social groups (i.e., women and youth) as a researcher or evaluator (national stakeholder). She is (co)author of more than 25 papers published in indexed journals and conferences, six chapters in books, one book, and one book's editor. Her primary research interests are organizational behavior, human resource management, and cultural studies. For her scientific work, Amra obtained a reward from the University of Sarajevo (2021). Some of her current projects are related to sustainability competencies in higher education and Global Leadership and Organizational Behavior Effectiveness (GLOBE) 2020 research.

Merima Činjarević is an Associate Professor at the Department of Microeconomics at the University of Sarajevo, School of Economics and Business, where she teaches microeconomics, managerial economics, and behavioral economics. She has published over 30 peer-reviewed articles in respected international journals, including the European Journal of Marketing, Journal of Knowledge Management, and the British Food Journal. Her work extends to book chapters with top academic publishers, including Springer and Emerald. She is the co-author of the textbooks Managerial Economics and Behavioural Economics. In recognition of her impactful research, she was twice awarded the prestigious Rector's Award for Excellence in Scientific Research by the University of Sarajevo (2020, 2021). In addition to her academic work, she has participated in numerous international and national projects, including those implemented within transnational cooperation programs. Through her project involvement, she has contributed to the development of strategies, policy papers, feasibility studies, and economic analyses aimed at enhancing the competitiveness and sustainable development of local communities in Bosnia and Herzegovina and the European region.

Adi Alić is an Associate Professor at the Department of Marketing at the University of Sarajevo, School of Economics and Business, where he teaches *Marketing Channels*, *Small Business Marketing,* and *Marketing Basics*. His fields of professional commitment include marketing, marketing channels, small business marketing, international marketing, and brand management. In his previous scientific and research work, independently or in co-authorship, he published more than 30 scientific and professional papers, most of which were peer-reviewed articles published in respected international journals. He is also the author of the textbooks Marketing Channels and Brand Equity of Store Brands and one of the co-authors of the book Small Business Marketing and Contemporary Topics in Business. Actively participates in domestic and international conferences, seminars, education programs, and workshops. He has reviewed scientific papers for several international and domestic scientific journals and scientific conferences with associated proceedings. In his varied scientific and professional career, he was a member of the project team on several international and domestic scientific research and commercial projects. He spends his free time hanging out with friends or in the virtual world of video games, which he has been a fan of since childhood. In addition, he is a fan of the seventh art, so he often spends his free time and escapes from everyday life watching movies or series. In life, one tries to be guided by the motto that kindness is virtues that people will never stop appreciating.

Hidden Champions of Bulgaria

Petar Petrov and Desislava Serafimova

Abstract This chapter explores the phenomenon of Hidden Champion companies in Bulgaria through two in-depth case studies: LEKS Group and Kinetik Automotive. Despite operating in vastly different industries, household appliances and electric mobility, both companies exemplify the core characteristics of Hidden Champions: market leadership in a narrow niche, international orientation, sustained innovation, and resilience in the face of market challenges. LEKS Group, a family-owned business founded in 1989, has grown into a regional leader in built-in kitchen appliances across five Balkan countries, developing strong proprietary brands and logistics networks. Kinetik Automotive, a high-tech startup founded in 2019, has rapidly gained international attention for its electric go-karts and education STEM kits, pioneering innovation in both motorsports and learning. The chapter analyzes the strategic approaches, competitive advantages, and leadership practices that have enabled these companies to succeed while remaining relatively unknown to the public. It also highlights key challenges related to talent retention, regulatory barriers, and financing constraints. The final section offers targeted recommendations to national governments, financial institutions, and higher education institutions on how to better support such companies. These include regulatory simplification. Tailored funding instruments and the development of educational programs aligned with small and medium size enterprises (SME) needs. The study underscores the importance of recognizing and investing in Hidden Champions as critical drivers of innovation, export performance, and sustainable economic growth in emerging European economies.

P. Petrov (✉)
Department of Management and Administration at University of Economics, Varna, Bulgaria

University of Economics Varna Accelerator, Varna, Bulgaria
e-mail: p.k.petrov@ue-varna.bg

D. Serafimova
Department of Management and Administration at University of Economics, Varna, Bulgaria
e-mail: serafimova_d@ue-varna.bg

D. Berberović, D. Purg (eds.), *Hidden Champions in Rising Economies*, Contributions to Management Science,
https://doi.org/10.1007/978-3-032-08263-3_15

Overview

Official name: Republic of Bulgaria
Type of government: Parliamentary democracy
Population in 2023: 6,445,481 (Source: National Statistical Institute of the Republic of Bulgaria)
Land area: 110,993.6 sq. km

History

681AD	The First Bulgarian Kingdom was founded.
864AD	The Christianization of Bulgaria.
Ninth to tenth century AD	The Cyrillic alphabet—a new writing system developed for Slavic-speaking peoples.
1018AD	The Byzantines conquered the First Bulgarian Kingdom.
1185AD	Liberation from Byzantian rule and establishment of the Second Bulgarian Kingdom.
1396AD	Bulgaria was conquered by the Ottoman Empire.
1878AD	Liberation from the Ottoman rule and establishment of the Third Bulgarian Kingdom.
1885AD	Unification with Eastern Rumelia.
1908AD	Bulgarian Declaration of Independence from the Ottoman Empire.
1944–1989AD	Communism dominance in Bulgaria—People's Republic of Bulgaria.
After 1990AD	Democratic development of the Republic of Bulgaria.
2007AD	Acceptance in the European Union.

1 Introduction: Context and History

Bulgaria is a parliamentary republic in Southeastern Europe, bordering the Black Sea. It has an area of about 111,000 square km and a population of just over 6.5 million people as of 2021. Bulgaria was established in 681, and different forms of government existed in different historical periods.

Until 1989, Bulgaria was part of the Council for Mutual Economic Assistance (CMEA), an ex-communist economic organization of socialist countries that existed from 1949 to 1991 under the influence of the Russian Soviet Union. During these 45 years, production, trade, and services were centralized and ruled only by the government of the only political party—the Bulgarian Communist Party. There is a lack of real democracy, market mechanisms, and private business initiatives; private property is severely limited. A free public sector exists in healthcare, education, and the state pension system.

After 1989, when Bulgaria left the CMEA, it fell into a deep economic and political crisis—a nonfunctioning economy, bankrupting large state-owned enterprises, huge unemployment, rapidly rising inflation, rising crime, corruption, and an inefficient judiciary. As a result of poor governance, inadequate economic development, insufficient domestic production, and limited imports, between 1990 and 1993, there were no essential products on the market, and 15 banks went bankrupt.

In 1996–1997, the country fell into a political and economic crisis, leading to hyperinflation—in February 1997, monthly inflation reached 242% or 4.19% on a daily basis.

Eight years after the start of the reforms, lasting financial stability has not yet been achieved in Bulgaria, which is why a currency board was introduced through the International Monetary Fund in 1997, and a fixed rate of the Bulgarian lev to the Deutsche Mark (in 2002 to the euro) began to be maintained. In the following years, economic growth accelerated, stimulated by foreign investment. The country became a political and military alliance NATO member in 2004 and a member of the European Union in 2007.

Some fundamental economic indicators characterizing the business environment in Bulgaria are presented in Exhibit 1.

Over the past decade, Bulgaria has demonstrated steady economic progress, positioning itself as an emerging player in the regional economy. GDP per capita has nearly doubled from 2017 to 2023, rising from $8,382 to $15,798. Despite the pandemic-induced drop in 2020, Bulgaria's economy returned to the path of improvement with an 8.5% GDP per capita growth in 2021 and 10.6% in 2022.

The export sector remains a key growth driver, consistently contributing a high share of GDP, reaching 69.2% in 2022. Manufactured goods form the majority of the merchandise exports (55% in 2023), complemented by notable shares of food (17.4%) and ores/metals (12.7%). High-technology exports remained relatively stable at around 10%.

Bulgaria's export-driven economy, combined with steady GDP growth and a robust manufacturing base, lays a strong foundation for nurturing potential Hidden Champions. The country's deep integration into high-income markets suggests potential for niche specialization and global competitiveness.

2 Characteristics of Hidden Champions from Bulgaria

The research focuses on two Hidden Champions in Bulgaria—LEKS Group and Kinetik Automotive, each representing a distinct industry yet sharing several defining characteristics that align with the Hidden Champions Model. These companies were selected based on a set of criteria tailored to the local context but consistent with the concept originally developed by Herman Simon. The key criteria included demonstrated market leadership within a specific niche, strong international operations, long-term resilience, innovative capabilities, and a tendency to remain relatively unknown to the general public despite their outstanding performance. Both LEKS Group and Kinetik Automotive meet these conditions, standing out as successful, founder-led enterprises with focused strategies and sustained growth.

Exhibit 1 Core economic indicators for Bulgaria

	2017	2018	2019	2020	2021	2022	2023
GDP per capita (current US$)	8381.88	9447.66	9874.34	10148.34	12219.34	13974.45	15797.60
GDP per capita growth (annual %)	3.50	3.44	4.77	−3.39	8.54	10.56	2.40
Long-term unemployment (% of total unemployment)	55.09	58.77	57.11	45.36	49.45	53.75	..
Foreign direct investment, net inflows (% of GDP)	3.38	2.73	3.22	5.11	2.97	3.56	..
GDP (current US$, mio)	59309.75	66370.13	68881.01	70368.76	84041.49	90346.17	101584.38
Exports of goods and services (current US$, mio)	39745.42	43611.50	44046.29	39498.55	51602.39	62514.13	61847.39
Exports of goods and services (% of GDP)	67.01	65.71	63.95	56.13	61.40	69.19	60.88
Merchandise exports (current US$, mio)	31438.00	33617.00	33340.00	31954.00	41157.00	49925.00	47854.00
Merchandise exports to high-income economies (% of total merchandise exports)	68.79	73.21	72.07	73.63	..	..	..
Merchandise exports to developing economies in Europe & Central Asia (% of total merchandise exports)	17.01	14.86	15.47	14.26	..	..	..
Ores and metals exports (% of merchandise exports)	14.18	14.06	12.78	14.75	15.28	13.12	12.65
Agricultural raw materials exports (% of merchandise exports)	1.21	1.30	1.17	0.95	0.92	0.82	0.72
Food exports (% of merchandise exports)	14.61	14.69	15.66	16.59	16.89	16.75	17.43
Fuel exports (% of merchandise exports)	9.91	8.89	9.53	4.64	6.00	12.19	7.89
Manufactures exports (% of merchandise exports)	55.29	57.42	57.84	59.75	58.19	52.18	55.02
High-technology exports (% of manufactured exports)	9.63	10.37	10.85	11.30	10.91	8.57	..

Source: Worldbank Group Databank (n.d.); National Statistical Institute (NSI) (n.d.)

LEKS Group, founded in 1989 in Botevgrad, exemplifies a traditional Hidden Champion. Over three decades, it has grown into a dominant regional player in the field of built-in household appliances and kitchen washing systems, operating in five Balkan countries. Initially leveraging its role as the exclusive importer of the Italian brand FABER, the company gradually shifted toward building its own brand identity and developing proprietary trademarks such as Eurolux and Lino. Its competitive advantage lies in the combination of product specialization, distribution excellence, after-sales service and customer trust. The company's development has been guided by a clear vision from its founder and strengthened by the succession of a new generation of family leadership, supported by continuous investments in employee development and transnational cooperation projects.

In contrast, Kinetik Automotive represents a new generation of Hidden Champions in Bulgaria's emerging high-tech sector. Established in 2019, it has quickly become a global pioneer in electric go-kart platforms and STEM educational kits. Kinetik's innovative business model bridges the gap between electric mobility, motorsports, and hands-on science education. Its approach combines affordability, sustainability, and technological sophistication through telemetry, cloud-based software, and in-house prototyping capabilities. Despite its recent entry into the market, the company has experienced rapid growth. Its success is grounded in continuous product iteration, strategic partnerships, and a strong commitment to environmental and educational impact.

We can learn several key lessons from the analysis of both companies. Firstly, market leadership in a narrow niche, whether regional or global, can be achieved through deep product focus, sustained innovation, and customer-centric strategies. Secondly, Hidden Champions exhibit a higher level of resilience, having successfully adapted to external shocks such as economic crises, pandemics, and resource disruptions. Thirdly, the strategic use of partnerships enables them to access knowledge, technologies, and markets otherwise out of reach. Fourthly, the development of leadership capacity remains a pressing need, especially in attracting younger professionals and building internal capabilities in specialized domains.

Through consistent investment in innovation, customer value and organizational development, LEKS Group and Kinetik Automotive demonstrate how niche excellence and long-term vision can underpin sustainable growth and international success. Their cases offer valuable insights for policymakers, educators, and business leaders.

3 Case Studies of Selected Hidden Champions

3.1 Case Study 1

3.1.1 LEKS Group

Overview
Address: Botevgrad, Industrial Zone, Tsar Osvoboditel Blvd. 28, Bulgaria
Phone: + 359 723 68 830
Fax: NAEmail: office@leksgroup.com
Website: https://www.leksgroup.com

Company Information
Industry: Trade in household goods (built-in household appliances and kitchen washing systems)
Year of establishment: 1989
Sales revenues for 2019—12.81 million euros, 2020—11.23 million euros, 2021—12.99 million euros
Sales revenue ten years before (2009 or 2011): for 2009—8.68 million euros
Average ROA/ROE in the latest year (2019): 7.6/8.3
Average ROA/ROE ten years before (2009): 2009 ROA/ROE—10.3/13.3
Latest debt-to-equity ratio: 0.28
Number of employees in the latest years (2019—109, 2020—97, and 2021—99)

3.1.2 Nature of Market Leadership

LEKS GROUP is a joint-stock company with over 30 years of experience (Creato. biz, n.d.). It was established in a small town near the Bulgarian capital city of Sofia. Thanks to the entrepreneurship, hard work, and leadership qualities of its founder, who is its active driver to this day, it has developed steadily over the years, maintaining its status as a family business. The two children of the company's founder gradually gained experience in its activity, completed appropriate higher education, and are currently involved in the management and ownership of the joint-stock company. Today, LEKS Group is the only international company in the Balkans with close specialization in importing and selling household electrical appliances for installation and washing systems on the territory of five countries—Bulgaria, Serbia, Macedonia, Montenegro, and Kosovo.

Initially, LEKS Group's market leadership was based on the fact that, since 1998, it has been the exclusive representative of one of the world's leaders in the production of hoods—the Italian company FABER, whose good production and management practices and know-how it borrowed and successfully applied. Subsequently, the company's market leadership was no longer due only to using the Italian company's brand name. LEKS Group has succeeded in gradually increasing its market presence and market share in the five Balkan countries by applying appropriate strategies for creating its own brands, product differentiation, product innovation, and improving customer relationships, emphasizing building an appropriate logistics network and after-sales service.

At the same time, the development vision of the company's founder adheres to the idea of imposing on the market a limited number of commercial brands for its most successful products, emphasizing their promotion and not so much on promoting the company's name itself. Therefore, we believe that LEKS Group can be described as the "hidden champion" of Bulgaria. It was established as a small and continues to develop medium-sized family company, which started in a small town near the capital, but achieved a successful international presence with dominant market positions in a narrow market niche in five Balkan countries with an annual turnover of millions of euros. The LEKS Group has been resilient to turbulences and economic downturns throughout its existence, including the hyperinflation in Bulgaria in 1996, economic crisis in 2009, the COVID-19 pandemic, and the resource crises caused by the war in Ukraine. The company achieves this by adhering to strategies of product innovation, geographic expansion, improving quality and customer relationships along the supply chain, and investing in continuous training and development of personnel.

3.1.3 Nature of Competitive Advantage

Over the years, LEKS Group has expanded the range of products and services offered, which, however, remains narrowly focused on satisfying a certain type of customer need—built-in appliances and washing systems in kitchen furniture. For this purpose, the company gradually registers two trademarks, invests in improving the product mix and appropriate marketing strategies, and improves quality and a system for its own service and logistics along the supply chain. LEKS group successfully manages customer relations, builds partnership relations, and gains the trust of its customers and partners in the furniture sector.

The company's head office from its creation until today is in the city of Botevgrad, 50 km from the capital Sofia, where LEKS Group has a modern material base consisting of closed warehouse areas, an administrative building, an exhibition hall, a building for the production of furniture and service laboratory. In 2004, LEKS Group patented the Eurolux trademark for all European countries, offering the largest range of built-in appliances for the modern kitchen. Two years later—in 2006—the company patented its second own trademark—LINO, which successfully established itself on the international markets where the group operates.

All products under the Faber, Eurolux, and Lino brands are realized both from the company's own sales offices in the larger cities of the countries in which it operates and through the established wide distribution network of partners—regional chains of furniture stores, leading furniture companies, and showrooms.

An exceptional competitive advantage for LEKS Group is its own service network built on the territories of Bulgaria, Macedonia, and Serbia, which the company is constantly expanding, improving, and developing. In 2012, LEKS Group was nominated as an honorary member of the "Council of the European Business Community." This can also be taken as public recognition of the company's international success—a hidden champion.

Over the years, another source of competitive advantage for the LEKS group is the systematic and constant investment in training and talent development activities. The company does this both independently and with the support of manufacturers and supply chain partners. In the period 2013–2014, in partnership with the world leader in the production of hoods—the Italian company Faber S.P.A., LEKS Group won and implemented a European project for "Development through transnational cooperation and exchange of experience" of its employees. It is fully financed by the Operational Program "Development of Human Resources," co-financed by the European Social Fund of the European Union. The project carried out various activities, including specialized training of 37 employees from the LEKS group team at Faber S.P.A. headquarters in Italy.

3.1.4 Core Lessons Learned on the Path to Success

We can outline several key lessons that led the company to its success. A key factor was maintaining a focused niche strategy. This enabled LEKS Group to build strong market positions without diluting its brand identity. Rather than expanding into unrelated product categories, the company invested in depth by refining its existing products. Equally important was the long-term commitment of the founder and the gradual integration of the next generation into the leadership roles, which ensured continuity and preservation of core values. Another pivotal element was the company's early engagement in international knowledge transfer. Through collaboration with FABER, LEKS was able to adopt world-class production and management practices. In addition, the strategic development of internal capabilities proved essential, particularly in areas such as logistics, after-sales service, and brand management. This was solidified by the recognition of the important role of human capital from an early stage and the ongoing investments in employee training.

3.1.5 Management and Leadership Development Needs

The main challenges facing LEKS Group stem from the lack of young and well-educated personnel who are motivated to make a long career in Bulgaria in companies in the researched sector. It would be useful for the development of LEKS group to have information from periodically conducting research among young people in Bulgaria to establish their attitudes towards work in Bulgarian companies, to identify the factors that contribute to their motivation and build attachment and loyalty to the companies, in which they work.

3.1.6 Financing and Regulatory Environment Development Needs

LEKS Group's development is constrained by limited access to flexible financing for expansion, innovation, and digitalization. While traditional bank loans are available, the company would benefit from easier access to EU and national funding tailored to mid-sized enterprises. Navigating complex grant procedures remains a challenge. Additionally, regulatory fragmentation in the Balkan region overcomplicates and increases the risks of cross-border operations.

3.1.7 Pandemics' Impact on "Hidden Champions" Business Approach

The COVID-19 pandemic reinforced LEKS Group's commitment to resilience, adaptability and long-term customer relationships. While the company had already built a solid foundation through logistics and service infrastructure, the crisis highlighted the importance of supply chain flexibility and strong local presence. The pandemic also highlighted the value of investing more in people and digital tools, prompting the company to enhance internal processes and workforce development.

3.1.8 Effects of the Ukraine War on "Hidden Champions" Business Operations

N/A.

3.1.9 "Quiet Power: The Rise of LEKS Group"

In the small Bulgarian town of Botevgrad, just outside Sofia, a family business quietly took root in 1989. With determination, foresight, and a deep understanding of customer needs, LEKS Group began its journey in the trade of built-in household appliances. Over the next three decades, this modest venture evolved into a regional market leader across five Balkan countries. Nevertheless, it remained largely unknown to the public.

At the heart of LEKS Group's success is the visionary leadership of its founder, who remains actively involved to this day. From the beginning, the company followed a clear path with a focus on quality, building lasting relationships, and growing steadily. This philosophy enabled LEKS Group to become the exclusive representative of the Italian brand FABER in 1998. This proved to be a turning points that opened doors to international best practices and product excellence.

But LEKS didn't stop here. Over time, it developed its own brands—Eurolux and LINO, tailored specifically for regional markets. The company expanded its product range while staying true to its niche vision: modern, reliable kitchen solutions. With strategic investments in logistics, after-sales service, and distribution networks, LEKS created a seamless customer experience that fueled its reputation.

What truly differentiates LEKS Group is its long-term mindset. It has withstood multiple economic crises, including hyperinflation in 1997, the 2008 global financial crisis, the COVID-19 pandemic, and recent resource shortages. Its strength lies in resilience, steady innovation, and a strong organizational culture. The involvement of the founder's children in the management team reflects a careful approach to leadership continuity, blending tradition with modern perspectives.

Additionally, LEKS has always placed a strong emphasis on employee development, launching training programs and participating in EU-funded transnational cooperation projects to build skills and loyalty within its workforce.

Today, LEKS Group is not just a household name in appliances. It is a symbol of how quiet determination, smart strategy and customer dedication can power success beyond borders.

3.2 Case Study 2

3.2.1 Kinetik Automotive

Overview

Address: Gledka Primorski, Perunika St, 9010 Varna. 28, Bulgaria
Tel: +359 882023636
Email: info@kinetikautomotive.com
Web: https://kinetikautomotive.com/

Company Information

Industry: 29.10 Manufacture of motor vehicles/85.60 Educational support activities
Electric vehicles/karts/educational kits—Kinetik Automotive creates highly customizable products that not only meet the specific needs and requirements of the clients but also match their personalities.
Year of establishment 2019
Sales revenues in 2019: 12600 BGN
Sales revenues in 2022: 412000 BGN
Average number of employees in 2023: 12
Brainer behind the company: Teodosiy Teodosiev

3.2.2 Nature of Market Leadership

Currently, there is a lack of Electric Go-Kart platforms and no base for pilots to start learning. Kinetik is one of the global pioneers to fill this gap. They represent a paradigm shift in the world of electric karting, redefining the standards of speed, control, and innovation. The pulse of innovation beats at the heart of Kinetik Karts' electric go-karts. Proprietary telemetry, user-friendly and integrated software control, and the potential incorporation of graphene battery technology exemplify their commitment to pushing technological boundaries (Kinetik Automotive, n.d.).

Kinetik Automotive aims to capture a 12.1% share of the global new sports kart market, which is valued at approximately 600 million EUR annually, with a steady growth rate of around 3.1%, within the first three years, projected to reach approximately 73 million EUR of revenue at a profit margin of nearly 17%.

Currently, there is a gap in electric motorsports, where there are high-level championships and no base from which the pilots can start learning. There is also a lack of Electric Go-Kart platforms, and Kinetik is one of the pioneers in this E-Moto sport.

In addition to that, in response to a prevailing issue in the educational system, Kinetik Automotive actively contributes to the development of STEM education. Their response involves offering electric karting kits designed for the STEM program, enabling students to assemble components and engage with electronics, mechatronics, physics, marketing, design, and more. This is a unique offering worldwide without any direct competitor.

To sum up, Kinetik Automotive addresses the following market needs:

- Accessible Entry Point: By offering a highly-integrated consumer-oriented solution for electric motorsports, Kinetik E-Karts bridges the gap between high-level championships and grassroots learning.
- Reduced Maintenance Costs: Kinetik's electric karts have significantly lower maintenance expenses compared to traditional internal combustion engine karts.
- Adaptability and Affordability: The karts' unique adaptability across divisions eliminates the need for multiple purchases, making the sport more affordable and versatile for pilots and teams.
- Environmental Responsibility: Through electric propulsion, Kinetik E-Karts play a pivotal role in reducing carbon emissions associated with motorsports, aligning with growing environmental concerns.
- Addressing Educational Gaps: Kinetik's engagement in STEM education fills the educational gap by providing students with hands-on experience in various fields, fostering skills vital for technological progress.
- Equitable Representation: With a commitment to gender balance, Kinetik Karts champions inclusivity in motorsports, encouraging equal participation and representation across all roles within the team.
- Technological Innovation: Incorporating telemetry and cloud-based technology, Kinetik E-Karts empower pilots with real-time data, propelling technological innovation within the sport.

3.2.3 Nature of Competitive Advantage

Currently, there are between five and seven competitors/manufacturers of performance/professional electric go-karts in the world.

Kinetik E-Karts revolutionizes the motorsport landscape by pioneering an exclusive electric division in a world predominantly dominated by Internal Combustion

Engine (ICE) vehicles. Unlike other alternatives in the entry motorsport sphere, Kinetik E-Karts breaks free from the conventional paradigm. It not only caters to the surging interest in eco-friendly alternatives but also fulfills the unmet demand from aspiring young racers eager to dive into the electrifying world of electric racing. No other brand, be it in karting, motorcycles, cars, or any other motorsport segment, provides the combination of affordability, collectability, ease of use, real-time data, and adjustable performance that Kinetik E-Karts offers.

In tune with the latest market trends, Kinetik E-Karts aligns seamlessly with the global surge in Electric Vehicle (EV) market share, a remarkable 56% increase in 2022 (EV-Volumes, n.d.). This not only underscores the robust appetite for sustainable transportation solutions but also highlights the forward-thinking nature of Kinetik E-Karts. It's not just a choice; it's a progressive decision that aligns with the shift towards greener mobility alternatives.

Furthermore, as society's fascination with motorsports surges, as evident by Formula 1's booming engagement on social media platforms, Kinetik E-Karts taps into this evolving societal interest. It offers an electrifying experience that profoundly resonates with the emerging generation of motorsports enthusiasts. The world is changing, and Kinetik E-Karts is at the forefront, offering a unique entry point into the motorsport world that transcends traditional boundaries.

One of the standout advantages of Kinetik E-Karts lies in its exceptional cost efficiency. Traditional ICE karts typically involve ongoing expenses, from regular engine replacements to chain repairs and filter maintenance. Electric karts, on the other hand, demand minimal upkeep, focusing on routine chain and driving component maintenance along with recharging. This shift results in significantly reduced maintenance costs over time, democratizing motorsports and making it accessible even to those without extensive financial backing or sponsorship. In an industry where every dollar counts, Kinetik E-Karts offers a clear advantage.

Competitors may exist, but none can match the comprehensive package that Kinetik E-Karts brings to the table. Direct rivals like Rotax E20 may confine pilots to specific championships without ownership rights, but Kinetik E-Karts breaks free from these limitations. The pilots not only have the option to purchase their electric go-karts but can also actively participate in championships through a specialized service. The disparities extend further in terms of functionality. Unlike Rotax E20, Kinetik's karts are equipped with real-time telemetry, enabling pilots to benefit not only during races but also during training sessions. This advanced feature contributes significantly to a comprehensive and effective learning experience, setting Kinetik E-Karts apart in the industry.

Among the contenders in the racing world, one standout competitor, Blue Shock Racing, may offer the appeal of ownership and the opportunity to participate in championships. However, when it comes to the technical aspects, Kinetik E-Karts clearly outperform in terms of weight, acceleration, and top speed. These advantages alone provide an enhanced racing experience.

But what sets Kinetik E-Karts in a league of its own is the incorporation of advanced real-time telemetry and user-friendly karting software that enables precise

	KINETIK	ROTAX	Blue Shock Race	OTL ElectraKart
Power	**40 kW**	24 kW	33 kW	23 kW
Weight	**115 kg**	142 kg	116 kg	120 kg
0–100	3.5 s	3.5 s	**~3.2 s**	5.7 s
TOP Speed	**135 km/h**	**135 km/h**	**135 km/h**	112 km/h
Telemetry	**Our own Telemetry!**	3rd party "MyChron" Telemetry by AIM	3rd party "MyChron" Telemetry by AIM	3rd party "MyChron" Telemetry by AIM
Championship as a Service	**Yes**	No	No	No

Source: Company data.

Exhibit 2 Competitors comparison. Source: Company data

control and learning. Unlike Blue Shock Racing, Kinetik E-Karts equips its machines with a sophisticated telemetry system, providing real-time data acquisition and analysis capabilities. With this feature, racers can fine-tune their karts' performance during training sessions and races, gaining an edge over the competition (Exhibit 2).

3.2.4 Core Lessons Learned on the Path to Success

Kinetik's success can be attributed to several key factors:

Innovation and Iteration
Kinetik's commitment to innovation has been a cornerstone of its success. The company has consistently sought to push the boundaries of electric karting technology, introducing new features and improvements with each iteration. This iterative approach has allowed them to learn from their experiences, refine their designs, and stay ahead of the competition. By embracing a culture of continuous improvement, Kinetik has been able to deliver products that meet the evolving needs of its customers and exceed industry standards.

Partnerships and Collaboration
Kinetik's strategic partnerships have played a vital role in their growth. Collaborations with industry leaders like Maranello and Nvidia have provided access to valuable expertise, resources, and testing facilities. These partnerships have enabled Kinetik to accelerate its development process, enhance its product offerings, and gain credibility in the motorsport industry. Additionally, Kinetik's participation in racing championships has allowed them to test their products in real-world conditions and gather valuable feedback from professional drivers.

Data-Driven Approach
Kinetik's use of telemetry has been instrumental in their ability to optimize performance and make data-driven decisions. By collecting and analyzing vast amounts of data, Kinetik has been able to identify areas for improvement, fine-tune its designs,

and enhance the driving experience. The real-time feedback provided by telemetry has also enabled drivers to make adjustments on the fly, improving their performance and reducing the need for costly mechanical interventions.

Sustainability and Environmental Focus
Kinetik's commitment to sustainability aligns with growing market trends and environmental concerns. By focusing on renewable energy infrastructure and developing electric go-karts, Kinetik is contributing to a cleaner and more sustainable future. This focus not only differentiates Kinetik from competitors but also appeals to a growing segment of environmentally conscious consumers.

Talent and Team Building
Kinetik's success is also a testament to their ability to attract and retain top talent. The company has assembled a diverse team of experts with a wide range of skills and experience. By fostering a collaborative and supportive work environment, Kinetik has been able to leverage the strengths of its team members and drive innovation. Additionally, the company's focus on employee development and retention has ensured that they have a skilled and motivated workforce.

Overcoming Challenges
Despite facing significant financial challenges, Kinetik has persevered and found creative solutions. The company's ability to navigate the complexities of fundraising and secure necessary capital has been crucial to its survival and growth. Additionally, Kinetik has demonstrated resilience in overcoming regulatory hurdles and adapting to the changing landscape of electric mobility.

In summary, Kinetik's success is a result of a combination of innovation, collaboration, a data-driven approach, sustainability focus, and a strong team culture. The company's ability to adapt, learn, and overcome challenges has been essential to its journey. By consistently striving to improve their products, leverage partnerships, and embrace emerging technologies, Kinetik has positioned itself as a leader in the electric karting industry.

3.2.5 Management and Leadership Development Needs

The reality is that e-mobility is a relatively new space, and there are very few people specialized in this space. For example, high-voltage systems, which are related to the automotive power train installations, are a specific domain, which is very crucial the product development process. The lack of knowledge and skills in high-voltage systems can lead to delays in the production time frame and project execution deadlines. For some areas trial and error approach is an alternative which is allowing the team to gain valuable experience until it reaches the most optimal approach, but when it comes to aspects related to health and safety of the potential customer, they need the right talent and skill set to execute those types of engineering systems in their product. That is why the company are approaching outside consultants who are specialized in the field.

3.2.6 Financing and Regulatory Environment Development Needs

Exploring avenues for grants, Kinetik turned its attention to EU structural (Bulgarian) funding possibilities. They encountered a roadblock, as these grants typically required companies to have a minimum of three years of operational history and are capped at maximum funding levels that would not make a big difference. This condition presented a barrier for Kinetik, given their relative novelty in the industry and R&D intensive engineering roadmap.

3.2.7 Pandemic's Impact on "Hidden Champions" Business Approach

Due to the broken supply chains and extended manufacturing production lifecycles, Kinetik were forced to develop new skills in order not to rely on external suppliers. This resulted in re-shaping what they can create/manufacture themselves in-house. Some of the solutions were pretty efficient. For example, they used 3d printing techniques and competencies to create their own parts and components and thus not to rely on 3rd party suppliers.

3.2.8 Effects of the Ukraine War on "Hidden Champions" Business Operations

The effect was similar to the one outlined in Sect. 3.2.7. We could add to the impact of the resource crisis, which changed the prices of some of the components, such as batteries or chassis parts (made from aluminum). This led to the need to rethink the product pricing and come up with more creative ways for additional upsell or revenue streams.

3.2.9 "Charging Ahead: The Kinetik Story"

In the coastal city of Varna, Bulgaria, a bold idea took shape in 2019, an idea that would revolutionize electric motorsports and reimagine how young people learn through technology. This idea became Kinetik Automotive, founded by visionary engineer Teodosiy Teodosiev. What started as a small team with limited resources soon evolved into one of the world's pioneers in electric go-karts and STEM mobility education.

Kinetik entered the market with a clear purpose: to fill the massive gap between elite motorsport and grassroots participation, especially in the electric vehicle segment. Their solution was both simple and groundbreaking: create adaptable, user-friendly, and high-performance electric karts, integrated with real-time telemetry and smart software. At the same time, the company introduced educational kits, allowing students to assemble and explore e-mobility systems hands-on, combining physics, engineering, design, and innovation in a single learning experience.

What set Kinetik apart was not just its technology, but its culture of innovation, agile leadership, and deep commitment to purpose-driven impact. The company thrived on iteration, constantly refining its products through real-world testing, customer feedback, and championship participation. Partnerships with global tech leaders and a data-driven approach to product development elevated its credibility and performance.

Kinetik's unique value proposition lies in offering more than a vehicle—it offers experience. The karts are not only fast and efficient but also educational and inclusive, designed for wide access. The company's forward-thinking mindset, environmental responsibility, and ability to overcome funding and supply chain challenges have turned it from a local startup into a global trendsetter.

Today, Kinetik continues to charge ahead—and make its impact on shaping the future of mobility, education and sustainable technology.

4 Conclusions and Recommendations

The research presented in this chapter highlights the significant role that Hidden Champion companies play in shaping competitive, resilient, and innovation-driven economies. The Bulgarian examples of LEKS Group and Kinetik Automotive demonstrate that even in smaller markets, companies can achieve remarkable success through focused strategies, entrepreneurial leadership, and sustained investment in product excellence and customer values.

While different in size, industry and maturity, both companies exhibit core characteristics typical of Hidden Champions: deep specialization in a narrow market niche, consistent international or regional orientation, high levels of innovation, and long-term strategic commitment. Their success is not driven by brand visibility or public recognition but by operational excellence, adaptability, and close relationships with customers and partners.

However, the findings also reveal important development needs. Both companies face barriers in accessing tailored financing, navigating complex regulatory environments and attracting and retaining skilled talent, particularly in high-tech or engineering-intensive domains. These challenges point to a gap between the potential of Hidden Champions and the level of institutional support available to them.

Given the strategic importance of such companies, targeted policy, financial, and educational measures are essential to help them scale, stay competitive, and build long-term capabilities. A coordinated approach involving governments, financial institutions and higher education is necessary in order to ensure that Hidden Champions not only survive but also thrive in the future. In the next section, we have prepared a set of recommendations for these groups of stakeholders.

1. Recommendations for Governments:

National governments play a critical role in shaping the regulatory and support environment in which Hidden Champions operate. Some ideas about the governmental support include:

- Streamline and harmonize regulations, particularly for cross-border trade, logistics, and certification, to reduce administrative burdens and promote regional expansion.
- Revise the design of public funding programs to account for the specific characteristics of Hidden Champions. This includes allowing younger companies or mid-sized family firms to access innovation, digitalization, and export support schemes.
- Promote visibility and recognition of Hidden Champions through national platforms, awards, or export promotion strategies, making them visible role models for entrepreneurship and competitiveness.
- Support talent retention practices such as tax reduction initiatives for hiring young professionals or programs encouraging return migration.

2. Recommendations for Financial Institutions:

Access to appropriate funding remains a critical bottleneck for many Hidden Champions. Financial institutions can play a transformative role by:

- Developing dedicated financial instruments for scaling SMEs, such as growth-oriented credit lines, innovation loans, or equity co-investment schemes that reduce risk for both parties.
- Offering blended financing and flexible terms.
- Providing nonfinancial support, such as business advisory services, international market access assistance and financial literacy training for SME management teams.
- Adapting risk assessment models to better value intangible assets such as proprietary technology, brand strength, or international networks.

3. Recommendations for Business Schools and Higher Education Institutions:

Higher Education Institutions, particularly business and engineering schools, are well-positioned to support the long-term development of Hidden Champions by preparing future leaders and enabling continuous learning. Here are some specific measures that can be taken:

- Develop tailored educational programs that address the real-world needs of SME and HC leaders with a focus on leadership, innovation management, internationalization and digital strategy.
- Strengthen cooperation with SMEs by involving students in internships, consulting projects and applied research that solve actual business challenges, thereby fostering mutual learning and increasing visibility of HCs among young professionals.

- Promote lifelong learning through executive education (still underdeveloped in Bulgaria) and modular programs for upskilling and reskilling existing employees.
- Encourage interdisciplinary education, combining business, technology and design thinking to equip graduates with the versatile skillset that innovation-driven companies like LEKS and Kinetik require.

Hidden Champions represent one of the most promising pillars of economic development for countries like Bulgaria. Their continued success requires a coordinated, long-term commitment from public, financial and academic institutions in building a supportive ecosystem.

References

Creato.biz. (n.d.). Leks Grup AD: Uredi za vgrazhdane. https://www.leksgroup.com/.
EV-Volumes. (n.d.). https://ev-volumes.com/.
Kinetik Automotive. Kinetik Automotive – Your vision. Produced. (n.d.). https://kinetikautomotive.com/.
National Statistical Institute. NSI. (n.d.). https://www.nsi.bg/en.
Worldbank Group DataBank. (n.d.). https://databank.worldbank.org/.

Petar Petrov, PhD, is a Chief Assistant Professor in the Department of Management and Administration at the University of Economics - Varna (UEV), Bulgaria. He is also the Coordinator of the university's student business accelerator, UEVA, where he actively supports the development of entrepreneurial skills and startup initiatives among students. Dr. Petrov holds a PhD in Social Management and two bachelor's degrees in Marketing and Management, alongside a master's degree in Management, all from the University of Economics - Varna.

His academic and professional work focuses on human resource management, talent development, internal marketing, HR information systems, intercultural competence, coaching, and online research methods. With over a decade of experience in higher education teaching, he has delivered courses and training in HRM, talent management, entrepreneurship, and digital learning. He has also provided consultancy and professional development workshops for both public institutions and private organizations.

Dr. Petrov has authored 33 scientific publications, including 10 in English, and has contributed as an expert, coordinator, or project leader in 15 projects, 7 of which have been international. He has played a key role in the development of joint international master programs and participates regularly as a trainer and jury member in European entrepreneurship initiatives. He is particularly engaged in EU-funded projects that foster innovation and capacity building in education and business.

Desislava Serafimova, PhD, is an associate professor and head of the Department of Management and Administration at the University of Economics - Varna (UEV), Bulgaria. She has delivered lectures in international and multicultural classrooms under the Erasmus+ mobility program in Portugal, Spain, Turkey, Algeria, Armenia, Kazakhstan, and Romania. She participated as a foreign research scholar and visiting professor at universities in India, Thailand, the UK, and Poland.

Dr. Serafimova provides guidelines to PhD students in Bulgarian and Kazakh universities and evaluates PhD theses of Bulgarian, Indian, and Pakistani scholars. She also provides consultancy and professional training to staff for business and public organizations.

Key areas of interest: Corporate Sustainability Management and Reporting, Sustainable Development, CSR, Digital Transformation in Higher Education, and Business Modelling.

She has contributed as an expert or project leader to two national and four international research projects, as well as to the development of one joint international master's program. She has published more than 70 works, including papers, books, and monographs on Management topics. Dr. Serafimova is a member of the Editorial Boards of national and international scientific journals.

Hidden Champions of China

Digitalization of Hidden Champions in China

Xiaobo Wu and Linan Lei

Abstract In 2024, the Chinese government's work report further emphasized the need to fully leverage innovation to drive industrial progress through scientific and technological advancements. The report aims to continuously shape new drivers and advantages for development, promoting a new leap in social productivity, and accelerating the development of new quality productive forces. Hidden champions, as the pioneers in digitalization, show their innovation in digital product development, digital business model design, digital process development or digital servitization. Two cases are analyzed in this chapter, revealing that hidden champions are undergoing digital transformation to explore innovations in supply chain operations and management. They are building digital platforms for networking, collaboration, and lean production to adapt to the constantly changing market environment and improve operational efficiency and innovation. Their lessons for digitization offer valuable insights for hidden champions in the world or other manufacturing enterprises.

Overview
Official name: People's Republic of China
Type of government: Socialism
Population in 2023: 1.410 billion
Land area: 9,634,057 km^2

X. Wu (✉)
School of Management, Zhejiang University, Hangzhou, China

International Research Center for Hidden Champions, International Campus, Zhejiang University, Jiaxing, China
e-mail: xbwu@zju.edu.cn

L. Lei
International Research Center for Hidden Champions, International Campus, Zhejiang University, Jiaxing, China
e-mail: leilinan@zju.edu.cn

D. Berberović, D. Purg (eds.), *Hidden Champions in Rising Economies*, Contributions to Management Science,
https://doi.org/10.1007/978-3-032-08263-3_16

History

2200–1700 BCE	The first non-mythical dynasty to rule China was the Xia (2200–1700 BCE), founded by Emperor Yu. It was succeeded by the Shang Dynasty (1600–1046 BCE), and then the Zhou Dynasty (1122–256 BCE).
618 CE	The Tang Dynasty was founded in 618 CE, and Chinese art and culture flourished. At the end of the Tang, China descended into chaos again in the "5 Dynasties and 10 Kingdoms" period.
1912	Revolutionary Sun Yat-sen becomes the first President of the Republic of China.
1927	The Ten Years Civil War occurs between the Kuomintang nationalists, led by Chiang Kai-shek, and the communist party, led by Mao Zedong.
1945	World War II comes to an end and Japan is defeated. The Civil War between the communists and the nationalists resumes.
1949	The communists win the war and the People's Republic of China is formed by Mao Zedong.
1978	China's reform and opening-up policy, launched under the leadership of Deng Xiaoping at the 1978 Third Plenum. This policy jump-started China's transformation from a poor and underdeveloped centrally-planned economy into an economic powerhouse, increasingly driven by the market.
2001	China entered into the World Trade Organization.
2008	The Olympic Games were held in Beijing.
2013	Chinese central government adopted a global development strategy "The Belt and Road Initiative" involving infrastructure development and investments in 152 countries and international organizations in Asia, Europe, Africa, the Middle East, and the Americas.
2015	The Chinese central government issued a strategic plan "Made in China 2025" to totally upgrade Chinese Manufacturing. With it, China aims to move away from being the "world's factory" and move to producing higher-value products and services. It is in essence a blueprint to upgrade the manufacturing capabilities of Chinese industries into a more technology-intensive powerhouse.
2016	The Chinese central government issued implementation of the Special Action to Cultivate and Enhance Single Champion Enterprises in the Manufacturing Industry. Aligned with the strategic goal of becoming a manufacturing powerhouse. This initiative focuses on enterprises as the primary drivers, adopting a market-oriented approach to cultivate and enhance single champion manufacturing enterprises. The goal is to guide enterprises to concentrate on long-term innovation in segmented product markets, striving for excellence and competitiveness and break-

	ing through manufacturing bottlenecks to enhance the quality and efficiency of the manufacturing industry. Single champions in the manufacturing sector play a vital role in supplementing and strengthening key areas of the industrial chain. They are entrusted with the mission of "filling the blank" and "addressing shortcomings," representing an indispensable force in the development of new quality productivity.
2021	The Chinese central government issued the Fourteenth Five-Year Plan for National Economic and Social Development and the Long-Range Objectives Through the Year 2035 of the People's Republic of China; this mainly focuses on high-quality development, emphasizing innovation-driven development, industrial upgrading, expansion of domestic demand, and supply-side reform.

1 Introduction: Context

In recent years, China has made remarkable progress in economic development and innovation capabilities, making it a global leader in multiple fields. As of 2024, the per capita gross domestic product (GDP) has reached $13,164, representing a significant increase compared with previous years. The growth rate of per capita GDP in 2024 was 4.36%, demonstrating a steady expansion of the economy. According to the data from the National Bureau of Statistics, the digital economy accounted for 44.6% of the GDP, indicating that the booming digital industry has contributed to the economic growth. In terms of innovation, the intensity of research and development (R&D) expenditure was 2.68%, reflecting a firm commitment to R&D. The total value of goods imports and exports reached 43.85 trillion yuan, an increase of 5% year-on-year, highlighting China's important role in global trade. These achievements highlight the effectiveness of China's economic strategies and China's position as a key player in the global economy. For more information on China's core economic indicators, please refer to Exhibit 1.

The trend of being "Specialized, Refined, Differentiated, and Innovative" is crucial for SME development. The following section outlines the national policy background related to SRDI enterprises. Since 2019, China has nurtured over 70,000 provincial-level "SRDI"enterprises and 15,970 national-level SRDI "Little Giants" enterprises. These "Little Giants" demonstrate strong innovation capabilities and have witnessed rapid growth in innovative outputs. On average, these enterprises have an R&D intensity of 9%, hold an average of 15.7 effective invention patents, establish 1.25 research and development institutions, and formulate 1.5 standards. The average patents per capita of the fourth batch of "Little Giants" enterprises is approximately 6%. "Specialized, Refinement, Differential, and Innovation" is the general trend and a necessary path for the development of small and medium-sized enterprises. The following outlines the national policy background related to SRDI enterprises.

Exhibit 1 Core economic indicators for China

	2018	2019	2020	2021	2022	2023	2024
GDP per capita (current US$)	9905.4	10143.9	10408.7	12617.5	12720.2	12614.1	13164.4
GDP per capita growth (annual %)	6.749773	5.950500	2.238638	8.448469	2.989084	–0.383183	4.363132
Long-term unemployment (% of total unemployment)	4.3	4.5	5	4.5	5	5	N/A
Foreign direct investment, net inflows (% of GDP)	1.69390530	1.31071878	1.72318379	1.88326294	N/A	N/A	N/A
GDP (current US$, mio)	13608151.9	14279968.5	14687744.2	17820459.5	17963171.5	18300000	18940000
Exports of goods and services (current US$, mio)	265,5609.1	262,8935.4	272,9871.5	355,3509.2	3590000.0	3379043.5	3577222.0
Exports of goods and services (% of GDP)	19.5148403	18.4099923	18.5861392	20.0377618	19.985335	18.2753783	18.5611596
Merchandise exports (current US$)	2.49E+12	2.50E+12	2.59E+12	3.36E+12	3.36E+12	2.99E+12	3.19 E+12
Merchandise exports to high-income economies (% of total merchandise exports)	69.8080032	67.8757362	68.8679937	N/A	N/A	N/A	N/A
Merchandise exports to developing economies in Europe and Central Asia (% of total merchandise exports)	4.07585148	4.32392840	4.13987749	N/A	N/A	N/A	N/A
Ores and metals exports (% of merchandise exports)	1.327561161	1.26063099	1.122069227	1.373866493	N/A	N/A	N/A
Agricultural raw materials exports (% of merchandise exports)	0.419092383	0.393780005	0.329770707	0.339609523	0.417099068	N/A	N/A
Food exports (% of merchandise exports)	2.910565147	2.87450637	2.68970992	2.293287385	N/A	N/A	N/A
Fuel exports (% of merchandise exports)	1.867644071	1.874653045	1.214368545	1.239561134	N/A	N/A	N/A

Source: World Bank, December, 2024

The "Guideline of the People's Republic of China on the Promotion of Small and Medium-sized Enterprises (SMEs)," which has been implemented since January 1, 2003, established a legal basis for encouraging and supporting the development of SMEs and provided guidelines for fostering and supporting the development of such enterprises in China. In 2003, inspired by the concept of "hidden champions" in Germany, the SMEs Administration of the State Economic and Trade Commission proposed the idea of SRDI, aiming to better guide and encourage the development of a vast number of small and medium-sized enterprises. In September 2011, SRDI was officially introduced into the "Twelfth Five-Year Plan for the Growth of SMEs." In April 2012, the State Council issued the "Opinions on Further Supporting the Healthy Development of Small and Micro Enterprises," which proposed to support the development of innovative, entrepreneurial, and labor-intensive small and micro enterprises, encourage them to pursue the path of SRDI and coordinated development with large enterprises, and accelerate the transformation from factor-driven to innovation-driven development. In April 2019, the General Office of the Central Committee of the Communist Party of China and the General Office of the State Council issued "Several Opinions on Promoting the Healthy Development of SMEs," reiterating the need to guide small and medium-sized enterprises to pursue the path of SRDI development, and to cultivate SRDI "little giants" in some key components, key basic industries, and key raw materials. In September 2022, President Xi Jinping wrote in a congratulatory letter to the 2022 National Conference on the Development of SRDI SMEs, calling for efforts to promote enterprise innovation, strengthen property rights protection, and stimulate the emergence of more SRDI SMEs. The Ministry of Industry and Information Technology (MIIT) proposed to strive to incubate one million innovative SMEs through small and medium-sized enterprise "double innovation" during the "14th Five-Year Plan" (2021–2025) period, cultivate 100,000 provincial-level SRDI SMEs, 10,000 national-level SRDI "little giants," and 1000 manufacturing industry single-item champions by 2025.

In the article titled "Continuously Strengthening, Optimizing, and Expanding China's Digital Economy" President Xi Jinping pointed out in 2022 that China's digital economy is currently in a stage of being large but not strong, fast but not optimal. He emphasized the need to "promote deep integration of digital technology and the real economy, empower the transformation and upgrading of traditional industries, foster new industries, new forms, and new models, and continuously strengthen, optimize, and expand China's digital economy." As the global trend of industrial digitization becomes increasingly clear, driving enterprise transformation with data as the driving force is a necessary path for SMEs to grow into SRDI enterprises and a key to the continuous strengthening of SRDI "Little Giants." Against this backdrop, the precise and effective implementation of top-level design and the construction of institutional mechanisms require the support of bottom-up multi-stakeholder participation and multi-level coordination.

The national policy guidelines for the digital development of SMEs are as follows: The National "14th Five-Year Plan for Promoting the Development of SMEs" and the "14th Five-Year Plan for Digital Economy Development" both clearly outline the strategic deployment to promote the digital transformation of SMEs. Various regions have also introduced policies to support the digital transformation and intelligent upgrading of SRDI enterprises. For example: The "Measures to Promote the High-Quality Development of SRDI SMEs in Beijing" propose support for companies applying for technology transformation projects related to digitization, intelligentization, and greenization. They also select no fewer than 30 benchmark enterprises for digital transformation annually. Tianjin city suggests organizing industrial internet platforms and digital transformation service providers to offer digital transformation assessment, diagnosis, and solutions for SRDI SMEs. Shanghai city aims to guide a wide range of SMEs, represented by SRDI enterprises, to recognize the development trends of the digital economy and master technological means in the digital field. The "Special Action Plan for Promoting the High-Quality Development of SRDI Enterprises in Chongqing (2022–2025)" aims to promote the digitalization, intelligentization, and greenization of SRDI enterprises. It plans to nurture 400 digital workshops, 50 smart factories, and 100 green factories. Guangdong province proposes supporting eligible SRDI SMEs, as well as technology-based and innovative SMEs, to participate in the construction of manufacturing innovation platforms at the provincial level or above.

Chinese Scholar Wu et al. (2021) identified specific keywords related to digital transformation. They employed text analysis methods to analyze the "Management Discussion and Analysis" section of the annual reports of SRDI listed companies in 2021. The total number of identified keywords was taken as an indicator of each company's focus on digitalization. Among the 719 SRDI listed companies, a total of 7674 mentions of digitalization keywords were found in their annual reports, with an average of 10.67 mentions per company. The top five most frequently mentioned keywords were all related to digital technologies, indicating that digital technology remains the primary focus of attention in the digital transformation efforts of SRDI enterprises. Furthermore, the study revealed that SRDI listed companies have a diversified focus on the application scenarios of digital technology. In addition to smart homes, smart grids, and autonomous driving, they also showed interest in areas such as wearable technology, intelligent robots, smart agriculture, and digital healthcare. This finding suggests that SRDI enterprises not only benefit from the broad applicability of digital technologies across various industries but also indicates their ongoing exploration of the commercial potential of digitalization from different perspectives.

2 The Hierarchical Cultivation System for China's Hidden Champions

In order to cultivate more single-item champions with the characteristics of hidden champions and SRDI "Little giants" enterprises, our country has established and continuously improved a "step-by-step" cultivation path and a "systematic" cultivation organizational structure. From the perspective of our country's policy system, a gradient cultivation system has been formed, targeting national small and medium-sized enterprises. It has initially developed a hierarchical development pattern from general small and medium-sized enterprises to SRDI enterprises (provincial and municipal level), to SRDI "Little giants" enterprises (provincial level), to national-level SRDI "Little giants" (key "little giants" enterprises), to national-level single-item champion enterprises and to leading enterprises. The gradient design of the small and medium-sized enterprise cultivation system helps embed the process of learning and capability enhancement of national small and medium-sized enterprises within the cultivation steps. It assists enterprises in clarifying their development goals and directions, and contributes to the formation of long-term competitiveness of small and medium-sized enterprises within the national innovation system (Table 1).

3 The Development Path of China's Hidden Champions

Since the Ministry of Industry and Information Technology (MIIT) first identified 248 national-level "Little Giants" enterprises in 2018, as of August 2023, MIIT has cumulatively publicized a total of 12,950 "Little Giants" enterprises, with the fifth batch adding 3671 new enterprises. These enterprises are spread across 31 provinces nationwide, with 20 provinces having more than 100 "Little Giants" enterprises each. Influenced by factors such as industrial foundations, the regional distribution of "Little Giants" enterprises shows a characteristic of "strong east and weak west," mainly concentrated in the more industrially developed eastern and central regions. Among the first five batches of "Little Giants," the provinces of Guangdong, Zhejiang, Shandong, and Jiangsu each have more than 1000 enterprises selected, with 1539, 1463, 1068, and 1509 enterprises respectively, leading the nation (Fig. 1).

Additionally, in terms of urban distribution, the five batches of national-level "Little Giants" enterprises are spread across 300 cities, with 12 cities hosting over 200 "Little Giants" enterprises each. Among the top 20 cities, there are 4 directly administered municipalities and 9 provincial capitals, while the remaining cities are all located in economically developed areas in the eastern region. This distribution reflects the advantages of these regions in industrial concentration and innovation capability (Fig. 2).

The five batches of nationally recognized "Little Giant" enterprises, manufacturing enterprises account for 78% of the total. Among them, the computer, communications, and electronic equipment manufacturing industry leads with 1499 enterprises, followed by specialized and general equipment manufacturing (1421 enterprises) and general equipment manufacturing (1259 enterprises), both industries having over 1000 "Little Giant" enterprises. The high concentration of industries such as computer, communications, and electronic equipment manufacturing, as well as specialized and general equipment manufacturing, reflects both the original intention of cultivating "Little Giant" enterprises—which are highly specialized

Table 1 China's hierarchical champion enterprise cultivation system

NO.	Business category	Evaluation criteria	Quantity available
1	SRDI enterprises (provincial and municipal level)	SMEs should strive to develop toward a path of SRDI. In the preceding year, these enterprises have witnessed growth in their core business revenue, with a focus on technological advancements, enhancements in process equipment, strengthened foundational management, thereby transforming into advanced manufacturing enterprises known for their dependable product quality, high added value, energy efficiency, environmental sustainability, and a commitment to safe production	About 140, 000 (By the end of 2024)
2	SRDI "little giants" enterprises (provincial level)	Emphasis on the selection of SMEs in the manufacturing sector, with priority given to strategic emerging industries, core foundational components (electronic components), crucial basic materials, advanced foundational industries, industrial technological foundations, and the field of basic software. These enterprises should have total assets of at least 30 million yuan by the end of the previous year, with comprehensive consideration given to their level of development in terms of specialization, refinement, distinctiveness, and innovation	About 70, 000 (As of the end of 2024)
3	National-level SRDI "Little giants" (key "little giants" enterprises)	In the previous year, the annual revenue should be 100 million yuan or more, and the proportion of R&D expenditure to annual revenue in the past two years should be no less than 3%. Alternatively, the annual revenue should be between 50 million yuan (inclusive) and 100 million yuan (exclusive), and the proportion of R&D expenditure to annual revenue in the past two years should be no less than 6%. Another option is that the annual revenue is less than 50 million yuan, but the enterprise meets the following criteria: There has been a new paid-in equity financing amount of 80 million yuan or more in the past two years, the R&D investment expenditure is 30 million yuan or more, the proportion of R&D personnel to total employees is 50% or more, and there have been significant breakthroughs in innovative achievements	15,970 companies (according to the first six batches of selection list)
4	National-level single-item champion enterprises	For enterprises with annual sales revenue above 400 million yuan: For enterprises with annual sales revenue below 400 million yuan, if they apply for the single-item champion status, they should already be selected as SRDI "Little giants" enterprises	1557 (based on the list of the first eight batches)
5	Leading enterprises	Industry-leading enterprises in the industrial chain have strong overall capabilities and hold significant influence, power, and international competitiveness in areas such as technology, standards, markets, and more, both domestically and internationally	–

Source: Sorted by authors

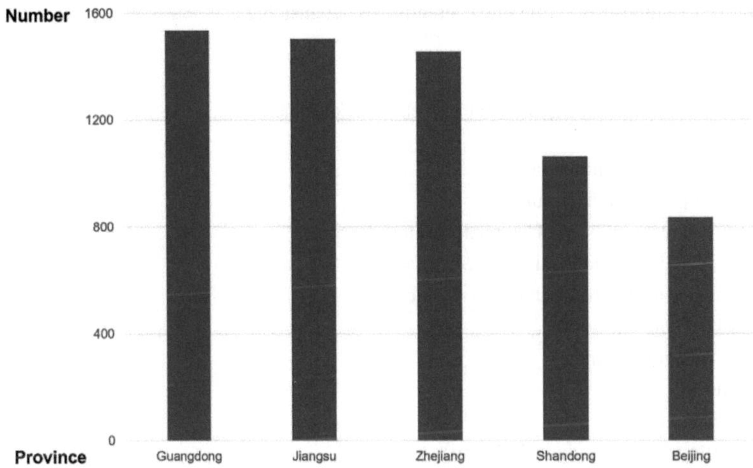

Fig. 1 The number of "little giants" enterprises in the top 5 provinces across five batches. (Source: MIIT)

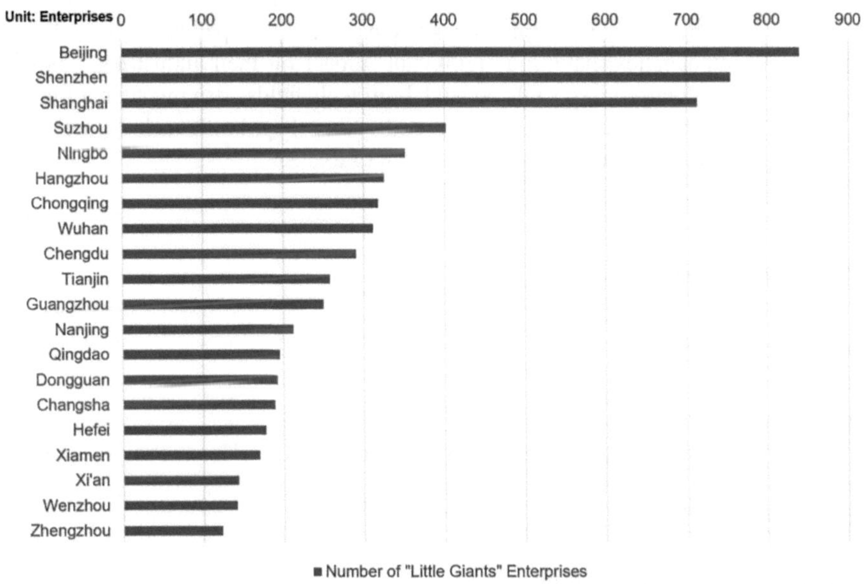

Fig. 2 Urban distribution of the five batches of "little giants" enterprises. (Source: MIIT, WIND)

SMEs that play a significant role in their respective industries, focusing on specific niche markets, innovating, producing key components or utilizing key technologies despite having a low public profile—and the core position of manufacturing in China's economic development. By analyzing their characteristics, this group of enterprises match well with the "hidden champions" proposed by German

Table 2 Top 10 industries "little giant" enterprises, August 2023

Industry Sector	Number of Enterprises
Computer, Communications, and Other Electronic Equipment Manufacturing	1499
Special Equipment Manufacturing	1421
General Equipment Manufacturing	1259
Chemical Raw Materials and Chemicals Manufacturing	995
Electrical Machinery and Equipment Manufacturing	939
Software and Information Technology Services	779
Automobile Manufacturing	688
Instrument Manufacturing	520
Manufacturing	505
Metal Products Industry	505
Non-metallic Mineral Products Industry	436

Source: MIIT, WIND

management scholar Hermann Simon, where these enterprises are not widely known but hold a leading position in their niche markets. "Little Giants" and "Hidden Champions" are both companies that excel in their specific fields and possess core competencies, having a significant impact on their industries. China's "Little Giants" focus on specialized and high-tech fields, driving technological advancements and industrial upgrades, addressing key bottleneck issues, and enhancing the resilience of the industrial chain (Table 2).

4 Case Study 1

4.1 DAESHIN

Overview

Address: 10 Xin 'an Road, Zhongmu County, Zhengzhou City, Henan Province, China
Tel: 86-400-659-7271
Fax: 86-0371-60862088
Email: 44549121@qq.com
Web: https://www.daeshin-china.com

Company Information

Industry: Manufacture of furniture
Year of Establishment: 1999
Brainer(s) behind the company: Mr. Xueyuan Pang

4.1.1 Nature of Market Leadership

DAESHIN is a design-focused professional enterprise specializing in the production, research and development, and supply of whole-house customization, household cabinets, wardrobes, kitchen and bathroom appliances, water equipment, mobile furniture, and home consumer goods. Currently, the company has more than 1800 DAESHIN Design Service Centers worldwide. In 2004, DAESHIN expanded from whole cabinets to kitchen appliances and pioneered the concept of integral kitchens in China. In 2005, DAESHIN invented the "dual distribution dual modular" production technology, forming DAESHIN's unique "ten-fold compatibility" and "five-dimensional industrial Internet manufacturing theory." The company also independently developed proprietary software. It is the only enterprise in the industry that has achieved unmanned order splitting, leading the way in the deep integration of informatization and industrialization. In 2023, DAESHIN was recognized as one of the top ten brands in China's integrated cabinet industry, ranking among the industry leaders. Additionally, DAESHIN received the prestigious TIA Original Design Brand Award and was named one of the top ten brands in China's home furnishing industry. Moreover, it ranked fifth in the 2021 Top Ten Integrated Cabinet Brands ranking. Its unique "Yi Jian" large-scale personalized customization model has successfully overcome four major challenges in custom furniture—high costs, long lead times, poor quality, and difficulties in mass production—reducing overall costs to half that of its peers.

4.1.2 Nature of Competitive Advantage

DAESHIN, through its independent and innovative "Easy Simplification" large-scale personalized customization model, utilizes the core components of "Dream Module + Dream Factory + Cloud Design" along with the "Dual Distribution Dual Module Intelligent Manufacturing" production method to make home design intelligent and simple.

4.1.3 Core Lessons Learned on the Path to Success

1. DAESHIN leverages digital business models and innovative production technologies to meet personalized customer needs and enhance efficiency. The company has transformed furniture customization by using "dual distribution and dual modularization" production methods, enabling the creation of diverse home furnishings through standardized components, supported by data from 100,000 households.
2. DAESHIN's intelligent manufacturing approach boosts material efficiency, reduces delivery time, and cuts costs. The company's smart manufacturing processes have raised material utilization from 76% to 94%, shortened delivery

cycles to under 4 days, and halved costs while maintaining an impressive product error rate of just 0.3%.

3. DAESHIN integrates industrial tourism and cultural marketing to enhance its brand's cultural depth. The company has established five museums, including the DAESHIN Kitchen Museum and the DAESHIN Living Museum, transforming these spaces into cultural landmarks that promote their custom home products.
4. DAESHIN's 500-acre industrial park and world-class museums attract millions of visitors annually, converting them into high-value customers. The company's industrial park, with five museums and an annual visitation of six million, has achieved high customer engagement, with a purchase conversion rate of one in six and an average transaction value exceeding 50,000 yuan.

4.1.4 Management and Leadership Development Needs

By leveraging the unique network thinking of the Chinese people and the rich cultural connotations of traditional Chinese culture, DAESHIN has developed a software system to achieve large-scale personalized customization of homes. Unlike traditional marketing approaches that focus on the company, DAESHIN places the user at the center of its marketing strategy. Through the digital empowerment of production, product, and management capabilities, the company redefines its brand positioning, predicts user demand, creates differentiated products, establishes personalized brands, and maximizes consumer value while facilitating the company's smooth transformation. In terms of future development, DAESHIN needs to further enhance its digital management capabilities to better integrate digital technology into production, product, and management processes. It also needs to cultivate leaders who have a deep understanding of both traditional culture and modern digital technology, and who can lead the company in its continuous innovation and transformation.

4.1.5 Financing and Regulatory Environment Development Needs

DAESHIN Furniture is a company with a heart, adhering to its original intentions and genuinely caring for its customers. As a result, the company offers cost-effective products and designs, allowing a 100-square-meter custom-made home to be completed for just 50,000 yuan, making DAESHIN's products accessible to most people around the world. DAESHIN Furniture also needs to secure sufficient funds to support its operations, such as production, marketing, and research and development. It might seek financing through various channels, including bank loans, equity financing, or government grants. The company needs to manage its cash flow effectively to ensure timely payments to suppliers and employees. DAESHIN Furniture needs to comply with relevant regulations in the furniture industry, such as product safety standards, environmental protection requirements, and labor laws. It should also follow regulations related to business operations, such as tax laws and consumer protection laws. The company needs to obtain necessary permits and licenses to operate legally.

(i) The Pandemic's Impact on "Hidden Champions" Business Approach.

The impact of the pandemic on China's furniture market is multifaceted. Initially, the production and logistics disruptions caused by epidemic prevention and control measures have directly affected the stability of the supply chain, prolonging the manufacturing and delivery cycles of furniture and impacting the normal operations of businesses. Secondly, the increased time spent at home by consumers during the pandemic has stimulated the demand for home environment improvement, prompting the differentiation and unique features of our products. Furthermore, due to the limitations on offline retail, the importance of online sales channels has significantly increased. DAESHIN's products allow customers to decorate without leaving home, with a 360-degree VR online experience of the home furnishing showroom, accelerating the digital transformation of furniture companies.

(ii) Effects of the Global Environment on "Hidden Champions" Business Operations.

The Russia–Ukraine war has had profound effects on the global economy, and it has also brought a series of challenges to China's furniture market. The war has triggered global increases in energy and raw material prices, adding pressure to the cost of furniture production. At the same time, trade restrictions and economic sanctions that may arise from the war have complicated the international trade environment for the furniture industry, affecting the operations of export companies. Exchange rate fluctuations have also brought additional financial risks to furniture companies that rely on imported raw materials or export products. For DAESHIN, this represents not only challenges but also opportunities. How to create differentiated products, focus on customer experience, and achieve digital transformation in the furniture industry has become particularly urgent.

4.1.6 Hidden Champion: DAESHIN

DAESHIN was established in 1999 and is located in Zhengzhou City, Henan Province, China. The company is dedicated to design leadership and is a professional enterprise specializing in the production, research and development, and supply of whole-house customization, household cabinets, wardrobes, kitchen and bathroom appliances, water equipment, mobile furniture, and household consumer goods. Currently, it has over 1800 DAESHIN Design Service Centers worldwide.

It was founded with the main focus on customized furniture, starting with the overall cabinet and exploring the path of achieving large-scale personalized modular production. In 2004, DAESHIN further extended its business to kitchen appliances and was the first in China to introduce the concept of integrated kitchens. In 2005, DAESHIN invented and created the "dual distribution and dual modular" production technology, forming its unique "ten-dimensional compatibility" and "five-dimensional industrial internet manufacturing theory." It independently developed software and is currently the only enterprise in the industry to achieve unmanned dismantling, achieving deep integration of information and industrialization.

In 2010, DAESHIN was first selected as one of the top ten leading enterprises in China's cabinet industry and was the first in the industry to launch the "industrial tourism" model. In 2015, it became the main drafting enterprise for the industry standard of whole-house customization. In 2017, Zhengzhou DAESHIN Home Furnishings Co., Ltd. was awarded the "Intelligent Manufacturing Pilot Demonstration Project Enterprise" and "Service-oriented Manufacturing Demonstration Enterprise" by the Ministry of Industry and Information Technology, becoming a model for intelligent manufacturing in the custom home furnishings industry. In 2018, based on the Inspur Cloud In-Cloud Industrial Internet Platform, DAESHIN launched a cooperation with Inspur to improve production efficiency.

Currently, the company uses unique Chinese network thinking and excellent traditional cultural connotations as its foundation, relying on independently developed software systems to achieve large-scale personalized customization of home furnishings. DAESHIN Home Furnishings Co., Ltd. is one of the first batch of service-oriented manufacturing demonstration enterprises, national intelligent manufacturing pilot demonstration project enterprises, and national high-tech enterprises. Its enterprise development model has been included in the case studies of the China Business Case Center at Tsinghua University. In November 2018, DAESHIN was selected to exhibit at the "Great Change–Celebrating the 40th Anniversary of China's Reform and Opening Up Exhibition" at the National Museum of China. It was featured in the "Great Country Atmosphere" exhibition section along with more than 40 other advanced enterprises such as China Railway High-speed, Huawei, Haier, and DJI, to jointly display the new achievements in China's modern industrial development.

In 2022, DAESHIN Furniture won the Gold Award in the Home Products category of the 2022 New York Design Awards. Additionally, DAESHIN has creatively built an AAA-level industrial tourism scenic area in its industrial park, which features advanced facilities and equipment systems such as the "Sky Garden Peacock Valley," "Big Data Cloud Waterfall," "Cloud Computing Center," "Global Eagle Eye Visual System," "Dual Distribution and Dual Modular," "Intelligent Manufacturing Production Workshop," "Intelligent Manufacturing Visual Hall," and "Non-mimic Robot."

5 Case Study 2

5.1 Shuanghuan

Overview

Address: Building 2, Hehe Building, No. 658-1 Jingchang Road, Wuchang Subdistrict, Yuhang District, Hangzhou, Zhejiang Province
Tel: +86-0571-8710 3999
Fax: +86-0576-87239867
Email: service@gearsnet.com
Web: https://www.gearsnet.com/about.html

Company Information

Industry: Manufacturing of Mechanical Parts Processing
Year of Establishment: 1980
Sales Revenues in 2017: 2639 million RMB
Sales Revenues in 2023: 8650 million RMB
Average number of employees in 2023: 7263
Brainer(s) behind the company: Mr. Changhong Wu

5.1.1 Nature of Market Leadership

Shuanghuan is an enterprise specializing in the research, development, manufacturing, and sales of core mechanical transmission components, gears, and their assemblies. The company has more than 7000 employees and over 10 subsidiaries. It has become one of the leading professional gear product manufacturers and service providers in China, with sales to Fortune 500 clients accounting for over 60% of its revenue. With its high-performance, high-speed rail gears, Shuanghuan has become a strategic supplier of high-speed rail gears to ZF. It has also completed innovative R&D and transitioned to the industrialization of industrial robot joints (RV reducers), becoming a leading brand in the domestic robot market. Additionally, its new energy vehicle gears cover half of the Chinese market.

Fig. 3 Shuanghuan's partial partners. (Source: Sorted by authors)

5.1.2 Nature of Competitive Advantage

Shuanghuan is a leading manufacturer of mechanical transmission gears, with strong partnerships with top global clients such as BorgWarner, a leader in powertrain solutions, and MAGNA, a global automotive supplier known for its technological expertise. The company's team of advanced engineers and cutting-edge technology enable it to design, process, and produce high-quality gear components. Shuanghuan's strategic collaboration with China FAW Group, one of China's largest automotive manufacturers, ensures a stable supply of gear components for advanced automotive transmission systems. Furthermore, the company's continuous investment in basic research and technology development translates its findings into practical products. Guided by customer needs, Shuanghuan has implemented a refined management model to achieve mutual success for all stakeholders (Fig. 3).

5.1.3 Core Lessons Learned on the Path to Success

1. Since 2005, Shuanghuan has introduced the concept of lean production. Faced with the problem of product quality traceability, it introduced the Toyota Lean Production Management Model (TPS) and information management systems such as U9 ERP, in order to integrate the information of various departments and build a high-speed information network within the Group.
2. In 2016, with the online MES system and the promotion of mobile office, Shuanghuan began to build a manufacturing operation management platform.
3. From 2019 to 2020, Shuanghuan deepened its digital transformation, independently developed an industrial Internet platform, and achieved data connectivity and transparency in the production process. Since 2021, Shuanghuan has established Huanzhi Yunchuang Technology Co., LTD., embraced 5G and industrial Internet technology, established the D-MOM platform, and promoted the ecological construction of a platform-type supply chain. In 2022, the Shuanghuan new energy auto parts factory was rated as a "future factory." Using the "1 + 5" new model, it integrated the enterprise intelligent brain and five platforms to achieve optimal allocation of resources and production cycle management.

5.1.4 Management and Leadership Development Needs

Shuanghuan adopts the "Lean Driven, Digitally Empowered" strategy, integrating digital practices to enhance production management experience. Since the introduction of the Lean Production Management System (TPS) in 2006, the company has continuously implemented quality management and information technology tools to improve product quality and efficiency, strengthen competitiveness, and establish a reliable brand image. The company has implemented a "localization of supporting facilities" strategy, with five major production bases located in Zhejiang, Jiangsu, Dalian, and Chongqing, ensuring rapid response to customer needs and guaranteeing product quality and delivery time. In terms of digitalization, starting from 2007, Shuanghuan has progressively adopted barcode management and MES systems. By 2023, it introduced the smart factory control platform (oWorks) to achieve online management of lean management, planning, operations, logistics, and quality, as well as efficient collaboration between production, supply, and sales. The company leverages digitalization to optimize management and empower business development. Additionally, Shuanghuan's future management needs focus on enhanced digital integration, evolving quality management, and supply chain optimization. Leaders must provide visionary guidance, fostering innovation and talent development. Digital tools like oWorks should be expanded to cover more processes, improving data flow and decision-making. Quality management will advance with AI-driven inspection systems and updated standards. Supply chain optimization involves closer collaboration with local suppliers and potential new production bases. Leadership requires a forward-looking vision to anticipate market trends and technological advancements, positioning Shuanghuan as an industry leader. Innovative leadership will encourage a culture of innovation, exploring new business models and partnerships. Talent development is crucial, with a focus on cultivating potential leaders and experts, and building a diverse workforce. These combined efforts will ensure Shuanghuan's continued success and growth.

5.1.5 Financing and Regulatory Environment Development Needs

The funds raised were invested in expansion projects at Shuanghuan, leading to increased production capacity and enhanced market power. This improved Shuanghuan's financing environment. Additionally, Shuanghuan has continually enhanced its board of directors, top management team, and organizational structure to establish a modern enterprise governance system.

5.1.6 Pandemic's Impact on "Hidden Champions" Business Approach

The automotive industry is under tremendous pressure due to factors such as chip shortages, rising raw material prices, the pandemic, and restrictions on electricity and production. Despite these adverse conditions, the company has rapidly scaled up several high-quality projects, effectively utilizing strategically planned production capacity. Leveraging years of experience and deep cultivation in the high-end gear sector, the company has seized the market initiative in the field of new energy vehicle drive system gears, promoting increased industry concentration. Consequently, the continuous rise in the penetration rate of new energy vehicles and the vigorous development of the industry are actively driving the growth of the Shuanghuan's performance. Independent innovation and technological upgrades continuously enhance the company's manufacturing capabilities, thereby reducing per-unit costs and improving competitive advantages in quality, delivery time, and cost. This, in turn, strengthens the cooperative cohesion between the company and its customers.

5.1.7 Effects of the Ukraine War on "Hidden Champions" Business Operations

The Russia–Ukraine war has caused fluctuations in the global supply chain, affecting the cost of raw materials and transportation efficiency in the gear industry. International sanctions may restrict trade, increasing market uncertainty. However, Shuanghuan's core strengths lie in three dimensions: product consistency and performance, cost reduction and efficiency enhancement in management, and technical and developmental capabilities in R&D. It has built a platform supply system fortified by products such as vehicle gears, robot reducers, and construction machinery gears, ensuring growth momentum. Continuous technological upgrades, process optimization, and management improvements are promoted as methods for cost reduction and efficiency enhancement (since raw materials for gears account for about 50% of the costs, there is significant room for cost reduction and efficiency enhancement), and the company's profitability is expected to gradually increase.

5.1.8 Shuanghuan: Digital Transformation

Since 2005, Shuanghuan has embarked on a digital transformation journey by introducing the Toyota Production System (TPS) and information management systems such as U9 ERP to streamline operations and build a robust internal information network. In 2016, the company advanced its digital capabilities with the launch of the MES system and mobile office initiatives, leading to the development of a comprehensive manufacturing operations management platform. Between 2019 and 2020, Shuanghuan deepened its digital transformation by independently developing an industrial Internet platform that ensured data connectivity and transparency in the production process. Furthering its commitment to innovation, in 2021, Shuanghuan established Huanzhi Yunchuang Technology Co., LTD, and integrated 5G and industrial Internet technologies to create the D-MOM platform, fostering a platform-based supply chain ecosystem. By 2022, the company's new energy auto parts factory was recognized as a "future factory," utilizing a "1 + 5" model that integrates an intelligent enterprise brain with five platforms to optimize resource allocation and production cycle management.

Shuanghuan's continuous implementation of quality management and information technology tools since the adoption of TPS in 2006 has significantly enhanced product quality, efficiency, and brand reliability. By 2023, the introduction of the

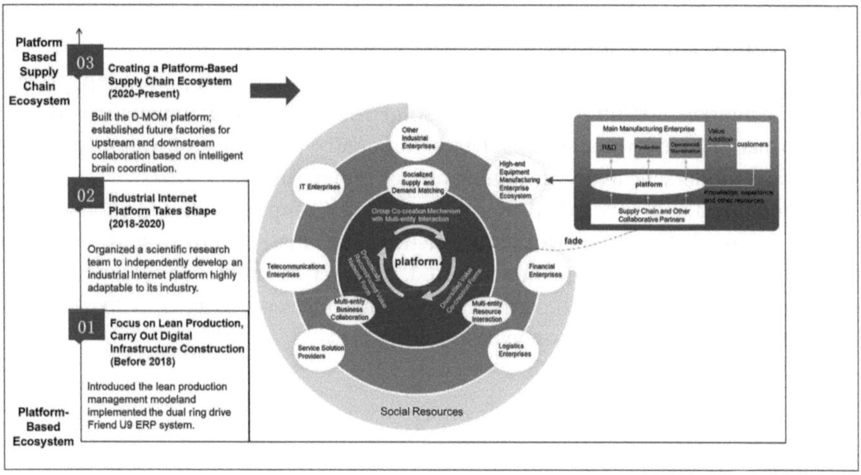

Fig. 4 Shuanghuan: The path to lean production with the construction of a digital platform supply system. (Source: Sorted by authors)

smart factory control platform (oWorks) enabled online management of lean practices, planning, operations, logistics, and quality, as well as efficient collaboration between production, supply, and sales. Leveraging digitalization, Shuanghuan optimizes its management processes, empowering the company's growth and development in the digital era (Fig. 4).

6 Conclusions and Recommendations

Based on the digital transformation practices of DAESHIN and Shuanghuan, as well as research on the development paths of SRDI firms, the following conclusions and recommendations are proposed.

6.1 Conclusions

Comprehensive Impact of Digital Transformation: Companies must undergo digital transformation to adapt to market changes. This involves not just technological applications, but also a revolution in organizational culture and management methods. Digital transformation is essential for enhancing personalized service capabilities, production efficiency, and cost control.

Core Role of Innovation: Innovation is the core driver of sustainable corporate growth. Companies like DAESHIN and Shuanghuan continuously optimize their products and services through relentless technological innovation, demonstrating the importance of integrating technological, organizational, and environmental factors for collaborative innovation.

Dual-Drive of Policy and Market Environment: Government policy support and favorable market conditions provide a solid foundation and impetus for digital transformation. Government subsidies significantly promote innovation in SRDI enterprises, underscoring the critical nature of policy support.

Personalized and Diversified Innovation Paths: Companies should choose innovation paths that suit their characteristics and market positioning, whether technology-driven, government-supported, market-oriented, or comprehensive development. The innovation paths of SRDI enterprises are diverse, with each path supported by successful corporate case studies.

6.2 Recommendations

Strengthen Technological R&D and Digital Application: Companies should continuously increase R&D investment, utilizing digital technologies such as big data and artificial intelligence to optimize production processes and enhance product quality. Emphasizing the integration of technological, organizational, and environmental factors can achieve collaborative innovation.

Build an Open Innovation Ecosystem: By establishing cooperation with universities, research institutions, and industry partners, companies can build an open innovation ecosystem that promotes knowledge sharing and technological exchange. Additionally, fully leveraging government policies, such as tax incentives and financial subsidies, is crucial.

Adapt Flexibly to Market and Policy Changes: Companies need to establish mechanisms to quickly respond to market and policy changes, reducing innovation costs and accelerating development. Fostering an open and inclusive innovation culture is essential to support long-term innovation development.

Focus on Talent, Brand, and Sustainable Development: Emphasizing talent cultivation and recruitment, strengthening brand building, and enhancing brand influence are critical. While pursuing economic benefits, companies should also focus on environmental protection and social responsibility, driving sustainable development and reflecting the importance of policy support in corporate growth.

References

Din, F. U., Dolles, H., & Middel, R. (2013). Strategies for small and medium-sized enterprises to compete successfully on the world market: Cases of Swedish hidden champions. *Asian Business & Management, 12*(5), 591–612.

Qi, P., Xu, C., & Sun, D. (2023). Research on the experience and countermeasures for promoting the digital transformation of "specialized, refinement, differential, and innovation" enterprises under the background of the smart innovation capital. *Ningbo Economy (Sanjiang Forum), 01*, 17–19+29.

Simon, H. (1996). You don't have to be German to be a "hidden champion". *Business Strategy Review, 7*(2), 1–13.
Tang, X., Yao, X., & Yu, L. (2023). Research on the innovation path of "little Giant" enterprises under the background of digitalization. *Science Research Management, 44*(12), 10–20.
Wu F, Hu H Z, Lin H Y, et al. Enterprise Digital Transformation and Capital Market Performance: Empirical Evidence from Stock Liquidity[J]. *Management World*, 2021, 37(7): 130–144+10.

Xiaobo Wu is Professor of Innovation and Strategic Management, School of Management, Zhejiang University. He is honored as Chang Jiang Scholar Professor by Ministry of Education, China for his outstanding achievements in innovation and entrepreneurship research and education. He is director of National Institute for Innovation Management, and also director of the International Research Center for Hidden Champions at Zhejiang University. He also serves as the vice-president of the The International Association for Management Development in Dynamic Societies (CEEMAN).

Linan Lei is an Assistant Professor of Innovation and Strategy at International Business School, Zhejiang University, and Deputy Director of the International Research Center for Hidden Champions.

Hidden Champions of Croatia

Slavica Singer, Sunčica Oberman Peterka, Mislav Ante Omazić, and Patricia Uroić

Abstract Croatia is a "catching up" country achieving 73% of EU GDP per capita in 2022, compared with 61% in 2013, when Croatia joined EU. Innovative minority of small and medium-sized businesses are crucial for contributing to the competitiveness on global markets. Eight identified hidden champions are from different sectors and different regions. Four presented cases confirm that innovativeness should and could be spread all over sectors (digitalization in agriculture, IT in financial planning, manufacturing of drones and manufacturing equipment for maintenance of traffic infrastructure) and territorial residence (capital city, industrial city in the most deprived region of Croatia, village). The research findings in 2023 closely mirror those identified in 2021, confirming the validity of the recognized patterns of characteristics, needs, and the business environment in which HC companies operate. HCs operate in niche markets, with global focus. It is positive that innovativeness remains a constant feature of Croatian HC companies. However, the stability in needs (access to venture capital, investment in R&D transfer, availability of educated people in STEM and entrepreneurial competences) and the persistence of identified obstacles in the business environment suggest these issues have not been resolved, raising the question of why this is the case. In line with those find-

S. Singer (✉) · S. O. Peterka
Faculty of Economics and Business in Osijek, J.J. Strossmayer University, Osijek, Croatia
e-mail: singer@efos.hr; suncica.oberman.peterka@efos.hr

M. A. Omazić
Department of Organisation and Management, Faculty of Economics and Business, University of Zagreb, Zagreb, Croatia

IEDC-Bled School of Management, Bled, Slovenia
e-mail: momazic@net.efzg.hr

P. Uroić
Department of Organisation and Management, Faculty of Economics and Business, University of Zagreb, Zagreb, Croatia
e-mail: puroic1@efzg.hr

D. Berberović, D. Purg (eds.), *Hidden Champions in Rising Economies*, Contributions to Management Science,
https://doi.org/10.1007/978-3-032-08263-3_17

ings, several recommendations to businesses, to the government, to the financial and higher education institutions were formulated.

Overview
Official name: Republic of Croatia
Type of government: Parliamentary democratic republic
Population in 2022: 3 855 600
Land area: 56,594 km2
GDPpc, current US$ 21,401.9 (2023, World Bank, Croatia)

History

1918	Shortly before the end of the First World War in 1918, the Croatian parliament severs relations with Austria-Hungary. On December, 1, 1918, the Kingdom of Serbs, Croats, and Slovenes was established.
1929	After a decade of unrest and political tensions, the country is renamed the Kingdom of Yugoslavia, and the system of government is further centralized under a royal dictatorship.
1941	Nazi Germany invades Yugoslavia. After the military collapse of the Kingdom of Yugoslavia, Croatia finds itself, along with Bosnia and Herzegovina, within the newly-established Independent State of Croatia (Nezavisna Država Hrvatska), with a Quisling regime, under German and Italian protection (Croatia.eu. (n.d.). Yugoslavia and World War II 1918–1990).
1943, June	The National Anti-Fascist Council of the People's Liberation of Croatia is founded at sessions of representatives of the Croatian partisans.
1943, November	The Anti-Fascist Council of the People's Liberation of Yugoslavia is established. The rulings of that session are considered the foundation act of post-war Yugoslavia.
1945	Croatia becomes one of the six constituent republics within the Federal People's Republic of Yugoslavia (renamed the Socialist Federal Republic of Yugoslavia in 1963), and Croatia's present-day borders are set.
1971	The early 1970s mark the beginning of a protest movement known as the nationalistic "Croatian Spring," during which many students and activists demand greater civil liberties and greater autonomy for Croatia.
1974	A new Yugoslav constitution emphasized federalism, meeting some of the demands for Croatian autonomy.
1980	After the death of President Tito, the process of disintegration of Yugoslavia begins as federal units (republics) assert their desire for more autonomy.
1991	Croatia declares its independence, followed by military interventions of the Yugoslav army and an armed insurgency by

	Serb separatists. They proclaim the "Autonomous Region of Krajina" over a quarter of the Croatian territory, which they intend to unite with Serbia. The Croatian War for Independence starts.
1992	The EU recognizes Croatia as an independent state. Croatia joins the United Nations.
1995	Croatian forces retake three out of four occupied areas and the war ends with the signing of the Dayton Agreement.
1996	UN administration of eastern Croatia starts, ending in January 1998, when the occupied territory is re-integrated with the rest of Croatia.
1996	Croatia joins the Council of Europe.
2003	Croatia submits a formal application for EU membership.
2009	Croatia joins NATO.
2013	Croatia becomes the 28th member state of the European Union.
2022	Croatia started the OECD accession process.
2023	Croatia adopts the single European currency, the euro.

1 Introduction: Context and History

As a member of the European Union from 2013, Croatia shares four principles of mobility—of people, money, goods, and services which define the broader context in which socio-demographic and economic activities take place. Additionally, the Croatian context is marked with consequences of two mega changes which happened at the same time, in the beginning of 1990s. The first change was the disintegration of the former Yugoslavia and the establishment of Croatia, which required building a new institutional infrastructure (pluralistic democratic political system and market economy). In the beginning, this aspect of transformation was marginalized, or even fully neglected. It led to a very corrupted privatization of previously socially owned (not state owned) companies and strongly negative feelings among the population. The second important change was the war 1991–1995. The war caused huge devastation in human resources, mined land (there were active minefields in 2019), destroyed houses, infrastructure, business facilities.

In order to provide consistent insight into the context framed with political, economic, sociological, technological, environmental, and legal factors, most of the data are used from the World Bank surveys. From 2008, Croatia is in the group of countries with high income.

Statistical Performance Indicators (SPI) are contributing to the country's transparency important for investors and entrepreneurs as well as for analyzing (identifying trends and patterns) and estimating potential changes. They are very relevant also for identifying different sustainable development goals: social (SDG 1–6), economic (SDG 7–12), environmental (SDG 13–15) and institutional (SDG 16–17). Croatia with the SPI score of 83.1 in 2022 (compared to 61.0 in 2017) is quite good placed to the fourth Quintile out of 186 countries, but the score also indicates a need for additional efforts to improve the performance of national statistical system in order to increase the country's transparency.

World Bank's Worldwide Governance Indicators (voice of accountability, rule of law, regulatory quality, political stability and absence of violence, government effectiveness, control of corruption) suggest moderate progress in 2022 compared to 2013 (OECD, 2024).

Consequences of the devastation caused by the war and corrupted privatization kept Croatia economic development at a very low rate, with high unemployment and lack of competitiveness, for quite long time (1991–2014). Only in the period after COVID-19, performance of Croatian economy is showing promising trends: GDPpc (current US$) started to rise with the expectations of 3% annual growth up to 2025 (from 61.4% of EU average in 2013, to 72.9% in 2022), unemployment rate started to decline, the share of exports of goods and services in GDP started to rise (see the Exhibit 1). The Gini index (deviation from perfect equality identified with the value of 0) slightly dropped to 28.9 in 2021. Despite Croatia being a small country, the regional development differences are significant and they are even

Exhibit 1 Core economic indicators for Croatia

	2019	2020	2021	2022	2023	2024
GDP per capita (current US$)	15,563.82	14,808.46	17,789.93	18,466.10	21,865.46	..
GDP per capita growth (annual %)	4.13	−7.49	13.65	7.94	3.19	..
Unemployment, total (% of total labor force) (modeled ILO estimate)	6.62	7.51	7.61	6.96	6.09	5.24
Foreign direct investment, net inflows (% of GDP)	6.47	2.54	7.43	5.52	3.96	..
GDP (current US$, mio)	61467.58	57963.37	69006.80	71198.64	84393.80	..
Exports of goods and services (current US$, mio)	31034.51	23925.56	34351.38	42361.03	44673.15	..
Exports of goods and services (% of GDP)	50.49	41.28	49.78	59.5	52.93	..
Merchandise exports (current US$, mio)	17180.00	17193.00	21878.00	25467.00	24937.00	..
Merchandise exports to high-income economies (% of total merchandise exports)	75.91	78.18	77.26	76.35	75.6	..
Merchandise exports to low-and middle-income economies in Europe and Central Asia (% of total merchandise exports)	19.78	18.78	19.13	21.3	21.44	..

(continued)

Exhibit 1 (continued)

	2019	2020	2021	2022	2023	2024
Ores and metals exports (% of merchandise exports)	4.05	4.39	4.97	4.49	4.01	..
Agricultural raw materials exports (% of merchandise exports)	4.34	4.06	4.18	4.25	3.63	..
Food exports (% of merchandise exports)	14.17	15.77	14.96	14.39	15.99	..
Fuel exports (% of merchandise exports)	9.48	9.04	11.87	19.39	11.99	..
Manufactures exports (% of merchandise exports)	67.34	65.91	63.46	56.69	63.88	..
High-technology exports (% of manufactured exports)	8.29	9.68	9.61	12.06	11.03	..

Source: World Bank, 2025

broadening (OECD, 2024)—e.g., the difference between City of Zagreb and the poorest Pannonian region is 5.2% of unemployment vs. 12.4% (2023), or GDPpc in Pannonian region is 66% lower than in the City of Zagreb (2021). Those regional differences are a challenge for the government policies in order to provide balanced quality of life in the whole country—what is the only way to reverse trends of increasing emigration of young people.

Economic backlash from 1991 to 2014 had and still has a strong influence on the social dimension of Croatian context, especially visible in the trends in poverty, shared prosperity, and demography. Human Capital Index (HCI) indicates how underinvestment in education and health for today's children reduces future incomes, or what should be done to empower people to achieve their potential and drives economic growth (WB, Human capital country brief: Croatia, October 2023). Croatia's value of HCI for 2020 (71%) is on the average of high-income countries (71%) and it says that a child born in Croatia will be 71% as productive when she grows up as she could be if she enjoyed complete education and full health. Net migration is negative (−2000 in 2023), as well as annual rate of the population growth (−0.605 in 2022). Negative demographic trends and a shortage of workforce require more investments in education and labor market policies.

Indicators on innovation, digitalization, and internet penetration describe if technological dimension of the Croatian ecosystem is supportive for working and living. The number of individuals using the Internet (% of population) is continuously rising (82.1% in 2022). In the period 2012–2022, R&D intensity in Croatia increased by 0.69% points, compared to 0.14 pp. in the EU. Despite that, the gross domestic expenditure on research and development (GERD) in Croatia (1.43%, 2022) is far below the EU average of 2.24%. There are also significant regional differences in the innovation performance, placing only the City of Zagreb in the category of a "strong innovator," all other three regions are "emerging innovators" (European

Commission, 2023). Having selected eight businesses as hidden champions from different regions is an important message that pockets of innovativeness can be found even on places which are lagging behind. Those hidden champions have important societal roles of being role models and change makers.

Croatia's policies and initiatives to promote renewable energy sources influence its energy independence and environmental sustainability. Electricity production from renewable sources (excluding hydroelectric) is showing a sharp increase (the last available data is 9.96% of total electricity production, 2015). The sustainability of the tourism industry, which is heavily reliant on Croatia's natural beauty, is crucial. Over-tourism and environmental degradation are significant concerns.

Numerous surveys (e.g., on competitiveness, on corruption, on entrepreneurial capacity) indicate that even stronger economic progress could be achieved if the institutional framework would be improved (OECD, 2024) and bottlenecks in the business environment to be eliminated. Fragility of business environment is identified as an obstacle for hidden champions in South-East Europe for long time (Berberović et al., 2019).

The Croatian economy is influenced by a combination of political stability within the EU context, a reliance on tourism, demographic challenges, and a need for technological advancement and environmental sustainability. This is the context in which innovative hidden champions are emerging. Strategic policies addressing these areas can enhance this process and contribute to their competitiveness through innovativeness.

2 Characteristics of Hidden Champions from Croatia

Croatia has participated in HC surveys from the start in 2011 and several lessons were learned in the time span of twelve years, analyzing selected hidden champions:

- 2011 cycle: Three businesses were identified as HCs, and presented in the publication McKiernan and Purg (2013). By the next cycle, only one business kept its HC status, two others lost it due to lack of innovative capacity and financial strength to keep and broaden their market base.
- 2018–2019 cycle: Three businesses were identified as HCs (one from 2011 cycle + two new HCs) and presented in the publication Braček Lalić and Purg (2021). All those three businesses had maintained their growth path, and became worldwide well-known businesses.
- 2022–2023 cycle: Eight new businesses were identified as HCs and four of them are presented in this publication.

In the 2022–2023 HC survey cycle, the following eight companies were identified as hidden champions:

Agrivi—digital agriculture, Zagreb; Alius Grupa—transportation of pharmaceutical products, Viškovo; Farseer—software production, Zagreb; SATO—graphic industry, Zabok; Croatian—umbrella—umbrella industry, Zaprešić; Kanaan—food production, Donji Miholjac; ORQA—electronics board, drones, Osijek; RASCO—production of equipment for the maintenance of traffic infrastructure, Kalinovac.

The selection of those HCs was based on three criteria defined by Hermann Simon (Braček Lalić & Purg, 2021): they should occupy top positions in the global/European market, must be small or medium-sized businesses, and must have a low visibility profile in the public domain. All identified HCs reserve to be presented in this publication, but the space limitation requested to select four. Selection criteria were combining sectors—services and production (digitalization in agriculture, IT in financial planning, manufacturing of drones and manufacturing equipment for maintenance of traffic infrastructure) and territorial residence (capital city, industrial city in the most deprived region of Croatia, village).

In all three cycles, identified HCs in Croatia which survived and become successful growing businesses are showing several common characteristics:

- Strong innovative capacity based on exceptional knowledge in IT, producing business models, analytical tools, and manufacturing highly functional products.
- Organizational culture based on team work and innovativeness.
- Visionary capacity to go global, from the beginning.
- Willingness to learn one's own mistakes.

These case studies collectively provide a comprehensive view of how digital solutions and innovative technologies can drive efficiency, sustainability, and growth in different industries, making them invaluable examples for the Hidden Champions book.

3 Case Studies of Selected Hidden Champions

3.1 Case Study 1[1]

3.1.1 Agrivi

Overview
Address: Ulica Grada Gospića 1/A, 10000 Zagreb, Croatia
Tel: +385 44 643 479
Fax: -
Email: info@agrivi.com
Web: https://www.agrivi.com

Company Information
Industry[2]: J.62 Computer programming, consultancy and related activities

[1] Interviews, analysis, and description of the case were conducted by Mislav Ante Omazić and Patricia Uroić.

[2] *According to NACE Rev. 2*

Year of Establishment: 2013
Sales Revenues in 2017: 250 thousand EUR
Sales Revenues in 2023: two million EUR
Average number of employees in 2023: 35
Brainer behind the company Matija Žulj

Nature of Market Leadership

Agrivi, among others, is emerging as a frontrunner, thanks to its strong global brand recognition and significant investments in product development. Agrivi's competitive edge is strengthened by its adaptability to serve diverse agricultural markets with tailored, IT comprehensive solutions focused on various crop types. This approach not only broadens its market presence but also ensures that farmers receive specialized support to optimize production and increase sustainability and profitability. Despite the market being fragmented, Agrivi estimates its global market share at 0.2%, exceeding competitors. The market landscape has changed notably due to the rise of agritech startups, prompting a consolidation phase. Over the past three to five years, Agrivi has increasingly focused on export, resulting in a higher share of export activities. The international business volume has been growing, while the willingness to embrace agricultural digitalization in Croatia could be faster.

Nature of Competitive Advantage

Agrivi initially stood out in the agritech industry due to its technological superiority. However, over the past three to five years, its competitive advantage has evolved. Today, Agrivi's strength lies in its technological capabilities, market approach, and exceptional customer support, crucial for successful digital transformation. In Europe, Agrivi faces limited competition from two to three pan-European rivals, setting it apart from single-country competitors. This signals a significant shift in the agritech competitive landscape, marked by consolidation and a stronger emphasis on customer-centric strategies. By prioritizing customer support and market approach, Agrivi has differentiated itself and solidified its position in the industry. Agrivi understands the importance of innovative technology and need for providing a guidance for effective implementation. In the increasingly competitive agritech sector, Agrivi's customer-centric focus and strategic market expansion set the stage for ongoing growth and success, spearheading the digital revolution in agriculture.

Core Lessons Learned on the Path to Success

For Agrivi, core lessons learned on the path to success can be summarized as:

- Start with the right target: Agrivi initially targeted SMEs but quickly recognized the need to shift focus as market conditions revealed slower adoption of digital solutions.
- Adapt to market realities: Agrivi learned to pivot toward value chains and enterprise growers who showed greater receptiveness to digital solutions.
- Strategic pivot drives growth: Agrivi adopted its strategy to capture emerging opportunities, leading to significant revenue growth. Stay aligned with the market: By focusing on the most receptive market segments, Agrivi positioned itself as a leading player in the digital agriculture industry.

Management and Leadership Development Needs

Agrivi emphasizes the continual enhancement of employees' skills, particularly in international B2B sales. Croatia's market lacks talent and experience in this area, presenting challenges for Agrivi's global growth. Unlike the traditional relationship-based sales approach common in the country, Agrivi requires a robust outbound B2B strategy. To bridge this gap, Agrivi is establishing an agritech education program, reflecting its commitment to continuous learning and development for all employees. In the rapidly evolving agricultural industry, ongoing education and learning are crucial to staying updated on the latest advancements, trends, and best practices. Agrivi acknowledges the need for continuous education to ensure its employees, managers and leaders remain well-informed and capable of contributing effectively to the company's success. By investing in the development of leadership and technical skills, Agrivi aims to cultivate a competent workforce capable of meeting the challenges of the dynamic agrotechnology market and driving the company's growth and innovation.

Financing and Regulatory Environment Development Needs

Agrivi recognizes the significant influence of agricultural subsidies on the pace of digitalization in Europe. Farmers predominantly purchase capital-intensive solutions only when subsidized by the EU. However, the EU now favors subsidy applications that include digital investments, encouraging farmers to embrace technology. The EU has allocated 10 billion euros through the Green Deal initiative to subsidize digital solutions from 2021 to 2027, driving stronger adoption of digital solutions in agriculture.

Another significant regulatory push is the ESG (Environmental, Social, and Governance) regulation, which requires companies with over 250 employees, including food companies that source from farmers, to report their environmental and social impact. The first reports under the Corporate Sustainability Reporting Directive (CSRD) is due in 2025 for the financial year 2024. To fulfill these reporting requirements, companies need to collect agricultural production data from farmers, making platforms like Agrivi invaluable in facilitating this process. Overall,

Agrivi anticipates that these regulatory demands for data will create additional opportunities and incentivize the industry to respond effectively to sustainability and transparency requirements.

In terms of collaboration, while specific financial institutions, governmental bodies, and international organizations are not mentioned, Agrivi has a strong track record of successful partnerships with various stakeholders in the industry.

Agrivi: The Hidden Champion

Agrivi, a leading company in the field of digital agriculture, has been at the forefront of tackling global food challenges since its establishment in 2013. Through their innovative technology solutions, they are dedicated to revolutionizing farming practices. By digitalizing agriculture, Agrivi provides farmers with real-time agronomic insights and promotes sustainable practices that contribute to a resilient and sustainable food supply chain. Their comprehensive suite of digital agriculture solutions covers every aspect of the food production process, empowering farmers with tools for efficient farm management and facilitating collaboration with stakeholders. Agrivi's holistic approach addresses critical issues such as food security, nutrition, climate change, soil health, and farmer livelihoods. With their commitment to making a positive impact on millions of people worldwide, Agrivi has already made significant strides in driving change within the industry. Their innovative solutions have empowered farmers to optimize production, reduce environmental impact, and increase overall efficiency. By leveraging technology and data-driven insights, Agrivi continues to be a trusted partner for farmers, enabling them to overcome challenges and unlock the full potential of sustainable agriculture.

Agrivi's success is driven by several key factors. Firstly, Agrivi's leadership demonstrates a clear vision for solving global food challenges through innovative technology solutions. They are committed to creating a resilient and sustainable food supply chain. Secondly, their agricultural technology, including farm management software and analytics, provides farmers with tools to optimize operations, positioning Agrivi as an industry leader. Additionally, Agrivi's emphasis on understanding and meeting customer needs through continuous engagement has built trust and loyalty among their growing customer base. Their strategic approach to market expansion, particularly into emerging markets like Latin America, the United States, and Asia, has diversified revenue streams and reduced dependence on any single market. Agrivi places a strong emphasis on strategic marketing, harnessing content marketing through various online channels such as its website, social media platforms, and newsletters. By prioritizing content marketing, SEO, and public appearances, Agrivi effectively promotes its brand and solidifies its market position. Continuously adapting its marketing approach enables Agrivi to overcome challenges and communicate its digital agriculture solutions to its target audience. Agrivi's commitment to continuous innovation and research ensures they remain at the forefront of agricultural technology advancements, delivering cutting-edge solutions that address evolving industry needs. With a dedicated team, industry expertise, and strategic partnerships, Agrivi is well-positioned for sustained growth in the agricultural technology sector. Finally, Agrivi has demonstrated adaptability and resilience by adjusting to changing market conditions during crises such as the COVID-19 pandemic and the resource crisis caused by the conflict in Ukraine. The COVID-19 pandemic significantly impacted Agrivi's business operations, leading to a shift toward online formats and digital communication channels. Initially, the company faced challenges as many companies adopted a wait-and-see approach, causing a temporary halt in ongoing discussions and projects. Despite this, Agrivi actively engaged in virtual conferences and events, leveraging online channels to generate leads, with the founder playing a prominent role as a speaker. While adapting to the new circumstances, Agrivi found success in maintaining communication with potential customers and generating new business opportunities through digital platforms. Agrivi also recognized the enduring importance of personal connections in the agricultural industry. While digital interactions facilitated initial research and interactions, the company realized that the subsequent stages of the sales process often required face-to-face engagement to build trust and strong customer relationships. Therefore, Agrivi emphasizes the need to strike a balance between digital interactions and maintaining personal connections to effectively meet the specific needs of its customers in the agricultural sector.

During the global resource supply crisis triggered by the conflict in Ukraine, Agrivi's business remained relatively unaffected due to its limited involvement in the region. However, the company observed broader impacts on the European market, characterized by a slowdown in new investments and heightened caution among businesses due to the high price growth of inputs. To adapt to these circumstances, Agrivi strategically shifted its focus to regions less affected by the resource crisis. Consequently, the company experienced improved performance and revenue generation in markets like Latin America, the United States, and Asia. This strategic pivot resulted in a larger portion of Agrivi's revenue now originating from these regions, rather than Europe. While the direct impact on Agrivi's operations was minimal, the ripple effects of the resource crisis and the cautious approach in Europe influenced the company's business strategy. By proactively adjusting their market focus and capitalizing on opportunities in less affected regions, Agrivi effectively navigated the challenges posed by the global resource supply crisis while sustaining its growth trajectory.

In conclusion, Agrivi exemplifies the essence of a hidden champion in the digital agriculture industry. Defined by Hermann Simon, hidden champions are niche market leaders, often unknown to the wider public but integral to global markets and innovation. Agrivi's global presence, robust export activities, and focused approach to modern agriculture solidify its hidden champion status. Under visionary leadership, Agrivi has pursued technological advancements and strategically navigated market dynamics to lead in the agro-tech sector. The company's commitment to empowering farmers with innovative digital solutions aligns with hidden champions' traits of dominating their segments and driving advancements behind the scenes. Agrivi's ability to adapt swiftly to changing conditions, such as the COVID-19 pandemic and global resource crises, underscores its agility and market influence. By maintaining a customer-centric approach and prioritizing sustainable agricultural practices, Agrivi continues to lead the industry, reflecting the hidden champion's focus on long-term performance over short-term visibility.

3.2 Case Study 2[3]

3.2.1 Farseer

Overview
Address: Bosanska 3, 10 000 Zagreb, Croatia
Tel: +385 99 448 6924
Fax: -
Email: info@farseer.io
Web: https://www.farseer.io/

Company Information
Industry[4]: 62.01 Computer programming activities
Year of Establishment: 2021
Sales Revenues in 2021: 87 thousand EUR
Sales Revenues in 2023: 954 thousand EUR
Average number of employees in 2023: 16
Brainers behind the company: Founders Matija Nakić, Luka Mijatović, Matej Trbara, and Zrinko Dolić

Nature of Market Leadership

Despite its current global market share being below 1%, Farseer is well-positioned for growth and poised to challenge the dominance of established players like Oracle, who command approximately 25% of the market share. With 9.6% of regional market—of former Yugoslavia countries—Farseer is among five top competitors (Oracle, IBM, and SAP). Farseer stands out in the market through its cutting-edge technological solutions and a strong commitment to customer-centricity, distinguishing itself from its competitors. This strategic approach not only

[3] Interviews, analysis, and description of the case were conducted by Mislav Ante Omazić and Patricia Uroić.

[4] *According to NACE Rev. 2*

positions the company for robust competitive advantage but also sets a solid groundwork for sustained growth and innovation in the future. Farseer is poised to reshape the financial planning and analysis market (FP&A) by continually innovating and aligning with industry trends. The company focuses on exceptional customer support and effective implementation strategies to cultivate strong client relationships and position itself as a trusted business growth partner. As Farseer expands its market presence and diversifies its product portfolio, it not only aims to serve a wider array of industries but also to tap into new revenue streams. Additionally, Farseer is strategically partnering with complementary technology providers and data sources, enhancing the value of its solutions and creating a more integrated analytics ecosystem for its clients. These efforts collectively strengthen Farseer's potential to emerge as a significant industry player and redefine the landscape of data analytics.

Through these initiatives, Farseer aims to steadily increase its market share and establish itself as a formidable player in the data analytics industry. As the demand for data-driven insights continues to grow, Farseer's strategic investments and commitment to innovation position it for long-term success and leadership in the ever-evolving data analytics landscape.

Nature of Competitive Advantage

In recent years, the industry has witnessed the emergence of the third generation of planning solutions, exemplified by Farseer. These solutions are exclusively cloud-based, offering expedited implementation processes and enhanced user experiences. Unlike their predecessors, third-generation solutions prioritize flexibility, user-friendliness, and adaptability to diverse business needs. Farseer's competitive advantage is further amplified with a high-level of user autonomy. Through a customer-centric approach, Farseer collaborates closely with organizations to understand their unique challenges and goals, tailoring models and processes accordingly. This personalized approach ensures that Farseer's highly relevant and impactful solutions enable businesses to extract maximum value from their data assets. With their AI expertise, advanced algorithms, and focus on customization, Farseer stands out as a trusted partner for businesses seeking to leverage the power of data analytics to drive growth and success in the competitive digital landscape. Due to all the aforementioned, Farseer has been included in the list of the best global third-generation FP&A solutions for two consecutive years (2022 and 2023). This list is compiled by the Business Partnering Institute in collaboration with some of the most influential figures in the FP&A domain.

Core Lessons Learned on the Path to Success

For Farseer, core lessons learned on the path to success can be summarized as:

- Trust in your vision: Farseer's journey demonstrates the power of self-trust, showing how a startup can successfully compete with industry giants like SAP, Oracle, and IBM by validating its potential through significant victories.
- Leverage innovation: Farseer's success is built on embracing cutting-edge technologies in AI, advanced algorithms, and data analytics, enabling the company to deliver groundbreaking solutions that secure a competitive edge.
- Prioritize customer needs: Farseer's customer-centric approach, focusing on understanding and addressing clients' unique requirements, has been crucial in establishing trust and building long-term relationships.
- Commit to continuous improvement: Farseer emphasizes ongoing research and development, along with strategic partnerships, ensuring their solutions remain cutting-edge and highly effective in the rapidly evolving digital landscape.

Management and Leadership Development Needs

In the company, one of the underdeveloped skills is the ability to generate SaaS (Software as a Service) demand and conduct sales on a larger scale. This is mainly due to the limited presence of established SaaS companies in Croatia, which requires more experienced professionals in these specific roles. To address this challenge, Farseer can proactively foster an internal SaaS expertise hub, creating a knowledge-sharing platform or community where employees can exchange insights, best practices, and industry trends related to SaaS demand generation and sales. This collaborative environment would empower employees to learn from one another and collectively develop their skills in these areas.

Farseer can cultivate external partnerships and collaborations to overcome the scarcity of experienced professionals. By partnering with established SaaS companies outside of Croatia, Farseer can tap into their expertise and gain valuable insights into demand generation and sales strategies. Collaborating with industry leaders could provide access to mentorship, training opportunities, and exposure to successful SaaS sales methodologies, enabling the company to scale its sales efforts more effectively. Continuous education is essential for all Farseer employees, with a collective commitment to self-improvement, emphasizing constant innovation and returning to work with enhanced knowledge. While there are no dedicated SaaS universities, individuals are advised to pursue technical disciplines like computer science, mathematics, or physics, and gain practical experience by working for startups in areas such as product development, sales, or marketing. Saastr.com is recommended for comprehensive insights into the SaaS industry.

By fostering an internal SaaS expertise hub, cultivating external partnerships, and promoting continuous education, Farseer can address the skills gap in SaaS demand generation and sales, strengthening its capabilities in these areas and positioning itself for growth in the evolving software industry.

Financing and Regulatory Environment Development Needs

Farseer operates as a Venture Capital-Backed entity. With a strategic roadmap that includes a planned series A funding round in 2025, following a successful seed round in 2023, the company is poised for the next phase of growth and advancement. However, Farseer recognizes that its development needs in terms of financing extend beyond the series A funding round. To sustain momentum, the company may explore additional avenues for capital infusion, such as strategic partnerships or debt financing, to drive further expansion and innovation. Furthermore, Farseer acknowledges the criticality of navigating the regulatory environment. By prioritizing up-to-date knowledge and compliance with evolving regulations on data privacy, cybersecurity, and industry-specific standards, Farseer aims to uphold trust, safeguard against potential risks, and ensure long-term success in its operations.

Farseer: The Hidden Champion

Farseer stands out as a leading data analytics company due to their expertise in developing advanced algorithms and leveraging machine learning techniques. Their intelligent and flexible solutions enable businesses to transform raw data into valuable insights, empowering decision-makers to make informed choices. By incorporating cutting-edge technologies such as natural language processing and computer vision, Farseer enhances the capabilities of organizations to extract meaningful patterns and trends from complex data sets. With their commitment to helping businesses thrive in the digital era, Farseer plays a pivotal role in enabling companies to stay ahead of the competition and drive sustainable growth.

The company's success can be attributed to several key leadership factors demonstrated by its founders. Their visionary mindset provides a clear and compelling vision of the future, effectively communicated to inspire and align the organization toward a shared purpose. The founders have cultivated a strong company culture, building a dedicated team that views the company as their own and works collaboratively to achieve its goals. This environment fosters high productivity and swift delivery of innovations. Additionally, the founders instill a sense of urgency and drive, ensuring rapid progress despite being a young player in the industry. They emphasize staying ahead by leveraging the latest technologies, enhancing user experience, and positioning the company as an innovator. In summary, the company's success stems from the founders' visionary mindset, strong company culture, relentless focus on execution, and commitment to cutting-edge technologies, driving continued growth and success.

Farseer recognizes the crucial relationship between product excellence and effective distribution. The company embraces continuous innovation, following Zuckerberg's mantra, "Move fast and break things." While maintaining agility, Farseer understands the enterprise software industry's demands and emphasizes enhancing user experience. Farseer is dedicated to exploring efficient distribution methods aligned with product development goals. The vision is to provide a high-quality solution for modeling complex enterprise planning scenarios, including seamless onboarding for industry giants like General Electric. Farseer aims to simplify the process, empowering users to create custom models and control panels, solidifying their market leadership. Recognizing the significance of strong partnerships, Farseer collaborates with technology resellers and implementation consultants to reach a broader customer base. By combining product excellence, continuous innovation, and efficient distribution, Farseer offers a seamless experience, enabling users to navigate complex enterprise planning scenarios with ease and confidence.

During Farseer's early stages, the COVID-19 pandemic posed significant challenges, particularly in acquiring users for meetings. Despite these disruptions, the pandemic's impact on the company was relatively mild. Over the past 3 to 3.5 years, it has become evident that Excel is inadequate for rapid business changes. Manual processes in Excel are time-consuming, taking weeks for tasks like what-if simulations and product additions. Additionally, the exponential growth in data has surpassed human resources' capacity for data management and analysis, fueling the rise of automation and platforms like Farseer, which prioritize leveraging data as a strategic asset. By adapting to crises, including the war in Ukraine, Farseer positioned itself for growth. The resource crisis increased demand for Farseer's services as businesses sought efficient planning and analysis tools. This crisis also accelerated the adoption of cloud-based solutions. Farseer's cloud-only platform provided businesses with flexibility, scalability, and accessibility, enabling deeper visibility into resource utilization and informed decision-making.

Farseer epitomizes a "Hidden Champion" by carving out a niche in enterprise software with innovative financial planning and analysis tools. Leveraging technological expertise and a customer-centric approach, Farseer anticipates business needs and adapts to market dynamics. Its specialized solutions, including enhanced data analytics and cloud-only platforms, appeal to startups and smaller businesses. By ensuring accessibility and inclusivity, Farseer solidifies its market position and expands its industry influence. As Farseer continues to innovate and pursue sustainable growth, it embodies the spirit of a "Hidden Champion," mastering its niche and setting new standards in business process digitalization and automation.

3.3 *Case Study 3*[5]

3.3.1 ORQA Ltd.

Overview

Address: J.J. Strossmayera 341, HR-31000 Osijek, Croatia
Tel: +385 98 9153798
E-mail: info@orqafpv.com
Web: www.orqafpv.com

[5] Interviews, analysis, and description of the case were conducted by Slavica Singer and Sunčica Oberman Peterka.

Company Information
Industry[6]: 26.12 Electronics boards manufacturing and R&D
Year of Establishment: 2018
Sales Revenues in 2018: 170,553 EUR
Sales Revenues in 2023: 6.5 m EUR
Average number of employees in 2023: 60
Brainers behind the company: Ivan Jelušić, CSO; Srđan Kovačević, CEO; Vlatko Matijević CTO; Anthony Cake, CTIO

Nature of Market Leadership

In a very short time, ORQA positioned itself as a global market leader in a tiny, highly technical but fragmented niche of products based on FPV technology. ORQA is one of few companies in the world (outside of Asia) that owns the entire technology stack required to implement a quadcopter FPV drone system. Whereas most of ORQA's competitors are focusing on higher-level integration, claiming the core set of drone technologies is (or soon will be) commoditized, ORQA has been pursuing the first-principles approach to building every critical component in the drone technology stack. ORQA has 7% market share in global FPV headsets market (2023) and is positioned among top five globally, or as Top one among non-china brands. Their biggest competitors are Chinese companies DJI, Skyzone, iFlight.

Nature of Competitive Advantage

ORQA competitive advantage is based on its products' portfolio which includes development and manufacturing of video headsets for drone pilots, remote controller units, drones, flight controllers, motor power management systems (ESCs), command and control solutions, ultra-low-latency video streaming solutions, remote vision systems, immersive headsets, and private 5G infrastructure solutions for low-latency video. ORQA is the only company outside of Asia that has vertically integrated portfolio of mission critical components for FPV quadcopter drones. With 80 products in portfolio and markets in 50 countries globally, ORQA produced and sold tens of thousands of units of their products by end of 2023.

Core Lessons Learned on the Path to Success

For ORQA, core lessons learned on the path to success can be summarized as:

- Innovation is key: Constantly strive to innovate and stay ahead of the curve in the rapidly evolving field of drone technology to meet the changing needs of the market and maintain a competitive edge.

[6] *According to NACE Rev. 2*

- Quality is paramount: Delivering high-quality components that meet or exceed industry standards is crucial for building trust with customers and establishing a strong reputation in the drone industry.
- Collaboration breeds success: Foster strong partnerships and collaborations with other industry leaders, drone manufacturers, and research institutions to leverage collective expertise and drive innovation.
- Customer-centric approach: Understand and anticipate the needs of drone manufacturers and operators, providing them with tailored solutions, excellent customer service, and ongoing support to build long-term relationships.

Management and Leadership Development Needs

Regarding management and leadership, ORQA identifies its development needs in the field of adding soft skills (e.g., communication skills, team work) to people involved in management as well to engineers who are core human resources in the company. Other important missing knowledge is understanding how to implement holistic approach, i.e., how to combine different technical knowledge with design, organization of production process, marketing and finance. Systematic workforce development is a major factor of keeping ORQA to be long-term competitive.

Financing and Regulatory Environment Development Needs

ORQA considers tax reliefs as a good mechanism to support growth of businesses, especially those with high growth potential. Regulatory environment supporting investments in R&D in order to keep innovative edge for companies with significant export potential would make ORQA's businesses even more competitive on a global stage.

ORQA—Team Visioning Pays off

ORQA was established in 2018 by three entrepreneurs, engineers by education, with the goal to make high performance FPV products for global drone racing community. The company evolved from making FPV headsets in early years, to having vertically integrated design, engineering, manufacturing and assembly line for more than 80 products. ORQA is on the mission to build complete value chain of drone hardware components Made in EU.

Main leadership factors which contributed to ORQA's success is a strong vision based on good knowledge of changes in technology and customers' needs, accompanied with a very effective communication skills and business integrity. ORQA's leadership culture is based on understanding that successful leaders have a clear and inspiring vision for their organizations. The process of envisioning involves the whole team, creating a sense of purpose and direction that motivates and aligns everyone toward common goals. The leading team of ORQA strongly believes that effective communication skills are vital for leaders. They must be able to convey their vision, expectations, and ideas clearly and concisely, while also actively listening to their team members and fostering open and transparent communication channels. ORQA learned that leaders who demonstrate honesty, transparency, and ethical behavior earn the trust and respect of their team. Maintaining high standards of integrity helps establish a positive work culture and fosters strong relationships with employees, stakeholders, and customers.

In the line of such organizational culture, ORQA is implementing a unique human resources approach where the majority of employees are company shareholders (around 80%—after some period of being employed, employees get the option to participate in Employee Option Pool) that helps company to keep very stable employee structure with minimal churn.

As main drivers of the company's success ORQA considers continuous improvement (innovation, quality), strong supply chain management (collaboration), high adaptability, and quick decision-making which contributes to fast reaction on changes in customers' needs. It was successfully exercised during the COVID-19 pandemic when ORQA experienced some problems in keeping work dynamics as it used to be. Their reaction was in introducing remote work, focus on supply chain management, optimization and digitalization. ORQA's experience showed that remote work significantly reduced productivity and introduced enormous need for online meetings to coordinate business activities. They quickly abandoned remote work mode and provided on-site working environment in the line of COVID-19 pandemic protection requirements, what paid off by bringing productivity up again.

The main current business challenge for ORQA is to establish credibility as a brand in new markets, outside of B2C market, especially in B2G and B2B markets. Introducing FPV drones and components for professionals (like police, fireworkers, security) as well for military usage made ORQA competitive on those markets, traditionally ruled by much bigger companies. Despite of high commitment of the work force to the company's vision and goals, ORQA expects that the main future business challenge will be how to keep top talents. There are more companies entering hardware R&D space and drone segment due to its growing specter of functionalities which will eventually lead to a more competitive environment for top talents. Based on ORQA's experience in working mostly with engineers, they strongly recommend to educational institutions to adopt experiential learning process (using project-based approach).

Having in mind global decoupling from Asian supply chains, ORQA's unique position as a Made in EU business is additionally contributing to the company's competitiveness due to recent economic and political geo context.

Ukraine war did not influence directly ORQA's business activities, but had a crucial impact on business strategy and the market ORQA is operating in. Before the Ukraine war, FPV drones and components were exclusive to hobby and consumer clients. Beginning of the war in Ukraine actually made this market dual-use by adding professional (military) users.

Combination of excellent engineering talent, great quality of products and low labor costs makes ORQA very competitive even toward Chinese costs of production, something that is difficult to achieve in Western countries and economies. With that in mind, it is likely that Central Eastern Europe could become an industrial base for developed countries, with ORQA leading the game in drone systems and components industry. In achieving this an effective collaboration with education system is crucial.

3.4 *Case Study 4*[7]

3.4.1 RASCO Ltd.

Overview
Address: Kolodvorska 120 b, HR-48361 Kalinovac Croatia
Tel: +385 48 883 112
Fax: +385 48 280 146
Email: rasco@rasco.hr
Web: https://rasco.hr/en/

Company Information
Industry[8]: 28.30 Manufacturing (production of equipment for the maintenance of traffic infrastructures)
Year of Establishment: 1990
Sales Revenues in 2017: 14,1 m EUR
Sales Revenues in 2023: 32,7 m EUR
Average number of employees in 2023: 345
Brainers behind the company: 3 Board members: Ivan Franičević, Ružica Petričec Fabijanec, and Mario Štefanec

Nature of Market Leadership

The market leadership evolved from continuous products' portfolio growth and market expansion. Portfolio of products broadened to 70 product lines in 2023 from 17 in 2010, and the market expanded to 43 countries, from 13 in 2010. RASCO is global number four in the industry niche of producing the communal equipment for winter and summer maintaining traffic infrastructure. On some markets the company is a market leader, for example in Norway, Ukraine, as well as in Central and Eastern Europe. Estimated market share of RASCO is 10% (in 2022) compared to 20% and 25% for their two largest competitors. In the observed period, RASCO's

[7] Interviews, analysis, and description of the case were conducted by Slavica Singer.
[8] *According to NACE Rev. 2*

market share doubled due to geographic market expansion, what resulted in more than tripled export.

Nature of Competitive Advantage

The nature or competitive advantage is continuously rooted in strong technological advancement and strong R&D investments. It resulted in leading positions on many markets and reduced the number of relevant competitors both on markets in Europe (four) as well as in North America (three). The technological shift to more advanced products for markets in western Europe is recently more emphasized, which is what resulted in increasing the share or RASCO on this market.

Core Lessons Learned on the Path to Success

For RASCO core lessons learned on the path to success can be summarized as:

- Strong and continuous technological advancement based on strong R&D investments contributes to production of high-quality products.
- Consistent long-term strategy implemented in phases.
- The competitive advantage of the company is based on the continuous improvement of the functionality of the product and simplicity in the production of machines which provides robustness in using and easiness in servicing them.
- Openness to changes, e.g., of further improvement of digital marketing.

Management and Leadership Development Needs

Regarding management and leadership, RASCO identified its development needs in the field of middle management and sales and customer services. The process of growing required changes in organizational structure, which opened the question of middle management and how to acquire people with such skills. Middle managers are supposed to have a deep understanding of operational processes, and to have management skills. The RASCO's growth depends on broadening portfolio of products and portfolio of markets, what requires upgraded knowledge related to sales and customer services based on deep understanding of product complexity and potential of customization. Based on its experience in managing the process of growth, RASCO will continue to invest in knowledge and skills of its employees, by offering training on the job inside the company and through collaboration with vocational educational institutions. For example, RASCO financially supports education of its present and future employees in different higher education institutions, like departments of electrical engineering and computing, or mechanical engineering at the University of Zagreb.

Financing and Regulatory Environment Development Needs

Keeping steady and un-interrupted manufacturing process requires significant levels of working capital, what position RASCO as a user of short-term financing. Therefore, attractive rates for short-term financing is an important development need for the company. In order to keep its competitive position on international markets, RASCO pleads for reducing tax and administrative burdens. By doing this, the government would free a significant amount of company's capital to be invested in innovative products and new markets.

RASCO

From two entrepreneurial engineers to an internationally recognized company,

RASCO emerged from a small craft business established in 1990 by two enthusiastic engineers, Frane Franičević and Darko Paviša. They identified a need for repairing and servicing agricultural mechanization, and started with their activities in a small, adapted space of 60 m^2. The company kept their basic business but expanded into manufacturing of own developed professional equipment for maintenance of traffic infrastructure, with strong aftersales support. In 1989, the founders withdraw from the leading roles in the company, but organizational culture based on innovativeness continued. RASCO's products portfolio results from dedicated continuous investments in developing new products or innovative improvements of the existing ones. Competitive advantage and worldwide presence have been achieved with advanced solutions for maintaining urban and suburban infrastructure, highways, mountain roads, airports and waterways (sweeping, de-icing, snow clearing, mowing, and washing). The leading idea was simplicity, effectiveness and ease of maintenance, what became a part of RASCO's organizational culture.

During the COVID-19 pandemic, RASCO experienced severe supply chain issues, on which the management responded by developing new supply modes: closer collaboration with suppliers, finding alternative suppliers and offshoring (in 2020 and 2021). The war in Ukraine additionally disrupted some supply chains. Both resource crisis changed numerous internal and supplier-facing processes, but the most important feature of it was strengthening a proactive approach in dealing with supply chain issues.

In RASCO, organizational culture based on personal initiative and responsibility, teamwork, productivity and quality are continuously supported with investments in human resource development. Due to its location (outside of major cities) and its highly technological profile, RASCO always paid attention how to attract specialized personnel in metal industry, what includes investment in education of own future employees. For that purpose, RASCO is participating in on-job training of vocational students (yearly, up to 50 vocational students). Such strategic approach toward human resources and organizational culture contributed that RASCO does not have problems with shortage of high-quality and committed human resources, what is linked to the capacity of RASCO to reach and maintain leadership position in their market niche, expressed through:

- Extreme focus on customer needs.
- Quick product improvement based on customer feedback.
- High speed in aftersales support, crucial given that functionality of RASCO's products is critical for customers.
- High investment in development of new products (2017 to 2023 over 10 m EUR in R&D).

Customer-centered policy, especially featured through aftersales support, requires that all RASCO distributors can respond to all customer needs and enquiries as quickly and efficiently as possible. To achieve it RASCO Academy offers training programs (sales training, user training and service training) based on examples from the usage of RASCO products. Such RASCO's customer-centered and innovation culture contributes to the company's competitiveness and profitability, but at the same time keeps company alert on business challenges, current and future ones. The current business challenges are:

- Supply chain—how to provide quality and stability along the chain.
- Talent availability (need for people with specific knowledge and skills required by new technology, robotized and digitalized—high demand for such skilled human resources not only in Croatia).

As future businesses challenges (in next five–ten years) RASCO expects to deal with opportunities emerging from climate change but as well to continue to struggle with talent availability.

Analyzing RASCO business history it is important to emphasize leadership factors which contributed to the company's success:

- Continuity of leadership—the vision of two founders and owners (Darko Paviša and Frane Franičević) was successfully continued with needed adjustments when they withdraw from the operational management. They still participate in the strategic discussions and follow on implementation results.
- Entrepreneurial organizational culture (innovative contributions by all, personal responsibility, teamwork) has a strong impact on the company's success.

Based on its experience in managing the process of growth from 1990, RASCO has two messages, one to educational institutions, other to the regulatory authorities. The most important message for educational institutions is to reconsider enrolment policy in order to avoid situation of shortage of expertise, e.g., in STEM areas. Additionally, educational institutions should focus on providing students with interpersonal and communications skills, team work, decision-making skills, diagnostic and analytical skills, conceptual skills. The message to regulatory authorities is related to reducing tax and regulatory burdens.

4 Conclusions and Recommendations

The research findings on Croatian HC companies in 2023 closely mirror those identified in 2021, confirming the validity of the recognized patterns of characteristics, needs, and the business environment in which HC companies operate. It is positive that innovativeness remains a constant feature of Croatian HC companies. However, the stability in needs and the persistence of identified obstacles in the business environment suggest these issues have not been resolved, raising the question of why this is the case.

From the analysis of eight case studies, four of which are presented in this chapter, several conclusions on the distinctive characteristics of their business models, which contribute to their exceptional performance and market dominance, as well as on the companies' needs and aspects of their business environment, emerge.

The most distinctive characteristic of Croatian HCs is a strong emphasis on innovation and continuous improvement, investing significantly in research and development to stay ahead of competitors. They successfully implemented innovative risk management approaches during COVID-19, addressing supply chain gaps, redesigning organizational procedures, and finding new solutions for markets lost due to the war in Ukraine. These companies predominantly operate in niche markets, achieving and maintaining leadership by offering highly specialized products and services. They leverage international markets to achieve growth and mitigate local market risks. Close relationships with customers allow HCs to tailor their offerings precisely to customer needs and foster strong loyalty. Additionally, HCs typically operate with a long-term perspective, prioritizing sustainable growth over short-term profits.

Regarding their needs, HCs require highly skilled employees with specific technical and managerial competencies to sustain their innovative edge. All interviewed companies expressed the need for additional training for management positions, project managers, and marketing and selling personnel in fields such as communication skills, teamwork, and selling skills. Using the concept of entrepreneurial competencies (Bacigalupo et al., 2016), which combines three groups of skills and knowledge (ideas and opportunities, resources, into action), it is clear that having only the skills to innovate is insufficient. This situation calls for higher education institutions to introduce education for entrepreneurial competencies across campuses, providing all students, regardless of discipline, with access to programs that contribute to their ability to transform innovative capacity into commercial actions. Adequate financing is essential for HCs to invest in R&D, expand globally, and upgrade their technological infrastructure. Furthermore, a stable and supportive regulatory framework is critical, enabling innovation and easing international trade barriers.

The business environment for HCs involves rapid technological changes, posing both opportunities and challenges, necessitating continuous investments to maintain leadership and adapt quickly. HCs face intense competition from both established players and new entrants, requiring constant vigilance and strategic agility. The educational systems are not providing adequate knowledge and skills related to entrepreneurial competencies. High-growth companies like hidden champions require access to appropriate types of capital (risk/venture capital), which is identified as a serious obstacle. Additionally, regulatory obstacles still limit the capacity of the business environment to fully support high-growth businesses.

Based on these conclusions, several recommendations are suggested for HC companies and selected actors in the business environment. HC companies, or those small businesses with ambitions to become HCs, should consider the business model which will guarantee a balance between operational and strategic focus and enable quick identification and closing gaps in knowledge and skills.

The government should develop and maintain a regulatory environment that supports innovation, reduces bureaucratic hurdles, and facilitates international trade. Investment in education systems that produce a skilled workforce tailored to the needs of businesses with growth potential, focusing on STEM fields, entrepreneurial competencies, and vocational training, is essential. Providing tax incentives, grants, and subsidies for R&D activities to encourage continuous innovation and technological advancement is crucial. Additionally, improving infrastructure, including digital infrastructure, is necessary to support the efficient operation and growth of HCs.

Financial institutions should develop financial products and services that cater specifically to the needs of businesses with growth potential, such as flexible loans, equity financing, and risk management solutions. Offering long-term financing options that align with the strategic horizons of businesses with growth potential enables sustained investment in innovation and global expansion. Providing specialized advisory services to help businesses with growth potential navigate financial challenges, optimize their capital structure, and enhance their financial strategies is important. Establishing venture capital funds or innovation hubs that focus on supporting HCs with high-growth potential and innovative business models is also recommended.

Higher education institutions should depart from traditional curriculum design and offer programs aligned with the specific needs of businesses with growth potential, based on the concept of relevant knowledge (OECD, 2019) and problem-based learning process. Fostering partnerships between academia and industry to facilitate practical learning experiences, internships, and research collaborations that benefit both learners and businesses with growth potential is essential. Providing executive education programs aimed at developing the leadership skills of HC managers and executives, focusing on strategic management, global market expansion, and innovation, is also important. Conducting and disseminating research on best practices, emerging trends, and challenges faced by businesses with growth potential can provide valuable insights that inform their strategic decisions.

By implementing these recommendations, businesses, governments, financial institutions, and higher education institutions can create a supportive ecosystem that enables businesses with growth potential, or Hidden Champions, to thrive and sustain their competitive edge in the global market.

References

Bacigalupo, M., Kampylis, P., Punie, Y., & Van den Brande, G. (2016). EntreComp: The entrepreneurship competence framework (EUR 27939 EN). *Publications Office of the European Union*. doi:https://doi.org/10.2791/593884

Berberović, D., Činjarević, M., & Kožo, A. (2019). Success despite lack of support: Lessons learned from hidden champions doing business in fragile business environments. *Sarajevo Business and Economics Review, 37*, 192–204.

Braček Lalić, A., & Purg, D. (Eds.). (2021). *Hidden champions in dynamically changing societies: Critical success factors for market leadership*. Springer Nature Switzerland. https://doi.org/10.1007/978-3-030-65451-1

Croatia.eu. (n.d.). Yugoslavia and World War II (1918–1990). *Croatia.eu.–online historical guide featured on the site Croatia.eu—Land and People, under its "History" section–The Miroslav Krleža Institute of Lexicography*. https://www.croatia.eu/index.php/en/home-en/history/yugoslavia-and-world-war-ii

European Commission (2023). Regional Innovation Scoreboard (2023), *Regional Profiles Croatia*, https://ec.europa.eu/assets/rtd/ris/2023/ec_rtd_ris-regional-profiles-croatia.pdf

McKiernan, P., & Purg, D. (Eds.). (2013). *Hidden champions in CEE and Turkey: Carving out a global niche* (Vol. 1). Springer. https://doi.org/10.1007/978-3-642-40504-4

OECD. (2019). Future of education and skills 2030: Concept note. *OECD Publishing*. https://www.oecd.org/content/dam/oecd/en/about/projects/edu/education-2040/1-1-learning-compass/OECD_Learning_Compass_2030_Concept_Note_Series.pdf

OECD. (2024). Towards balanced regional development in Croatia: From strategy design to implementation (OECD Multi-level Governance Studies). *OECD Publishing*. https://doi.org/10.1787/3c0779cf-en

World Bank. (2023). Human capital country brief: Croatia, October. *The World Bank*. https://thedocs.worldbank.org/en/doc/64e578cbeaa522631f08f0cafba8960e-0140062023/related/HCI-AM23-HRV.pdf

Slavica Singer is Professor Emerita at the Josip Juraj Strossmayer University of Osijek, Croatia (Faculty of Economics and Business). UNESCO recognized her academic and professional contribution in developing education for entrepreneurial competences, and from 2008 she is a holder of the UNESCO Chair in Entrepreneurship Education.

Slavica's research focus is on connecting holistic approach with understanding of entrepreneurship as a mindset, the role of small businesses in the economic development, gender gap in entrepreneurship, entrepreneurship ecosystem and the role of the entrepreneurial university in the Quintuple Helix model (academia, government, business, civil society and environment).

From 2010 she leads the interdisciplinary doctoral program ENTREPRENEURSHIP AND INNOVATIVENESS designed by collaborative efforts of five universities (Osijek, Croatia; Turku, Finland; Maribor, Slovenia; Klagenfurt, Austria and Durham, UK). Next to students from Croatia, there are doctoral students from Bosnia and Herzegovina, Canada, China, Germany, Ghana, Greece, Kosovo, Nigeria, Oman, Pakistan, Spain, USA.

Slavica participates as guest speaker or panelist on numerous international conferences, and she is very active in researching different perspectives of entrepreneurship in international research teams, funded by EU funding schemes. She initiated participation of Croatia in Global Entrepreneurship Monitor (GEM) and from 2002 she leads the Croatian GEM team. Slavica is often engaged by the OECD as a consultant/expert in the field of reviewing national policies on entrepreneurship, inclusivity and entrepreneurship education. In 2010 she was awarded with the honorary doctorate by the University of Turku, Turku School of Economics. In 2021, she was awarded with the European Entrepreneurship Education Award, by the Lund University (School of Economics and Management), Sweden.

Sunčica Oberman Peterka is a full professor at the Josip Juraj Strossmayer University of Osijek, Faculty of Economics and Business, where she teaches courses in entrepreneurship and strategy at the undergraduate, graduate, and postgraduate levels. She is also a member of the UNESCO Chair in Entrepreneurship Education, Before joining the University, she was a project manager, trainer, and consultant at the Osijek Centre for Entrepreneurship, and she currently serves as a member of its Assembly.

She has been a member of the Global Entrepreneurship Monitor (GEM) research team for Croatia since 2002 and is also part of the research team of the CEPOR–policy center for small and medium-sized enterprises and entrepreneurship. She is a member of the European Council for Small Businesses and Entrepreneurship (ECSB), the Croatian Society of Economists and Croatian Corporate Governance and Management Society.

Sunčica Oberman Peterka has participated in numerous EU-funded projects related to entrepreneurship and entrepreneurial education, and regularly conducts workshops and lectures on these topics. She has also participated in multiple accreditation processes organized by the Agency for Science and Higher Education of the Republic of Croatia.

Her areas of interest include entrepreneurship education, entrepreneurial universities, authentic leadership, new venture creation, small business management, gender and entrepreneurship, and the quality of higher education.

Mislav Ante Omazić is a Full Professor of Management at University of Zagreb, Faculty of Economics and Business, and currently serves as President of the Management Board at IEDC-Bled School of Management. With over two decades of academic experience, he holds a PhD in business with a focus on corporate social responsibility, change management, leadership and business strategy.

Professor Omazić has taught extensively at undergraduate, graduate, postgraduate, and doctoral levels. He has developed and led a wide range of courses, including Strategic Change Management, Leadership, Business Ethics, Corporate Social Responsibility, and Project Management. His teaching has consistently received the highest student evaluations.

He has mentored over 350 theses, including doctoral dissertations, and is deeply engaged in curriculum development and pedagogical innovation. As an active scholar, he has authored numerous peer-reviewed publications and participated in leading national and EU-funded research projects, particularly in the fields of sustainability, digital transformation, and social innovation in higher education.

His international academic footprint includes training and collaboration with institutions such as INSEAD, Case Western Reserve University, and IEDC-Bled. He is also a contributor to prominent initiatives like the Hidden Champions project and serves on editorial boards of international academic journals. His dual roles in academia and management education leadership reflect a deep commitment to bridging theory and practice on a global scale.

Patricia Uroić mag. oec., works as a teaching and research assistant at the University of Zagreb, Department of Organization and Management at the Faculty of Economics and Business. She is involved in teaching courses in the areas of management, leadership, business ethics, change management and corporate social responsibility, both in Croatian and in English, as part of undergraduate and graduate study programs.

Her professional interests include sustainable business practices, leadership development, and the role of ethics in organizational settings. She participates in international and national research projects, most notably the Hidden Champions project, where she has co-authored several case studies focused on successful, export-oriented companies. Her work has been published in academic journals and edited volumes, dealing with topics such as sustainable development, blockchain technology, and transformative learning.

In addition to her teaching and research activities, she has contributed to the organization of various professional and scientific events, such as the fintech conference Money Motion and the World Skills Croatia competition. She is also a co-author of several textbooks and workbooks used in secondary schools and higher education.

She has received several recognitions for her work, including an award for excellence in seminar teaching and a commendation from the Ministry of Science and Education for her contribution to the development of the education system.

Hidden Champions of Estonia

Meelis Kitsing

Abstract The Estonian business ecosystem has fostered the creation of 10 technology unicorns and numerous startups. By integrating the concept of hidden champions with empirical evidence on innovative Estonian companies, this chapter examines the cases of Milrem, Starship Technologies, and Ready Player Me. Each of these companies has established global market niches that did not exist a decade ago. These hidden technology champions have pushed industry boundaries by combining high-end manufacturing with services, as seen in the cases of Milrem and Starship Technologies. Additionally, they have integrated the business-to-business and business-to-consumer segments, exemplified by Starship Technologies and Ready Player Me. The broader business ecosystem has been a key enabler of these innovative business models. To provide a deeper understanding of the evolution of Estonia's business environment, this chapter highlights major economic reforms of recent decades and essential components of the current ecosystem. The final section presents key lessons drawn from the Estonian experience.

Overview
Official name: Republic of Estonia
Type of government: unitary parliamentary republic
Population in 2022: 1348, 80
Land area: 45,340 sq. km

History

1918	Estonian Declaration of Independence.
1918–2020	Estonian War of Independence.
1920	Treaty of Tartu establishes peace with the Soviet Russia.
1940	Unlawful incorporation of Estonia into the Soviet Union.
1941	Occupation by the Nazi Germany.

M. Kitsing (✉)
Estonian Business School, Tallinn, Estonia
e-mail: meelis.kitsing@ebs.ee

D. Berberović, D. Purg (eds.), *Hidden Champions in Rising Economies*, Contributions to Management Science,
https://doi.org/10.1007/978-3-032-08263-3_18

1944	Territory of Estonia is captured by the Red Army. Restoration of Soviet occupation.
1991	The restoration of Estonian independence.
1996	The internet banking is introduced.
2000	The online declaration of taxes becomes possible.
2002	The ID card is introduced.
2004	Estonia joins the EU and NATO.
2005	The first Estonian unicorn is born. Skype is sold to EBay for 2.6 billion US dollars. The first online voting takes place in municipal elections.
2007	The mobile ID is introduced.
2008	Skype is sold to Microsoft for 8.5 billion US dollars.
2011	Estonia joins the eurozone.
2021	The most valuable Estonian unicorn is born. The IPO of Wise at London Stock Exchange values the company at 11 billion US dollars.
2023	Another Estonian unicorn Bolt is valued at 8.4 billion US dollars in the financing round.

1 Introduction: Context and History

The emergence of a vibrant business ecosystem in Estonia can be traced back to reform efforts that have been among the most radical and far-reaching in Central and Eastern Europe (CEE) since the breakup of the Soviet Union. The fight against corruption and the push for increased transparency have been central to the comprehensive reforms carried out by the Estonian government. Over the decades, these reforms have significantly reshaped economic, trade, fiscal, and monetary policies, as well as overall governance, by enforcing the rule of law, enhancing efficiency, and embracing digitalization.

Recent years have been more challenging due to the COVID-19 pandemic, the full-scale war in Ukraine, a rapid increase in consumer prices, and a decline in key export markets, all of which have negatively impacted Estonia's macroeconomic performance. However, Estonia possesses key ingredients to overcome these temporary setbacks. The International Institute for Management Development (IMD) World Competitiveness Booklet (2023) reveals that decades of reform efforts have resulted in high government efficiency, an open business environment, and advanced infrastructure. These developments did not occur overnight but are the result of long-term evolution over the past decades. Understanding this evolution is crucial for explaining the current competitiveness of Estonia's business ecosystem, which has directly contributed to the emergence of hidden technology champions.

Five key reforms were essential for Estonia's transition from a socialist planned economy with a challenging Soviet legacy to one of the most democratic and freest economies in the world:

First, Rule of Law and Privatization—In the 1990s, Estonia implemented the rule of law, securing property rights and enforcing hard budget constraints (Abrams

& Fish, 2015; Laar, 1996). This prevented politically connected individuals from enriching themselves at the expense of taxpayers. As a result, corruption levels in Estonia are the lowest among former Soviet and socialist countries. A credible commitment to the rule of law enabled rapid and large-scale privatization, attracting foreign direct investment. Estonia now has the highest net inflows of FDI per capita in Central and Eastern Europe.

Second, Monetary Policy Reform—Estonia introduced its new currency, the kroon, in 1992, backed by a currency board and pegged to the German mark (later to the euro) (Freytag, 2003). This policy, which lasted until Estonia joined the eurozone in 2011, was implemented despite the International Monetary Fund's recommendation to remain in the ruble zone.

Third, Trade Liberalization—Estonia carried out one of the most extensive trade policy liberalizations in history (Feldmann & Sally, 2001). From 1993 until EU accession in 2004, Estonia unilaterally adopted free trade, including for agricultural goods. This allowed businesses to reorient rapidly toward Western markets. By 2000, only 2% of Estonian exports went to Russia, whereas most trade was conducted with EU countries.

Fourth, Fiscal Policy—Since the early 1990s, Estonia has pursued a conservative and prudent fiscal policy (Feldmann & Sally, 2001; Freytag, 2003). During economic expansions, reserves were built to be used in downturns. Until the COVID-19 pandemic, Estonia's public sector debt-to-GDP ratio remained below 10%. Even after emergency measures, the ratio rose to just 20%, the lowest in the EU. Estonia also introduced a simple, proportional tax system with no corporate income tax on reinvested or undistributed profits. However, recent crises have led to adjustments, including tax increases and more progressive elements in tax policy.

Fifth, Digitalization—Estonia has been at the forefront of digital transformation in both the public and private sectors (European Commission, 2024; Eurostat, 2024; Kitsing, 2017, 2021; Martens, 2010). Internet banking was introduced in 1996, online tax declarations became possible in 2000, and e-voting was implemented in 2005, with nearly half of all votes now cast online in some elections. Estonia has also pioneered e-residency, allowing global citizens to access its digital infrastructure without residing in the country.

The impact of these reforms is evident in Estonia's productivity, price levels, and GDP per capita, which have steadily converged toward the EU average. In 1996, Estonia's per capita GDP and labor productivity per employee were less than 40% of the EU average. By 2014, both indicators had risen to 75% of the EU average (Estonian Government Office, 2016). However, as Estonia has grown wealthier, progress has slowed. While the country's overall per capita GDP remains below the EU average, Tallinn and its surrounding areas exceed 120% of the EU average, whereas other regions remain at about half of that level.

Recent data from the IMD Competitiveness Study reflects negative changes in Estonia's macroeconomic performance. Nevertheless, Estonia improved its ranking from 36th in 2019 to 26th in 2023. Among European countries and nations with populations under 20 million, Estonia ranks 19th. The following table provides an

Exhibit 1 Ranking of Estonia in comparison with selected countries in the IMD Competitiveness Index

Country/Year	2019	2020	2021	2022	2023
Denmark	8	2	3	1	1
Estonia	36	28	26	22	26
Finland	15	13	11	8	11
Latvia	40	41	38	35	51
Lithuania	29	31	30	29	32
Poland	38	39	47	50	43
Sweden	9	6	2	4	8

Source: Composed by the author on the basis of IMD (2023)

overview of Estonia's rankings from 2019 to 2023 and compares them with regional counterparts (Exhibit 1).

Overall, Estonia's performance has been better than that of the other two Baltic states and Poland. However, Nordic countries have outperformed Estonia. The rankings of Finland and Sweden worsened in 2023, as did Estonia's ranking compared to 2022.

The IMD assessment of Estonian government efficiency is particularly strong, with Estonia ranking fifth in business legislation, 14th in public finance, and 17th in institutional framework among the 64 countries studied. There is a direct connection between these rankings and the reforms outlined at the beginning of this chapter. In the societal framework and tax policy categories, Estonia ranked 23rd and 39th, respectively. While taxes in Estonia are not low, the tax base is broad, and tax collection is efficient.

In the infrastructure category of the IMD assessment, Estonia ranked 14th in education, 23rd in health and environment, 27th in technological infrastructure, 34th in basic infrastructure, and 41st in scientific infrastructure. The IMD takes a broad approach to infrastructure, including education and human capital development. Estonia's education system can be considered a form of soft infrastructure, as it has consistently been ranked the best in Europe and one of the best in the world by the OECD PISA study (Mehisto & Kitsing, 2023).

A similarly broad approach to infrastructure was taken by the author while developing scenarios for Estonia's future until 2035 at the Foresight Centre of the Estonian Parliament (Arenguseire Keskus, 2020; Kitsing, 2021). These studies cover digital, energy, and transport infrastructure, as well as both physical and knowledge-based aspects—often referred to as hardware and software. The key issue is not just the availability of technology but also the willingness, capability, and capacity to implement and manage it. This will be discussed in greater detail in the following sections of this chapter, using specific case studies.

Furthermore, infrastructure development is not merely an internal matter for states, communities, and organizations. The networked nature of infrastructure means it extends across national, local, regional, and other borders. Consequently, infrastructure development depends on multiple actors and the ability to ensure collective action. Various levels of collaboration are possible, including global,

EU-wide, or national approaches. The following discussion on hidden champions will illustrate how hidden technology champions have successfully built global networks into their business models.

2 Characteristics of Hidden Champions from Estonia

New business models and hidden champions have been emerging in the Estonian economic environment, even as macroeconomic indicators have shown weak performance in recent years. In this context, necessity could be the mother of both invention and innovation in Estonia.

As Exhibits 2 and 3 illustrate, Gross Domestic Product (GDP) growth declined in 2022, 2023, and 2024. However, GDP growth for 2025 is forecasted to be around 1.7%, with an expected increase to over 2% for the years 2026–2029 (Exhibit 3). Furthermore, Estonia experienced a rapid rise in the Consumer Price Index (CPI) in 2022–2023. The IMD grouped Estonia with other countries classified as "inflation losers" (IMD, 2023, p. 29). According to the IMD study outlined in the previous section, Estonia performed worst in the category of domestic economy, ranking 61st out of 64 countries included in the report. In other categories, Estonia ranked 42nd in employment, 36th in international trade, 35th in international investment, and 32nd in prices.

The low ranking in employment is somewhat unclear, as the unemployment rate has only slightly increased, as shown in Exhibit 2. According to the Estonian Ministry of Finance's forecast (Exhibit 3), the unemployment rate is expected to decline gradually between 2025 and 2028. Exhibit 3 provides an overview of Estonia's key macroeconomic variables for 2023 and forecasts for 2024–2028, suggesting a modest economic recovery. The Estonian CPI is expected to stabilize, GDP growth is projected to return, driven by productivity gains that do not exceed real wage growth, and exports are anticipated to contribute positively starting in 2025. The unemployment rate is also expected to decline gradually.

At the same time, the export of services has increased due to globally competitive technology companies. Estonia has produced 10 unicorns and numerous start-ups, resulting in the highest ratio of unicorns and venture capital investments per capita.

While Estonia does not perform remarkably well in basic and scientific infrastructure, as revealed in the IMD study (2023), the country's education system has provided the necessary skills and knowledge for success in non-R&D innovation. Estonia ranks highly in business efficiency, placing 17th in management practices (IMD, 2023). The ability to manage the transition to a cleaner, greener economy is one of the fundamental challenges for Estonia, where strong management practices can make a significant impact. Estonia also ranks 21st in attitudes and values and 26th in productivity and efficiency (IMD, 2023).

The significance of these broad indicators can be seen in the development of innovative business models, where the skillful combination of existing technologies has led to the emergence of 10 unicorns, including Skype, Wise, Bolt, and Veriff. Many of Estonia's innovative breakthroughs have been knowledge-based process innovations rather than science-based innovations. Instead of developing entirely new technologies, Estonian companies have successfully combined and applied existing technologies in novel ways. In other words, intellectual capital matters more than physical infrastructure.

However, the rapid growth of Estonia's technology sector has not been sufficient to offset the decline in exports from traditional manufacturing industries, which still dominate the country's exports (Exhibits 2 and 3).

Nevertheless, this chapter does not focus on statistically significant trends in the Estonian economy but rather on emerging trends that can be classified as "weak

Exhibit 2 Core Economic Indicators for Estonia

	2018	2019	2020	2021	2022	2023	2024
GDP per capita (current US$)	23,166	23,425	23,595	27,944	28,247	30,133.30	..
GDP per capita growth (annual %)	3.8	3.7	−0.6	8	−1.3	−4.54	..
Long-term unemployment (% of total unemployment)	5.4	4.5	6.8	6.2	5.6	6.38	7.83
Foreign direct investment, net inflows (% of GDP)	4	9.9	12	20.3	4.3	12.96	..
GDP (current US$, billions)	30.92	31.08	31.47	37.19	38.1	41291.25	..
Exports of goods and services (current US$, billion)	22.8	23.0	21.7	29.1	32.6	32148.42	..
Exports of goods and services (% of GDP)	74.3	73.9	69.3	78.3	85.5	77.86	..
Merchandise exports (current US$, billions)	17.0	16.1	16.3	21.5	22.4	19,674	
Merchandise exports to high-income economies (% of total merchandise exports)	84.9	86.3	84.5	N/A	N/A	91.45	..
Merchandise exports to low- and middle-income economies in Europe and Central Asia (% of total merchandise exports)	9.0	9.1	9.0	N/A	N/A	4.87	..
Ores and metals exports (% of merchandise exports)	2.8	2.4	2.1	2.9	2.2	2.14	1.87
Agricultural raw materials exports (% of merchandise exports)	8.1	7.6	7	7.9	7.6	6.59	6.55
Food exports (% of merchandise exports)	9	10.4	10.6	9.1	10.0	11.67	13.61
Fuel exports (% of merchandise exports)						8.41	7.77
Manufactures exports (% of merchandise exports)	70.5	71.1	71.7	69.8	63.9	66.06	64.43
High-technology exports (% of manufactured exports)	18.2	16.9	20.6	20.6	17.7	16.58	..

Source: World Bank, June, 2024

Exhibit 3 Estonian key macroeconomic indicators and forecast in percentages in comparison with the previous year

Indicator/Year	2023	2024	2025	2026	2027	2028
GDP growth	−3.0	−0.3	1.7	2.5	2.2	2.2
Consumer Price Index	9.2	3.4	3.9	3.3	2.4	2.2
Exports (real)	−6.9	−1.1	2.5	3.0	3.0	2.9
Current account balance	−2.1	−1.6	−1.5	−1.6	−1.0	−0.8
Investments	−3.4	−6.7	7.6	1.1	2.0	0.4
Unemployment rate	6.4	7.6	7.1	6.6	6.4	6.3
Growth of real wages	2.1	4.4	0.0	1.7	2.3	2.2
Productivity growth	−5.4	−0.9	1.8	2.0	2.1	2.2
Government sector real growth	0.9	0.3	0.0	2.0	0.0	0.3

Source: composed by the author with the data from Estonian Ministry of Finance (2024–2025)

signals." The rise of technology-intensive companies spans multiple sectors and extends beyond both traditional manufacturing firms and the highly visible 10 technology unicorns. The recovery of Estonia's export industry depends on turning these emerging companies into globally scalable business platforms. Over time, weak signals will become strong signals, and these new businesses will become statistically significant in export and macroeconomic indicators.

To better understand the nature of rapidly emerging technology companies and their market leadership, three semi-structured interviews were conducted. Interviews were held with Jüri Pajuste, Chief Operating Officer of Milrem UAE; Haver Järveoja, Chief Operating Officer of Ready Player Me; and Pepe Aaviksoo, Senior Vice President of Operations at Starship Technologies. These one-hour, in-person interviews took place between June 7 and 11, 2024, in Tallinn, Estonia, and were recorded. The insights from these interviews serve as the primary source of research findings throughout the following sections.

The three hidden technology champions selected for this study—Milrem, Ready Player Me, and Starship Technologies—have all been in operation for over 10 years. Each company entered a global market niche that did not exist when they were founded. They have not only created their own markets but also established a globally dominant position within them. All three companies have a particularly strong presence in Europe and the United States and have successfully raised equity investments on a global scale.

Additionally, all three hidden champions have developed a strong presence in the business-to-business (B2B) segment, although Ready Player Me and Starship Technologies also interact frequently with end consumers.

Ready Player Me is a software company that initially experimented with 3D printing under the name Wolf3D when it was founded in 2013. After exploring various fields, the company pivoted to focus on the metaverse by developing cross-platform avatars—long before the metaverse gained widespread attention through Meta (formerly Facebook). Meta's strategic shift, along with the impact of the COVID-19 pandemic, provided a strong boost to Ready Player Me's business.

Two of the hidden technology champions, Milrem and Starship Technologies, combine both manufacturing and services. Milrem classifies itself primarily as a manufacturing company with a strong service component, while Starship Technologies considers itself a service company with a strong manufacturing base. These companies represent a new, emerging technology sector where services and high-skilled manufacturing are seamlessly integrated into business models that are difficult to categorize according to standard business studies, hidden champions literature, or NACE codes.

The blurring of industry boundaries and traditional business models is particularly intriguing for this study. At present, these hidden champions may seem like "extreme cases" (see Seawright, 2016, on extreme cases). However, these companies are likely to establish new business model standards, potentially rendering current business models extreme—or even obsolete.

3 Case Studies of Selected Hidden Champions

3.1 Case Study 1

3.1.1 Milrem

Overview
Address: Betooni 1, Talllinn 13619, Estonia
Tel: +372 6620865
Email: info@milrem.com
Web: www.milremrobotics.com

Company Information
Industry: manufacturing NACE code 29 (motorized vehicles: detailed NACE code 29101)
Year of Establishment: 2013
Sales Revenues in 2017: 2.5 million euros
Sales Revenues in 2023: 19.1 million euros
Average number of employees in 2023: 250
Brainer(s) behind the company: Kuldar Väärsi and rotating team of engineers.

Nature of Market Leadership

Milrem is a defense robotics company in the world offering unmanned ground vehicles and integrated autonomous systems. In the essence, Milrem is a platform where through cooperation with partners various military as well as civilian solutions can be integrated. Depending on the assessment the company has either first or second position in the world market. By simply measuring the sales of units Milrem is number 1 provider of unmanned defense vehicles in the world (Pajuste, 2024).

The main competitors are German company Rheinmetall, US company General Dynamics and Israeli company IAI. Overall, 100 companies operate in this global market niche. The main markets for Milrem are Europe and United States. Since EDGE Group PJSC from United Arab Emirates purchased 54% of Milrem's equity, then Milrem is in the process of establishing also a strong presence the Middle East and Africa.

Nature of Competitive Advantage

Milrem has the first mover advantage in rapidly developing field of unmanned ground vehicles by starting to build such solutions and systems already in 2013. The first unmanned vehicle was demonstrated in 2015 when the defense industry considered such approach unimportant. Startup culture allows us to be agile and more flexible in the industry characterized by slow-moving traditional defense companies. As with other technology companies in Estonia such as Skype, Bolt and Wise, Milrem's strength relies on ability to apply innovative technological solutions to specific area. It is driven by non-Research and Development innovation rather than pure R&D innovation.

Core Lessons Learned on the Path to Success

Milrem has been throughout its operations sales and client focused. This means that company has had a lot of flexibility in adjusting to the needs of clients and environment. If large defense companies are not likely to be interested in dealing with small quantities, then Milrem has often supplied only one-two vehicles to its clients and constantly adjusting to their needs. Such an approach has made it possible to receive constant feedback from end-users and integrate their insights into research and development of new products. Milrem has been open to developing its core technology and concepts in cooperation with partners and clients. Participation in various international development programs with different partners in Europe and the Middle East has been key for the success of Milrem's vehicles. The use of vehicles in real-life situations has been instrumental for sales and R&D. For instance, Milrem's unmanned vehicle was used by Estonian units in Mali where they were part of French troops. Such real-life use cases demonstrate the reliability and relevance of Milrem's unmanned vehicles (Pajuste, 2024). In a nutshell, Milrem offers following four lessons:

- Client-centric flexibility: Milrem's adaptability to client needs, including supplying small quantities, has strengthened its market position.
- Continuous feedback integration: Constant interaction with end-users has enhanced research and development, leading to improved products.
- Collaborative innovation: Partnerships with international players have contributed to the evolution of Milrem's core technology and concepts.
- Real-life validation: Deploying vehicles in operational environments has reinforced their reliability and boosted sales and R&D.

Management and Leadership Development Needs

The main development need is recruitment. As Milrem is growing rapidly its staff must grow at least two times to meet current demand. Company plans to increase its workforce to 300 people by the end of 2024 and to 400 by the end of 2025 from the current staff of 250. They have built new production facility in Tallinn, Estonia, which allow us to produce 500 vehicles per year, which is represents increase of 10 times. The expansion of R&D and manufacturing is also the core aim of new unit in the United Arab Emirates. Company has offices in Finland and Sweden with primary goal of recruiting engineers from the defense industry. It has also office in the Netherlands which was the first client. A small marketing focused office is in the United States.

Financing and Regulatory Environment Development Needs

Since Milrem received a significant equity injection from the UAE EDGE Group, then financing needs are met for expansion. The main issues concern regulatory environment as the company has basically created a new field in traditionally complex and conservative defense industry. Estonian regulations still create difficulties for integration of different weapons systems on the Milrem platforms. For this reason, some of the experiments have been done outside of Estonia. However, Estonian regulations might change as the government is the process of updating the laws. Nevertheless, the equity stake of 54% by the UAE company can create further regulatory barriers in Europe and United States—even though company has been granted independence and autonomy in its daily operations by investors. Further regulatory uncertainty is created by the EU regulations on artificial intelligence and robotics which have conflicting goals. It is unclear how abstract concepts in the EU AI Act will be implemented and how it will affect so-called narrow AI in the form of machine learning that Milrem exploits.

Pandemic's Impact on "Hidden Champions" Business Approach

The COVID pandemic had a negative impact on company's sales and staff was reduced. The sales of unmanned vehicles require in-person meetings and demonstration which was not possible during the pandemic. Particularly, military clients prefer to meet in-person in order to complete sales which was not possible during the pandemic (Pajuste, 2024).

Effects of the Russian War in Ukraine on "Hidden Champions" Business Operations

The effect of the full-scale war by Russia in Ukraine has been positive on Milrem's operations. Firstly, overall importance of defense industry has increased in Estonia and in Europe. This development affects all aspects of business operations in terms of financing, recruitment, marketing and R&D. Secondly, the war is important input for research and development. Milrem's vehicles are present in the battlefield, which allows us to collect constant feedback about the solutions and adjust vehicles and systems accordingly. Thirdly, the presence in the battlefields is a reference point for sales. It shows that the vehicles can be used in the extremely difficult conditions of war (Pajuste, 2024).

It should be noted that the war also poses risks for Milrem. One Milrem's unmanned vehicle has been captured by the Russian military. Milrem has considered the risks associated with reverse engineering. It is relatively easy to copy hardware but reverse engineering software and integration of hardware and software should create a major obstacle. Whether this risk assessment holds will be seen in the future (Pajuste, 2024).

3.1.2 Attracting Diverse Talent to Milrem

In the current environment of Russia's full-scale war in Ukraine and the increasing risks of military conflict worldwide, the defense industry has garnered significant interest, and Milrem has certainly benefited enormously from this trend. However, it is important to remember that this was not the case just a few years ago, particularly when Milrem was founded in Estonia in 2013.

Milrem was one of the first defense startups in Estonia. Since regaining its independence, Estonia had not developed a significant defense industry, with the main focus being on cybersecurity. Therefore, the emergence of a defense startup in the manufacturing sector was not a natural development. Milrem essentially came out of nowhere. In retrospect, the lack of legacy companies and systems in this area was beneficial, as it allowed the company to attract diverse talent.

Milrem's founder, Kuldar Väärsi, worked with various groups of engineers who had backgrounds in the Formula Student Competition, an international product development competition aimed at students of engineering and automotive technology. In addition to creative engineers, Milrem has recruited from the Estonian military. The Chairman of Milrem's Council for many years was General Riho Terras, the former head of the Estonian military and a current member of the European Parliament.

Former Estonian military officer Jüri Pajuste, who served two tours in Afghanistan as a unit commander, is the new Chief Operations Officer of Milrem in the United Arab Emirates. Pajuste has also served as Research and Development Director, head of the sales department, and project manager at Milrem. Pajuste was interviewed for this chapter.

When the military vehicle systems provider BAE Systems Hägglunds in Sweden made many engineers redundant through restructuring, Milrem established a presence in Northern Sweden specifically to recruit this engineering talent. In many ways, Milrem was an underdog, recruiting new engineers for a defense company at a time when the established defense industry was struggling with decreasing military expenditure and demand for weapons systems.

Milrem's capability and capacity to recruit talents with diverse professional backgrounds from different nationalities and operate the company in various locations certainly demonstrate foresight and strong execution by the leadership team. Building a successful company and creating a new market niche is foremost about people.

3.2 Case Study 2

3.2.1 Ready Player Me

Overview
Address: Telliskivi 60/2, Tallinn 15073, Estonia
Tel: 372 56214070
Email: info@readyplayer.me
Web: readyplayer.me

Company Information
Industry: Information and communication, NACE code 62 (62,011 Programming)
Year of Establishment: 2014
Sales Revenues in 2017: 1,971 euros
Sales Revenues in 2023: 486,925 euros[1]
Average number of employees in 2023: 66
Brainer(s) behind the company: Timmu Tõke, Kaspar Tiri, Rainer Selvet and Haver Järveoja.

Nature of Market Leadership

Ready Player Me (RMP) is a metaverse company which provides cross-platform avatars in gaming industry. The gaming industry consists of games played through different devices (smart phones, computers, consoles) and market size is estimated to be 180–190 billion US dollars annually. There are different participants such as large platforms (Meta, Google, and others) and small- and medium-sized developers. RMP focuses on providing cross-platform avatars to small- and medium-sized developers to save them from development costs of creating own avatars that can be used in different platforms. RMP is a market leader in this global niche. In addition to developers, RMP another target group is end-users who want to take their avatars across different platforms. The main markets are Europe and the United States and most competitors are based in the United States (Järveoja, 2024).

[1]The sales figure for 2023 represents roughly 80% of Ready Player Me sales globally as the data is based on the activities of Estonian unit and not consolidated (Järveoja, 2024). The consolidated data is not publicly available.

Nature of Competitive Advantage

The main competitive advantage is development of avatars which can be used across different platforms. RMP takes more open approach than other market participants which tend to create avatars for closed systems within particular platform. Another source of competitive advantage is focus on small- and medium-sized developers which potentially could create a new breakthrough game in the market (Järveoja, 2024).

Core Lessons Learned on the Path to Success

The main lesson is good team synergy. The core team studied together at the Estonian Business School and has worked together in RMP for 10 years. They are different individuals but they complement each other with skills in visionary leadership, operations management, creativity and technology. They have gone through different phases of creative maze experimenting with different ideas and pilots. Each pivot has led them to the next level of building a business (Järveoja, 2024).

RMP offers following four lessons for success:

- Cross-Platform Innovation: RMP's success stems from developing avatars usable across different gaming platforms, offering a unique and open alternative to closed-system competitors.
- Targeted Market Strategy: By focusing on small- and medium-sized developers, RMP provides cost-effective solutions that support emerging game creators and niche market expansion.
- Strong Team Synergy: A cohesive team with complementary skills in leadership, operations, creativity, and technology has been crucial for navigating challenges and driving growth.
- Iterative Growth Through Experimentation: Continuous pivots and experiments with different ideas and pilots have enabled RMP to refine its business model and scale effectively.

Management and Leadership Development Needs

The main management and leadership needs relate to expansion of the business. One of the key challenges is how to reduce its dependence on developers with unsustainable business models. One option is to increase the quality of selection process for partners in development community. Another challenge is diversification of revenue sources which implies development of own games as possible new ventures in the area of cryptocurrencies and NFTs. Furthermore, about half of RMP staff is based in New York, United States, and about half in Tallinn, Estonia. This creates also challenges for managing a diverse team across two continents.

Financing and Regulatory Environment Development Needs

RMP had a successful financing round in 2022 when 55 million euros was raised in equity investments from the consortium led by the leading Silicon Valley venture capital firm Andreessen Horowitz. This has secured funding for research and development and expansion until 2027. The current regulatory environment has not affected RMP as gaming does not receive significant regulatory scrutiny in Europe and the United States.

Pandemic's Impact on "Hidden Champions" Business Approach

The COVID pandemic had a strong positive effect on RMP as the use of gaming increased and metaverse started to develop more rapidly. This was followed by the decision by Facebook to focus on metaverse and change its name to Meta which gave an additional boost to RMP as an early metaverse company.

Effects of the Russian War in Ukraine on "Hidden Champions" Business Operations

RMP has four employees based in Ukraine. Initially, their safety was a huge concern but business-as-usual has returned where their Ukrainian developers see the opportunity to work as a good distraction from the miserable reality. Otherwise, the effects of Russian war in Ukraine are limited on the operations of RMP.

From the 3D Printing to Avatar Economy

The core RMP team has spent 10 years experimenting in various fields before focusing on the metaverse and the development of cross-platform avatars. Initially, the company was named Wolfprint 3D and concentrated on 3D printing, modeling, and scanning. With a small grant of 5,000 euros from Enterprise Estonia and investments from the Estonian Business School, the company purchased 3D printers in 2014. They created a service called DollyMe3D, which allowed people to create 3D images of themselves.

Following this, the company developed a business idea to print 3D images of unborn babies based on ultrasound scans, targeting European clinics and hospitals. This initiative gained worldwide attention, with coverage from the Daily Mail and Washington Post. However, revenue growth did not follow.

The company then gradually shifted toward creating avatars. RMP started by developing avatars for large platforms, with clients such as H&M, Verizon, Vodafone, and the leading Chinese technology platform Tencent. Negotiations also took place with Huawei. Fortunately, the cooperation with Chinese companies ended before geopolitical turmoil escalated, allowing RMP to focus on the American and European gaming industries.

Successful financing rounds, totaling 72 million US dollars from various venture capital firms in Estonia, Europe, and the United States, enabled RMP to reshape its business model. The company now focuses on developing an open ecosystem for cross-platform avatars. RMP has recruited key team members from Estonian unicorns Wise and Pipedrive, as well as from global players like Epic Games.

By April 2024, the number of monthly active developers relying on RMP had reached almost 4000, compared to about 1,000 in April 2022. Additionally, 2,241 companies had signed up for RMP in April 2024, up from 369 in April 2022. The latter figure refers to the B2B market segment of mid-sized and large companies with whom RMP signs contracts, while small developers are self-served.

RMP benefits from a 10–25% revenue share from the avatar economy on different platforms. Exclusive avatar assets have been developed for diverse organizations such as Angry Birds, Manchester City, New Balance, and Walt Disney.

In summary, after a decade of experimenting with various business ideas, the core team has stayed together and created a market and business ecosystem that did not previously exist. In this emerging ecosystem, RMP benefits from network effects typical of technology platforms, where a circular relationship between more avatar content, more developers, and more users reinforces growth.

3.3 *Case Study 3*

3.3.1 Starship Technologies

Overview

Address: Teaduspargi 8, Tallinn 12618, Estonia
Tel: 372 5292999
Email: info@starship.co
Web: https://www.starship.xyz/

Company Information

Industry: Professional, scientific and technical activities NACE code 72 (research and development in other natural and technical sciences NACE code 72191)
Year of Establishment: 2014
Sales Revenues in 2017[2]: N/A
Sales Revenues in 2023[3]: N/A
Average number of employees in 2023: 400
Brainer(s) behind the company: Ahti Heinla, Jaanus Friis and the engineering team.

[2] The company does not reveal its consolidated sales revenue publicly. Indicators are available for the sales revenue from Estonian unit through business registry but it represents only a fraction of actual sales.

[3] The company does not reveal its consolidated sales revenue publicly. Indicators are available for the sales revenue from Estonian unit through business registry but it represents only a fraction of actual sales.

Nature of Market Leadership

The main market is last-mile food and hot-meal delivery solutions. If the market is considered in its entirety, including both couriers and technological solutions (sidewalk robots, drones), Starship's position is practically negligible. However, if the focus is solely on technological solutions, Starship is clearly number one in the world in terms of the number of deliveries and kilometers traveled, which is a crucial metric for technological solutions. Today, Starship's lead over the nearest competitor is several-fold, if not ten-fold.

Unfortunately, it is not possible to obtain this information on competition in a very reliable form today. One of Starship's competitors, Serve, recently went public, and their documents revealed that they have made fewer than 100,000 deliveries. Starship's total number of deliveries today exceeds six million, and the company has traveled more than 12 million kilometers. Cartgen, Serve, and Kiwibot are notable competitors. Of these, Cartgen is the only one who also has commercial operations in Europe, not just pilot projects (Aaviksoo, 2024).

Nature of Competitive Advantage

Starship Technologies holds a dominant position in the autonomous last-mile delivery market, particularly in sidewalk robot solutions, where it far surpasses competitors in deliveries and kilometers traveled.

In the market for autonomous vehicles, the valuable "currency" is kilometers traveled. At the end of the day, this is where Starship's systems improve through various challenges. With over six million deliveries and 12 million kilometers covered, Starship has amassed unparalleled operational experience, which strengthens its AI and navigation systems.

Another important advantage is its experience in very different markets and business models, not as pilots but as working commercial services. Unlike competitors that are still in pilot phases, Starship operates fully commercial services in multiple countries, demonstrating a proven business model. The company's presence in 75+ locations across six countries and its three distinct business models provide flexibility and scalability.

Additionally, its ambition to double revenue annually drives continuous innovation, reinforcing its competitive edge. Starship's growth ambition, put simply, is to double the revenue every year. Historically, Starship has both exceeded and fallen short of this goal, but it is the daily objective that they work toward as a company to fulfill this promise to our investors.

Starship has been in this field for nearly 10 years, its market share has been relatively unaffected so far. Real competition has only begun to emerge in the last 2–3 years, and in the landscape of US universities, this is particularly important.

Starship exploits three different business models:

As a full-service provider to end consumers and merchants in US universities.
As a partner to merchants providing autonomous delivery solutions in Finland and the United States.
As an industrial partner providing autonomous delivery solutions in Germany and Denmark.

Core Lessons Learned on the Path to Success

It is important to be critical in understanding the stages of the company's development—each new phase requires new approaches and sometimes new types of people. What brought Starship here might not take them forward. Recognizing when a phase change is occurring and sensing it at the right time is a major challenge.

Starship's strength has certainly been in the field of innovation. The company has been fortunate that develop an attractive product to many people, making it somewhat easier to find good talent than one might expect for a small country like Estonia.

Creating world-changing technology is challenging, but people at startups generally enjoy solving difficult problems. Starship works to ensure that their ambitious plan aligns with the ambitions of these individuals, which is certainly one of the key strengths (Aaviksoo, 2024).

In a nutshell Starship offers four lessons for success:

- Adaptability to Growth Stages: Recognizing when the company enters a new phase and adjusting strategies and talent accordingly has been crucial for sustained success.
- Strong Innovation Culture: Starship's ability to attract top talent and foster a problem-solving mindset has been key to advancing autonomous delivery technology.
- Market Leadership Through Experience: A vast number of completed deliveries and extensive real-world operational experience provide Starship with unmatched industry expertise.
- Scalable Business Models: Operating across multiple markets with different business models ensures resilience and the ability to expand strategically.

Management and Leadership Development Needs

Starship is a geographically very widespread company, and this is only growing. Although it has been like this from the beginning, it remains a challenging issue in terms of successful communication, cooperation models, and the simplest everyday work processes.

Financing and Regulatory Environment Development Needs

The lack of a regulatory environment is a clear obstacle Starship has to overcome daily. Their advantage is perhaps the experience Starship has gained over the years in various countries and the ability to contribute to shaping regulations. As a growth company, it depends on the ability to raise capital, and building this business has been very capital-intensive. The difficult capital market situation in recent years has certainly also affected Starship. The existing investors know that they are developing world-changing technology, and they know it works. Once the product has proven itself in market conditions, the day will come when Starship can solve funding challenges on market terms (Aaviksoo, 2024).

Pandemic's Impact on "Hidden Champions" Business Approach

Mostly positively, as COVID quickly changed customers' consumption habits, and the market for food/grocery delivery only grew because of it. Robots also provided a very clear solution for contactless delivery, which helped Starship to establish a strong market position on US university campuses.

Effects of the Russian War in Ukraine on "Hidden Champions" Business Operations

Estonia's location and geopolitical situation have certainly affected Starship's ability to raise capital, both directly and indirectly, due to deteriorated capital markets. Just before the war, the Russian technology platform Yandex seemed to be one of the companies making rapid progress in last-mile robot courier development. The war essentially halted the development of this business vertical in the United States. However, today this business has been separated from the parent company associated with Russia and is trying to establish a new market position (Aaviksoo, 2024).

From Skype to Starship

Starship Technologies was founded in 2014 by Ahti Heinla and Jaanus Friis, both of whom were part of the founding team of Skype. Before Skype, they worked on projects such as the Estonian portal Everyday.com and the peer-to-peer file-sharing platform Kazaa, which gained widespread popularity but faced legal challenges. Skype was launched in 2003 and sold to eBay for $2.6 billion in 2005, making it Estonia's first unicorn. Due to intellectual property disputes, some of Skype's founders later repurchased the company before selling it to Microsoft for $8.5 billion in 2008 (Kitsing, 2021). Following their success with Skype, Heinla, and Friis shifted their focus to robotics and founded Starship Technologies.

Starship exemplifies the so-called Skype effect in the Estonian technology ecosystem. First, Skype inspired many entrepreneurs by demonstrating that it was possible to build global technology companies in Estonia. Second, Skype provided its employees with valuable experience in scaling such businesses, with Heinla and Friis being prime examples. Additionally, former Skype employees went on to establish other successful Estonian startups and unicorns, including Bolt and Wise. Third, Skype's acquisition generated venture capital, which was later reinvested into new startups like Starship.

Starship also signifies a shift in Estonia's tech landscape, proving that Estonian entrepreneurs are willing to take on more complex challenges beyond software development. Starship is a robotics company that seamlessly integrates both hardware and software. Currently, all Starship delivery robots are assembled in Estonia. However, hardware alone is not enough—robot autonomy is made possible by artificial intelligence (AI) and the seamless integration of AI with robotics. Starship began its AI development a decade ago, long before the general public became widely aware of AI through technologies such as large language models like ChatGPT and Google Gemini (Aaviksoo, 2024).

All of Starship's autonomous systems are developed in-house, with no reliance on external contributions. In other words, Starship functions as a large-scale AI laboratory, which is why its NACE classification falls under research and development in other natural and technical sciences. Notably, Amazon attempted to develop a similar autonomous delivery robot under the name Amazon Scout but eventually abandoned the project.

With nearly a decade of experience in the field, Starship has maintained a strong market position, largely unaffected by competition until recent years. Significant competitors have only begun to emerge within the past 2–3 years, particularly within US universities, a crucial landscape for this technology. Starship's growth ambition is to double its revenue each year. While the company has at times both exceeded and fallen short of this target, this remains its guiding objective as it continues to deliver on its promise to investors and other stakeholders.

4 Conclusions and Recommendations

The development of a technology ecosystem that enables both established and emerging companies to thrive is multidimensional, with outcomes often being overdetermined—many factors contribute to results simultaneously. Consequently, drawing simple recommendations for governments, financial institutions, and business schools is challenging. The relevance of the Estonian experience can also be questioned due to the country's small size, with a population of just 1.3 million. Nevertheless, despite differences in institutional contexts, some of Estonia's lessons can certainly be relevant for its current government and scalable if adapted properly to specific circumstances.

First, Estonia's reforms, initiated in the 1990s, help explain the country's current success in the technology ecosystem and business creation. The comprehensive and radical nature of these reforms makes Estonia an extreme case among the countries that joined the EU in 2004. For nations transitioning from a centrally planned economy to a competitive market-based ecosystem, comprehensive and bold reforms are essential. A gradual or stop-and-go approach is ineffective, particularly in the face of multiple overlapping challenges. Estonia implemented simultaneous reforms in the areas of rule of law, privatization, trade, and monetary and fiscal policy. Simply focusing on a few policy measures or relying on targeted industrial policy is insufficient.

Comprehensive reforms require both strong leadership and clear ownership of the reform process. A deep understanding of structural reform needs is essential, along with the willingness to make decisive choices based on a long-term vision. Success also depends on a well-designed strategy that leverages scenario planning and focuses on effective execution. Often, the "how" is more important than the "what" when defining a strategy. There must be a firm commitment to the reform process, with an emphasis on rapid implementation.

Second, digitalization in both the private and public sectors has been crucial in enhancing government and business efficiency. Estonia's digital transformation began in the mid-1990s with the introduction of internet banking, which fostered a culture of using complex digital services in everyday life. This, in turn, served as a foundation for continuous digital innovation in both sectors. Today, Estonia stands as a global leader in digitalization, boasting highly digitalized public services and the highest number of unicorn startups and venture capital investments per capita. Through the e-Residency program, individuals worldwide can access Estonia's digital infrastructure without being physically present in the country.

Third, Estonia has fostered a business-friendly environment, as highlighted by the 2023 IMD study. The country offers a simple and efficient process for starting a company, along with a transparent and entrepreneur-friendly tax system. The Estonian government has consistently taken a long-term approach to fostering its business ecosystem. Over the decades, a strong implicit consensus has existed on key economic development goals, including reintegration with the West, trade, and monetary and fiscal policy, despite changes in coalition governments.

The 2023 IMD study placed Estonia in relatively modest positions in terms of labor market and financial sector competitiveness, ranking 34th and 32nd out of 64 countries, respectively. However, the discussion of Estonia's hidden champions demonstrates that successful companies have overcome these challenges by raising capital from the United States, Europe, and the United Arab Emirates. While competition for talent remains fierce, these companies have successfully recruited employees from around the world, allowing them to build globally competitive businesses.

Fourth, education and management practices play a crucial role in Estonia's success. The 2023 IMD study ranked both relatively high in Estonia, emphasizing the importance of lifelong learning. Business schools must provide relevant education throughout individuals' careers. For example, Milrem's Chief Operating Officer is a graduate of the micro-degree program at the Estonian Business School, while Starship's Senior Vice President for Operations is an alumnus of the EMBA program at the same institution. Additionally, all four founders of Ready Player Me earned their undergraduate degrees from the Estonian Business School. However, business schools can contribute beyond education. The Estonian Business School was an early investor in Ready Player Me and still retains a significant stake. In addition to teaching and research, business schools can engage in venture building, incubation, and startup acceleration. This approach creates a circular relationship between teaching, venture building, and research and development, where all elements complement and reinforce one another.

References

Aaviksoo, P. (2024). Semi-structured interview with Pepe Aaviksoo, Senior Vice President of Operations at Starship Technologies. June 10, Estonian Business School, Tallinn, Estonia.

Abrams, N. A., & Fish, S. M. (2015). Policies first, institutions second: Lessons from Estonian economic reforms. *Post-Soviet Affairs, 31*, 6.

Arenguseire Keskus. (2020). *Globaalsed jõujooned 2035. Stsenaariumid ja tähendus Eesti jaoks*. Tallinn, Estonia.

Estonian Government Office. (2016). Estonian labor productivity, per capita GDP and price level in relation to EU average (1996-2014), Tallinn, Estonia.

Estonian Ministry of Finance. (2024–2025). Spring Forecast, Tallinn, Estonia.

European Commission. (2024). *The digital economy and society index*. European Commission. https://ec.europa.eu/digital-single-market/en/digital-economy-and-society-index-desi

Eurostat. (2024). *Data on individuals using internet for internet banking*. Eurostat.

Feldmann, M. & Sally R. (2001). From the Soviet Union to the European Union: Political economy of Estonian trade policy reforms, 1991–2000. *Bank of Finland BOFIT Online* (January), Helsinki.

Freytag, A. (2003). Challenges for Estonia's economic policymaking at the eve of EU-enlargement. *Demokratizatsiya, 11*(4), 535–554.

IMD World Competitiveness Booklet. (2023). International Institute of Management Development, Lausanne, Switzerland, June.

Järveoja, H. (2024). Semi-structured interview with Haver Järveoja, Chief Operating Officer of Ready Player Me. Ready Player Me, Tallinn, Estonia, June 7.

Kitsing, M. (2017). The internet banking as a platform e-government. In *The proceedings of 7th international conference on innovation and entrepreneurship* (pp. 99–107). Singapore, GSTF.

Kitsing, M. (2021). *The political economy of digital ecosystems: Scenario planning for alternative futures*. Routledge.

Laar, M. (1996). Estonia's success story. *Journal of Democracy, 7*(1), 96–101.

Martens, T. (2010). Electronic identity management in Estonia between market and state governance. *Identity in the Information Society, 3*(1), 213–233.

Mehisto, P., & Kitsing, M. (2023). *Lessons from Estonia's education success story: Exploring equity and high performance through Pisa*. Routledge.

Pajuste, J. (2024). Semi-structured interview with Jüri Pajuste, Chief Operating Officer of Milrem UAE. Milrem, Tallinn, Estonia, June 11.

Seawright, J. (2016). The case for selecting cases that are deviant or extreme on the independent variable. *Sociological Methods and Research, 45*(3). https://doi.org/10.1177/0049124116643556

World Bank. (2024). Data on Estonia. Accessed June 10, 2024, from https://data.worldbank.org/country/estonia?view=chart

Meelis Kitsing is the Rector at the Estonian Business School (EBS), where he also serves as a Professor of Political Economy. He is a member of the boards of the Estonian Council on Foreign Relations, the Estonian Service Industry Association, and Eurofound, a European Union research agency based in Dublin, Ireland.

Kitsing has been Head of Research and Acting Director at the Foresight Center, a think tank within the Estonian Parliament; Adviser at the Strategy Unit of the Estonian Government Office; and Head of Economic Analysis at the Estonian Ministry of Economic Affairs and Communications. Additionally, he has served as President of the Estonian Economic Association and chaired the supervisory boards of the public-sector companies.

Kitsing is the author of The Political Economy of Digital Ecosystems (Routledge, 2021 and 2023). His research has been published by Springer, IEEE, ACM, Leuven University Press, and MIT Press. He has conducted research and taught at universities across Asia, Europe, and North America, such as the University of Massachusetts, Central European University, Harvard University, the University of Connecticut, the Stockholm School of Economics, and the Institute of Management Technology (Dubai and Ghaziabad campuses).

Meelis Kitsing earned his PhD from the University of Massachusetts, Amherst (USA), and his MALD degree from the Fletcher School at Tufts University (USA) as a Fulbright scholar. He also holds an MSc from the London School of Economics (UK), where he studied as a Peacock scholar. Before transitioning to academia, Kitsing worked for multinational corporations and founded an e-commerce startup.

Hidden Champions of Georgia

Amashukeli Maia, Surmanidze Natia, and Tskhadadze Keti

Abstract This chapter examines the phenomenon of hidden champions in Georgia, focusing on enterprises that, while relatively unknown to the general public, hold leading positions in their industries and contribute significantly to the country's economic competitiveness. The study draws on Hermann Simon's conceptual framework of hidden champions and applies it to the Georgian context, analyzing companies that meet the criteria of global niche leadership, sustained growth, and innovation capacity. Methodologically, the research combines secondary data analysis with case study investigation to identify and assess firms that exemplify the hidden champion model. Two Georgian companies, Tbilvino in the wine sector and Tegeta Motors in the automobile service industry, are presented as illustrative cases. The findings reveal that both companies demonstrate strong international orientation, adaptive strategies in response to crises such as COVID-19 and regional instability, and a consistent focus on quality and customer relationships. These cases highlight how firms in small, emerging economies can achieve global competitiveness by leveraging niche markets, innovation, and resilient leadership. The chapter contributes to the broader literature on hidden champions by extending the concept to the South Caucasus region and providing insights into how Georgian firms enhance national economic visibility and competitiveness.

Overview
Official name: Georgia.
Type of government: Parliamentary representative democratic republic.
Population in 2013: 3,728,282.
Land area: 69,700 km^2.

*Corresponding author.

A. Maia · S. Natia · T. Keti (✉)
School of Business and Administrative Studies, University of Georgia, Tbilisi, Georgia
e-mail: m.amashukeli@ug.edu.ge; n.surmanidze@ug.edu.ge; k.tskhadadze@ug.edu.ge

D. Berberović, D. Purg (eds.), *Hidden Champions in Rising Economies*, Contributions to Management Science,
https://doi.org/10.1007/978-3-032-08263-3_19

History

1801	Alexander I, Emperor of Russia, signs a manifest on the incorporation of East Georgia (Kingdom of Kartli-Kakheti) within the Russian Empire.
1810	Russia incorporates West Georgia into the Russian Empire, and the Kingdom of Imereti becomes part of it.
1918	Georgia proclaims the establishment of the independent Democratic Republic of Georgia (DRG) in the wake of the Russian Revolution of 1917.
1921	The Russian Red Army invades Georgia and occupies the country. The Georgian government is forced to flee.
1922–1991	The Socialist Soviet Republic of Georgia as a part of the Soviet Union.
1989, April 9	Soviet troops are used to break up a peaceful demonstration in Tbilisi.
1991, April 9	The Georgian Supreme Council declares secession from the Soviet Union according to a referendum on independence of Georgia, which is approved by 98.9% of the votes.
1991–1992	The Georgian coup d'état: an internal military conflict against the first democratically elected President of Georgia, Zviad Gamsakhurdia. A Military Council removed Gamsakhurdia as president, who died in circumstances that are still unclear.
1992–1993	Georgia–Abkhazia War: Georgia sends troops to Abkhazia to halt moves for secession. Fierce fighting ends with Georgian forces, and more than 250,000 Georgians and others are expelled from Abkhazia.
1999	Georgia joins the Council of Europe.
2003	After the peaceful Rose Revolution, Georgia vigorously pursued a pro-Western foreign policy, introducing a series of democratic and economic reforms aimed at integration into the European Union and NATO.
2008	The Russo-Georgian War. Russia continues to occupy parts of Georgia and recognizes both South Ossetia and Abkhazia as independent states.
2014	The European Union and Georgia sign an association agreement—a far-reaching trade partnership deal.
2023, December 14	The European Union grants Georgia candidate status, acknowledging the nation's ongoing efforts toward EU integration.

1 Introduction: Context and History

Georgia is a small, open economy characterized by a small domestic market with significant import dependence, resulting in a negative trade balance of 6.8 billion USD in 2023 (National Statistics Office of Georgia—Geostat). This is somewhat mitigated by the service sector's positive balance, particularly tourism, which contributed 4.0 billion USD in 2023 (Geostat, 2024). The 2023 current account deficit amounted to 2.5 billion USD (Geostat, 2024).

Georgia's geography is a mix of mountains and flat areas, with the country divided into several regions, each with its own distinct economic profile. Over the past two decades, this economic landscape has been marked by a stark contrast. While certain regions, particularly rural areas, have grappled with economic stagnation and depopulation, urban centers like Tbilisi and Batumi have thrived, experiencing significant economic growth and development.

Georgia's current social, political, and economic tendencies are deeply rooted in its complex and often turbulent history. Before the dissolution of the Soviet Union in 1991, the country was marked by significant political and social instability, a result of its strategic location and historical conflicts. The post-Soviet period was no less challenging, with economic hardships and political turmoil, including civil strife in the early 1990s. However, since the early 2000s, Georgia has been on a path of relative stability and economic growth, a journey that was accelerated by the Rose Revolution in 2003, which ushered in significant political and economic reforms.

Since 2003, Georgia's GDP has grown considerably, increasing from approximately 4.1 billion USD to 28.2 billion USD in 2023, or around 7,500 USD per capita (World Bank, 2024). The key macroeconomic indicators summarizing Georgia's economic performance over the past five years are presented in Exhibit 1.

The structure of Georgia's economy has changed dramatically since the socialist period. After the dissolution of the Soviet Union in 1991, the economy transitioned from a centrally planned system to a market-oriented one. During the Soviet era, Georgia's economic growth was primarily based on industry, with significant state support for factories and production facilities. However, many of these enterprises have since closed or gone bankrupt due to the challenges of transitioning to an open market economy without state support.

Today, Georgia's economy largely depends on tourism, the small and medium-sized enterprise (SME) sector, agriculture, the financial sector, and trade. Infrastructure investments have supported GDP growth since the early 2000s, contributing to the development of these sectors.

Tourism remains a significant driver of Georgia's economy, contributing approximately 4.0 billion USD or around 16.2% of the national GDP in 2023 (National Statistics Office of Georgia—Geostat, 2024). Since the early 2000s, the number of tourists visiting Georgia has increased significantly, reaching over nine million in 2023 (Geostat, 2024). Several essential investment projects, including new resorts, hotels, and significant infrastructural developments in various parts of Georgia, are

Exhibit 1 Core economic indicators for Georgia

Indicators	2018	2019	2020	2021	2022	2023	2024
GDP per capita (current US$) billion	4722.04	4696.15	4255.74	5023.27	6674.95	8283.67	..
GDP per capita growth (annual %)	4.88	5.16	−6.82	10.88	10.27	7.75	..
Unemployment, total (% of total labor force) (modeled ILO estimate)	11.57	11.73	11,851	11,683	11,749	11.54	11.48
Foreign direct investment, net inflows (% of GDP)	7.4	7.9	3.5	6.86	8.6	6.78	..
GDP (current US$) billion	17.6	17.47	15.84	18.63	24.78	30777.83	..
Exports of goods and services (current US$) billion	8.9	9.58	5.91	8.05	13.11	15163.33	..
Exports of goods and services (% of GDP)	50.6	54.8	37.3	43.2	52.9	49.27	..
Merchandise exports (current US$) billion	3.38	3.8	3.34	4.24	5.58	6,091	..
Ores and metals exports (% of merchandise exports)	26.5	31.7	36.9	32.4	33.1	28.33	..
Agricultural raw materials exports (% of merchandise exports)	0.75	0.65	0.52	0.698	0.68	61.99	..
Food exports (% of merchandise exports)	31.03	31.06	31.82	30.11	26.3	21.85	13.57
Fuel exports (% of merchandise exports)	1.97	0.71	0.37	0.79	2.62	0.83	0.69
Manufactures exports (% of merchandise exports)	36.08	32.30	25.85	33.48	34.32	39.16	45.67
High-technology exports (% of manufactured exports)	2.88	2.07	2.12	1.60	3.11	4.2	2.33
						29.63	33.97
						3.78	3.74

Source: World Bank, 2024

expected to boost tourism further, attract first-time visitors, extend the tourism season, and reduce seasonal inequality. By 2030, the travel and tourism industries are expected to contribute even more significantly to the national GDP.

Besides tourism, SMEs are crucial for Georgia's economic development. Over 99% of companies in Georgia fall into the SME category, employing around 68% of the total workforce (Government of Georgia, 2023a, 2023b). Further steps are needed to foster an entrepreneurial spirit and support the development of entrepreneurship in Georgia. Critical areas for development include finance (through credit lines and the establishment of a guarantee fund, which is critical for the internationalization of SMEs), entrepreneurial infrastructure (business centers, incubators, etc.), and entrepreneurial knowledge (organization of training and education, promotion of lifelong entrepreneurial learning, etc.).

Foreign direct investments (FDIs) are also a vital source of economic growth in Georgia, helping to reduce the deficit in the current account. In 2023, FDIs amounted to approximately 2.0 billion USD, constituting about 7.1% of GDP (Geostat, 2024). FDIs are particularly significant for tourism (investments in marinas and luxury resorts) and energy (renewable sources and distribution), two crucial sectors of the Georgian economy. A substantial portion of FDIs is achieved by establishing new foreign-owned entities and reshaping, improving, and expanding the economy by bringing international business standards, know-how, technology, and new business cultures to Georgia.

Due to the small domestic market, successful Georgian companies have identified foreign markets as essential for growth and development. For most Georgian enterprises, internationalization is a prerequisite for long-term success.

Georgia's market size and economic structure have presented challenges for companies aspiring to attain a leading position on the global stage. However, despite these hurdles, a select group of enterprises has emerged as hidden champions, showcasing exceptional capabilities within their respective industries.

Our quest for hidden champions in Georgia was guided by research methodologies inspired by seminal works such as "Hidden Champions: Lessons from 500 of the World's Best Unknown Companies" by Hermann Simon (2009). Initially, we focused on six enterprises with a strong international orientation. Through extensive field research and market analysis, three companies were identified as meeting the stringent criteria set for hidden champions.

Based on comprehensive market share analysis and industry expertise, each of these companies holds the coveted number-one position in its regional market. All three companies have demonstrated remarkable potential.

These findings are underscored by the World Economic Forum's reports on global competitiveness, particularly the "Global Competitiveness Report" (2023), which highlights the crucial role of thriving businesses in enhancing a nation's competitiveness index.

These companies have significantly contributed to Georgia's enhanced competitiveness index, as outlined in reports by the World Economic Forum. Despite their relatively young age, as they were founded after Georgia declared independence in 1991, their rapid prominence highlights their agility, innovation, and strategic foresight.

These Georgian hidden champions embody the resilience and ingenuity of the country's business community, illustrating how success can be achieved even in challenging environments through astute market insights, strategic positioning, and unwavering commitment to excellence. Two companies stood out for their exceptional performance and dominance in their regional markets: Tbilvino and Tegeta.

Tbilvino, a leading name in the wine industry, has achieved unparalleled success by combining traditional craftsmanship with modern techniques. Focusing on producing high-quality wines that resonate with both domestic and international consumers, Tbilvino has secured its position as the premier wine producer in Georgia, contributing significantly to the country's reputation as a hub for fine wines.

Tegeta Motors Georgia, a prominent entity in the automotive sector, has established itself as a leading force, leveraging its extensive expertise and strategic alliances to become the premier choice for automotive solutions in the region. Through its unwavering commitment to quality, efficiency, and customer satisfaction, Tegeta Motors has garnered a reputation as a hidden champion, propelling innovation and advancement in Georgia's automotive industry. Georgian hidden champions have demonstrated exceptional vision, agility, and commitment to excellence. By understanding market dynamics, responding swiftly to emerging trends, and investing in talent development, they have achieved market leadership and played a pivotal role in enhancing Georgia's competitiveness on the global stage.

2 Case Study 1

2.1 Tbilvino

Overview
Address: Tbilisi, Sarajishvili Avenue #2, 0153
Telephone: +0322651625
Email: info@tbilvino.ge
Web: https://tbilvino.ge/

Company Information
Industry: Wine Production
Year of establishment: 1962
Sales revenue in 2022: 9.6 (USD, millions)
Sale revenue in 2019: 12,682 (USD, millions)
Number of employees in 2022: 351
Brain(s) behind the company: Founders and Visionaries Mr. Zurab Margvelashvili and Mr. Giorgi Margvelashvili.

Tbilvino, a distinguished name in the wine production industry, was established in 1962 and has since risen to prominence as one of Georgia's leading wine producers. Renowned for its unwavering commitment to quality and innovation. According to its latest annual report (Tbilvino, 2022), the company employed 351 professionals and recorded a sales revenue of 9.6 million USD in 2022. Under the visionary leadership of its founders, Mr. Zurab Margvelashvili and Mr. Giorgi Margvelashvili, Tbilvino continues to thrive and achieve international recognition.

Nature of Market Leadership
Tbilvino holds the number-one position in Georgia's wine market segment, particularly in the production and export of high-quality Georgian wines. Known for its diverse range of wines that cater to various tastes and preferences, Tbilvino has established itself as a leading name in the industry. Its vineyards, spanning across the fertile regions of Kakheti, provide the ideal conditions for producing exceptional wines that have garnered international acclaim.

Tbilvino's unwavering commitment to quality and innovation has set it apart from competitors. The company's extensive portfolio includes both traditional Georgian wines and modern blends, making it a unique player in the market. This combination of heritage and innovation has made Tbilvino the preferred choice for wine connoisseurs both locally and globally.

Tbilvino's Competitive Advantage

Tbilvino's competitive advantage lies in its strategic focus on quality and tradition, combined with innovation in wine production. By concentrating on high-quality Georgian wines, Tbilvino has carved out a niche market that is both significant and underserved on a global scale. This niche primarily consists of wine enthusiasts, sommeliers, and premium wine collectors who seek authentic, indigenous varieties with a rich history. It also includes health-conscious consumers drawn to the natural and traditional winemaking methods, such as the use of qvevri fermentation, which aligns with the growing global interest in organic and biodynamic wines. The company's strategy involves targeting discerning wine consumers who appreciate the unique characteristics of Georgian wines.

Every functional policy at Tbilvino is developed with this strategic focus in mind. The founders recognized the growing international interest in authentic and traditional wines and positioned Tbilvino to meet this demand effectively. By prioritizing quality and authenticity, Tbilvino has differentiated itself from competitors, offering wines that reflect the rich heritage and unique terroir of Georgia.

This strategy is further bolstered by Tbilvino's investment in state-of-the-art production facilities and sustainable practices, ensuring that each bottle meets the highest standards of quality. Additionally, Tbilvino leverages its deep understanding of the local viticulture and winemaking traditions to create wines that are both innovative and rooted in tradition.

Moreover, Tbilvino benefits from Georgia's favorable legal framework for wine exports, which allows for competitive pricing and easier access to international markets. This advantage, combined with Tbilvino's commitment to excellence, enables the company to serve its strategic target market more effectively and efficiently than many of its competitors.

Tbilvino's Core Lessons Learned on the Path to Success

Tbilvino's journey to success has been shaped by four core lessons, each rooted in the company's commitment to quality, responsibility, teamwork, and innovation. These guiding principles have fortified Tbilvino's position as a market leader in the wine industry.

1. Clear Vision and Strategic Leadership.

Tbilvino's success is anchored in a well-defined vision and strong leadership. The founders, Mr. Zurab Margvelashvili and Mr. Giorgi Margvelashvili, played a pivotal role in shaping the company's direction with their intuition, strategic foresight, and passion. Their positive reputation in the business world fostered trust and credibility, enabling the company to build strong partnerships and expand globally. Maintaining leadership continuity ensured long-term strategic coherence and sustained growth.

2. Commitment to Quality and Responsibility.

At the heart of Tbilvino's ethos is an unwavering dedication to quality and responsibility. From vineyard to bottle, the company meticulously upholds the highest standards, ensuring that every wine reflects Georgia's rich heritage. Recognizing its role as a steward of tradition, Tbilvino embraces sustainability through environmentally friendly practices, responsible land management, and social responsibility initiatives. This commitment not only enhances brand credibility but also fosters lasting customer trust.

3. Market Adaptation and Innovation.

In an industry steeped in tradition, Tbilvino thrives by balancing heritage with innovation. The company has successfully identified and targeted an underserved market segment—wine consumers who value authentic, high-quality Georgian wines. By continuously adapting to market demands and embracing new winemaking techniques, Tbilvino remains competitive and relevant. Its culture of creativity and adaptability ensures that it stays ahead of industry trends and continues to set new standards in the global wine market.

4. Investment in People and Teamwork.

Tbilvino recognizes that success is a collective endeavor. By fostering a culture of teamwork, respect, and empowerment, the company harnesses the diverse talents of its workforce to drive innovation and excellence. Investing in human resources—through employee development, engagement, and satisfaction—has been instrumental in maintaining the high level of service and quality that Tbilvino's clients expect. A unified and motivated team has been key to the company's sustained success.

In essence, Tbilvino's journey is not just about producing exceptional wines—it's about embodying values that resonate deeply with its stakeholders. Through a steadfast commitment to vision, quality, innovation, and people, Tbilvino has not only achieved market leadership but has also set an inspiring example for the industry.

Management and Leadership Development Needs

As Tbilvino continues to expand its presence in the global wine market, the company faces new leadership and management challenges that will shape its future growth. To sustain its competitive edge, Tbilvino must strengthen its leadership capabilities, enhance decision-making agility, and develop a strategic approach to talent management.

One of the primary leadership challenges is navigating market volatility, including fluctuating production costs, shifting consumer preferences, and evolving trade regulations. Future leaders at Tbilvino must be equipped with the skills to anticipate industry changes, respond to economic pressures, and drive innovation while maintaining the company's core values of quality and tradition.

Additionally, as Tbilvino increases its international footprint, leadership development must focus on cross-cultural management and global market adaptation.

Expanding into diverse markets requires leaders who can understand and respond to regional consumer behaviors, regulatory environments, and competitive dynamics. Strengthening leadership capabilities in international business strategy will be essential for Tbilvino's sustained success.

Furthermore, investing in talent development and succession planning will be crucial to ensuring long-term leadership stability. As the company grows, nurturing future leaders from within the organization will help maintain strategic continuity and reinforce the company's mission. This includes leadership training programs, mentorship initiatives, and fostering a culture of innovation and collaboration.

By proactively addressing these management and leadership development needs, Tbilvino can continue to navigate the complexities of the global wine industry while upholding its legacy of excellence.

Impact of COVID-19 on Tbilvino

The COVID-19 pandemic presented significant challenges for Tbilvino, affecting both domestic operations and international sales. As lockdowns and economic uncertainty disrupted global markets, the wine industry faced shifting consumer behaviors, logistical constraints, and financial instability.

Market and Sales Disruptions

During the pandemic, many international markets restricted imports and imposed lockdown measures, limiting the demand for premium wines. The hospitality and tourism industries—key drivers of wine sales—were among the hardest hit. With restaurant closures and reduced travel, sales channels for high-end Georgian wines, including Tbilvino's exports, declined temporarily.

Operational and Supply Chain Adjustments

To navigate the crisis, Tbilvino implemented remote work solutions where possible and adopted strict safety protocols at its production facilities to ensure business continuity. Despite global supply chain disruptions, the company diversified its sourcing strategies to mitigate delays in packaging materials and transportation bottlenecks.

Financial Impact and Strategic Response

Revenue fluctuations required cost optimization measures, including streamlining operational expenses and adjusting production schedules to align with shifting demand. However, the crisis also accelerated Tbilvino's digital transformation, leading to an increased focus on direct-to-consumer sales through online platforms.

Lessons Learned and Opportunities

Despite the hardships, the pandemic underscored the importance of market diversification and e-commerce adaptation. Tbilvino strengthened its digital marketing efforts, expanded its presence in online wine marketplaces, and enhanced relationships with retailers that adapted to changing consumer behaviors. These strategic shifts positioned the company for stronger post-pandemic recovery.

Impact of the Russia-Ukraine War on Tbilvino

The Russia-Ukraine war introduced new geopolitical and economic challenges for Tbilvino, impacting key export markets and supply chain operations.

Export Market Challenges
Before the war, Russia and Ukraine were among the largest importers of Georgian wine, making the conflict particularly disruptive. Economic sanctions, trade restrictions, and declining consumer purchasing power in these regions led to a decline in sales. Additionally, instability in neighboring markets like Poland, Estonia, Latvia, and Lithuania further complicated the situation.

Supply Chain Disruptions
The war also caused logistical difficulties, including delays in shipments and increased transportation costs due to regional instability. Rising fuel prices and supply chain inefficiencies placed additional financial pressure on Tbilvino, requiring strategic adaptations to maintain smooth operations.

Financial and Market Strategy Adjustments
In response to these disruptions, Tbilvino:

- Diversified its export destinations, reducing reliance on the affected markets.
- Strengthened partnerships with European and Western distributors, expanding its footprint in stable markets.
- Adjusted pricing strategies to account for inflation and rising costs in global trade.

Opportunities Amidst Crisis
Although the war created immediate economic difficulties, it also prompted European consumers to explore alternative wine producers, creating an opportunity for Georgian wines, including Tbilvino, to increase market share in Western Europe. Additionally, with many Russian-affiliated brands facing sanctions, Tbilvino leveraged its position as an independent Georgian producer to reinforce its presence in global markets.

Long-Term Strategic Outlook
The war highlighted the need for risk management, geopolitical awareness, and flexible supply chain strategies. By prioritizing resilience, diversifying revenue streams, and building relationships with stable, long-term trading partners, Tbilvino continues to strengthen its position despite global uncertainties.

Tbilvino Financing and Regulatory Environment Development Needs
Tbilvino faces challenges within the financial sector due to operating in a market with limited lending capacity. The relatively small size of Georgia's financial market restricts local banks' ability to provide long-term financing, impacting companies like Tbilvino that require capital for growth and expansion.

To create a more conducive financing environment, several key measures could be implemented:

1. Expansion of alternative financing options—Developing capital markets, such as expanding corporate bond offerings with longer maturities (beyond the current five-year cap), would provide companies with more sustainable financing options.
2. Government-backed loan guarantees and subsidies—Introducing state-supported loan programs specifically designed for agricultural and wine industries would enhance access to affordable credit.

3. Collaboration with international financial institutions—Encouraging foreign investment and partnerships with global financial institutions could help mitigate the limitations of local banking capacity.

Additionally, Tbilvino faces several regulatory complexities that impact its financial and operational strategies:

- Taxation policies—Fluctuating excise taxes on wine products, both domestically and in key export markets, create financial unpredictability and affect pricing strategies.
- Import-export regulations—Stringent certification requirements and evolving international trade agreements require continuous adaptation to regulatory changes, increasing operational costs.
- Access to EU financial frameworks—While Georgia has strengthened ties with the EU through trade agreements, navigating European regulatory frameworks remains complex, affecting market entry and expansion efforts.

Tbilvino's winemaking industry operates with an inherently long-term operational cycle, necessitating long-term financing options and products. Unfortunately, Georgia's capital market remains underdeveloped, with commercial banks serving as the primary source of financing. In recent years, a more structured alternative debt financing bond market has emerged, yet the maximum duration of available financial instruments remains capped at five years—falling short of the industry's long-term needs. Expanding financial products with longer maturities would greatly benefit both the wine sector and agriculture in general.

Beyond debt markets, developing derivative markets and financial instruments could play a crucial role in price stabilization and risk management. By enabling hedging mechanisms, such as commodity futures and currency hedging tools, wine producers could better manage financial volatility caused by fluctuating exchange rates and global wine market conditions.

Addressing these needs will help Tbilvino strengthen its access to capital, mitigate financial risks, and foster sustainable growth in the competitive global wine industry. Additionally, the company's ability to adapt to external disruptions—such as the COVID-19 pandemic and the Russia–Ukraine war—will be crucial in maintaining stability and ensuring long-term resilience in the global market.

Tbilvino: A Visionary Journey Transforming Georgian Winemaking and Global Recognition

Tbilvino has not only revitalized Georgia's winemaking industry but has also become a coveted destination for wine enthusiasts and connoisseurs worldwide. Its commitment to excellence and dedication to sustainable practices have earned it acclaim as a beacon of Georgia's vinicultural heritage, offering a compelling blend of tradition and innovation in every bottle.

In the dynamic world of Georgian winemaking, Tbilvino stands as a testament to the vision and leadership.

The company's unwavering commitment to excellence, coupled with its sterling reputation and international recognition, has not only attracted a loyal clientele but also garnered the trust and support of investors and stakeholders. Keen insight into the market landscape allowed Tbilvino to carve out a niche within the wine industry, catering to a discerning clientele seeking quality and authenticity.

At the heart of Tbilvino's success lies its strategic approach, characterized by a laser focus on meeting the needs of a specific market segment. By tailoring its offerings to the tastes and preferences of its target audience, Tbilvino has been able to differentiate itself and maintain a competitive edge in an increasingly crowded market.

From vineyard to bottle, Tbilvino's commitment to innovation is evident in every aspect of its operation. By leveraging cutting-edge technology and sustainable practices, the winery has been able to produce wines of exceptional quality while minimizing its environmental footprint.

Central to Tbilvino's success is its steadfast leadership, which has remained consistent despite changes in ownership. This continuity has enabled the winery to maintain its momentum and drive forward with ambitious expansion plans, including the development of new vineyards and facilities.

Moreover, Tbilvino prides itself on fostering a culture of trust, respect, and collaboration among its owners, managers, and employees. By investing in the professional development and well-being of its workforce, the winery has cultivated a team of passionate individuals dedicated to pushing the boundaries of Georgian winemaking.

In essence, Tbilvino's success story is a testament to the transformative power of visionary leadership, strategic innovation, and a steadfast commitment to excellence. As it continues to evolve and grow, Tbilvino remains a beacon of Georgia's rich winemaking heritage, captivating enthusiasts around the globe with its exceptional wines and unwavering dedication to quality.

In the realm of Georgian winemaking, Tbilvino's success is not only attributed to its competitive advantages but also to its robust collaboration with governmental bodies, public authorities, and the local community. This synergy has yielded mutual benefits, fostering economic growth, boosting employment rates, and elevating the region's standing within the global wine industry.

Tbilvino's journey began with its establishment in 1962, and since then, it has become a beacon of excellence in Georgian winemaking. Over the years, Tbilvino has forged strong partnerships with governmental entities and local communities, recognizing the symbiotic relationship between business prosperity and societal advancement.

The impact of Tbilvino's initiatives on the local economy and tourism sector is palpable. Through strategic collaborations and investments, Tbilvino has contributed to a surge in tourist arrivals in the Kakheti region, home to the winery. This growth surpasses the national average, underscoring the transformative influence of Tbilvino on regional tourism dynamics.

Furthermore, Tbilvino's success has spurred further developments in the region's viticultural landscape, inspiring the establishment of modern wineries and vineyards. These endeavors, influenced by Tbilvino's trailblazing example, have augmented Georgia's reputation as a premier wine destination, attracting wine enthusiasts and connoisseurs from around the globe.

In essence, Tbilvino's collaborative approach to business, coupled with its unwavering commitment to excellence, has not only propelled the winery to international acclaim but has also catalyzed broader economic growth and development in the Kakheti region. As Tbilvino continues to thrive and innovate, its impact on the local community and Georgian winemaking industry is poised to endure for generations to come.

3 Case Study 2

3.1 Tegeta Motors

Overview
Address: Tbilisi, D. Aghmashenebeli Alley #129
Telephone: +995 32224 44 44
Email: info@tegetamotors.ge
Web: https://www.tegeta.ge

Company Information
Industry: Automotive aftermarket
Year of establishment: 1995
Sales revenue in 2021: 797,152 (USD, thousands)
Sale revenue in 2019: 630,021 (USD, thousands)
Number of employees in 2022: Up to 2000
Brain(s) behind the company: Konstantine Patsatsia, Director at Tegeta Automotive Imports, head of product development at Tegeta Retail.

Tegeta Motors was established in 1995 and has become one of Georgia's leading automotive service providers. Known for its unwavering commitment to quality and innovation, Tegeta Motors has set the industry standard. By 2023, the Company employed up to 2,000 dedicated professionals (Tegeta Motors, 2022). Under the visionary leadership of its founder, Mr. Konstantine Patsatsia, Tegeta Motors continues to thrive, achieving national and international recognition for its exceptional service and customer satisfaction.

Nature of Market Leadership
Tegeta Motors is a leader in the Georgian automotive aftermarket business, which refers to the industry that provides vehicle parts, accessories, and services after the initial sale by the manufacturer. Offering a comprehensive range of products and services for passenger cars and trucks, Tegeta Motors has established itself as a key player in vehicle maintenance, repair, and enhancement. Since its establishment in 1995, the company has been dedicated to innovation and growth, setting and implementing numerous worldwide standards within Georgia.

Since 2011, Tegeta Motors has become even more vital, capturing an increasingly significant market share. The Company has a vision to be innovative and quality-oriented, investing significantly in technology, human capital, and infrastructure. This strategic investment helps Tegeta Motors stay ahead of competitors and maintain its market leadership. As the market leader in tire, lubricant, battery, and spare parts sales, Tegeta Motors represents up to 300 global brands, providing customers with top-tier products and services. The Company employs over 2,000 people and operates 30 service stations nationwide, ensuring extensive coverage and accessibility for its clientele.

Tegeta Motors holds an approximate 25%-30% market share in Georgia, while its closest competitor holds only around 5%. This dominant position in the local automotive aftermarket industry is a result of the company's strategic expansion of product ranges and service offerings, along with the construction of numerous service stations across the country. Tegeta's unwavering commitment to quality and customer satisfaction has solidified its position as the leading player in Georgia's automotive industry, contributing to the sector's advancement and setting new benchmarks for service excellence.

Tegeta Motor's Competitive Advantage

Tegeta Motors' competitive advantage is built on continuous innovation, modern technology, strategic partnerships, and exceptional customer orientation. These elements collectively ensure the Company's dominance in the Georgian automotive aftermarket business.

- Continuous Innovation and Modern Technology.

Tegeta Motors focuses on continuous innovation and the use of modern technology in the car service business. By integrating cutting-edge technology into physical infrastructure and digital operations, the Company remains at the forefront of the industry. In 2009, Tegeta Motors implemented SAP, the renowned German software, which significantly scaled its business operations. Furthermore, in 2017, Tegeta became the first Georgian Company to offer online purchasing of its products, demonstrating its commitment to digital innovation. Projects like the Tire Hotel, TAX-Free project, and mobile service further exemplify Tegeta Motors' innovative approach. As of 2024, Tegeta Motors continues to expand its operations and strengthen its online services (Tegeta Motors, 2024).

- Strategic Partnerships.

Partnerships with global brands and suppliers ensure that Tegeta Motors' workshops have high-standard equipment. This lets the Company promptly address any vehicle problems, guaranteeing top-quality service. By partnering with world-leading manufacturers known for their product safety and reliability, Tegeta Motors upholds its key message centered on quality and trust.

- Customer Orientation and Quality Management.

Customer orientation is a defining feature of Tegeta Motors. The Company believes that putting customers first is crucial to business success. Service excellence and quality management training programs equip employees with the skills to serve clients effectively. A dedicated Quality Management Department researches customer satisfaction, ensuring continuous improvement in service delivery.

- Tegeta Academy.

Understanding the importance of well-trained individuals, Tegeta Motors established the Tegeta Academy. Initially a regular training center, it has evolved into a full-fledged college. To work as a salesperson or mechanic at Tegeta, candidates must study and pass exams. The academy also offers numerous on-the-job training sessions conducted by technicians, with additional training provided by many suppliers online or offline.

- Strategic Alliances.

Tegeta Motors' strategic alliances with global trade groups, such as Group Auto International (2024), enhance its competitive edge. As a Group Auto International member and a Group Auto Caucasus founder, Tegeta Motors builds strong business relationships with leading suppliers. These alliances help maintain its leadership position in the automotive service industry and enable the company to offer cutting-edge solutions to customers.

In summary, Tegeta Motors' competitive advantage lies in its relentless pursuit of innovation, strategic partnerships, customer-first approach, comprehensive training programs, and strong industry alliances. These factors ensure that Tegeta Motors continues to lead the Georgian automotive aftermarket business, providing outstanding quality and convenience to consumers.

Tegeta Motors' Core Lessons Learned on the Path to Success

Tegeta Motors' journey to becoming a leader in the Georgian automotive aftermarket business has been guided by several core lessons that have shaped its strategic approach and long-term success.

1. Embracing a Growth Mindset, Long-term Vision, and Innovation.

A fundamental lesson for Tegeta Motors is the importance of a growth mindset and a long-term vision, ensuring that the company remains proactive in an ever-evolving market. By continuously striving to implement progressive solutions and technological innovations, Tegeta Motors has positioned itself as an industry leader. This future-oriented approach, coupled with a competitive and positive attitude, has fueled the company's sustained expansion, enabling it to navigate market changes with agility and foresight.

2. Investing in People, Technology, and Best Practices.

Tegeta Motors recognizes that success is built on continuous investment in human capital, technology, and operational excellence. By enhancing employee skills through training and professional development, the company ensures a highly qualified workforce that meets evolving customer demands. Simultaneously, Tegeta Motors actively adopts cutting-edge technologies and implements industry best practices, allowing it to maintain a competitive edge and improve operational efficiency.

3. Building Strong Global and Local Partnerships.

Strategic collaborations have been instrumental in Tegeta Motors' growth. By forging strong partnerships with renowned global brands and key local players, the company has expanded its access to high-quality products, advanced technologies, and innovative solutions. These relationships have strengthened Tegeta's market reputation and service offerings, further reinforcing its leadership position.

4. Differentiating Through Quality, Customer Loyalty, and Market Leadership.

Tegeta Motors has successfully distinguished itself through a commitment to service quality, adherence to safety standards, and a diverse product assortment. The company prioritizes customer loyalty programs, creative marketing strategies, and innovative service models, ensuring that it remains the top choice for consumers. By consistently enhancing the customer experience, Tegeta Motors has built long-term trust and strong brand recognition, solidifying its dominance in the automotive industry.

In conclusion Tegeta Motors' success is built on a growth-oriented mindset, strategic investments, strong partnerships, and a focus on differentiation. By continuously evolving, adapting to market needs, and prioritizing sustainable development, the company has solidified its position as a leader in the automotive service industry, setting new benchmarks for quality and innovation.

Management and Leadership Development Needs

Tegeta Motors recognizes the critical importance of developing its staff's skills to maintain and enhance its leadership in the automotive aftermarket business. The company's management and leadership development needs to focus on several key areas to ensure continued success and growth.

- Enhancing Customer Service Skills.

One of the most vital skills for retail companies, including Tegeta Motors, is superior customer service, known internally as "service plus." This aspect of the business is always challenging and requires continuous improvement to meet and exceed customer expectations.

Service excellence training: Tegeta Motors must invest in comprehensive training programs focusing on customer interaction, problem-solving, and service excellence. These programs equip employees with the skills needed to provide outstanding service consistently.

Customer Feedback Integration: Regularly gathering and integrating customer feedback into training programs will help ensure the staff is always aligned with customer needs and expectations.

- Developing Technical Skills for Workshop Mechanics.

Workshop mechanics and technical staff are the backbone of Tegeta Motors' service operations. However, a limited number of study programs are available for individuals aspiring to become car repair mechanics.

In-house training programs: Establishing robust in-house training programs that offer both theoretical knowledge and hands-on experience is crucial. These programs can bridge the gap left by the limited external study options.

Partnerships with Educational Institutions: Technical schools and universities can help develop specialized curricula and certifications that align with Tegeta Motors' standards and requirements.

- Leadership and Management Development.

To ensure that Tegeta Motors continues to thrive, developing strong leaders who can drive the Company's vision and manage teams effectively is essential.

Leadership training: Providing leadership training programs that cover strategic planning, decision-making, team management, and innovation will prepare potential leaders to take on greater responsibilities.

Mentorship programs: Establishing mentorship programs where experienced leaders guide and support emerging leaders can help transfer valuable knowledge and skills.

- Continuous Professional Development.

Tegeta Motors must focus on the continuous professional development of its staff to keep up with industry advancements and evolving customer needs.

Ongoing education and certification: Encouraging employees to pursue ongoing education and certification in their respective fields can ensure they stay updated with the latest industry trends and technologies.

Access to industry conferences and workshops: Providing opportunities for staff to attend industry conferences and workshops can enhance their knowledge and bring new ideas into the Company.

- Investment in Technology and Digital Skills.

With the integration of modern technology into Tegeta Motors' operations, the staff must be proficient in using these technologies effectively.

Digital literacy training: Implementing training programs focused on digital literacy and modern tools and software will ensure that all employees can utilize technology to improve efficiency and service quality.

Advanced technical training: To maintain high service standards, technical staff will need advanced training on new diagnostic tools, repair techniques, and automotive technologies.

In summary, Tegeta Motors' management and leadership development needs include enhancing customer service skills, developing technical skills for workshop mechanics, fostering leadership and management capabilities, promoting continuous professional development, and investing in technology and digital skills. By addressing these needs, Tegeta Motors can ensure that its staff remains highly skilled, motivated, and capable of driving the Company's continued success.

Tegeta Motor's Financing and Regulatory Environment Development Needs
Tegeta Motors, as a leading company in the Georgian automotive aftermarket business, operates in an environment where both financing and regulatory compliance are critical (Government of Georgia, 2024). Several development needs must be addressed to ensure sustained growth and adherence to industry standards. Strict control over automobile air pollution is necessary to improve environmental quality (United Nations Environment Programme, 2024).

Impact of COVID-19 on Tegeta Motors
The COVID-19 pandemic presented unprecedented challenges for Tegeta Motors, disrupting operations, straining financial resources, and reshaping customer demand. As a leading player in Georgia's automotive industry, the company had to act swiftly to adapt to the evolving situation while maintaining its commitment to service quality and business continuity.

One of the immediate priorities for Tegeta Motors was ensuring the safety of its employees and customers. The company implemented strict health and safety protocols across its service stations, showrooms, and warehouses to mitigate risks and maintain operations. Recognizing the critical role of vehicle maintenance during the pandemic, Tegeta prioritized servicing government and emergency vehicles, including ambulances, police cars, and utility trucks, ensuring that essential transportation remained uninterrupted.

Financially, the pandemic led to a shift in consumer spending behavior, with a decline in discretionary purchases and an increased focus on vehicle maintenance rather than new car acquisitions. To navigate the economic downturn, Tegeta Motors optimized costs and streamlined expenses while preserving its core services. Supply chain disruptions posed another major challenge, as global factory shutdowns led to shortages in auto parts and delays in delivery times. In response, the company diversified its sourcing strategies, expanding partnerships with alternative suppliers to ensure continued product availability.

Despite these challenges, the pandemic accelerated digital transformation at Tegeta Motors. The company strengthened its online presence by developing e-commerce platforms for auto parts, launching digital payment systems, and introducing remote booking services for maintenance appointments. This shift to digital operations not only helped Tegeta maintain customer engagement during lockdowns but also positioned the company for future growth in an increasingly digital marketplace.

Ultimately, the pandemic underscored the importance of business agility, proactive risk management, and digital innovation. Tegeta Motors emerged from the crisis with a stronger technological infrastructure and a more resilient business model, better equipped to navigate future disruptions.

Impact of the Russia-Ukraine War on Tegeta Motors
The Russia-Ukraine war introduced new economic and operational uncertainties for Tegeta Motors, impacting supply chains, financial stability, and consumer demand. As one of Georgia's leading automotive companies, Tegeta faced challenges related

to inflation, rising costs of raw materials, and logistical bottlenecks, all of which required swift strategic adaptations.

One of the most immediate consequences of the war was its effect on the supply chain. Ukraine and Russia were key trade partners for many industries, and disruptions in these markets created shortages in essential automotive components. The increased costs of transportation, driven by rising fuel prices and shipping constraints, further complicated logistics. Tegeta Motors responded by strengthening relationships with European and Asian suppliers, expanding its procurement network, and adjusting inventory management strategies to ensure stable product availability despite external uncertainties.

The economic impact of the war also affected consumer behavior, with inflation and reduced purchasing power leading to shifts in market demand. Vehicle owners prioritized essential repairs and maintenance over discretionary upgrades, prompting Tegeta to focus more on after-sales services and customer retention initiatives. The company adapted its pricing strategy to account for fluctuating costs while maintaining affordability for customers. Additionally, Tegeta Motors explored new market segments, including eco-friendly automotive solutions, as the war highlighted the global need for energy efficiency and alternative transportation options.

Despite the economic volatility, the crisis also presented opportunities. As some foreign competitors scaled back operations due to geopolitical instability, Tegeta Motors strengthened its market position by expanding its regional presence and deepening relationships with key stakeholders. The company also reinforced its risk management strategies, incorporating geopolitical assessments into long-term planning to better anticipate and respond to similar crises in the future.

Through a combination of strategic adaptation, supply chain resilience, and market diversification, Tegeta Motors has continued to navigate the challenges of the war. The company remains focused on maintaining operational efficiency, exploring new growth opportunities, and reinforcing its leadership position in Georgia's automotive sector, even in the face of global uncertainty.

Financing Development Needs

A. Access to Capital.

Expansion Funding: As Tegeta Motors continues to expand its service stations and product offerings, access to sufficient capital is essential. This includes securing loans, attracting investors, and exploring alternative financing options to support growth initiatives.

Technology Investment: Investing in cutting-edge technology requires significant capital. To stay competitive and innovative, financing options for technology upgrades and digital transformation projects must be explored.

Financial Management

Efficient Financial Planning: Implementing advanced financial planning and management systems will help allocate resources better and manage cash flow effectively. This includes utilizing financial software that integrates with existing systems like SAP to streamline operations.

Cost Management: Continuous evaluation and optimization of costs, including operational expenses and supply chain management, are crucial for maintaining profitability. Strategies for cost reduction without compromising on quality should be developed.

Regulatory Environment Development Needs

A. Enhancing Safe Driving Regulations.

Prohibition of Outdated Tires: Implementing regulations prohibiting outdated tires is essential to enhance road safety. Tegeta Motors can advocate for and support the enforcement of these regulations by providing education and inspection services to ensure compliance.

Regular Tire Inspections: Encouraging regular tire inspections and replacements can significantly reduce the number of collisions caused by tire failures. This initiative can be promoted through customer awareness campaigns and partnerships with regulatory bodies.

B. Control Over Automobile Air Pollution.

Emission Standards: Strict control over automobile air pollution is necessary to improve environmental quality. Tegeta Motors can support the implementation of stringent emission standards and provide services, such as emission testing and maintenance, that help vehicles meet these standards.

Eco-friendly products and services: Promoting the use of eco-friendly products, such as low-emission tires and green lubricants, can help reduce the overall environmental impact. Tegeta Motors can lead by example by incorporating these products into its offerings.

C. Compliance and Advocacy.

Regulatory Compliance: Ensuring full compliance with all local and international regulations is critical for Tegeta Motors. This includes regular audits, employee training on compliance matters, and staying updated with regulatory changes.

Advocacy for Better Regulations: Tegeta Motors can actively advocate for better regulations that enhance road safety and environmental protection. By collaborating with government agencies and industry groups, the Company can influence positive regulatory changes.

D. Training and Awareness Programs.

Employee Training: Regular training programs on regulatory compliance, safety standards, and environmental protection are necessary. This ensures that the staff is well-informed and capable of adhering to regulatory requirements.

Public Awareness Campaigns: Conducting public awareness campaigns on the importance of using safe, up-to-date tires and maintaining low vehicle emissions can drive community support for regulatory measures.

In summary, Tegeta Motors' financing and regulatory environment development needs include:

- Securing capital for expansion and technology investments.
- Enhancing financial management practices.
- Advocating for and complying with regulations that promote safe driving and reduce air pollution.
- Conducting training and awareness programs.

Addressing these needs will help Tegeta Motors sustain its growth and leadership position while contributing to safer and more environmentally friendly driving conditions in Georgia. Additionally, by strengthening its resilience to external challenges—such as the economic impact of the COVID-19 pandemic and the geopolitical instability caused by the war in Ukraine—Tegeta Motors can better navigate uncertainties, maintain financial stability, and continue to drive innovation in the automotive sector.

Tegeta Motors: Driving Safety, Inclusivity, and Innovation Through Challenges

Tegeta Motors, a stalwart in the automotive industry, has long been dedicated to promoting safety guidelines and enhancing car care practices. Recognizing the importance of seasonal tire changes, high-quality braking products, and superior engine oils to reduce air pollution, Tegeta has raised awareness about these crucial aspects.

Moreover, Tegeta has made significant strides in fostering inclusivity by empowering women to pursue careers in the traditionally male-dominated auto industry. Tegeta has contributed to a more diverse and inclusive workforce by breaking down barriers and providing opportunities.

During the challenging pandemic, Tegeta rose to the occasion by implementing rigorous safety measures to protect its employees while continuing to provide essential services. Focusing on servicing government vehicles, including ambulances and police cars, Tegeta ensured that critical vehicles remained operational, supporting the community during unprecedented times.

Navigating through the financial challenges brought about by the pandemic required resilience and strategic planning. Tegeta demonstrated its ability to adapt and thrive, maintaining financial liquidity and overcoming obstacles with determination and efficiency.

The pandemic also accelerated Tegeta's digital transformation journey, underscoring the importance of embracing technology in the Company's strategy. Leveraging digital solutions has not only enhanced operational efficiency but has also provided valuable insights into navigating through stressful situations.

Furthermore, the resource crisis highlighted the importance of having a diversified supplier portfolio and the ability to respond swiftly to market changes. Tegeta's proactive approach to managing resources and adapting to market dynamics has positioned the company for continued success amidst uncertainty.

In essence, Tegeta Motors' commitment to safety, inclusivity, resilience, and innovation has fortified its position in the automotive industry and exemplified its dedication to serving the community and driving positive change. As Tegeta continues to evolve and embrace new challenges, its impact on the automotive landscape is poised to endure for years.

4 Conclusions and Recommendations

Tbilvino's journey from its establishment in 1962 to its current position as a global leader in the wine industry is a testament to the power of vision, innovation, and steadfast commitment to quality. Founded by Mr. Zurab Margvelashvili and Mr. Giorgi Margvelashvili, Tbilvino has not only revitalized Georgia's winemaking heritage but has also become a symbol of excellence in the global wine market.

Through its strategic focus on quality, tradition, and innovation, Tbilvino has secured its position as the premier wine producer in Georgia, dominating both the domestic and international markets. By leveraging Georgia's rich viticultural heritage and embracing modern winemaking techniques, Tbilvino has created a diverse portfolio of wines that cater to the discerning tastes of consumers worldwide.

Furthermore, Tbilvino's commitment to sustainability, responsible business practices, and community engagement has earned it acclaim as a leader in corporate social responsibility and contributed to broader economic growth and development in the Kakheti region. By fostering collaborations with governmental bodies, public authorities, and the local community, Tbilvino has played a pivotal role in elevating Georgia's standing within the global wine industry while simultaneously stimulating tourism and economic activity in the region.

As Tbilvino continues to evolve and innovate, its impact on the local community and Georgian winemaking industry is poised to endure for generations. By staying true to its core values of quality, responsibility, teamwork, and innovation, Tbilvino will undoubtedly continue to shape the future of Georgian winemaking and inspire others with its visionary leadership and commitment to excellence.

Tegeta Motors is a beacon of excellence in the Georgian automotive aftermarket industry, driven by a commitment to quality, innovation, and customer satisfaction. Since its inception in 1995, under the visionary leadership of Mr. Konstantine Patsatsia, Tegeta Motors has continually pushed boundaries, setting new standards and solidifying its position as a market leader. Through strategic investments in technology, human capital, and infrastructure, Tegeta Motors has not only expanded its market share but also enhanced the overall customer experience.

The company's success can be attributed to its relentless pursuit of continuous innovation, strategic partnerships, customer-centric approach, comprehensive training programs, and strong industry alliances. By embracing a growth mindset, investing in its employees, seeking the best partners, differentiating itself in the market, and maintaining a long-term vision, Tegeta Motors has carved a niche in the automotive service industry.

Furthermore, Tegeta Motors has recognized the importance of addressing its management and leadership development needs to sustain its growth trajectory. By focusing on enhancing customer service skills, developing technical expertise, nurturing leadership capabilities, promoting continuous professional development, and investing in technology and digital skills, Tegeta Motors is poised to remain at the forefront of the industry.

Recommendations

1. Diversification and Expansion: Tbilvino should continue to explore opportunities for diversification and expansion into new markets and product lines. By leveraging its strong brand reputation and expertise, Tbilvino can capitalize on emerging trends and consumer preferences to strengthen its position in the global wine market further.
2. Investment in Human Resources: Investing in its workforce's professional development and well-being is crucial for Tbilvino's long-term success. By nurturing talent, fostering a culture of innovation, and empowering employees to take ownership of their roles, Tbilvino can enhance productivity, creativity, and employee satisfaction.
3. Sustainable Practices: Tbilvino should prioritize sustainability across its operations, from vineyard management to production and distribution. By adopting environmentally friendly practices, reducing waste, and minimizing its carbon footprint, Tbilvino can reduce costs, enhance efficiency, and strengthen its brand reputation as a responsible corporate citizen.
4. Strategic Partnerships: Collaborating with governmental bodies, industry associations, and other stakeholders is essential for Tbilvino's continued success. By forging strategic partnerships, Tbilvino can access resources, expertise, and market insights that will enable it to navigate challenges, seize opportunities, and drive innovation in the wine industry.
5. Market Research and Innovation: Tbilvino should invest in market research and innovation to stay ahead of evolving consumer preferences and market dynamics. By understanding emerging trends, identifying untapped market segments, and developing innovative products and marketing strategies, Tbilvino can maintain its competitive edge and sustain long-term growth in the global wine market.
6. Continued Innovation: Tegeta Motors should focus on continuous innovation, leveraging emerging technologies to enhance operational efficiency and customer experience. Regularly assessing market trends and consumer preferences will help the company stay ahead of the competition.
7. Investment in Human Capital: Tegeta Motors should continue to invest in developing its employees through comprehensive training programs and opportunities for professional growth. By nurturing talent and empowering its workforce, the company can ensure a high standard of service delivery and maintain its competitive edge.
8. Strategic Partnerships: Tegeta Motors should actively seek strategic partnerships with global brands and suppliers to access cutting-edge technologies and

expand its product offerings. Collaborating with industry leaders will enable the company to enhance its service quality and stay abreast of industry trends.

9. Compliance and Advocacy: Tegeta Motors should remain vigilant in complying with regulatory requirements related to road safety and environmental protection. Additionally, the company should advocate for better regulations that promote safer driving practices and reduce air pollution, contributing to a sustainable automotive ecosystem.
10. Digital Transformation: Tegeta Motors should continue its digital transformation journey, embracing digital solutions to streamline operations, improve efficiency, and enhance customer engagement. Investing in advanced digital tools and platforms will position the company for future growth and success.

References

Geostat. (2024). National Statistics Office of Georgia. Retrieved from https://www.geostat.ge

Government of Georgia. (2023a). SME development strategy 2023.

Government of Georgia. (2023b). Regulatory framework for wine production in Georgia.

Government of Georgia. (2024). Automotive industry regulations. Retrieved from [URL]

Group Auto International. (2024). About us. Retrieved from https://www.groupauto.com

Simon, H. (2009). *Hidden champions: Lessons from 500 of the world's best unknown companies*. Harvard Business Review Press.

Tbilvino. (2022). Annual report 2022.

Tegeta Motors. (2022a). About us. Retrieved from https://www.tegetamotors.ge

Tegeta Motors. (2022b). Our leadership. Retrieved from https://www.tegetamotors.ge

Tegeta Motors. (2024). Contact us. Retrieved from https://www.tegetamotors.ge

United Nations Environment Programme. (2024). Air quality and mobility. Retrieved from https://www.globalfueleconomy.org/media/597569/ab-day-one.pdf

World Bank Data. (2024). https://data.worldbank.org

World Bank Group. (2024). Financing for sustainable development. Retrieved from [URL]

World Economic Forum. (2023). Global competitiveness report. https://www.weforum.org/publications/annual-report-2022-2023/

Maia Amashukeli holds a master's degree in Physics from Ivane Javakhishvili Tbilisi State University (TSU). Currently serving as the Vice-Rector for Institutional Development at the University of Georgia. She brings extensive experience to her role as the director of the School of Business and Administrative Studies since 2006. Throughout her career, Maia has undertaken numerous international trainings, contributed to several research papers, and amassed significant expertise in scientific endeavors, consulting, and conducting trainings in Finance and Business.

Dr. Natia Surmanidze is an Associate Professor of Economics at the School of Business and Administrative Studies, University of Georgia. She holds a PhD in Economics from Ivane Javakhishvili Tbilisi State University, where she also earned her Master's in Economics and Bachelor's in Business Administration. Dr. Surmanidze teaches a range of undergraduate and graduate courses, including Research Methods, Business Communications, and Economic Research Methods. Her academic and teaching focus is complemented by an active research agenda that covers public procurement, entrepreneurship, financial literacy, and digitalization. She has authored over 30 scholarly publications, many of which are indexed in Scopus and other international databases. Notably, her 2022 open-access article, “Financial Literacy Exchange and Its Challenges in Post-Soviet Georgia,” was published in Knowledge & Performance Management. In addition to Georgian publications, she contributes regularly to international journals and conferences. Dr. Surmanidze is also a member of editorial boards for several peer-reviewed international journals and is frequently invited to present her work at international academic forums. Her professional activities reflect a commitment to high-quality education, rigorous research, and active participation in the global academic community.

Dr. Keti Tskhadadze is a Professor of Economics at the Faculty of Business and Administrative Studies at the University of Georgia. She holds a doctoral degree in Economics earned from Ivane Javakhishvili Tbilisi State University (TSU), a master’s degree in Economics from International School of Economics at TSU (ISET), and a bachelor’s degree in Business from the University of Georgia. Dr. Tskhadadze is an accomplished Professor at the Faculty of Business and Administrative Studies. Since 2016, Dr. Tskhadadze has been an esteemed educator, offering her expertise in courses such as Microeconomics, Macroeconomics, Public Finance, and Managerial Economics. Her commitment to advancing education is further demonstrated through her leadership roles. As the head of the Business Analytics program, conducted in both Georgian and English languages, she guides students towards a comprehensive understanding of the subject matter. Dr. Tskhadadze also serves as the international accreditation manager, contributing significantly to the recognition and enhancement of academic standards. Dr. Tskhadadze’s multifaceted career showcases a dedication to both theoretical knowledge and practical application in the field of Business and Economics.

Hidden Champions of Hungary

Miklós Stocker, Dániel Kostyal, Péter Koncz, and Levente Mikes

Abstract The hidden champions of Hungary so far have been characterized as small yet remarkably innovative companies operating in niche markets. This trait still stands true with the new round of companies in 2024. These companies still excel in industries that have been traditionally strong in Hungary. Compared to previous research, we have observed a shift in entrepreneurial mindset as talent retention and building stronger teams are prioritized by hidden champions, although some still rely on centralized leadership practices.

This chapter lays the foundation of our research with a brief introduction to Hungary's economic overview. We have identified four new hidden champions this year. Julius-K9 is a market leader in Europe in the quality dog harness market thanks to its patents, high-quality and flexible technology solutions, and prominent use of materials. Mcule.com Kft. operates as an online marketplace for chemical compounds, offering services in molecular docking and compound preparation. They rank among the top three providers in the EU and top four in the world with almost 10% market share. Mertcontrol Group offers testing, inspection, and certification of agricultural produce. As an integrated company, the Group has achieved a dominant leading market share in Central-Eastern Europe. Pallet Solution Kft. is a market leader in the sales and rental of used pallets and GitterBox products. The company has nearly 50% market share in the Central-Eastern European region. The identified hidden champions excel in their respective niche market, offering tailored solutions to their customers.

M. Stocker (✉)
Institute of Strategy and Management, Corvinus University of Budapest, Budapest, Hungary
e-mail: miklos.stocker@uni-corvinus.hu

D. Kostyal · P. Koncz · L. Mikes
Strategic and International Management Research Centre, Corvinus University of Budapest, Budapest, Hungary
e-mail: daniel.kostyal@uni-corvinus.hu; peter.koncz@uni-corvinus.hu; levente.mikes@uni-corvinus.hu

D. Berberović, D. Purg (eds.), *Hidden Champions in Rising Economies*, Contributions to Management Science,
https://doi.org/10.1007/978-3-032-08263-3_20

Overview

Official name: Hungary.
Type of government: Parliamentary Democratic Republic.
Population in 2017: 9,797,561.
Land area: 90,530 km^2.

History

1920	After the collapse of the Austro-Hungarian Monarchy and signing the Treaty of Trianon, Hungary loses two/third of its territory and more than half of its population.
1940	Hungary joins World War II.
1945	At the end of the war, Hungary loses its regained territory.
1949	Hungary becomes a People's Republic under the influence of the Soviet Union.
1989	Hungary becomes a republic.
1999	Hungary admitted to NATO.
2004 (May)	Hungary is one of 10 new states to join the EU.
2011 (January)	Hungary takes over the EU presidency for the first time in its history.
2022	Viktor Orbán is elected as prime minister for the fifth time and FIDESZ-KDNP is elected as governing alliance with two-third majority for the fourth consecutive time.

1 Introduction: Context and History

After the Second World War, Hungary's economic system was a planned economy under the influence of the Soviet Union and the country was one of the founding members of the Council of Mutual Economic Assistance (COMECON), an economic organization led by the Soviet Union. One of the crucial policies of this organization was the specialization of its members, which meant that in the member countries some selected industries were developed, while others withered. Hungary had a special focus on pharmaceuticals, the chemical industry, food processing, agricultural machinery, bus production, and electronics, while other industries were developed in other member countries (Stocker & Szlávik, 2013).

Hungary started its economic and political transition is 1989 to change the planned economy into a market economy and to shake off the Soviet influence. Foreign investors were invited to the country and leading industrial companies were sold to international corporations. Hungary had the most intensive foreign direct investment of all transition economies of Central and Eastern Europe. As a result, the number of foreign-owned companies increased substantially in the transition period and the traditional openness of the Hungarian economy increased further as foreign companies drove exports and imports (Chikán & Czakó, 2002).

After the privatization, some of the world's leading companies invested significantly in their Hungarian subsidiaries: e.g., General Electric, General Motors, Nokia, Samsung, TEVA, and Audi. They were attracted by the well-educated and inexpensive workforce, industrial tradition and experience, good infrastructure, and investment incentives (Stocker & Szlávik, 2013).

Because of these processes, economic growth was relatively stable in Hungary from 1997 to 2006. Annual GDP growth was around 3–4%, and a relatively small number of large companies created almost 50% of the added value in the country. According to Román (2009), 49.7% of the added value was created in 2009 by 870 large companies, which was significantly higher than the EU average of 42.1%. The economic development pattern differed not only in terms of company size but in ownership as well, as foreign companies operated much more efficiently than Hungarian ones. According to Reszegi and Juhász (2014), in 2011 the added value per capita of foreign companies was 11.3 million HUF, compared to 4.5 million HUF of companies with only Hungarian ownership.

The Hungarian economy stumbled in 2007. This situation was worsened by the financial and economic crisis and resulted in −6.7% GDP growth in HUF in 2009 and −1.5% in 2012. GDP growth rates were even worse in US dollar terms as the Hungarian forint was significantly weakening (Központi Statisztikai Hivatal, 2019). Because of the negative trends, high unemployment rate, and even worse expectations, tens of thousands of Hungarians left the country to work in Austria, Germany, the United Kingdom, or other countries. According to Hárs and Simon (2017), in the period from 2006 to 2016 the Hungarian labor market lost 260,000 people who were employed in other countries and the return rate was significantly lower than the emigration rate.

In the 2 years following the change of government in 2010, the focus was on rebalancing, but after that, from 2013, the Hungarian economy started to expand on a sustained basis. A significant increase in foreign direct investments, the government's strategic agreements with large multinational companies and EU funds have played a key role in achieving growth.

In an increasingly favorable macroeconomic environment, the government and the central bank started to pursue expansive economic policy, which also contributed to growth. The Hungarian government also reinvigorated the Hungarian EXIM Bank in 2012 to facilitate internationalization-based growth with relatively inexpensive financial solutions. The Hungarian National Bank initiated the Funding for Growth Scheme, with which it supplied interest-free credit to retail banks, offered at a fixed 2.5% interest rate to companies financing their growth. Because of all these initiatives, the Hungarian economy returned to growth in 2013 and another stable growth period started. Hungary even over performed almost all EU countries in 2018 according to the World Bank, with its 5.1% annual GDP growth (Stocker, 2021). Thanks to the high-pressure economy, the expansion continued in 2019 with 4.9% annual GDP growth.

In 2020, following the outbreak of the pandemic, shutdowns, disrupted supply chains, declining consumption and export activity, and general uncertainty led to an economic slowdown in Hungary, as in the global economy. In the following year, expansive monetary and fiscal policy, base effects and a positive change in the macroeconomic environment put the Hungarian economy back on a growth path, which continued in the first half of 2022, but the outbreak of the Russian-Ukrainian war caused serious problems. The high-pressure economy alone put the economy under inflationary pressure, exacerbated by the depreciation of the forint, the sharp increase in energy prices and the dependence on Russian energy. These factors, combined with productivity problems, led to inflation of 14.5% in 2022 and 17.6% in 2023 (Központi Statisztikai Hivatal, 2024a). The high inflation resulted in a sharp increase in the base rate and a decline in consumption and market investments, which pushed the Hungarian economy into recession. The recovery started in 2024, but it will take longer to recover in the steady economic growth above 4%.

Between 2020 and 2024, interest rate conditions in Hungary fluctuated notably due to various shocks. The impact of the pandemic further eased the already loose monetary conditions by lowering the base rate from 0.9% to 0.6%. In response to rising inflationary risks, the Monetary Council started its rate hike cycle in the summer of 2021, bringing the base rate in Hungary to 13.0% by September 2022, but the end of the cycle proved premature. In order to halt the process, the Hungarian National Bank opened the ceiling of the interest rate corridor and launched new overnight tenders at 18%, which served as the reference rate in Hungary for 6 months. The move drought market lending, only the state-supported Baross Gábor Reindustrialization Programme could support lending processes. Since spring 2023, the Monetary Council has been steadily easing monetary conditions, but the higher-than-regional-average interest rate environment has made it difficult for market lending to recover.

Since 2012, unemployment in Hungary has been falling steadily due to rapid economic growth, job creation programs and the significant FDI inflow supported by the government: unemployment fell from 12.5% in January 2012 to 3.5% in March 2020 (Központi Statisztikai Hivatal, 2024b). Regardless of the difficulties, there has been no significant increase in unemployment in the following period, with the rate remaining below 5% (Exhibit 1). A tight labor market also improved the bargaining power of employees and resulted in a steady rise in real wages except in 2022 and 2023. Rising wages led Hungary to a substantial increase in the cumulative financial wealth of the citizens.

The education in Hungary is based on the Prussian-based educational culture, which does not truly motivate entrepreneurship. It is far easier and less difficult for a Hungarian to be employed or to go abroad to get a job than start his own enterprise even if he has the knowledge to do it. The educational system does not really support entrepreneurship (Stocker, 2021).

Despite the difficulties, the Hungarian economy has made a significant progress over the past decade, but it is also clear that the economic model based on extensive growth is starting to face barriers due to the low unemployment rate. The path to the sustainable economic growth lies in productivity growth. For this transformation, Hungary's hidden champions can provide an excellent example for other companies.

Hidden champions in Hungary are usually in industries where a high level of knowledge is transformed into solutions for customer needs. Most Hungarian

Exhibit 1 Core Economic Indicators for Hungary

	2014	…	2017	2018	2019	2020	2021	2022	2023	2024
GDP per capita (current US$)	14,294		14,621	16,425	16,786	16,131	18,775	18,353	22,142	..
GDP per capita growth (annual %)	4.23		4.27	5.36	4.91	−4.28	7.51	5.29	−0.37	..
Unemployment, total (% of total labor force) (modeled ILO estimate)	7.73		4.16	3.71	3.42	4.25	4.05	3.61	4.11	4.43
Foreign direct investment, net inflows (% of GDP)	9.26		−8.48	−40.09	59.91	106.43	18.39	−1.12	−34.01	..
GDP (current US$, mio)	141,034		143,112	160,566	164,020	157,288	182,110	177,006	212,389	..
Exports of goods and services (current US$, mio)	122,874		122,961	134,482	133,725	123,747	145,581	160,041	172,469	..
Exports of goods and services (% of GDP)	87.12		85.92	83.76	81.53	78.68	79.94	90.42	81.2	..
Imports of goods and services (% of GDP)	81.27		79.31	79.51	79.22	76.78	79.76	95.52	76.27	..
Merchandise exports (current US$, mio)	110,622		113,806	124,705	123,796	120,654	141,830	151,672	160,720	..
Merchandise exports to high-income economies (% of total merchandise exports)	85.53		86.06	86.55	89.49	89.46	88.75	89.01	89.32	..
Merchandise exports to low- and middle-income economies in Europe and Central Asia (% of total merchandise exports)	9.99		9.48	9.33	6.65	6.73	7.03	7.13	6.87	..
Ores and metals exports (% of merchandise exports)	1.5		1.38	1.48	1.31	1.23	1.54	1.62	1.35	1
Agricultural raw materials exports (% of merchandise exports)	0.71		0.63	0.62	0.65	0.52	0.7	0.65	0.58	0.61
Food exports (% of merchandise exports)	8.31		8.36	7.77	7.98	8.57	8.3	8.56	8.55	9
Fuel exports (% of merchandise exports)	3.34		2.5	2.81	2.62	2.19	3.2	4.27	3.14	3.32
Manufactures exports (% of merchandise exports)	83.49		86.73	86.57	86.86	86.85	85.71	82.81	86.16	..
High-technology exports (% of manufactured exports)	16.69		17.18	16.81	17.36	17.43	16.25	17.72	17.89	..

Data from database: World Development Indicators Last Updated: 05/30/2025. World Bank (2025)

hidden champion internationalize very quickly after their inception, which qualifies most of them as international new venture (Oviatt & McDougall, 1994). Early internationalization is very helpful as Hungarian companies which internationalize early create more added value per employee, employ more people and grow faster than those which do not (Stocker, 2019). In this chapter Mcule is a prominent example, which is even a born global company with their platform solution.

In the 2024 hidden champions research round, eight potential new hidden champions were identified with the help of research organizations, industry organizations and personal connections. Four of them accepted our request and participated in the actual research. The analyzed companies are diverse in terms of corporate maturity and industry, and therefore have different characteristics.

Regardless of the differences, there are common strengths of the Hungarian hidden champions. In the case of companies, it can be said that Hungarian hidden champions have achieved outstanding international success primarily in traditionally strong industries. In addition, all of them are well-capitalized companies that have been key players in their industry for a long time, not only in Hungary but also throughout Europe, due to their skilled workforce and highly innovative solutions.

2 Case Studies of Selected Hidden Champions

2.1 Case Study 1

2.1.1 MCULE.COM KFT

Overview
Address: Bartók Béla út 105–113. 1115, Budapest, Hungary
Tel: +36302932064
Email: info@mcule.com
Web: https://www.mcule.com

Company information
Industry[1]: 46.75 Wholesale of chemical products
Year of Establishment: 2011
Sales Revenues in 2017: 0.199 million euros
Sales Revenues in 2023: 3.996 million euros
Average number of employees in 2023: 27 full-time employees
Brainer(s) behind the company: The Team, each person and their cohesion is of key importance

Nature of Market Leadership

Mcule.com Kft. operates as an online platform/marketplace for molecules as raw materials for pharmaceutical research. Additionally, they offer services in molecular docking and compound preparation. Within this niche, they rank among the top three providers in the EU and the top four in the world, holding nearly a 10% market share globally. Their impressive growth has garnered international attention, with The Financial Times listing Mcule.com Kft. among the 1,000 fastest-growing European companies in 2021, 2022, and 2023.

Nature of Competitive Advantage

Mcule is a highly innovative company with specialized expertise in a niche field. The founders, who come from research and chemical informatic backgrounds, leverage this perspective to connect with aspiring researchers, who often become buyers. These connections sometimes evolve into strategic partnerships. After a few years in the market, they became known as a company that can be relied upon, which provide a solution for challenging problems. Most of their competitors have no expertise in chemical IT and focus on trading, whereas Mcule focuses on solutions which includes trading as well, which differentiates them from the others.

Mcule's commitment to innovation remains strong as they continually explore new directions for the company. They offer a fully integrated service, providing not only the highest quality compounds but also molecular modeling tools, design unique compounds unavailable elsewhere, have molecular docking services, and give assistance with customs clearance and logistics.

Core Lessons Learned on the Path to Success

1. Leveraging their backgrounds in research, Mcule maintains an innovative mindset to connect more freely to fellow researchers and innovators, enhancing their ability to sell compounds.
2. The success of the company is rooted in their human resources, as they cultivated a closely knit team of young, high-achieving professionals that are committed to the company.
3. Mcule fosters a culture of innovation and collaboration to enable the team to drive the company forward and ensure that they stay at the forefront of the industry.

Management and Leadership Development Needs

The company heavily relies on the expertise of its team members. This reliance was a significant strength in the early stages, as the team possessed all the necessary knowledge. However, as the company gradually grows, it has become essential to document these processes for future use.

Recognizing the critical role of their team, the company strives to maintain an ideal size from collaboration and cost perspective as well, by being highly selective in their hiring process and investing in retaining existing talent. Whenever possible, they prioritize automating processes instead of hiring additional staff. Implementing knowledge management systems and prioritizing employee engagement and retention are the key future needs of the company.

Financing and Regulatory Environment Development Needs

The company no longer relies on external investors for funding. Instead, they secure capital through grants from the state or the European Union for R&D projects. Additionally, if necessary, they can depend on financial injections from the owners. This approach provides them with greater financial independence and flexibility.

Pandemic's Impact on "Hidden Champions" Business Approach

While the COVID-19 crisis negatively impacted many companies, Mcule experienced a different trajectory. Initially, labs were closed, and R&D projects were halted in the industry, funding for these projects dried up. However, after a few months, the pharmaceutical and biotech industries received an unprecedented influx of capital. This financial boost resulted in significantly increasing demand to market players like Mcule, and especially their solution-based focus led to even higher growth, which resulted in a highly successful year for the company.

Effects of the Ukraine War on "Hidden Champions" Business Operations

Historically, most companies manufacturing chemical compounds in the region are based in Russia or Ukraine. This posed significant logistical challenges for many businesses. However, Mcule distinguished itself by capitalizing on this situation and generating value. Unlike several large pharmaceutical companies that faced bureaucratic hurdles when ordering molecules directly from manufacturers, Mcule demonstrated agility in resolving these issues swiftly. This ability to overcome obstacles allowed them to enhance their services and add value to their offerings. Mcule's approach is characterized with the highest possible level of transparency, in this way buyers can decide whether they order from Russian or Ukraine based manufacturers or not. One of Mcule's competitors Chemspace, which is a Ukraine based company could solve several of their war-based problems with relocation of some activities to the European Union.

From Researcher Roots to a Global Innovation Leader, Based on "The Team" Founded by a group of researchers, Mcule has always embraced an innovative mindset that has been integral to its success. This approach not only helps the sale of compounds to diverse biotech companies with leaders that are also researchers, but also establishes Mcule as an innovator within the global industry. This mindset has proven invaluable in navigating and thriving amidst challenges such as the COVID-19 pandemic and geopolitical disruptions like the Ukrainian War, enabling the company to emerge stronger and more profitable.

Mcule's primary revenue stream stems from supplying chemical compounds to researchers of pharmaceutical firms, particularly burgeoning biotech enterprises. Beyond their robust compound search platform, Mcule extends its service offering with additional solutions including molecular docking and comprehensive logistics support. They place significant emphasis on maintaining a wide-ranging product portfolio and ensuring swift service delivery. Mcule differentiates itself by developing and offering exclusive compounds that are unavailable elsewhere, leveraging their advanced technical capabilities to outpace competitors. Furthermore, their operational capabilities include cold room storage facilities, enabling rapid distribution across the EU within a day and to the USA within 2–3 days, which is a feature highly valued by their customers.

A cornerstone of Mcule's success, as highlighted by the company, lies in their exceptional team, where members go the extra mile for each other and company by default. As Mcule continues to expand, they recognize the critical importance of documenting processes beyond individual expertise. They remain committed to recruiting top-tier talent and fostering an environment that nurtures and retains employees that are crucial to the company's growth and achievements.

With a strong dedication to innovation, Mcule is well-positioned to drive advancements in the pharmaceutical industry and maintain its market leading role in the coming years.

2.2 *Case Study 2*

2.2.1 MERTCONTROL Group

Overview
Address: Móricz Zsigmond út 51, 2151 Fót, Hungary
Tel: +36 14554010
Fax: -
Email: sales@mertcontrol.com / gparkanyi@mertcontrol.com
Web: https://www.mertcontrol.hu

Company Information

Industry[1]: 74.90 Other professional, scientific and technical activities n.e.c
Year of Establishment: 1996
Sales Revenues in 2017: 577 thousand euros
Sales Revenues in 2023: 7.293 million euros
Average number of employees in 2023: 93 full-time employees
Brainer(s) behind the company: Csongor Kállay, founder and co-CEO of Mertcontrol Group & Gábor Párkányi, co-CEO of Mertcontrol Group

Nature of Market Leadership

Mertcontrol Group has longstanding market experience in the field of testing, inspection, and certification (in short: TIC activities) of agricultural crops and produce. Mertcontrol offers its TIC service portfolio to food and agriculture producers. As an integrated company, Mertcontrol has achieved a dominant leading market share in Hungary and Slovakia besides sustaining a strong foothold in Romania, thus holds a significant position in the Central-Eastern European market too.

Nature of Competitive Advantage

Mertcontrol's predecessor legal entity was founded in the 1950s which means the company has accumulated deep industry expertise throughout decades. As an established player in its field, Mertcontrol has a wide clientele and expert network in the form of strategic partnerships. Today, Mertcontrol successfully covers testing, inspection and certification which is perceived as a unique value proposition on the market. Besides having an integrated portfolio, Mertcontrol offers consultancy services as well.

Core Lessons Learned on the Path to Success

1. In a high-risk industry, Mertcontrol prioritizes caution over rapid growth, maintaining a careful balance between prudent management and business expansion.
2. Despite having the potential to triple its revenue, Mertcontrol chooses stability, recognizing the industry's low tolerance for error.
3. The company sees human resource management as key to success, valuing proactive behavior and strong team collaboration.
4. Mertcontrol distinguishes itself by anticipating client needs and initiating solutions early, even before receiving official requests.

[1]According to NACE Rev. 2—please check the technical instructions included in this document (pg. 9).

Management and Leadership Development Needs

On the market and in the CEE region, especially in Hungary, maintaining personal relationship with clients and the partner network is essential. Executives lay strong emphasis in PR and management should always take care of maintaining an expert image of Mertcontrol. The company upholds a liveable, friendly atmosphere at work where colleagues are not pressured to perform. Leaders and even CEOs (as they operate with three CEOs) know each of their subordinates and their motivations, their personal background, how they like to work and how they perform at their best. Mertcontrol desires to keep it that way and avoid getting too big in size as it is one of the core lessons learned. Today, acquiring and retaining talented employees is challenging and Mertcontrol has recognized that substantial effort is needed toward keeping the skilled workforce.

Financing and Regulatory Environment Development Needs

As part of its prudent management practices, Mertcontrol mostly opts for equity finance. What they would like to get better in is how they perform with Hungarian tenders and proposals. Keeping up to date with regulatory changes also poses a challenge for Mertcontrol.

Pandemic's Impact on "Hidden Champions" Business Approach

Regarding operations, Mertcontrol's laboratories in Komárom, Kerepes, and Debrecen worked in a well-organized manner and the risk was mitigated well. Employees worked in flexible schedules and separation was perfect. Border crossing and crop transportation was difficult, also to determine who to work with during the virus spreading as transportation was banned in some cases to avoid spreading disease. In the first year, the pandemic caused major disruption, but Mertcontrol was fueled to find a solution and they managed to alter the transportation routes, which are still used to this day. The hardships experienced during the pandemic and the service disruptions of courier and transportation demanded Mertcontrol create their own fleet and operations. Today, this in-house capability is greatly appreciated on the market, because with this the company can provide additional value as it is more careful and focused than using independent transportation providers.

Effects of the Ukraine War on "Hidden Champions" Business Operations

Food safety and quality assurance of produce became crucial during the Ukraine War. Mertcontrol hasn't experienced significant disruption as many similar hurdles were mitigated during the pandemic (road alterations, longer waiting times). Crop inspection was executed near the Ukraine border, surprisingly imports from Ukraine mostly remained intact and on time. To further widen its service offerings, Mertcontrol has started to lay a stronger focus on handling food products besides agricultural produce, providing a truly value chain-spanning solution portfolio to its clientele.

Value Chain-Spanning Service Portfolio Paired With Market Expertise at Mertcontrol Group

Mertcontrol Group was established in 1996; however, the preceding legal entity has been in the agricultural crop testing market for more than 60 years. Throughout these decades, the company has gathered deep industry knowledge and a network of expert partners. Today, Mertcontrol offers a value-chain spanning service portfolio for agricultural companies and food producers as testing, inspection, and certification coupled with consultancy services.

In the last decade, Mertcontrol has experienced stable growth in its operations. This growth has remained strong despite the challenges generated by the COVID-19 pandemic and the Ukraine War. These crises have strengthened the need for food and produce safety, creating further demand for Mertcontrol's services: in 2023, Mertcontrol achieved twofold growth in net revenue compared to 2020.

Many different factors have contributed to this success, such as the thoughtful management practice that kept the balance between sustaining growth and avoiding getting too big in size, too soon. Team effort and collegiality are recognized and rewarded at Mertcontrol which allows employees to maximize their efficiency without pressure. The company sustains a friendly atmosphere and focuses on maintaining a close relationship with each colleague. The importance of personal relationships is also utilized in how Mertcontrol markets its services and keeps contact with clients.

Looking ahead, Mertcontrol prepares to focus on retaining its highly skilled workforce and applying for Hungarian financial subsidies, besides keeping the ideal size where the business can grow but the current positive atmosphere is still sustained at Mertcontrol.

2.3 *Case Study 3*

2.3.1 PALLET SOLUTION KFT

Overview

Address: Koronafürt utca 22, 1165 Budapest, Hungary
Tel: +36 20 665 6052
Fax: -
Email: info@palletsolution.hu
Web: https://www.palletsolution.hu

Company information

Industry[2]: 46.13 Agents involved in the sale of timber and building materials
Year of Establishment: 2001
Sales Revenues in 2017: 3.385 million euros
Sales Revenues in 2023: 13.847 million euros
Average number of employees in 2023: nine full-time employees
Brainer(s) behind the company: Gábor Lévai, Chief Executive Officer, and Ádám Lévai, Sales Director of Pallet Solution Kft

Nature of Market Leadership

Pallet Solution Kft. is a market leader in the sales and rental of used pallets and GitterBox products, targeting automotive businesses, logistics companies, retailers, pharmaceutical companies, and food & beverage companies. The company has nearly 50% market share in the Central Eastern European region in the rental of used GitterBoxes. In recent years, the economic downturn somewhat helped Pallet Solution to expand as production didn't cease and excess inventory required clients to store finished goods with the help of GitterBoxes. Pallet Solution's efforts are recognized on an international level too: *The Financial Times* has selected the company among the 1,000 fastest-growing European companies in 2022 and 2023.

Nature of Competitive Advantage

Pallet Solution has remained a family-focused company, where brothers Gábor Lévai and Ádám Lévai both work devotedly and build trust with their partners. Today, Pallet Solution Kft. managed to place itself in the role of system integrator, upholding a wide network of domestic and international partners and stable suppliers. This integrator role helps the company to maximize efficiency in its core activities and outsource other activities to reliable partners. In this network model, Pallet Solution receives a transaction fee after the sales or rental of its products, so export is indirect through clients.

Core Lessons Learned on the Path to Success

1. Coming from a family business, Pallet Solution has always believed in organic growth and careful cost management as keys to long-term success.
2. A stable and reliable network provides the company with a strong sense of security and stability in the market.

[2]According to NACE Rev. 2—please check the technical instructions included in this document (pg. 9).

3. During the COVID-19 pandemic, the founders learned to navigate crisis situations effectively and recognized that their industry remains essential and resilient in any economic climate.

Management and Leadership Development Needs

With such a background as Pallet Solution, the company follows a prudent management practice, focusing on organic growth. However, due to the recent expansion, the company has also recognized a need for a second managing director and the development of Pallet Solution's sales capabilities to ensure future market success. Also, the need for proper company branding is required, to which a planned new showroom facility and new leadership can bring success.

Financing and Regulatory Environment Development Needs

The company follows the practice of equity financing and only takes bank loans with small interests. As a system integrator in the sales of used storage products, Pallet Solution often opts for acquisitions. The company acknowledges that a better business environment and pricing would favor such acquisition practices.

Pandemic's Impact on "Hidden Champions" Business Approach

As downturns tend to favor Pallet Solution and similar businesses, the COVID-19 pandemic contributed to the company's growth in the past 3 years. However, at the beginning of the pandemic, business processes in the industry were disrupted and recovery was slow. Transportation routes were also delayed, and the market experienced shortages. Due to the pandemic, Pallet Solution had to create a resilient form of operations in which its strong, reliable supplier network turned out to be crucial. This learning point strengthened the company's belief in organic growth and the importance of a stable partner network.

Effects of the Ukraine War on "Hidden Champions" Business Operations

At the time of the outbreak of the conflict, wood supply was disrupted which is an essential ingredient to wood pallets. Supply did not cease in 2022 and recovery did not take long for supply to be reliable again. The pandemic and the conflict caused fluctuation in prices, which was hard to handle for Pallet Solution and its clientele.

From Family Business to Regional Market-Leading Presence as a Network Integrator
Led by people coming from a longstanding family business, Pallet Solution has slowly become a leading network integrator in the sales and rental of used pallets and GitterBox products. The company has a wide range of clientele, operating in markets such as retail, the automotive sector, pharmaceuticals, and logistics. Through an increased focus on organic growth and cautiously managing expenses, Pallet Solution has achieved a stable position on the market, securing nearly 50% market share in the Central Eastern European region in the rental of used GitterBoxes. The pandemic and the Ukraine War fueled demand for the company's products as many businesses were forced to increase inventory as overall demand and consumption fell during the time of these crises. Also, many businesses seek cheaper and more sustainable solutions like used pallets and storage products. Pallet Solution managed to capitalize on this growth opportunity, which was so successful that The Financial Times recognized its effort among the top 1,000 fastest-growing companies in 2022 and 2023.

As a network integrator, Pallet Solution lays strong emphasis on maintaining a strong supplier and partner network which allows the company to outsource non-crucial business activities to its partners and keep its core activity in-house to maximize efficiency and contain the costs.

Despite sustaining its strong position in the market, Pallet Solution faces challenges in building out its sales capabilities and increased visibility as a brand. Management is considering the appointment of a new executive to handle the expansion and to create a new showroom facility which would help the company's branding efforts. These steps would further fuel the growth of Pallet Solution.

2.4 *Case Study 4*

2.4.1 Julius-K9

Overview
Address: Ipar utca 10–12, 2310 Szigetszentmiklós, Hungary
Tel: +36 20 252 1816
Fax: -
Email: info@julius-k9.com
Web: https://www.julius-k9.com

Company information
Industry[3]: 15.12 Manufacture of luggage, handbags and the like, saddlery and harness
Year of Establishment: 1997

[3] According to NACE Rev. 2—please check the technical instructions included in this document (pg. 9).

Sales Revenues in 2017: 15.262 million euros
Sales Revenues in 2023: 14.802 million euros
Average number of employees in 2023: 322 employees
Brainer(s) behind the company: Anikó Bakos, Founder, and Gyula Sebő Founder, Chief Executive Officer of Julius-K9 Kft

Nature of Market Leadership

Julius-K9 is the European market leader in the quality dog harness market thanks to its patents, high-quality, and flexible technology solutions, and prominent use of materials. In the coming period, the company plans to strengthen its market position by increasing its market share in the USA.

Nature of Competitive Advantage

Julius K-9 sets itself apart with more than 20 years of experience, industry embeddedness, expertise and continuous innovation, enabling it to produce goods of higher quality than its market competitors. As a result of high-quality manufacturing, Julius-K9 products are described as a positive example by international intellectual property organizations. The brand name stands for quality, reliability, and innovative solutions in the market.

Core Lessons Learned on the Path to Success

1. In an increasingly competitive market, you need to constantly innovate and strive for flexible production.
2. The only way to move forward is through relentless consistency and making the tough decisions.
3. Without strong textile industry background it is difficult to maintain competitiveness.

Management and Leadership Development Needs

In the face of fierce price competition in the European market, management needs to cut costs and streamline operations. Implementing organizational change is a challenge for management. To increase cost efficiency, the existing production structure must be transformed, and the organization must be made leaner and more flexible in order to handle the challenges of a rapidly changing environment.

Financing and Regulatory Environment Development Needs

In many cases, inferior products from non-EU manufacturers enter the EU market, which is even supported by store chains as they sell them as private label brands. This brings about a challenge for European high-quality manufacturers and looks to set a future, where the market will be divided to quality brands and value brands, with value brands cannibalizing the previous high share of quality brands. According to the company, it would be important to strengthen the common European customs regulations as well as the whole European textile industry.

In its current situation, the company's own resources are not sufficient for expansion, so a long-term loan would be necessary. However, the current high interest rate environment prolongs the return on investment, which is why various state-supported export incentive programs could also provide a solution.

Pandemic's Impact on "Hidden Champions" Business Approach

The pandemic has caused the company to deal with significant fluctuations in demand. The rise of web shops has also challenged the company, as the competitive advantage of high-quality products can be better exploited through a physical presence.

Effects of the Ukraine War on "Hidden Champions" Business Operations

After the outbreak of the war, a sharp rise in energy and raw material prices caused cost challenges for Julius-K9, which became even more pronounced with the expansion of imported low-cost products.

Julius-K9: Innovation and Quality in the Dog Harness Market
Julius-K9 has been a leading player in the dog accessories market for more than 20 years. Founded by Anikó Bakos and Gyula Sebő, the company has grown over the years from a garage company to one of Europe's most renowned high-quality dog harness manufacturers. The products manufactured by the company outperformed their competitors in terms of shape, color, and durability even in the early 2000s; moreover in the last decade thanks to their continuous innovation capabilities, they have become one of the biggest players in the European dog harness market. All of the company's product developments have been elaborated on in the field of patent and design protection, resulting in more than 160 trademarks and numerous other patents worldwide.

Before the outbreak of the pandemic, Julius-K9 had a market share of almost 50% in Europe, but macroeconomic and geopolitical events have challenged the company: significant growth in online trade has been difficult for a company that relied on a physical presence, but the main problem has been the uncontrolled influx of cheaper import goods into the European market. Energy and raw material prices also rose sharply following the outbreak of the war, posing a further challenge in the race to sustain competitiveness.

Despite the difficulties, Julius-K9 has secured its leading position in the European high-quality dog harness market, although the value segment of the market rose steeply in the past few years. Furthermore, their innovative capabilities permanently help them to compete with Asian manufacturers. By broadening its product portfolio and increasing its market share in the USA, the company still has significant potential to contribute to the re-growth of Julius-K9.

3 Conclusions and Recommendations

Hungarian hidden champions are predominantly small yet exceptionally innovative companies. While some emphasize strong, centralized leadership, a new generation of entrepreneurs places greater emphasis on building strong teams. Many of these companies operate within industries historically significant to Hungary, yet some have distinguished themselves in saturated markets through innovative products or services. These hidden champions excel in carving out competitive advantages in specialized niches within larger industries.

The recent years that were marked by the COVID-19 crisis and the Ukraine War have significantly impacted the Hungarian market, affecting each player differently. Hidden champions demonstrated resilience by swiftly adapting to challenges, thereby maintaining their leadership positions in their respective markets.

The role of the local government and the European Union is pivotal for the hidden champions. They can support fostering a culture of innovation by implementing policies that incentivize research and development. Also, grants and financial support could enable companies to invest in innovation, technological advancements, and market expansion. Government support is also needed in managing competitive pressures ensures fair competition, which is crucial for the sustained success of these companies.

Although the number of hidden champions in Hungary is relatively low, those that exist are highly innovative and successful. There is optimism that continued support for innovation will nurture a greater number of hidden champions in the future, fostering economic development and enhancing Hungary's competitiveness with Western economies over the long term. These companies have the potential to drive innovation, stimulate economic growth, and propel Hungary forward on the global stage.

References

Chikán, A., & Czakó, E. (2002). Competitiveness of small economies in the global economy—The case of Hungary. In A. Chikán, E. Czakó, & Z. Zoltay-Paprika (Eds.), *National competitiveness in global economy—The case of Hungary* (pp. 23–33). Akadémiai Kiadó.

Hárs, Á., & Simon, D. (2017). A külföldi munkavállalás és a munkaerőhiány. In K. Fazekas & J. Köllő (Eds.), *Munkaerőpiaci Tükör 2016* (pp. 94–109). MTA Közgazdaság- és Regionális Tudományi Kutatóközpont Közgazdaság-tudományi Intézet.

Központi Statisztikai Hivatal. (2019). 3.1.1. A bruttó hazai termék (GDP) értéke, volumenindexe és implicit árindexe (1995–). Retrieved from Központi Statisztikai Hivatal https://www.ksh.hu/docs/hun/xstadat/xstadat_eves/i_qpt001.html

Központi Statisztikai Hivatal. (2024a). 1.2.1.2. A fogyasztóiár-index fogyasztási főcsoportok szerint, és a nyugdíjas fogyasztóiár-index, havonta (2020–). Retrieved from Központi Statisztikai Hivatal https://www.ksh.hu/stadat_files/ara/hu/ara0040.html

Központi Statisztikai Hivatal. (2024b). 20.2.1.2. A 15–74 éves népesség gazdasági aktivitása nemenként, havonta (2009–). Retrieved from Központi Statisztikai Hivatal https://www.ksh.hu/stadat_files/mun/hu/mun0097.html

Oviatt, B., & McDougall, P. (1994). Toward a theory of international new ventures. *Journal of International Business Studies, 25*, 45–64. https://doi.org/10.1057/palgrave.jibs.8490193

Reszegi, L., & Juhász, P. (2014). *A vállalati teljesítmény nyomában*. Alinea Kiadó.

Román, Z. (2009). *Statisztikai Tükör 2009/109*. KSH.

Stocker, M. (2019). Survival, growth, and performance of Hungarian international new ventures. *Society and Economy, 41*, 47–64. https://doi.org/10.1556/204.2019.41.1.4

Stocker, M. (2021). Hidden champions of Hungary. In A. Lalic & D. Purg (Eds.), *Hidden champions in dynamically changing societies* (pp. 195–213). Springer.

Stocker, M., & Szlávik, P. (2013). Hidden champions of Hungary. In P. McKiernan & D. Purg (Eds.), *Hidden champions in CEE and Turkey* (pp. 201–217). Springer.

World Bank. (2025). Data; countries and economies. https://data.worldbank.org/country/hungary

Dr. Miklós Stocker is a habil. Associate Professor at Corvinus University of Budapest, Hungary. Dr. Stocker earned PhD and Habilitation in Management and Business Administration from Corvinus University of Budapest, and he also studied in short programs at Harvard Business School, HEC Paris, IEDC Bled, ESADE Barcelona, IESE Barcelona and Universität Bayreuth.

Miklós is the Head of the Institute of Strategy and Management at Corvinus University, a member of the University Senate, and oversees the institution's Case Track program.

Miklós has extensive managerial and consulting experience, having served as General Secretary of the Hungarian Table Tennis Association, Head of Department at the Ministry of Human Capacities, and worked over a sustained period as a management consultant.

Miklós is a member of Academy of International Business, the European International Business Academy, the Hungarian Academy of Sciences, the Hungarian University Sport Federation and the Hungarian Society of Sport Science. His research is interdisciplinary, with a particular emphasis on strategy, international strategy, competitiveness, knowledge management, sport strategy.

Miklós was the Chairman of the 2024 AIB-CEE Chapter Conference and served in the organizational board of several conferences and world championships.

Miklós is in the editorial board of the Hungarian Review of Sport Science and the Sports and Health Sciences Notebooks and has guest editor experience from International Business Review, European Management Studies and the Budapest Management Review.

Dániel Kostyal is a Ph.D. student at Corvinus University of Budapest, currently also working as a lecturer and researcher at the Institute of Entrepreneurship and Innovation, Department of Business Studies. For over a year now, Dániel has also been part of the advisors' team at the University's Case Track program, coaching undergraduate and graduate teams to participate in international case competitions. Besides activities as a researcher, Dániel also takes part in teaching for several undergraduate freshman and final year courses in management and financial planning.

Dániel also has several years of consulting experience in the fields of management and sustainability, having served as the Managing Director of Ingenium Alliance, a certified training centre and ESG consultant, with a focus on Hungarian and other European markets. He also acted as project manager for organizing scientific conferences for the Circular Economy technology Platform, sponsored by the Ministry of Energy, Hungary.

Péter Koncz is a researcher at the Strategic and International Management Research Centre and Ph.D. student, seminar instructor at the Institute of Strategy and Management, Corvinus University of Budapest. He earned his degrees with distinction from the Budapest University of Technology and Economics and Corvinus University of Budapest. During his studies, he was twice awarded the Excellence Scholarship of the Central Bank of Hungary.

He began his professional career at OTP Bank, and since the summer of 2022, he has been working as a senior consultant at one of Hungary's leading think tanks. As a project manager, he collaborates with Hungary's leading retail and FMCG companies on various consulting projects and also leads projects for the Ministry of National Economy. In addition to his professional activities, he regularly publishes opinion articles in Hungary's leading economic newspapers.

Levente Mikes is a researcher at the Strategic and International Management Research Centre and Ph.D. student, seminar instructor at the Institute of Strategy and Management, Corvinus University of Budapest. He earned his bachelor's and master's degrees with distinction from Corvinus University of Budapest.

Levente began his professional career at K&H Bank, gaining foundational experience in the financial sector. Since March 2024, he has been working as a consultant in the Strategy & Transformation division at Mastercard Data & Services. In this role, he collaborates with leading banking and payments industry clients, leveraging data-driven insights to drive strategic growth, enhance operational efficiency, and address various complex business challenges.

Hidden Champions of India

T. Revathi, Revanth Kumar Guttena, and K. Hemachandran

Abstract The chapter delves into the concept of Hidden Champions in India with reference to two outstanding companies in India: Vijayalaksmi, which is a dominant player in the home appliances industry, and Metalok, an originator of blockchain solutions. Essentially, these firms owe their success to being ahead of competitors at all times, constantly coming up with new ideas, having unique features that customers want more than anything else and never compromising on quality. By specifically examining them, this section seeks to bring out what has made each of these organizations highly prosperous within their narrow fields. It also suggests some key takeaways we can learn from such organizations about how prosperous companies are led and managed. The research indicates that concentrating on segments of a market, ensuring high standards of goods or services, keeping clients satisfied, and using methods that do not harm the environment are critical for sustainable achievements over many years.

Overview

Official name:	Republic of India
Type of government:	Federal Parliamentary Democratic Republic
Population in 2023:	Approximately 1.4 billion
Land area:	3.287 million square kilometres

History

1947: India gained independence from British rule, marking the beginning of its journey as a sovereign nation.

1950: The Constitution of India came into effect, establishing the country as a republic.

T. Revathi (✉) · R. K. Guttena · K. Hemachandran
Woxsen University, Hyderabad, India
e-mail: revathi.t@alliance.edu.in; revanth.kumar@woxsen.edu.in; hemachandran.k@woxsen.edu.in

D. Berberović, D. Purg (eds.), *Hidden Champions in Rising Economies*, Contributions to Management Science,
https://doi.org/10.1007/978-3-032-08263-3_21

1991: Economic liberalization reforms were introduced, leading to significant growth and integration into the global economy.
2020: India became one of the world's largest digital markets, with rapid advancements in technology and infrastructure.

1 Introduction: Context and History

1.1 Business Context in India for Hidden Champions

India has a highly dynamic yet fast-growing economy that lends a helping hand to the growth of its Hidden Champions. In this chapter, the two hidden champions to be explored are Vijayalaksmi (a home appliance company) and Metalok (a blockchain company). These are small to middle-sized companies and have achieved much success throughout the years. This study is of the business landscape in which these Hidden Champions excel, using the PESTEL framework which analyses the Political, Economic, Social, Technological, Environmental, and Legal factors of these two companies.

1.1.1 Political Environment

Indian governance is based on a centralized parliamentary democracy. The government puts efforts into several pro-business measures to rouse economic development, including the Make in India campaign to promote native production and investment. The country's political stability and procedures enhance business-friendly conditions and have established a beneficial environment for the success of enterprises.

1.1.2 Economic Environment

India has one of the most rapidly growing economies in the world. Though in the COVID-19 pandemic, the country faced many economic challenges, the nation showed strength and a clear path for the recovery of the economy. Efficient measures like GDP growth, foreign direct investment, and export performance highlight the effective economic landscape. The government concentrates on digital modernization and infrastructure expansion which also strengthens economic growth.

1.1.3 Social Environment

Indian country has a diverse people with a young population, where the mean age is 28 years old. The young population is attracted to new technology, thereby gradually adopting more digital technologies and providing a large and dynamic population of consumer support. Ongoing development and rising income levels are also thrusting demand for a wide range of products and services. Social developments, such as raising internet access and spreading awareness of universal brands, contribute to a favourable market for Hidden Champions.

1.1.4 Technological Environment

India is well known for their IT and software service sector. In this environment, smart gadgets with internet penetration take the digital business to bigger heights. These efforts support technological growth by improving online infrastructure through its Digital India programme (Sindakis & Showkat, 2024). To face the competitive world, Indian companies are adopting emerging technologies like AI, blockchain and internet of things.

1.1.5 Environmental Environment

The state of the environment in India is now more of interest than ever before. Indian companies have suggested adopting sustainable practices to meet customer needs and expectations for healthy environmental practices. Various steps are also being taken by the government to introduce environmentally friendly policies into businesses and to encourage the use of renewable energy sources.

1.1.6 Legal Environment

There is an active legal framework in place in India, making for a robust system with regard to business functionalities supported by strong intellectual property laws alongside rules that are conducive to investors. Tax systems are made more straightforward through Goods and Services Tax which also goes ahead to convenience trade operations so that even more can take place thus leading towards economic growth at large. Additionally, corporate governance is encouraged by the government through various legal provisions, hence all companies ought not only to be established well but also run in accordance with set regulations otherwise licence may be revoked anytime without notice creating fairness among the competition as much as possible.

1.2 Recent Economic Development and Hidden Champions

In the past few years, there has been huge growth and diversity in Indian economic development. One key shift was India's economic liberalization and reforms in 1991. This series of reforms broadened India's economy into the international market through tax reductions and encouragement of foreign investment. It signifies the move towards a market-oriented economy which sets the stage for future progress (Kotwal et al., 2011). A second development was the "Make in India" initiative which began in 2014. This initiative aims at making India a global manufacturing hub where companies are encouraged to produce their goods within the country. It has resulted in a significant inflow of foreign direct investments thereby giving a boost to the manufacturing sector (Mehta & Rajan, 2017). Lastly, the Digital India Initiative was introduced in 2015. Its main objective is to make all government services available to the citizens electronically by establishing online infrastructure and increasing internet connectivity. Many industries have adopted digital technology widely because of this programme (Agrawal et al., 2022).

Hidden Champions in India have emerged as key players within this context, leveraging the country's economic strengths and navigating its unique challenges. Often overlooked in mainstream business conversations these enterprises are leading players within their niches due to their innovation, and strategic foresightfulness not to mention resilience across markets of various sizes.

1.3 Characteristic of Hidden Champions: The Indian Context

This research identifies two hidden champions in India which are pioneers in their market, namely VL Appliances, a home appliances company and Metalok, a blockchain solutions provider. The interesting fact about hidden champions is that they are hidden, yet popularly known in their niche market. This conveys that there would be many hidden champions that should come into the limelight as these champions are evolving in their markets.

There are three characteristics of VL Appliances and Metalok that make each company a hidden champion in their sectors. The first characteristic the companies possess is market leadership. The two hidden champions each lead their niche markets in their unique ways that are both true to the companies' values and deliver quality services and products to consumers. While VL Appliances has become a trusted household name across the country with its innovative designs and high-quality products, Metalok positioned itself as a leading player in the Indian tech landscape through its blockchain solutions transforming industries. The second characteristic of these hidden champions is ongoing innovation. Each company models ongoing innovation that ensures that the companies sustain their market positions. For example, VL Appliances has been investing in research and development continuously and incorporating smart technology in their home appliances to enhance their customer experiences and meet market demands. Similarly, Metalok has prioritized technological advancements to innovate scalable and secure blockchain frameworks that cater to industry expectations; one feature that maintains their competitive advantage. Finally, these companies both have the characteristics of consumer trust and loyalty. VL Appliances has a deep understanding of the target market segment and uses an extensive distribution and pricing strategy to build a strong customer base that is loyal to their company and products. Likewise, Metalok, through its technical expertise and strong security commitment offers customized blockchain solutions and builds trust in its clients, which gives the company a competitive advantage over its competitors.

Core Lessons Learned

There are several core lessons from these hidden champions such as their strategic play of focusing on niche markets, innovation as a key driver, commitment to quality, and strong customer relationships. The secret of these champions lies in their urge to innovate technology and company processes with relentless efforts that keep them competitive within the dynamically evolving market landscape. Both companies are specialized in their niche markets with deep expertise through which they have established a leadership position. This was possible with their commitment to quality and credibility which built trust in their customers. But the most important lesson to be learned from these two hidden champions of India is their dedication to customer satisfaction with personalized solutions that have facilitated strong customer bonding and ongoing brand loyalty.

Management and Leadership Development Needs

Appreciating their efforts and achievements, the two champions need to have a clear strategic vision that aligns with each company's values and that capitalizes on market opportunities. Both companies can adapt to the market turbulences and ever-changing marketing complexities, maintain recruiting of talented employees, and develop expertise through skill training so that they are updated to the market demands. Finally, cultivating a customer-centric culture and co-creating products and services with customers will help them retain their customer base and attract new customers, which is an ongoing expectation for leadership at each company.

Selection Criteria for Hidden Champions

The selection criteria for selecting the hidden champions included their commitment to innovation, market position in their niche markets, consistent financial performance, high levels of customer satisfaction and loyalty, and sustainable practices to be environmentally friendly. These criteria ensure that the selected companies exemplify the qualities and characteristics of Hidden Champions. The below provides a PESTLE analysis of both companies that gives a profound understanding of the company's environmental profiles (Exhibit 1).

Exhibit 1 Core Economic Indicators for India

Year	2017	2018	2019	2020	2021	2022	2023
GDP per capita (current US$)	1983	2104	2104	1929	2099	2254	2389
GDP per capita growth (annual %)	7.2	6.1	4.2	−7.3	8.9	6.7	6.4
Long-term unemployment (% of total unemployment)	3.6	3.5	3.5	4.1	4.0	3.9	3.8
Foreign direct investment, net inflows (% of GDP)	2.0	1.9	2.0	1.5	1.8	1.9	2.1
GDP (current US$, mio)	2,650,725	2,726,321	2,869,134	2,622,984	2,937,764	3,186,345	3,425,302
Exports of goods and services (current US$, mio)	498,000	538,000	557,000	478,000	549,000	638,000	685,000
Exports of goods and services (% of GDP)	18.8	19.7	19.4	18.2	18.7	20.0	20.3
Merchandise exports (current US$)	299,000	322,000	330,000	277,000	320,000	391,000	424,000

Merchandise exports to high-income economies (% of total merchandise exports)	41.2	40.8	40.5	39.9	41.0	42.3	43.5
Merchandise exports to developing economies in Europe & Central Asia (% of total merchandise exports)	12.7	12.4	12.6	13.0	12.8	12.5	12.3
Ores and metals exports (% of merchandise exports)	8.4	8.1	8.0	7.6	7.8	8.0	8.2
Agricultural raw materials exports (% of merchandise exports)	2.5	2.4	2.3	2.2	2.3	2.4	2.5
Food exports (% of merchandise exports)	10.2	10.1	10.0	10.1	10.2	10.4	10.5
Fuel exports (% of merchandise exports)	12.0	11.8	11.7	11.5	11.6	11.8	11.9
Manufactures exports (% of merchandise exports)	55.4	55	70	70	72	73	74

2 Case Study 1

2.1 VL Appliances

Overview
Address:
VL Appliances Pvt. Ltd.,
90 VK Road, Kanakka Pillai Street
Peelamedu, Coimbatore—641,004, Tamil Nadu, India.
Tel: +91-80-4661-4661
Fax: +91-80-4661-4655
Email: info@vlappliances.com
Web: www.vlappliances.com

Company Information
Industry: Home Appliances
Year of Establishment: 1990.
Sales Revenues in 2017: ₹100 Crores
Sales Revenues in 2023: ₹ 110 Crores
Average number of employees in 2023: 1500
Brainer(s) behind the company: Natarajan Rajanbabu, Karunanidhi, Natarajan Suryaa Mani Shyaam, Sumathi.

2.1.1 Nature of Market Leadership

VL Appliances leads the Indian market in home appliances for their innovation, quality, and customer-centric approach. The company consistently offers high quality products aligned with the distinct needs of Indian customers. They set industry standards across the country for their efficiency and durability. Their leadership quality exhibits a strong brand reputation throughout the market.

2.1.2 Nature of Competitive Advantage

VL Appliances vision states: "To deliver a world class and affordable kitchen appliance, which is a result of relentless research and consistent quality standards, to every house in the country."

Their dedication to the perfection of each of their products gains the consumer's trust and loyalty. Vijayalakshmi Appliances' main focus on innovation creates new value for its customers. By regularly upgrading new technology and innovative solutions, the company leads the home appliances sector across India, proposing innovative products that meet customers' transforming needs. VL products are mainly focused on quality, innovation, and affordability. Vijayalakshmi Appliances brings together high-quality materials and innovative strategies with cost-effective manufacturing processes to construct the best products at the lowest cost. This allows Vijayalakshmi to deliver premium home appliances at an affordable price to provide for a wider range of customers.

2.1.3 Core Lessons Learned on the Path to Success

First, continuous innovation fuelled by R&D and new technologies keeps this company ahead of the curve. Second, a customer-centric approach focused on understanding evolving needs fosters customer loyalty to the brand. Finally, building high-quality products and services strengthens brand reputation, ensuring long-term success.

2.1.4 Management and Leadership Development Needs

VL Appliances makes consistent progress in its management and leadership needs. The organization arranges training programmes focusing on customer relationship management, which includes modernized thinking and innovation management. Developing skills in digital transformation and supply chain optimization is also critical for steering the modern company landscape.

2.1.5 Financing and Regulatory Environment Development Needs

To sustain its growth curve, VL Appliances must pay attention to obtaining various financing solutions, such as stock and loan mechanisms. Compliance with regulatory standards, particularly safety rules and environmental needs, is critical. The company also plans to strengthen its financial planning and risk-managing capabilities to ease any market uncertainty.

2.1.6 Pandemic's Impact on "Hidden Champions" Business Approach

The COVID-19 pandemic significantly impacted the business landscape globally, including "hidden champions" like VL Appliances. The pandemic forced companies to reassess their business models, operations, and strategies to ensure resilience and sustainability. For VL Appliances, the pandemic emphasized the importance of digital transformation and e-commerce. With lockdowns and social distancing measures in place, there was a substantial shift towards online shopping. VL Appliances quickly adapted by enhancing its digital presence and expanding its e-commerce capabilities. This shift not only helped maintain sales during the pandemic but also opened new growth avenues for the future.

2.1.7 Effects of the Ukraine War on "Hidden Champions" Business Operations

The Ukraine war has had far-reaching effects on global business operations, including for "hidden champions" like VL Appliances. While the direct impact on VL Appliances may not be as significant as for companies with direct exposure to the region, there are several indirect effects to consider. There are Supply Chain Disruptions, Rising Costs, Market Uncertainty, and Focus on Sustainability. While the Ukraine war has posed several challenges for VL Appliances, the company has leveraged its agility and resilience to adapt to the evolving business environment. By focusing on supply chain diversification, cost management, market stability, and sustainability, VL Appliances continues to navigate the complexities of the current geopolitical landscape.

2.1.8 Innovation at the Heart of Home Comfort

Introduction

VL Appliances, commenced in 1990 by visionary entrepreneur Mr. Natarajan Rajan Babu, has grown from a small home appliance company to a major competitor in the Indian industry. The story of the company shows the strength of invention, persistence, and an ongoing commitment to quality. VL Appliances is known for its quality and innovative technology throughout India. Their success shows how a company can grow through focusing on customer benefit plans and maintaining strategic leadership.

Early Days and Visionary Leadership

VL Appliances has been recognized for developing breakthrough solutions that meet the unique issues that Indian homes face. With this strategic expertise, the organization discovered a market-specific for durable and energy-efficient appliances that can withstand all climatic conditions. The launching of these appliances immediately captured the hearts of consumers and established VL Appliances as a reliable brand in the Indian market.

The leadership of the management and employees across the company plays a critical role in the company's major success. Their ability to predict industry trends and adapt to changing consumer and economic dynamics has led the company through several stages of growth. VL Appliances has constructed a strong supply chain and distribution network under their leadership, ensuring the products reach even the most remote places of India. This approach has been critical in sustaining the company's competitive edge.

Innovation as a Cornerstone

VL Appliances has always prioritized innovation in its operations. One example of the company's commitment to research and development (R&D) is seen in its cutting-edge R&D centre. In this centre, engineers and designers work diligently work together to create innovative technologies that improve home comfort for their customers. From energy-efficient refrigerators to smart washing machines, VL Appliances has constantly produced products that established industry benchmarks for efficiency and performance.

Sustainable Methods

One of the primary innovations that distinguishes VL Appliances from their competition is their emphasis on sustainability. The company has pioneered the use of energy-efficient technologies in its products, in line with global trends towards environmental responsibility. For example, two specific sustainable solutions of VL are the development of energy-efficient gadgets and using recyclable materials in manufacturing. This commitment to sustainability not only meets regulatory requirements but also appeals to the expanding proportion of environmentally sensitive consumers. VL Appliances has also introduced green manufacturing procedures to reduce waste and minimize the environmental impact of its production operations. These measures have not only improved their brand recognition but also reduced costs and increased operational efficiency.

Success in the Indian Market

VL Appliances has established itself as a top brand in India by constantly offering high-quality goods that consistently meet the expectations of Indian consumers. Three significant variables that contribute to their ongoing success are the diversity of their products, extensive distribution network, and a strong brand reputation. The first variable that contributes to VL Appliances' ongoing success in the Indian market is that it provides a diverse selection of products for its customers, such as refrigerators, washing machines, air conditioners, kitchen appliances, and others. This diversified group of products appeals to a wide range of consumers, from budget-conscious buyers to those looking for high-end products. Another variable that contributes to the company's ongoing success is VL the established distribution network that ensures its products are available throughout the country, including in isolated and rural places. This extensive reach has been important to the company's market penetration and growth. Finally, years of consistent quality and dependable after-sales support have earned VL Appliances a strong brand reputation among Indian customers. Their dedication to customer satisfaction has increased brand loyalty and trust over time.

Success in the Global Market

VL Electronics has also been successful in the international market. Various strategic measures have contributed to their success in the international market, and we will briefly explore four of these. First, the export strategy VL Appliances has helped to not only create international success in sales, but also ongoing plans for exports across the world. The company exports its products to many countries including North America, Europe, and Asia, and they have successfully created a world of value by understanding the needs of each region and designing its products accordingly. This commitment to quality and customization is crucial to building trust with customers around the world. Another strategic measure is partnership with local partners. VL Appliances collaborates with local sales offices and stores in many countries, using their local knowledge to succeed and serve customers more effectively. These partnerships are necessary to manage the complexities of global trade. VL Appliances' innovative and energy-saving products are popular with environmentally friendly customers worldwide and as a result, the company continues its international journey and continues to compete at an international level. The company also quickly adapts to the trends in the market.

VL Appliances' success story is also known for its versatility. The company continues to update its product line to reflect changing consumer preferences and technology. Whether it is the transition to smart home appliances or the importance of sustainable development, VL Appliances has always been at the forefront of business development and continues to be a pioneer in the field of adapting to consumer preferences and changes in the market. Finally, a last strategic measure for success in the global market is that the company has capitalized on the emergence of smart home appliances that include advanced features, such as remote control and voice assistance via smartphone apps. In addition to the convenience that these features afford, these products with advanced technology integration also appeal to tech-savvy consumers. The company's ability to incorporate technology into its equipment gives it a competitive advantage over other companies.

Culture and leadership

VL Appliances' success can be attributed to its excellent leadership and its ongoing leadership development. The organization oversees technical development and fosters a culture of innovation amongst all employees. The employees are encouraged to think creatively and empowered to submit ideas that will help the organization move forward. The organization has also invested in training to help its managers foster critical thinking, innovation management, and customer relations skills. This continuous improvement ensures that the company is ready to meet the challenges of today's business world, from ideas and innovation to meeting customer needs.

Financial Growth and Business Expansion

Financial expansion has been an important part of VL Products' journey. Since its humble beginnings, the company's sales revenue has increased, demonstrating its strong business and operational efficiency. VL Appliances' sales revenue in 2017 was Rs. 5 billion and is expected to reach Rs. 8 billion by 2024. Like all successful companies, VL Appliances faces its share of problems. Competition in the building materials market, financial reform, and legislative change are now major challenges to the company, however, the company's determination and approach continue to overcome these problems and allow it to continue growing.

One overwhelming hurdle for the company was the COVID-19 virus, which created a big problem for the company in various areas. First, lockdowns affected production as well as created product disruptions, and negatively affected sales. VL Electronics, however, used this obstacle as an opportunity to forge ahead by expanding its digital offerings and using e-commerce to connect with customers. This rapid response and innovation of the company not only reduced the burden of the pandemic but also created new growth and ongoing opportunities for the company.

Future Outlook

VL Products tends to maintain its growth curve by focusing on innovation, customer satisfaction, and business expansion. The company plans to increase its research and development investments to develop new-generation home appliances that will meet the changing needs of consumers. Sustainability will continue to be a priority and efforts will be made to reduce the environmental impact of its products. The company also plans to expand its digital capabilities by using technologies such as artificial intelligence and the Internet of Things to create and better use smarter devices. This digital transformation will keep VL Appliances at the forefront of the home appliances industry and also help continue to deliver great value to customers.

3 Case Study 2

3.1 Metalok

Overview

Address: fifth Floor, C9RP + 6RJ Trendz Axis, Vittal Rao Nagar, HITEC City, Hyderabad, Telangana 500,081.
Tel: +919908200056
Fax:
Email: mohitgoel@metalok.io
Web: https: //www.metalok.io/

Company Information

Industry: Metaverse Web3.0 IT industry.
Year of Establishment 2021
Sales Revenues in 2017: N/A.
Sales Revenues in 2023: 3.0–7 cr.
Average number of employees in 2023: 39
Brainer(s) behind the company: Mohit Goel, Founder & CEO

3.1.1 Nature of Market Leadership

Metalok has built a solid business around solving real problems in two key sectors—real estate and healthcare. In real estate, they create virtual property tours that let buyers walk through homes and commercial spaces without being physically there. For healthcare, they've developed training simulations where doctors and nurses can practise medical procedures in a safe, virtual environment before working with actual patients. They also offer blockchain solutions for property transactions, making buying and selling more transparent and secure. What sets them apart is how they work closely with each client to understand their specific needs and then build custom solutions rather than offering one-size-fits-all products. This hands-on approach and their focus on these two industries has helped them become recognized leaders in applying metaverse technology to solve actual business challenges.

3.1.2 Nature of Competitive Advantage

Metalok's main advantage comes from how they package their services. Instead of selling individual products, they bundle everything together—the software, the platform access, and ongoing support. They offer three different subscription models: Platform-as-a-Service (PaaS), Software-as-a-Service (SaaS), and Landing-as-a-Service (LaaS). This gives their business clients flexibility to choose what fits their budget and needs. Since they work exclusively with companies (B2B market), they understand that different businesses have different requirements and financial constraints. What really gives them an edge is that they let potential clients essentially "test-drive" their technology before making big commitments. For companies that are new to metaverse or blockchain technology, this removes a lot of the risk and helps them get to market faster with their Go-to-Market (GTM) strategy. They're competing against established players like Trezi, PropVR, AugRay, FlippAR, Quytech, Plutomen Technologies, and Tata Elxsi in the Indian market, but their bundled approach and trial options help them stand out.

3.1.3 Core Lessons Learned on the Path to Success

Metalok's journey has taught them several valuable lessons. First, staying ahead of the technology adoption curve—meaning they invest in and master new technologies before their competitors do—has paid off big time. While others were still figuring out what metaverse meant, Metalok was already building solutions. Second, they've learned that adapting their company culture to match industry trends and keeping an eye on multiple industries (not just their main focus areas) has been crucial for staying competitive. Third, they discovered that building strong relationships with clients during the trial phase often leads to long-term partnerships. When companies feel supported while learning new technology, they're more likely to stick around. Fourth, being flexible with their business model has been essential. The ability to offer different subscription options means they can work with startups on tight budgets as well as larger corporations with different needs. These lessons have helped them survive in a crowded market where new competitors seem to pop up every month.

3.1.4 Management and Leadership Development Needs

One of the greatest company needs is the marketing of their services. The company's expertise lies in the entrepreneurial mindset and technological solutions. The management believes that every employee in the company must be at least aware of the domain expertise and solutions for potential problems.

3.1.5 Financing and Regulatory Environment Development Needs

The company plans to distribute finances of projects approved to recruiting resources for software and hardware as required. Initiatives under Skill India & MSMEs can help prosper real use cases creating employability, skill training, and adoption in the real market.

3.1.6 The Pandemic's Impact on the "Hidden Champions" Business Approach

During the COVID-19 pandemic, the primary obstacles disrupted were client engagement, delays in project implementation, and uncertainty surrounding the adoption of new technologies in the Metaverse and Web 3.0 domains. The sudden shift to remote work initially hurt their ability to showcase immersive experiences and interactive training modules in person. However, it also created unexpected opportunities as companies became more open to virtual solutions. Many of their clients had to rethink their priorities during the pandemic, with some putting technology projects on hold while others accelerated their digital transformation plans.

3.1.7 Effects of the Ukraine War on "Hidden Champions" Business Operations

The global resource crisis presented challenges in securing key technology components and managing increased costs. The supply chain disruptions affected the availability of software and hardware components for immersive experiences, while inflationary pressures impacted their operational costs.

3.1.8 "From Solopreneur to Metaverse Leader: The Hidden Champion Journey of Metalok"

The case study explores the rise of a hidden champion "Metalok", a young Indian company pioneering advanced simulation technology in the burgeoning Metaverse and Web 3.0 space. Founded in 2021 by Mohit Goel, a seasoned leader with over 20 years of experience in digital transformation, Metalok has carved a niche for itself despite its short existence.

The case study delves into the company's success factors, exploring how innovative leadership, a focus on industry-specific solutions, and a commitment to adaptation have propelled Metalok to the forefront of this rapidly evolving field.

Company Background

In 2021, Mohit Goel, a seasoned leader with a history of driving digital transformation across industries, embarked on a solo venture—Metalok. Fuelled by a vision to democratize advanced simulation technology, Metalok set out to develop cutting-edge virtual environments. These immersive experiences transcended mere entertainment; they offered realistic and scalable training scenarios designed to empower professionals in healthcare, real estate, and sports. Metalok's mission extended beyond its own success. They aspired to be a guiding force, ushering businesses of all sizes into the burgeoning world of Web 3.0 and the Metaverse. Transparency and accountability were paramount, ensuring businesses could confidently navigate this transformative landscape. Metalok envisioned a future powered by digital solutions, fostering a decentralized and globally accessible environment that benefited everyone. At the heart of their philosophy lay a core set of values, especially those of innovation and customer focus. Innovation, with a focus on harnessing the power of cutting-edge technology, was paramount while an unwavering customer focus ensured their solutions prioritized user needs. They championed niche competence and valued in-depth expertise within the industries they served. Finally, a futuristic outlook permeated every aspect of Metalok, ensuring they were constantly building for the future.

Metalok: A Hidden Champion

Metalok's rise stemmed from a potent combination of leadership, vision, and a unique approach to the burgeoning Metaverse and Web 3.0 landscape. Mohit Goel's extensive experience was not simply a collection of years; it was a proven track record of pioneering digital solutions across diverse industries. This experience instilled in him not only the ability to innovate but also the foresight to identify and capitalize on emerging trends. Metalok's unique offering wasn't just another Metaverse company; it was a company that understood the specific needs of various sectors and developed targeted solutions to address those needs. This laser focus not only filled a critical gap in the market but also positioned Metalok as a leader with the potential to revolutionize the way learning and development are conducted. In short, Metalok wasn't just riding a wave; it was shaping the wave itself. Thus, making it a hidden champion.

Metalok had carved out a significant niche for itself within the Web 3.0 and Metaverse space and their competitive edge was multifaceted. Unlike some of their competitors who offered one-size-fits-all solutions, Metalok understood the importance of flexibility. By providing subscription-based access through PaaS, SaaS, and LaaS models, they catered to a diverse range of clients with varying needs and budgets. This ensured a wider client base and fostered long-term relationships. Moreover, Metalok didn't just offer generic Metaverse experiences; they focused on developing industry-specific solutions. These targeted solutions acted as a springboard for clients new to the technology, essentially offering a "test drive" that de-risked adoption and accelerated their integration strategy. Finally, Metalok wasn't content to rest on its laurels in real estate and healthcare. They continuously expanded their service offerings, exploring and developing solutions for a wider range of industries. This diversification ensured their continued relevance and growth potential in the ever-evolving Metaverse landscape.

The Crisis Impact

The COVID-19 pandemic threw a curveball at Metalok's early growth trajectory. Disrupted client engagement, project delays, and a general climate of uncertainty surrounding the adoption of emerging technologies threatened to stall their momentum. The sudden shift to remote work posed a particular challenge for the company because Metalok's core offerings relied heavily on in-person demonstrations of immersive experiences and interactive training modules. Furthermore, with many clients refocusing priorities due to the pandemic, the company struggled to showcase immersive experiences and interactive training modules in person.

However, Metalok's adaptability proved to be its saving grace. The company pivoted swiftly, embracing virtual demonstrations and webinars. Leveraging their expertise in immersive technologies, they were able to effectively engage clients remotely. Moreover, they recognized the growing need for remote collaboration and training solutions. By developing new virtual experiences specifically tailored to the Metaverse and Web 3.0, Metalok not only addressed this need but also strategically aligned itself with the evolving demands of the market. This strategic shift wasn't simply about maintaining relevance; it also necessitated the development of new skill sets within the team. Metalok invested in training for virtual reality, augmented reality, communication systems, and domain-specific expertise. These investments proved highly efficient. The virtual demonstrations and webinars garnered significant interest, and the new remote collaboration and training solutions resonated with clients adapting to a remote work environment. In essence, the pandemic, rather than hindering Metalok's progress, became a catalyst for innovation and a strategic shift towards virtual and remote technologies. This newfound focus not only ensured business continuity but also propelled Metalok further along the path of establishing itself as leader in the Metaverse and Web 3.0 learning and development space.

As the company started recovering from the pandemic, the war in Ukraine created ripple effects that reached Metalok in the form of a global resource crisis. Securing essential technology components became a hurdle, as supply chain disruptions impacted the availability of both software and hardware crucial for creating immersive experiences. Furthermore, inflationary pressures squeezed their operational costs, threatening to derail their growth trajectory.

Metalok, however, wasn't one to be easily discouraged. They tackled these challenges head-on with a multi-pronged approach. First, they diversified their supplier base and explored alternative technology solution providers which broadened their options and fostered resilience against future disruptions. Additionally, they embraced a collaborative partnership approach, fostering connections with other companies in the industry. Internally, Metalok implemented cost-saving measures while simultaneously investing in strategic areas. Software optimization, virtual reality development, and decentralized solutions in the Web 3.0 domain were prioritized. These investments not only enhanced the performance of existing hardware, reducing reliance on new components but also yielded unexpected benefits. The improved efficiency and focus on mixed reality solutions ultimately led to the development of new product offerings, further strengthening their competitive edge.

In essence, the resource crisis, like the COVID-19 pandemic before it, served as a crucible for Metalok. It pressured them to adapt and innovate, ultimately reshaping their business in profound ways. Operational efficiency, supply chain resilience, and technological innovation in the Metaverse and Web 3.0 space became paramount. Investing in software solutions that maximized hardware performance led to new product lines. The crisis also solidified their commitment to developing key skillsets, and domain expertise, and fostering a culture of innovation—all of which positioned Metalok to not only weather the storm but emerge stronger and even more competitive.

The Road Ahead

Despite its impressive early growth, Metalok recognized the need for continued development in two key areas. First, they acknowledged the importance of bolstering their marketing efforts. While their solutions were demonstrably valuable, effectively communicating that value proposition to a wider audience remained a challenge. Metalok sought to strengthen its marketing expertise by recruiting a seasoned professional who could craft and execute targeted campaigns that resonated with potential clients. Secondly, Metalok prioritized employee education. They understood that a well-informed workforce was a critical asset. Equipping all employees with a foundational understanding of their domain expertise and the intricacies of their solutions would foster a more collaborative and innovative environment. This focus on employee development wasn't simply about internal knowledge sharing; it was about empowering every member of the Metalok team to become a brand ambassador, capable of effectively explaining the company's value proposition to clients and potential partners. The goal was to illuminate the power of simulated learning experiences within the Metaverse and Web 3.0 landscape.

4 Conclusions and Recommendations

Conclusion

Hidden champions in India, often overlooked by the mainstream, achieve remarkable success within their chosen niches both in India and globally. By delving into their world, we can illuminate the key characteristics that propel them forward, alongside the challenges they navigate in a dynamic business environment.

A relentless pursuit of innovation lies at the heart of every hidden champion. They don't settle for mediocrity; they constantly refine their offerings to address specific market needs. A leading household appliance manufacturer, for instance, prioritizes research and development to develop energy-efficient and user-friendly products tailored to the unique needs of their target market. Similarly, a pioneering company in the Metaverse and Web 3.0 space creates industry-specific training solutions, ensuring their virtual environments offer superior value compared to generic offerings. This focus on innovation ensures they remain at the forefront of their field, delivering solutions that resonate with evolving demands.

These hidden champions cultivate a deep understanding of their chosen niche. An appliance manufacturer, for example, understands the nuances of their target market, from climate needs to budget constraints. This allows them to develop products with features and functionalities that resonate with their audience. Likewise, a company in the Metaverse space focuses on the specific training requirements of industries like healthcare and real estate. This niche expertise allows them to tailor their virtual environments to address these specific challenges, offering targeted solutions with superior value.

The ability to adapt and pivot strategies is another defining characteristic of our hidden champions. An appliance manufacturer, for instance, navigated a changing regulatory environment by adopting sustainable practices in their manufacturing processes. They also recognized the need to expand their distribution network beyond urban centres to reach remote areas, demonstrating their agility in adapting to evolving market dynamics. Similarly, a company in the Metaverse space swiftly pivoted to virtual demonstrations and webinars during the COVID-19 pandemic, ensuring business continuity. When the global resource crisis threatened their supply chain, they explored alternative technology solutions and diversified their supplier base, showcasing their ability to adapt even in the face of unforeseen challenges.

Strong leadership with a clear vision and a deep understanding of the industry is crucial for hidden champions. A leading appliance manufacturer thrives under strategic leadership that focuses on market trends and customer satisfaction. Their leadership team plays a crucial role in guiding the company through periods of growth and ensuring their products remain relevant to evolving consumer needs. Similarly, a company in the Metaverse space is propelled forward by a leader with extensive experience in digital transformation. This leadership fosters a culture of innovation and drives strategic decision-making. Furthermore, the leader's focus on building a strong industry network opens doors to new opportunities and fosters collaboration, allowing the company to stay ahead of the curve.

Despite their strengths, hidden champions also face unique challenges. Attracting and retaining top talent with the necessary skills and expertise can be difficult, especially in these niche markets. An appliance manufacturer, for instance, invests in employee training to bridge skill gaps and foster a culture of innovation within its workforce. Similarly, a company in the Metaverse space identifies the need for training in virtual reality, augmented reality, and domain-specific expertise to stay at the cutting edge of their field.

Effectively communicating their value proposition to a broader audience is another common hurdle. An appliance manufacturer seeks to expand its reach beyond its established customer base, requiring targeted marketing campaigns. Similarly, a company in the Metaverse space, despite its pioneering solutions, acknowledges the need for a seasoned marketing professional to craft compelling messaging that resonates with potential clients. The success of hidden champions often attracts new players, intensifying competition. An appliance manufacturer faces competition from other manufacturers in the market. Similarly, a company in the Metaverse space, despite its early mover advantage, grapples with increasing competition in this rapidly evolving landscape. This constant state of competition necessitates continuous innovation and strategic decision-making to maintain a competitive edge.

Hidden champions must also remain vigilant in the face of potential disruptions to resource availability. An appliance manufacturer navigated fluctuations in financial regulations, while a company in the Metaverse space encountered supply chain disruptions during the global resource crisis. These examples highlight the importance of building resilience and exploring alternative solutions to ensure uninterrupted operations.

Hidden champions operate in dynamic environments characterized by rapid technological advancements. An appliance manufacturer needs to adapt to evolving consumer preferences and integrate new technologies into their products. Similarly, a company in the Metaverse space needs to stay abreast of rapid advancements in the field and adapt its solutions accordingly. By embracing continuous learning and adaptation, hidden champions can ensure their continued success in a dynamic and ever-changing world.

The journey of hidden champions is one of innovation.

Recommendations

Hidden champions are often unheard of as they operate under the radar, achieving remarkable success within their specialized fields. To ensure their continued growth, a comprehensive support system is necessary. This framework outlines recommendations for three key stakeholders: governments, financial institutions, and educational institutions.

Governments as Facilitators

First, national governments can act as catalysts for hidden champion growth. Targeted funding programmes offering grants, tax breaks, or subsidized loans specifically for research and development within niche markets can incentivize continuous innovation. Collaborations with educational institutions can lead to specialized programmes that equip graduates with the skillsets needed for these niche sectors. Furthermore, implementing flexible regulations tailored to hidden champions' unique needs, alongside recognition and visibility programmes that showcase their success stories, can attract future talent and collaborators. By enacting these initiatives, governments can cultivate an environment that fosters and nurtures the innovative spirit of hidden champions.

Financial Institutions as Enablers

Financial institutions can become crucial partners in supporting the growth aspirations of hidden champions. Specialized loan facility with longer repayment terms, flexible collateral requirements, or financing options can address their specific financial needs. Additionally, risk-sharing mechanisms that mitigate perceived risks could encourage banks and other institutions to invest in these companies. Offering investment banking services that connect hidden champions with investors or venture capitalists specializing in niche sectors can unlock essential capital for expansion or acquisitions. Finally, mentorship programmes pairing hidden champions with experienced financial professionals can provide valuable guidance on financial planning, risk management, and growth strategies.

Academic Institutions as Incubators

Business schools and higher education institutions can play a vital role in nurturing the next generation of hidden champions. Integrating case studies and research focused on these companies into the curriculum exposes students to their unique challenges and strategies. Specialized courses in niche marketing, research and development management, or navigating niche-specific regulations can equip students with the necessary skillsets to thrive in these markets. Collaboration through joint research projects, internships, or guest lectureships fosters knowledge exchange and allows students to gain practical experience within these niche markets. Additionally, establishing entrepreneurship incubators specifically focused on hidden champions can provide crucial mentorship, funding opportunities, and networking connections, propelling promising niche companies towards success.

By working collaboratively, governments, financial institutions, and academic institutions can create a supportive ecosystem that empowers hidden champions to continue thriving and driving innovation within their chosen markets.

References

Agrawal, A., Khan, R. A., & Ansari, M. T. J. (2022). Empowering Indian citizens through the secure e-governance: The digital India initiative context. In *Emerging Technologies in Data Mining and Information Security: Proceedings of IEMIS 2022, volume 3* (pp. 3–11). Springer Nature.

Kotwal, A., Ramaswami, B., & Wadhwa, W. (2011). Economic liberalization and Indian economic growth: What's the evidence? *Journal of Economic Literature, 49*(4), 1152–1199.

Mehta, Y., & Rajan, A. J. (2017). Manufacturing sectors in India: Outlook and challenges. *Procedia Engineering, 174*, 90–104.

Sindakis, S., & Showkat, G. (2024). The digital revolution in India: bridging the gap in rural technology adoption. *Journal of Innovation and Entrepreneurship, 13*(1), 29.

T. Revathi Assistant Professor at Woxsen University, specializes in Machine Learning, Deep Learning, and Computer Vision. With 7+ years of experience and a PhD from Anna University, she has worked across prestigious institutions including VIT University and IITDM. A passionate researcher, she has published extensively in international journals and conferences, receiving best paper awards for her contributions to artificial intelligence and computer vision applications.

Revanth Kumar Guttena Assistant Professor in Marketing at Woxsen University, holds international postgraduate degrees from Netherlands and Taiwan. With 10+ years of teaching and research experience, he combines engineering background with business innovation expertise. His PhD in Marketing from National Dong Hwa University, Taiwan, and Master's in Imagineering from Breda University uniquely position him in consumer behavior, social media, design thinking, and systems thinking research.

K. Hemachandran Director of the AI Research Centre and Vice Dean at Woxsen University, is a globally recognized AI expert with expertise in Natural Language Processing, Computer Vision, and Autonomous Robotics. He serves as UNESCO Expert, ATL Mentor of Change, and holds advisory roles with international companies. A prolific researcher and inventor, he has authored 4 books, edited 17 books, and created multiple patented AI systems including healthcare and agricultural intelligence platforms.

Hidden Champions of Kazakhstan

Daniyar Medetov and Vadim Novikov

Abstract The chapter offers a deep dive into the burgeoning landscape of "Hidden Champions" in Kazakhstan, spotlighting the unique success stories of SMEs like Parqour and Clockster. It explores how these companies, despite operating in a challenging post-Soviet economic environment, have leveraged innovation and adaptability to achieve market leadership in their respective niches. The chapter also examines the critical role of government policies, financing mechanisms, and cultural attitudes in shaping Kazakhstan's evolving entrepreneurial ecosystem, offering valuable insights for both policymakers and aspiring entrepreneurs. The case studies of Parqour and Clockster provide concrete examples of how Kazakhstani companies can overcome obstacles such as skills shortages and regulatory complexities to achieve remarkable growth and international expansion. The chapter underscores the immense potential of Kazakhstan's SME sector and offers actionable recommendations for further fostering its development.

Overview

Official name:	Republic of Kazakhstan.
Type of government:	Presidential Republic.
Population in 2023:	20 mln persons.
Land Area:	2,724,900 km^2.

D. Medetov (✉) · V. Novikov
School of Entrepreneurship and Innovation, Almaty Management University, Almaty, Kazakhstan
e-mail: d.medetov@almau.edu.kz; v.novikov@almau.edu.kz

D. Berberović, D. Purg (eds.), *Hidden Champions in Rising Economies*, Contributions to Management Science,
https://doi.org/10.1007/978-3-032-08263-3_22

History

II-I centuries BC:	Formation of the first states on the territory of Kazakhstan.
VI-VII centuries AD:	The blossoming of Turkic Khaganate.
1860s:	Completion of Kazakhstan's accession to the Russian Empire.
1916:	Uprising of Kazakhs against tsarist rule.
1917–1920:	Establishment of Soviet power.
1930s:	Collectivization of agriculture, mass famine, which led to the death of about 40% of the indigenous population.
1936:	Formation of the Kazakh SSR.
1930–1950s:	Mass deportations to Kazakhstan of peoples recognized as "unreliable" by the Soviet authorities, including Koreans, Germans, Poles, Chechens, Ingush, Balkars, Crimean Tatars, Meskhetian Turks, and Kurds.
1991:	Kazakhstan is the last of the union republics to declare independence.
1991–2019:	Nursultan Nazarbayev is the first president of Kazakhstan.
1997:	Akmola (Tselinograd) is renamed to Astana and becomes the new capital.
2001:	Establishment of the SCO together with China, Russia, Kyrgyzstan, Tajikistan.
2015:	Kazakhstan joins the WTO.
2015:	Establishment of the Eurasian Economic Union (EAEU).
2019:	Kasym-Jomart Tokayev is elected President of Kazakhstan.
2022:	"January events," Constitutional referendum and early presidential elections.

1 Introduction: Context and History

Kazakhstan's market economy emerged amidst significant economic turbulence following the dissolution of the Soviet Union. The post-communist transition period was characterized by severe economic contraction, chronic capital shortages, and the collapse of existing trade networks (Sadyrova et al., 2021). The economic landscape was further shaped by global trends, including increasing financial and economic integration, technological advancements, and shifting geopolitical dynamics (Saiymova et al., 2020). Despite these challenges, Kazakhstan successfully leveraged its resource wealth to sustain robust economic growth, particularly from the late 1990s onward, largely due to rising global demand for its primary export commodities (OECD, 2018).

The country has made substantial progress in developing an innovation-driven economy. Government initiatives, such as the "Kazakhstan 2030" and "Kazakhstan 2050" strategies, have been instrumental in promoting economic diversification and technological advancement (Saiymova et al., 2020). However, the country's innovation ecosystem remains underdeveloped compared to global standards, with relatively low levels of R&D investment and significant regional disparities in innovative capacity (OECD, 2017). The PESTEL framework is used in this chapter to look at the bigger picture of Kazakhstan's Hidden Champions (HCs) and find the most important political, economic, social, technological, environmental, and legal factors that affect their growth. Using the PESTEL framework, this chapter tries to find the main outside factors that are affecting the growth of Kazakhstan's Hidden Champions. The findings will help readers see where they can improve and grow. This comprehensive analysis will help stakeholders better understand the challenges and opportunities faced by these innovative companies in the context of the broader economic landscape.

1.1 Political Environment

Kazakhstan's political stability has played a crucial role in shaping its business environment. While upholding strict regulatory oversight, the government has aggressively supported economic liberalization. Key policy initiatives, such as the Business Roadmap 2025 and the State Program on Industrial and Innovation Development, have provided financial and institutional support to small and medium-sized enterprises (SMEs) and high-growth firms (HGFs) (GEM Kazakhstan Report, 2021). However, regulatory inefficiencies, corruption, and bureaucratic obstacles remain persistent challenges (OECD, 2018). These issues hinder the full potential of the business landscape, creating barriers that can stifle innovation and deter foreign investment. To address these challenges, ongoing reforms and a commitment to transparency will be essential for fostering a more conducive environment for both local and international businesses. The government's efforts to attract foreign direct investment (FDI) through economic reforms, such as the establishment of the Astana International Financial Centre (AIFC), reflect its commitment to fostering a more competitive business climate. By implementing such reforms, the government aims to enhance its appeal to foreign investors, ultimately leading to increased economic growth and diversification. This proactive approach strengthens the local economy and positions the country as a key player in the global market.

1.2 Economic Environment

Kazakhstan's economy is characterized by its dependence on the extractive sector, particularly oil and gas, which accounted for approximately 30% of GDP (Reuters, 2020). While SMEs constitute 96.9% of all registered businesses, their contribution to GDP remains relatively low, at 30.2% in 2023 (Statistics Kazakhstan, 2024). This divergence from global trends highlights the dominance of large state-owned enterprises and multinational corporations in key industries. Despite efforts to diversify the economy, challenges such as limited access to financing, high interest rates, and an underdeveloped venture capital ecosystem continue to constrain SME growth. The government has introduced tax incentives and loan guarantees to mitigate these barriers, but further structural reforms are required to enhance economic competitiveness.

Additionally, technological advancements, particularly in artificial intelligence (AI), present new economic opportunities for Kazakhstan. AI-driven business processes and automation have the potential to improve efficiency across industries. The "Digital Kazakhstan" program has been pivotal in driving AI adoption, with initiatives such as smart traffic management and predictive analytics in public services (Ashimova & Alzhanova, 2023). However, limited AI infrastructure, regulatory uncertainties, and a shortage of skilled professionals remain key barriers to AI-driven economic transformation.

1.3 Social Environment

Kazakhstan's entrepreneurial culture has evolved significantly, with increasing societal acceptance of entrepreneurship as a viable career path (GEM, 2021). According to recent surveys, over 90% of the adult population perceives good business opportunities in their immediate environment, although fear of failure remains a major deterrent to venture creation. Entrepreneurship education has gained prominence with the integration of business-related curricula in vocational institutions since 2016 (OECD, 2018). However, regional disparities persist, with entrepreneurial activities concentrated in major urban centers like Almaty and Astana, while rural areas lag behind in business development.

AI adoption in Kazakhstan's social landscape is also increasing, with significant investments in e-government services, AI-driven healthcare solutions, and digital public services. Projects such as PneumoNet, which utilizes AI to diagnose lung diseases, demonstrate the potential societal benefits of AI integration (Ashimova & Alzhanova, 2023). However, digital literacy gaps and unequal access to digital infrastructure continue to pose challenges to AI-driven societal development.

1.4 Technological Environment

Kazakhstan has made strides in fostering an innovation ecosystem, but significant challenges remain. R&D expenditure as a percentage of GDP was only 0.14% in 2015, significantly below the OECD average of 2.4% (OECD, 2017). Innovation hubs, such as Nazarbayev University and the Alatau Innovation Technology Park, have been established to bridge the gap between research and industry (Saiymova et al., 2020). However, the lack of venture capital funding and a weak startup support infrastructure hinder the commercialization of new technologies (Abazov & Salimov, 2016). To address these limitations, the government has launched several business incubators and accelerators, although concerns regarding their effectiveness persist (MOST Business Incubator 2019). These initiatives aim to foster a more conducive environment for entrepreneurship and innovation, yet the challenge remains in effectively connecting emerging businesses with the necessary resources and mentorship. Strengthening collaboration between academia and industry could further enhance the potential for successful technology transfer and commercialization.

AI is emerging as a key technological driver, with Kazakhstan investing in AI-powered automation, machine learning, and predictive analytics. However, the country remains dependent on foreign AI technologies, and there is a need to strengthen local AI research and talent development initiatives (Ashimova & Alzhanova, 2023). Government initiatives supporting AI research, such as the establishment of the National AI Cluster, seek to enhance local capabilities, but progress remains slow. Slow progress can hinder the country's ability to fully capitalize on AI's potential benefits, making it imperative for stakeholders to collaborate closely. By fostering partnerships between academia, industry, and government, Kazakhstan can accelerate innovation and create a robust ecosystem that nurtures homegrown AI solutions.

1.5 Environmental Considerations

Sustainability has become an increasingly important consideration for Kazakhstan's business environment. The country has committed to reducing its reliance on fossil fuels and enhancing energy efficiency as part of its Green Economy Strategy (Doskaliyeva et al., 2016). However, the extractive industries continue to dominate the economy, posing significant environmental challenges (OECD, 2018). Government-led initiatives promoting renewable energy and sustainable business practices aim to create a more balanced economic model, but their impact remains limited in the short term. In the long term, successful implementation of these initiatives could pave the way for a diversified economy that embraces innovation and sustainability. Additionally, fostering public-private partnerships may enhance investment in green technologies, ultimately supporting the country's transition toward a more resilient and eco-friendly future.

AI technologies also present opportunities for environmental monitoring and resource optimization. AI-driven climate modeling, smart grid solutions, and precision agriculture have the potential to enhance sustainability efforts in Kazakhstan. However, the integration of AI in environmental policies remains limited, and more government support is needed to harness AI for sustainability (Ashimova & Alzhanova, 2023).

1.6 Legal and Regulatory Environments

Kazakhstan has undertaken several legal reforms to improve the ease of doing business. The country ranked 25th in the World Bank's Doing Business 2020 report, reflecting improvements in business registration, property rights, and contract enforcement (World Bank, 2020). However, regulatory inefficiencies and inconsistencies in policy implementation continue to pose challenges for SMEs and HCs (OECD, 2019). The absence of a well-defined venture capital regulatory framework further constrains the growth of high-potential firms. Strengthening the legal infrastructure for business incubation, intellectual property protection, and investor rights will be critical for fostering a more dynamic entrepreneurial ecosystem. Additionally, enhancing access to financing options and providing targeted support for innovation can empower SMEs and HCs to thrive in a competitive market. By addressing these regulatory gaps and fostering collaboration among stakeholders, the economy can unlock its full potential and drive sustainable growth.

1.7 Summary

Kazakhstan's economic transformation has created a fertile ground for the emergence of Hidden Champions. However, several structural barriers, including limited access to finance, regulatory inefficiencies, and low levels of innovation activity, hinder their full potential. Taking on these problems needs a multifaceted approach that includes changing policies, improving financial support, and investing strategically in people, AI technologies, and digital infrastructure.

2 Characteristics of Hidden Champions from Kazakhstan

We identified two key Hidden Champions in Kazakhstan through extensive research: Parqour and Clockster. These companies exhibit strong market leadership, innovation-driven strategies, and unique competitive advantages that distinguish them in their respective industries. Both Parqour and Clockster leverage advanced technology and customer-centric approaches to drive growth and maintain their edge. Their success stories not only highlight the potential within Kazakhstan's market but also serve as inspiring examples for emerging businesses in the region. The selection of Hidden Champions was based on a structured methodology that considered several key factors. These factors included revenue growth, market share, and the ability to adapt to changing market conditions. By focusing on these criteria, the selection process aimed to identify companies that excel in their current operations and demonstrate the potential for sustainable development and long-term success. Market leadership was a crucial determinant, focusing on companies that hold dominant positions in niche markets, demonstrating strong brand recognition and customer loyalty. This focus not only highlights the importance of competitive advantages but also emphasizes the need for innovation and responsiveness in a rapidly evolving business landscape. The objective was to identify organizations that thrive today and are ready for tomorrow's challenges. Innovation was another key criterion, emphasizing firms with a strong commitment to research, technological advancement, and product differentiation that provides them with a competitive edge. Sustained growth was also essential, with companies required to show resilience, continuous expansion, and long-term viability despite market challenges. Competitive advantage played a significant role in selecting firms with unique value propositions that create high barriers to entry for potential competitors. Finally, scalability was a critical factor, as Hidden Champions are not only influential within their domestic markets but also have the potential to expand into regional and global markets, reinforcing Kazakhstan's presence in the international business landscape.

Hidden champions in Kazakhstan demonstrate a clear pattern of strategic positioning and resilience. They maintain their market leadership by emphasizing innovation, quality, and specialized offerings that consistently outperform competitors. Both Parqour and Clockster illustrate how cutting-edge technology, such as AI, automation, and digital solutions, can enhance operational efficiency and improve customer satisfaction. Resilience and adaptability are crucial, as these companies have successfully navigated economic uncertainties and regulatory challenges by continuously evolving their business models. Management and leadership development is another key takeaway, as these firms invest in leadership training and foster a culture of continuous learning, ensuring that managerial competencies remain aligned with business growth. Expansion and internationalization further distinguish these companies, as they have successfully extended their market reach beyond Kazakhstan, demonstrating the scalability potential of local enterprises and their ability to compete on a global stage. The overarching lesson from these Hidden Champions is that a combination of technological innovation, strong leadership, market positioning, and strategic adaptability is fundamental to long-term success in emerging economies like Kazakhstan.

Exhibit 1 illustrates the key economic indicators related to GDP, unemployment, and foreign direct investment, further highlighting the economic context of Kazakhstan. The table presents Kazakhstan's key economic indicators over the period from 2014 to 2023, sourced from World Development Indicators of the World Bank. It provides insights into key macroeconomic metrics such as GDP per capita, GDP growth rates, unemployment figures, foreign direct investment (FDI) inflows, and trade-related indicators. This dataset reflects the economic resilience and challenges Kazakhstan faces, particularly its reliance on commodity exports, fluctuating FDI inflows, and the need for further economic diversification. The insights from these indicators are valuable in understanding the broader business environment in which Kazakhstan's Hidden Champions operate.

Exhibit 1 Core Economic Indicators for Kazakhstan

	2014	2015	2016	2017	2018	2019	2020	2021	2022	2023
GDP per capita (constant 2015 US$)	10,539.04	10,510.77	10,476.35	10,758.52	11,053.36	11,402.76	10,974.24	11,186.28	11,283.42	11,700.84
GDP per capita growth (annual %)	2.68	−0.27	−0.33	2.69	2.74	3.16	−3.76	1.93	0.87	3.70
Unemployment, total (% of total labor force) (national estimate)	5.06	4.93	4.96	4.90	4.85	4.80	4.89	..	4.86	..
Unemployment with advanced education (% of total labor force with advanced education)	..	..	..	3.49	..	..	..	..	..	..
Foreign direct investment, net inflows (% of GDP)	3.30	3.57	12.55	2.85	0.20	2.05	4.21	2.32	2.18	..
GDP (current US$)	221,415,613, 595.47	184,388,404, 706.04	137,278,320, 084.17	166,805,788, 827.23	179,339,977, 690.49	181,667,184, 854.50	171,082,365, 861.42	197,112,255, 360.61	225,496,328, 925.49	261,421,121, 085.57
Exports of goods and services (BoP, current US$)	77,108,811, 971.28	47,824,824, 676.90	43,106,088, 497.30	55,974,348, 709.74	66,345,230, 456.64	67,295,793, 717.67	49,273,351, 002.69	71,725,659, 997.85	93,598,361, 221.93	90,167,457, 991.52
Exports of goods and services (% of GDP)	39.34	28.52	31.84	32.40	37.63	36.44	30.53	33.64	41.78	..
Merchandise exports (current US$)	79,460,000, 000.00	45,956,000, 000.00	36,685,000, 000.00	48,304,000, 000.00	60,956,000, 000.00	57,309,000, 000.00	46,447,000, 000.00	60,625,000, 000.00	84,593,000, 000.00	78,533,000, 000.00
Merchandise exports to high-income economies (% of total merchandise exports)	67.57	64.77	63.61	63.50	66.97	58.22	56.89	..	..	..

Merchandise exports to low- and middle-income economies in Europe and Central Asia (% of total merchandise exports)	16.81	20.28	19.87	19.62	17.59	22.27	23.20	..	..	..
Ores and metals exports (% of merchandise exports)	8.97	12.71	15.59	16.17	12.35	14.78	19.15	18.96	14.90	14.60
Agricultural raw materials exports (% of merchandise exports)	0.15	0.18	0.30	0.31	0.26	0.28	0.22	0.26	0.15	0.23
Food exports (% of merchandise exports)	3.28	4.61	5.72	4.94	5.04	5.61	6.97	6.18	6.55	6.69
Fuel exports (% of merchandise exports)	76.39	67.72	60.73	63.33	70.03	66.24	57.63	57.73	61.38	58.93
High-technology exports (% of manufactured exports)	39.26	43.43	32.10	24.21	23.57	29.29	33.37	27.96	32.16	..
Manufactures exports (% of merchandise exports)	10.88	14.31	17.57	15.20	12.30	13.08	16.01	16.81	16.91	18.98

Source: World Bank (2024)

3 Case Studies of Selected Hidden Champions

3.1 Case Study 1

3.1.1 Parqour

Overview

Address: Almaty, Shevchenko, 144, Astana, Tursynbek Kakisheva street, 13, Dubai, One Central Dubai World Trade Center, Tashkent, Ahmad Donisha, 20A
Fax: 516468–1202
Email: hello@smart-parkings.com
Web: https://parqour.kz/eng/

Company Information

Industry: Parking Management Industry
Year of establishment: 2020
Sales revenues in 2024: N/A
Average number of employees in 2024: over 200
Brain(s) behind the company: Amirkhan Omarov, CEO, Founder

3.1.2 Nature of Market Leadership

Urbanization and high-density developments have increased the demand for structured parking, particularly in cities with limited public transit options. As urban expansion replaces surface parking lots with new buildings, parking facilities gain value for both consumers and investors. The industry remains monopolistic, with a few dominant operators, further driving up demand.

Parqour leads the smart parking industry in the SPECA subregion, offering number-recognition-based solutions in Central Asia, the USA, Saudi Arabia, and CIS countries. As the largest and sole major exporter of smart parking solutions, the company differentiates itself through advanced technology, extensive experience, and strong marketing strategies. From 2020 to 2024, Parqour expanded its market share from 60% to 90%, solidifying its dominance in the sector.

3.1.3 Nature of Competitive Advantage

Parqour's automated parking systems (APS) optimize space usage, enhance efficiency, and improve the user experience in urban environments where parking is scarce. These systems stack vehicles vertically or horizontally, reducing land requirements while minimizing congestion and emissions. APS technology streamlines parking operations, making it more convenient for drivers while promoting environmental sustainability.

Parqour integrates advanced technologies such as license plate recognition, sensor-based vehicle guidance, and digital signage to automate vehicle entry, exit, and space allocation. This reduces the time spent searching for parking spots, easing traffic congestion and improving air quality. The system's efficiency benefits both businesses and consumers by enhancing operational productivity and reducing parking-related stress. With its innovative solutions, Parqour continues to set industry standards, reinforcing its competitive edge.

3.1.4 Core Lessons Learned on the Path to Success

Parqour's journey to becoming a market leader highlights the critical role of continuous innovation. The company's commitment to impactful innovation ensures that it meets evolving market demands while maintaining a competitive edge. A deep understanding of the parking industry, gained through extensive research, has allowed Parqour to identify and address key challenges such as limited parking availability, outdated payment methods, and inefficient user experiences. By proactively adapting its technology and services, the company remains ahead of industry trends.

Another crucial lesson is the importance of building a diverse and skilled team. Parqour's success is driven by a multidisciplinary workforce that brings expertise across technical, operational, and marketing domains. This well-rounded team enables the company to develop cutting-edge solutions while effectively positioning itself in the market. Additionally, collaboration with local authorities has proven essential in shaping policies that benefit both users and the broader community. By engaging in policy discussions and advocating for smart parking initiatives, Parqour has strengthened its industry leadership and contributed to the modernization of urban mobility solutions.

3.1.5 Management and Leadership Development Needs

To sustain its market leadership and drive future growth, Parqour must focus on strengthening its management and leadership capabilities. As the company scales, its leadership team will need to deepen its understanding of global market trends, competitive landscapes, and advancements in smart parking technology. Founders and executives must continuously refine their strategic vision to align with emerging industry shifts and customer demands. As smart parking solutions evolve, Parqour should prioritize research and development to stay ahead of technological advancements, particularly in artificial intelligence (AI), the Internet of Things (IoT), and data analytics. Enhancing technical knowledge across leadership levels will ensure the company remains at the forefront of digital transformation in the parking industry.

Moreover, Parqour should develop strategies to streamline workflows, optimize resource allocation, and minimize operational expenses while maintaining service quality. Strengthening decision-making and analytical capabilities will be essential for scaling operations effectively without compromising efficiency or customer satisfaction. Furthermore, as Parqour expands into international markets, its leadership team must enhance its global business acumen. The task includes understanding regulatory frameworks, cultural nuances, and business environments in target markets. Strengthening partnerships with local authorities and stakeholders will also be crucial in navigating policy discussions and advocating for smart parking initiatives that align with urban development goals.

Investing in leadership development programs and executive training will help equip Parqour's management team with the skills needed to drive sustainable growth, foster innovation, and maintain a competitive edge in an increasingly dynamic industry. By addressing these development needs, Parqour will be well-positioned to scale its operations, enhance customer experiences, and lead the future of smart parking solutions.

3.1.6 Financing and Regulatory Environment Development Needs

As Parqour continues to expand, securing the right financial resources and navigating regulatory frameworks will be critical to its success. The company should explore diversified funding strategies, including venture capital investments, strategic partnerships, and government-backed financial incentives. Access to long-term financing will enable Parqour to scale its operations, invest in advanced R&D, and enhance technological capabilities.

In addition to financing, regulatory compliance remains a key area of focus. The smart parking industry is subject to evolving regulations regarding data privacy, urban mobility policies, and environmental sustainability. Parqour should strengthen its ability to adapt to varying international legal frameworks while proactively engaging with policymakers to shape regulations that support innovation in parking technology.

Developing an agile approach to compliance will be essential, particularly as the company expands into markets with different regulatory requirements. By building up its own legal staff and working together with government agencies, Parqour can stay ahead of legal problems and establish itself as a reliable partner for smart city projects. By addressing these financing and regulatory needs, Parqour can reinforce its growth trajectory and sustain its position as a leader in the smart parking industry.

3.1.7 Pandemic's Impact on Parqour's Business Approach

The COVID-19 pandemic profoundly influenced the way businesses operate, forcing companies to reassess their strategies, resilience, and adaptability. For hidden champions like Parqour, the pandemic underscored the importance of agility, digitalization, and risk management in sustaining long-term growth. During the pandemic, Parqour experienced disruptions in operations due to fluctuating demand, lockdown restrictions, and changes in urban mobility patterns. With fewer people commuting and a decline in demand for parking services in certain sectors, the company faced an immediate challenge in maintaining revenue streams. However, Parqour quickly adapted by accelerating its digital transformation efforts. The company strengthened its focus on automation, contactless payments, and AI-driven parking management to align with shifting consumer behaviors and urban infrastructure needs. The crisis also reinforced the importance of financial resilience. Parqour optimized its operational expenses, ensuring financial stability while continuing its R&D investments. The pandemic highlighted the need for diversified revenue streams, prompting the company to explore new market segments, such as logistics and smart city partnerships, where its automated solutions could be deployed beyond traditional parking systems.

Moreover, the pandemic underscored the necessity of proactive leadership. Parqour's management swiftly implemented strategic shifts, reinforcing a culture of innovation and adaptability. The company strengthened relationships with local governments and urban planners, advocating for smart parking solutions as an integral component of post-pandemic urban mobility planning. Overall, the pandemic shifted Parqour's approach to business by emphasizing resilience, technological advancement, and proactive market adaptation.

3.1.8 Effects of the Ukraine War on "Hidden Champions" Business Operations

The war in Ukraine has had significant geopolitical and economic repercussions, affecting businesses worldwide, including Parqour. Given Parqour's expansion into CIS markets, the conflict has introduced challenges related to supply chain disruptions, regional economic instability, and regulatory uncertainty. One of the most immediate impacts has been on logistics and procurement. With supply chains disrupted due to sanctions, currency fluctuations, and trade restrictions, Parqour has had to adapt its sourcing strategies. The company has sought alternative suppliers outside of traditional CIS markets, diversifying its supply base to mitigate risks associated with geopolitical tensions. Moreover, financial volatility in the region has also affected Parqour's pricing strategies and contract negotiations. Currency depreciation in affected markets, alongside inflationary pressures, has required the company to reassess its financial models to maintain profitability while ensuring affordability for customers. Additionally, shifting regulatory landscapes in response to the war have posed compliance challenges. Parqour has had to navigate evolving trade policies, sanctions, and investment restrictions, requiring enhanced legal expertise and a more proactive approach to regulatory engagement.

3.1.9 The Quiet Giant of Smart Parking: Parqour's Unwavering Ascent

In the dynamic landscape of urban mobility, where securing a parking space often poses a formidable challenge, Parqour has emerged as an industry leader, redefining parking solutions through technological innovation. Founded by Amirkhan Omarov, Parqour has evolved from a basic parking application into an advanced smart parking ecosystem, demonstrating a steadfast commitment to enhancing urban infrastructure. Parqour's remarkable growth and industry leadership can be attributed to several critical success factors, including visionary leadership, innovation, unique value propositions (UVPs), and strategic market positioning.

Under the stewardship of Amirkhan Omarov, Parqour has fostered a strong culture of innovation, adaptability, and customer-centricity. Omarov's ability to anticipate industry trends and proactively address parking challenges has played a pivotal role in shaping the company's trajectory. His strategic vision has guided Parqour's expansion into international markets while maintaining its commitment to cutting-edge technological advancements.

At the core of Parqour's success is its relentless pursuit of technological innovation. The company's dynamic pricing model, a pioneering advancement within the parking sector, optimizes space utilization by adjusting tariffs based on real-time demand. This strategy not only maximizes the efficiency of available parking spaces but also enhances revenue generation for facility owners. Further strengthening its technological capabilities, Parqour has developed an advanced system for recognizing vehicle dimensions, streamlining the parking process by eliminating the need for manual measurements and reducing the risk of vehicle damage. Additionally, the integration of AI-driven analytics and IoT-enabled parking management solutions has positioned Parqour at the forefront of smart urban mobility solutions.

Beyond its technological advancements, Parqour has successfully differentiated itself through its unique value propositions. The company's intuitive interface and integrated payment solutions ensure a frictionless parking experience for motorists. Meanwhile, its comprehensive management platform provides parking operators with real-time data and analytical insights, enabling informed decision-making, operational efficiency, and enhanced customer satisfaction. These features set Parqour apart from traditional parking operators and reinforce its competitive edge.

Parqour's ability to identify and capitalize on gaps in the smart parking sector has significantly contributed to its success. By targeting urban centers with high congestion levels and outdated parking infrastructure, the company has established itself as a crucial player in modernizing urban mobility. Moreover, its expansion into Central Asia, the USA, Saudi Arabia, and CIS countries demonstrates its ability to scale its solutions while adapting to diverse regulatory and business environments.

Parqour's success exemplifies the synergy of innovation, customer focus, and strategic leadership. As the company continues its expansion, it is poised to redefine urban parking experiences, reinforcing its status as a hidden champion in the field of smart parking solutions.

3.2 *Case Study 2*

3.2.1 Clockster

Overview
Address: 50/3 Turan Avenue, Suite 4, Astana, Kazakhstan
Fax: +7 74 8608719
Email: info@clockster.com
Website: https://www.clockster.com/

Company Information
Industry: Staff Management Solutions
Year of Establishment: 2018
Sales Revenues in 2023: N/A
Average Number of Employees in 2023: N/A
Brain(s) behind the company: Yerjan Ryskali, CEO & Co-Founder

3.2.2 Nature of Market Leadership

Clockster has established itself as a market leader in Kazakhstan in the domain of time tracking and shift automation. Based on insights from interviews with Yerjan Ryskali, the company was a pioneer in this sector within Kazakhstan and has significantly outpaced its competitors in terms of product functionality over 6 years of operation. By focusing on addressing the comprehensive needs of clients in the HoReCa (Hotel, Restaurant, Café) and retail sectors, Clockster has evolved beyond a mere time-tracking solution to offer a fully integrated Human Resource Management (HRM) system. This strategic differentiation sets it apart from competitors that typically provide only fragmented workforce management tools.

The company's leadership position extends beyond Kazakhstan, with successful operations in Kyrgyzstan and an entry into the Saudi Arabian market. This geographical expansion underscores Clockster's ability to compete beyond national borders, demonstrating both its scalability and international growth potential. Despite being the most premium-priced solution in the Kazakhstani market, Clockster remains the preferred choice for clients due to its extensive functionality, deep customization capabilities, and high product quality. The company's partnerships with leading firms in Kazakhstan and Southeast Asia further reinforce its reputation as a superior solution provider.

The demand for advanced personnel management systems in Kazakhstan has surged recently, driven by the rapid expansion of coffee shop chains, restaurants, and other HoReCa enterprises. The sector's persistent challenges, such as labor shortages and high employee turnover, have necessitated sophisticated workforce management tools, positioning Clockster as a critical enabler of operational efficiency.

In other markets where Clockster operates, the competitive landscape varies significantly. In the Philippines, the company identifies substantial growth potential in the HoReCa sector due to the absence of dominant market players. Conversely, in Indonesia, while the market presents opportunities, intense competition and price sensitivity pose challenges to immediate investment. In Uzbekistan, Clockster has adopted a remote operational model, recognizing the country's large market size yet constrained by low average income levels, which limit purchasing power.

What distinguishes Clockster as a hidden champion is its ability to provide an all-encompassing workforce management solution tailored to frontline employees. The platform integrates time tracking, shift automation, leave management, task assignment, checklists, and payroll processing into a singular system. In contrast, competing providers predominantly offer isolated functionalities, such as basic time-tracking tools. This holistic approach enhances operational efficiency for businesses, reinforcing Clockster's competitive advantage and its status as a leading innovator in the sector.

3.2.3 Nature of Competitive Advantage

Clockster does not publicly disclose its market share; however, the company asserts that it is the most premium-priced solution in its sector, with costs averaging two to three times higher than those of its competitors. This pricing strategy makes sense because the company offers a lot more than just basic time tracking. It offers a fully integrated Human Resource Management (HRM) system as well. The superior functionality and depth of the platform are evidenced by its adoption among leading clients in Kazakhstan and Southeast Asia, who recognize its capacity to enhance operational efficiency and workforce management.

Clockster's primary markets include Kazakhstan, where it holds a leading position; Uzbekistan, where it operates remotely; Indonesia, where it strategically focuses on large enterprise clients; and the Philippines, where it identifies significant potential for rapid expansion.

The company's competitive advantage is rooted in its holistic approach to personnel management automation and its capacity for profound product customization to meet client-specific needs. Yerjan Ryskali highlights that Clockster is designed to comprehensively serve the HoReCa and retail sectors, differentiating itself from competitors that primarily offer isolated workforce management tools. Rather than limiting its functionality to time tracking, Clockster provides a complete HRM ecosystem, integrating multiple modules to support business operations seamlessly.

Key features of Clockster's HRM system include time tracking and shift automation, advanced scheduling functionalities that allow businesses to manage employee shifts dynamically, ensuring flexibility and minimizing operational disruptions. The system also enables real-time monitoring of attendance and late arrivals.

This integrated approach positions Clockster as a superior solution within its market, reinforcing its status as a hidden champion by delivering a sophisticated and adaptable workforce management platform that meets the evolving needs of businesses across multiple regions.

3.2.4 Core Lessons Learned on the Path to Success

Several critical lessons, each highlighting key strategic and operational considerations in scaling a technology-driven business, have shaped Clockster's journey toward market leadership. One of the most significant insights has been the strategic value of product customization. In its early stages, the company faced considerable challenges in competing with larger, more established players, particularly in Southeast Asia. However, its commitment to deep product adaptation emerged as a defining strength. By tailoring its HRM system to address the specific needs of businesses in the HoReCa and retail sectors, Clockster was able to distinguish itself from competitors offering more generic workforce management solutions. Focusing on being flexible and adaptable helped the business get important clients who needed custom features. This proves that investing in making your products stand out can give you a big edge in markets with lots of competition.

Another crucial lesson learned was the importance of market selection in shaping growth trajectories. The company's early internationalization efforts underscored the significance of rigorous market evaluation before expansion. While Indonesia appeared to offer substantial opportunities, the high level of competition and market-wide price sensitivity made scaling more challenging than initially anticipated. In contrast, Clockster achieved faster traction in the Philippines, where competition was less intense and market conditions were more favorable for the company's product. This experience highlighted the necessity of prioritizing expansion based not only on market size but also on competitive dynamics, customer readiness, and the feasibility of establishing a sustainable presence.

Clockster also encountered difficulties in building a proficient B2B sales team, particularly in Kazakhstan. In the initial phases, it was a significant challenge to find and train sales professionals with enough technical expertise to effectively communicate the product's value proposition. This limitation impeded early scaling efforts and underscored the necessity of investing in sales force development from the outset. Recognizing this, the company shifted its focus toward recruiting and training in-house talent, which subsequently improved its market penetration and overall sales performance. This experience made me realize again how important human capital is for growing tech companies and how important it is to give sales teams both technical and business skills.

Another key challenge in Clockster's expansion strategy was navigating the regulatory complexities of international markets. As the company sought to establish operations in Southeast Asia, it encountered significant legal and compliance hurdles, particularly in relation to payroll and labor legislation. In several cases, local regulations proved more intricate than initially expected, leading to delays in client onboarding and operational inefficiencies. This experience reinforced the importance of conducting thorough legal due diligence before entering new markets and establishing partnerships with local experts to navigate complex regulatory landscapes effectively. Ensuring compliance with country-specific labor laws and tax regulations emerged as a critical factor in sustaining long-term business operations and mitigating the risks associated with international expansion.

Collectively, these lessons illustrate that sustainable growth in the HRM technology sector requires a combination of strategic product development, informed market entry decisions, investment in human capital, and regulatory preparedness. Clockster's ability to adapt to these challenges and refine its approach has reinforced its position as a hidden champion in workforce management, demonstrating resilience and agility in an evolving competitive landscape.

3.2.5 Management and Leadership Development Needs

There is a significant demand for B2B sales professionals with technical expertise, yet the labor market in Kazakhstan faces a shortage of such specialists. As Clockster expands into new markets, the need for skilled sales personnel will continue to grow, alongside the necessity of strengthening teams of developers and product customization specialists to meet diverse market requirements. The company's least developed capability remains B2B sales in the technical products sector, a challenge exacerbated by the relative immaturity of the HRM system market in Kazakhstan and the scarcity of experienced professionals. The founder emphasizes that priority should be given to training sales managers, as their effectiveness directly influences client acquisition and revenue growth. Simultaneously, continuous investment in the professional development of developers and customization specialists is essential to maintaining the product's competitive edge in a rapidly evolving market.

3.2.6 Financing and Regulatory Environment Development Needs

Clockster's development trajectory as a Hidden Champion (HC) is closely linked to its ability to secure adequate financing and navigate the regulatory environment effectively. As the company seeks to scale operations and enhance its technological capabilities, access to growth capital is a critical requirement. Clockster is currently pursuing a Series A funding round of $2–5 million, aimed at accelerating its expansion in Southeast Asian markets and further advancing its product development. Given the competitive nature of the HRM solutions market, securing investment from venture capital funds in Southeast Asia and beyond is essential to sustaining its growth momentum and strengthening its market positioning.

From a regulatory perspective, the most significant development affecting Clockster's business is the introduction of new legislation in Kazakhstan concerning platform employees. This legal reform simplifies taxation for businesses working with freelance workers, potentially increasing demand for HRM solutions among SMEs that previously found tax compliance too complex. This regulatory shift could serve as a catalyst for Clockster's client base expansion within Kazakhstan.

However, the company has not identified any major regulatory challenges in other markets where it operates. However, as it continues to expand internationally, regulatory due diligence will remain crucial, particularly in jurisdictions with complex labor laws and payroll regulations, which could affect its product's adaptation and implementation.

Overall, Clockster's sustained development as a Hidden Champion depends on a strategic balance between securing investment and anticipating regulatory changes. How quickly it develops new technologies and grows its market will depend on how well it can get funding. Foresight in regulatory matters will be very important for making sure operations run smoothly and reducing the risks that come with international growth.

3.2.7 Pandemic's Impact on "Hidden Champions" Business Approach

The COVID-19 pandemic had a profound impact on Clockster's business, reshaping its strategic approach and reinforcing key lessons on resilience, adaptability, and market diversification—factors that are increasingly central to the outlook of Hidden Champions (HCs). With government-imposed restrictions leading to the closure or downsizing of many HoReCa establishments, which constitute Clockster's primary client segment, the company faced a severe decline in revenue, threatening its long-term viability. In response, Clockster adopted a multi-pronged strategy to mitigate risks and reposition itself for sustainable growth.

A key adjustment was the exploration of alternative monetization strategies, including offering the application for free while focusing on revenue generation through additional services targeted at employees. Although this approach did not yield the expected financial returns, it demonstrated the company's willingness to experiment with new business models. More significantly, Clockster accelerated its expansion into Southeast Asian markets, where pandemic-related restrictions were less severe and demand for HRM systems remained stable. This shift highlighted the importance of geographical diversification as a risk mitigation strategy for HCs operating in niche markets.

Another critical response was continued investment in product development, with enhancements aimed at attracting new clients and retaining existing ones despite the challenging economic environment. This strategic focus reinforced the company's competitive positioning and strengthened customer loyalty in a time of uncertainty. While some short-term measures, such as free product offerings, proved less effective, the emphasis on international market entry and continuous innovation emerged as the most impactful solutions, enabling Clockster not only to withstand the crisis but also to sustain its growth trajectory.

The broader implication of Clockster's experience aligns with an evolving perspective among Hidden Champions globally. The pandemic underscored the need for agility in business models, proactive internationalization, and an unwavering commitment to innovation. Companies that successfully navigated the crisis demonstrated a capacity to pivot rapidly, seize emerging opportunities in new markets, and enhance their value proposition to ensure long-term resilience. While no direct impact of the war in Ukraine on Clockster's business was noted in interviews with Yerjan Ryskali, the company's pandemic response exemplifies the necessity for HCs to anticipate and adapt to external shocks by fostering strategic flexibility and reinforcing their global competitiveness.

3.2.8 The Clockster Story: Pioneering Time and Attendance Solutions in Kazakhstan

Clockster has established itself as a leading innovator in workforce management, evolving from a simple time-tracking tool into a comprehensive HRM system. Founded in 2018 by Yerzhan Ryskali, the company caters primarily to the HoReCa and retail sectors, addressing workforce efficiency challenges through shift automation, leave management, task tracking, and internal communication tools.

A key driver of Clockster's success is its commitment to customization, enabling businesses to tailor HRM solutions to their specific needs. This flexibility has set it apart from competitors relying on generic time-tracking tools, positioning it as a market leader in personnel management automation. Additionally, strategic market selection has been crucial—after an initial broad expansion attempt, the company refocused on markets with high demand and lower competition, ensuring sustainable growth.

Despite its success, Clockster has faced challenges, particularly in building a skilled B2B sales force in Kazakhstan, where experienced professionals in tech sales are scarce. The company addressed these issues by investing in internal training, reinforcing the importance of a strong sales strategy in scaling operations. Expanding internationally also required navigating complex regulatory landscapes, highlighting the need for compliance research and local partnerships.

The COVID-19 pandemic further tested Clockster's resilience, as the HoReCa sector faced widespread closures. In response, the company pivoted its business model, accelerated its expansion into Southeast Asia, and enhanced product development, emerging stronger and more diversified.

Clockster's growth reflects the critical role of innovation, adaptability, and customer focus in building a hidden champion. Its ability to anticipate market needs, refine its offerings, and strategically expand positions it as a key player in HRM technology, driving workforce efficiency for businesses in Kazakhstan and beyond.

4 Conclusions and Recommendations

Looking into Kazakhstan's Hidden Champions, especially the businesses Parqour and Clockster, can teach us a lot about their traits, needs, and difficulties. These are high-growth, innovation-driven companies. Kazakhstan has made significant progress in promoting entrepreneurship, yet certain structural issues still hinder healthcare companies from realizing their full potential. Hiring the right people, adhering to regulations, and expanding internationally are the main challenges. A defining feature of Hidden Champions is their focus on highly specialized niche markets, where they achieve leadership through product innovation, customer-centricity, and sustained investment in R&D. However, their ability to scale and compete on an international level is contingent upon a supportive business environment, access to highly skilled professionals, and financial resources to facilitate expansion.

The case of Parqour highlights the increasing demand for technology-driven solutions, reinforcing the importance of fostering innovation-based entrepreneurship. In contrast, Clockster exemplifies the structural obstacles encountered by Kazakhstani HCs, including labor market shortages, outdated payroll regulations, and difficulties in expanding into foreign markets, particularly in regions where Kazakhstan lacks a strong business reputation. Of particular concern is the predominance of gray payroll practices, with approximately 90% of companies in Kazakhstan engaging in informal employment arrangements. The situation underscores the need for regulatory reforms, educational improvements, and skills development initiatives to enhance the competitiveness of the labor market. In light of these findings, targeted recommendations for key stakeholders are necessary to support the long-term growth and global competitiveness of Hidden Champions.

Recommendations for National Governments

Governments play a fundamental role in fostering an environment conducive to the growth and internationalization of Hidden Champions. To strengthen their development, policymakers should:

1. Simplify regulatory frameworks and reduce administrative barriers that hinder business operations and limit access to global markets.
2. Reform payroll and employment regulations, encouraging the transition to formalized employment structures and reducing reliance on gray payroll practices.
3. Enhance international market access by fostering trade partnerships, improving the global perception of Kazakhstan as an innovation hub, and supporting companies in expanding into new markets.
4. Invest in the national innovation ecosystem by providing targeted financial incentives, expanding incubator and accelerator programs, and fostering stronger collaboration between industry and research institutions.
5. Strengthen human capital development through educational reforms that equip the workforce with the skills required in high-growth sectors, particularly in areas such as B2B sales, technology, and international business management.

Recommendations for Financial Institutions

Access to growth capital remains a key challenge for Hidden Champions, particularly when seeking to expand operations or enter new markets. Financial institutions should modify their support mechanisms as follows:

1. We are developing specialized financial instruments, including venture debt, revenue-based financing, and growth-stage equity investments to support HCs in their expansion efforts.
2. Facilitating access to international investment, strengthening ties with venture capital funds and strategic investors that focus on high-growth enterprises in emerging markets.
3. Enhancing financial support for export-oriented businesses, including targeted financial incentives and risk mitigation mechanisms to support market entry abroad.
4. Make businesses more official by tying better loan terms to following the rules. This gives companies a reason to switch to clear and organized ways of handling payroll and hiring employees.

Recommendations for Business Schools and Higher Education Institutions
Given the pivotal role of human capital in the success of Hidden Champions, higher education institutions must adapt their curricula and industry engagement strategies to better equip professionals with the skills necessary for technology-driven, export-oriented enterprises. To address these needs, business schools and universities should:

1. Expand training in B2B sales, international business strategy, and technology entrepreneurship, ensuring that graduates possess the skills required by high-growth firms.
2. Strengthen collaboration between academia and industry, incorporating applied research, internships, and startup incubation programs to bridge the gap between theoretical learning and real-world business challenges.
3. Develop executive education programs tailored to entrepreneurs and senior managers in HC firms, providing insights into international expansion strategies, innovation management, and high-growth leadership.
4. Foster an entrepreneurial culture by integrating practical entrepreneurship training across disciplines and encouraging the development of early-stage innovation projects and startup competitions.

Kazakhstan's Hidden Champions have the potential to drive economic diversification, global competitiveness, and long-term innovation-led growth. To reach this potential, though, governments, financial institutions, and the education sector need to work together to fix inefficient regulations, make it easier for people to get access to capital, and put money into developing the workforce. By implementing these targeted reforms, stakeholders can create an environment in which Hidden Champions can scale effectively, compete internationally, and contribute to Kazakhstan's positioning as a hub for high-growth, technology-driven enterprises.

References

Abazov, R., & Salimov, U. (2016). Technoparks in Kazakhstan: Will they help develop the innovation sector? *The Central Asia-Caucus Analysists, 2*(3), 12–15.

Ashimova, A., & Alzhanova, A. (2023). SWOT and PEST analysis of current state and prospects for the development of artificial intelligence in Kazakhstan. *SSRN Electronic Journal*. https://doi.org/10.2139/ssrn.4366721

Doskaliyeva, B. B., Orynbassarova, Y. D., Karibaev, Y. S., & Baimukhametova, A. S. (2016). Development of the system of investment support of projects in the industrial-innovative development of Kazakhstan. *International Journal of Environmental and Science Education, 11*(12), 5109–5127.

GEM Kazakhstan Report. (2021). *Global entrepreneurship monitor: Kazakhstan.*

MOST Business Incubator. (2019). *MOST business incubator: Programs and initiatives.* https://mostbi.com

OECD. (2017). *Small, medium, strong. Trends in SME performance and business conditions.* OECD.

OECD. (2018). *SME and entrepreneurship policy in Kazakhstan.* OECD.

OECD. (2019). *SME and entrepreneurship outlook.* OECD.

Sadyrova, M., Yusupov, K., & Imanbekova, B. (2021). Innovation processes in Kazakhstan: development factors. *Journal of Innovation and Entrepreneurship, 10*(1), 36.

Saiymova, M., Shakharova, A., Rakaeva, A., Serikova, M., Tasmaganbetov, A., Tyurina, Y., & Bimagambetova, Z. (2020). Energy security, economics and environment in the Eurasian economic union: Current and future scenarios. *International Journal of Energy Economics and Policy, 10*(4), 293–299.

Statistics, B.o.. (2024, July 20). *Qazstat.* Industry statistics: https://stat.gov.kz/en/industries/business-statistics/stat-org/publications/70137/#:~:text=1%2C471.9%20thousand%20units.-,The%20number%20of%20people%20employed%20in%20SME%20as%20of%20April,of%

World Bank. (2020). *Doing business 2020 report.* World Bank.

Daniyar Medetov is Director and Assistant Professor in Entrepreneurship at the Institute for Entrepreneurship Almaty Management University (AlmaU), Kazakhstan. He holds a PhD in Entrepreneurship from Henley Business School, University of Reading, United Kingdom. His academic work focuses on business incubation, institutional theory, and the development of entrepreneurial ecosystems in emerging economies, with a particular emphasis on Central Asia. Dr. Medetov has extensive experience in designing and leading experiential entrepreneurship education programs, as well as consulting for early-stage ventures and innovation support organizations. He has collaborated on a range of internationally funded projects, including initiatives supported by the British Council, UNECE, UNDP, and QazInnovations, aimed at fostering youth entrepreneurship, supporting institutional transformation, and advancing inclusive innovation practices. His scholarly contributions explore the role of institutional intermediaries in shaping entrepreneurial outcomes and innovation capacity in underdeveloped regions. His work combines qualitative research methodologies with a practitioner-oriented perspective, bridging academic inquiry with policy and ecosystem development. Dr Medetov is the recipient of national and institutional awards for his research and academic leadership.

Vadim Novikov is an Assistant Professor and Presidential Advisor at Almaty Management University (AlmaU), Kazakhstan. At AlmaU, he teaches courses on entrepreneurship and the applications of artificial intelligence in data analysis. Before his academic career in Kazakhstan, Vadim worked for over a decade as an expert witness in high-profile commercial litigation cases in Russia, specializing in competition law and economic policy. He holds a Master of Laws in Commercial Law (with distinction) from the University of Manchester and a Master's degree in Economics from the Higher School of Economics in Moscow.

References

Hidden Champions of Kosovo

Florentina Dushi and Dafina Turkeshi Ballanca

Abstract The chapter on Kosovo presents a comprehensive analysis of the nation's economic landscape, focusing on the evolution and characteristics of Hidden Champions (HCs) in its emerging market. It details Kosovo's transformation from a centrally controlled economy to a dynamic free-market system, emphasizing the country's significant growth since declaring independence in 2008. The chapter highlights key economic indicators, including robust GDP growth and notable improvements in private sector investment driven by economic reforms and international support. The young, well-educated workforce, favourable tax system, and strategic location are identified as critical factors contributing to Kosovo's economic potential.

Through detailed case studies, the chapter explores exemplary HCs like Koshi Group LLC, a leading manufacturer of carbon fibre products. These companies demonstrate exceptional market leadership, innovation, and resilience, maintaining competitive advantages through advanced technologies, strategic global partnerships, and continuous investment in employee development. The analysis underscores the importance of innovation, customer-centricity, and strategic management in sustaining growth.

The chapter concludes with tailored recommendations for various stakeholders, including government policies to support innovation, financial institutions' role in facilitating access to capital, and the contribution of educational institutions in providing relevant skills training. This holistic approach aims to foster a conducive environment for the sustained growth of HCs in Kosovo.

F. Dushi (✉) · D. T. Ballanca
Business Development Group, Prishtina, Kosovo
e-mail: florentina@bdgroup-ks.com; dafina@bdgroup-ks.com

D. Berberović, D. Purg (eds.), *Hidden Champions in Rising Economies*, Contributions to Management Science,
https://doi.org/10.1007/978-3-032-08263-3_23

Overview[1]

Official name:	Republic of Kosovo
Type of government:	Parliamentary Republic
Population in 2023:	1.8 million
Land area:	10,908 km^2

History

15th–twentieth Century	Ottoman Empire
1912–1913	First Balkan War
1912–1913	Albanian Independency (including Kosovo Territory)
1913	Treaty of London, recognizing Albania's independence, excluding Kosovo
1913	Second Balkan War and Treaty of Bucharest
1913–1941	Kingdom of Serbia and Kingdom of Montenegro (Dukagjini), with increase in Serb settlements (colonization) and expulsion of Albanian population
1946–1974	Autonomous Province of SFRY
1974–1989	Self-governance under SFRY constitution
1989–1998	Reversal of self-governance, repression, violence, self-declared independence
1998–1999	Kosovo War
1999–2008	Kosovo administered by the United Nations Interim Administration Mission in Kosovo (UNMIK) under the United Nations Security Council Resolution 1244.
2008	Kosovo declared independence
2013	The EU opened negotiations with Kosovo on an SAA
2017	Kosovo growth is estimated at 4.4%, the top growth rate in the Western Balkan
2018	Parliament passed legislation to transform the Kosovo Security Force into a regular army.
2019	The European Parliament endorsed visa liberalization for Kosovo citizens; meanwhile, economic reforms boosted private sector growth and investment
2020	Kosovo and Serbia signed economic normalization agreements facilitated by the United States.
2022	Kosovo continued efforts towards European Union integration by meeting required criteria.

1 Introduction: Context and History

The Kosovo economy is a transition economy. Being new and dynamic, its foundation has been transformed form a centralist and controlled economy, to a free-market economy. Kosovo was the poorest province of the former Yugoslavia with a modern

[1] World Bank, April, 2024.

economy established only after a series of federal development subsidies in 1960s and 1970s (World Bank, 2017). Growth in 2017 was estimated at 4.4%, the top growth rate in the Western Balkans, due to investment and the export-driven recovery in external demand, which also improved external indicators (World Bank, 2017). The relatively good growth performance was related to international community and the diaspora of Kosovo. Kosovo's population is the youngest in Europe, with an average age of 26 years. A well-educated workforce, enviable natural resources such as mining, agriculture, low taxes and a transparent tax system, custom free access to the markets of CEFTA, the EU, and the USA, as well as the Euro as the official currency are believed to be a comparative advantage and key resource for economic growth in Kosovo (World Bank, 2017). Additionally, World Bank statistics of 2017 show that there is great potential for the IT Sector, as well as the textile and wood processing industries in Kosovo.

A historic overview of Kosovo shows that during most of its history Kosovo has been under foreign rule. Foreign powers and regional neighbours have ruled over the territory, which reinforced a mentality of and created incentives for parallel structures and economic informality, the reliance on extended family relationships, and a widespread scepticism towards government and the public sector (Malcolm, 2010).

The historic overview of the Illyrian region of Dardania included the territory of modern Kosovo, which is why most Kosovars see themselves as descendants of the Illyrians. After the Romans had conquered the Illyrian tribes in 168 BC, the region experienced a period of development as a transit point for the most of the Balkan's trade routes. Ulpiana, located a few kilometres from where Prishtina stands today, became an important trade centre and was promoted to the status of a Roman municipium (Dushi, 2002). Since then, the major depended industries of Kosovo were (a) mining, as it has large reserves of lignite, lead, zinc, silver, nickel, cobalt, copper, iron, and, (b) agriculture. In addition, mine lead, silver and gold have been the most important articles of export during the medieval period (Dushi, 2002). The archaeological explorations show that Trepça (also Tripça, Trebza) have been used since the Roman Empire period. However, its name had been previously used in the year 1303 (Dushi, 2002).

The Ottoman Empire ruled over the area for approximately 500 years and left the region economically ruined and in poverty. In Ottoman times, Kosovo's agriculture was a vital industry; the main production was of cereal and meat. After the Ottoman Empire collapsed, Serbia regained control over the region and seeing Kosovo incorporated into the Kingdom of Serbs, Croats, and Slovenians (later named Yugoslavia) (Malcolm, 2010). There is little information of the condition of the mining fields left behind by the Ottoman Empire. Nevertheless, research conducted since 1924 shows the extensive possession of mining fields in Kosovo (Dushi, 2002).

After World War II, the present day boundaries of Kosovo were established. Kosovo became an autonomous province in the Socialist Federal Republic of Yugoslavia. Under Yugoslavia a significant degree of Kosovo Industrialism was achieved. Manufacturing played a significant part in the economy, developing urbanization of Kosovo (Malcolm, 2010). Small market towns like Peja and Gjakova developed on Ottoman trade routes, expanded when local industry surfaced. Transport, telecommunications were very under-resourced in Yugoslavia's Kosovo, this was mainly due to political consequences. Regardless, it slowed down the economic development of the rural area of Kosovo significantly. The impact is noticeable to date (Malcolm, 2010).

According to Mustafa (2017); in 1974, Kosovo gained political and economic autonomy and direct representation in the federal government of Yugoslavia. Kosovo recorded the highest rate of economic growth in 1965–1975, when substantial and qualitative changes were made in the production structure as well as moderate growth during 1976–1980. The economic and political system of that time was decentralized to some extent, while Kosovo's constitutional position in the economic and political system of the former Yugoslavia was identical to other federal units (Mustafa, 2018). After the political reforms of the 1970s, Kosovo reached the point when it became more independent in the field of self-government in politics, economics, social development, and especially in the areas of budget, finance and taxation. Kosovo at that time had the right and power to plan and finance economic strategies and enter contractual relations with international financial institutions (Mustafa, 2018).

After the end of the Cold War and the fall of Yugoslavia, the Serb Communist Leadership changed the Yugoslav Constitution to revoke Kosovo's autonomy. This ignited Albanian nationalism in Kosovo, generating protests and calls for Kosovo's independence. In the early 1980s, as a result of political and economic crises, the situation in Kosovo deteriorated. Domestic production in the period 1981–1989 increased by 1–1.8% (Mustafa, 2018). These political and economic events resulted with the "Kosovo Declaration of independence" in September 1991 the creation of a parallel political, legal and economic structure, beginning in the 1992. However, the Declaration was not widely supported at the international level (Mustafa, 2018).

The 1990s was a lost decade, followed by Yugoslavian violent disintegration, Kosovo resulted in a sharp drop of output and trade; large-scale destruction of infrastructure; severe deterioration of the enterprise, financial, and social sectors; worsened social indicators and increased poverty and inequality (World Bank, 2017). In Kosovo, the decade saw an accelerating rate of economic neglect and destruction, the increasing discrimination against citizens of Albanian-ethnic origin (including in education), and an intensifying conflict that led to greater violence and—following the failed negotiations of Rambouillet—it culminated with the Kosovo War of 1998–99. The war ended on 12 Jun 1999 after a 78-day bombing campaign led by North Atlantic Treaty Organization (NATO) over Serb military, paramilitary and police forces (World Bank, 2017).

After the war, which came to a formal end through the adoption of UN Security Council Resolution 1244 of June 1999, Kosovo was placed under the administration of the UN Interim Administration Mission in Kosovo. The war caused a massive humanitarian crisis for such a small country (Perrit, 2004). Kosovo declared independence from what was left of Yugoslavia, on 17 February 2008, the year globally known as economic recession year. It is recognized as an independent country by 114 of 193 United Nations members and by 23 of 28 European Union (EU) members. Kosovo is a potential candidate for EU membership, a process that was accelerated with the signing of the Stabilization Association Agreement in October 2015, in force since April 2016 (European Commission, 2017).

With no formal economic ties to the global financial and trade market, the 2008 global economic crises had barely any impact on Kosovo's steady growing economy. The structure of Kosovo's economy to date is linked to remittances from migrants in Europe and Switzerland, which depends heavily on private consumption and investment. Hence, the net export in period 2008–2014 contributed negatively to the growth due to larger expansion of imports than exports. This was partially as a result of the absence of a government for 6 months in 2014. However, in 2015, private investment, fuelled by recovery in the inflow of foreign direct investment (FDI), was the key driver of growth recovery. Only in the last few years have net exports contributed positively to growth (World Bank, 2017).

During the period from 2018 to 2020, Kosovo continued to experience robust economic growth, averaging around 4% annually. The government implemented several structural reforms aimed at improving the business climate and attracting foreign direct investment. The IT sector, in particular, saw substantial growth, driven by a young, tech-savvy population and increasing interest from international investors. Infrastructure projects, especially in transportation and energy, were prioritized to support economic activities and enhance connectivity within the region.

Kosovo's political landscape also saw significant developments, with efforts to normalize relations with Serbia through EU-facilitated dialogue. The signing of economic normalization agreements in 2020 was a critical milestone, aimed at boosting regional cooperation and economic integration.

From 2021 to 2023, Kosovo's focus shifted towards consolidating economic gains and ensuring sustainable development. The new government under Albin Kurti's leadership emphasized anti-corruption measures, judicial reforms, and enhanced transparency to improve governance and build investor confidence. The country's strategic location and free trade agreements with the EU, CEFTA, and other regions continued to position it as an attractive destination for businesses looking to expand in the Balkans.

Despite challenges such as high unemployment rates and the need for further diversification of the economy, sectors like renewable energy, tourism, and digital services showed promising potential. The government's efforts to align its policies with EU standards and invest in education and vocational training aimed to equip the workforce with skills relevant to emerging industries, thereby supporting the growth of Hidden Champions in Kosovo.

2 Characteristics of Hidden Champions from Kosovo

Throughout our research in Kosovo, conducted in 2018/2019 and continuing into 2024, we identified several Hidden Champions—companies that have demonstrated exceptional market leadership, innovation, and competitive advantage in their respective industries. Among these, MOEA LLC was part of our earlier research in 2018/2019, while Koshi Group LLC has been recognized as our Hidden Champion (HCH) for 2024.

Koshi Group LLC, a manufacturer of carbon fibre products for the automotive and marine industries, has been acknowledged for its significant contributions and advancements in its field. MOEA LLC, a leading fruit grower and natural juice producer in the Central and East European market, continues to maintain its status as a Hidden Champion identified in our earlier research. Additionally, we have identified potential Hidden Champions in the IT sector and the niche of the aftermarket automotive industry.

Koshi Group LLC has established itself as a global leader in aftermarket carbon fibre products, exporting 100% of its products worldwide. The company specializes in a broad range of vehicles, including high-end brands like Alfa Romeo, Fiat, Lamborghini, and Porsche. It has also ventured into marine products with innovations like the Interstellar 32 fishing vessel. MOEA LLC is the top fruit grower and natural juice producer in the Central and East European market, known for its advanced fruit processing technology and commitment to producing unique and healthy fruit drinks under the Frutomania brand.

Koshi Group LLC utilizes advanced materials such as prepreg carbon Fibre and employs Autoclave technology to ensure the highest quality of its products. The company continuously invests in proprietary technology to create unique and innovative products. MOEA LLC has adopted cold juice extraction techniques and emphasizes the inclusion of all fruit fibres, vitamins, and antioxidants in its products. The company focuses on using the healthiest and freshest fruits to produce its juice.

Koshi Group LLC's competitive edge lies in the quality of materials used, advanced manufacturing techniques, and strategic partnerships with luxury car brands. The company's focus on innovation and customer needs has enabled it to stand out in the highly competitive automotive aftermarket industry. MOEA LLC's competitive advantage comes from its commitment to quality and health, transparent partnerships with local farmers, and the adoption of international quality standards. The company's unique business model and leadership style have been crucial in maintaining its market position.

Key lessons from Koshi Group LLC include the importance of innovation, customer-centricity, and strategic global partnerships. Continuous investment in employee development, especially in technology and management skills, has also been critical. For MOEA LLC, the significance of fair treatment of suppliers and employees, transparent business practices, and a strong marketing strategy that emphasizes health and environmental consciousness have been pivotal.

Koshi Group LLC has focused on enhancing management and leadership skills among its staff, recognizing the need for continuous development to sustain growth. Similarly, MOEA LLC has invested in training and developing its workforce, particularly in production and agriculture, to ensure high-quality output and business sustainability.

The selection criteria for identifying Hidden Champions included market leadership, innovation, competitive advantage, growth potential, and strong management and leadership. Companies were chosen based on their significant market share and influence within their industry, commitment to innovation in products, services, and processes, clear and sustainable competitive advantage, and potential for growth and expansion both domestically and internationally. Additionally, companies with strong leadership and effective management practices that contribute to their success were prioritized. These criteria ensured that the selected companies not only excelled in their current markets but also had the potential to sustain and grow their competitive advantage over time.

Exhibit 1 Core economic indicators for (insert the country)

	2017	2018	2019	2020	2021	2022	2023
GDP per capita (current US$)	3948	4281	4440	4320	4580	4810	5050
GDP per capita growth (annual %)	3.4	3.3	4.0	−2.7	4.1	3.8	3.5
Long-term unemployment (% of total unemployment)	27.5	28.0	29.0	29.5	28.0	27.0	26.5
Foreign direct investment, net inflows (% of GDP)	4.5	3.0	2.8	3.2	3.5	4.0	4.2
GDP (current US$, mio)	7.2	7.9	8.3	8.0	8.5	8.9	9.2
Exports of goods and services (current US$, mio)	1926	2203	2300	2100	2250	2400	2550
Exports of goods and services (% of GDP)	26.65	27.88	27.71	26.25	26.47	26.97	27.72
Merchandise exports (current US$)	400	430	460	440	460	490	520
Merchandise exports to high-income economies (% of total merchandise exports)	30.30	32.0	33.5	30.0	31.0	32.0	33.5
Merchandise exports to developing economies in Europe and Central Asia (% of total merchandise exports)	50.0	48.5	49.0	48.0	49.0	50.0	51.0
Ores and metals exports (% of merchandise exports)	15.0	16.0	15.5	14.0	15.0	16.0	17.0
Agricultural raw materials exports (% of merchandise exports)	5.0	5.5	6.0	6.0	6.5	6.8	7.0
Food exports (% of merchandise exports)	10.0	11.0	11.5	11.0	11.5	12.0	12.5
Fuel exports (% of merchandise exports)	3.0	2.5	2.0	1.8	2.0	2.2	2.5
Manufactures exports (% of merchandise exports)	55.0	53.0	52.5	52.0	52.5	53.0	54.0
High-technology exports (% of manufactured exports)	5.0	5.5	6.0	6.5	7.0	7.5	8.0

Source: World Bank, April, 2024

3 Case Study

Koshi Group LLC

Overview
Address: Str Tirana Nn. 20,000, Prizren, Kosovo
Tel: +383 (0) 49 428 910
Fax: N/A
Email: info@koshigroup.com
Web: www.koshigroup.com

Company Information
Industry:[2] Manufacturer of Carbon Fibre Products
Year of Establishment: 2014
Sales Revenues in 2017: 672,000.00
Sales Revenues in 2023: 1,644,424.00
Average number of employees in 2023: 62
Brainer(s) behind the company: CEO and founder Shkamb Koshi

3.1 Nature of Market Leadership

KOSHI is established and operates in Kosovo, but it exports 100% of its products worldwide. KOSHI, established in 2014, has rapidly ascended to become the global frontrunner in aftermarket carbon fibre products. This dominance is built on a foundation of over a decade of pre-founding experience. The company specializes in a broad range of vehicles including Alfa Romeo, Fiat, Lamborghini, Porsche, and others. KOSHI excels in transforming vehicles not only aesthetically but also enhancing their performance, a feat that has garnered widespread admiration. The company's product line-up is extensive, encompassing accessories, jewellery, body kits, interior decals, and performance parts both for interiors and exteriors. They pay attention even to the minutest details, such as button covers. For enthusiasts seeking to impart a distinctive carbon fibre flair to their cars, motorbikes, or even jewellery, KOSHI stands out as the premier choice.

Additionally, KOSHI Marine produced Interstellar 32, the newest innovation in offshore fishing vessels. This vessel stands as a technological marvel, setting new standards in the maritime world with its blend of superior performance, lightness, and enduring durability. Crafted entirely from 100% carbon fibre and epoxy resin, the Interstellar 32 is designed to excel in the demanding environment of offshore fishing. Its construction emphasizes innovation and excellence, ensuring that every aspect of the vessel contributes to a superior fishing and maritime experience. The

[2]According to NACE Rev. 2—please check the tecnical instructions included in this document (pg. 9).

use of advanced materials not only reduces the overall weight but also enhances the strength and longevity of the vessel, making it a standout choice for enthusiasts and professionals alike.

Newest project in process is the production of Koshi 51′ monohull boat, 15 × 3.6 m to reach speed of more than 100 knods.

3.2 Nature of Competitive Advantage

KOSHI is renowned for utilizing the most advanced technology and the latest materials in its manufacturing processes. This commitment to quality is highlighted by their use of prepreg carbon fibre material sourced from Delta-Preg, the same supplier for prestigious brands such as Ferrari and Lamborghini. They further enhance their products with top-tier finishes, including a clear coating with a long-lasting finish (PPG-D880) and a Ceramic clear coat (PPG-D8122). These components are expertly cured using autoclave technology, which involves a specific combination of high temperature and pressure (130 °C, 6 bar), to ensure durability and strength. Through these sophisticated techniques, KOSHI transforms standard carbon fibre products into exceptional pieces of art that are both beautiful and functional.

3.3 Core Lessons Learned on the Path to Success

The following are the core lessons learned on the path to success:

- Koshi Group, operating within a rapidly expanding industry, has recognized the significant market demand for bespoke automotive products, reflecting a robust growth in customer interest. The company has leveraged this opportunity by forging global partnerships with numerous salons and securing various agreements, although these opportunities also pose unique challenges.
- Innovators within Koshi are continually encouraged to remain receptive to customer needs and preferences.
- Over its years of operation, Koshi Group has developed proprietary technology for production. This in-house technology has enabled the creation of unique and innovative products, with the company now boasting a portfolio of 101 products that cater to the diverse requirements of its clientele.
- As a family-run business, Koshi Group has taken substantial strides in its growth. Over the past year, the company has made significant investments in staff development, focusing on technology training as well as enhancing management and leadership skills. This strategic focus on employee development is aimed at sustaining its trajectory of growth and innovation in the coming years.

3.4 Management and Leadership Development Needs

Koshi Group LLC has focused on enhancing management and leadership skills among its staff, recognizing the need for continuous development to sustain growth. Mr. Shkamb Koshi, the founder and intellectual force behind Koshi Group LLC, epitomizes innovation. His genius extends not only to the inception of new products but also to the strategic frameworks he devises for them. To maintain and advance their competitive edge, the company focuses on continuous development in the following areas:

Keeping abreast of the latest advancements in carbon fibre technology and market trends is crucial. This involves ongoing education and training programmes for employees to stay updated with industry innovations and best practices. It ensures that the company can continue to innovate and produce cutting-edge products that meet market demands.

Developing advanced manufacturing skills and techniques among employees is essential to maintain high-quality production standards. This includes specialized training in the use of materials like prepreg carbon fibre and mastering processes such as autoclave technology. By enhancing these competences, Koshi Group ensures that its products remain at the forefront of performance and aesthetic excellence.

3.5 Financing and Regulatory Environment Development Needs

Koshi Group imports its raw material and exports its products. They complain on exporting policies for being costly for this type of industry. On the trade front, Koshi Group faces additional challenges due to high costs imposed by export policies. Given their need to import raw materials and export finished products, these fiscal burdens are particularly impactful. Finally, testing fishing vessels in Kosovo presents a unique challenge primarily because the country is landlocked, lacking direct access to a sea or ocean where maritime activities typically take place.

3.6 Pandemic's Impact on "Hidden Champions" Business Approach

During the COVID-19 pandemic, automobile factories faced a unique challenge primarily related to adhering to new health and safety regulations, rather than operational capacity issues. Despite these constraints, factories generally operated at normal levels of production. Interestingly, the pandemic period saw an increase in automobile sales, attributed largely to a shift in consumer behaviour towards online purchasing.

3.7 *Effects of the Ukraine War on "Hidden Champions" Business Operations*

The war in Ukraine has not had a direct effect on the business operations of Koshi Group LLC. However, the company has remained vigilant about potential indirect impacts, such as disruptions in supply chains or changes in the global economic environment. By maintaining flexible and resilient business strategies, Koshi Group continues to mitigate any potential risks arising from global geopolitical events.

3.8 *"Title for the Story About the Hidden Champion"*

The Innovative Journey of Koshi Group LLC: A Hidden Champion

Koshi Group LLC, founded in 2014 and headquartered in Prizren, Kosovo, has established itself as a global leader in manufacturing carbon fibre products for the automotive and marine industries. Known for its innovative approach and high-quality products, the company exports 100% of its production worldwide. This story delves into the factors that have propelled Koshi Group to its prominent position, focusing on leadership, innovation, unique value propositions (UVPs), and other key elements of its success.

Koshi Group LLC was founded by Shkamb Koshi, whose vision was to create superior carbon fibre products that not only enhance the aesthetic appeal of vehicles but also improve their performance. Leveraging over a decade of experience prior to the company's establishment, Shkamb Koshi set out to revolutionize the aftermarket automotive industry with products that cater to high-end brands such as Alfa Romeo, Fiat, Lamborghini, and Porsche.

The leadership at Koshi Group LLC is characterized by a clear vision and a relentless drive for innovation. Shkamb Koshi, the CEO and founder, is a quintessential innovator whose strategic frameworks have guided the company towards global recognition. His leadership style emphasizes continuous improvement, strategic partnerships, and a deep understanding of market needs.

Innovation is at the core of Koshi Group's operations. The company utilizes advanced materials such as prepreg carbon fibre and employs autoclave technology to ensure the highest quality of its products. This technological prowess is evident in their broad range of products, from automotive accessories and body kits to performance parts and the recently developed Interstellar 32 fishing vessel. The company's commitment to innovation extends to developing proprietary technologies that enhance both the functionality and aesthetic appeal of their products.

Koshi Group LLC's UVPs lie in the superior quality of their materials and the advanced manufacturing techniques they employ. By sourcing prepreg carbon fibre from the same suppliers as Ferrari and Lamborghini, Koshi Group ensures that their products meet the highest standards of excellence. The meticulous finishing processes, including clear coating with long-lasting finishes and ceramic clear coats, further distinguish their products in the market. These UVPs not only attract luxury car brands but also appeal to enthusiasts seeking unique, high-performance modifications.

The leadership's vision for continuous innovation and excellence has been pivotal in Koshi Group's journey. Shkamb Koshi's strategic direction has fostered an environment where innovation thrives, allowing the company to stay ahead of industry trends and maintain a competitive edge. The unique value propositions, rooted in high-quality materials and advanced manufacturing processes, have solidified the company's reputation as a leader in the carbon fibre products industry.

Koshi Group LLC's success can be attributed to several core lessons. The importance of understanding customer needs and continuously innovating to meet those needs cannot be overstated. Koshi Group's product development is deeply influenced by customer feedback and market trends. Forming strategic partnerships with luxury car brands and other key stakeholders has been crucial. These partnerships have not only enhanced the company's credibility but also expanded its market reach. Continuous investment in the development of employees' skills, particularly in technology and management, has been essential in maintaining high production standards and fostering a culture of excellence.

To sustain its growth and continue leading in its industry, Koshi Group LLC focuses on the following areas for management and leadership development. Keeping abreast of the latest advancements in carbon fibre technology and market trends is crucial. This involves ongoing education and training programmes for employees to stay updated with industry innovations and best practices. Developing advanced manufacturing skills and techniques among employees is essential to maintain high-quality production standards. This includes specialized training in the use of materials like prepreg carbon fibre and mastering processes such as Autoclave technology. Enhancing management and leadership skills to foster a culture of innovation and excellence within the company is also critical. Training programmes focused on strategic thinking, effective communication, and leadership development are pivotal in empowering managers and leaders to drive the company's vision forward.

The war in Ukraine has not had a direct effect on the business operations of Koshi Group LLC. However, the company remains vigilant about potential indirect impacts, such as disruptions in supply chains or changes in the global economic environment. By maintaining flexible and resilient business strategies, Koshi Group continues to mitigate any potential risks arising from global geopolitical events.

Koshi Group LLC exemplifies the qualities of a Hidden Champion through its unwavering commitment to innovation, high-quality production, and strategic leadership. The company's journey from a small start-up in Kosovo to a global leader in carbon fibre products serves as an inspiration for other enterprises aiming to achieve similar success. Through strategic foresight and continuous development, Koshi Group LLC continues to set benchmarks in the automotive and marine industries.

4 Conclusions and Recommendations

The research on Hidden Champions (HCs) in Kosovo has revealed that these companies exhibit remarkable characteristics of market leadership, innovation, and competitive advantage, even in a challenging business environment. Key findings indicate that these HCs have successfully leveraged their unique value propositions (UVPs) and have shown exceptional resilience and adaptability. The HCs have not only sustained their competitive positions but also advanced their operational capabilities and market reach.

From the research conducted in 2018/2019 and the current study, it is evident that there have been notable differences in the characteristics and progress of HCs. Initially, these companies focused heavily on establishing a solid market presence and developing their product portfolios. Since then, they have shifted towards enhancing technological capabilities, forging strategic partnerships, and investing significantly in employee development. This evolution reflects their growing maturity and sophistication in managing both local and international business challenges.

The primary characteristics of the identified HCs include a strong focus on innovation. HCs continuously invest in R&D to stay ahead of industry trends, which is crucial for developing unique products that meet evolving market demands. Another key characteristic is customer-centricity. A deep understanding of customer needs and preferences drives product development and service delivery, ensuring high satisfaction and loyalty. Forming strategic partnerships with other industry leaders and stakeholders has been essential for expanding market reach and enhancing credibility. Furthermore, a relentless pursuit of quality in products and processes distinguishes HCs from their competitors, with a commitment to excellence being a core aspect of their value proposition. Lastly, the ability to adapt to market changes and global economic conditions has been pivotal. This resilience is particularly evident in their response to the COVID-19 pandemic and geopolitical events like the Ukraine war.

The progress of HCs highlights several key areas for management and leadership development. Keeping up with technological advancements and market trends through ongoing education and training programmes is crucial. Developing advanced manufacturing skills and techniques among employees to maintain high production standards is essential. Enhancing strategic thinking, effective communication, and leadership skills is vital for fostering a culture of innovation and excellence.

To ensure the continued success and growth of Hidden Champions in Kosovo, several recommendations are made for different stakeholders. For governments, implementing policies that support innovation and R&D, including tax incentives and grants for technology development, is critical. Investing in infrastructure, particularly in transportation and energy, will enhance connectivity and support business operations. Simplifying regulatory processes and reducing bureaucratic hurdles can facilitate smoother business operations and international trade. Financial institutions can support HCs by providing easier access to financing, especially for SMEs and start-ups, enabling them to invest in growth and innovation. Developing financial products tailored to the specific needs of HCs, such as flexible loans and venture capital funding, can further assist. Offering advisory services to help HCs with financial planning, risk management, and expansion strategies is also beneficial. Business schools and higher education institutions can contribute by designing curricula that address the specific skills needed by HCs, including advanced manufacturing techniques and strategic management. Fostering partnerships between academia and industry can facilitate practical learning experiences and research collaborations. Developing leadership programmes focused on innovation management, strategic thinking, and effective communication will prepare future leaders.

References

Dushi, M. (2002). *Trepca*. Academy of Science and Arts of Kosovo.

European Commission. (2017). Kosovo progress report. Retrieved from https://ec.europa.eu/neighbourhood-enlargement/kosovo-progress-report

Malcolm, N. (2010). *Kosovo: A short history*. Macmillan.

Mustafa, M. (2017). Kosovo's economic growth and development. *Journal of Balkan Studies, 12*(3), 45–60.

Mustafa, M. (2018). Political and economic reforms in Kosovo. *Economic Transition Review, 5*(2), 110–130.

Perrit, H. H. (2004). *The Kosovo Liberation Army: The inside story of an insurgency*. University of Illinois Press.

World Bank. (2017). Kosovo economic outlook. Retrieved from https://www.worldbank.org/en/country/kosovo/publication/kosovo-economic-outlook-2017

World Bank. (2024). Kosovo economic report. Retrieved from https://www.worldbank.org/en/country/kosovo/publication/kosovo-economic-report-2024

Florentina Dushi is a PhD candidate in Entrepreneurship and Innovativeness at Josip Juraj Strossmayer University in Osijek, Croatia. With over 20 years of experience in human resources, research, teaching, and training, she has worked extensively in Kosovo, Western Europe, and Latin America across the banking, private, and non-governmental sectors. Her academic research focuses on Corporate Entrepreneurship and Leadership in SMEs, particularly within the Kosovan context.

Florentina has designed and delivered a wide range of training programs on topics such as communication, sales strategy, customer service, performance and stress management, and HR systems development. She has also led internationally funded projects supporting SME development and is currently engaged in regional research on entrepreneurship.

She holds an MA in Organizational Psychology and is a graduate of ProCredit Bank's Academy with a focus on financial management. In addition to her professional work, she is a co-founder of the Kosovo HR Association and an active guest speaker on HR-related topics. Within Rotary, she has held several leadership roles and currently serves as District Governor 2026–2027 for Rotary District 2485 (Albania–Kosovo).

Dafina Turkeshi Ballanca is a PhD candidate in Entrepreneurship and Innovativeness at Josip Juraj Strossmayer University, Osijek, Croatia. With over 20 years of experience in Human Resource Management, training, and consulting, she specializes in Corporate Entrepreneurship and HR practices, focusing on strengthening SME development in Kosovo. Dafina has led internationally funded projects and is currently conducting regional research on entrepreneurship.

She is a certified trainer in sales and soft skills, having trained staff in international and local banks, enterprises, and institutions, using modern methodologies and maintaining excellent feedback from participants. Dafina is also experienced in market research, salary surveys, HR policy development, and business proposal drafting. Earlier in her career, she trained over a hundred client advisors and front-desk officers at ProCredit Bank Kosovo and held key roles in commercial banking and junior management.

She holds a Master's degree in Management, Organization, and Business Economics from Universitat Autònoma de Barcelona and a Bachelor's in Management and Informatics from the University of Pristina. Dafina also lectures on Organizational Culture and Management of Technological Innovation at Universum College, Kosovo. She is an active mentor in the UNDP peace-building program and a Rotary Club Prishtina 2025–2026.

Hidden Champions of Latvia

Galina Zilgalve and Irina Sennikova

Abstract The chapter explores the emergence and development of hidden champion companies in Latvia, small to mid-sized enterprises that have achieved significant global market leadership in specialised niches while remaining largely under the radar. Building on prior regional research, the study examines the evolution of previously identified hidden champions. It introduces new ones, analysing their key success factors, innovation strategies, and resilience in times of crisis. Utilising a PESTEL framework, the chapter contextualises the Latvian economic and political environment that shapes business opportunities and constraints. Two detailed case studies of Primekss SIA and SIA Peruza illustrate how innovation, leadership, export orientation, and adaptability have enabled these firms to thrive despite challenges such as geopolitical instability, labour shortages, and the COVID-19 pandemic. The findings highlight common characteristics across firms: strong and visionary leadership, commitment to innovation, focus on high-quality customised products, and a strong export orientation. The chapter concludes with recommendations for governments, financial institutions, and higher education institutions to nurture and support the hidden champion ecosystem in Latvia. The study underscores the pivotal role these companies play in driving economic resilience, technological advancement, and sustainable growth in small, open economies like Latvia.

Overview[1]
Official name: Latvia
Type of government: Parliamentary republic
Population in 2023: 1,874,000
Land area: 64,573 km^2

[1] Please provide World Bank data and a history overview of your country.

G. Zilgalve (✉) · I. Sennikova
RISEBA University of Applied Sciences, Riga, Latvia
e-mail: Galina.zilgalve@riseba.lv; irina.sennikova@riseba.lv

D. Berberović, D. Purg (eds.), *Hidden Champions in Rising Economies*, Contributions to Management Science,
https://doi.org/10.1007/978-3-032-08263-3_24

History

1918 Following the end of the First World War on 18 November 1918, Latvia was proclaimed an independent state for the first time in its history.

1920 A peace treaty is signed with Russia, and some 200,000 refugees return to Latvia. The Latvian economy begins to grow, focusing primarily on the export of agricultural products.

1937 Latvia had repaid all its external debts and raised some 6 tons of gold in various banks in the United Kingdom, Switzerland and the United States, during Latvia's economic boom.

1940 (June 17th) Latvia is entirely occupied by the Soviet Union. "Sovietization" of Latvia (i.e. transforming Latvia into a Soviet republic) begins.

1941 Holocaust on the territory of Latvia: some 70,000 Jews were murdered. Latvians were recruited into both the Soviet Union's army and the German SS Legion. Some 200,000 Latvians perish on both sides.

1944/45 Renewed Soviet occupation leads to a large influx of inhabitants from other Soviet republics into Latvia, mainly Russians, Ukrainians, and Belarusians.

1949 To prevent resistance from the local intelligentsia and workers in rural areas to collectivism (the establishment of the kolkhoz), the largest deportation of Latvians was carried out in March 1949. 42,125 Latvians were deported to Siberia and the Far East. Large factories were also built during this period, including those in the chemical industry, machinery, textiles, building materials, pharmaceuticals, and the electrical and electronic industries, all of which are present within the relatively small territory of Latvia. Additionally, there was development in the agricultural sector.

1985 With the onset of perestroika, the idea of independence in Latvia grew in popularity.

1991 (August 21st) Latvia regains independence (Parliamentary Democratic Republic). The transition from socialism to a market economy begins with the implementation of various reforms, marked by the collapse of most large factories and a reorientation towards a service economy.

1994 Bank crisis in Latvia.

1998 The Russian Crisis hit the Latvian economy.

2001/07 Years of rapid economic growth. Latvia, Lithuania, and Estonia are labelled as the "Baltic Tigers".

2004 (March 27th) Latvia joins NATO and the European Union.

2008 Latvia was hit hard by the world financial crisis.

2010 The recovery of the Latvian economy begins with a 3.3% GDP growth already forecast for 2011.

2011 The International Financial Support Programme was successfully completed, and Latvia was recognised as having recovered from the economic crisis.

2014	Latvia joined the Eurozone when the Euro replaced its national currency, the Lat.
2011–2014	Steady annual economic growth of 3.8% yearly average.
July 2016	Latvia became a member of the OECD.
End of 2017	The Latvian economy reached its pre-crisis level.
2018	One of the fastest-growing economies in Europe.
2020	COVID-19 Global pandemic outreach.
2022	Energy crisis caused by the unstable geopolitical situation in the region.

1 Introduction: Context and History

Latvia is a small, open economy in the Baltic region that has made significant progress in transitioning to a market economy since regaining independence in 1991. Although it went through a severe recession in 2008–2010, Latvia has since achieved consistent economic growth and integration into the European Union. To understand the context in which hidden champions operate in Latvia, we will provide a brief analysis of the broader political, economic, social, technological, environmental and legal factors that influence the business environment for hidden champions in Latvia, using the PESTEL framework.

1.1 Political Factors

Latvia is a parliamentary republic with a democratically elected government. The country joined the European Union in 2004 and the Eurozone in 2014, indicating a stable political system aligned with Western institutions. However, the government has been somewhat fragmented, with a multiparty system and frequent leadership changes.

Political tensions with Russia remain due to Latvia's support for Ukraine and efforts to reduce Russian influence, such as restricting the Russian language in education and banning Russian TV broadcasts. This geopolitical instability creates some uncertainty for businesses.

1.2 Economic Factors

Latvia has a small, open economy that is highly integrated with the European single market. The country is ranked 14th globally in the World Bank's Ease of Doing Business Index, suggesting a relatively business-friendly environment. Key economic strengths include:

- Rapid GDP growth of over 10% annually in 2006–2007 before the recession
- Privatisation of state-owned enterprises, with the private sector accounting for 70% of GDP
- Highly developed transit and logistics sectors due to Latvia's strategic location
- Competitive manufacturing industries like wood processing, machinery, and electronics

However, challenges remain, such as labour shortages, a small domestic market, and potential market saturation. The economy contracted sharply from 2008 to 2010 and has only gradually recovered since then. Achieving the government's ambitious goal of doubling GDP by 2035 will require sustained high growth rates, which may be challenging to attain. Overall, while Latvia has made significant economic strides, it still faces hurdles in becoming a fully developed, high-income economy.

1.3 Social Factors

Latvia has a small population of just 1.9 million people. The country faces demographic challenges, including an ageing population, low birth rates, and high emigration rates, especially among young, educated workers. This shrinking labour force creates skills shortages for businesses.

Income inequality is also a concern, with the risk of poverty or social exclusion higher in Latvia than the EU average. Improving social inclusion and public trust in institutions is a key priority for the government.

1.4 Technological Factors

Latvia has made progress in developing its technological capabilities in recent years. The country has a relatively high rate of internet usage at 80% of the population. Key technology sectors include information and communication technologies, renewable energy, and transportation infrastructure.

Major technology projects underway include:

- Connecting Latvia's electricity grid to the European system by 2025
- Constructing the European Rail Baltica high-speed rail line
- Developing a 115 MW solar park project

However, more investment is needed in research, development and innovation to drive productivity growth. Strengthening the digital skills of the workforce is also a priority.

1.5 Environmental Factors

Latvia has a relatively clean environment, with 50% of its territory covered by forests. The country is ranked among the top 10 globally in the Environmental Performance Index. Key environmental strengths include:

- Compliance with most UN and EU environmental regulations
- Low levels of air and water pollution, with only localised issues
- Commitment to reducing land-based pollution into the Baltic Sea

However, Latvia faces several environmental challenges, including managing transboundary air and water pollution from neighbouring countries. Transitioning to a low-carbon economy and adapting to climate change will require further policy action.

1.6 Legal Factors

Latvia has a civil law legal system and has made progress in aligning its legislation with EU standards since joining the bloc in 2004. Key legal factors impacting businesses include:

- Intellectual property rights protection, which is vital for innovative companies
- Regulations on labelling and packaging, which can create additional costs
- Insolvency procedures and the court system, which some view as slow and inefficient

Corruption remains a concern, with the government working to enhance the independence of anti-corruption agencies. Overall, the legal environment is generally favourable for business activity but could be improved in certain areas.

1.7 Innovation Policies and Framework

The Latvian government has established various policies aimed at enhancing innovation. The National Industrial Policy for 2021–2027 emphasises innovation as a key priority, outlining 12 tasks to improve the innovation ecosystem. These tasks include promoting investments in R&D, enhancing collaboration between public and private sectors, and creating legal frameworks for innovation zones. Additionally, the Science, Technology Development, and Innovation Guidelines for 2021–2027 further support these objectives by focusing on the development of human capital and fostering an environment conducive to innovation. The government aims to increase funding for innovative projects and improve the overall business environment to attract investments.

1.8 Current Innovation Landscape

According to the European Innovation Scoreboard 2023, Latvia is classified as an "Emerging Innovator", with an innovation performance score of 52.5% of the EU average. While there have been improvements in areas such as public-private co-publications and employment in knowledge-intensive sectors, the country continues to lag in R&D expenditures and government support for business innovation. Notably, Latvia has a high share of non-innovators, indicating a significant potential for growth in innovation activities. The Latvian Bioeconomy Strategy 2030 also highlights the importance of innovation in sustainable resource management and the efficient exploitation of natural resources. This strategy aims to position Latvia as a leader in bioeconomy sectors, promoting innovative practices that balance economic growth with environmental sustainability.

1.9 Challenges and Opportunities

Despite these initiatives, Latvia's innovation system faces several challenges. The fragmentation of research institutions, insufficient collaboration between academia and industry, and underfunding in the science sector are significant barriers to enhancing innovation capacity. Addressing these issues will require targeted policy interventions and increased investment in research and development. Moreover, the shift towards a knowledge-based economy necessitates a cultural change within educational institutions to foster entrepreneurship and innovation. Enhancing the entrepreneurial culture among universities and supporting the commercialisation of research outputs are critical for leveraging Latvia's innovation potential. In conclusion, while Latvia's economy shows promise with its focus on innovation, Significant efforts are required to overcome current challenges and unlock its full potential as a competitive player in the global market. The government's commitment to fostering an innovation-driven economy through strategic policies and investment will be essential for sustainable growth.

2 Characteristics of Hidden Champions from Latvia

Latvia offers both opportunities and challenges for hidden champions. The country's strategic location, educated workforce, and integration with the European market provide a solid foundation. However, the small domestic market, demographic pressures, and lingering corruption issues create headwinds. To succeed, hidden champions in Latvia must navigate this complex business environment while leveraging the country's strengths. With continued reforms and investment, Latvia can further improve its competitiveness and attract more innovative, high-growth firms.

The current research builds upon the findings of the previous study, "Hidden Champions in CEE and Dynamically Changing Environments". The primary objective of this investigation is to examine the evolution of previously identified hidden champions, as well as to identify and characterise new hidden champions, elucidating their shared attributes, market leadership positions, success factors, challenges, and developmental requirements. As Latvia transitions from an efficiency-driven economy to an innovation-driven one, an increasing number of enterprises are emerging that meet the criteria of hidden champions.

To identify potential hidden champions, the research methodology involved a comprehensive examination of various enterprise support agencies and initiatives, including:

- Latvian Investment and Development Agency
- Latvija Var! (Latvia Can!)
- Magnetic Latvia
- Labs of Latvia

Particular attention was directed towards export-oriented companies that have been nominated for or received recognition through various accolades, such as local export awards or European Business Awards. This methodological approach enables the systematic identification and analysis of hidden champions within Latvia's economic landscape, providing a deeper understanding of their role in the country's transition towards an innovation-driven economy.

Exhibit 1 Core economic indicators for (Insert the country)

	2017	2018	2019	2020	2021	2022	2023
GDP per capita (current US$)	15695.1	17,865	17883.3	18096.2	20930.4	21508.4	23184.3
GDP per capita growth (annual %)	3.3	4	0.6	−3.5	6.7	3	−0.3
Long-term unemployment (% of total unemployment)	37.67	41.69	38.18	27.33	30.33	29.07	27.6
Foreign direct investment, net inflows (% of GDP)	3.7	1.2	3.3	2.8	9.4	2.9	4
GDP (current US$, mio)	30.46	34.85	34.23	34.39	39.44	40.42	43,63
Exports of goods and services (current US$, mio)	18,814	21,134	20,535	20,931	25,429	29,373	27,947
Exports of goods and services (% of GDP)	61.1	58.9	60.0	60.8	64.6	72.9	64.1
Merchandise exports (current US$)	14.13	16.16	15.70	16.33	20.83	24.10	22.65
Merchandise exports to high-income economies (% of total merchandise exports)	74.4	76.2	74.5	74.8	n/a	n/a	n/a
Merchandise exports to developing economies in Europe & Central Asia (% of total merchandise exports)	20.7	19.24	20.6	19.1	n/a	n/a	n/a

Exhibit 1 (continued)

	2017	2018	2019	2020	2021	2022	2023
Ores and metals exports (% of merchandise exports)	2.0	2.2	1.8	1.8	2.6	1.9	1.7
Agricultural raw materials exports (% of merchandise exports)	10.0	12.0	12.0	11.0	13.0	12.0	9.0
Food exports (% of merchandise exports)	19.9	18.2	20.8	21.7	18.0	19.5	16.5
Fuel exports (% of merchandise exports)	5.2	5.0	5.0	4.0	6.0	12.0	7.0
Manufactures exports (% of merchandise exports)	60.5	60.7	59.1	60.4	58.9	52.1	56.4
High-technology exports (% of manufactured exports)	17.7	20.5	17.2	20.0	17.0	16.4	18

Source: World Bank, July 2024, OECD July 2024

3 Case Studies of Selected Hidden Champions

3.1 *Case Study 1*

3.1.1 PRIMEKSS SIA

Overview
Address: 76 Gustava Zemgala gatve, Rīga, LV - 1039, Latvia
Tel: +371-67801120
Fax: n/a
Email: info@primekss.com
Web: www.primekss.com

Company Information
Industry[2]: 43.33 FLOOR AND WALL COVERING
Year of Establishment: 1997
Sales Revenues in 2017: 18.4 mln EUR
Sales Revenues in 2023: 49 mln EUR (2022)
Average number of employees in 2023: 280
Brainer(s) behind the company: CEO and owner Janis Ošlejs

Nature of Market Leadership

SIA PRIMEKSS is recognised as a leading authority in concrete production in the Baltic and Northern European markets. The company is actively broadening its export network, securing new contractual agreements across various regions,

[2]According to NACE Rev. 2—please check the tecnical instructions included in this document (pg. 9).

including Israel, the United States, and India. PRIMEKSS faces competition mainly from companies such as XTM, Twintec Group, and Linatel.

Nature of Competitive Advantage

The competitive advantage of SIA PRIMEKSS can be attributed to several key factors. One of the most significant is their innovative technology. PRIMEKSS has developed a proprietary technology called PrimeComposite, which is a high-performance, fibre-reinforced concrete solution. This technology significantly reduces the need for traditional steel reinforcement and minimises the occurrence of shrinkage cracks.

Cost efficiency is another crucial factor. The PrimeComposite technology enables thinner slabs and reduced material usage, resulting in cost savings in both materials and labour. This efficiency allows for their products to be highly competitive in terms of price without compromising on quality.

Sustainability also significantly enhances their competitive advantage. PRIMEKSS's solutions are environmentally friendly because they lower the carbon footprint by using less concrete and steel. The company's emphasis on sustainable building practices appeals to the increasing market demand for green construction solutions.

Quality and durability are additional key benefits. The high performance of PrimeComposite floors guarantees superior durability, with enhanced resistance to wear and tear, making them ideal for heavy-duty applications such as warehouses, industrial facilities, and retail spaces.

PRIMEKSS has also established a strong presence in the international market, delivering projects across Europe, North America, and other regions. Their proven track record and reputation for quality work bolster their competitive edge.

Customisation and flexibility further boost their appeal. The company provides tailored solutions to meet specific client needs, offering customised floor designs that cater to unique project requirements. This flexibility makes them attractive to a broader range of customers.

Lastly, technical expertise is a significant competitive strength. PRIMEKSS's team comprises highly skilled professionals with deep expertise in concrete technology and construction. Their ability to deliver technically challenging projects adds to their competitive strength.

By leveraging these factors, SIA PRIMEKSS maintains a competitive advantage in the construction industry, particularly in the niche of high-performance concrete floors.

Core Lessons Learned on the Path to Success

The core lessons learned by SIA PRIMEKSS on their path to success encompass several strategic and operational insights that have contributed to their leadership in the concrete production industry.

- One of the most significant lessons is that innovation is key. Embracing and developing technology, such as their proprietary PrimeComposite, has been crucial. This innovation has enabled PRIMEKSS to differentiate its products, offering superior performance and cost advantages.

- Another critical lesson is the importance of a customer-centric approach. Tailoring solutions to client needs and offering customised and flexible solutions have enhanced client satisfaction and loyalty. Understanding and addressing specific client requirements is essential for competitive differentiation.
- Additionally, the entrepreneurial spirit of the company owner has been a pivotal factor in the success of SIA PRIMEKSS. This entrepreneurial drive has fostered a culture of innovation, risk-taking, and proactive problem-solving, which has been instrumental in the company's growth and its leadership in the market.

Management and Leadership Development Needs

To sustain its current growth trajectory, SIA PRIMEKSS recognises the need to enhance the managerial and delegation skills of its middle-level managers. Most of these managers are internally developed specialists who have advanced alongside the company's growth. While they possess high-level technical expertise, there is a critical need for them to acquire additional managerial competencies, specifically in areas such as delegation and project management.

Additionally, the company should establish an internal training system focused on the utilisation of its proprietary technology, ensuring consistent and effective application across all projects.

Financing and Regulatory Environment Development Needs

Regarding regulatory needs, the company has advocated for tax reductions for stable market participants and consistent taxpayers. No further financial or regulatory obligations have been specified.

Pandemic's Impact on "Hidden Champions'" Business Approach

During the COVID-19 pandemic, restrictions enacted to curb the spread of the coronavirus remained in force in the Republic of Latvia and many other countries, resulting in a significant slowdown in economic growth both locally and internationally. The management of Primekss continuously evaluated the situation, recognising its inherent unpredictability. As a result, the company's turnover was not greatly affected. The management remained confident that the company could manage the crisis effectively by reducing both administrative and direct project costs.

Financially, Primekss benefited from strategic support during the pandemic. The company secured an €8 million financing deal from the Altum investment fund, specifically aimed at helping large companies adapt to the new realities of life and business. This funding not only assisted Primekss in navigating the immediate challenges posed by the pandemic but also enabled ongoing investment in product development and market expansion.

One significant benefit came from the increased emphasis on sustainability and efficiency. Primekss's PrīmX technology, known for its reduced CO_2 emissions and material efficiency, became even more appealing as businesses and governments sought greener solutions. The pandemic accelerated the shift towards sustainable practices, and Primekss was well-positioned to meet this growing demand.

The pandemic also underscored the importance of flexibility and rapid construction. Primekss's technology, which allows for faster installation and reduced labour costs, provided a competitive edge. As construction projects faced delays and budget constraints, the ability to complete projects more quickly and cost-effectively became a crucial advantage.

As a result, SIA Primekss was able to capitalise on its innovative, sustainable, and efficient concrete solutions to navigate the crisis. The company's ability to adapt to changing market demands, coupled with strategic financial support, enabled it not only to survive but also to strengthen its competitive position in the industry.

Effects of the Ukraine War on "Hidden Champions" Business Operations

SIA Primekss ceased its operations in Russia and Belarus on 28 February 2022, as a show of solidarity with the international community and in response to the changing geopolitical situation. This decision meant that Primekss had to halt its business activities in these markets, which had historically been important for many Latvian companies. The end of operations in these regions forced Primekss to seek alternative markets to compensate for the loss of revenue from Russia and Belarus.

Building Strength from the Ground Up: The Story of Primekss

The company was established in 1997 by the young entrepreneur Jānis Ošlejs. Initially, the business focused on coatings, specifically on how to improve poor floor surfaces by covering them with plastic material that makes the floor look visually appealing and easy to maintain for food companies, among others. Although the business experienced rapid growth, problems soon emerged—the coating material began to detach from the floor surface.

After investigating the problem, the team concluded that the problem lay not in the material, but in the poor concrete substrate. This led the team to reassess their approach and explore ways to enhance the quality of the concrete. After conducting intensive research, they developed and patented a product called Primekss Composite, which became the company's flagship product.

Primekss Composite offered an innovative solution for industrial floors and structures, reducing concrete rusting and cracking. This unique product enabled the company to become a global leader in the industrial floors and structures market.

With its technology, the company helped customers save costs by offering thinner, yet stronger, concrete.

The company's growth was rapid, and it established two main business lines: manufacturing with its workforce and selling the technology through licensing. With its team, the company carried out projects in Scandinavia, the Baltic states, Israel, the United States, Belarus, India, and Africa. The licence allowed customers to use the technology with training and support.

"We realised quite quickly that the Latvian market was small and that growth opportunities were limited, so we turned to exports as early as 2002. We started with the geographically closest countries - Lithuania and Estonia," says Mr. Ošlejs. Later, when Latvia joined the European Union and job opportunities opened in the single European market, the company started exporting to Sweden. The rest of Scandinavia and other countries gradually followed this. Scandinavia is the company's biggest export market today, but it also exports to Asia, India, Israel and other European countries, including the United Kingdom. The United States and even South Africa are important export destinations. Before the Russian invasion of Ukraine, the company was also active in Russia and Belarus—these markets are now closed.

For many years, the company has demonstrated annual growth of 30–35% and continues to expand, strengthening its position in the market and reaching a turnover of 90 million euros in 2023, with 95% of this turnover stemming from production and licence export. There are several key factors that contribute to the company's success.

One of the main factors is continuous innovation and investment in R&D. While researching defects in concrete production, Primekss developed a unique, patented steel fibre-reinforced self-stressing concrete (SFRSSC) technology known as PrīmX. This technology enables the construction of jointless, dimensionally stable concrete floors and structural elements, which are essential for high-precision environments like gigafactories. The PrīmX system is also designed to be future-proof, offering flexibility in modifications and load placements. The innovative concrete technology developed by Primekss results in floors that are 50% stronger than traditional concrete. This increased strength contributes to the durability and long life of the floors, making them suitable for heavy-duty industrial applications. Primekss has demonstrated a strong commitment to research and development (R&D), allocating significant resources to promote continuous product innovation. The company has established collaborations with multiple technical universities, both in Latvia and abroad, to enhance its research capabilities. In a notable advancement of its R&D infrastructure, Primekss opened its Research and Development Centre in 2023. The centre is the most modern and largest private concrete research centre in the Baltics and Eastern Europe, representing a significant milestone in the company's dedication to scientific progress in concrete technology. The Research and Development Centre serves multiple functions, including concrete mix design development, material testing, and the advancement of concrete solutions for robotics and automation applications. The company's annual investment in R&D activities, approximately 2 million euros, underscores its commitment to remaining a leader in concrete innovation.

Additionally, the company demonstrates a strong commitment to sustainability. Operating in an industry with high pollution levels, Primekss has made sustainability a fundamental part of its business, notably impacting its operations, product development, and corporate culture. Here's how their dedication to sustainability influences their business. Primekss has developed PrīmX, a patented concrete technology that is 50% stronger than traditional concrete and generates up to 70% less CO2 emissions.

Client focus and a strong emphasis on quality are additional success factors. The organisation invests in educating its clients through various webinars, workshops, and direct training sessions. The company prioritises not only achieving results but also fostering strong, long-term relationships with its clients. Primekss offers full-service design-build project partnerships, supported by meticulous planning and high-quality standards. The company's structural-engineering department ensures that all projects are delivered with a full warranty, covering materials, design, and execution.

To guarantee the high quality of its products, Primekss established its own quality control system, PrimeQuality.com, which enables real-time monitoring of critical floor parameters. This ensures that the highest quality standards are consistently upheld across all projects. The use of sensor-equipped slabs further improves the ability to monitor and maintain floor quality over time.

Above all, the key to success is the company's leadership and team. The entrepreneurial spirit of the company owner fuels steady growth and attracts motivated employees with similar mindsets, thereby creating a strong and united team.

Nevertheless, the main success factor for Primekss is its leadership and team. The entrepreneurial spirit of the company's owner acts as a catalyst for steady and sustained growth, attracting like-minded, motivated individuals who together make a strong and united team. This dynamic leadership encourages a corporate culture that highlights innovation, commitment, and a shared vision for the company's future, thereby supporting Primekss's ongoing success and competitive position in the concrete technology industry.

3.2 *Case Study 2*

3.2.1 SIA PERUZA

Overview

Address: 'Lejasrandoti', Mucenieki, Ropazu novads, LV-2137, Latvia
Tel: +371-67240836
Fax:
Email: info@peruza.com
Web: www.peruza.com

Company information

Industry[3]: 28.93, Manufacture of machinery for food, beverage and tobacco processing.
Year of Establishment: 1991
Sales Revenues in 2017: 3,6 mln EUR
Sales Revenues in 2023: 6,2 mln EUR
Average number of employees in 2023: 67
Brainer(s) behind the company: Roberts Dlohi, board member; Arnis Petranis, owner

Nature of Market Leadership

SIA PERUA has established itself as a prominent global player in the production line solutions sector, with a particular focus on fish processing machinery. While the company's core expertise lies in the development and manufacturing of fish processing equipment, it has diversified its portfolio to include a wider range of food industry applications. These include, but are not limited to, pumpkin processing lines, spinach washing systems, box conveying mechanisms, and weight batching solutions. The company's international footprint is considerable, with exports reaching various regions including the European Union, Brazil, China, Japan, and Thailand. Notably, South East Asia has become a key growth market for PERUZA, with the Philippines showing particular promise. In terms of market position, PERUZA maintains a significant market share of 10–15% within the global small fish processing industry.

Nature of Competitive Advantage

The company is renowned for the superior quality of its products and exceptional individualised customer support. Emphasising innovation and continuous improvement—embodied by the motto "Improvement is our passion"—the company persistently enhances its production lines, focusing on core aspects and refining areas of potential advancement. The industry requires ongoing engagement with both potential and existing clients while maintaining high service support standards, making a high level of client orientation crucial. Adhering to the principle of "keeping your word/promise", the company commits to working diligently until the equipment operates correctly.

Furthermore, the company invests in educating young specialists by collaborating with educational institutions, frequently inviting second- and third-year students for internships or employment and dedicating substantial time and effort to their training and development.

[3]According to NACE Rev. 2—please check the tecnical instructions included in this document (pg. 9).

Core Lessons Learned on the Path to Success

A key success factor is the company's dedication to continuous improvement. This mindset, described as "looking into the core and improving what can be improved", is embedded throughout the organisation and drives both technological progress and problem-solving. This culture is underpinned by a deliberate strategy to develop young engineering talent. Peruza actively recruits students from university engineering and technical programmes, invests in their practical training, and supports their professional development over a 2-year mentoring period. This long-term commitment to nurturing internal talent has established a pipeline of highly capable and loyal engineers who contribute significantly to the company's innovation capacity.

Closely related to this is Peruza's non-punishing approach to mistakes, which the company regards as learning opportunities. Leadership encourages experimentation and tolerates failure when it results from genuine effort. This cultural element is vital for fostering innovation, as it ensures that employees are not afraid to explore new solutions. The support provided to those who show initiative, regardless of rank or role, reinforces a workplace environment based on trust, empowerment, and respect.

Another key success factor is the involvement and empowerment of employees at all levels. Over time, the company has shifted from a founder-led structure to one where functional managers and specialists operate independently. Employees are trusted with decision-making, planning, and operational responsibilities. This change has been supported by clear, equal rules for everyone, whether an owner or a cleaning staff member, fostering a culture of fairness, professionalism, and mutual accountability. The symbolic importance of traditions like awarding an "Employee of the Year", which has previously been given to a cleaning staff member, demonstrates the value placed on all contributions and strengthens inclusive recognition.

The role of leadership has been to establish a strong foundation, exemplify ethical behaviour, and gradually step back to enable new leaders to emerge. The founders set the company's values and direction but now mainly act in a mentoring or strategic advisory role. This slow transfer of authority has enabled employees to develop into leadership positions, further embedding a culture of initiative and responsibility.

Finally, one of the key lessons Peruza has learned is the importance of consistency in values and discipline. The company enforces a strict code of conduct that applies equally to everyone, fostering an environment of integrity and high standards. This level of consistency not only promotes internal cohesion but also builds external trust with customers, partners, and the wider business community.

Management and Leadership Development Needs

As the rapidly growing company, one of the challenges involves recruiting, developing, and retaining technically skilled employees, especially in robotics and software programming. These skills are crucial for expanding in-house capabilities, particularly since many projects involve highly customised solutions that are not fully defined at the start. While outsourcing remains a temporary measure, the long-term plan clearly emphasises the need for dedicated internal teams capable of handling complex and evolving technical tasks.

Equally important is the need to foster a work culture centred on responsibility and deep commitment to results. The company places a high value on the principle of delivering fully functional solutions—"we work until it works"—which necessitates a team of professionals who are not bound by rigid working hours but are instead motivated by shared accountability for performance.

The operational environment further emphasised the need for strong project management. The organisation manages multiple ongoing projects that differ in complexity, duration, and scope. This variability creates continuous challenges in resource distribution and task prioritisation, especially when some tasks require specialised expertise. Effective project coordination, proper task sequencing, and flexible planning are therefore crucial. Project managers are expected to demonstrate not only technical skills but also strong communication and organisational abilities. In response, the company regularly invests in project management training and encourages staff to continually enhance their planning skills.

Financing and Regulatory Environment Development Needs

Perusa has historically relied on financing from Altum, a state financial institution, which has played a critical role in the company's survival during past economic downturns. Unlike commercial banks, Altum has taken a more supportive and flexible approach to loan restructuring and repayment, allowing the company to navigate financial difficulties without the risk of sudden loan recalls.

One of the main financial challenges stems from the need to produce and deliver sample equipment for testing at client sites. Although this practice was not initially part of Peruza's business model, it has become an industry expectation largely driven by larger competitors. Since clients do not pay for these trial units upfront, Peruza must fund the production and delivery of test equipment through loans. This also includes additional costs related to adapting and improving the equipment based on site-specific conditions and client feedback. These expenses are incurred before any sale is made, creating a financial gap that must be filled through external funding.

A second major financial pressure arises from a change in industry payment practices. Previously, the company followed a standard payment structure: 50% deposit, 40% before delivery, and 10% after commissioning. However, leading companies in the sector have started to demand lower advance payments and defer final payments, forcing Peruza to adapt in order to stay competitive. This change has heightened the company's need for working capital to cover production costs and operational expenses over extended payment cycles.

Pandemic's Impact on "Hidden Champions'" Business Approach

No employees have been laid off or wages cut, despite a significant drop in turnover due to the impact of the virus. However, the company has borrowed a substantial amount of money to meet payroll obligations, reflecting the owners' commitment to their staff, from whom loyalty, quality, and efficiency are expected in return.

The main goal was to keep the company afloat during the difficult times of the COVID-19 pandemic. At first, the crisis was managed well, but problems arose with securing new orders. Some foreign clients, discouraged by the pandemic's economic impact and the reduced demand for their products, delayed projects to buy new equipment. Additionally, other clients faced loan rejections from their banks, which had become more cautious. These factors have presented challenges for PERUZA.

To address these challenges, the company has diversified its production profile, moving beyond manufacturing equipment solely for the fish processing sector to include the robotisation of production and packaging lines and solutions for waste sorting. This diversification requires employees to develop new skills as the company ventures into new business areas. The company is now more actively promoting its offerings globally than ever before, confident that proactive measures will enable it to withstand the crisis and achieve significant growth in the future.

Effects of the Ukraine War on "Hidden Champions'" Business Operations

At the beginning of the Ukraine war, the company and food processing industry continued to face a complex and evolving set of challenges stemming from the aftershocks of the COVID-19 pandemic, which were further intensified by geopolitical and economic instability.

One of the most significant issues caused by the Ukrainian war was the extended delivery times for food processing equipment and its components. Where manufacturers and clients once expected machinery to be delivered within 2–3 months, the average wait has increased to 4–6 months. The delay was largely due to unresolved supply chain disruptions, which began during the pandemic and have been worsened by political tensions in Europe. Specific contributing factors included a global shortage of truck drivers, limited capacity of logistics providers, higher freight costs, shipping delays, inventory shortages, and labour shortages. The global energy crisis has also further destabilised the delivery process, indicating that a full recovery of the supply chain remains out of reach.

Another significant challenge was the sharp increase in inflation, which directly affects the total cost per product across the industry. Over the past year, the material cost per product has risen from 11% to 17%. This increase was caused not only by higher manufacturing costs but also by rising prices for ingredients and raw materials.

From Fish to Robotics: The Evolution of Peruza as a Process Engineering Innovator

Founded in 1991, SIA PERUZA has expanded from a modest enterprise into a significant player in the field of industrial automation and process engineering. Based in Latvia, the company initially gained recognition as a specialist in fish processing equipment. However, from its earliest days, PERUZA's philosophy has never been about simply imitating what had already been done. Instead, the company adopted a strong commitment to continuous improvement, innovation, and customer-focused development. As one of the company's representatives noted, "Even at the very beginning of the company, we were very much about not just repeating but improving every time we got an order to do."

This ethos of improvement was not solely technical; it was driven by a broader mission. PERUZA sees its work as helping to solve global food challenges. A large part of worldwide food loss does not stem from a lack of resources, but from poor processing, preservation, and storage capacity. By providing producers with more efficient and dependable machinery, PERUZA aims to improve the global food supply chain. As the company states, "Equipment to profit is the goal why our customers are buying our equipment. And even higher value is that for the world, it means more quality food."

Although fish processing equipment remained the company's main focus for many years, PERUZA made a strategic choice to expand into new sectors some years ago. Today, the company describes itself more broadly as a process engineering firm, providing customised technological solutions across various industries, including meat, dairy, fruits and vegetables, and beverages. A particularly significant development has been the company's growth into robotic and computer-controlled production lines, demonstrating a deeper integration of artificial intelligence and machine vision into their designs.

This transformation from a niche manufacturer to a multidimensional engineering firm has been supported by a lean but dynamic workforce of around 65 specialists. The company operates through a balanced structure, with its engineering and manufacturing capacities split nearly evenly between a team of experienced technicians and a younger generation of innovative thinkers. This organisational model enables PERUZA to respond swiftly to market needs, develop bespoke solutions, and support continuous technical iteration.

Despite its relatively small size, PERUZA has achieved a significant global presence. In recent years, the company has expanded to Chile, Norway, Iceland, Thailand, China, and Japan. Traditionally known for its fish processing solutions in coastal markets, the company now operates in over 30 countries across multiple continents. Importantly, all equipment is sold under the PERUZA brand, emphasising a global identity built on proprietary expertise. Rather than acting as an anonymous subcontractor, PERUZA positions itself as a direct partner with its clients, relying heavily on word-of-mouth reputation and customer referrals to foster international growth.

The company's technological path is sharply aimed at the future of processing industries, especially considering workforce shortages and increasing demands for automation. PERUZA considers robotic vision systems, artificial intelligence networks, and collaborative robots (co-bots) vital to the development of modern production environments. These technologies are especially relevant in food processing, where product shapes, sizes, and quality can differ significantly, challenging traditional automation. PERUZA has created hybrid systems that combine machine precision with human oversight, enabling nuanced decision-making in sorting and processing materials such as fish, potatoes, and fruits.

One notable example of PERUZA's innovation is in the Philippines, one of the company's fastest-expanding markets. Here, PERUZA replaced entire lines of manual fish graders with robotic vision systems capable of identifying and sorting fish from overlapping, indistinct piles. Previously, these tasks required up to ten manual workers; PERUZA's equipment now accomplishes the same with just two operators and a robotic system processing up to 300 fish per minute. This level of innovation is seen across their range of products, which includes automated can fillers, high-speed weighing systems, and modular packaging lines.

The company's expansion into Europe has presented similarly complex challenges. In Latvia, for example, PERUZA developed a robotic system for the Cēsu alus brewery, designing an automated glass bottle handling unit to fit into a narrow space rejected by other European firms. The solution involved advanced programming and mechanical design to ensure that fragile bottles could be safely separated and delivered to the filling line. Other examples include automated packing systems for dairy producer Tukuma Piens and spinach washing lines for baby food manufacturer Spilva, each representing unique engineering solutions tailored to specific food sector requirements.

What unites all of these projects is PERUZA's approach to process engineering. The company believes that even proven technologies can—and should—be improved. This conviction drives its investment in customised solutions that go beyond off-the-shelf machinery, offering clients greater efficiency, adaptability, and long-term value.

In a broader context, PERUZA reflects the challenges and opportunities faced by what scholars call "hidden champions"—small to mid-sized firms that operate globally in niche markets, often without widespread recognition. Latvia, as a national context, provides a mixed environment for such firms. Its strategic location, educated workforce, and integration into the European Union offer a strong platform for innovation and export-led growth. At the same time, firms like PERUZA must navigate demographic pressures, a limited domestic market, and occasional regulatory or institutional constraints.

Despite these challenges, PERUZA has not only survived but thrived, establishing itself as one of Latvia's most forward-looking industrial firms. With a clear vision, a strong technical foundation, and a commitment to long-term innovation, the company continues to shape the future of food processing—not only in Latvia but across the globe.

4 Conclusions and Recommendations

Over the past decade, Latvia has seen the steady rise and solidification of a group of enterprises recognised as "hidden champions": small to mid-sized companies with specialised market leadership, strong innovation capabilities, and consistent international expansion. These firms come from various sectors, including manufacturing, high-tech construction, and food processing equipment, and share core traits that set them apart from the broader SME landscape.

The research confirms that the main driving force behind hidden champions is strong, dedicated leadership. In most cases, founders or long-term CEOs lead the companies with vision, resilience, and adaptability. These leaders foster cultures that emphasise innovation, operational excellence, and customer focus.

Another common feature is the integration of innovation into the company's core strategy. While not always driven by formal R&D departments, innovation in hidden champions is often based on practical problem-solving, iterative product improvement, and responsiveness to customer feedback. This kind of "embedded innovation" allows firms to deliver highly customised, value-added solutions in global niche markets.

The business environment in Latvia offers both opportunities and challenges for such companies. EU membership, proximity to major markets, access to funding channels, and a growing innovation ecosystem have supported their growth. However, shortages of skilled talent, bureaucratic inefficiencies, and relatively underdeveloped collaboration between academia and industry remain significant hurdles.

Compared to the 2018/2019 HC research findings, Latvian hidden champions have made significant progress. They are now more internationalised, more structured in their management approaches, and more integrated into global value chains. Many have shifted from founder-driven start-ups to scalable, mid-sized companies with dedicated teams for R&D, export management, and product development. At the same time, managing rapid growth has introduced new challenges, such as the need for managerial upskilling, development of internal systems, and governance structures.

Despite these challenges, Latvian hidden champions have demonstrated strong resilience. During the COVID-19 pandemic and the geopolitical disruptions caused by the war in Ukraine, most showed agility by adapting their business models, supply chains, and client engagement strategies to maintain performance and explore new markets. This resilience is further supported by their operational flexibility, sustainable practices, and technological adaptability.

To promote the continued growth of hidden champions and develop a larger ecosystem of internationally competitive SMEs, the following recommendations are suggested.

1. Recommendations for National Governments:

To support the sustainable growth of hidden champions, national governments should prioritise policy continuity and focus on reducing regulatory uncertainty, thereby creating a more stable and predictable business environment. It is equally important to expand targeted support programmes for innovation and export promotion, while ensuring that application and compliance procedures are streamlined and accessible for small and mid-sized enterprises. Addressing labour shortages remains a crucial task, which can be tackled by revising immigration policies to attract high-skilled talent and by providing stronger incentives for students to study science, technology, engineering, and mathematics (STEM). Governments should also strengthen support for collaboration between companies and universities, particularly in technology transfer and applied research. Additionally, improving the international visibility of hidden champions through coordinated trade missions, strategic nation branding, and diplomatic engagement would help these firms access new markets and partnerships more effectively.

2. Recommendations for Financial Institutions:

Financial institutions play a vital role in supporting the growth and innovation capacity of hidden champions. They should develop financial instruments specifically designed for the needs of innovation-driven small and medium-sized enterprises, including options such as scale-up capital, export credit guarantees, and specialised lines of credit for research and development activities. Additionally, existing risk assessment frameworks should be enhanced to better evaluate intangible assets like intellectual property, brand equity, and workforce skills—key factors in knowledge-based businesses. Lending practices also need greater flexibility, allowing repayment structures and investment horizons that match the long development cycles often required for product innovation and international growth. Finally, closer collaboration between private financial institutions and publicly supported development banks, such as Altum, could enable joint financing of early-stage innovation projects, reducing risk and speeding up the market readiness of new technologies.

3. Recommendations for Business Schools and Higher Education Institutions:

Business schools and universities should proactively support Latvia's hidden champion ecosystem. An important step is to incorporate case studies of hidden champions into business and engineering courses, enabling students to engage with real-world examples of innovation, strategy, and global expansion. Expanding executive education programmes focused on innovation management, internationalisation, and digital transformation would further aid the development of current and future leaders in these firms. Additionally, establishing incubators and innovation labs can encourage collaboration among students, researchers, and small-to-mid-sized enterprises, providing a practical platform for experimentation and applied research. Creating structured mentorship networks would enable students to connect directly with hidden champions, offering meaningful internship opportunities and pathways to future employment. Finally, higher education institutions should emphasise interdisciplinary learning and foster entrepreneurial thinking, equipping graduates with diverse skills and mindsets needed to lead and expand complex, high-performing firms in dynamic global markets.

In conclusion, hidden champions play a critical role in Latvia's economic transformation. Their continued success depends not only on internal capabilities but also on the quality of external support they receive from the public sector, financial ecosystem, and educational institutions. A coordinated multi-stakeholder approach is essential to build a thriving environment where innovation-driven firms can scale globally while contributing to sustainable national growth.

References

https://databank.worldbank.org/reports.aspx?source=2&series=TX.VAL.TECH.MF.ZS&country=LVA.

https://www.oecd.org/en/data/indicators.html?orderBy=mostRelevant&page=0&facetTags=oecd-policy-areas%3Apa5.

https://data.stat.gov.lv/pxweb/en/OSP_PUB/START__POP__IR__IRS/IRS010m/table/tableViewLayout1/.

https://www.latvia.eu/our-dna/key-facts/.

https://www.liaa.gov.lv/lv.

Ministry of Economics of Latvia, Latvia Macroeconomic Review, April 2024. https://www.em.gov.lv/lv/media/19029/download?attachment

www.primekss.lv.

www.peruza.lv.

Galina Zilgalve is the Head of External Relations at RISEBA. With educational background in European Business and Human Resource management, Galina is responsible for the development and implementation of the university's internationalisation policy, expansion of the university's partner network, supervision and provision of the University's participation in international accreditations and ratings, as well as international students' recruitment and well-being at the university.

Prior to taking the position of Head of External relations, Galina has been working as Erasmus and double degree programme manager, working on daily basis with international exchange students, ensuring their integration into university life and study process. Galina also organised cultural events for international students and international partners, e.g. international weeks, summer schools, etc.

Irina Sennikova is a distinguished academic leader and researcher specialising in entrepreneurship and innovation. She currently serves as Rector, a Board Member, and Professor at RISEBA University of Applied Sciences in Riga, Latvia. Irina holds an MA in English Philology from the University of Latvia, an International Executive MBA, and an MSc in Management from IEDC-Bled School of Management (Slovenia), as well as a PhD in Management from Kozminski University (Poland). Her doctoral thesis focused on the phenomenon of intellectual entrepreneurship, a subject she has continued to explore extensively. Irina's research interests mainly encompass intellectual entrepreneurship, entrepreneurial leadership and leadership development, gender diversity, corporate governance, and the advancement and internationalisation of business education. She actively participates in international projects on entrepreneurship and innovation, serving as Vice President of CEEMAN, a network of management development institutions in dynamic societies.

Hidden Champions of Lithuania

Erika Vaiginiene, Laimute Urbšienė, and Jurgita Butkevičienė

Abstract Lithuania has undergone a profound economic transformation, evolving from an agrarian society to a knowledge-based economy driven by innovation. The most recent data from the World Bank illustrates the expansion of high-technology exports, a modest contribution from agricultural raw materials exports, and a relatively high proportion of exports destined for high-income economies. In addition, policymakers have taken steps to enhance the business environment in Lithuania, thereby rendering the Lithuanian economy an attractive proposition for developing hidden champions. This chapter reviews the development of the Lithuanian economy in the context of the success of hidden champions in Lithuania. In addition, the chapter presents the market leadership and competitive advantages of Lithuanian hidden champions, discussing their success stories, lessons learned, and the management and leadership development needs that have emerged. The case study results demonstrate that for market leadership success, sensitivity to customer problems and their needs, the power of teamwork and a high appreciation of employees is of great importance.

Overview
Official name: Republic of Lithuania
Type of government: Unitary semi-presidential system
Population in 2017: 2808.9 (thousands)
Land area: 65300 (sq. km)

History
Lithuania, a Baltic state with a rich history, has undergone significant economic and political transformations, particularly since regaining its independence from the Soviet Union in 1990. Here are some key events in Lithuanian economic and political life:

E. Vaiginiene (✉) · L. Urbšienė · J. Butkevičienė
Vilnius University, Vilnius, Lithuania
e-mail: erika.vaiginiene@cr.vu.lt; laimute.urbsiene@evaf.vu.lt; Jurgita.butkeviciene@evaf.vu.lt

D. Berberović, D. Purg (eds.), *Hidden Champions in Rising Economies*, Contributions to Management Science,
https://doi.org/10.1007/978-3-032-08263-3_25

1009	First time Lithuanian name was mentioned in documents.
1815	Lithuania together with Poland was occupied by Russian Empire.
1918	Lithuania regained its independency.
1918	the first bank of Trade and Industry was established.
1921–1924	first production companies (mainly in food industry) were established.
1922	The Bank of Lithuania started operating.
1944	Lithuania was occupied by Soviet Union.
1990	Lithuania regained its independence, the Bank of Lithuania re-established, market economy was started to be implemented "and state-owned companies started to be privatized".
1991	Lithuania joins the United Nations.
1992	Lithuania joined the International Monetary Fund and the World Bank.
1994	Lithuania economy survives private banks' collapse.
1997	The fight against black economy was started.
2004, May	Lithuania becomes a member of the European Union (EU).
2004	March Lithuania joins NATO, enhancing its security and defence.
2008	Financial crisis.
2015	Lithuania adopted the euro as its official currency, replacing the litas. This move further integrated Lithuania into the EU's economic framework and aimed to ensure greater economic stability.
2018	The law of Innovation and technologies was issued.
2018	Joined the OECD.
2020–2022	COVID-19 pandemic.
2022, February	Russia launched a full-scale invasion of Ukraine, marking a significant escalation in the conflict.

1 Introduction: Context and History

Lithuania is located in Northern Europe, on the eastern shore of the Baltic Sea. 2.8 million inhabitants live in an area of 65,300 sq. km. between Latvia, Belarus, Poland, and Russia.

1.1 Economic History and Current State of the Art of Lithuania

The economic history of Lithuania until the re-establishment of independence in 1990 has been thoroughly analysed in works such as *Hidden Champions in Dynamically Changing Societies* (Vaiginiene et al., 2021). Under Soviet rule, Lithuania's technological advancement and attention to environmental, health, and labour standards lagged significantly behind Western norms. Industrial production remained below pre-war levels until the 1960s, with systemic inefficiencies persisting throughout the

Soviet period. The economic and societal losses during the Soviet occupation have been estimated at approximately $800 billion, with direct damages, including genocide, deportations, and property confiscation, accounting for $20 billion, as calculated by UN-recognised methodologies (Ziemele, 2003).

In 1990, Lithuania became the first Baltic state to declare independence, rapidly transitioning from a centrally planned economy to a market-oriented system. The nation implemented comprehensive liberal economic reforms, including privatising state-owned enterprises and establishing a legal framework conducive to market operations. These reforms facilitated the development of a highly open economy characterised by increasing trade and investment liberalisation, fiscal responsibility, and financial independence.

1.1.1 Privatisation and Economic Reform (1990–2000)

Privatisation occurred in two stages. During the initial phase (1991–1995), Lithuanian citizens received investment vouchers worth €3.1 billion, enabling asset privatisation participation. Approximately 5700 enterprises, representing €2 billion in state capital, were privatised through share offerings and auctions (Vilkas, 1997). The second phase (1995–1998) introduced more diverse privatisation mechanisms, selling 526 entities for over €0.7 billion. By 2000, private sector contributions to GDP exceeded 70%.

Monetary reform was another cornerstone of economic stability. The introduction of the Lithuanian litas in 1993 and its subsequent peg to the US dollar in 1994 curbed hyperinflation. This currency stability promoted foreign trade and investor confidence, further enhanced by pegging the litas to the euro in 2002 until full euro adoption in 2015.

1.1.2 Shifting Trade Patterns and Growth (2000s)

Lithuania's economy suffered from the 1998 Russian financial crisis, prompting a shift in trade orientation from Russia to Western markets. By 2006, exports to EU countries accounted for 63% of total exports, while those to the Commonwealth of Independent States dropped to 21%. The establishment of the Vilnius Stock Exchange in 1993 (later part of the NASDAQ OMX Group in 2008) signalled growing integration into global financial markets.

1.1.3 Recovery and Diversification (Post 2008)

The global financial crisis in 2008 and 2009 precipitated a sharp economic contraction in Lithuania. However, austerity measures and structural reforms facilitated a swift recovery. Exports, foreign direct investment, and innovation drove robust growth during the 2010s. Lithuania's energy independence initiatives, such as the Klaipėda LNG terminal (operational in 2014) and synchronisation with the

Continental European power grid (expected completion by 2025), highlight the nation's focus on long-term sustainability.

1.1.4 Challenges and Adaptations (COVID-19 and Beyond)

The COVID-19 pandemic tested Lithuania's economic resilience, causing a GDP contraction of 0.8% in 2020. However, government interventions, including subsidies, grants, and digital transformation initiatives, helped mitigate long-term damage. The war in Ukraine in 2022 further impacted Lithuania through disrupted trade routes, rising energy costs, and inflation. In response, the government prioritised investments in energy independence, defence, and high-tech sectors, aiming for greater economic diversification.

Lithuania leads the Baltic states with the highest GDP per capita, reaching €25,700 in 2023. Since regaining independence in 1990, its economy has grown over 600%, earning it the nickname "Baltic Tiger". The nation is recognised for its openness to trade and investment, resulting in high business and financial freedom. Despite a 6.2% unemployment rate in 2023, wage growth remains strong, driven by long-term economic expansion. The government is actively promoting innovation and infrastructure development, supported by the European Resilience and Recovery Fund. However, challenges persist, including labour market imbalances and a shrinking workforce. The agricultural sector has seen significant changes, dropping employment from 19.2% in 1998 to 3.97% in 2022. Lithuania's integration into global value chains has boosted exports, particularly in medium and high-tech sectors. The country has also emerged as a leading exporter of life sciences.

Lithuania's economic strategy underscores the importance of resilience, innovation, and sustainability. Key priorities include strengthening the digital economy, fostering the fintech sector, and reducing reliance on geopolitically vulnerable industries. By leveraging EU recovery funds and its strategic location, Lithuania continues to position itself as a regional economic and technological integration leader.

1.2 Socio-Political Environment of Lithuania

Lithuania's contemporary socio-political environment reflects its efforts to balance social welfare, economic growth, and regional security challenges.

President Gitanas Nausėda has prioritised the development of a welfare state. His vision emphasises reducing social inequality, enhancing regional and family-oriented support, and creating inclusive education, healthcare, and cultural development policies.

Government focuses on fiscal responsibility, digital transformation, and environmental sustainability. It also works on enhancing Lithuania's position within NATO and the EU, reflecting concerns over regional security and Lithuania's proximity to geopolitical tensions in Eastern Europe.

Lithuania's political climate features active debates about social justice, economic modernisation, and its role in European and global politics. It also aims to harmonise domestic welfare ambitions with broader strategic security and international relations goals.

1.3 *Business Environment of Lithuania*

A dynamic and supportive approach to business characterises the business environment in Lithuania. A number of factors contribute to this positive environment, including strong economic fundamentals, technological advancement, and government incentives for innovation and investment.

The following are the principal characteristics of the business environment in Lithuania:

1. Economic Stability and Growth:

Lithuania exhibits one of the EU's highest GDP per capita growth rates, indicative of robust economic progress. The inflationary pressures that had emerged in recent years have been effectively managed, with forecasts indicating that this will continue to be the case soon (Allianz Trade Corporate, Invest Lithuania). The country's stable financial outlook is also reflected in its credit ratings from major agencies (Fitch, Moody's, and S&P), reinforcing its reputation as a reliable investment destination (Invest Lithuania).

2. Ease of Doing Business:

Lithuania is ranked highly in international indices for business regulation. It offers a streamlined company registration process, with new businesses often established within 1–3 days. The tax system is both efficient and modern, and it is further complemented by the use of digital tools for tax administration (Invest Lithuania).

3. Support for Foreign Direct Investment (FDI):

The government has implemented several initiatives, including establishing Free Economic Zones and providing tailored support for investors, collectively enhancing Lithuania's attractiveness as a destination for FDI. Notable sectors include manufacturing, fintech, biotechnology, cybersecurity, and renewable energy (Green Reporter, Invest Lithuania).

4. Technological Innovation and Start-up Ecosystem:

Lithuania is a hub for technology and innovation, with a robust start-up ecosystem bolstered by initiatives such as Startup Visa Lithuania. Success stories such as Vinted and Nord Security exemplify the country's capacity to foster the growth of high-performing companies (Green Reporter). It is distinguished globally for its proficiency in digital skills and electronic security infrastructure, reinforcing its aspirations to become a leading technology hub (Invest Lithuania).

5. The labour market in Lithuania is characterised by a highly educated and multilingual workforce, which is an attractive quality for global businesses. Furthermore, the government has implemented incentives and initiatives to address labour shortages and enhance workforce adaptability (Green Reporter).
6. Sustainability and Green Growth:

Lithuania has made notable progress in energy efficiency and climate risk preparedness, which collectively demonstrate the country's commitment to sustainability. Nevertheless, there is potential for enhancement in renewable energy and recycling initiatives (Allianz Trade Corporate).

Lithuania's business environment is strategically positioned for growth and innovation, rendering it an appealing destination for entrepreneurs and multinational corporations seeking to expand in the Baltic region and beyond.

Exhibit 1 Core economic indicators for Lithuania

	2018	2019	2020	2021	2022	2023	2024
GDP per capita (current US$)	19089.7	19615.5	20381.9	23849.6	25078.7	26428.1	..
GDP per capita growth (annual %)	4.99	4.94	−0.05	6.06	1.33	−1.73	..
Long-term unemployment (% of total unemployment)	32.24	30.6	29	36.67	38.91	na	7.5
Foreign direct investment, net inflows (% of GDP)	1.63	6.27	7.91	4.45	1.05	2.84	..
GDP (current US$. bil.)	53.251	54.809	56.965	66.799	71.014	74.622	..
Exports of goods and services (current US$. bil.)	43.998	42.34	41.64	53.48	61.64	64.39	..
Exports of goods and services (% of GDP)	82.29	77.24	73.10	80.07	86.80	86.29	..
Merchandise exports to high-income economies (% of total merchandise exports)	71,59	70,26	71,04	n/a	n/a	n/a	..
Merchandise exports to developing economies in Europe & Central Asia (% of total merchandise exports)	24,69	25,61	24,26	n/a	n/a	n/a	..
Ores and metals exports (% of merchandise exports)	1.87	1,90	2,18	2,94	2,11	1,79	..
Agricultural raw materials exports (% of merchandise exports)	2.98	2,98	2,94	3,16	3,12	2,55	1.86
Food exports (% of merchandise exports)	16.32	17,32	20,19	16,55	16,62	18,56	2.45
Fuel exports (% of merchandise exports)	14.61	13,13	6,91	9,86	16,67	14,30	19
Manufactures exports (% of merchandise exports)	62.33	63,36	66,51	66,34	59,87	60,92	14.04
High-technology exports (% of manufactured exports)	12.11	12,03	12,01	11,51	13,00	14,40	60.46

Source: The World Bank, 2025, Trading Economics, Eurostat

As evidenced by the review of the development of the Lithuanian economy, Lithuania is undergoing a significant economic transformation, evolving from an agrarian nation to an innovation-driven economy. As illustrated in Exhibit 1, data from the World Bank reveal a notable expansion in high-technology exports, a relatively modest contribution from agricultural raw materials exports, and a considerable proportion of exports destined for high-income economies. In addition, policymakers have taken steps to enhance the business environment in Lithuania (Business Reforms in Lithuania), making the Lithuanian economy an attractive location for developing hidden champions.

2 Characteristics of Hidden Champions from Lithuania

A more extensive list of Lithuanian Hidden Champions was presented by Vaiginiene et al. (2021) in the book Hidden Champions in Dynamically Changing Societies: Critical Success Factors for Market Leadership. Seven hidden champions (Deeper, 8 Devices, CGTrader, Ekspla, Game Insight, Light Conversion and Telesoftas) and two potential hidden champions (Fidens and Parkis) were identified. Some Vaiginiene et al. (2021) presented Hidden Champions (such as Ekspla, Light Conversion, Telesoftas and Deeper) grow up to the level when they are not hidden any more (Žuolytė, 2019)). During the 2023/2024 hidden champions research, we revealed two new companies as hidden champions—J&C Aero and JSC "TV Zaidimai". JSC "TV Zaidimai", with its product BetGames, is a leading game provider in the live dealer online gaming industry.[1] This section presents two more Hidden Champions: VILIMED (former Fidens) and J&C Aero.

3 Case Studies of Selected Hidden Champions

3.1 *VILIMED (Former Fidens) (ViLim Ball)—Potential Hidden Champion*

Overview

Address: Kaunas Science and Technology Park, Maironio str. 6–1, Kaunas, Lithuania
Tel: n.d.
Email: n.d.
Web: https://vilimed.com/

[1] https://www.betgames.tv/

Company information
Industry: Other manufacturing n.e.c., Medical devices
Year of Establishment: 2014
Sales Revenues in 2024: 0.51 M Eur
Average number of employees in 2024: 10
Brainer(s) behind the company: Dr. Mantas Venslauskas and a team

3.1.1 Nature of Market Leadership

ViLim Ball is a therapeutic device that reduces essential tremors, Parkinson's disease, and rheumatoid arthritis symptoms. It helps to reduce hand tremors by at least 20% for most patients. Furthermore, ViLim Ball reduces morning stiffness caused by rheumatoid arthritis. According to pre-clinical trials, nine out of ten reported less stiffness after 10 min of therapy. There are no direct competitors globally. However, there are some substitutes with less functionality. The device was launched in 2017 and certified in 2021. Around 70% of purchases are made by buyers from European Union countries, followed by 15% from the Middle East, 10% from the USA, and 5% from Lithuania.[2] In 2022, it attracted risk capital and business angels' investment of 300,000 euros, which was used to accelerate sales.

3.1.2 Nature of Competitive Advantage

– Innovative product which solves painful health problems.
– Scientists with a background in medicine and information technologies developed the product.
– The product is patented.
– Acquired CE certificate.

3.1.3 Core Lessons Learned on the Path to Success

1. A product should solve an actual human problem.
2. Understand the related decisions which can improve the product.
3. The product should be a "must-have", not a "nice to have" product.
4. Have close relationships with your clients.

[2] https://www.delfi.lt/login/technologijos/naujienos/medicinos-inovaciju-kureja-vilimed-pritrauke-investicija-kuria-specialu-terapini-irengini-sumazinanti-ranku-drebejima-92148195

3.1.4 Management and Leadership Development Needs

The central management and leadership concerns relate to questions such as creating a market for a new product, introducing it to the client, and informing him about opportunities to buy it. In general, new product marketing competencies are needed.

3.1.5 Financing and Regulatory Environment Development Needs

Vilimed managed to attract risk capital investment in 2022. Currently, they do not meet any financial or regulatory problems. However, they have just achieved the break-even point, so they will be interested in getting finances for the production expansion.

3.1.6 "Vilimed"

Vilimed (former Fidens) founder Mantas Venslauskas has a PhD in technology, and his inspiration for developing hand tremor technology came during his PhD studies. Vilimed created a thoroughly new technology and concept of a device for reducing hand tremors and stiffness by communicating with a researcher from the Neurologic Clinic.[3]

Mantas says that the key to their company's success is the timely testing of a new product (even a prototype) with consumers. Whatever the "crooked" product, if it solves a significant customer problem, the customer will come and help you find a solution to the problem. It is essential to see if the customer recognises the benefits. It is vital to test a new product as early as possible rather than wait for it to be completed. In medicine, it can take many years to develop a final product, and if it turns out to be less than what the client needs, it could result in huge time and financial losses.

Another success factor is a good team. According to Mantas, a business owner (manager) has to be continuously interested in innovation, have competence in many areas, understand what other colleagues do, the needs of colleagues, and the needs of people, and is also a very relevant communication skill. It is challenging to be a leader if energy does not converge between the manager and his/her subordinates or colleagues. Because then, at best, you can only lead, i.e., to be a manager who delegates tasks. Undoubtedly, the manager must represent himself and the company appropriately; he must see the progress and the quality, and the employees must recognise that their work is not in vain and that their efforts are valued and appreciated.

[3] https://en.delfi.lt/business/lithuanian-scientists-solution-for-shaky-hands-condition-hits-the-market.d?id=76934829

Critical factors for successful innovation include meeting the client's needs, addressing the client's immediate and painful problem, collaborating with scientists and scientific consultants, and having a good team.

One of Vilimed's biggest challenges is creating a market for a new product, introducing it to the customer, and informing the customer that it is already available for search and purchase.

The COVID-19 period caused a shortage of microchips, which led to the stoppage of the production of VILIM balls. Due to these consequences, they started developing a mobile app-based solution for tremor monitoring and diagnostics, Steady Hands. Currently, Vilimed is running clinical trials that are needed for certification and commercialisation. What specific lessons does Vilimed teach us? The key to a start-up company's success is addressing the client's immediate and painful problems, timely testing of a new product (even a prototype) with the client, a good team, and a climate inside the organisation.

3.2 J&C Aero

Overview

Address: Terminalo str. 14, Kuprioniškės, Vilniaus region, Lithuania, LT-13279
Email: info@jcaero.com
Web: https://jcaero.com

Company Information

Industry: Manufacture of air and spacecraft and related machinery (NACE 30.30—Manufacture of air and spacecraft and related machinery, which includes the manufacture of aircraft, spacecraft, and their components and 33.16—repair and maintenance of aircraft and spacecraft). The company is an EASA-certified international cabin interior hub and end-to-end interior solutions provider.
Year of establishment: 2012
Sales revenue in 2023: 18.5 mil Euro
Average number of employees in 2023: 163
Brains behind the company: Laurynas Skukauskas (Co-founder and CEO) and Maxim Duskof, Head of Design

3.2.1 Nature of Market Leadership

The Jump Seat Duo,[4] developed by J&C Aero's R&D team, is a product that sets a new benchmark for in-flight accessibility, supporting both the comfort of passengers with reduced mobility (PRM) passengers and airlines' operational efficiency. Its integration into standard cabin equipment helps optimise space, streamline

[4] https://jcaero.com/we-care/jump-seat-duo/

operations, and remove barriers to accessibility. There are no global competitors for this innovative product yet.

The aviation industry has long been by intense competition and has historically been dominated by large multinational corporations. However, the sector is undergoing a period of consolidation among major market players, creating opportunities for more flexible and agile services offered by small and medium enterprises (SMEs).

Over the years, shifts in the supply chain have become increasingly evident, with key players like Airbus and Boeing facing persistent challenges, particularly in the aftermath of the COVID-19 pandemic. These disruptions have impacted manufacturing and supply chain processes, creating an opportunity for SMEs to leverage their agility and adaptability. For example, while customers may order aircraft from a major manufacturer, they might seek aircraft interiors from specialised companies like J&C Aero, which can deliver tailored solutions more efficiently.

J&C Aero has emerged as a leading player in the evolving aviation industry, ranking among the top five aircraft interior companies in the EU and establishing itself as the market leader in the CEE region. The company offers a broad range of services, including aircraft interior design and CAMO engineering, manufacturing, maintenance, special projects, and research and development. Its primary strength lies in certified engineering activities, particularly the modification and repair of aircraft engineering systems. These services are highly specialised and customised, requiring the expertise of the Head of Design, who holds the necessary certifications and competencies to develop engineering solutions and accompanying documentation. This core capability sets J&C Aero apart, solidifying its market leadership.

Operating in a highly regulated industry, J&C Aero has demonstrated a strong commitment to compliance with rigorous aviation standards. The company has achieved significant milestones in certification, including:

EASA Part 21J Design Organisation Approval (DOA) in 2014–2015
EASA Part 21G Production Organisation Approval (POA) in 2016–2017
EASA Part 145 Certification in 2021

These certifications have enabled J&C Aero to expand its service offerings and achieve sustainable growth. By 2023, the company had scaled its capacity to handle over 3500 projects annually, established a representative office in Ireland, and, in 2024, inaugurated a 3600 sqm state-of-the-art facility near Vilnius Airport. This facility consolidates all services under one roof, further enhancing operational efficiency and reinforcing the company's market position.

3.2.2 Nature of Competitive Advantage

J&C Aero began its journey by identifying an untapped market niche in aircraft interior design and repair services, emphasising flexibility and a customer-centric approach. Recognising the global nature of the aviation industry, the company adopted an international operational scope from its inception, without limitations from the size of the local market. The founders quickly realised the value of prioritising customer needs, which became a cornerstone of their business strategy.

The company's competitive edge lies in its vision: to enhance the capabilities of the aviation industry through expertise, dedication, and unwavering professionalism, contributing to its sustained growth and success. Regardless of a project's profitability, J&C Aero consistently upholds a commitment to excellence, delivering high-quality results and honouring its commitments.

A unique aspect of the company's operations is its focus on the leasing companies that own most aircraft. For these clients, the preparation of documentation, meticulously aligned with aviation safety regulations, is as critical as the technical services provided. Precision and compliance in documentation are integral to the company's service offering.

Today, J&C Aero's competitive advantage is firmly rooted in the expertise of its certified employees, a track record of successfully executed projects, and the leadership of its Head of Design. This core team member brings extensive experience, a high degree of responsibility, and certifications from aviation authorities, ensuring the company continues to excel in a highly regulated and demanding industry.

3.2.3 Core Lessons Learned on the Path of Success

1. **The power of teamwork**: Effective teamwork is essential for success in business and manufacturing. Managers emphasised that a well-prepared team can tackle challenges more efficiently through collaboration. By understanding and leveraging each team member's strengths, the team achieves its goals more effectively and provides innovative solutions. The combination of diverse cultural perspectives, technical skills and expertise, and a shared commitment to excellence enables the team to consistently produce high-quality results while fostering a culture of continuous improvement, innovation, and agility. Moreover, when a team is united, each member experiences accelerated learning, acquiring new skills and growing more effectively in their roles. By fostering a strong sense of unity, team members can achieve greater success and overcome obstacles together.
2. **Diversity and inclusion matters**: Diversity is a powerful asset in any team. J&C Aero's team is strengthened by a mix of nationalities and cultural backgrounds, bringing unique perspectives that foster innovative problem-solving. This diversity, combined with expertise, enables a deeper understanding of the global aviation industry. A culture of knowledge-sharing, constructive communication, and mutual respect helps drive success and continuous improvement.

This inclusive and collaborative approach drives innovation and plays a crucial role in maintaining the company's competitive edge, particularly in the aviation industry.

3.2.4 Regulatory Environment Development Needs

Workforce Shortage

In recent years, the company has experienced rapid growth; however, it now faces challenges due to a shortage of skilled workforce rather than a lack of client orders. This issue is prevalent across the entire engineering sector at a national level, compounded by Lithuania's geographical location, which does not provide any particular advantage in attracting skilled professionals.

To address this, the company has tried to recruit talent globally, including attempts to employ specialists from Sri Lanka and other regions. Despite these efforts, Lithuania's limited pool of engineers remains a challenge. While the company has developed some of its skilled employees through internal training programmes and partnerships with technical universities, this approach alone is insufficient to meet the growing demand.

Further complicating the situation is Lithuania's national migration legislation, which does not adequately support the recruitment of foreign professionals in the aviation sector. Current exemptions are better suited to industries like IT or logistics, leaving aviation companies disadvantaged.

The company has taken a strategic step to overcome these hurdles by establishing a business unit in Ireland. Ireland's long-standing traditions in aviation, along with a larger pool of skilled professionals and more favourable conditions for international employment, including the ability to relocate employees with their families, make it a more viable location for workforce expansion. This move ensures the company can maintain its growth trajectory while accessing the necessary talent to support its operations.

3.2.5 J&C Aero Hidden Champion

The company's CEO has always wanted to establish his own business, driven by a desire to push boundaries and challenge his ambitions. A natural salesperson, he quickly recognised that sales expertise alone would not suffice; industry-specific engineering competencies were essential for the successful development of a start-up in the aviation sector. Understanding the power of complementary skills, he joined forces with an experienced engineering professional, forming a partnership that combined the core competencies critical for success in this specialised industry.

The company's primary competitive advantage lies in its ability to transcend boundaries and deliver professional services, flexibility, and a customer-centric approach. Each client is treated with responsibility, care, and attention, ensuring a unique and tailored experience that sets the company apart in the market.

Innovation has been a cornerstone of the company's growth. Recognising its transformative potential, they established an R&D department to develop cutting-edge products that address industry needs and align with social sustainability trends. Among their recent breakthroughs is the Jump Seat Duo—a convertible jump seat and wheelchair designed for Passengers with Reduced Mobility (PRM). This innovative solution addresses accessibility challenges in aviation, combining advanced design with practical functionality. The Jump Seat Duo integrates seamlessly into standard cabin equipment, optimising space, enhancing operational efficiency, and removing barriers to in-flight accessibility. Offering a dual-purpose solution sets a new benchmark for PRM comfort and inclusivity while also supporting the operational needs of airlines. This pioneering product has already been showcased at leading industry exhibitions in collaboration with their partner, Airbus.

Social sustainability is a core value for the company, which strives to build an inclusive community and develop solutions that address the needs of individuals with limited mobility. Their commitment extends to creating opportunities for professionals with disabilities, ensuring that mobility challenges do not hinder career prospects. This dedication is reflected in their innovative solutions, developed through close collaboration between industry experts and academic professionals. By merging innovation, inclusivity, and functionality, the company demonstrates its unwavering commitment to enhancing accessibility and fostering a more equitable aviation industry.

3.2.6 What Specific Lessons Does J&C Aero Teach us?

J&C Aero's management emphasises that the skills and competencies of their employees are the company's greatest competitive advantage. Given the highly specialised nature of the business, they prioritise the development of talent from within the organisation. The managers believe that the company's most valuable asset is its loyal and skilled workforce, not its physical infrastructure—such as buildings, machinery, or office spaces.

To retain and nurture this key asset, the company focuses on creating a positive work environment that aligns with shared values and fosters a sense of belonging. They prioritise continuous professional development for their employees, ensuring that skill enhancement is matched with appropriate monetary rewards. The workplace reflects this commitment to employee well-being, featuring modern, thoughtfully designed spaces filled with flowers and art to enhance the overall work atmosphere.

J&C Aero's leaders also emphasize the importance of morality in business. CEO Laurynas Skukauskas places integrity, empathy, and social responsibility at the heart of the company's values. As he puts it, "Morality is fundamental; it should be the foundation for building businesses—not just profit."

The company honestly seeks to support underprivileged individuals, especially those with mobility challenges who haven't yet been able to enjoy the freedom of travel. J&C Aero is working to create innovative solutions that ensure equal access to air travel for everyone, including people with disabilities, fostering a more inclusive aviation industry.

In addition to these efforts, the company actively supports disadvantaged communities in Lithuania. By combining innovation with social responsibility, J&C

Aero aims to make a positive and lasting impact within aviation and the broader community.

However, recently, J&C aero has met two disruptive crises. COVID-19 has been extremely difficult for the aviation industry, and during the COVID lockdown, the turnover of J&C Aero dropped by 97%. Thus, it required a quick reaction and bold decisions. However, thanks to innovative solutions and customer segment diversification, the company immediately reviewed their activities and focused on cargo transportation instead of passenger aviation. They were able to offer an innovative and newly developed and certified product—cargo containers for wide-body passenger cabins, which allow to change the seats with containers and vice versa—another innovative and globally unique product to meet the high demand for vaccine transportation. Thus, the innovations and diversification of activities allowed them not only to survive that challenging period but also to become even stronger and more competitive in the market, meeting the demands of new customers and entering new markets worldwide such as India, Chile, Africa, and others.

The war in Ukraine caused a shortage and price increase of precious metals and raw materials. Still, the impact on J&C Aero business has been minimal due to relatively low quantities compared with big players in the industry. Although they have seen price rises and longer supply timelines, these issues have not posed significant challenges. They have increased warehouse capacity and made strategic investments to address the situation. The company's organic growth has enabled it to expand smoothly without the need for external investments.

The company had a chance to participate in the notably ambitious project of modifying and refurbishing the cabin of Ukraine's presidential Airbus A319 Corporate Jet (Orban, 2023). Given the aircraft's designation as the Presidential Airbus A319, this distinctive project necessitated careful attention to detail, adaptable problem-solving, and a dedication to confidentiality. The modifications involved incorporating a new In-Flight Entertainment system and enhancements to the Cabin Management System, which received EASA certification. J&C Aero also played a critical role in installing a KA-BAND Satcom navigation system. Furthermore, J&C Aero thoroughly refurbished the aircraft's interior, including fabric coverings, executive seating, veneers, carpets, laminates, and additional cabin components. These elements were manufactured in-house by J&C Aero, with installation and maintenance managed by Magnetic MRO at Tallinn Airport. CEO Laurynas Skukauskas highlighted the deep engagement and commitment of the J&C Aero team in ensuring the success of this important project.

4 Conclusions

Lithuania is experiencing a significant economic transformation, shifting from an agrarian base to an innovation-driven economy. This shift is marked by significant growth in high-technology exports, a relatively small share of exports from agricultural raw materials, and a substantial focus on exporting to high-income economies.

Furthermore, policymakers have implemented reforms to improve the business environment, making the Lithuanian economy an attractive location for developing hidden champions.

A favourable regulatory environment, incentives for FDI, and a thriving start-up ecosystem have positioned Lithuania as a competitive player in the EU. Notable successes include innovative companies like Vilimed and J&C Aero, demonstrating Lithuania's potential to cultivate "Hidden Champions" in niche markets. Both companies leverage their competitive advantages to address global needs, from health solutions to aviation inclusivity, while emphasising customer-centric approaches, interdisciplinary teamwork, and social responsibility.

Lithuania should consider addressing labour shortages through targeted education and training programmes, especially in high-demand sectors such as engineering and technology. It is also important to simplify immigration policies to attract skilled international professionals, particularly for niche industries like aviation and biotech.

References

Allianz. Consumer spending drives gradual recovery in 2024-2025. Allianz | Country Risk Report Lithuania.

Green Reporter. Business in Lithuania: explore investment opportunities. Accessed on 6 December 2024 Green Reporter green-reporter.com.

Invest Lithuania. Lithuania's business environment is primed for FDI. Accessed on 6 December 2024 Invest Lithuania — Lithuania's business environment is primed for FDI | Invest Lithuania investlithuania.com.

Jump Seat Duo: a Convertible Jump Seat/Wheelchair for Passengers with Reduced Mobility (PRM) https://jcaero.com/we-care/jump-seat-duo/.

Lithuanian Department of Statistics. Retrieved 5 October 2019, from https://osp.stat.gov.lt/statistiniu-rodikliu-analize#/.

Lithuania Country Study Guide Volume 1. (2015). World Country Study Guide Library) by Ibp, Inc. https://www.amazon.com/Lithuania-Strategic-Information-Developments-2015-01-31/dp/B01A64SCE0

"Lithuania – Official Gateway to Lithuania – History". Lietuva.lt.

Lithuanian scientists' solution for shaky hands condition hits the market. (2018). https://www.delfi.lt/en/business/lithuanian-scientists-solution-for-shaky-hands-condition-hits-the-market-76934829

Medicinos inovacijų kūrėja "Vilimed" pritraukė investiciją—kuria specialų terapinį įrenginį, sumažinantį rankų drebėjimą. (2022). https://www.delfi.lt/login/technologijos/naujienos/medicinos-inovaciju-kureja-vilimed-pritrauke-investicija-kuria-specialu-terapini-irengini-sumazinanti-ranku-drebejima-92148195

NASDAQ. Completes OMX Transaction to Become The NASDAQ OMX Group, Inc. https://www.nasdaq.com/about/press-center/nasdaq-completes-omx-transaction-become-nasdaq-omx-group-inc.

Norman Davies. (1997). *Europe: A history*. Pimlico.

OECD Economic Surveys, Lithuania 2022, June 2022. https://www.oecd-ilibrary.org/economics/oecd-economic-surveys-lithuania-2022_0829329f-en

OECD. (2023). Basic statistics of Lithuania, 2021. In *OECD economic surveys: Lithuania 2022*. OECD Publishing. https://doi.org/10.1787/177cfafd-en

Orban, A. (2023). J&C Aero completes cabin modification and refurbishment of Ukraine's presidential Airbus A319. Retrieved from: https://www.aviation24.be/military-aircraft/ukrainian-air-force/jc-aero-completes-cabin-modification-and-refurbishment-of-ukraines-presidential-airbus-a319/#:~:text=The%20project%20involved%20modifying%20and%20renewing%20the%20cabin,Management%20System%20%28CMS%29%2C%20which%20received%20certification%20from%20EASA
US Department of State. 2024 Investment Climate Statements: Lithuania. Accessed on 6 December 2024 Lithuania - United States Department of State.
Vaiginienė, E., Paulienė, R., & Urbšienė, L. (2021). Hidden champions of Lithuania. In A. Braček Lalić & D. Purg (Eds.), *Hidden champions in dynamically changing societies*. Springer. https://doi.org/10.1007/978-3-030-65451-1_17
Vilkas, E. (1997). *Experience and challenges of privatisation in Lithuania*. Warsaw School of Economics.
The World Bank DataBank. Retrieved 28 July 2024, from https://databank.worldbank.org/home.
Ziemele, I. (Ed.). (2003). *Baltic yearbook of international law* (Vol. 3). Brill | Nijhoff. Retrieved from https://brill.com/view/title/11025
Žuolytė, J. (2019, March 5). Trys lietuviškos kompanijos pateko į "Financial Times" reitingą. Delfi. https://www.delfi.lt/m360/naujausi-straipsniai/trys-lietuviskos-kompanijos-pateko-i-financial-times-reitinga.d?id=80531937

Erika Vaiginiene is an associate professor at Vilnius University Faculty of Economics and Business Administration. She is an experienced researcher and consultant with a proven track record of working in the higher education sector. Her research and consulting areas encompass topics such as higher education management, entrepreneurship and innovation management, change management, and foresight development. She is the Head of the Millennium Project Node in Lithuania and a member of CEEMAN, AOM, EMRBI and FEN. Erika holds a PhD in Social Science with a focus on Business Administration and Management. She is a certified change manager. She possesses strong skills in quantitative and qualitative research methodologies, as well as the development of valid survey questionnaires and foresight methodologies.

Laimute Urbšienė is an associate professor at Vilnius University Faculty of Economics and Business Administration. She is an experienced researcher and the director of the study programme. She has experience in both academia and as a finance practitioner. Before she began her academic career, she served as Vice Minister of Finance in Lithuania.

Jurgita Butkevičienė is an associate professor at Vilnius University, Faculty of Economics and Business Administration. Highly skilled professional with experience in academic research on institutional change, social sustainability, diversity and inclusion, entrepreneurship, and digital transformation. Excellent understanding of various industries, businesses, stakeholder management, and entrepreneurial ecosystems. Sound interdisciplinary knowledge and an advanced university degree in social sciences and industry engineering.

Hidden Champions of Moldova

Dumitru Slonovschi

Abstract This chapter describes the economic, socio-political, and business environments in which Moldova's potential hidden champions operate. It explores how these companies, originating from a small Eastern European country, manage to expand regionally and globally, building a worldwide customer base.

Through interviews with key company figures and analysis of secondary sources, the chapter identifies the developmental needs and success factors of these potential hidden champions. The discussions highlight the continuous efforts in automation, production enhancement, and employee investment, which drive their recognition and strong market positions both locally and globally.

The chapter also examines the impact of recent events such as the COVID-19 pandemic and the war in Ukraine on these companies, noting some disruptions in the logistical chain, increased costs for raw materials, and anxiety among employees. In response, companies are strategizing to diversify their export markets and enhance customer cooperation. The analysis underscores the dual influence of external and internal factors on company operations, including economic instability and energy crises, and discusses the risk mitigation strategies implemented by the companies.

The chapter concludes with recommendations for stakeholders to support the ongoing prosperity of Moldova's potential hidden champions in the future.

Overview
Official name: Republic of Moldova
Type of government: Parliamentary republic
Population on 1st January 2023: 2.51 million
Land area (in sq. km): 33,850 km^2

D. Slonovschi (✉)
Magenta Consulting, Chisinau, Moldova
e-mail: d.slonovschi@consulting.md

D. Berberović, D. Purg (eds.), *Hidden Champions in Rising Economies*, Contributions to Management Science,
https://doi.org/10.1007/978-3-032-08263-3_26

History

1991 Moldova became an independent and sovereign state.
1992 Transnistrian Conflict (a war between Moldovan and Transnistrian separatist forces).
1992 Moldova joined the United Nations and the Organisation for Security and Co-operation in Europe.
1994 The Constitution was adopted, which granted substantial autonomy to Transnistria and Gagauzia.
1995 Moldova became a full member of the Council of Europe.
1998 The Partnership and Cooperation Agreement with the European Union (EU) came into force in July.
2001 Communist Party won the elections and Moldova became the first former Soviet republic to return unreformed communists to power.
2005 The European Union Border Assistance Mission to Moldova was launched.
2009 The Alliance for European Integration (AEI) formed by four pro-West parties came to power.
2009 Moldova joined other five countries in the Eastern Partnership initiative.
2014 The EU–Moldova Association Agreement was signed in June.
2014 The Schengen area visa waiver for short stays was applied to citizens of the Republic of Moldova holding a biometric passport.
2015 Banking scandal, in which one billion US$ (12% of Moldova's annual GDP) vanished from the central bank.
2017 The mixed electoral system was voted by the Parliament, replacing the proportional one.
2019 The Parliament canceled the mixed electoral system.
2020 The oligarchic and corrupt regime fell and the process of eradicating corruption at the highest level began.
2020 For the first time in the history of the republic, the president is elected a woman, with pro-Western views.
2021 Early parliamentary elections. The pro-European party obtained 63 of the 101 mandates in the new Parliament.
2022 The post-COVID crisis, the war in Ukraine, the refugee crisis, the energy resource crisis generated the contraction of the economy and the declaration of the state of emergency.
2022 Moldova is granted EU candidate status.
2023 EU opens accession negotiations with Moldova.

1 Introduction: Context and History

Moldova is a small country with an area of 33,850 km^2 situated between Romania and Ukraine, with a population of 2.5 million.

In 1991 Moldova gained independence as a result of the Soviet Union's collapse and embarked on ambitious structural reforms aimed to implement a market-driven economy.

In 2020, for the first time in the history of the Republic, the president is elected a woman with pro-Western views. According to different statistics, between 500,000 and one million Moldovans live and work in other countries, and approximately 93% of them expressed their support for Maia Sandu. Maia Sandu assumed office amid deep distrust in state institutions and significant challenges in both domestic and foreign policy. In her victory speech, Sandu pledged to rebuild a united society and heal political divisions (Negura, 2021).

In 2019, the Parliament canceled the mixed electoral system, which was adopted in July 2017 and drew criticism from Western partners (Necsutu, 2019). In 2020, the oligarchic and corrupt regime fell and the process of eradicating corruption at the highest level began. (Cenusa, 2019) In Moldova, two of the parties have joined forces in order to help the country recover after an oligarchic-focused political system. This seemed to receive positive feedback from residents of the country, as well as other partners and the EU.

Early parliamentary elections were held in 2021 where the pro-European party obtained 63 of 101 mandates in the new Parliament. For the first time since April 2009, a party (PAS) obtained the parliamentary majority. In fact, PAS obtained the highest electoral score ever recorded by a party in the Republic of Moldova, in relation to the number of voters present at the polls—52.80% of validly cast votes (Central Electoral Commission, 2021).

In terms of the coronavirus pandemic's impact on Moldova, almost 70,000 jobs were lost, predominantly in trade, HORECA, industry, and transport, based on forecasts growth and different surveys made during 2020. Chisinau was the most affected area, with almost 30% of total job losses, followed by the Northern and Central regions. Young workers (25–34 years) would bear the brunt of the crisis and, together with workers aged 35–44, represented more than half of the total job losses. (World Bank, 2022).

The year of 2022 was marked by the post-pandemic crisis, the war in Ukraine, the refugee crisis, and the energy resource crisis; events that generated the contraction of the economy and the declaration of the state of emergency.

The Ukrainian war and the refugee crisis had an enormous impact on Moldova, as the country was not ready for the influx of Ukrainian residents:

- Almost 750 thousand refugees who crossed the border into the Republic of Moldova, of which over 100 thousand remained in the country;
- 59 million euros, the amount of humanitarian support provided by Team Europe for managing the flow of refugees;

- 150 million euros granted by the EU to alleviate the energy crisis generated by the war which helped approximately 600 thousand citizens to benefit from compensation for energy consumption;
- 150 million euros of financial assistance provided in the form of loans and grants;
- 112 million euros for economic resilience and business support;
- Over 400 million euros for strategic areas such as border management, investments in energy efficiency projects, modernization of the defense sector, cyber security, etc. (Delegation of the European Union to the Republic of Moldova, 2023).

The year 2022 was one of the most difficult for the country's economy, being marked by an economic decline of 5.9% and a record inflation of 34.6% reached in October 2022.

The National Institute for Economic Research stated that the economy of the Republic of Moldova decreased sharply in 2022, as a result of the secondary effects of the war, the energy crisis, and the drought. Thus, the GDP contracted by 5.9% in real terms compared to the previous year and amounted to 272.5 billion lei. Agricultural production decreased by 29.8% compared to 2021. The volume of money transfers from abroad through banks in favor of individuals amounted to 1.75 billion US$, being 8.6% higher than in 2021. At the same time, the total value of international trade in goods registered increases by 31.3% compared to 2021 and amounted to 13.5 billion US$, with increases recorded in both exports and imports (Stratan et al., 2023).

It was also pointed out that in 2022, the disposable income of the population registered an increase in nominal terms of 21.2%, reaching 4252 MDL (over 200 euros) per person, per month. The most important source of income remains salaries, with a share of 50%, followed by social benefits and remittances from abroad. At the same time, the population's expenses also increased by 22.1%, reaching an average of 3711 lei per person, per month.

The information and communication technology sector is an economic sector in which the Republic of Moldova is making significant progress. 2314 companies with over 29 thousand employees operate in the sector, and the share of the ICT sector in the country's Gross Domestic Product (GDP) is about 7%. The IT industry has significant intake, which is on a positive development trend and ensured an increase in income from 2.4 billion MDL in 2016 to 6.6 billion MDL in 2019, while the volume of exports of IT services increased during 2015–2018, from 64 million USD to 258 million USD in the year 2020.

In order to support the digital innovations and technological startups, there is a need of funds. As the limited access to financing of companies in the IT industry was identified as one of the main problems in the socio-economic development of the Republic of Moldova, the Ministry of Economy and Infrastructure created an action for grant fund for IT startups. The action emerged from the Information Technology Industry Development Strategy and an ecosystem for digital innovation for the years 2018–2023 (Ministry of Economy and Infrastructure, 2021). For the implementation of the measure, approximately 60 million US$ were allocated, of whichhalf came from resources development partners and another half from the state budget. The implementers of the action were Moldova IT park, ODIMM, and the development partners.

2 Characteristics of Hidden Champions from Moldova

The companies that were nominated as potential hidden champions have a low visibility on the local market, have registered high growth in recent years, and have expanded to other markets. All companies identified as potential hidden champions are present on the global market, this feature considered important for the companies' development and growth.

The companies that were identified as hidden champions mentioned their nature of market leadership and what they considered to be their competitive advantages. Companies that participated in the research report mention that the diversification of the activity and the future implementation of innovative products and services are the aspects that will ensure success.

Another tendency that is attested is the fact that companies seem to understand social and environmental responsibility and try to implement products or services that also benefit the environment.

Respondents highlighted several key lessons on the path to business success, emphasizing the importance of time management, adaptability to market demands, and staying attuned to customer feedback. They stressed the need for continuous product development, automation, and investment in both staff and infrastructure. Monitoring competitors, especially larger industry players, helps anticipate trends, while building a strong image and relationships is crucial in large markets. Companies should aim for independence from external suppliers and financial institutions, especially in agriculture, where feed preservation is vital. Continuous employee training, performance improvement, and ongoing research and modernization were also seen as essential for long-term growth and competitiveness.

Companies in Moldova currently face a range of challenges, including navigating complex international contexts and legal systems, which often require costly legal advice. There is a notable lack of government support for business development and international promotion, with high costs for participating in foreign exhibitions. Access to capital remains limited due to perceptions of high risk and unattractiveness, and many financial instruments are unavailable. Additional obstacles include a shortage of qualified workers, unstable market conditions, VAT complications (particularly for agricultural inputs), the ongoing energy crisis, and bureaucratic delays in obtaining quality and compliance certifications from the National Food Safety Authority.

Exhibit 1 Core economic indicators for Moldova

	2013	2014	2015	2016	2017	2018	2019	2020	2021	2022	2023	2024
GDP per capita (current US$)	2668.68	2674.12	2179.23	2272.23	2724.49	3189.36	4405.33	4375.78	5274.61	5738.42	6729.41	..
GDP per capita growth (annual %)	9.07	5.06	−0.27	4.47	4.77	4.10	5.22	−7.26	15.66	−2.49	3.69	..
Long-term unemployment (% of total unemployment)	–	–	–	–	–	–	1.47	1.19	0.79	0.9	1.56	1.43
Foreign direct investment, net inflows (% of GDP)	2.55	3.59	2.79	1.17	1.66	2.05	4.44	1.35	2.82	4.04	2.16	..
GDP (current US$, mio)	9496.70	9510.20	7745.20	8071.50	9669.80	11309.10	11736.80	11530.75	13691.87	14510.49	16539.44	..
Exports of goods and services (current US$, mio)	3047.73	2964.40	2460.38	2607.82	3007.18	3440.58	3660.83	3218.73	4196.39	5984.20	5877.85	..
Exports and goods of services (% of GDP)	32.09	31.17	31.90	32.31	31.10	30.42	31.19	27.91	30.65	41.24	35.54	..
Merchandise exports (current US$, mio)	2428.00	2340.00	1967.00	2045.00	2425.00	2707.00	2779.00	2467.00	3144.00	4332.00	4049.00	..
Merchandise exports to high-income economies (% of total merchandise exports)	34.14	38.74	40.94	39.95	41.76	n/a	81.41	82.39	79.27	68.83	73.92	..
Merchandise exports to developing economies in Europe & Central Asia (% of total merchandise exports)	63.88	57.97	53.21	53.13	52.70	n/a	14.5	14.98	17.82	27.95	23.32	..
Ores and metals exports (% of merchandise exports)	4.11	2.32	1.74	1.30	1.45	1.37	1.16	1.75	3.81	2.5	1.91	2.31
Agricultural raw materials exports (% of merchandise exports)	0.68	0.81	0.95	0.84	0.64	0.64	0.49	0.42	0.48	0.38	0.39	0.39
Food exports (% of merchandise exports)	57.60	64.10	62.69	64.94	63.86	57.93	56.1	52.98	55.59	60.55	57.37	56.11
Fuel exports (% of merchandise exports)	0.19	0.25	0.13	0.06	0.06	0.05	0.02	0.07	0.08	0.84	1.64	2.38
Manufactures exports (% of merchandise exports)	37.40	32.51	34.48	32.91	33.96	40.41	42.17	44.74	40	35.6	38.45	38.71
High-technology exports (% of manufactured exports)	2.36	4.81	3.99	3.10	5.14	2.52	2.96	2.24	2.24	2.14	2.62	..

3 Case Studies of Selected Hidden Champions

3.1 Noction

Overview
Address: Lev Tolstoi 63, Chisinau, Moldova
Tel: +373,600 65,333
Email: sales@noction.com
Web: https://www.noction.com/

Company Information
Industry: Information and communication
Year of Establishment: 2011
Sales Revenues in 2017: Confidential
Sales Revenues in 2022: Confidential
Average number of employees in 2022: 75
Brainer(s) behind the company: CEO John Strong, director Victor Bordian

3.1.1 Nature of Market Leadership

Noction provides cutting edge network intelligence technologies, enabling organizations of all sizes to take full advantage of maximum network performance for their business-critical applications such as e-commerce, VoIP, and media streaming across IP networks.

Noction has developed an intelligent Internet routing platform to significantly improve network performance, thus meeting the most complex needs of its customers. The core product has kept its market position as one of the most cost-effective solutions in the global market for the last 4 years.

Noction currently offers a competitive price in the market, as the development cost is much cheaper than that of their competitors, that are located in the USA and have enormous expenses, compared to Noction.

The company representative indicated that it is difficult to say whether Noction's product is still the leader from 2018 to the present, because the software market is constantly developing new and complex products to meet the needs and expectations of the market. According to the company's internal estimates, Noction and its competitors combined currently cover less than 15% of the market's potential which according to them, is expected to grow by 15–20% annually.

Also, there are specific aspects of Noction's product and their competitors' products that are different—some of the competitors' products rely on gathering information from their large network, while Noction's product has a more advanced algorithm for monitoring and troubleshooting a Border Gateway Protocol network. Moreover, Noction is continuously working on the development of a much better performing algorithm and software than other similar products on the world market. The representative mentioned their customers test multiple products and say Noction is the leader for that product.

3.1.2 Nature of the Competitive Advantage

The representative indicated that it is difficult to talk about leadership positions when discussing a niche product but said that Noction's product is one of the most advanced in the BGP network performance optimization market. Noction believes they became the market leader as soon as the product was offered because it was better than anything else on the market at the time.

Noction's field of activity is a niche that is difficult for competitors to break into. The cost and time needed for obtaining patented technology is another barrier for penetrating the field.

One of the competitive advantages, according to a spokesperson, is that the company only hires highly skilled professionals to produce products that meet market demands.

The company also launched Noction Flow Analyzer (NFA)—a new network traffic analysis product designed to excel in a competitive market. NFA stands out with its top-notch performance and cutting-edge real-time analysis capability. Unlike other products that may offer delayed or limited insights, NFA uses advanced algorithms and databases to instantly analyze network flows, identifying patterns and anomalies on the fly.

Another key feature of NFA is its intuitive user interface (UI) and user experience (UX), which require minimal learning time. Customizable reports and visualizations provide actionable intelligence in a user-friendly format, making it easy to make proactive decisions and manage resources efficiently.

NFA is compatible with all major network devices and protocols, ensuring easy deployment in diverse network environments. Its scalability means it can accommodate networks of all sizes, from small companies to large-scale service providers. With an optimal capabilities-to-price ratio, NFA offers exceptional value, making advanced network analysis accessible to most businesses.

3.1.3 Core Lessons Learned on the Path to Success

- The most important lesson is that you have no time to waste.
- It is important to work hard on new developments. The company has a development plan for 5 years ahead. This constant pressure is updated in real time based on market demand.
- Keeping an eye on the market and requesting feedback from customers is key. The company requests feedback from the customers about the functionality of the product; knowledge that they later use for product design. Accordingly, the company enters the market with a product based on needs and not according to the company's own interpretation and analysis. The company is always at the customer's disposal for their complaints.
- An interesting lesson was to realize the impact of the company's product on the world. The company was forced to rethink its security protocols as a result of a

client's use of their software, which, following manipulations on internet networks, crashed Cloudflare (the platform where half of the world's websites are kept and on that day half of the world's websites went down).

3.1.4 Management and Leadership Development Needs

The company faces challenges with the IT talent pool due to intense competition from other companies and investors opening branches in Moldova, which has led to a fierce battle for candidates, sometimes resulting in excessive efforts to attract talent.

3.1.5 Financing and Regulatory Environment Development Needs

The representative indicated that one of the primary challenges is navigating the international landscape and associated legal factors. Given the company's extensive market presence across multiple jurisdictions, customers often incorporate jurisdiction-specific clauses into their contracts.

Additionally, the company is required to conduct thorough legal research to ensure compliance with diverse regulatory requirements. This necessitates incurring additional costs for legal consultation and advisory services.

3.1.6 Noction: Behind the Bytes

Founded in 2011, Noction emerged as a notable player in its industry, carving its niche in the network intelligence technologies. The company's flagship product—an intelligent Internet routing platform — has become integral for businesses, enabling them to maximize the potential of their critical applications across various sectors including e-commerce, VoIP, and media streaming. In a competitive market, Noction has learned to make proactive adjustments informed by real customer feedback rather than speculative assumptions.

Amidst the ever-evolving regulatory landscape and international complexities, Noction navigated with poise, leveraging legal expertise to ensure compliance across jurisdictions.

Noction managed to overcome also the challenges posed by the COVID-19 pandemic through swift adaptation to the changes imposed by the global context. Not only did the company not suffer business-wise throughout the pandemic, but also its online presence increased, and interest in their services amplified.

Another significant crisis, the war in Ukraine, has impacted the company's day-to-day business operations. In 2022, the company faced considerable challenges related to ensuring energy supply to its offices and securing the safety of its employees. Due to international sanctions, the company had to curtail its transactions with Russia, resulting in missed opportunities in that market.

As Noction's footprint expanded, so did their aspirations—beyond their core offerings, they ventured into new frontiers, unveiling a network analysis product poised to redefine optimization standards. Fueled by a team of skilled professionals, Noction's journey is not just about innovation, but also about empowerment—capacitating businesses to transcend limitations, allowing industries to redefine benchmarks, and ultimately, empowering the digital ecosystem to thrive.

3.2 Santino-Service

Overview
Address: Feredeului 12, Chisinau, Moldova
Tel: +373 22 548 986; +373 78330027
Email: info@santino.md; santino.quality.chief@gmail.com;
Web: https://santinoshop.md/

Company Information
Industry: Plastic products manufacturing and trade
Year of Establishment: 2003
Sales Revenues in 2017: Undisclosed
Sales Revenues in 2022: Undisclosed
Average number of employees in 2022: Undisclosed
Brainer(s) behind the company: Founders Vladimir Imbirovski, Serghei Odobescu

3.2.1 Nature of Market Leadership

Santino is the Moldovan market leader in the production and sale of household plastic (polypropylene) products. According to the company's calculations and sales statistics, approximately 80% of the entire Moldovan market belongs to Santino. The company is also expanding its international presence, the biggest market being Romania, where they cover 20% of the market. Santino also exports their products to Ukraine, which has a high demand, as well as to the European market and the USA.

3.2.2 Nature of the Competitive Advantage

Santino's competitive advantage comes from two main factors: the company operates in a niche market with a clear unmet need and the company always brings innovation to the market. Santino's core team noticed that there was an unrealized gap in the product offering in the market: there was no middle segment between low-cost and premium products. Using industrial design expertise, innovative and forward-thinking solutions, as well as strong intellectual property protection, Santino has created a successful middle segment.

In addition to continuously improving its product, Santino streamlines and improves production quality, thereby increasing production volume and establishing a reputable brand name.

The company constantly focuses on identifying the causes of problems, as well as those causes that affect their occurrence. The company strives to improve the quality and efficiency of its production, conducts new research and experiments with new components and raw materials.

Santino has become a monopolist on the market in Moldova. The strengths of the company are many years of experience, innovative solutions, patents for their products and intellectual innovations, and a thorough analysis of their actions and market research. In the present, the company is focused on automating the manufacturing process.

3.2.3 Core Lessons Learned on the Path to Success

- The main lesson is that a company should not skimp on its staff, but rather invest in them and compensate accordingly. Leadership training for staff is very important.
- Automation of the production process is necessary in order to become more competitive and diversify the product.
- Tracking the competition is another key lesson. The biggest players in the field, although less flexible and more conservative, can predict market trends at early stages.

3.2.4 Management and Leadership Development Needs

Santino has realized the significance of talent retention and the cost associated with losing key employees. Therefore, the company needs to further develop skills in talent management, including strategies for employee retention, succession planning, and creating a positive work environment that fosters employee growth and development.

3.2.5 Financing and Regulatory Environment Development Needs

There is a significant lack of support from the Government in promoting and strengthening promising businesses. Moldovan companies are not as exposed as they should be due to the lack of resources to promote themselves internationally, and the Government fails to help with the exposure. Another need relates to access to capital and financial resources, which is a significant unmet need in Moldova due to the overall perceived unattractiveness and riskiness of the country. Some financial instruments are simply unavailable in Moldova, limiting the growth potential of promising domestic enterprises. To solve the problem, Santino opened subsidiaries in other countries and had access to their capital resources. Although market conditions have not been particularly favorable over the past 3 years, Santino has managed to pull through and plans to get back on track with their goals by 2024.

3.2.6 Santino: Crafting Convenience

Founded in 2003, Santino has emerged as the undisputed national market leader, having an 80% share of the Moldovan household plastic market, shaping the narrative of success in its industry.

Santino's journey is defined by a deep understanding of unmet market needs and a commitment to innovation. Recognizing a void between low-cost and premium products, the company seized the opportunity to introduce a middle segment, blending industrial design expertise with forward-thinking solutions. This strategic positioning, coupled with robust intellectual property protection, helped Santino to establish a strong presence not just within Moldova but in Romania.

Amidst the lessons learned on the path to success, Santino emphasizes the value of investing in its workforce, recognizing that trained employees are the cornerstone of sustainable growth. Automation is another key element that drives competitiveness and diversification.

However, amidst triumphs lie challenges. Despite its rise, Santino grapples with a lack of government support, hindering its potential for international exposure and growth. Access to capital remains a pressing concern, exacerbated by Moldova's perceived riskiness in the global financial landscape.

The company faced significant logistical challenges during the COVID-19 pandemic, particularly regarding supply chain disruptions. However, the company swiftly identified opportunities in the market and adapted their production to meet the increased demand for medical products. This proactive approach not only allowed Santino to maintain a competitive edge but also capitalized on emerging trends in the industry. Another key component of the company's plan was their personnel management strategies and implementation of new standards and protocols to ensure the well-being of their workforce during the uncertain times of the pandemic. Santino's focus on nurturing a supportive team culture further contributed to the resilience of the organization.

Furthermore, the war in Ukraine disrupted supply chains and heightened market volatility, leading to challenges in forecasting and pricing. Santino had to navigate through these uncertainties by implementing flexible strategies and closely monitoring market trends.

4 Conclusions and Recommendations

Potential Hidden Champions of Moldova are fast-growing companies that provide services and products to global brands worldwide. Based on the interviews with the potential Hidden Champions, it appears that the majority don't have local competitors that are as developed as them. This advantage allows them to maintain a strong position on the market, being recognized both locally and globally. This recognition is motivated by continuous development and innovation.

Faced with challenges, the companies are striving to make processes automatic, to increase production lines, and to continue to invest in their employees.

Because of the latest events like COVID pandemic and war in Ukraine, potential Hidden Champions have suffered changes, such as decrease in export level or in production of goods and services. This is the reason why companies are planning to increase exports to other countries and to improve the cooperation with customers.

Analyzing the challenges that companies encounter, it is apparent there are both external and internal factors that influence companies' activity. Economic instability and energy crisis directly influence the cost of production, and therefore the prices on the market. For mitigating these, the companies have implemented different strategies for risk situations and uncertainties that will help them to continue their activity. Most companies would appreciate help from the government in supporting local companies by promoting them abroad in different exhibitions and projects, as lack of visibility is a barrier encountered by many of the companies. Meantime, legislation and political instability are some other challenges the companies face, and which directly influence business development. In the companies' opinion, the government should implement strategies that encourage investing in local businesses.

Another challenge that potential Hidden Champions face is lack of workforce. In respondents' opinion, existing educational programs are not sufficient for creating a professional. It is important to hire people that are experts in a specific domain, which is hard to come by nowadays. A method of improving the professional qualities of a potential employee is implementing, in all educational institutions, specific programs and activities where students can participate and can be motivated to choose a profession that seems right for their future. By implementing extracurricular activities sponsored by local companies, students could be encouraged to learn about new possibilities when provided accurate information. Thus, future workforce would have the chance to meet entrepreneurs and learn about businesses in Moldova.

While it is important to focus on potential workforce, it is equally important for companies to maintain their current workforce and to invest in their continuous improvement. These initiatives will lead to an improvement of the company's internal culture, as well as employee welfare. Constant improvement in employees' skills and happiness will directly influence the company's success.

References

Central Electoral Commission. (2021). Parliamentary elections in Moldova. https://web.archive.org/web/20210712190912/https://pv.cec.md/parlamentare2021-rezultate.html

Cenusa, D. (2019). State capture downfall: Case of Moldova. *New Easter Europe, Issue 6 2019.* https://neweasterneurope.eu/2019/11/13/the-downfall-of-a-captured-state/

Delegation of the European Union to the Republic of Moldova. (2023). One year of war in Ukraine. How did the Republic of Moldova deal with the challenges generated by Russia's invasion of the neighboring country? https://www.eeas.europa.eu/delegations/moldova/one-year-war-ukraine-how-did-republic-moldova-deal-challenges-generated-russia%E2%80%99s-invasion_en?s=223

Ministry of Economy and Infrastructure. (2021). List of proposals to finance policy actions/measures in the field of information and communications technology in the context of elaborating the medium-term budgetary 2022–2024. https://old.mei.gov.md/sites/default/files/lista_de_propuneri_de_finantare_a_masurilor_de_politica_pe_domeniul_tehnologiei_informatiei_si_comunicatiilor_pentru_anii_2022-2024_1.pdf

Necsutu, M. (2019). Moldova votes to scrap much criticised electoral system | Balkan insight. https://balkaninsight.com/. https://balkaninsight.com/2019/07/31/moldova-votes-to-scrap-much-criticised-electoral-system/

Negura, P. (2021). Moldova's thirty-year search for independence. *Current History, 120*(828), 268–273. https://www.jstor.org/stable/48637965

Stratan A., Ianioglo A., Ceban A., Timofei O., Popa V., Iatisin T., Novac A., Colesnicova T., Ciobanu M., Toaca Z. (2023). *Trends in the economy of Moldova. The National Institute of Economic Research.* nr. 48 (trim. IV, 2022). https://doi.org/10.36004/nier.met.2023.48

World Bank. (2022). Moldova: Assessing the impact of COVID-19 and drought on jobs, companies and households. https://thedocs.worldbank.org/en/doc/453701608708692970-0080022020/original/MoldovaEconomicUpdateSpecialFocusDec22Romanian.pdf

Dumitru Slonovschi is a sociological researcher and strategic marketing consultant based in Moldova. He is the founder and general director of Magenta Consulting, a leading research and strategy firm with over 2000 implemented projects across the public and private sectors. With more than two decades of experience, he has provided consultancy to government institutions, international organizations, and businesses, focusing on market analysis, public policy, and strategic communication. Dumitru has also contributed to the development of Moldova's entrepreneurial ecosystem as co-founder of the Dreamups accelerator and has mentored over 300 startups. He holds a PhD in International Business and master's degrees from universities in Sweden and Moldova. In addition to his consultancy work, he teaches Marketing and Research Methods at the Academy of Economic Studies in Chisinau. His expertise lies in combining data-driven research with actionable strategy, particularly in transitional and emerging markets.

Hidden Champions of Mongolia

Zolbayar Jargalsaikhan, Zolzaya Gankhuyag, Khosbayar Nyamsuren, Odgerel Batsaikhan, and Jargalmaa Ganbaatar

Abstract Mongolia has a unique civilization that merges nomadic and settled traditions. Its economy is dominated by mining, animal husbandry, and agriculture, with mining minerals constituting the majority of its exports. The development of production began in 1924, and most factories were privatized during the 1990 Democratic Revolution. This study aims to highlight hidden champions operating in Mongolia. Enterprises were selected based on three main criteria defined by research scientist Simon, and individual interviews were conducted. In recent years, Mongolian brands have made significant strides in the global market, marking a major advancement for a developing country. The number of companies aiming to compete internationally has risen, with many showing rapid development—a positive indicator for the economy. Lately, small and medium-sized enterprises in Mongolia have increasingly turned to foreign markets to sell their products and services, driven by the shrinking domestic market and the impact of the pandemic. For Mongolia's hidden champions, the intensified focus on e-commerce and services during the pandemic has proven successful. Looking ahead, the expansion into foreign markets is set to further encourage the growth of e-commerce and broaden their activities across more countries. Following the COVID-19 pandemic, many small and medium-sized enterprises are focusing on recovering their losses and paying off debts. Simultaneously, the pandemic has spurred an increase in e-commerce abroad, presenting new opportunities for Mongolian businesses.

Z. Jargalsaikhan · Z. Gankhuyag · K. Nyamsuren (✉) · O. Batsaikhan · J. Ganbaatar
Otgontenger University, Ulaanbaatar, Mongolia
e-mail: Zolbayar@otgontenger.edu.mn; Zolzaya@otgontenger.edu.mn; Khosbayar@otgontenger.edu.mn; Odgerel@otgontenger.edu.mn; Jargalmaa@otgontenger.edu.m

D. Berberović, D. Purg (eds.), *Hidden Champions in Rising Economies*, Contributions to Management Science,
https://doi.org/10.1007/978-3-032-08263-3_27

Overview

Official name: Mongolia
Type of government: Parliamentary Republic
Population in 2023: 3,504,741 (Mongolian Statistical Information Service, 2024a, 2024b)
Land area: 1,564,116 km^2

History

209 BCE	Modun Shanyu founded the Hun Dynasty, the first Mongolian state.
1206	Chinggis Khan established Great Mongolia, creating the largest empire in the world history.
1271	Khubilai established the Yuan Dynasty and moved the capital to Beijing.
1368	The Mongolian Yuan Dynasty fell in China, and King Togoontumor returned to Mongolia.
1691	The Manchu-Qing State officially approved the administration of Khalkh Mongolia at the Dolnuur Assembly, which included Khalkh and Inner Mongolian princes.
1911	The National Liberation Revolution led to the end of Manchu rule. Mongolia declared independence, and the eighth Bogd Javzandamba was enthroned.
1921	The People's Revolution succeeded, making Mongolia the second socialist country in the world.
1924	The first Constitution was approved, the Monarchy was abolished, and the Republic was declared.
1961	Mongolia became a member of the United Nations.
1990	The democratic revolution succeeded, establishing a democratic regime. The first free and democratic elections were held, and the People's Assembly was reformed.
1992	The democratic Constitution was approved, and Parliamentary rule was declared. The first election of the Great Khural of Mongolia was organized using the majority system.
1997	Mongolia joined the World Trade Organization as its 130th member.

1 Introduction: Context and History

Mongolia is a lower-middle-income, landlocked, and resource-rich open economy that is in transition. These features, together with the country's rich history, have defined its development trajectory in the recent past and are shaping its economic future. With the looming collapse of the Soviet Union in the late 1980s and the withdrawal of Soviet troops form Mongolia, largely peaceful demonstrations demanding democracy gathered momentum from late 1989 in Ulaanbaatar's

Sukhbaatar Square and other major points of public assembly. (Helble, 2020) In the early twentieth century Mongolia regained independence from the Chinese Empire and continued as a feudal-theocratic state. The old feudal social and political structure was preserved and even reinforced, together with the extraordinarily strong position of the Lamaist church. Society was highly stratified with high-ranking feudal lords and lamas, followed by herders who were their feudal subjects, and herders who were subjects of the state. (Potkanski, 1993) Mongolia has faced tremendous external pressures in the twentieth century but has remained a sovereign state. The Mongols' strong national identity and great power politics have prevented the erosion of its independence, although it has been compelled to rely first on the Soviet Union and, at the moment, on China, Russia, and the international financial agencies for economic assistance, which has translated into foreign influence on politics and society. (Irina Y. Morozova, 2009) Tremendous mineral reserves, agricultural endowments, and proximity to Asia's vast markets make Mongolia an attractive destination for medium to long-term foreign direct investment (GRATA International Mongolia, 2023).

Landlocked between its giant neighbors, Russia and China, Mongolia was the first Asian country to adopt communism and the first to abandon it. When the Soviet Union collapsed in the early 1990s, Mongolia turned to international financial agencies—including the International Monetary Fund, the World Bank, and the Asian Development Bank—for help in compensating for the economic changes caused by disruption in the communist world (Rossabi, 2005). The transformation from single-party dictatorship to multi-party democracy has marked the major swing in the Mongolian state. It facilitated the shift from monolithic Communism to pluralism. So far, democracy has been firmly implanted in the new political system, with several elections held for the "Hural," local government, and President (Bedeski, 2006). In the period following the end of socialism, to balance the influence of China and Russia, Mongolian politicians developed the idea of "third neighbors" by inviting other powers to protect Mongolia from the political domination of Russia and China (Bumochir, 2020).

The rapid rate of industrialization in the 1970s and early 1980s contributed to mounting internal and external imbalances. Domestic prices, in particular those of petroleum products, were not adjusted to reflect higher costs of imported inputs. Resulting in a distorted structure of investment and output (Padej Sukachevin, 1991). Although the annual decrease in gross domestic production (GDP) slowed down in 1993 to 1.3%, over the period 1990–1993 GDP contracted in total by 25.2%. More comprehensive policy reforms were introduced from 1993 onward, in particular in banking and government finance, although a substantial state-dominated "soft budget" sector still remained (Spoor, 1996). Since the 1990s revolution, the change in the state of Mongolian exports reflects the change in the state of the political landscape. In accordance with the National Statistics Office, 81% of the exports were to Russia and 0.7% to China in 1990; and in 2018, 92% of the total exports were to China versus only just 1% to Russia. As of now, the main export products (as a percent of total exports) are coal (40%), copper concentrate (29%), gold (2%), crude oil (6%), iron ore (5%), and cashmere (5%) (UHY, 2023).

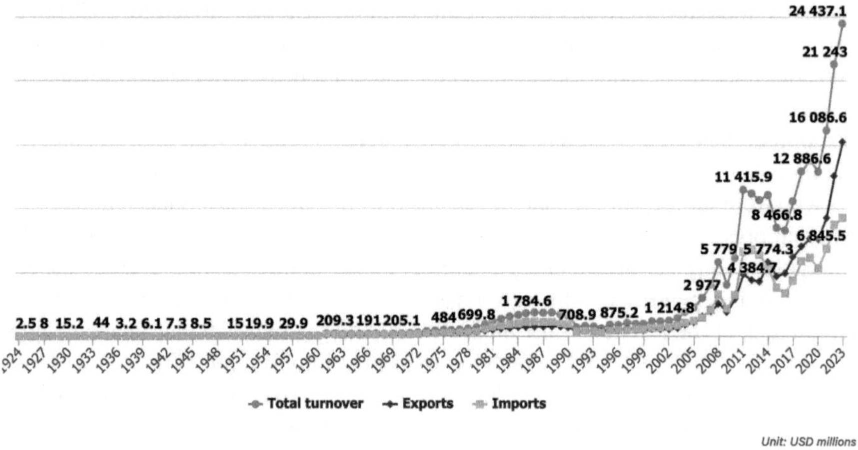

Fig. 1 Foreign Trade turnover, Exports and Imports, by year (Mongolia N. S., 2024b). Source: National Statistics Office of Mongolia, www.1212.mn

As shown in Fig. 1, from 1924 to 2005, foreign trade turnover grew from \$2.5 million to \$214.8 million. From 2006 to 2023, it further increased significantly to \$24,437.1 million.

Its recovery from the economic slowdown caused by the pandemic and the impacts of the war in Ukraine has been challenging due to several factors: First, Mongolia's high dependency on commodity exports makes its economy highly vulnerable to external price shocks in commodity markets. Second, Mongolia has a low level of trade integration with the world and is highly dependent on trade with its neighbors. Economic recovery is therefore strongly contingent on border openness and port capacity. Third, Mongolia's economy also depends significantly on imports of goods from other countries: boosting domestic production would reduce its reliance on imports (Borodyna Olena, 2023).

Mongolia's economic freedom score is 60.6, making its economy the 76th freest in the 2024 in Index of Economic Freedom. Its rating has decreased by 1.1 points from last year, and Mongolia is ranked 15th out of 39 countries in the Asia-Pacific region. The country's economic freedom score is higher than the world and regional averages. Mongolia's economy is considered "moderately free" according to the 2024 Index (Economic Freedom Index, 2024). Economic growth in Mongolia has been robust but uneven, with the mining sector driving the economy while the non-mining sector lags. Growth reached 6.2% in the first half of 2023 (up from 5.0% in 2022) (Bank, Mongolia Economic Update: Robust but Unbalanced Growth, 2023). A rebound in mineral production and transportation services for mineral exports were key drivers of growth in 2023. With coal production more than doubling and copper production increasing by 17.3%, mining output expanded by 23.4% y-o-y on 2023 (The World Bank, 2004).

The society of Mongolia is composed of two different cultures: nomadic and urban. More than two thirds of the population is settled in an urban area, but animal husbandry is still a significant component of the economy (Campi, 1997). As of 2023, there are 983,485 households in Mongolia (Mongolian Statistical Information Service, 2024a, 2024b).

Mongolia has the opportunity to put in place a best-in-class Beneficial Ownership (BO) regime that contributes to the government's policy priorities—especially the creation of a digital economy (Digital Nation), which would include digitized government services. A regime that makes BO information accessible to citizens and investors would also contribute to a more open and competitive economy and help combat corruption, money laundering, and other illicit financial flows (Michael Barron, 2022). In 2023, the global innovation index for Mongolia was 28.84 index (Knoema, 2023).

As already mentioned, Mongolia is a landlocked East Asian country with a vast territory of 1.6 million square kilometers that borders Russia to the North and China to the South. It is surrounded by mountain ridges in the transition zone between the Siberian taiga and Central Asia's dry steppes and semi-desserts (USAID, 2023). The land is predominantly characterized by semi-arid grass steppes and hardly arable. With around 85%, most of the country lies more than 1000 meters above sea level (WBG, 2015). Mongolia has significant exposure to environmental risk factors because of poor environmental management, population behaviors, and the harsh climate. During winter (December–February), the monthly average temperatures are usually very high, with night temperatures falling as low as –40 °C. In the past two decades, levels of environmental pollutants in rural and urban areas have increased because of rapid urbanization and industrialization, adding to Mongolia's harsh climate and geographical location (Amarzaya Jadamba, 2015). As a signatory to the Paris Agreement in 2016, Mongolia committed to reducing greenhouse gas emissions and helping to limit global warming (Development, 2023).

The 1992 constitution provides for a separation of powers, restricting any individual or institution from acquiring excessive power. The Mongolian legal system is a hybrid of civil and common law systems. Although judges may take notice of prior rulings in similar cases, Mongolian laws lack the specificity needed for consistent interpretation and application (Bertelsmann Stiftung, 2024).

Mongolia, like many other countries, faces the challenge of modernizing and constantly simplifying its business environment, following the adoption of increasingly complex and numerous standards and obligations in legislative texts (World Bank, 2022). In 2019, global competitiveness rank for Mongolia was 53. In 2020, the ease of doing business for Mongolia was 67.8 score. According to a survey conducted by the Mongolian National Chamber of Commerce and Industry in 2022, during the pandemic, 49% of Mongolian enterprises reduced their workforce, 43% made no changes, and 8% increased the number of employees. Additionally, 83% of enterprises experienced supply chain disruptions, leading to an average cost increase of 43.7%. The average delay in receiving inventory was 17 days or more, with some cases showing no clear timeline for delivery. Supply disruptions during the pandemic impacted business operations by increasing the price of raw materials and goods and services (66%), making it difficult to obtain raw materials (45%), and preventing timely delivery of goods and services to customers (3%) (Mongolian

National Chamber of Commerce and Industry, 2022). Since February 2022, the operation of small and medium enterprises has faced multiple challenges. Due to the war in Ukraine, transportation through China, the leading trade partner of domestic businesses, has been slow due to its Zero-COVID policy a situation that creates difficulties for the manufacturing and trade sectors (United Nations, 2023).

Today, its economy, heavily reliant on mining and commodity exports, faces challenges from global disruptions, such as the COVID-19 pandemic and the Ukraine war. Despite robust growth driven by mining, the country struggles with high dependency on imports, environmental risks, and a complex regulatory environment. With a moderate economic freedom score and ongoing efforts to modernize, Mongolia continues to balance its historical influences with contemporary economic demands.

2 Characteristics of Hidden Champions from Mongolia

The industry in Mongolia is not highly developed, with the economy primarily sustained by mining and its export. However, recently, many companies have successfully operated in various fields. While many of these companies have not yet met the requirements to become Hidden Champions, it is noteworthy that they have achieved significant sales and growth in a short period. More than 2000 companies in Mongolia export products and services to foreign markets. Apart from a small number of large corporations, the majority are small and medium-sized enterprises (SMEs) focusing on specific countries. Although Mongolia's production history began relatively late compared to other nations, some companies have rapidly and effectively organized their activities.

One example of such an emerging enterprise is URICA LLC, a start-up with the potential to compete not only regionally but also globally. The company offers innovative environmental solutions, making it unique in its contribution to climate change mitigation while also providing additional income opportunities for low-income communities (Exhibit 1).

3 Case Studies of Selected Potential and Hidden Champions

3.1 Case Study 1: URECA LLC

Overview

Address: #1208, 12th floor, Shangri-La Office, Olympic Street, Sukhbaatar District, Ulaanbaatar City, Mongolia 14241
Tel: (+976) 7716-0303
Fax: (976) 7716-0303

Exhibit 1 Core economic indicators for Mongolia

	2017	2018	2019	2020	2021	2022	2023
GDP per capita (current US$)	3708.2	4165	4394.9	4041.2	4566.1	5045.5	5764.8
GDP per capita growth (annual %)	3.4	5.4	3.4	−6.4	0	3.5	5.5
Long-term unemployment (% of total unemployment)	8.80	7.80	–	–	–	–	–
Foreign direct investment, net inflows (% of GDP)	13	14.8	17.2	12.9	14.2	14.6	–
GDP (current US$, mio)	11.48	13.18	14.21	13.31	15.29	17.15	19.87
Exports of goods and services (current US$, mio)	6,79	7,67	8,41	7,68	8,95	11,16	15,50
Exports of goods and services (% of GDP)	59.2	58.2	59.2	57.7	58.5	65.1	78.0
Merchandise exports (current US$)	6.2	7.01	7.62	7.58	9.24	12.54	15.19
Merchandise exports to high-income economies (% of total merchandise exports)	13.5	5.4	9.5	5.9	–	–	–
Merchandise exports to developing economies in Europe and Central Asia (% of total merchandise exports)	1.2	1.4	1	1.1	–	–	–
Ores and metals exports (% of merchandise exports)	38.6	42	38.9	40.1	49.4	30.9	–
Agricultural raw materials exports (% of merchandise exports)	5	5	5	3	4	4	–
Food exports (% of merchandise exports)	2	3	2	2	2	1	–
Fuel exports (% of merchandise exports)	43	46	46	30	33	54	–
Manufactures exports (% of merchandise exports)	2	2	3	1	1	1	–
High-technology exports (% of manufactured exports)	3	5	19	3	22	31	–

Source: World Bank Data (2024)

Email: Contact@ureca.com
Web: www.URECA.mn

Company Information

Industry: Environmental Services
Year of Establishment: 2022
Sales Revenues in 2023: Operating with investment income
Average Number of Employees in 2023: 50
Leadership: Managed by a management team or three founders and directors

3.1.1 Nature of Market Leadership

URECA is a climate tech start-up pioneering the use of artificial intelligence to simplify greenhouse gas reduction measurement and verification. It is currently executing the groundbreaking "Coal to Solar" project in Ulaanbaatar, enabling families in traditional Mongolian homes to shift from coal to renewable energy for heating. This initiative not only reduces emissions but also generates additional income for households. Ureca trades carbon credits[1] globally, uniquely positioned without direct competitors in its field, offering targeted solutions to combat climate change. The company innovatively addresses global challenges and leveraging technological solutions for profit.

The management team, characterized by diverse personalities and perspectives, excels in risk assessment and opportunity identification through collaborative efforts. Their strategy includes recruiting seasoned industry professionals, pivotal in opening new global markets.

3.1.2 Nature of Competitive Advantage

Few companies globally are actively combatting climate change. URECA stands apart with its unique initiatives, operating independently in the global market and pioneering new markets. Unlike similar companies, Ureca focuses on groundbreaking projects like the "Coal to Solar" initiative, facilitating household-level transitions to renewable energy. While technologies exist for calculating greenhouse gas absorption in rainforests, using AI drones and satellite imagery to protect the Amazon, these methods aren't universally applicable—for instance, they may not be suitable for regions like Central Asia.

3.1.3 Core Lessons Learned on the Path to Success

1. As the company expands its activities, it aims to systematize operations and enhance work organization.
2. The company is committed to fostering innovation
3. Maintaining high ambitions at all times
4. Always study and use your resources, no matter how small

3.1.4 Management and Leadership Development Needs

There is an urgent need to elevate the company's operations to the next level, emphasizing rapid and robust expansion and development. This growth phase requires continuous improvement, activation of the team, and effective leadership.

[1] It is a monetary equivalent of one ton of greenhouse gas emissions.

Additionally, expanding operations into international markets necessitates cultural and environmental understanding. Moreover, enhancing corporate governance, management practices, teamwork, and risk management through international ISO certification is crucial. Lastly, there is a significant imperative to raise awareness of the company's initiatives among large organizations and decision-makers.

3.1.5 Financing and Regulatory Environment Development Needs

In the future, the company aims to secure investments for establishing subsidiaries in countries like Kyrgyzstan, Kazakhstan, and Australia. Mongolia currently lacks a conducive legal environment for start-up businesses. While new technologies and ventures are emerging rapidly, there is insufficient momentum and collaborative effort to regulate them effectively. Current tax laws are particularly challenging for new companies, lacking flexible arrangements. Viewing these issues from the perspective of developing countries presents a flawed approach for international financial institutions, given the distinct contexts and challenges they face.

3.1.6 "URECA for the Story About the Potential Hidden Champion"

URECA operates on the premise that countries' development challenges can be addressed while combating climate change through the use of "Carbon Credits,"[2] a global mechanism aligned with the Paris Agreement. Globally, countries have committed to reducing greenhouse gas emissions by 2030 to limit temperature rise to 1.5 °C, necessitating a reduction of approximately 27 million tons of greenhouse gases.

The company offers consulting services to organizations to calculate greenhouse gas emissions, analyze environmental data, and develop targeted reduction strategies. Ureca's flagship "Coal to Solar" project aims to facilitate a complete energy transition for ger[3] district households in Ulaanbaatar,[4] particularly Mongolian homes.[5]

The "Coal to Solar" project by our company aims to facilitate a complete energy transition for households in ger district areas of Ulaanbaatar, with a particular focus on Mongolian yurt. The company has introduced a solution to minimize heat loss in yurt by installing solar systems outside and battery systems inside, enabling cost-effective electric heating as an alternative to coal. We've developed and patented a smart meter that monitors energy sources, distinguishing between coal and solar

[2] A carbon credit represents the monetary equivalent of one ton of greenhouse gas emissions.

[3] Yurt.

[4] Ulaanbaatar is the coldest capital city in the world and one of the most polluted. As a result, various diseases are spreading, adversely affecting people's health. Additionally, about 70% of the city's total population (1.7 million) lives in ger district.

[5] The majority of these residents have low incomes and typically come from rural areas. They often migrate to the city after losing their livestock to natural disasters such as droughts.

energy usage. The company has invented and patented a smart meter that monitors whether a household is using coal or solar energy. By tracking temperature and humidity, the system collects heat data to ensure the household is not making a fire. Each household's transition prevents approximately 15 tons of greenhouse gases from entering the atmosphere. If a household prevents the release of about 15 tons of greenhouse gases, it earns 15 carbon credits, with each credit representing the avoidance of one ton of greenhouse gas emissions. These carbon credits are verified through artificial intelligence and authentication systems and are then purchased by companies. Approximately 60% of the world's largest publicly traded companies have made commitments to reduce greenhouse gas emissions as part of their operations. However, even if a company with 100,000 employees reduces its emissions, a certain percentage of 30–40% may remain. To offset these remaining emissions, companies can buy carbon credits through the Voluntary Carbon Market, which facilitates the trade of such credits equivalent to thousands of tons of reduced emissions.

The Coal to Solar project is currently in its pilot phase. If it reaches 50% of the 90,000 households, it will significantly reduce smoke-related problems. This initiative also helps achieve 7 out of the 17 Sustainable Development Goals (SDGs). This means that even though one carbon credit corresponds to the reduction of one ton of greenhouse gases, there is a difference between carbon credits from renewable energy sources like wind farms and those from the energy transition of households in Ulaanbaatar.

The Coal to Solar project supports the implementation of numerous Sustainable Development Goals (SDGs). For instance, the living standards of families in Mongolia's ger district are being improved through the revenue generated from carbon credit sales. The company's IoT sensors collect data, which is then verified by artificial intelligence and securely recorded on the blockchain, ensuring data integrity. This approach enables the company to address various issues, such as reducing emissions in Ulaanbaatar and providing additional income to citizens. Additionally, it allows major global companies to meet their commitments to reducing coal power emissions without impacting their profits or normal operations. In November 2022, the company raised its first investment of $1.5 million.

3.2 Case Study 2: MONOS Cosmetics LLC

Overview

Address: Sambuu street, Chingeltei District, Ulaanbaatar city, Ulaanbaatar 15172, MN

Tel: +976 77373737

Fax: (976-11) 315908, 314532

Email: Cosmetics@monos.mn
Web: www.Monoscosmetics.mn

Company information

Industry: Beauty Industry
Year of Establishment: 1990
Sales Revenues in 2014: $529,000 (at current exchange rates)
Sales Revenues in 2023: $4.7 million
Average Number of Employees in 2023: 150
Key Individuals: Chairman and CEO

3.2.1 Nature of Market Leadership

Monos Cosmetics is one of the few mass production companies in Mongolia and is a leading cosmetics manufacturer that owns about 60% of the domestic production market. The company's products are always based on technological innovation. For example, they offer consumers the combination of organic, best ingredients and raw ingredients such as sheep's tail oil and sea buckthorn, traditionally used by Mongolians, with modern beauty technology.

3.2.2 Nature of Competitive Advantage

Monos Cosmetics manufactures beauty products specifically designed for extreme climates. The sale of organic raw materials rich in biologically active substances, such as various vitamins, amino acids, and proteins, combined with modern technology, positions the company to become a leader in the Central Asian region. Currently, Monos Cosmetics exports to Kyrgyzstan and is recognized as a Potential Hidden Champion, with plans to expand its foreign trade to STAN countries in the future.

3.2.3 Core Lessons Learned on the Path to Success

1. In the case of a small market, concentrating on production is more important than diversifying product lines. Introducing many types of products and variations in packaging can lead to financial problems. Therefore, it is crucial to carefully select the right product when developing or inventing new offerings.
2. Open and participatory management is an effective approach that positively impacts employee productivity. By involving employees in decision-making processes, the company can foster a more engaged and motivated workforce.

3.2.4 Management and Leadership Development Needs

Consumer trust in the Mongolian beauty industry is insufficient because it is not well known to the public. Although Mongolian-produced beauty products are competitive with, and sometimes superior to, those of foreign factories, consumers need to be informed about their quality. Employees possess the necessary knowledge and skills to perform their responsibilities effectively. It is essential to identify their training needs and determine the necessary skills based on that assessment. Additionally, there should be a focus on improving interpersonal understanding, relationships, and attitudes. The new generation of graduates often faces responsibility issues, such as irregular attendance and poor communication regarding leave. Therefore, human resource management must work with the younger generation to train them and instill a sense of responsibility.

3.2.5 Financing and Regulatory Environment Development Needs

In Mongolia, the beauty industry is often treated as a sub-category and is not recognized as a separate industry. As a result, there is minimal government regulation or support for the beauty industry at the policy level. If the industry were given proper consideration and policy support, it could develop further. For instance, the government has exempted light industries from customs duties, but this exemption currently only applies to the garment and food sectors. Including the cosmetic industry in this exemption would provide significant support. Additionally, the government recently issued loans with a very low interest rate of 6% per annum through Food Industry. Similar support is needed for other industries, including the beauty industry.

3.2.6 "Monos Cosmetics LLC for the Story About the Potential Hidden Champion"

In 2017, Monos Cosmetics Company reformed the Mongolian cosmetics industry and was certified by the AFNOR Group of France, one of the world's top five certification organizations, for implementing the ISO 9001-2015 quality management system. In 2020, the company also achieved the ISO 14001 environmental management system standard and continues to uphold these standards in its operations.

In collaboration with researchers from the R&D team of a major university's beauty institute in South Korea, Monos Cosmetics introduced nanostructured sunscreen into production in 2017. In 2018, the company successfully exported its Biomon brand shampoo to China and Japan, marking the first such export from Mongolia.

Monos Cosmetics fosters a culture of open and democratic leadership, which significantly boosts employee productivity. Encouraging participation through organizational culture forms the basis for productive work and job satisfaction.

Annual employee satisfaction surveys demonstrate that employees feel more comfortable and satisfied, especially when working in harmony with direct management. Consequently, the company focuses on measuring employee productivity and maintaining high satisfaction levels in its annual strategic plan.

From 2016 to 2022, Monos Cosmetics made several attempts to enter foreign markets, including China, but faced challenges such as lengthy registration processes. After studying Central Asian markets, the company identified Kyrgyzstan as a suitable target and, following product registration preparations in 2023, officially began exporting there in January 2024.

During the COVID-19 pandemic, demand for hand sanitizers skyrocketed. Although the company stocked up on packaging and raw materials due to the high demand, the pandemic's shorter-than-expected duration turned this into a short-term challenge. Nonetheless, in September 2021, Monos Cosmetics commissioned Mongolia's largest cosmetics factory, meeting international GMP (Good Manufacturing Practice) standards. As a result, production capacity increased fourfold, the workforce doubled, and chard production output increased by three to four times.

3.3 *Case Study 3: LHAMOUR LLC*

Overview

Address: Baga toiruu 13-1, 6 khoroo, Sukhbaatar district, Ulaanbaatar, Mongolia
Tel: +976 77120256
Fax: (976) 77120256
Email: info@lhamour.mn
Web: www.lhamour.mn

Company information

Industry: Beauty
Year of Establishment: 2014
Sales Revenues 2017: $200,000
Sales Revenues 2023: $500,000
Average Number of Employees (2023): 36
Key Person: Founder and CEO, Khulan D.

3.3.1 Nature of Market Leadership

"Lhamour" company started as a household production aimed at solving skin problems but has now become a brand used by young people in many countries. It is Mongolia's first organic and handmade cosmetics factory. The main advantage of

"Lhamour" is its product quality. By combining unique raw materials, they produce organic products suitable for people with dry and sensitive skin. Notable ingredients include the internationally valued rosehip, sea buckthorn, pure yak milk, and pure goat's milk. Since 2016, Lhamour has been exporting its products to foreign markets. Before the COVID-19 pandemic, it exported to nine countries, including Australia, India, Japan, Thailand, Taiwan, Kuwait, the United States, and Singapore. After the pandemic, exports have decreased; continuing to the United States, Japan, and Taiwan. Although it's been a year since selling products on Amazon, Lhamour has not only established a company and opened a warehouse in the United States but also has warehouses in Asian countries.

Another priority from the very beginning was benefiting society through the company. Even 10 years ago, when profits were low, many community-focused activities were organized. In 2016, Japan's NHK World TV made a documentary about Mongolia's first beauty factory. Following that, Germany's Deutsche Welle and Singapore's Channel News Asia also reported on the company and studied its practices, which is a clear sign of its leadership.

3.3.2 Nature of Competitive Advantage

In recent years, the competitiveness of organic and handmade cosmetics in the global market has been rapidly improving. As the first company in Mongolia in this field, Lhamour has distinguished itself. However, in other Asian countries, organic production has also been carried out using their own unique raw materials.

3.3.3 Core Lessons Learned on the Path to Success

1. It is easier to progress to the next stage when you start your production with a vision. Since the company was able to standardize its products and operations from the beginning, it was able to export directly. In this sense, it became the first official Mongolian brand on Amazon.
2. There is always a way to overcome any problem. As the first organic product in Mongolia, the company adopted an attitude of overcoming challenges, even in the absence of a legal framework and standards. This involved working toward creating those standards and releasing products that had never been produced in Mongolia before.

3.3.4 Management and Leadership Development Needs

By constantly learning and developing, the management team will demonstrate better leadership to other employees. In the future, we should promote our company and products in the foreign market.

3.3.5 Financing and Regulatory Environment Development Needs

In Mongolia, it is very difficult for a small or medium-sized company to become a large company. SMEs are not supported by the government, nor are they provided with opportunities to grow and develop. Livestock farmers, due to the nature of their production, often cannot submit tax returns, yet there is a lack of understanding and flexibility in this situation. There are no standards for imported goods, resulting in many people using unhygienic products that harm their health and beauty. Conversely, there is little protection and support for local producers. Limited discounts are offered, but they last for a very short period. Additionally, there is a need to streamline government processes and paperwork requirements, ensure exams are reviewed by professionals, and reduce bureaucracy.

Working internationally is also challenging due to political and policy instability. Rising inflation and the weakening exchange rate of the MNT exacerbate these issues, leading to significant problems, such as difficulties in securing financial investments.

3.3.6 "Lhamour LLC for the Story About the Hidden Champion"

Organic cosmetic products are produced by hand using special raw materials grown in Mongolia, such as sea buckthorn, rosehip, nettle, sheep's tail oil, beeswax, goat's milk, and yak's milk. The organization also supports eco-friendly production and offers consumers a Zero Waste corner, in addition to using recycled paper and accepting back the packaging of finished products. This approach is not only cost-effective but also produces less waste.

In 2016, the company was selected as a "Responsible Small and Medium Enterprise" at the ACES-2016, or "Asia's Most Exemplary and Sustainably Developing Enterprise" award ceremony.

Another goal of the company is to positively influence the lifestyles and opinions of others through its products, spreading the philosophy of self-love, love for others, and love for the earth. For example, in 2017, Women in Business organized its first major event for 450 women. "Finding Your Passion" training was conducted to help teenagers discover their interests and choose the right career. The "Girls in STEM" initiative was organized to inspire girls in the fields of science, technology, engineering, and mathematics.

In 2018, we introduced a "Zero Waste" corner in our store, allowing customers to bring their own containers and fill them directly with products. By 2021, our initiative was recognized on the prestigious Asia 100 list of young start-ups by Forbes magazine, highlighting our growing impact and commitment to positive global change.

During the pandemic, our organization encountered significant challenges due to prolonged curfews in Mongolia, which disrupted our operations. However, this period also fostered a more dedicated and resilient attitude among our employees, leading to positive changes such as expanding our product offerings.

Since 2024, we have transitioned away from relying on official distributors and launched our own global website. Within just 14 days of this transition, we received orders from the United States, Sweden, Italy, France, Malaysia, Korea, Germany, and other countries, reflecting a successful start to our direct international sales approach.

4 Pandemic's Impact on "Hidden Champions" Business Approach

At the onset of the pandemic, the Mongolian government, like many others, implemented strict restrictions on citizens' activities, imposed a curfew that was extended 17 times, and shifted the public preparedness level five times. These measures led to the closure of many businesses. Hidden Champions in the business world faced significant challenges as well. For instance, curfews disrupted the supply chain, halting the withdrawal of raw materials, which in turn led to price increases, decreased sales, and other related issues.

For URICA LLC, the pandemic heightened global awareness of energy issues and environmental pollution, making it easier for business partners and investors to understand and support our company's activities and goals.

The COVID-19 pandemic posed severe challenges for Lhamour LLC, threatening its operations and pushing it toward bankruptcy. However, the company managed to secure loans and navigate economic hardships. As a manufacturing business, its reliance on in-person work limited the feasibility of remote operations.

To mitigate financial difficulties, Lhamour introduced price discounts on previously undiscounted products and offered free shipping. Employees also played an active role in finding creative ways to boost sales, fostering a stronger team atmosphere and increasing their appreciation for the workplace.

Market demands shifted during the pandemic, prompting the company to expand its product line to include hand sanitizers, sprays, and pocket soaps. Post-pandemic, consumer interest in health-conscious products grew, driving demand for organic and high-quality goods.

Monos faced significant supply chain challenges during COVID-19. Raw materials imported from China and Korea were delayed due to border closures, causing indefinite delivery disruptions that affected production not only in Mongolia but also in the United States. Additionally, transportation costs surged by nearly 4–5 times, directly impacting product costs and profitability.

To address these challenges, Monos revised its procurement strategy, shifting from quarterly to annual raw material reservations. This proactive approach helped mitigate supply chain uncertainties. While the pandemic did not fundamentally alter the company's core business, it led to the adoption of flexible work arrangements, including remote meetings and adjusted schedules. These changes are believed to have positively impacted both employee productivity and overall organizational efficiency.

To navigate post-pandemic challenges, Hidden Champions have adopted several key strategies. First, we analyzed our cost structure and implemented cost-saving measures to mitigate the impact of price increases and maintain normal business operations. Discounts and incentives were also offered to retain customers. Second, new policies and strategies were introduced to retain employees, including the adoption of global standards for electronic work.

5 Effects of the Ukraine War on "Hidden Champions" Business Operations

Mongolia relies heavily on Russia for fuel, energy, consumer goods, and certain raw materials. Fuel shortages result in higher prices for fuel, which in turn drive up the cost of goods and services. In response to the ongoing conflict, the Mongolian government exempted the excise duty on AI-92 gasoline, the most widely used fuel, to mitigate the impact. Due to this swift government action, the war has not significantly disrupted the business activities of Mongolia's hidden champion, unlike the pandemic.

6 Conclusions and Recommendations

In the evolving landscape of leadership and management in Mongolia, there is a growing emphasis on cultivating a positive brand image and promoting Mongolian-made products and brands in both regional and global markets. As businesses navigate this dynamic environment, developing a robust and recognizable brand identity has become a crucial factor in differentiating themselves from competitors and capturing the attention of international consumers.

A significant challenge for Mongolian companies is addressing human resource issues. There is a notable decline in interest among young people in pursuing factory work, driven by factors such as the perception of factory jobs as less desirable compared to other career paths and the allure of urban and digital professions. To counter this trend, companies need to invest in the professional growth and development of their employees. This includes implementing comprehensive training programs, creating clear career progression pathways, and fostering an inclusive and supportive workplace culture. Additionally, promoting intergenerational connections and understanding within the workforce can bridge the gap between experienced workers and younger employees, facilitating knowledge transfer and enhancing overall organizational cohesion.

Mongolian producers are carving out a competitive advantage by emphasizing their commitment to clean and organic products. This focus on sustainability not only aligns with global consumer trends but also distinguishes Mongolian products in the international market. By leveraging this niche, producers can appeal to increasingly eco-conscious consumers and gain a foothold in markets where environmental and health considerations are paramount. The rise of e-commerce has been a transformative development for Mongolian businesses, partially alleviating the challenges associated with the country's landlocked geography and underdeveloped infrastructure. E-commerce platforms have enabled companies to reach broader markets without the constraints of physical logistics, thereby enhancing their competitive position and facilitating international trade. This shift has also provided a valuable avenue for businesses to diversify their revenue streams and mitigate the risks associated with traditional trade barriers.

The COVID-19 pandemic has had a profound impact on Mongolia's economic landscape, severely disrupting operations and sales across all sectors. The imposition of prolonged and stringent government curfews led to significant financial challenges, as businesses faced halted operations while continuing to bear the costs of employee salaries and rent. In response, many enterprises have been focused on recovering from the financial losses incurred during the pandemic. This period of upheaval, however, has also led to several notable shifts. The pandemic accelerated the growth of online shopping, expanding its reach into international markets and highlighting the importance of digital transformation. This shift has underscored both the opportunities and vulnerabilities within Mongolia's production capabilities. The challenges revealed during the pandemic have pointed to the need for robust strategies to address economic weaknesses, such as improving supply chain resilience, enhancing digital infrastructure, and investing in innovative technologies.

National governments could undertake a set of activities to support these companies:

- Ensuring stability is crucial for the government, as it directly influences policies and decisions that shape a positive environment. Without stability, negative perceptions of the country's reputation can significantly hinder entrepreneurial activities in the international arena. Thus, proactive measures to maintain stability are essential for fostering a conducive environment for business growth and international engagement. In Mongolia, changes in policies and laws often follow election results, leading to challenges in the business environment.
- Maintaining a strong domestic currency is crucial as fluctuations in exchange rates directly impact purchasing power and the economic value of goods. Addressing fundamental issues such as enhancing economic potential and ensuring stable inflation rates is essential. These efforts help mitigate financial challenges that organizations often face due to fluctuations that weaken the exchange rate, affecting foreign investments and loan repayments. Therefore, a stable currency is vital for fostering economic resilience and attracting sustainable investment.
- Implement flexible policies to support and empower business owners. Collaborate with companies to promptly and effectively establish legal frameworks and necessary policy regulations for emerging industries.

- Streamline the multi-layered bureaucratic state apparatus, transitioning to a more efficient governance system. Businesses have observed that while legal regulation is relatively strong in established and traditional industries, there is a lack of adequate legal frameworks for newly established start-ups and small and medium enterprises (SMEs). The government's ability to respond quickly and efficiently in these emerging sectors is limited. Despite the multi-level structure of inspections, their effectiveness remains low, and public services often lack the supportive attitude needed to foster entrepreneurship.
- The support of financial institutions should also be adjusted. It should be avoided exclusively seeking solutions to problems from international organizations and the experiences of developed countries. Given the distinct circumstances in developing countries, gaining local insights can significantly enhance the success of businesses in these regions.

As for Universities, they should accelerate development by observing and comparing how top global schools prepare their students, rather than limiting competition to domestic arenas. In educating the next generation, it's crucial to systematically train them in soft skills such as effective communication, responsibility, independent work, and creativity.

In summary, national governments have a crucial role in fostering a supportive environment for business growth and development. Ensuring stability is paramount, as it directly affects the formulation and execution of policies that shape a positive business climate. In Mongolia, where policy and legal frameworks can be subject to changes based on election outcomes, maintaining stability is particularly important. A stable environment reduces negative perceptions and enhances entrepreneurial activities, both domestically and internationally. It's noteworthy that companies integrating sustainable development into their operations and actively engaging in this field have a positive impact on the business sector.

References

Amarzaya Jadamba, J. S. (2015). The impact of the environment on health in Mongolia: A systematic review. *Asia-Pacific Journal of Public Health, 27*(1), 45–75.

Bedeski, R. (2006). Mongolia as a modern sovereign nation-state. *The Mongolian Journal of International Affairs, 13*, 77–87.

Borodyna Olena, E. M. (2023). *Mongolia: Towards sustainable economic recovery*. http://www.jstor.org/stable/resrep51276.8

Bumochir, D. (2020). The reification of the National Economy. In *The state, popular mobilisation and gold mining in Mongolia: Shaping 'neoliberal' policies* (pp. 21–39). UCL Press.

Campi, A. J. (1997). *Moving Mongolian Nomadism into the 21st century: Cultural and ecological preservation coupled with economic vitality and national security*. Research thesis.

Development, G. P. (2023). *Economy-wide impacts of climate change and adaptation in Mongolia*. GIZ.

Economic Freedom Index. (2024). *Economic Freedom Country Profile Mongolia*. Retrieved from Index of Economic Freedom https://www.heritage.org/index/pages/country-pages/mongolia

Helble, H. H. (2020). The economy: An overview. In M. H. Magee (Ed.), *Mongolia's economic prospects: Resource-rich and landlocked between two Giants*. Asian Developments Bank.

Knoema. (2023). *Mongolia world rankings*. Retrieved from KNOEMA Data Hub https://knoema.com/atlas/Mongolia/topics/World-Rankings/World-Rankings/Global-competitiveness-rank

Michael Barron, T. L. (2022). *Beneficial ownership transparency in Mongolia: Tackling complex implementation issues*. LTRC.

Mongolia, G. I. (2023). *Doing business in Mongolia-2023*. GRATA International Mongolia.

Mongolian National Chamber of Commerce and Industry. (2022). *Post-pandemic business situation study*.

Mongolian Statistical Information Service. (2024a, May 24). *Population of Mongolia*. National Statistics Office of Mongolia. Retrieved March 2024, from Mongolian Statistical Information Service https://www2.1212.mn/tables.aspx?tbl_id=DT_NSO_0300_003V1&SEX_select_all=0&SEXSingleSelect=_1&AGE_GROUP5_select_all=0&AGE_GROUP5SingleSelect=_1&YearY_select_all=0&YearYSingleSelect=_2023&viewtype=table

Mongolian Statistical Information Service. (2024b, May 2). *Foreign trade turnover, exports and imports, balance, by month (cumulative) and year*. National Statistics Office of Mongolia. Retrieved from Mongolian Statistical Information Service https://www2.1212.mn/tables.aspx?tbl_id=DT_NSO_1400_001V1&GH1_select_all=0&GH1SingleSelect=_2_3&YearM_select_all=0&YearMSingleSelect=&YearY_select_all=1&YearYSingleSelect=&viewtype=linechart

Morozova, I. Y. (2009, November 1). Socialist revolutions in Asia: The social history of Mongolia in the twentieth century. *The Journal of Asian Studies, 68*(4), 172.

Padej Sukachevin, J. E. (1991). *The Mongolian people's republic: Toward a market economy*. International Monetary Fund.

Potkanski, T. (1993). Decollectivisation of the Mongolian pastoral economy (1991-92): Some economic and social consequences. *Nomadic Peoples, 24*(1), 123–135.

Rossabi, M. (2005). *Modern Mongolia: From khans to commissars to capitalists*. University of California Press.

Spoor, M. (1996, June). Mongolia: Agrarian crisis in the transition to a market economy. *Europe-Asia Studies, 48*, 615–628.

Stiftung, B. (2024). *BTI 2024 country report: Mongolia*. Bertelsmann Stiftung.

The World Bank. (2004). *Mongolia economic update*. World Bank.

The World Bank. (2022). *Mongolia business environment and competitiveness assessment report*. Online.

The World Bank. (2023). *Mongolia economic update: Robust but unbalanced growth*.

The World Bank Data. (2024, May). Retrieved 2024, from data.worldbank.org https://data.worldbank.org/country/MN

UHY. (2023). *Doing business in Mongolia*. UHY.

United Nations. (2023). *The socioeconomic impacts of the war in Ukraine on Mongolia*.

USAID. (2023). *USAID climate risk analysis for Mongolia*. USAID.

WBG. (2015). *Mongolia: Agricultural sector risk assessment*. The World Bank Group.

Dr. Zolbayar Jargalsaikhan is a higher education professional with over a decade of experience leading policy development and institutional reform in the education sector of Mongolia. She has been closely involved in strengthening the role of universities in national development, with a focus on improving governance, curriculum design, and strategic planning.

She currently serves in a leadership role at Otgontenger University, the first private university established in Mongolia, where she has worked to build stronger links between the public and private sectors in education. Her efforts have contributed to advancing a more collaborative approach to education reform through public–private partnerships.

Dr. Zolbayar is the Global Coordinator of the Erasmus+ RETEACH project, an EU-funded initiative that supports the reform of teacher education programs in Mongolia, with a focus on digital and green transitions. She previously coordinated the MONGWBL project, which introduced and helped institutionalize work-based learning models within Mongolian higher education—bringing academic training closer to labor market needs.

She holds a Ph.D. in Political Science and has a particular interest in education policy, governance, and international cooperation. Her work continues to focus on building inclusive and responsive higher education systems that are aligned with both national goals and global developments.

Dr. Zolzaya Gankhuyag has been a university lecturer since 2018 and currently serves as the Head of the Department at Otgontenger University. She holds a Ph.D. in Political Science and has authored around 15 academic articles. Her scholarly contributions include presenting at over 10 national and international academic conferences. She has actively participated as a researcher in several prestigious international projects, including Erasmus+ Jean Monnet and RETEACH. Her research interests span public policy, governance, and political analysis, with a strong emphasis on applied, impact-driven research.

Nationally, she has contributed to approximately 10 policy-oriented research projects, offering evidence-based insights to inform and support decision-making processes. Her academic and professional journey reflects a commitment to advancing political science through both teaching and research, while fostering meaningful collaboration between academia and policy institutions.

Dr. Khosbayar Nyamsuren is the Head of the International Relations and Cooperation Office at Otgontenger University, Mongolia. She holds a Ph.D. in Linguistics and the academic title of Associate Professor. Dr. Khosbayar has published over 20 academic articles, including several in high-impact, peer-reviewed journals.

She has co-led multiple Erasmus+ Capacity Building in Higher Education projects—such as RETEACH and MONGWBL at both the international and national levels, and ARTEST, EUIF, ARROW, and C3QA at the institutional level.

In 2024, she was appointed as the Erasmus+ National Focal Point in Mongolia by the European Education and Culture Executive Agency.

Dr. Odgerel Batsaikhan is the Vice Rector of Otgontenger University in Mongolia. She holds a Ph.D. in Political Science and a Master's degree in Education. Her doctoral research explored "Women's Participation in Political Decision-Making in Mongolia: Current Status and Emerging Trends." With over 18 years of teaching experience and more than 9 years in academic administration, Dr. Batsaikhan has been a key figure in program development, policy planning, and academic leadership. She has successfully led the development of four academic programs and introduced five new subjects, including gender studies. She also has extensive experience managing and implementing EU-funded Erasmus+ projects, enhancing international academic collaboration.

A committed advocate for gender equity, she is an active member of the Gender Consortium, a nationwide platform that unites Mongolian universities to promote gender-responsive education. She was selected to serve on a national team that conducted gender analysis of liberal arts curricula in Mongolian higher education institutions.

In 2025, she was elected Vice President of the Mongolian Political Science Association. In 2023, she was awarded a Hubert H. Humphrey Fellowship, spending the 2023–2024 academic year at Penn State University (USA). During her fellowship, she focused her research on higher education reform, women's political participation, and gender policy.

Dr. Odgerel is the author of several books, handbooks, and academic articles on gender, education, and political engagement. She continues to be a strong voice for academic equity and women's leadership in Mongolia.

Jargalmaa Ganbaatar, a lecturer of International Relations at Otgontenger University in Ulaanbaatar, Mongolia, and a dedicated freelance researcher specializing in foreign policy, regional cooperation and international development. Currently, I am advancing my graduate studies in Management and Data analytics in the United States, focusing on data-driven policy analysis and strategic decision-making to address complex global challenges.

With a Master's degree from Shanghai International Studies University and a Bachelor's degree from the National University of Mongolia, my academic background integrates international cooperation, economic development, and higher education sector. I have contributed to various national and international projects, including ERASMUS+ and published work on international cooperation, politics, and education.

At Otgontenger University, I teach undergraduate courses in international law studies, diplomacy, and research methodologies. I have also contributed in international initiatives such as the "EUIF" module by Jean Monnet and the "EDGE" project in collaboration with Penn State University, co-teaching USA and Mongolian students in an interdisciplinary and cross-cultural context.

Fluent in Mongolian Chinese, and English, I combine qualitative research skills with growing expertise in data analytics. My work centers on fostering interdisciplinary collaboration, promoting educational development, and supporting Mongolia's engagement within global academic networks.

Hidden Champions of Montenegro

Milorad Jovović, Bojana Femić-Radosavović, Nikola Mišnić, Jovan Đurašković, and Ksenija Jovović

Abstract Montenegro is a small, open economy characterized by a small domestic market. Montenegro has a significant import dependence that results in a negative trade balance, which is somewhat mitigated by the positive balance in the service sector. Montenegro is a credible NATO member with a good prospect of becoming a member state of the EU shortly.

We have identified two Hidden Champion (HC) companies in Montenegro: Marina Porto Montenegro (Tourism sector) and Domen (ICT sector).

Marina Porto Montenegro is a luxury marina for yachts, super yachts, and mega yachts, located in Tivat (the Bay of Kotor). In the target market segment of superyachts and mega yachts, Marina Porto Montenegro is the market leader in the Adriatic Sea region.

Domen is a joint venture that was founded in 2008 by Afilias Limited, GoDaddy.com (foreign partners), and ME-net (a domestic partner) which does business as a ".ME" Registry. Domen is the market leader in the region according to the number of Country Code Top-Level Domains registered (CCTLD) and is ranked at first place in Europe according to the number of CCTLDs registered outside of their home country.

Both HC companies were founded after the Montenegrin Declaration of Independence in 2006. In a relatively short period of time, they have achieved a leading position in competition with companies from other regional countries. The clear visions of both companies' founders, operationalized through a well-chosen and implemented strategy based on a differential focus, led these companies to success. In their business success, it was of extreme importance that they identified excellent business ideas with high market potential in a timely manner.

M. Jovović · N. Mišnić · J. Đurašković
Faculty of Economics, University of Montenegro, Podgorica, Montenegro

B. Femić-Radosavović (✉) · K. Jovović
Innovation Fund of Montenegro, Podgorica, Montenegro
e-mail: ksenija.jovovic@fondzainovacije.me

D. Berberović, D. Purg (eds.), *Hidden Champions in Rising Economies*, Contributions to Management Science,
https://doi.org/10.1007/978-3-032-08263-3_28

Overview

Official name: Montenegro
Type of Government: Parliamentary Democracy
Population in 2021: 617,683
Land area: 13,812 km^2

History

1878	Montenegro is recognized as an independent and sovereign state at the Congress of Berlin.
1910	Montenegro becomes a Kingdom during the rule of King Nikola Petrovic I.
1918	Shortly after the end of World War I, Montenegro became part of the newly formed Kingdom of Serbs, Croats, and Slovenes, a parliamentary monarchy whose capital was in Belgrade, Serbia.
1945	After the great human loss and economic devastation of World War II, Montenegro became one of the six constituent republics of the Socialist Federative Republic of Yugoslavia ruled by the Communist Party.
1980	The death of the post-war Yugoslavia leader Tito marks the starting point of Yugoslavia's slow dissolution during the 1990s.
1992	After Slovenia's, Croatia's, Macedonia's, and Bosnia and Herzegovina's declaration of independence, the Federal Republic of Yugoslavia was formed, consisting of Serbia and Montenegro.
1999	Still being part of FR Yugoslavia, Montenegro officially introduced a dual currency system, consisting of the German mark and dinar. After 1999, Montenegro starts introducing its own laws on main political and economic issues (e.g., laws on taxes and customs), different from those in Serbia. This paves the way to independence.
2001–2002	The German mark became the only legal tender in Montenegro from 2001 to 2002 when the Euro replaced the German mark. The adoption of the German mark and the Euro brought greater stability, predictability, and lower inflation (Fabris, 2015).
2003	The Federal Republic of Yugoslavia disintegrated and a new state was established under the State Union of Serbia and Montenegro.
2006	An independence referendum is held in Montenegro. Montenegro officially declared its independence after the clear victory of the people voting in favor.
2007	The Stabilisation and Association Agreement (SAA) was signed in October 2007 and has been in force since May 2010. This agreement lays the groundwork for enhanced economic and political ties with the EU, symbolizing Montenegro's strides toward European norms and standards.
2011	After fulfilling the required conditions, Montenegro became a candidate country for EU membership.

2016	Montenegro became a member of NATO. This offers a good prospect of becoming a member state of the EU shortly.
2020	Regarding European integration, as of November 26, 2020, Montenegro is the only candidate country that has thus far opened all and provisionally closed three negotiating chapters.
2024	Montenegro is determined to accelerate its legal, political, and economic alignment with the EU, aspiring to attain full membership status as the 28th member state by 2028.

1 Introduction: Context and History

Montenegro has a small open economy characterized by a small domestic market with significant import dependence, resulting in a negative trade balance of 2983.1 million euros (Central Bank of Montenegro (CBCG, 2024). This is somewhat mitigated by the positive balance in the service sector (1695 million euros) (CBCG, 2024). According to the new methodology, the 2021 total current account balance amounted to −782.32 million euros (CBCG, 2024).

Montenegro is a predominantly mountainous country, but flat in a significant part of the central region, with a total coastline length of 293 km. The country is divided into three regions: the northern, central, and southern parts of Montenegro. In the last two decades, the northern part of Montenegro has experienced economic stagnation and depopulation, while the central and southern parts are growing at a significant pace.

The current social, political, and economic tendencies are shaped by the country's turbulent history. Before World War II, Montenegro had suffered a lot from political and social instability as a consequence of the country's relatively small territory and strategically important location.

The period after World War II was a period of stability and economic development, interrupted by the disintegration of Yugoslavia in the 1990s. By the beginning of the twenty-first century, another period of relatively general stability occurred. At that time, Montenegro achieved its EU accession frontrunner status and was determined to accelerate its legal, political, and economic alignment with the EU, aspiring to attain full membership status as the 28th member state by 2028. Apart from that, Montenegro today is a credible NATO ally and partner.

Montenegro's freedom status, as reported by Freedom House (2024), is classified as "Partly Free" with a Global Freedom Score of 69 out of 100. With the insignificant score increase from the previous year, Montenegro remains "Partly Free," indicating that while there have been some positive developments, significant challenges to full political rights and civil liberties persist.

Since the beginning of the twenty-first century, we have witnessed the acceleration of economic growth in Montenegro, especially after it gained its independence in 2006. Economic growth was partially slowed down by the World Economic Crisis of 2008/09 and then again in 2020 due to the COVID-19 crisis, with a negative GDP growth rate in 2020 (−15.30%), topping the previous negative record from 2009 (−5.8%). Nevertheless, since 2006, Montenegrin's GDP has increased from 2170 million euros to 5700.4 million in 2022 (CBCG, 2023). GDP per capita is projected at 9228 euros in 2022.

The structure of the country's economy has changed dramatically since the socialist period. After World War II, Yugoslavia's economic growth was based primarily on industry and the country's economy was centrally planned and organized rather than being liberal and free-market oriented. Nowadays, many factories and production facilities from that period are closed and bankrupt as a consequence of a difficult transition period toward an open-market economy and companies' inability to face the open market without State support. The current Montenegrin economy is largely dependent on tourism, the Small and Medium-sized Enterprise (SME) sector, energy production, the financial sector, and trade. With the support of investments in infrastructure, these sectors, have contributed to GDP growth since 2006.

Tourism remains the strongest driver of the Montenegrin economy. According to World Tourism & Travel Council—WTTC (2022), this sector accounts for 1556 million euros, or 30.8% of the national GDP in 2019, the last year before COVID-19 crisis. Due to the COVID-19 crisis, in 2022 tourism contributed to the national GDP by 25.3% (WTTC, 2023). The number of tourists visiting Montenegro supports additionally, the importance of tourism in the Montenegrin economy. Since Montenegro gained independence in 2006, the total number of tourists has more than doubled, reaching 2.61 million in 2023 (Monstat, 2024). We hope several important investment projects—new resorts, hotels, and significant infrastructural projects in southern and northern parts of Montenegro—will reshape tourism in Montenegro, increasing the number of first-time visitors, extending the tourism season, and reducing seasonal inequality. It is expected that in 2025, the travel and tourism industries will contribute 25% to the national GDP in Montenegro (MNE Tourism Development Strategy, 2022–2025).

Besides tourism, SMEs are very important for Montenegro's economic development. Over 99% of companies in Montenegro are in the SME category, employing around 75% of the total workforce (Government of Montenegro, 2020). Further steps are needed to encourage an entrepreneurial spirit and support the development of entrepreneurship in Montenegro. The primary fields that must be developed are finance (through credit lines, the establishment of the Guarantee Fund, which is of extreme importance for the internationalization of SMEs), entrepreneurial infrastructure (business centers, incubators, etc.); and entrepreneurial knowledge (organization of training and education, promotion of lifelong entrepreneurial learning, etc.).

Foreign Direct Investments (FDIs) are also a significant source of economic growth in Montenegro, reducing the deficit in the current account. Total FDI inflow in 2022 amounted to 1151.42 million euros (a growth of 24.07%) as a result of an increase in equity investments and investments in the form of intercompany debt (CBCG, 2023). FDI is especially important for tourism (investments in marinas and luxury resorts) and energy (renewable sources and distribution), which are two very important sectors of the Montenegrin economy. A significant part of FDIs is achieved through the formation of new foreign-owned entities. Those companies are reshaping, improving, and additionally expanding the economy by bringing in international business standards, know-how, technology, and new business cultures to Montenegro.

Because of the small domestic market, successful companies from Montenegro have identified foreign markets as a source for growth and development. Thus, for most Montenegrin enterprises, internationalization is a prerequisite for their long-term success.

The socio-cultural environment in Montenegro, characterized by a blend of traditional and collectivist cultures, significantly influences the behavior and interactions of its people, fostering strong community ties and a deep sense of shared identity.

As of 2023, internet usage in Montenegro shows considerable progress but still lags behind the EU average. About 90% of individuals in the EU aged 16–74 used the internet within the last 3 months, with 81.3% using it in Montenegro (Freedom House, 2024). Moreover, only 18.4% of individuals in Montenegro reported purchasing goods or services online in 2022, which is significantly lower than the EU average of 56.1%.

Traffic congestion is a significant bottleneck in Montenegro. However, the Government has identified the issue and is making substantial efforts to develop new projects and construct roads and highways. This initiative impacts long-term economic development and dynamics but also poses risks to the country's macroeconomic performance, particularly concerning public debt.

2 Characteristics of Hidden Champions from Montenegro

Taking into account the size of the Montenegrin market and the structure of its economy, it was not realistic to expect that there would be a large number of companies in Montenegro that had achieved a leading position in the international market. As a consequence, in an earlier study from 2019, our initial list of companies worth interviewing in search of HC consisted of six enterprises that have been dominantly focused on foreign markets. At the end of our field research, three companies were identified as meeting the hidden champion criteria (Simon, 2009). Each of them occupies the number-one position in their regional market, as measured by market share. Since one of them is regarded as part of a foreign entity, that company was excluded from the list. In the end, just two out of six initially interviewed companies met all criteria. We are sure that all of them have had an important role in helping Montenegro improve its Competitiveness Index in 2020 in comparison to 2008 (World Economic Forum—WEF, 2020). It is important to note that HC from Montenegro might be regarded as young companies (founded after Montenegro declared its independence in 2006). Using the same methodology, we did research on HC in Montenegro in 2023, and after analyzing the collected data and information, we found that there had been no significant changes compared to the prior study. Thus, we have concluded that the previously identified HC from Montenegro have maintained and somewhat improved their competitive position and that these two companies still meet the HC criteria. At the same time, we did not identify new HC from Montenegro, despite the notable advancements some companies have made in the ICT (information and communications technologies) sector, yachting, and hotel industry.

We strongly believe that the two companies that we present here are true Montenegrin hidden champions. One—Marina Porto Montenegro, which is part of the Adriatic Marinas Ltd.—is from the tourism sector. The other one—Domen—is in the information and communication technologies sector.

Marina Porto Montenegro is a luxury marina for yachts, superyachts, and megayachts, located in Tivat, in the Bay of Kotor, with a capacity of 450 berths. In order to provide a premium service to Marina's clients, a luxurious settlement was built around the Marina, including deluxe residential facilities, hotels, restaurants, and more, providing services that satisfy the needs of a very demanding high-income target group, whose price sensitivity is relatively low. Today, Marina Porto Montenegro is the market leader in the Adriatic Sea in its market segment of superyachts and megayachts. In the period after the first conducted study, through the buyout process, the shipyard in Bijela was also included in the portfolio of Porto Montenegro, which expanded its offer, enabling them to provide maintenance and service of yachts for their clients, which will undoubtedly strengthen their competitive position.

Domen Ltd. is a joint venture founded in 2008 by Afilias Ltd., GoDaddy.com (foreign partners), and ME-net (a domestic partner), that does business as a .me registry. After a formal public request for proposals was issued by the Government of Montenegro to find a registration agent who could provide a world-class registry platform, run operations for an international registry, and deliver marketing expertise to make .me a globally successful CCLTD, the contract was awarded to Domen. Now, this company is a market leader in the region in terms of numbers of registered CCTLDs and is third in Europe in terms of the number of CCLTDs registered outside one's home country. After the Government's decision in 2023 not to renew the 15-year contract with the company Domen, a legal dispute has been opened. Hopefully, this will lead to clearing up doubts and enable the continuation of this, so far very successful arrangement.

Both companies were founded after the Montenegrin Declaration of Independence in 2006. In a relatively short time, they have achieved a leading position in competition with companies from other countries in the region. To obtain a leading position in the market, identifying a business idea with high market potential based on a full understanding of the needs of potential customers promptly was of extreme importance. The clear visions of the founders, operationalized through well-chosen and implemented strategies, and based on a differential focus, led these companies to success. They demonstrate that, in a fast-changing environment, the readiness of companies to adapt and their adaptation speed is crucial for business success. The companies' employees also had a special role in this process. Aware of their employees' importance, these companies constantly invest in the development of skills of managers and other employees (Exhibit 1).

Exhibit 1 Core economic indicators for Montenegro

	2017	2018	2019	2020	2021	2022	2023
GDP per capita (current US$)	$7784.07	$8760.69	$8909.65	$7677.15	$9465.70	$10,093.43	n/a
GDP per capita growth (annual %)	4.70%	4.86%	40.96%	−15.21%	12.81%	6.40%	n/a
Long-term unemployment (% of total unemployment)	n/a	15.20%	15.10%	17.90%	16.50%	15.30%	14.40%
Foreign direct investment, net inflows (% of GDP)	11.57%	8.91%	4.69%	6.92%	7.33%	14.00%	n/a
GDP (current US$, mio)	$4844.59	$5452.17	$5542.05	$4769.86	$5861.27	$6229.80	n/a
Exports of goods and services (current US$, mio)	$1988.96	$2356.26	$3906.58	$1995.81	$4054.57	$3208.35	n/a
Exports of goods and services (% of GDP)	41.06%	43.22%	43.85%	26.00%	42.83%	51.50%	n/a
Merchandise exports (current US$, mio)	$421.00	$472.00	$465.00	$419.00	$515.00	$742.00	n/a
Merchandise exports to high-income economies (% of total merchandise exports)	44.62%	44.82%	46.70%	40.90%	42.13%	43.14%	n/a
Merchandise exports to low- and middle-income economies in Europe and Central Asia (% of total merchandise exports)	49.04%	n/a	n/a	n/a	n/a	n/a	n/a
Ores and metals exports (% of merchandise exports)	37.75%	31.21%	27.92%	29.10%	32.65%	30.70%	n/a
Agricultural raw materials exports (% of merchandise exports)	8.02%	7.30%	8.30%	8.64%	8.47%	8.10%	n/a
Food exports (% of merchandise exports)	12.88%	11.78%	11.99%	13.66%	13.55%	n/a	n/a
Fuel exports (% of merchandise exports)	12.38%	20.81%	21.41%	16.65%	18.52%	30.00%	n/a
Manufactures exports (% of merchandise exports)	28.69%	28.76%	30.39%	31.94%	26.82%	n/a	n/a
High-technology exports (% of manufactured exports)	2.54%	3.15%	6.89%	7.57%	9.44%	8.00%	n/a

Source: World Bank, May, 2024

2.1 *Case Study 1: Marina Porto Montenegro (Part of Adriatic Marinas Ltd)*

Overview

Address: Blaža Jovanovića 1, 85320 Tivat, Montenegro
Telephone: +38232660700
Fax: +38232674656
Email: marinaoffice@portomontenegro.com
Web: www.portomontenegro.com

Company Information

Industry: Amusement and recreation activities (yacht homeport with berths)
Year of establishment: 2006
Sales revenue in 2017: 20.9 million euros (Adriatic Marinas Ltd)
Sales revenue in 2023: 42.9 million euros (Adriatic Marinas Ltd)
Number of employees in 2023: 480 in Adriatic Marinas Ltd
Brains behind the company: Founder Mr. Peter Munk (1927–2018);
Current owner: Investment Corporation of Dubai (ICD) (2016–)
CEO and project leader David Margason.

2.1.1 Nature of Market Leadership

Marina Porto Montenegro (part of Adriatic Marinas Ltd) still occupies the number-one position in the Adriatic Sea in the market segment of superyacht and megayacht accommodation measured by market share. Despite facing numerous challenges, including the COVID-19 pandemic's negative impact on tourism, the repercussions of the war in Ukraine, and sanctions against Russia that impacted the operations of this company during the period between the two studies, Porto Montenegro, a homeport for the largest berths of up to 250 m, remains the only and leading marina with this kind of facility in the Adriatic Sea.

2.1.2 Nature of the Competitive Advantage

The competitive advantage of Marina Porto Montenegro is its well-selected and consistently implemented focus strategy (Porter, 1998), focusing on a particular buyer group and serving them very well. Consequently, each functional policy is developed with this focus in mind. Since its establishment, PM has been focused on a significant yet underserved market segment of super and megayacht owners who are looking for a home port for their yachts in the Adriatic Sea. Marina Porto Montenegro identified this segment as a great opportunity and made a clear choice to focus on the needs of superyacht and megayacht owners already in the process of project design and marina planning. By doing so, Adriatic Marinas built a new marina that is completely adapted and equipped to serve its narrow strategic target more effectively and efficiently than its competitors do. An additional advantage has been achieved by taking over the Shipyard in Bijela, near the marina, to expand its offer with services of maintenance, repair, and refurbishment of yachts to clients.

This good competitive strategy is additionally supported by the fact that, according to the Montenegrin legal framework, Marina's clients' yachts may remain in the waters of Montenegro without time constraints or import taxes. That gives Marina a significant competitive advantage over marinas in EU countries, Montenegro's key competitors.

Apart from that, the beauty of the environment, and characteristics of the Boka Bay as a natural marina providing both the serene sea with appropriate sea depth (which are uncommon to be seen together), gave additional competitive advantage to Marina Porto Montenegro. Another factor influencing the selection of this Marina was its proximity to the airport in Tivat, which significantly facilitates the easy arrival of guests.

This effective competitive strategy in the past (until 2024) had been additionally supported by the fact that, according to the Montenegrin legal framework, Marina's clients had the ability to use the benefits of low VAT (only 7%), which represented a significant competitive strength of Porto Montenegro. However, recent changes in the tax regulation, which increased VAT to 15% for Marina's clients, as well as the volatility of excise taxes, which for a certain period of time eliminated the possibility for Marina's clients to provide fuel bunkering services tax-free, might jeopardize competitiveness of Porto Montenegro.

Relatively low crew prices compared to EU marinas give Marina another significant competitive advantage over other marinas in EU countries—Montenegro's key competitors.

At this moment, Marina Porto Montenegro is a hub with all necessary amenities (exclusive retail, office space, restaurants, hotels, international schools, first class real estate, entertainment, and culture, etc.). As a consequence, yachts stay in the Marina all year round.

It is worth mentioning that Porto Montenegro has received the first in the world Platinum Marina status. This accomplishment demonstrates their ability to establish and set industry standards. After that, only three other marinas in the world obtained this status (available at: https://www.portomontenegro.com/news-2/platinum-marina-montenegro/).

2.1.3 Core Lessons Learned on the Path to Success

The company's first years of experience highlights the importance of the following factors in their path to success:

- A clear vision and strategy that led the company to success, which was supported by financial strength of the founders and investors due to the high investments that marina construction and the accompanying real estate business necessitate.
- Carefully selecting an underserved target market, and continuous adaptation of the offers to the demands of the selected target market.
- Good cooperation with the Government and public authorities, and in particular with the local community.
- Investing in human resources and employee satisfaction as these are prerequisites to the premium service that the clients of Porto Montenegro Marina expect, strengthened by strong leadership.

2.1.4 Management and Leadership Development Needs

When Marina Porto Montenegro started doing business in Montenegro, it faced a problem: insufficient management and leadership skills and a lack of expertise across most employees. This was a consequence of an outdated educational system. At that time, it was almost impossible to find companies in Montenegro that provided education services for managers, leaders, and other employees. Therefore, the company has decided to put in place an in-house training program in general skills, such as project management, time management, leadership effectiveness, and more. The company also identified a need for additional training for employees who are in direct contact with customers. For those employees, specific customer relationship management training has been provided. Additionally, for certain employees from the legal and accounting departments, the company covered the costs of certified training and courses organized by other institutions.

A significant gap still exists between the educational system and the real demands of the market in terms of employees' skills. Although the official statistics show significant numbers of unemployed people, the experience of Porto Montenegro management has been that it is difficult to find well-qualified and skilful workers. This HR management problem has been identified not only in top management positions, but also at lower levels, such as carpenters, builders, and painters. Porto Montenegro has realized that blue-collar jobs, which have been neglected for a long time, also warrant attention. This phenomenon seems to be very pronounced in Montenegro. As a consequence, competition, which usually revolves around customers, is shifting more and more toward human resources; further impacting management's role. As a result, investing in human resources and employee satisfaction are the prerequisites of the premium service that the clients of Porto Montenegro Marina expect.

As a consequence of the mentioned activities of the company, Marina Porto Montenegro has developed a substantial base of equipped staff members. However, despite that, they are constantly investing in developing employees for a variety of specific industries. They have developed an HR strategy, which relies on expats for knowledge transfer, while attracting, investing in their development, and retaining quality Montenegrin employees (80% of their employees are from Montenegro and

50% from the Boka Bay region). As a result, employees are showing a high level of satisfaction and loyalty.

2.1.5 Financing and Regulatory Environment Development Needs

Adriatic Marinas Ltd. has a good relationship with banks in Montenegro since they are willing to cooperate with the company due to its reputation and financial stability. However, the financial sector in Montenegro represents a challenge for the company because the market is relatively small, meaning that local banks are limited in their lending capacity. This company has financing needs higher than the maximum amount local banks can provide, based on their capital constraints. Therefore, Adiratic Marinas Ltd. is working with their headquarters abroad, as well as with international financial institutions (IFC, EBRD, DEG) on syndicated financing. This issue could be improved if banks had a better understanding and were willing to cooperate and supply syndicated loans.

Moreover, partial financing of Porto Montenegro Marina's further development comes from ICD, as a shareholder dedicated to this unique project.

2.1.6 Porto Montenegro: From an Abandoned Military Boatyard to a Unique and Exquisite High-Class Marina

The Porto Montenegro project started with the clear idea and vision of Canadian entrepreneur Peter Munk, who made use of the exquisite natural environment and central Mediterranean location in the Bay of Kotor, one of the most beautiful bays of the Adriatic Sea. Long-term concession agreements on the former Yugoslav military boatyard in Tivat, in the Bay of Kotor, were made in 2006 with the Government of Montenegro. A unique marina with state-of-the-art facilities that could accommodate superyachts and megayachts, with a length of up to 250 m is built. With backing from some of the world's most respected business figures and institutions, the largest private-sector investment in Montenegro, the ex-military base was transformed into a beautiful marina. Today, Marina Porto Montenegro is a super attractive and financially advantageous destination and the only marina in the Adriatic Sea with berths that can accommodate superyachts and megayachts while satisfying the needs of this kind of high-income market segment. Since 2016, Porto Montenegro has been owned by the Investment Corporation of Dubai, which continues developing this project. The company invested in facilities for maintenance, repair, and ship-building in Bijela (a former state-owned shipyard close to Tivat), based on a signed concession agreement with the Government of Montenegro, which made their offer even more competitive.

In the case of Marina Porto Montenegro, the founder, innovator, and leader Mr. Peter Munk's crucial role can clearly be seen. The vision, passion for the project, great international recognition, positive reputation, and trust in the business world, as well as the financial strength and reputation of the company, its leaders, and its investors, were important prerequisites for the business's success, especially because of the huge investments that marina construction, business development, and the accompanying real estate business require.

A key factor of Marina Porto Montenegro's business's success is the exceptionally competitive strategy, which was based on a differential focus on a defined underserved market segment. Starting the marina project almost as a greenfield investment allowed the company to adapt its market offer—facilities and services—perfectly to the needs of the selected target market. The fact that the company both designed and constructed the Marina enabled the introduction of state-of-the-art technology compatible with the market segment's needs and the characteristics of contemporary superyachts and megayachts.

It is clear that leadership plays a crucial role and represents an important basis for the market success of Porto Montenegro. For that reason, it has been of extreme importance to maintain continuity and consistency in leadership, even after changes in company ownership. New investments in Porto Montenegro, new hotels and buildings,—and connected businesses—a shipyard, which occurred after the change in ownership structure, are proof that Porto Montenegro Project has sustained the same pace in development.

Furthermore, relationships of mutual trust and respect have been built between owners, managers, and employees, leading to the development of a positive organizational culture. Porto Montenegro has developed a specific task-based and customer-oriented organizational culture, which is different from most other companies in Montenegro. This company regards organizational culture as an important element of its success. Investments in the development of employee knowledge, skills, and growth, resulted in high levels of employee satisfaction and enthusiasm. This is especially important because business strategy was firstly defined by their focus on customer service, which involved the inclusion of complementary services. In doing so, the top management is mostly comprised of ex-pats with experience, while middle management is from Montenegro, whose career has been developed in Marina Porto Montenegro.

With such an approach, Marina Porto Montenegro has managed to develop a substantial base of equipped staff members.

The Focus of Marina Porto Montenegro's strategy is also aimed at sustainability and integrating the best ESG (Environmental, Social, and governance) practices into its operations. In this sense, the standards that are adhered to are significantly ahead of Montenegrin regulation.

Marina Porto Montenegro leaders have a good understanding and cooperation with the Government, public authorities, and the local community in particular. For the company and the local and public authorities, the benefits are mutual: increased public revenues, increased volume of exports, growth in the employment rate, development of supporting companies and suppliers, development of entrepreneurship, and growth of the real estate prices in the wider area of the Municipality of Tivat.

Porto Montenegro opened its doors in 2009. The changes that have occurred between 2008 and today clearly show the impact that Porto Montenegro has had on the development of tourism in the Municipality of Tivat and the Bay of Kotor. Namely, the number of foreign tourist arrivals in 2018 in Montenegro grew by 101.4% during that period (Monstat, 2019). As an illustration of the influence Porto Montenegro opening had on Tivat municipality, in the same period, the number of foreign tourist arrivals in the Municipality of Tivat grew by 278.1% (Monstat, 2019). This difference suggests that the number of tourist arrivals in Tivat grew 2.74 times faster than general tourism in Montenegro as a whole. Consequently, we found that the share of foreign tourists visiting Tivat rose from 3% in 2008 to 5.6% in 2018. In 2019, which was the last pre-pandemic year, an additional increase in the number of tourists occurred, and the share of foreign visitors to Tivat rose to 6.2% (Monstat, 2024). After a sharp drop in the number of foreign tourist arrivals during COVID-19 pandemic, there were signs of a significant recovery in the years 2022 and 2023, with an annual growth rate of 30.7% and 19.6%, respectively. In 2023, number of foreign tourist arrivals was near the pre-pandemic level achieved in 2019. The number of foreign tourists in Tivat follows a general post-pandemic trend to that in Montenegro.

Additionally, after the opening of Porto Montenegro, two more modern internationally competitive marinas—Porto Novi and Luštica Bay—were open in the Bay of Kotor, with more than 400 berths in total. These marinas will further increase the quality of tourist offers and the international positioning of Montenegro as an important yachting tourism destination. Investments in new marinas were spurred by the example that Marina Porto Montenegro had set.

Although the period between the two studies was extremely challenging, especially because of the COVID-19 pandemic, as well as global issues caused by the war in Ukraine, Marina Porto Montenegro not only improved its financial indicators but also currently holds an even stronger position on the market, than in 2019. This was certainly influenced by the successful change of ownership and management that occurred just prior to the pandemic, which led to changes and improvements in business. The management of Marina Porto Montenegro is particularly satisfied with the success they have achieved by receiving the first in the world Platinum Marina status. Today, Marina Porto Montenegro is setting standards in the industry. At the same time, new markets for Porto Montenegro are open: the USA, Scandinavia, and countries from the region (Serbia mostly). Unlike other Marinas, such as those in Barcelona or Monaco, which adopt a conservative approach, Porto Montenegro provides extra services and amenities for yachts, yacht owners, and yacht crews, hence offering clients greater value.

As already mentioned, the COVID-19 pandemic brought significant problems and challenges for businesses, especially in the tourism sector. During the first phase, business activities diminished in 2020 (mostly since the borders were closed). That also happened to Porto Montenegro in the year 2020. However, it seems that it brought positive consequences for this company in the long term. It turned out that one of the long-term effects of COVID-19 is reflected in the fact that rich and ultra-rich individuals are increasingly valuing their privacy. As a result, some luxury industries have shown a trend of growth. One of them is the boom in super and megayacht construction, as well as a significant upsurge in demand for super yachts and megayachts in shipyards and consequently for the marina berths. That had a very positive effect on Porto Montenegro. In addition, even though, due to sanctions against Russia as a result of its war with Ukraine, in 2022 Russian owners left the Mediterranean and this marina as well with their super and megayachts; Porto Montenegro managed to avoid negative consequences with a quick reaction. Namely, by reorienting to other market segments, this part of the market that has been reduced is compensated by focusing on new markets, as well as by attracting owners of smaller yachts (in significantly larger numbers).

2.2 Case Study 2: Domen Ltd.

Overview

Address: Vojvode Maša Đurovića, Lamela 3/1, Podgorica, Montenegro
Tel: +382 77 300 070
Fax: +382 77 300 079
Email: info@domain.me
Web: www.domain.me

Company Information

Industry: Data processing, hosting and related activities (Internet domain registration)
Year of establishment: 2008
Sales revenue in 2017: 6.5 million euros
Sale revenue in 2023: 9.18 million euros
Number of employees in 2023: 8
Brain behind the company: CEO Predrag Lešić

2.2.1 Nature of Market Leadership

Domen Ltd. is the market leader in terms of total number of CCTLDs registered (1.28 million domains), in the region which consists of ex-Yugoslav countries plus Albania, Bulgaria, and Greece. Domen is also number 1 in Europe, in terms of the numbers of CCTLDs registered outside their home country.

2.2.2 Nature of the Competitive Advantage

The main competitive advantages of Domen are as follows:

– The attractiveness of the .me domain because of multiple meanings and limitless wording possibilities in multiple languages, allowing personalization (e.g., text. me, travel.me, pay.me, about.me, etc.). Today two main markets are domains

that: "Call to action" (e.g.: love.me) or are "Personalized" (e.g.: namesurname.me).
- A competitive strategy based on differentiation through marketing and promoting domains directly to customers.
- The creation of a safe environment for customers who are developing their own businesses in the digital world, using domains and platforms provided by Domen.

Since new digital customers need a secure and trusted registry for their domains, the company has positioned itself as a reliable and trusted partner and has successfully created strong relationships with customers.

2.2.3 Core Lessons Learned on the Path to Success

The most important lessons that the company learned on the path to success can be summed up in four pillars:

- In the digital era, it is of extreme importance to identify and operationalize business ideas with a high market potential promptly. This process must also be based on a deep understanding of the needs, behavior, and expectations of potential customers. Domen believes that this is also true of companies that are not directly involved in the ICT sector.
- For the company, differentiation is the foundation of business success. Since the need for personalization is one of the most important characteristics of a new digital customer, opening the space for differentiation through personalization lies at the core of Domen's business strategy.
- Domen has developed a positive organizational culture that emphasizes employee strengths, individual vitality, and growth. The organizational culture is task-oriented and is accompanied by a flat organizational structure. As a consequence, the employees show a high level of satisfaction and enthusiasm, which are important success factors.
- The company points out that another important lesson was learned in the period between the two studies. Namely, the Company has become more aggressive in targeting the market, and since 2020 an insufficient level of aggressiveness led to a drop in overall performance.

2.2.4 Management and Leadership Development Needs

Knowing that the nature of the market and the environment are changing very fast, Domen realized that it is very important to have up-to-date skills. Therefore, it provides intensive training opportunities for employees. The company asserts that it is necessary to invest continuously in the development of managerial and employee skills. Domen relies on numerous online courses to stay up-to-date because the necessary training is very hard to acquire locally.

The company strongly believes that Montenegro's educational system should emphasize preparing students for work in the digital economy era, with an emphasis on programming. Despite significant advancements in this area that have taken place in Montenegro in the meantime, due to the growing importance of digitalization in everyday life and business, there is still a great need for further improvement in this field. In this regard, they emphasize that new employees are not equipped for digital marketing when entering the organization (education is lagging behind) and that there is a great demand for this type of skills in companies.

University students as well as employees in Montenegro still need more leadership courses dealing with developing, inspiring, guiding employees and teams, and effectively influencing stakeholders across an organization. In addition, the company indicates that the educational system should do more to stimulate group problem-solving orientation, as well as work and openness to unfamiliar things.

The CEO believes that his role should be to encourage risk-taking from their employees. Fear within young people should be recognized, for instance, fear of making a mistake. Nevertheless, not making decisions and taking risks is also an enormous mistake in the ever-changing business environment. According to him, informal communications within the organization and with the CEO is very important for their business success.

2.2.5 Financing and Regulatory Environment Development Needs

In terms of the regulatory environment, very soon the Montenegrin government will be obliged to implement some new EU regulations. The one that may have an impact on Domen is the General Data Protection Regulation on data protection and privacy for all individuals.

2.2.6 Domen: Limitless Opportunities Behind the Limitless Wording Possibilities

Understanding that "me" has multiple meanings and has mass appeal as a word in numerous languages, the Government of Montenegro embarked on generalizing the .me name space so that anyone could obtain a .me. As a result, in November of 2007, a formal public request for proposals was issued to find a registration agent who could provide a world-class registry platform, run operations for an international registry, and deliver marketing expertise to make .me a successful CCTLD worldwide. The contract was eventually awarded to Domen. Due to its deep inherent meaning in multiple languages (English, French, Spanish, Dutch, Italian, Portuguese, Bulgarian, and languages spoken in former Yugoslavia) and limitless wording possibilities, just 3 days after its official launch, .me recorded its 100,000th registration. Me has continued its success through the years with a continuous and stable rise in registrations and more and more big brands connecting to .me and its development program. Despite being a CCTLD, .me is very similar to generic TLDs in terms of policies, domain cycle, and search engine optimization benefits. Most importantly, according to the company's CMO, Google treats it like any other generic TLD.

Since the company sees differentiation as the foundation of business success, Domen started the business with a huge awareness-raising campaign. The company wanted to be seen and recognized by its customers as different. It is trying to satisfy the need for personalization, which is one of the most important characteristics of a new digital customer. An understanding of customer needs and opening of space for both company and individual personalization on the Internet lies at the core of Domen's business strategy.

Domen also differentiates itself by diverging from the usual marketing approach that the competition was using and by starting to market and promote domains directly to customers. That approach was the innovation that gave the company a special strength and a competitive advantage. Due to a lack of internationally competitive local marketing agencies, the company has mostly outsourced and acquired these services outside of Montenegro. However, it would be much easier for Domen to outsource its marketing to the domestic market, which highlights a potential business opportunity for the marketing industry in Montenegro.

The company has also created a safe environment for its customers who are developing their own businesses in the digital world on platforms provided by Domen Ltd. New digital customers need a secure and trusted registry for their domains, and Domen has positioned itself as a reliable and trusted partner, successfully creating strong relationships with customers.

Like many successful companies, Domen believes that the most important factor behind its success is the motivated employees. This company has developed a positive organizational culture that emphasizes employee strengths, individual vitality, and growth. The organizational culture is task-oriented and accompanied by a flat organizational structure. As a consequence, the employees are showing high levels of satisfaction and enthusiasm. This creates a great atmosphere in the company and reflects the leadership continuity.

Another important factor is that the company leaders have a great vision, a lot of knowledge of the market and marketing, and good intuition. They have used appropriate tools for targeting customers, creating brand awareness and image, and maintaining strong relations with customers and partners.

After the first HC research in Montenegro, as a result of the impact of the pandemic caused by the COVID-19 virus and the war in Ukraine, it turned out that the market has changed significantly. On one hand, the trend of digitalization has increased demand for CCTLDs generally. On the other, the demand for domains reflects overall market conditions. This is a consequence of the speculative part of the market—investors are purchasing domains in bulk aiming to sell some of them afterward with a premium. However, in times of crisis, they are rejecting some of the domains in their "portfolio" due to the high costs of holding them. But despite that, it didn't take long until there was a growth trend in the number of sold CCTLDs on an annual level, followed by a similar growth in annual income. This arose from the fact that the Company has become more aggressive in targeting the market because it turned out that previously an insufficient level of aggressiveness led to a drop in overall performance in 2020. Another leadership challenge during and after the pandemic was the inclusion of new employees in Domen when working remotely, which judging by the results, the company has handled successfully. In addition, the crisis period from 2020 has shown that the Domain's main strength lies in its organizational culture because if the organization is adaptable, it can overcome the obstacles ahead.

New trends in the market are positioning the domain as an extension of a specific industry/market niche. For instance, the .io extension is the prime location for the programming industry. Domen ltd. aims to create a niche related to their domain and one of the possible extensions would be influencers when extending from social media to personal websites.

Nevertheless, the Company continues to take into account the consequences of the war in Ukraine, the energy crisis, inflation, dollar–euro ratio and aims to be ready to adapt to the new environment and market conditions.

However, the Company is mostly concerned about the decision of the Government of Montenegro to initiate the procedure of termination of the contract without negotiating the conditions for renewal it, which resulted in an ongoing legal process. The Company hopes that this legal challenge will eventually be resolved to the satisfaction of both parties involved.

3 Conclusions and Recommendations

The clear visions of the founders of Montenegrin's hidden champions were the starting points of the companies' successes. Those visions were the basis for well-chosen and consistently implemented strategies and were developed on a good understanding of their target market customers. The Montenegrin hidden champions' leaders, characterized by strong personalities, intuition, and vision, as well as a passion for the project, led the companies toward the leading market position that they hold in the region. These companies' histories emphasize leadership as a crucial element for market success.

They also see differentiation as the foundation of business success. Because of that, differentiating themselves from their competitors is at the core of the strategies that they have applied. In both companies, managers understand and implement elements of personalization and an individual approach in the service that they provide, knowing that this personalization is an almost mandatory customer request nowadays. This necessity is highlighted by the fact that all the basic instruments utilized for the marketing mix were well-suited to the needs of every single customer. Their new and different approach to customers and promotion, as well as their consistent adaptation of their services to meet their customers' demands, were especially poignant. An additional lesson learned in the recent past, characterized by COVID-19 crises as well as the war in Ukraine, is the need to be more aggressive in targeting the market. In 2020 and 2021, an insufficient level of aggressiveness has led to a drop in overall performance, especially in the case of Domen.

They both regard organizational culture as a very important element of their success. Their task and customer-oriented organizational culture that emphasizes employee strengths and growth resulted in high levels of employee satisfaction and enthusiasm. Both Marina Porto Montenegro and Domen perceive investing in human resources and employee satisfaction as prerequisites to the service that clients expect. The leadership challenge in Domen during the COVID-19 pandemic was the inclusion of new employees in Domen when working remotely. The role of the CEO in that situation is to encourage risk-taking from their employees. Especially because fear within young people could be recognized, for instance, fear of making a mistake. Nevertheless, not making decisions and taking risks is also an enormous mistake in the ever-changing business environment. Informal communication within the organization and with the CEO is of crucial importance in Domen. This understanding is very important since they think that the competition, which usually revolves around customers, is shifting outward to the area of human resources. This problem was initially typical of higher-level positions only but now exists at lower-level positions as well.

The companies also have a good understanding of the local political and legal frameworks and their easy cooperation with the Government and public authorities strengthens their market position. The benefits for companies and public and political authorities are mutual due to the increase in public revenues, volume of exports, decrease in import dependence, growth in the employment rate, development of supporting companies and suppliers, development of entrepreneurship, and promotion of Montenegro. The benefits have led both Marina Porto Montenegro and Domen to be recognized as socially responsible companies. Their corporate social responsibility programs are mainly implemented in the sphere of education, contributing to the development of a new digital generation of customer-oriented employees.

Although they regard the business environment in Montenegro as favorable in general, the financial sector in Montenegro represents a challenge because local banks are limited in their lending capacity, which forces companies to work with foreign banks in case they need to make bigger investments.

Because of the differences in the sectors that they belong to (tourism vs. ICT), these companies have a different understanding of the key business challenges that they face and expect. As Montenegro is one of the fastest-growing tourist destinations and tourism is one of the most important industries in Montenegro, we find it very important to mention some challenges that companies like Marina Porto Montenegro face. They pointed out that infrastructure problems, especially roads, and airports, as well as long lines at border crossings, have a negative impact on the tourism industry in Montenegro.

In the beginning, both companies faced the same challenge, related to the fact that Montenegro was insufficiently recognized in the international market. We are sure that Marina Porto Montenegro and Domen have both helped to elevate the image of Montenegro internationally.

Moreover, both companies find that formal education should be more focused on developing the skills needed for jobs that are essential today (i.e., digital marketing skills) and should stimulate group work and openness to unfamiliar things, especially when it comes to the service industry and ICT: programming and other skills that are important in the era of the digital economy. Thus, we found that a stronger link should exist between educational institutions and the labor market.

In this respect, both companies continuously invest in different educational programs in their local communities through various CSR activities. We identified their pioneer role in promoting the concept of education as a lifelong process as particularly important. It is to be expected that this kind of approach, deeply embedded in their organizational cultures, will motivate other companies in Montenegro to follow in their footsteps.

This study of the hidden champions of Montenegro has resulted in recommendations for key stakeholders, based on key conclusions summarized below.

Summarizing the interviews with the top management of the hidden champions, it is possible to provide several highly important recommendations to the Government. Most of these recommendations relate to the need to solve infrastructure problems that have direct consequences for the quality of Montenegro's business offers, primarily in tourism. In that sense, it is suggested that the Government continues its investments in road infrastructure, airports, and especially border crossings, so as to do away with the bottlenecks that have a negative impact on tourist satisfaction. The hidden champion in the tourism sector also emphasized the intensification of investment in the electrical energy system, water supply, and waste and wastewater treatment systems, especially given the Government's tendency to position Montenegro as an ecological state. In addition, it was recommended that the rate of the reinvested income tax be reduced, as this would certainly greatly stimulate investment, and bring benefits for all.

Focusing on education, inevitably more emphasis should be put on preparing students for work in the era of the digital and service economy. This particularly refers to the development of usable knowledge and skills in the field of management, leadership, and establishing quality relationships with customers. Although certain business schools have made some progress in this area, the hidden champions estimate that it is not enough to meet the needs of successful companies, especially in terms of offering programs for improving the specific knowledge and skills of employees. A special role in this respect belongs to the Government, which should pursue modernization of the educational system at all levels so that it meets the needs of the labor market. In this regard, it would be important to influence, through the education system, the development of an entrepreneurial spirit, as well as information, economic, and financial literacy, and more strongly support the concept of lifelong learning.

These companies recommend that the Government continue to promote Montenegro, aiming to increase recognition in the international market. This is especially important for Porto Montenegro, as how Montenegro is promoted as a tourist destination, affects Porto Montenegro's individual marketing strategy. Although in the post-independence period, major advancements have been made in this respect, and the hidden champions have played an important role, these activities should be continued.

A key recommendation to banks concerns the problem of their limited credit potential, identified in this study as a significantly limiting factor in the banking system. It could be solved by increasing the degree of openness to cooperation with other banks by offering syndicated loans. Therefore, we believe that, whenever it is deemed necessary and mutually beneficial, banks should include elements of cooperation in their competitive struggle, combining competition and cooperation in the way suggested by Brandenburger and Nalebuff (1996) in their book Co-opetition.

Business schools should intensify their cooperation with companies, especially the most successful ones because the benefits of such cooperation are multiple. Through cooperation, problems in companies would be easier to solve, business schools would improve their knowledge, experience, and programs, and graduates would be better prepared to face every day professional problems.

The lack of local consulting agencies in different fields (marketing, programming, human resource management, etc.) can pose an additional challenge for business schools to expand the range of their consulting services. Some of them already use this market niche, but if we take into account the estimate that the demand for this type of service will only increase; a significant market space will continue to exist.

References

Brandenburger, A. M., & Nalebuff, B. (1996). *Co-opetition*. HarperCollins Business.

Central bank of Montenegro official web-site. (2024). Retrieved May 14, 2024, from https://www.cbcg.me/me/publikacije/redovne-publikacije/makroekonomski-izvjestaj-cbcg

Dolasci i noćenja u kolektivnom smještaju 2023. (Monstat, 2024). *Monstat—Statistical office of Montenegro*. Retrieved January 14, 2025, from http://www.monstat.org/userfiles/file/turizam/din2023/12/SAOPSTENJE%20decembar%202018.pdf

Economic impact 2021 Montenegro. (2022). *World Travel & Tourism Council*. Retrieved December 4, 2023, from www.wttc.org/economic-impact/country-analysis/country-reports/

Economic impact 2022 Montenegro. (2023). *World Travel & Tourism Council*. Retrieved August 4, 2024, from www.wttc.org/economic-impact/country-analysis/country-reports/

Fabris, N. (2015). The history of money in Montenegro. *Journal of Central Banking Theory and Practice, 4*(1), 5–18.

Freedom House. (2024). *Montenegro. In Freedom House*. https://freedomhouse.org/country/montenegro/freedomworld/2024?utm_

Gardašević-Slavuljica, A., Lazović, G., Mugoša, J., Kovaćević, M., & Todorović, A. (2022). Montenegro Tourism Development Strategy 2022-2025 with the Action Plan.

Macroeconomic report I-XII 2022. (2023). *Central Bank of Montenegro*. Retrieved May 14, 2024, from www.cbcg.me/en/publications/regular-publications/cbcg-macroeconomic-report/annual-report

Porter, M. E. (1998). *Competitive strategy: Techniques for analysing industries and competitors*. The Free Press.

Porto Montenegro official web-site. Retrieved October 14, 2023., from www.portomoontenegro.me

Schwab, K., Zahidi, S., & World Economic Forum. (2020). The Global Competitiveness Report Special Edition 2020: How Countries are Performing on the Road to Recovery. *World Economic Forum*. https://www3.weforum.org/docs/WEF_TheGlobalCompetitivenessReport2020.pdf
Simon, H. (2009). *Hidden champions of twenty first century*. Springer.

Prof. Dr. Milorad Jovović is a Full Professor of Management and Marketing at the Faculty of Economics, University of Montenegro in Podgorica. He was born on January 18th, 1966.

He completed his undergraduate studies at the Faculty of Economics in Podgorica. He finished his Master's studies at the Faculty of Economics, University of Belgrade, and obtained his PhD in 2004 at the Faculty of Economics, University of Montenegro.

He has participated in numerous research and professional development programs at several universities across Europe and the United States, where he also held lectures.

From 2006 to 2012, he served as the Dean of the Faculty of Economics. Throughout his career, he has held high-level positions in the Government of Montenegro (such as Secretary General of the Ministry of Foreign Affairs and Deputy Chief of Mission of Montenegro to the European Union 1998–2001), the Central Bank of Montenegro (as a member of the Council 2010–2025), and several business enterprises (as a member of the Board of Directors).

He has also been active in the NGO sector, working with the American NGO IREX (International Research & Exchanges Board) at their office in Podgorica. Additionally, he worked as a lead researcher in public opinion research agencies.

His primary areas of interest include research into business practices of companies in Montenegro, particularly in the fields of customer satisfaction and employee satisfaction. He has published a significant number of scientific and research papers in reputable international journals. He speaks, reads, and writes English and Italian fluently.

Bojana Femić-Radosavović is the Executive Director of the Innovation Fund of Montenegro since the establishment of that institution in September 2021. She is also a member of the National Council for Sustainable Development of Montenegro and a Vice-Chairperson of the Bureau of the Committee on Innovation, Competitiveness and Public–Private Partnerships (CICPPP) at the United Nations Economic Commission for Europe (UNECE). Additionally, Bojana is a Visiting Lecturer at the University of Montenegro, teaching at the Faculty of Political Sciences. She holds a PhD in Economics. As a PR manager, Bojana has strong communication skills. She has participated in many conferences and seminars and published several articles. She speaks English and has good knowledge of Spanish.

Nikola Mišnić is a Teaching Assistant at the Faculty of Economics, University of Montenegro, where he has worked since 2015. He teaches courses in management, organization, and marketing, and is actively involved in academic research and international collaboration. Currently, he is pursuing a PhD focusing on project management in renewable energy, with an emphasis on solar power development in Montenegro.

Nikola has participated in academic exchanges and research programs at institutions across Europe, including the University of Natural Resources and Life Sciences, Vienna (BOKU), the University of Covilhã (Portugal), the University of Life Sciences in Warsaw (Poland), and the University of Ljubljana (Slovenia). These experiences have contributed to his interdisciplinary research approach and broadened his international academic engagement.

His scholarly contributions include articles and conference papers in the fields of energy economics and organizational behavior. Selected works include: "Financial viability of integrating storage capacity within a solar power plant" (2023), "The Economic Viability of PV Power Plant Based on a Neural Network Model of Electricity Prices Forecast" (Energies, 2022), and "Analysis of public attitudes and perceptions towards renewable energy sources in Montenegro" (Energy Reports, 2020). He also co-authored a chapter in the Springer monograph Hidden Champions of Montenegro. In addition to his academic work, Nikola provides consulting services in the areas of business planning, feasibility analysis, and cost–benefit evaluation, primarily focused on sustainable energy and infrastructure projects.

Jovan Đurašković is an Assistant Professor and Vice Dean for Scientific Research and Strategic Development at the Faculty of Economics, University of Montenegro. He earned his PhD in Macroeconomic Theory and Policy from the same institution in 2014. His research focuses on economic analysis and policy, with particular interest in state interventionism, health economics, labor markets, and social policy. He is also interested in the development and transformative potential of Montenegrin companies, especially in the context of structural change and sustainable growth. During his doctoral studies, he completed a research stay at the City University of New York (The Graduate Center). He has also delivered guest lectures through Erasmus+ exchange programs at the University of Beira Interior (Portugal) and the University of Rijeka (Croatia). Dr. Đurašković has authored numerous scientific articles, monographs, and conference papers. He has led or participated in international research projects funded by UNDP, UNICEF, ILO, Erasmus+, and Horizon programs, contributing to the study of the Montenegrin economy and broader issues of economic policy.

Ksenija Jovović was born in Cetinje in 1999. She completed her primary education at "Maksim Gorki" Elementary School and graduated from "Slobodan Škerović" High School as a recipient of the "Luča" award for outstanding academic achievement. She earned her bachelor's degree from the University of Donja Gorica, Faculty of International Economics, Finance and Business, with an average grade of 9.71. During her undergraduate studies, she participated in numerous faculty projects and was a member of the Operational Team at the Student Business Center. She completed her Master's studies at the University of Ljubljana, School of Economics and Business, in October 2023, defending her thesis with the highest grade (10). Her thesis topic was: Application of Neuroscience in Human Resource Management: Evidence from Companies Operating in the Western Balkans. In March 2025, she received the Prešeren Award from the University of Ljubljana, School of Economics and Business. Since May 2025, she has been a member of the Beta Gamma Sigma honor society. She is fluent in English and holds a Cambridge English Level 2 Certificate in ESOL International (Advanced C1). She also has a working knowledge of Italian, both spoken and written. She began her professional career in 2021 at APEX Capital Partners, where she worked as an assistant in the Economic Citizenship Program. Since September 2023, she has been employed as an Assistant Manager at the Innovation Fund of Montenegro. As of May 2025, she holds the position of Senior Advisor in the Department of Applicant Support.

Hidden Champions of Morocco

Oumaima Chamchati, Sofia Arougay, and Mohamed Nabil El Mabrouki

Abstract This chapter focuses on hidden champions from Morocco, a North African country that has undergone remarkable developments and transformations in recent decades. It examines three enterprises operating in distinct industrial sectors: lighting and electricity, the plastics industry, and construction and public works.

These companies share common attributes that distinguish them as true hidden champions in Morocco. They primarily operate in B2B sectors, have strong entrepreneurial origins, demonstrate exceptional strategic resilience, adopt a customer-centric approach, show high adaptability, and employ effective risk management strategies.

The chapter begins with an overview of Morocco's historical context and economic landscape, followed by an exploration of the unique characteristics that define Moroccan hidden champions. Each case study is meticulously analyzed, highlighting their individual paths to success and their significant impact within their respective industries.

O. Chamchati (✉)
HEM Research Center, Rabat, Morocco
e-mail: Oumaima.Chamchati@lcieducation.onmicrosoft.com

S. Arougay
Cadi Ayyad University, Marrakesh, Morocco
e-mail: s.arougay.ced@uca.ac.ma

M. N. El Mabrouki
HEM Research Center, Rabat, Morocco

Cadi Ayyad University, Marrakesh, Morocco
e-mail: mo.elmabrouki@uca.ma

D. Berberović, D. Purg (eds.), *Hidden Champions in Rising Economies*, Contributions to Management Science,
https://doi.org/10.1007/978-3-032-08263-3_29

Overview

Official name: The Kingdom of Morocco

Type of government: Parliamentary constitutional monarchy

Population in 2023: 37,840,044

Land area: 710,850 km^2

History

788–1666	Morocco was ruled by the following dynasties: Idrisid (788), Almoravid (1070), Almohad (1147), Marinid (1269), Saadian (1578), and Alaouite (1666 to today).
1912	Signing of the treaty of fez, establishing the French protectorate in Morocco.
1927	Mohammed V becomes sultan of Morocco.
1930s–1940s	Development of commercial agriculture, especially citrus and cereal cultivation, as well as mining, particularly phosphates.
1956	Independence of Morocco from France and Spain.
1961	Hassan II becomes king of Morocco after the death of Mohammed V.
1960s–1970s	Policies of industrial and agricultural development, with the creation of large public companies.
1973	Start of the *Moroccanization* of foreign companies, aiming to transfer their ownership to Moroccan citizens.
1975	Green march, a peaceful march for the recovery of Western Sahara.
1993	Reforms of the financial sector and opening of the Casablanca stock exchange to foreign investments.
1999	Mohammed VI becomes king of Morocco.
2000	Launch of the emergence plan, aiming to diversify the Moroccan economy and promote industrial and technological sectors.
2004–2005	Reform of the family code (Moudawana), strengthening women's rights in marriage, divorce, and child custody, and the launch of the National Initiative for human development (INDH), aiming to reduce poverty, social inequalities, and promote sustainable development.
2007	Start of the implementation of major industrial projects, notably with the arrival of Renault-Nissan in Tangier.
2008	Inauguration of the Tanger-med port, becoming a major logistics hub for international trade.
2011	Revision of the Moroccan constitution, introducing reforms to increase civil liberties, human rights, and strengthen democracy.
2013	Launch of the green Morocco plan, aiming to modernize the agricultural sector and improve agricultural production, and the launch of Morocco's African strategy, aiming to strengthen economic and political relations with African countries.
2014	Adoption of the renewable energy development strategy, with major projects such as the Noor solar complex in Ouarzazate.
2016	Launch of the industrial development strategy (PNEI), aiming to strengthen industrialization and attract FDI.
2017	Official reintegration of Morocco into the African union, marking a turning point in its African policy.

2018	Signing of the African continental free trade area (AfCFTA) agreement, underscoring its commitment to promoting intra-African trade.
2020	Launch of the special fund for the management of the COVID-19 pandemic, raising billions of dirhams to support economic sectors and vulnerable populations.
2022	Announcement of the National Green Hydrogen Strategy, aiming to position Morocco as a key player in the production and export of green hydrogen.

1 Introduction: Context and History

Nestled at the north-western tip of Africa, Morocco's geographical diversity and rich historical heritage are two essential factors in defining the nation's identity. From a geographical standpoint, the Moroccan Kingdom is marked by a striking diversity of landscapes. Its borders cover a coastline that runs along both the Atlantic Ocean and the Mediterranean Sea, turning it into a crucial crossroads between Africa and Europe (El Khanchoufi et al., 2024). The Atlas Mountains across Morocco embodies the High Atlas, Middle Atlas, and Anti-Atlas, split the nation into distinct areas, each with its own climate and topography. The fertile plains along the coast contrast with the arid expanses of the Sahara Desert to the south. Covering a diverse area of 710,850 km^2, Morocco contains 12 different regions, each with its own unique charm (High Commission for Planning, 2019). The capital Rabat is steeped in history and culture; while Casablanca, the largest city, boasts a dynamic modernity. More than 37 million inhabitants live in Morocco and are mostly Muslim Arabs and Berbers known for their family' attachment and warm hospitality (World Bank, 2023). Marrakech for example, stands out as an emblematic tourist destination. Known as the "Red City," Marrakech is a crossroads of crafts, music, and traditional architecture, offering an immersive experience of Moroccan culture. Hence, tourism plays a significant role in the Moroccan economy. In 2023, Morocco welcomed 14.5 million tourists, a remarkable increase of more than 34% compared to 2022 (Ministry of Tourism, Crafts and the Social Solidarity Economy, 2024).

From an economic history standpoint, Morocco bridges harmoniously the ancient and modern coexist offering visitors a captivating immersion in its evolving thousand-year-old history. Despite being double colonized by France and Spain for 45 years (from 1912 to 1956), Morocco has not only regained its independence, but has also reshaped its economic landscape and strengthened its strategic position over the years. Morocco's economic environment is relatively liberal, guided by the forces of supply and demand. From the 1990s onward, Morocco embarked on a policy of privatizing public economic sectors. As a result, it has become a major player in the African entrepreneurial world, as evidenced by its position as the continent's fifth-largest economy in terms of Gross Domestic Product (GDP). State policies and steady annual growth averaging 4–5% between 2000 and 2007, including an impressive 4.9% year-on-year growth in the period 2003–2007, have boosted the Moroccan economy from its previous state. Today, Morocco ranks in fourth place among 48 African countries in terms of GDP (World Bank, 2023). Despite the challenging COVID-19 situation and its economic consequences resulting in a 7.2% decline in GDP growth by 2020, Morocco has regained its footing by 2021, recording growth of around 8%. According to World Bank data, Morocco's GDP has grown steadily from around US$43.02 billion in 2000 to over US$121.35 billion in 2020 and US$141.11 billion in 2023. This progression attests to Morocco's ongoing efforts to stimulate its economic activity.

In terms of foreign trade, Morocco has established strong economic ties, with a particular focus on imports and exports. Morocco's exports have seen an intense increase of 4.4% in Mai 2024 compared to Mai 2023, and reach US$19.41 billion (Foreign Exchange Office, 2024). Exports, particularly in the agri-food, phosphates and automotive sectors, have made a significant contribution to economic growth. In 2023, Morocco's exports of goods and services have generated more than 44% of GDP. Interestingly, the services sector accounts for just over half of GDP, while industry, which includes mining, construction and manufacturing, contributes a further quarter. The most important growth sectors are tourism, telecommunications, information technology and textiles; highlighting Morocco's diverse and dynamic economic landscape. This strategic diversification and steady growth underline Morocco's commitment to fostering a robust and resilient economic environment and most importantly, a paradise for foreign investors.

Morocco has introduced reforms to improve its business climate, as illustrated by its position in the World Bank's "Doing Business" ranking. The country ranked 53rd out of 190 economies in 2020, reflecting continued improvements in the ease of doing business (Doing Business, 2020). Consequently, fiscal taxation is one of the reforms adopted to balance revenue mobilization and growth support. The tax revenues portray 19.7% of Morocco' GDP.

All these economic advantages make Morocco particularly attractive as a location for a wide range of businesses, from large corporations to small- and medium-sized enterprises (SMEs) and very small enterprises. SMEs, innovation and employment driven, have become an increasingly important part of the Moroccan economic landscape. According to the High Commission for Planning (2019), SMEs account for 95% of the national economic fabric, making them the backbone of our nation's development. Among these SMEs, a particular type of company with specific features is emerging as global successfully economic leaders, able not only to compete with large corporations but also to maintain their leadership position over the very long term. Despite their economic, social, and political significance power in their own countries, these companies remain little known to the general public, and are known as hidden champions (Exhibits 1 and 2).

Exhibit 1 Core economic indicators for Morocco

	2015	2016	2017	2018	2019	2020	2021	2022	2023	2024
GDP per capita (current $US)	3139.23	3132.95	3288.50	3492.67	3498.58	3258.27	3767.52	3442.0	3771.45	…
GDP per capita growth (annual %)	4.30	0.50	5.10	3.10	2.90	−7.20	8.00	1.30	2.34	…
Unemployment rate (% of total unemployment)	9.50	9.30	9.20	9.20	9.20	11.11	10.50	9.50	9.04	8.94
Foreign direct investment, net inflows (% of GDP)	2.90	1.90	2.30	2.80	1.30	1.20	1.60	1.70	0.76	…
GDP (current $US m)	110,413.8	111,572.9	118,540.6	127,341.1	128,920.3	121,353.6	141,817.8	130,912.6	144417.10	…
Exports of goods and services (current $US m)	33,119.57	34,291.49	38,651.89	43,077.52	43,952.86	37,369.77	47,060.55	58,661.45	61741.32	…
Exports of goods and services (% of GDP)	29.91	30.73	32.60	33.82	34.10	30.80	33.20	44.80	42.75	…
Merchandise exports (current $US m)	22,334.00	22,661.00	25,272.00	28,609.00	29,132.00	27,159.00	35,843.00	41,481.00	41,642	…
Merchandise exports to high income economies (% of total merchandise exports)	70.75	73.64	73.92	73.35	73.84	75.83	n/a	n/a	78.15	…
Merchandise exports to low- and middle-income economies in Europe & Central Asia (%of total merchandise exports)	4.31	4.71	4.43	3.15	3.42	3.50	n/a	n/a	3.01	…
Ores and metals exports (% of merchandise exports)	8.16	6.41	7.03	6.17	5.43	5.49	5.89	5.90	4.41	…
Agricultural raw materials exports (% of merchandise exports)	0.95	0.94	0.83	0.71	0.78	0.83	0.65	1.00	0.62	…
Food exports (% of merchandise exports)	20.30	20.87	21.12	20.62	21.17	23.09	20.70	19.00	18.9	…
Fuel exports (% of merchandise exports)	1.93	0.85	0.91	1.16	1.51	0.51	0.69	1.00	1.21	…
Manufactures exports (% of merchandise exports)	68.22	70.39	69.83	70.94	70.89	69.90	71.94	73.00	74.75	…
High-technology exports (% of manufactured exports)	3.70	3.74	4.00	4.00	5.00	4.00	4.00	4.00	5.43	…

Source: World Bank (2025)

Exhibit 2 Moroccan Hidden Champions

Name	Market leadership definition	Revenue 2021 (in €m)	Revenue 2012 (in €m)	Average employees 2021
Inadis	One among the leaders in the lighting market in Morocco. The market share exceeds 10% nationwide.	12.20	1.5	80
PlastikPack	Moroccan leader in the manufacture of plastic packaging. It is part of the European group, PlasticPack, leader in the field of extrusion, blow molding and injection. The market share is over 30% in Morocco.	11.00	n/a	60
Seprob	The first manufacturer of engineering structures in Morocco. The company is one of the oldest companies in the construction sector in Morocco.	16.00	37.00	600

Source: Data published and reported by the company

2 Characteristics of Hidden Champions from Morocco

Hidden champions are generally small- and medium-sized enterprises, often considered family businesses (Simon, 1996). They are described as innovation-driven, single-product makers with long-term goals and visions. Although their success, strong export performance, global orientation and excellent market position, most of these companies are unknown to the large public. Thus, the research on hidden champions have become constantly more central, fundamental, and relevant recently. Several papers have contributed importantly to the hidden champions' literature; however, to the best of our knowledge, no previous study was undertaken in the African context. Hence, we especially lack evidence on the emergence and development of hidden champions in Morocco—a rising economy. The following section provides a thorough analysis of three Moroccan hidden champions: Inadis, Seprob, and PlastikPack. To identify our sample, we have followed the SME definition in Morocco. According to the national SME agency (ANPME), currently known as Maroc-PME, there are three types of enterprises: very small enterprise (sales revenues is less than three million MAD), small enterprise (sales revenues is sales revenues is between 3 and ten million MAD), and medium-sized enterprise (between 10 and 175 million MAD). In our case, we analyzed the top Annual ranking of Moroccan industrial, financial, and service companies published by Economie Entreprises in 2022, focusing more on the following selection criteria: sales revenues less than 175 million MAD, operating in a niche market, existence for more than 5 years, low visibility and leading some exports activities. We were able to identify 63 companies that matched our criteria, and after contacting them, three Hidden champions agreed to welcome us to take part in the study. More details on these companies are provided in Appendix 2.

The literature on hidden champions states that this concept is widely used to describe a specific category of SMEs that not only succeed on a global scale, but also outperform large corporations with their sustained profitability and high growth rates (Venohr & Kamp, 2019). Simon (2009) points out that hidden champions often share more similarities with each other than with large companies in their own countries. Our analysis of three medium-sized Moroccan hidden champions—Inadis, Seprob, and PlastikPack—confirms this observation, highlighting common characteristics with their global counterparts. These companies illustrate how Moroccan businesses can not only survive, but also thrive in competitive sectors through strategic planning and continuous innovation.

Hidden champions always distinguish themselves by specializing in specific market segments rather than engaging in broader competition (Simon, 2009). They target specialized and often overlooked niches in order to better understand their customers' unique needs, enabling them to provide highly customized products or services. This focus permits them to build customer loyalty and maintain a significant competitive edge. Indeed, Inadis specializes in customized customer relationship management solutions tailored to the particular requirements of the Moroccan market, emphasizing responsiveness and adaptability in service delivery. Seprob excels in the niche sector of complex infrastructure and industrial civil engineering projects, thanks to its technical expertise and meticulous project management capabilities that set it apart from its major competitors; whereas PlastikPack, dominates the niche market for high-quality HDPE packaging solutions, exploiting advanced technologies and sustainable practices to respond effectively to specific industry requirements. Hence, operating in niche markets enables hidden champions to differentiate themselves from their more generalist competitors and reinforce their perception as experts in their chosen field.

Interestingly, hidden champions seek to expand their activities abroad, but in a well-considered way. Their strategy is based on a dual paradigm: concentration on a niche market and international expansion (Johann et al., 2022). At the same time, the three cases of this study have adopted unique approaches to effectively penetrate global markets, ranging from strategic partnerships and alliances to participation in international projects, as well as investment in overseas production facilities to meet the needs of foreign markets. Above all characteristics of hidden champions, innovation is at the heart of their growth strategy (Din et al., 2013). These companies have integrated cutting-edge technologies and developed tailor-made solutions to meet the specific requirements of the Moroccan market, strengthening their competitiveness and resilience in the face of economic fluctuations and regulatory changes. Their competitive edge is based on efficient resource management and operational excellence.

There are many lessons to be learned from these hidden champions. They have learned to be agile and responsive to market changes, investing in the continuous development of their internal capabilities and strengthening their capacity for innovation in order to maintain a sustainable competitive edge. What's more, these companies recognize the crucial importance of strong management and leadership, particularly in crisis management and international expansion.

The following section will allow us to further explore the characteristics of these companies.

3 Case Studies of Selected Hidden Champions

3.1 Inadis

Overview

Address: 29, Rue Al Oukhouane, Beauséjour, Casablanca, Morocco
Tel: +212522360898
Fax: +212522360906
Email: fathi.benhatira@inadis.ma
Web: http://www.amlashpk.com

Company Information

Industry: Lighting and electricity
Year of establishment: 2012
Sales revenues in 2021: € 12.2 MIO
Sales revenues in 2012: € 1.5 MIO
Average number employees in 2021: 80
Brain(s) behind the company: The founder Fathi Benhatira

3.1.1 Nature of Market Leadership

Inadis or Inara Distribution is a Moroccan small- and medium-sized company that specialized in the sale of lighting products. It is one of the leaders in the lighting market in Morocco. After a long experience, as an employee in the field of import/export of lighting fixtures, its founder decided in 2012 to embark on the adventure of entrepreneurship in partnership with two brothers Mohamed and Abdelouahed Filali Chahad, owners of the Bricoma Group specialized in DIY (Do it yourself) in Morocco. The lighting sector was flourishing at the time and the three young entrepreneurs seized the opportunity. The co-founder of the company Mr. Fathi estimates that the market share of Inadis is now 10% at the national level. Their products are exposed through two points of sales: Luxalight and Bricoma, and they have 10 franchises across Morocco and three stores in Casablanca. Yet, the company no longer markets its products only in Morocco; but in partnership with its German supplier Brillant and its local partner Bricoma. Inadis has decided to enter the sub-Saharan market. This market represented, in 2022, 5% of its global turnover.

3.1.2 Nature of Competitive Advantage

Inadis sets itself apart from competitors by two criteria. The first criterion is the offer. Inadis offers a wide range of products and services at reasonable prices. The second criterion is a strong business network. The company has established long-term partnerships with the best operators in its field. Brilliant, a supplier of quality German lighting products and Bricoma, a locally and internationally recognized distributor of DIY products.

3.1.3 Core Lessons Learned on the Path to Success

- **Embrace the Philosophy: Your Success is Our Success.** Ensuring customer satisfaction is synonymous with entrepreneurial satisfaction. Prioritizing the customer's advantage builds loyalty, ultimately securing the business's success. Taking complete responsibility for the offered product is essential in this regard.
- **Motivate Employees with a Bonus Policy.** Fostering employee motivation through a bonus policy plays a crucial role in the company's long-term viability. A motivated team actively engages in their work, leading to enhanced overall performance.
- **Focus on Local Growth Before International Expansion.** Instead of seeking international markets prematurely, focus on significant growth opportunities within your own country. Pursuing foreign growth prematurely can undermine the stability of the business; capturing local potential should be prioritized over global expansion.

3.1.4 Management and Leadership Development Needs

Benhatira, highlights the crucial need for management and leadership development in his company. There is a clear gap between the skills provided by business schools and those required in the workplace. More specifically, graduates often lack the skills adapted to the job market, often limiting themselves to sales techniques without any real understanding of market needs. Benhatira insists on the importance of recruiting salespeople not only for their technical skills, but also for their intrinsic passion and ambition, stressing that sales success stems from a passion for the job, not simply the pursuit of immediate profit. Benhatira identifies sales staff as a department requiring further training, particularly when it comes to their interactions with customers in the front office, where specific interpersonal and behavioral skills are crucial. Finally, although his company prefers bank financing, he recognizes the importance of self-financing to ensure financial sustainability and long-term growth.

3.1.5 Financing and Regulatory Environment Development Needs

According to Benhatira, there is no need for any specific development in terms of financing or regulatory environment. He firmly defends self-financing through results as the main driving force behind the growth and development of his company, Inadis. His commitment is reflected in his close collaboration with banking institutions, facilitating loans of several million dirhams, thus strengthening Inadis' ability to invest substantially in the expansion and optimization of its activities. This strategy significantly multiplied Inadis' initial capital. Benhatira emphasizes that this financing model, anchored in operational viability, not only ensures growth but also consolidates the company's financial stability, positioning it favorably in a competitive and dynamic economic environment.

3.1.6 Resilience and Strategic Adaptation Amid Global Crises: COVID-19 and the War in Ukraine

The company has demonstrated remarkable resilience and strategic adaptability in the face of two major global disruptions: the COVID-19 pandemic and the ongoing Russia–Ukraine conflict. During the COVID-19 crisis, the company experienced cash flow constraints due to the mandatory closure of its retail outlets for 2 months, despite receiving support from government financial assistance programs, specifically Oxygène and Relance. However, through prudent management, the company continued its import activities while many competitors suspended theirs, building substantial inventory. This decision, aligned with the non-perishable nature of lighting products, positioned the company advantageously when markets reopened, allowing it to respond swiftly to renewed demand. Consequently, the company recorded only a limited revenue decline of 6%, significantly outperforming the broader market, which faced declines of 20–30%, before rebounding with a 28% growth in 2021. Furthermore, the company proceeded with a strategic investment in a new facility worth 26 million dirhams during the pandemic, reflecting its confidence in long-term growth prospects, and maintained stable pricing despite rising transport costs, thereby retaining customer loyalty while expanding its market share.

Similarly, the Russia–Ukraine war has impacted the company indirectly, primarily through significant increases in raw material costs driven by global energy disruptions and supply chain constraints. Key materials such as glass, steel, and aluminum experienced sharp price hikes, with glass prices increasing by up to 60%. While the COVID-19 pandemic primarily affected the company through rising logistics costs, the Ukraine conflict disrupted gas supplies, further intensifying production cost pressures for the company's suppliers. In response, the company has reinforced its managerial philosophy of prioritizing the enterprise's long-term sustainability over short-term personal gains. This approach is evident in its compensation strategy, favoring performance-based bonuses over fixed salary increases, thereby aligning employee incentives with the company's financial health while preserving operational flexibility in volatile environments. The company also employs a nuanced performance evaluation system across its 10 Luxalight stores and franchise network in Morocco, assessing relative performance against broader market trends to maintain motivation and accountability.

Overall, the key lesson derived from both the COVID-19 pandemic and the Ukraine conflict is the necessity for business leaders to prioritize the reinforcement of their enterprise's foundation to ensure long-term viability. By maintaining a forward-looking, disciplined management approach, the company has preserved its resilience, captured market opportunities, and strengthened its position as a hidden champion within the lighting sector, even amid global crises.

3.1.7 Inadis: A Discreet Leader in Lighting Solutions

Inadis' success story is rooted in the entrepreneurial spirit of its founder, Fathi Benhatira, a former sales and export director at Ingelec, a Moroccan electrical equipment company. The inception of Inadis stems from a personal experience, where Benhatira, facing challenges in equipping his apartment, identified a gap in the market. In the late 1990s, the Casablanca market offered limited choices at exorbitant prices, prompting him to seek alternatives overseas. During a business trip to Italy, he discovered the vibrant world of lighting, inspiring him to bring a similar experience to Morocco. This led to the creation of his first venture, Promodel, which specialized in lighting and became the market leader for a decade. However, due to mismanagement, Promodel eventually failed. Undeterred by setbacks, Benhatira made a comeback by founding Inadis (short for Inara Distribution), a company exclusively dedicated to lighting.

What makes Inadis a hidden champion lies in its unique competitive advantages and effective strategies. The company excels in managing product life cycles, keeping its offerings dynamic and responsive to changing market trends by introducing 300 to 350 new products annually and thoughtfully retiring those at the end of their life cycle. Inadis strengthens its market presence by strategically combining the Luxalight and Bricoma networks and utilizing feedback and efficient delivery systems to meet customer demands effectively. Additionally, Inadis adopts a prudent approach to international expansion, maintaining a modest export rate of 5% to consolidate its dominance in Morocco before venturing abroad. The company's resilience and adaptability, especially during the COVID-19 pandemic, are evident through strategic investments in new premises and maintaining optimal stock levels to prepare for market resurgence. Furthermore, Inadis' financial management, characterized by close collaboration with banks and strategic reinvestment of profits, highlights its sound fiscal practices. This comprehensive approach underscores Inadis' position as a hidden champion in the Moroccan business landscape.

3.2 PlastikPack

Overview
Address: 207-1 PARC, Sidi Bou Othmane 43303, Marrakech, Morocco
Tel: +212682232605
Email: contact@plastikpack com
Web: https://plastikpack.ma/

Company Information
Industry: Plastics industry
Year of establishment: 2015
Sales revenues in 2021: € 11 MIO
Sales revenues in 2015: € 1.2 MIO
Average number employees in 2021: 60
Brain(s) behind the company: Members of two families: LAKHMIRI and ARMANDO

3.2.1 Nature of Market Leadership

PlastikPack Morocco is a small- and medium-sized enterprise founded in 2015, specializing in the manufacture of plastic packaging. It is part of the European Plastic Pack group, a leader in extrusion, blow molding, and injection. The group also has locations in France, Poland, Slovenia, Italy, Germany, and one soon in Spain. PlastikPack Morocco operates on a Business-to-Business basis, serving large companies in the oil, chemical, and food industries, primarily manufacturing drums and crates. In Morocco, the founders estimate that they currently hold 30% of the market, with around 10% in injection molding and 20% in blow molding. Recently, PlastikPack Maroc has been investing in renewable energy, planning to replace a significant portion of its energy consumption with greener alternatives. This initiative aims to reduce its carbon footprint by 1253 tons of CO_2 per year, positioning the company as a sustainable player in the market.

3.2.2 Nature of Competitive Advantage

PlastikPack Maroc stands out in Morocco's plastic packaging industry thanks to its strong partnership with a leading French group known for advanced technology in blow molding and injection. This partnership enabled a crucial technology transfer that kickstarted PlastikPack's operations. The Moroccan founders' industry connections and family background in a similar B2B market were also key in building their customer base.

With the support of international institutions such as the European Bank for Reconstruction and Development, PlastikPack expanded its production capabilities to meet growing customer needs. Their competitive edge lies in producing lighter products, using faster and more energy-efficient machinery, and increasing storage capacity. These factors set PlastikPack apart from other Moroccan companies in the same sector.

3.2.3 Core Lessons Learned on the Path to Success

1. In niche markets like PlastikPack's, setting up subsidiaries abroad to serve foreign customers requires having local partners who can assist with administrative tasks, navigate regulatory requirements, and foster relationships with local stakeholders effectively.
2. Location is crucial in industrial sectors; it must offer affordable costs and access to nearby human resources.
3. Even if the company is family-owned, recruitment should prioritize meritocracy over familial connections.

3.2.4 Management and Leadership Development Needs

PlastikPack originated from SC Pack, a European holding active in countries like France, Poland, and Germany, with plans to expand to Spain. It manufactures drums for oil and chemicals and crates for sectors like agri-food and beverages, serving clients such as Coca-Cola and Pepsi. The company grows internationally via subsidiaries—PlastikPack France, Germany, Morocco, and soon Senegal—favoring local setups over exports due to logistical efficiency. Its consistent global strategy relies on the same French partner, with Senegal chosen for its cultural and geographic advantages to attract and support international clients. PlastikPack faces significant challenges, including informal business practices, financial stability concerns, and the need to meet growing demand for high-quality, technically sophisticated products in a capital-intensive industry. Situated in Sidi Bou Othmane, 40 km from Marrakech, the company benefits from lower land costs and ample space availability. Despite these advantages, CEO Saad underscores ongoing developmental needs, particularly in enhancing technical capabilities and attracting skilled human resources. Attracting qualified professionals to Sidi Bou Othmane remains an ongoing priority and challenge for the company.

3.2.5 Financing and Regulatory Environment Development Needs

In terms of financing and regulatory environment development needs, PlastikPack adopts a balanced financial strategy, leveraging a combination of bank loans and internal funds. CEO Lakhmiri Saad indicates that approximately 35–40% of investments are self-financed, underscoring the company's financial robustness and strategic foresight. Recently, the company also secured approval for a loan from the EBRD, which supports PlastikPack's expansion and the establishment of new industrial units, emphasizing a commitment to integrating eco-friendly practices through the use of recycled materials.

In light of these development projects, company leaders acknowledge strong governmental support. Local authorities, notably the Regional Investment Center (CRI) and the municipality, have demonstrated receptiveness and sensitivity toward the company's development initiatives, expressing a genuine willingness to provide support. This support is reflected in continuous encouragement, the facilitation of administrative procedures (particularly regarding land acquisition), and the absence of significant obstacles, despite a slight level of bureaucracy deemed normal. Overall, this engagement has created a favorable and enabling institutional environment, which has encouraged the company to pursue its new projects while reinforcing its satisfaction with its relationship with local public actors.

3.2.6 Resilience and Growth Amid Global Crises

The company, operating in the industrial plastics sector with a focus on food packaging, demonstrated notable resilience and growth during the COVID-19 crisis. Contrary to many industries that faced severe disruptions, the company experienced two exceptional years in terms of revenue, driven by a significant surge in demand for food products in Morocco, fueled by consumer fears of shortages and increased consumption patterns during the pandemic. This heightened demand translated into an increased need for packaging among the company's clients, resulting in substantial growth in sales and unprecedented levels of investment during the COVID-19 period. As a result, the pandemic did not represent a crisis for the company but rather an opportunity to strengthen its market position and expand its operational capacities in response to heightened demand.

In contrast, the ongoing Russia–Ukraine conflict has exerted indirect pressures on the company, primarily through price volatility in raw materials. The conflict led to speculation and fluctuations in material prices, with instances of price increases reaching 20% within short periods. To maintain stable margins, the company has passed these price variations onto its customers while ensuring the continuity of supply by strategically managing its raw material inventory. Despite global uncertainties, the company reported no significant disruptions in its supply chain and maintained operational continuity, emphasizing that the demand for essential products persists regardless of macroeconomic conditions, thereby sustaining the need for packaging solutions.

Overall, the company's experience during these global crises highlights the importance of agile supply chain management and market responsiveness in maintaining operational resilience. By anticipating fluctuations in raw material availability and aligning investment decisions with market demand, the company has not only preserved but also strengthened its market position within the industrial plastics sector, demonstrating the sector's critical role in supporting essential goods supply chains during periods of global instability.

3.2.7 Hidden Champion: PlastikPack's Rise in Plastic Packaging Excellence

PlastikPack, a family-owned enterprise situated in the Marrakech region since its inception in 2015, has emerged as a notable force in the plastic packaging industry. A collaborative venture between the Lakhmiri and Armando families, the company's foray into blow molding and injection processes signifies a commitment to diverse plastic transformation methods. PlastikPack's exclusive use of high-density polyethylene (HDPE) as its primary raw material underscores its focus on quality and standardization.

Delving into market dynamics, PlastikPack navigates distinct markets, producing drums and crates. While estimating market share in blow molding proves challenging due to the parallel nature of the market, the company approximates a significant 30% market share among players of similar size in injection molding. Expansion plans in Africa, starting with Senegal, indicate a strategic vision to replicate domestic success on a broader scale. In fact, the key catalysts for PlastikPack's rapid market penetration lie in fortuitous technical alliances and substantial investments. The company's association with PlastikPack France, recognized as one of Europe's premier blow-molding facilities, positioned it advantageously. This advantageous network, coupled with continuous and substantial investments, enabled PlastikPack to swiftly gain market share.

PlastikPack' competitive advantage not only lies in its partnership with the French group and above its strong network relations but also stems from its internal resources. Above all, innovation stands as a cornerstone of PlastikPack's operations. The company pioneers lighter, more efficient packaging with superior technical–mechanical qualities. The deployment of faster and more productive machines, coupled with a focus on energy efficiency, positions PlastikPack competitively in terms of pricing. Beyond financial metrics, PlastikPack's success is intertwined with its human resources. The company boasts a small yet versatile team, comprising, consisting of around 60 individuals encompassing technicians, engineers, administrators, packers, guards, couriers, and supply chain personnel. The emphasis on customer-centricity, flexible delivery, and continuous improvement showcases a commitment to holistic customer satisfaction. With young individuals proficient in their respective domains, PlastikPack operates as a cohesive unit applying a participatory management style.

Looking ahead, PlastikPack remains optimistic about Morocco's economic development, envisioning it as a favorable environment for growth. The company's hope is anchored in the belief that large corporations, particularly exemplified by OCP (Phosphate Office), will catalyze a supportive ecosystem. While OCP currently represents a minor percentage of Plastique Pack's sales, there is a strategic optimism that future developments will lead to increased collaboration.

Reflecting on what makes PlastikPack a hidden champion, we point out the company's low public visibility due to operating entirely in the B-to-B sector, specializing in secondary products, and being located in an industrial zone rather than a renowned city. PlastikPack's role is clarified as not pure subcontracting but rather manufacturing packaging for clients, including a range of customer-specific molds and a line of German products for multiple clients. Thus, the company' success story unfolds as a multifaceted journey encompassing strategic partnerships, technological prowess, financial acumen, and a commitment to sustainability. The company's evolution from a nascent enterprise in 2015 to a key player in the plastic packaging industry is a testament to its ability to navigate complexities, innovate consistently, and align with the broader economic vision of Morocco. The lessons to be learnt from this PlastikPack' journey are the importance of strategic partnerships for international subsidiaries' success, the critical significance of a cost-effective and proximate location in industrial operations, and the essential prioritization of meritocracy over familial ties in recruitment campaigns even within family-owned businesses.

3.3 Seprob

Overview
Address: 6, avenue of Omar Slaoui, Casablanca, Morocco.
Tel: +212 666 960 826
Fax: +212 522 885 170
Email: elbada@seprob.com
Web: http://seprob.com/

Company Information
Industry: Construction and public works
Year of establishment: 1947
Sales revenues in 2021: € 16 MIO
Sales revenues in 2015: € 1.2 MIO
Average number employees in 2021: 600
Brain(s) behind the company: The founder Younes Laraqui

3.3.1 Nature of Market Leadership

Leveraging over 55 years of experience, Seprob stands as one of the most established companies in Morocco's construction sector. Today, the company is recognized as the leading manufacturer of engineering structures in Morocco. Seprob boasts extensive expertise across a wide array of public works domains, including civil engineering, dam construction, building construction, port works and water stations, as well as the fabrication of silos and tanks, and highway project design. Notably, Seprob was the first company to join Morocco's highway projects program.

The company's leadership in the field is attributed to its technical proficiency, innovative capabilities, and distinguished know-how, which set it apart from competitors. Committed to becoming internationally competitive, Seprob prioritizes quality and competitiveness as its primary objectives. It has successfully completed a major construction project in Libya in partnership with a Libyan firm and is currently engaged in another significant project in Ethiopia.

3.3.2 Nature of Competitive Advantage

Seprob differentiates itself from competitors through its notable reputation and over 55 years of experiential knowledge. Additionally, the company prides itself on having highly competent and qualified employees. Seprob's extensive expertise in the construction sector, combined with its innovation-oriented approach, helps it maintain a strong market position.

Notably, Seprob's commitment to Health, Safety, and Environment (HSE), along with its ISO 9001 certification, underscores its dedication to employee safety and the implementation of a robust quality assurance plan.

3.3.3 Core Lessons Learned on the Path to Success

- **Select Reputable Suppliers:** Choose suppliers known for offering an excellent quality-to-price ratio and strive to build robust, long-term relationships with them. Despite the construction industry's reputation for high costs, leverage your purchasing power to secure more competitive prices through increased volume.
- **Prioritize Speed and Precision:** Stand out in the construction sector by emphasizing both speed and precision. Adopt a collaborative management approach that empowers every team member to contribute to decision-making, share innovative ideas, and propose efficient work methods. This approach fosters an environment conducive to meeting tight deadlines without compromising on quality.
- **Implement a Comprehensive Risk Management System:** Develop an internal and customer-oriented risk management system to proactively identify potential risks. This strategy not only helps anticipate challenges but also ensures that stakeholders are well-informed about the potential consequences. Such preparedness is invaluable in navigating crises like the COVID-19 pandemic or geopolitical events, such as the Ukraine–Russia war.

3.3.4 Management and Leadership Development Needs

SEPROB, as a growing industrial company, faces critical needs in terms of managerial and leadership development. The rapid evolution of its activities, particularly at the national and potentially regional level, requires a more advanced structuring of managerial functions. The organization remains marked by a high degree of centralization of decision-making around the founder-CEO, which limits delegation and hinders the emergence of middle managers capable of carrying out the strategic vision. The need for professionalization of management is evident, both in the establishment of autonomous teams and in the strengthening of cross-functional skills (project management, change management, strategic management). In addition, the lack of formal continuing education programs limits the ability of managers to adapt to changes in the sector. The development of agile leadership, capable of combining entrepreneurial culture and organizational discipline, is therefore a key lever for ensuring SEPROB's sustainability.

3.3.5 Financing and Regulatory Environment Development Needs

SEPROB's development also faces constraints related to the financial and regulatory environment. Access to financing, although partially facilitated by public measures, remains insufficiently adapted to the specific needs of family-owned industrial companies. Guarantee requirements, processing times, and the limited diversity of financing instruments slow down expansion and innovation projects. Furthermore, the national regulatory framework remains unstable and sometimes unsuited to the operational realities of industrial SMEs, particularly with regard to taxation, customs standards, and import-export procedures. SEPROB therefore expresses a need for clarification, simplification, and above all regulatory stability. The introduction of incentives targeting productive investment and exports would be a factor in accelerating its development. Better coordination between public and private actors would also help create an ecosystem more conducive to industrial growth.

3.3.6 Adapting Business Practices Amid the COVID-19 Pandemic and Ukraine War

SEPROB has undeniably felt the repercussions of the COVID-19 pandemic and the ongoing Russia–Ukraine conflict, which have created intertwined challenges for its operations. During the COVID-19 crisis, the company experienced significant price increases in raw materials, a trend that has persisted and even intensified with the Ukraine conflict, leading to further volatility in material and fuel prices. These increases, averaging around 5%, have placed considerable strain on the company, especially as most of its clients are public administrations and state-owned entities with fixed-price contracts, making price adjustments difficult and limiting the company's ability to attract new clients. The rising fuel prices have also impacted supply chains and project timelines, creating additional pressure in a sector where strict adherence to deadlines is critical for maintaining credibility and ensuring project success.

Financially, the company has faced increased financial charges, further tightening its operational flexibility. In response, the company has adopted a negotiation-based approach with clients, engaging in transparent discussions to adjust project budgets by explaining the current market prices and the reasons behind these increases. Additionally, the company has pursued price revisions for specific key materials, such as cement and concrete, through the support of the National Federation of Construction and Public Works (FNBTP). Affiliated with the CGEM and established in the 1980s, the FNBTP plays a crucial role in representing and defending the interests of construction companies in Morocco, serving as an intermediary to negotiate with government authorities during crises. The company also benefited from the Daman Oxygène program, providing essential financial support to navigate liquidity constraints during the pandemic.

Beyond immediate operational measures, these crises have prompted the company to rethink its management practices and organizational culture. Recognizing the inevitability of future crises, the company has established an internal risk management system aimed at enhancing preparedness and responsiveness. This system emphasizes proactive communication for clients, ensuring they remain informed about market dynamics and potential impacts on project execution.

3.3.7 Seprob: Morocco's Hidden Champion in Construction and Civil Engineering

Seprob, a leading force in the building and civil engineering sector, embodies a compelling story of entrepreneurial achievement within the Moroccan landscape. The company's roots trace back to 1947, when it operated as a subsidiary of a French company. A significant transformation occurred in 1963, marking its transition to a common-law entity. In 1982, the Omar Laraki Group acquired the company, renaming it Seprob (Boussiron Process Operating Company) and solidifying its unequivocal Moroccan identity.

The company's field of activity covers the industrial and construction sectors, with a complete specialization in building and civil engineering. What sets Seprob apart is the breadth of its portfolio, which includes iconic projects such as the Zevaco Dome in Casablanca, freeway construction, industrial civil engineering, and major infrastructure initiatives.

Seprob's differentiating factor lies in its unwavering commitment to quality, innovation, and technical prowess. While it may not hold the largest market share, the company is at the cutting edge of technology and expertise. With a workforce boasting over six decades of collective experience, Seprob is extending its expertise beyond national borders and making a notable impact in Africa. In a landscape marked by formidable competition from the likes of Somagec and SGTM, Seprob's success is attributed to a culture of innovation, the use of high-quality equipment, and a participative management style. This ethos fosters a problem-solving mindset, fueling a continuous cycle of innovation and resilience.

Seprob's international engagements, exemplified by ongoing projects in Ethiopia, highlight its global presence. The company's strong commitment to Health, Safety, and Environmental (HSE) standards, underscored by its ISO 9001 certification, aligns seamlessly with its corporate social responsibility (CSR) principles. Morocco's stable economic and political environment, combined with its receptivity to foreign investment, has significantly contributed to Seprob's achievements. The company's capacity to adapt, innovate, and prosper in the face of challenges solidifies its standing as a hidden champion within Morocco's vibrant construction and civil engineering industry.

4 Conclusion and Recommendations

In early 1990, Hermann Simon an allemande professor was interested in examining the economic prosperity of Germany. By that time, Germany was a major exporter to the world despite its small size. On a snapshot, Simon came to the conclusion that small- and medium-sized businesses were the key to this outstanding success (Audretsch et al., 2021; Schenkenhofer, 2022). These companies are extremely profitable businesses that rule niche marketplaces globally; yet, they are relatively unknown to the large public, hence the concept "Hidden Champion." Per definition, Hidden champions are often SMEs typically seen as family firms (Simon, 2009; Johann et al., 2022). They are characterized as single-product, innovation-driven manufacturers with long-term objectives and visions. Even with their great market position, global orientation, prosperity, and export performance, the majority of these businesses are unknown to the general public (Lehmann & Schenkenhofer, 2023; Audretsch & Lehmann, 2016). Although the hidden champions phenomenon has garnered a notable interest by researchers in distinct fields, few is known about these companies; especially in the African context. The reason why the current study prompts to fill this gap by deeply analyzing three Moroccan Hidden champions: Inadis, PlastikPack, and Seprob; each operates within a distinct industry and specializes in a unique segment.

By deep-diving into Simon's hidden champions, we conclude that the three Moroccan hidden champions' traits are strikingly similar to those identified in Germany. All three companies showcase an entrepreneurial spirit, with founders who identified market gaps and seized opportunities. Inadis, under Fathi Benhatira, capitalized on the lighting market, PlastikPack emerged in plastic packaging under the collaboration of two family-owners, and Seprob, initially a subsidiary, transformed under the ownership of the Omar Laraki Group into a leading force in building and civil engineering. Interestingly, the companies demonstrated strategic resilience. Inadis for example, despite the mismanagement of its predecessor Promodel, orchestrated a comeback and evolved into a niche leader. In parallel, PlastikPack strategically partnered with PlastikPack France, leveraging technical alliances and investments for rapid market penetration. And Seprob, despite facing formidable competition, thrived through innovation, high-quality equipment, and a participative management style. In addition, customer-centricity and adaptability characterize these hidden champions. For 10 years, Inadis became a one-stop-shop for home essentials, offering transparent pricing and emphasizing service. In its part, PlastikPack prioritized innovation, eco-friendly practices, and a versatile team, ensuring customer satisfaction. And Since 1947, Seprob's commitment to quality, innovation, and problem-solving positioned it at the forefront of technology and know-how. Last but not least, the three Moroccan companies strategically managed challenges, showcasing financial acumen and risk management. Inadis wisely invested during the COVID-19 pandemic, PlastikPack navigated price fluctuations and supply chain disruptions and Seprob, facing global events like the Russia–Ukraine conflict, implemented robust risk management strategies. However, despite these similarities, there are evidently some distinctions between Moroccan hidden champions and Simon's hidden champions. Inadis, PlastikPack, and Seprob are leading market players in Morocco. Nevertheless, their size may not match that of the international hidden champions identified by Simon, who often have a larger market share exceeding 50%. Moreover, the international expansion strategies of Morocco's hidden champions also differ; in particular, PlastikPack, as a family-owned company specializing in plastic packaging, stands out for its notable international presence and strategic partnerships. The company's dependence on a coherent partnership model, particularly with a French group, is a departure from the autonomous internationalization generally associated with Simon's hidden champions.

To sum up, the Moroccan hidden champions generally align with the characteristics of Simon's hidden champions. Their entrepreneurial origins, strategic resilience, customer-centric approach, adaptability, and effective risk management underscore their global competitiveness within their respective niches. These companies exemplify the essence of hidden champions, thriving in the global marketplace while maintaining a degree of discretion and focusing on excellence within their markets.

References

Audretsch, D. B., & Lehmann, E. (2016). *The seven secrets of Germany: Economic resilience in an era of global turbulence*. Oxford University Press.

Audretsch, D. B., Lehmann, E. E., & Schenkenhofer, J. (2021). A context-choice model of niche entrepreneurship. *Entrepreneurship Theory and Practice, 45*(5), 1276–1303.

Din, F., Harald, D., & Rick, M. (2013). Strategies for small and medium-sized enterprises to compete successfully on the world market: Cases of Swedish hidden champions. *Asian Business & Management, 12*(5, SI), 591–612.

Doing Business 2020: Comparing business regulation in 190 economies. Washington, DC: World Bank.

Économie Entreprises. (2022). *The 500—Environment, social, governance*.

El Khanchoufi, M., Ammi, A., & Ouhejjou, O. (2024). The dynamics of the establishment of multinational firms in Morocco: New geopolitical and geoeconomic factors. *International Journal of Accounting, Finance, Auditing, Management & Economics, 5*(2), 86–104.

Haut-Commissariat au Plan. (2019). *Enquête nationale auprès des entreprises*. https://www.hcp.ma/Enquete-nationale-aupres-des-entreprises-2019_a2405.html
Johann, M., Müller, S., & Becker, H. (2022). Hidden champions and the dynamics of innovation in emerging markets. *Journal of Business Research, 145*, 312–324.
Lehmann, E. E., & Schenkenhofer, J. (2023). The evolution of hidden champions as niche entrepreneurs. *Foundations and Trends in Entrepreneurship, 19*(4), 340–446.
Ministère du Tourisme, de l'Artisanat et de l'Économie Sociale et Solidaire. (2024). *Chiffres clés*. https://mtaess.gov.ma/fr/tourisme/chiffres-cles/
Office des Changes. (2024). *Indicateurs mensuels des échanges extérieurs*. https://www.oc.gov.ma/fr/actualites/indicateurs-des-echanges-exterieurs-a-fin-mai-2024#
Schenkenhofer, J. (2022). Hidden champions: A review of the literature and future research avenues. *Management Review Quarterly, 72*(2), 417–482.
Simon, H. (1996). You don't have to be German to be a hidden champion. *Business Strategy Review, 7*(2), 1–13.
Simon, H. (2009). *Hidden champions of the twenty-first century: The success strategies of unknown world market leaders*. Springer.
Venohr, B., & Kamp, B. (2019). Global niche market leaders in emerging Asia and the necessity to become market insiders. *Ekonomiaz, 95*(1), 111–133.
World Bank. (2023). *Data: Countries and economies—Morocco*. https://data.worldbank.org/country/morocco.
World Bank. (2025). World Development Indicators 2025: DataBank. Washington, DC: World Bank.

Oumaima Chamchati holds a PhD in Management Sciences from Cadi Ayyad University in Marrakech and currently serves as a lecturer and researcher at HEM Business & Engineering School. Her research focuses on international management, with a particular pathways on intra-African internationalization strategies.

Driven by a commitment to advancing knowledge through cross-border collaboration, she has enriched her academic career through postdoctoral research at the University of Littoral Côte d'Opale (France) and visiting fellowships at the University of Pisa (Italy) and HEC Liège (Belgium).

Her scholarly work has been featured in leading academic journals, including Emerald Emerging Markets Case Studies and Thunderbird International Business Review. She has also contributed to collective volumes published by prestigious academic editors such as Palgrave Macmillan and Routledge.

Beyond academia, Oumaima Chamchati has played a key role in consultancy and research projects led by the HEM Research Center, in collaboration with major institutional and corporate partners such as the Regional Investment Center (CRI) of the Marrakech-Safi region, LCI Education, and the Attijariwafa Bank Group.

Sofia Arougay is a doctoral student at Cadi Ayyad University, affiliated with the Laboratory for Research in Organizational Management (LAREGO) at the National School of Commerce and Management (ENCG) in Marrakech, Morocco. Her research focuses primarily on hidden champions in emerging countries, with an emphasis on the Moroccan context.

She is interested in understanding the growth trajectories, dynamic capabilities, and key success factors of these low-profile but high-performing companies. Her goal is to fill the scientific gap regarding hidden champions in North Africa and to enrich the existing literature with an analysis based on the Moroccan context.

Mohamed Nabil El Mabrouki is a full Professor at Cadi Ayyad University in Marrakech and a senior research associate at HEM Research Center. He teaches strategy, corporate social responsibility, and research methodology. His research primarily focuses on the internationalization strategies of companies from the Global South, as well as on competitive intelligence practices. He is the author of several peer-reviewed scientific publications and regularly contributes to ranked academic journals. He also co-leads the "International Management and Society" chair.

Hidden Champion of Nigeria

Louis Nzegwu and Raymond Onuoha

Abstract This chapter presents a case of West African Soy Industries Limited (WASIL) as a Hidden Champions in an emerging economy context—Nigeria. The Nigerian business environment is domiciled within a macro economy that has been declining in growth within the last two decades. Contextually, the institutional environment is a critical constraint on the innovative structures and capacities of firms operating within. Despite this business environment handicap, WASIL has emerged as a key leader in the production and export of soy products in the ever-expanding African market with a current production facility that processes half a million tons of soy in capacity, with expansion efforts targeting sales revenues of 500,000 USD by 2024. WASIL is a Hidden Champion that exemplifies an agro-processing manufacturing and export business model with an internal resource focus rather than an external focus. The company's internal resource focus with respect to raw materials sourcing, processing capabilities, people, and export contributes significantly to their success story. The case of WASIL exemplifies the imperative of supporting the local agro-processing industry to improve utilization of local raw materials, improve local technology, diversify the economy, increase government revenue, and abate foreign exchange shocks with greater level of agro-based exports.

Overview

Official name: Federal Republic of Nigeria
Type of government: Presidential System
Population in 2023: ~ 202 million people
Land area: 923,768 km^2

L. Nzegwu (✉)
Lagos Business School (LBS), Pan-Atlantic University, Lagos, Nigeria
e-mail: lnzegwu@lbs.edu.ng

R. Onuoha
Wits Institute for Social and Economic Research (WiSER), University of the Witwatersrand, Johannesburg, South Africa
e-mail: ronuoha@lbs.edu.ng

D. Berberović, D. Purg (eds.), *Hidden Champions in Rising Economies*, Contributions to Management Science,
https://doi.org/10.1007/978-3-032-08263-3_30

History

1860–1960 Corresponds about the period of colonial rule in Nigeria. "In 1900, the British government took over the administration of the northern territories from the Royal Niger Company and proclaimed the area the Protectorate of Northern Nigeria, with Sir Frederick Lugard as the first High Commissioner. At the same time, the Protectorate of Southern Nigeria was created to replace the Niger Coast Protectorate. In 1914, the Northern and Southern Protectorates were amalgamated to become Nigeria" (Ekundare, 1973: 12).

1960 The Federal Republic of Nigeria became a sovereign nation on first October 1960 within the British Commonwealth. "On 1 October I963 a republican constitution was introduced into Nigeria by the federal parliament, and it operated until January I966. Following a series of political crises in I965, the Prime Minister of the Federation, the Western Region Premier, the Northern Region Premier and the Federal Minister of Finance were assassinated on I5 January I966 in a coup d'état led by some army officers. On the day following the coup, the administration of the country was handed over by the remaining members of the federal cabinet to the General Officer Commanding the Nigerian Army, Major-General T. U. Aguiyi Ironsi, who suspended the office of President, the Prime Minister and Parliament, and vested legislative and executive powers in the federal military government comprising a Supreme Military Council and a Federal Executive Council. He also appointed military governors to administer the regions. On 29 July I966 Major General Aguiyi-Ironsi was assassinated in a counter coup in which the Military Governor of the Western Region, Lt-Colonel Adekunle Fajuyi, also lost his life. After the few days of confusion which followed the counter coup, General Yakubu Gowon (then a Lt. Colonel) took over on 1 August 1966 as Supreme Commander of the Armed Forces and Head of State. The two coup d'états in 1966 created a deep rift between the Hausa and Ibo army officers. Following a series of clashes between Hausa and Ibo civilians in Northern and Eastern Regions, some of the Ibo leaders led by Emeka Ojukwu, who was then a Lt-Colonel and the military governor of Eastern Region, felt that the Ibos as a group should constitute themselves into a separate country. However, one of the major political issues in Nigeria, that of the creation of more states in order to protect minority interests, was solved by the creation of twelve states out of the existing four regions, on 27 May 1967. Three days later, Ojukwu announced that the territory comprising the former Eastern Region had seceded from the Federation of Nigeria. He gave the name "Biafra" to this area. As a result of this event the civil war broke out in July 1967. It lasted for about 30 months and ended on 12 January 1970, after Lt-Colonel Effiong, the man to whom Ojukwu handed over power after he fled the country on the night of January 1970, made a radio broadcast announcing the surrender of the rebels. Effiong ordered an orderly disengagement of the rebel troops and led a delegation to Lagos to negotiate a peace settlement. On the night of 13 January 1970, General Gowon welcomed the surrender of the rebels, and thus Nigeria was kept together as a Federation. At the celebration of the tenth anniversary of Nigerian independence on 1 October 1970, General Gowon announced that "military rule in Nigeria was to continue until 1976, and that the military government would endeavour to surrender power to a civilian government through an orderly constitutional process" (Ekundare, 1973: 14–15).

1970 Oil boom of the 1970s began, which led to a decline in the country's other economic sectors; Majorly Agriculture and manufacturing, including the palm oil industry, cocoa, groundnut, and cotton exports, and the garments and textile industries, respectively. The oil boom "led to an overvalued naira made it cheaper for Nigeria to import consumer goods—from soap and pencils to fruit juice—rather than produce them locally" (Usman, 2022: 5), effectively making Nigeria a "rentier economy". Nevertheless, Nigeria continued to post strong economic growth in the following three decades, peaking between 2003–2015 during the commodities super cycle at an average growth rate of 5–7%. According to Usman, "although this growth happened at the time of an oil boom, it was driven by non-oil economic sectors."

1999 till date. Transition to democratic rule. Basking on the non-oil growth of the 2000s, Nigeria's economy became more diversified, and expanded to become Africa's largest economy in 2014. However, this phenomenon did not translate to wider export basket beyond the oil sector, as industrialization and the country's manufacturing capabilities continued to stagnate (Usman, 2022).

1 Introduction: Context and History

The Nigerian business environment is domiciled within a macro economy that has been declining in growth within the last two decades (Fig. 1).

This economic decline has largely been driven by monetary and fiscal policy distortions, lower oil production, rising insecurity, and external global shocks. While Nigeria is one of Africa's largest economies, it is however, currently ranked 131 out of 190 economies according to the 2022 World Bank annual ratings on ease of doing business.[1] This position is congruent with the country's innovation system, which is not as well-developed (Jegede et al., 2012; Chukwudifu, 2021). A snapshot of Nigeria's key economic indicators in relation to its innovation ecosystem from 1995 to the recent, relative to comparator African countries (Ghana and South Africa) according to the World Bank database is given in Fig. 2.

[1] https://businessday.ng/news/article/boosting-nigerias-ranking-on-ease-of-doing-business-via-standards/#:~:text=Nigeria%2C%20Africa's%20largest%20economy%2C%20is,latest%20World%20Bank%20annual%20ratings

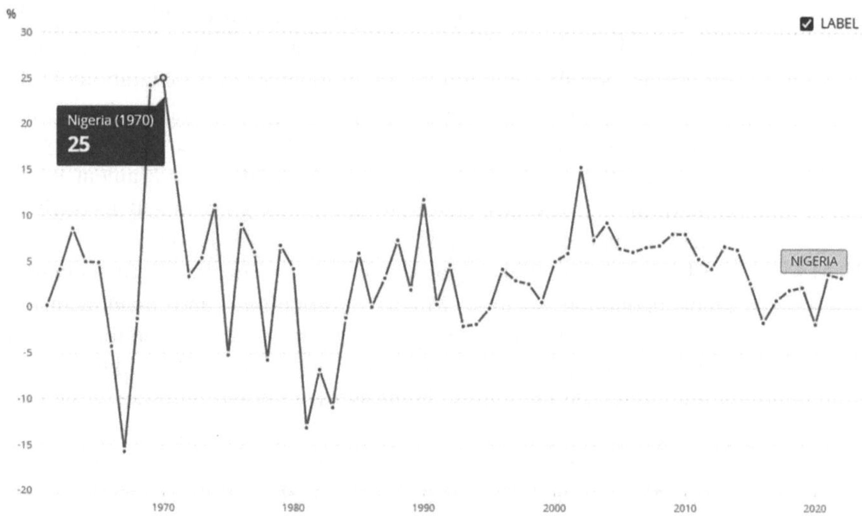

Fig. 1 GDP growth (annual %)—Nigeria. Source: The World Bank Database

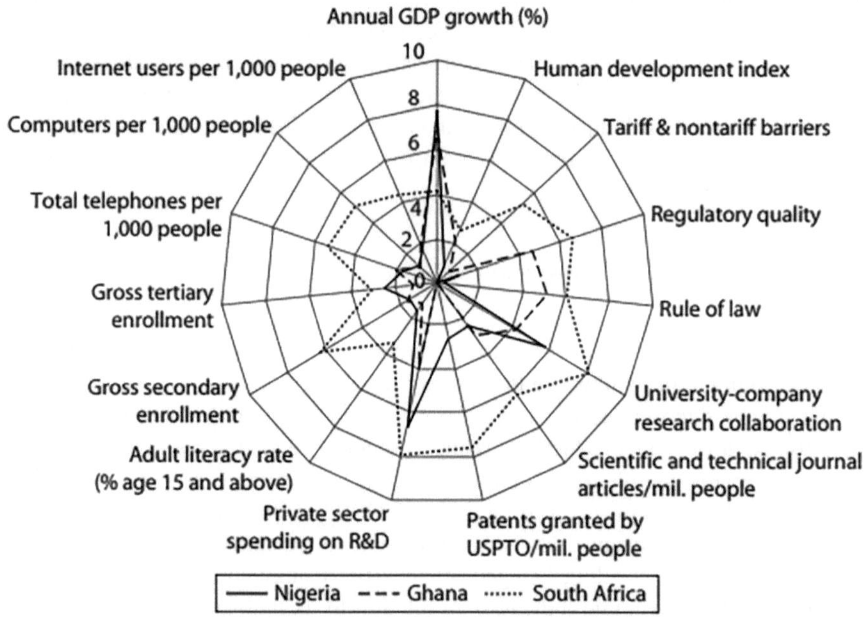

Fig. 2 Economic innovation indices for Nigeria, in comparison to Ghana and South Africa (1995—recent). Source: World Bank database

Nigeria's ranking on the Global Innovation Index (GII) 2023[2] shows a general poor performance—placing 82nd and 127th out of 132 economies on the Business and Market Sophistication parameter respectively. This performance was below the lower-middle income group and Africa regional averages. Contextually, the above institutional environment is a critical constraint on the innovative structures and capacities of firms operating within it, especially considering the economic size and level of development at the country level (Allred & Steensma, 2005; Jackson & Deeg, 2008; Alam et al., 2019; Edeh et al., 2020). To bridge this impediment in most African market environments, firms often adopt a geographical portfolio internalization strategy in Africa's digital ecosystem. This position is strategically to leverage cross-country competitive advantages in ameliorating their significant liability of foreignness within countries and overcoming institutional voids—especially with regards to infrastructure and regulatory environments—that create market uncertainties for innovation activities (Abereijo et al., 2007; Zhou, 2007; Terjesen & Elam, 2009; Cuervo-Cazurra & Gene, 2011; Adeleye & Boso, 2016). This internationalization mechanism has increased significantly across Africa over the last two decades (Ibeh et al., 2012; Boso et al., 2016; Boso et al., 2019). For firms that are able to navigate the institutional voids within the region, this mechanism provides a source of long-term competitive advantage, but for those that can't find pathways to overcoming the institutional voids, the contextual market imperfections become a serious impediment to doing business innovatively (Gao et al., 2017). The above phenomenon is a fundamental problem for smaller buisinesses operating witin the Nigerian environment. In this regard, these businesses find it difficult to integrate innovation into their business practices to enhance their overall performance (Chukwudifu, 2021).

2 Characteristics of the Hidden Champion from Nigeria

Two Hidden Champions were identified within the Nigerian business context—West African Soy Industries Limited (WASIL) and Interswitch. These companies were selected based on their primus market position in Africa relative to their strongest competitors across their respective markets—agro-processing and financial technology services—respectively, although they currently maintain a relatively low visibility profile in the public domain. However, this chapter presents a case of only one of the identified companies—WASIL—as the researchers were not able to get an official written consent from Interswitch for the publication of a case study at this time (Exhibit 1).

[2] https://www.wipo.int/edocs/pubdocs/en/wipo-pub-2000-2023/ng.pdf

Exhibit 1 Core economic indicators for Nigeria

	2019	2020	2021	2022	2023	2024
GDP per capita (current US$)	2334	2075	2066	2163	1596.64	…
GDP per capita growth (annual %)	1.5	−4.0	5.3	2.3	0.72	…
Long-term unemployment (% of total unemployment)	–	–	–	–	3.07	2.99
Foreign direct investment, net inflows (% of GDP)	0.5	0.6	0.8	−0.4	0.51	…
GDP (current US$, mio)	474.5	432.2	440.8	472.6	363846.33	…
Exports of goods and services (current US$, mio)	69.9	39.9	50.9	69.1	…	…
Exports of goods and services (% of GDP)	–	–	–	–	…	…
Merchandise exports (current US$)	62.5	35.6	46.9	63.1	55182.00	…
Merchandise exports to high-income economies (% of total merchandise exports)	39.3	36.7	–	–	64.15	…
Merchandise exports to developing economies in Europe & Central Asia (% of total merchandise exports)	0.01	0.02	–	–	1.81	…
Ores and metals exports (% of merchandise exports)	0.3	0.3	0.9	1	1.18	…
Agricultural raw materials exports (% of merchandise exports)	–	–	–	–	0.38	…
Food exports (% of merchandise exports)	2	3	3	3	3.78	…
Fuel exports (% of merchandise exports)	87	89	89	91	91.61	…
Manufactures exports (% of merchandise exports)	11	8	6	5	2.83	…
High-technology exports (% of manufactured exports)	–	–	–	–	3.53	…

Source: World Bank, 2025
https://data.worldbank.org/indicator/NY.GDP.PCAP.CD?locations=NG

3 Case Study of Selected Hidden Champion

3.1 West African Soy Industries Limited (WASIL)

Overview

Address: Flowergate Mixed Development Scheme Sagamu, Ogun State, Nigeria.
Tel: 01 – 903 – 9000
Email: info@wasil.ng
Web: https://www.wasil.ng

Company Information

Industry: Manufacturing
Year of Establishment: 2019
Sales Revenues in 2020: 100,000 USD
Sales Revenues in 2023: 350, 000 USD
Average number of employees in 2023: 600

Brainer(s) behind the company:

- Group Managing Director—Rahul Savara.
- Managing Director—Mahendra Kumar Vaidh.

3.1.1 Nature of Market Leadership

The African leader in the production and export of soy products. The market is now expanding. WASIL currently has a production facility that processes half a million tons of soy in capacity, with expansion efforts targeting sales revenues of 500,000 USD by 2024. The main competitors in the midterm are Olam (with a presence across Africa) and Flour Mill of Nigeria.

3.1.2 Nature of Competitive Advantage

- Processing facility siting at strategic location—Sagamu, near the port location in Lagos, which provides a strong logistics advantage.
- Significant investment in research and development, and a best-in-class laboratory in a factory, products going out of the factory is fully tested and are certified 100% sure about with respect to quality. That is why they are able to do the export in the European market, as is relatively challenging to export to the European market.
- WASIL is not dependent on imports for their production. The company depends on a 100% local supply of raw materials, shielding it from market shocks in the global supply value chain and forex fluctuations.

3.1.3 Core Lessons Learned on the Path to Success

As a local player with a global expansion vision, do not take any shortcut in terms of the quality of production, in terms of technology adoption, and in terms of the recruitment of the right personnel. We have not compromised on those. That is an important factor.

1. The adoption of innovative technologies in soy processing and export by WASIL as a local manufacturer with a global expansion vision enables it to compete effectively with imported goods. Smart technology adoption makes their busi-

ness processes to be highly effective and smooth-running on a continuous in order to meet the strategic goals of the company within a continuously evolving global market.

2. Another key requirement for WASIL's success is a strong personnel recruitment and retention model, which at its centrality is an enhanced employee engagement system. The effects of strong employee engagement are significant for the company with respect to employee retention, productivity and loyalty, which ultimately enhances the company's reputation and overall stakeholder value as a competitive advantage for sustained profitability. WASIL's employee engagement model focuses on social cohesion, employee–supervisor relationships, and corporate information sharing, which ultimately engenders trust and an enhanced sense of personnel value within the business environment.

   Apart from those, we review ourselves on a frequent basis. We are continuously thinking about how we can go ahead from this level to the next level if we are to reach our global standposts.
3. WASIL's developed evaluation culture is hinged on a results-based monitoring and evaluation (M&E) system with a long-term focus, in response to varying frequencies of internal, and more importantly, external business pressures within the global business environment. The results-based M&E has significantly increased the levels of enterprise accountability and transparency within WASIL's business ecosystem in relation to its various stakeholders—across the private and public sectors, as a critical basis for its continuous business innovation with respect to the company's products and services.
4. WASIL's result-based M&E system is built around the principle of Total Quality Management (TQM) concerning the quality of products and manufacturing processes, with particular respect to operations, inspection, and quality control.

3.1.4 Management and Leadership Development Needs

A crucial short-term need of WASIL is the development of their local talent and skills base. Currently, the company's internal operations—Logistics, Security, Health, Safety and Environment (HSE), and Human Resources (HR) are run by local staff, while some external operations are handled by expatriate staff. In the future, the company wants to handle 100% of its total operations local staff, but these require critical appropriate training programmes, in particular, with respect to technology management, to fill the strategic personnel void, thereby reducing dependency on expatriates to the barest minimum.

3.1.5 Financing and Regulatory Environment Development Needs

WASIL will require more local backing from the financial institutions in Nigeria in the area of trade and export finance logistics. This will help the firm to achieve its long-term strategic business and production expansion targets. The company stresses its demand on the significance of engendering an enabling business environment that protects local industries who are creating local jobs and wealth in the country. This perspective is with particular reference to the agro-processing and export sector that has significant potential to earn foreign exchange for the country through the export of processed agricultural products, thereby diversifying the country's non-oil export earnings significantly. Through initiatives like the Anchor Borrowers' Program and export stimulation facilities, the Central Bank of Nigeria (CBN) can provide concessional loans and credit guarantees for agro-processors via the Non-Oil Export Stimulation Facility (NESF) and Export Development Fund (EDF) which both support export-oriented businesses in Nigeria. The Nigerian Export-Import Bank (NEXIM) may also provide export financing, guarantees, and trade facilitation for agro-processed goods. Bank of Industry (BOI): Offers medium-to-long-term loans for industrial and agro-processing projects. Commercial and microfinance banks should also develop partnerships to create tailored trade and export finance products that address the needs of local agro-processors as well. In addition, the Presidential Enabling Business Environment Council (PEBEC) should advocate for reforms that simplify the processes for obtaining permits, licenses, and trade financing for the agro-processing sector work with agencies like the Nigerian Ports Authority (NPA) to improve export logistics and reduce turnaround times at ports. By addressing these areas, WASIL can secure the local financial backing and enabling environment necessary to achieve its long-term goals while contributing to Nigeria's non-oil export diversification.

3.1.6 Impact of COVID-19 and the Ukrainian War

During the COVID-19 pandemic, WASIL stopped their manufacturing plant for just about 1½ months during the very early stages of the malaise, specifically in the months of April and May 2020. The company felt that it would not allow its team members to be infected with COVID, so they shut down their plant during that period. Then later on, when the company realized that the pandemic was not going to be over soon, the company made unique accommodation arrangements within the factory itself. The company team members were staying within this arrangement helping with the productions, while the company provided complementary food, entertainment, and sporting arrangement for them. This bootstrap makeshift arrangement helped the company team members to bond well with themselves while the company took care of their accommodation needs. According to the company, when other companies' staff were coming and going back on a vehicle on a daily basis, their own team members were staying there [in the plant] and were helping to drive production non-stop in a healthy environment. So, in the end, the pandemic did not affect WASIL's plant operations in anyway significant, even their supply chain, because the company's raw materials sourcing for 2020 was already completed in the month of February 2020 just before COVID [in March 2020]; so, 2021 operations was not that disturbed at the height of the pandemic.

In addition, since the company was not dependent on imports, but rather on local supply for their productions, they were also isolated from the global supply chain disruptions as a result of the war in Ukraine. Even when the global supply chain challenges were there, they were still doing export from Nigeria unconstrained.

3.1.7 WASIL: "Agro-Processing Manufacturing and Export Business Model with an Internal Resource Focus Rather than an External Focus"

WASIL is a Hidden Champion that exemplifies an agro-processing manufacturing and export business model rooted in an internal resource focus rather than an external dependency. This unique approach is central to the company's operations, ensuring sustainable growth and resilience in a competitive and often volatile market. WASIL's strategy prioritizes the optimal use of local resources, from raw material sourcing and processing capabilities to workforce development and internal decision-making processes. This model stands in stark contrast to traditional approaches that heavily rely on imported inputs or foreign expertise.

A cornerstone of WASIL's success is its robust integration with local agricultural communities. The company actively collaborates with local farmers through organized cultivation schemes, ensuring a steady supply of high-quality raw materials for its production processes. By working closely with these farmers, WASIL not only secures its input needs but also fosters economic empowerment and community development. This partnership transforms farmers into stakeholders in the company's value chain, creating a mutually beneficial relationship that strengthens local agricultural ecosystems and enhances the livelihoods of farming communities. This internal sourcing strategy also mitigates the risks associated with global supply chain disruptions, reinforcing WASIL's operational stability.

Beyond raw materials, WASIL places significant emphasis on its internal workforce. The company relies on its employees to make collective corporate decisions, prioritizing internal expertise over external or foreign consultancy. This approach fosters a culture of inclusivity, ownership, and innovation among its workforce. By tapping into the knowledge and skills of its employees, WASIL ensures that its business decisions are aligned with its core values and long-term strategic objectives. This internal reliance also reduces costs associated with hiring external consultants and reinforces a sense of shared purpose and commitment among the staff.

From a financial perspective, WASIL's success story is closely tied to strategic internal resource management. The company's journey was significantly bolstered by the early intervention of the Central Bank of Nigeria (CBN), which provided an intervention fund to establish its manufacturing plant and facilities in Nigeria. This financial support played a critical role in enabling WASIL to set up a robust local production infrastructure. The company has since maintained a 100% local production effort, deliberately avoiding dependency on imported materials or equipment. This approach not only reduces foreign exchange expenditure but also aligns with Nigeria's broader economic goals of promoting local content, industrialization, and economic diversification.

WASIL's internally focused model extends its impact beyond the company to the national economy. By operating a fully localized production and export business, the company contributes significantly to Nigeria's foreign exchange earnings through the export of agro-processed goods. This is particularly vital in a country seeking to diversify its earnings base away from oil dependency. The company's efforts align with Nigeria's economic diversification strategy, showcasing the transformative potential of agro-processing industries in driving sustainable economic growth.

Moreover, WASIL's commitment to internal resources underscores the broader principle of self-reliance and sustainable development. In a global economic environment characterized by uncertainties, the company's model serves as a blueprint for resilience. It demonstrates that businesses can thrive by leveraging local resources, investing in human capital, and fostering strong partnerships within the local economy.

In summary, WASIL's agro-processing manufacturing and export business model is a testament to the power of internal resource optimization. By focusing on local raw materials, workforce capabilities, and indigenous decision-making processes, the company has achieved remarkable success. Its reliance on local resources not only ensures operational stability but also contributes to broader economic and social development goals. WASIL's story is an inspiring example of how businesses can create sustainable value by prioritizing internal resources and aligning their strategies with the needs of their local ecosystems.

4 Conclusions and Recommendations

While the 2022 World Bank annual ratings on ease of doing business ranked Nigeria 131 out of 190, the Country's innovation ecosystem and corporate innovation have evolved, encompassing technological advancement, process, product and service. WASIL is the African leader in soy product production and export, with a production facility in Sagamu, near Lagos port, providing a logistics advantage. The company has invested in research and development, ensuring high product quality and allowing them to export to the European market. By looking at the West African Soy Industries Limited (WASIL), this study established that the company's success is highly attributed to the adoption of innovative technologies in Soy processing and export, and the development of an evaluation culture through a monitoring and evaluation system amongst others. However, the business is still faced with present challenges which affect the business; despite the production facility being located in Sagamu, near Lagos port providing a logistics advantage, logistics still presents a challenge due to the high cost compared to neighbouring countries. Also, the security problem impedes farmers from cultivating, which presents future challenges. This suggests that while WASIL has invested in research and development, innovative technologies, and human resources, it is important to consider the wider business environment in which the company operates. The challenges of high logistics cost and insecurity may pose a great risk to the growth as well as disrupt the ease of operating successfully. To create a thriving environment, aid through local financial backing will be required as the company moves to develop programs that address their needs.

Despite its enormous potential in producing huge raw materials from the abundance of natural resources, Nigeria is still importing a lot of processed foods. Despite the enormous production potentials of soya beans in Nigeria, the country is still a net importer of the commodity with a net trade of almost $30 million in 2022.[3] The country's industrial policy has not prioritized the processing of locally grown crops (Abdullahi et al., 2021). The case of WASIL examplifies the imperative of supporting the local agro-processing industry to improve utilization of local raw materials, improve local technology, diversify the economy, increase government revenue, and abate foreign exchange shocks with greater level of agro-based exports. The potentials of local agro-processing in Nigeria can only be achieved when an enabling policy environment is created for large-scale production and consequent export. This proposition comprises the provision of adequate access to low-interest loans and optimal knowledge and skills required for local agro-processing at the highest levels. Achieving this require a tenacous commitment from policy stakeholders at all levels. Beyond the government, improving the processing of locally grown crops such as soya bean requires a symbiotic relationship between research Institutions and private sector operators such as WASIL to bridge technology transfer in local operations and production processes (Abdullahi et al., 2021). These institutions can also partner with the local companies in retrofitting their marketing campaigns especially in the export segment and in maintaining good business relationships with suppliers and foreign consumers. Institutions can also provide tailor-made training on financial risk management that is crucial for long-term sustainability of these local producers.

References

Abdullahi, N., Badau, M. H., Shuaib, A. U., & Bako, N. S. (2021). Promoting local agro-processing in Nigeria: Way forward. *Nigeria Agricultural Journal, 52*(3), 34–45.

Abereijo, I. O., Ilori, M. O., Taiwo, K. A., & Adegbite, S. A. (2007). Assessment of the capabilities for innovation by small and medium industry in Nigeria. *African Journal of Business Management, 1*(8).

Adeleye, I., & Boso, N. (2016). Africa-to-Africa internationalization: Future trends and research avenues. In I. Adeleye, L. White, & N. Boso (Eds.), *Africa-to-Africa internationalization: Key issues and outcomes* (pp. 35–65). Palgrave Macmillan.

Alam, A., Uddin, M., & Yazdifar, H. (2019). Institutional determinants of R&D investment: Evidence from emerging markets. *Technological Forecasting and Social Change, 138*, 34–44.

Allred, B. B., & Steensma, H. K. (2005). The influence of industry and home country characteristics on firms' pursuit of innovation. *MIR: Management International Review, 45*(4), 383–412.

[3] https://oec.world/en/profile/bilateral-product/soybeans/reporter/nga

Boso, N., Adeleye, I., & White, L. (2016). Africa-to-Africa internationalization: Emerging trends and key issues. In I. Adeleye, L. White, & N. Boso (Eds.), *Africa-to-Africa internationalization: Key issues and outcomes* (pp. 3–34). Palgrave Macmillan.

Boso, N., Adeleye, I., Ibeh, K., & Chizema, A. (2019). The internationalization of African firms: Opportunities, challenges, and risks. *Thunderbird International Business Review, 61*(1), 5–12.

Chukwudifu, J. N. (2021). *Strategies to integrate innovation into business practices in the Nigerian private sector* (Doctoral dissertation, Walden University). https://search.proquest.com/openview/6ffdb75cf42571c3eb4d38f368cc960f/1?pq-origsite=gscholar&cbl=18750&diss=y&casa_token=wH5dmZYbbH8AAAAA:IM_XLH7oN1ETTCMLuUd_WIpd8YFE-msUuTo7CrtP2ubC4yUkVJVxmr9JgAwjhhaEyY2p6ZnDK8s

Cuervo-Cazurra, A., & Gene, M. E. (2011). Obligating, pressing, and supporting dimensions of the environment and the non-market advantages of developing-country multinational companies. *Journal of Management Studies, 48*(2), 441–455.

Edeh, J. N., Obodoechi, D. N., & Ramos-Hidalgo, E. (2020). Effects of innovation strategies on export performance: New empirical evidence from developing market firms. *Technological Forecasting and Social Change, 158*, 120167.

Ekundare, R. O. (1973). *An economic history of Nigeria, 1860-1960*. Methuen. https://www.sahistory.org.za/sites/default/files/archive-files3/r._olufemi_ekundare_an_economic_history_of_nigerbook4you.org_.pdf

Gao, C., Zuzul, T., Jones, G., & Khanna, T. (2017). Overcoming institutional voids: A reputation-based view of long-run survival. *Strategic Management Journal, 38*(11), 2147–2167.

Ibeh, K., Wilson, J., & Chizema, A. (2012). The internationalization of African firms 1995–2011: Review and implications. *Thunderbird International Business Review, 54*(4), 411–427.

Jackson, G., & Deeg, R. (2008). Comparing capitalisms: Understanding institutional diversity and its implications for international business. *Journal of International Business Studies, 39*(4), 540–561.

Jegede, O. O., Ilori, M. O., Sonibare, J. A., Oluwale, B. A., & Siyanbola, W. O. (2012). Factors influencing innovation and competitiveness in the service sector in Nigeria: A sub-sectoral approach. *Management, 2*(3), 69–79.

Terjesen, S., & Elam, A. (2009). Transnational entrepreneurs 'venture internationalization strategies: A practice theory approach. *Entrepreneurship Theory and Practice, 33*(5), 1093–1120.

Usman, Z. (2022). *Economic diversification in Nigeria: The politics of building a post-oil economy*. Bloomsbury Academic. https://library.oapen.org/bitstream/handle/20.500.12657/58886/1/9781786993960.pdf

Zhou, L. (2007). The effects of entrepreneurial proclivity and foreign market knowledge on early internationalization. *Journal of World Business, 42*(3), 281–293.

Louis Nzegwu is a Professor of Marketing at the Lagos Business School. Prior to joining the Lagos Business School Faculty, Professor Nzegwu was a Professor of Marketing and the Executive Director of the International Business Resource Center (IBRC) at the University of Wisconsin–Platteville (UW–Platteville), for over two decades and on the faculty of Business Administration at Alcorn State University, Lorman, Mississippi from 1981 until 1991.

Louis Nzegwu teaches a variety of marketing courses, including Sales Management, Marketing Management, Pricing Marketing Research, and Global Marketing courses, amongst others. Nzegwu earned his Doctorate Degree in Business Administration from Nova Southern University, MBA from Morgan State University, M.Ed. from University of Southern Mississippi, and MSc in Agricultural Economics from Alcorn State University.

He was also awarded the 2004 UW–Platteville Teaching Excellence Award and 2005 College of Business, Industry, Life Science and Agriculture (BILSA) Thomas and Lee Ann Lindahl Teaching Excellence Award. In 2002, and in 2003, the American Marketing Association honored Nzegwu with the distinguished Teaching Innovation Service Award. In 2002, Wisconsin Governor Scott McCallum recognized Nzegwu as one of Wisconsin's 100 top researchers.

His research interest is in the areas of marketing strategy, product development, marketing entry strategy, consumer behavior, and sales enablement. He has served on the editorial board of The Journal of African Business, as Associate Editor of the Emerald Emerging Market Case Studies as well as on the advisory board of the Academy of World Business, Marketing & Management. Nzegwu is an Emeritus Professor of Marketing with the University of Wisconsin, USA and fellow of The National Institute of Marketing of Nigeria.

Dr. Raymond Onuoha is a Technology Policy Scholar and Consultant specializing in the digital economy and innovation in developing countries, particularly Africa. His work spans digital transformation, internet governance, fintech regulation, digital trade, e-governance, digital public infrastructure, open data, and AI policy. He serves as a Research Consultant with global think tanks such as Caribou (UK), Research ICT Africa (South Africa), and The Portulans Institute (USA), focusing on evidence-based policy for inclusive digital development.

Dr. Onuoha has advised prominent organizations including The World Bank, African Union Commission, GIZ, APC, CBN, AFI, ILO, BMGF, UNESCO, Microsoft Nigeria, IGF, CIPESA, NIC.br, NITDA, and AfriSIG. He was a 2024 AfOx Fellow at the Oxford Internet Institute, an Open Fellow at the Weizenbaum Institute in Berlin, and is currently a Post-Doctoral Fellow at WISER, South Africa, where he researches digital ID systems and trust-building in Africa.

Hidden Champions of North Macedonia

Violeta Cvetkoska, Martin Kiselicki, Filip Peovski, and Bojan Kitanovikj

Abstract Being the regional frontrunner in supporting a favorable environment for businesses, boasting a highly liberalized foreign trade and tax policy, a stable monetary environment, and a member of NATO and a EU candidate country, North Macedonia represents a favorable ground for developing and investing in hidden champions. This book chapter gives comprehensive research and an overview of hidden champions in North Macedonia, highlighting these companies' nature of market leadership and competitive advantage, development needs, best practices, challenges, and strategies for overcoming them, especially in turbulent times post-COVID and facing rising geopolitical tensions. Considering this, the book chapter analyzes four hidden champions, which operate in diverse industries—Korab Trnica, Mermer Imperijal, Ading, and Mikrosam. Through semi-structured interviews with management members from the hidden champion companies, it was found that export orientation, leadership through innovation and uniqueness, family business style of operations, continuous learning, and a focus on originality in a niche market can lead to business success in this type of companies.

Overview
Official name: Republic of North Macedonia
Type of government: Parliamentary Democratic Republic
Population in 2023: 2,097,319[1]
Land area: 25,220 km^2

[1] According to the latest census by the State Statistical Office in 2021

V. Cvetkoska (✉) · M. Kiselicki · F. Peovski · B. Kitanovikj
Faculty of Economics - Skopje, Ss. Cyril and Methodius University in Skopje, Skopje, North Macedonia
e-mail: vcvetkoska@eccf.ukim.edu.mk; martin.kiselicki@eccf.ukim.edu.mk; peovski@eccf.ukim.edu.mk; bojan.kitanovikj@eccf.ukim.edu.mk

D. Berberović, D. Purg (eds.), *Hidden Champions in Rising Economies*, Contributions to Management Science,
https://doi.org/10.1007/978-3-032-08263-3_31

History

1918 The modern Republic of Macedonia joined the Kingdom of Serbs, Croats, and Slovenes following the fall of the Austro-Hungarian Empire.

1929 The kingdom adopted the name Yugoslavia.

1941 During World War II, Nazi Germany, Bulgaria, and Italy occupied the modern Republic of Macedonia.

1945 Following the war, the present-day Republic of Macedonia became a constituent republic of socialist Yugoslavia.

1991 In a referendum, 95.26% of voters in the Republic of Macedonia supported breaking away from Yugoslavia, making the country an independent one.

1992 The Republic of Macedonia became a member of the International Monetary Fund (IMF).

1993 The Republic of Macedonia became a part of the United Nations (UN) as "the former Yugoslav Republic of Macedonia," serving as an interim name.

1995 Greece and the Republic of Macedonia signed the Interim Accord.

2001 (Spring) Insurgency in the Republic of Macedonia.

2001 (August) The Ohrid Framework Agreement was signed, signaling the end of the conflict.

2003 The Republic of Macedonia formally joined the World Trade Organization (WTO).

2005 The Republic of Macedonia gained the status of a candidate country for membership in the European Union (EU).

2008 (April) Greece blocked the Republic of Macedonia's admission to the North Atlantic Treaty Organization (NATO).

2009 Visa-free travel within EU's Schengen zone came into effect for Macedonian citizens.

2011 The International Court of Justice in The Hague ruled that Greece was wrong to block Macedonia's bid to join NATO in 2008 because of the row over its name.

2012 (December 24) The Macedonian political opposition was forcefully removed from the Parliament upon voting for the controversial Government budget for 2013. Political tensions escalate and reach their peak.

2013 (April) Positive EU report in all areas on Macedonia's path toward membership, despite domestic political tensions.

2015 (February) Massive wiretapping scandal emerged as the prime minister and the ruling party were accused of a mass surveillance program and interfering in the judiciary.

2016 The Republic of Macedonia was categorized as a hybrid regime based on the Democracy Index. Colorful Revolution protests began, demanding the political resignation of key figures. The country was facing a political crisis.

2017 The Bloody Thursday occurred on 27 April, when about 200 Macedonian nationalists stormed the Macedonian Parliament, severely injuring several politicians. Strong condemnation from the international community, the EU, and NATO. After 11 years, a major governmental change occurred.

2018 (June) The Prespa Agreement between the Republic of Macedonia and Greece was signed, replacing the 1995 Interim Accord.
2018 (July) NATO invited the Republic of Macedonia to start accession talks in a bid to become the Euro Atlantic alliance's 30th member.
2019 The Republic of Macedonia officially changed its constitutional name to the Republic of North Macedonia.
2020 North Macedonia becomes the 30th NATO member.
2021 After 5 years of a hybrid regime, the Republic of North Macedonia was categorized as a flawed democracy based on the Democracy Index.
2021 (June) At the Economic Forum on Regional Cooperation held in Skopje, leaders of Albania, North Macedonia, and Serbia unveiled a new name for what was colloquially known as Mini-Schengen, which, from then on, would be officially called the Open Balkan initiative.
2021 (December) Bulgaria again blocked EU accession talks for the Republic of North Macedonia.
2022 The Republic of North Macedonia finally started accession talks with the EU.

1 Introduction: Context and History

The Republic of North Macedonia is a small and open, but landlocked, country located in the heart of the Western Balkan region in Southeastern Europe. The modern-day geographic territory of North Macedonia has served as a junction throughout its history for explorers, traders, and conquerors traveling between Europe and Asia Minor, which left their own cultural mark. It arose as one of the prominent ancient civilizations alongside the Greeks, Persians, and Egyptians, followed by being one of the structural jurisdictions under the Roman and Byzantine empires. As the geographical area fluctuated, North Macedonia eventually ended up as a Slavic nation, with Slavic tribes moving into the area between the sixth and eighth century A.D. Its vibrant historical nexus was elevated during its nearly half-a-millennia occupation by the Ottoman Empire, lasting until 1912. Since Macedonia lacked governance of its own ethnic region covering an area of approximately 67,000 km^2 (about twice the area of Belgium), the Second Balkan War resulted in its division between Greece, Serbia, and Bulgaria. Consequently, due to its jurisdiction under the Serbian Kingdom, the present-day area of the Republic of North Macedonia was incorporated into the formed Kingdom of Serbs, Croats, and Slovenes. Only after the end of World War II, did the Republic of North Macedonia become one of the six constituent republics of the new Socialist Federal Republic of Yugoslavia (SFRY), finally achieving formal and nationwide establishment.

The then-called Republic of Macedonia entered the SFRY as the poorest and least developed country. During the SFRY period, the Republic of Macedonia started the process of industrialization and establishing its infrastructure. Besides its naturally agricultural economic setting, the Yugoslavian government substantially invested in North Macedonia's light industry such as food, tobacco, and textile, after which came the agricultural machinery and household appliances factories. The focus of the Macedonian economy was to supply the Yugoslav market with agricultural products, tobacco, steel plates, textiles, and semi-finished products, consequently finalized for export in the other republics. Following the breakup of former Yugoslavia, this reliance of the Macedonian economy on Yugoslav markets had disastrous effects.

A peaceful declaration of independence was stated on 8 September 1991 regarding the referendum conducted, maintaining peaceful separation from SFRY amid violent separation and conflicts in the other Yugoslav republics. Monetary independence was declared in 1992, introducing the Macedonian denar as a national currency. Due to Greece's objection to using the term *Macedonia* in the country's constitutional name, North Macedonia experienced a political rollercoaster upon finally joining the UN in 1993. However, Greece unilaterally imposed a trade embargo against the Republic of Macedonia (i.e., FYROM for international usage) in 1994 after which the Interim Accord of 1995 was adopted. The Accord stipulated, among other things, that Greece would not object to FYROM's admission to international organizations under its new name, but such an agreement was broken multiple times in the following years. In 2003 North Macedonia officially became a member of the WTO. In 2004, the Stabilization and Association Agreement entered into force, and North Macedonia started the application process to join the EU in 2005. Since 2006, the nation has belonged to both the European Free Trade Association (EFTA) and Central European Free Trade Agreement (CEFTA) but failed to institutionalize itself in the EU and NATO.

Since its formal entrance into the SFRY, North Macedonia has been regarded as the least developed Western Balkan country (excluding Kosovo from the analysis). Classified as a country with high human development, North Macedonia ranks 78th in the World, with the Human Development Index (HDI) estimated at 0.770 for 2021, four places below Bosnia and Herzegovina with HDI of 0.780 (UNDP, 2022). Its GDP per capita grew approximately 171.3% in the last 30 years (The World Bank, 2022), with an average geometric GDP growth rate of 1.31%, and an average arithmetic growth rate of 1.38%. For the period between 2011 and 2021, the average geometric growth rate of the GDP is 1.86% and the arithmetic average is 1.9%. Having in mind the impact of the COVID-19 pandemic in 2020 and its structural break in countries' growth rates, the average geometric growth rate of the Macedonian GDP between 2011 and 2019 is 2.55%, annually.

Unemployment levels have come a long way since 2011, dropping from 31.38% to 14.3% in the third quarter of 2022, with youth unemployment still high at 32.6% (State Statistical Office, 2022a). Furthermore, after a series of increases since 2018, the minimum net wage stands at 18,000 MKD (or 291.78 EUR) while the national average is 32,553 MKD (or 527.68 EUR) according to the State Statistical Office (2022a). So far, a government announcement has been made that the minimum wage should be estimated at approximately 20,000 MKD (or 324.2 EUR) until the second quarter of 2023.

The average inflation levels since 2011 are estimated at 2.79% and are influenced by the foreign supply shocks of oil, gas, and electricity prices, and the EU-level inflation. The low inflation rates excluding exogenous shocks are achieved through the monetary stability of the economy, impacted by the central bank's de facto fixed exchange rate anchor. The current account balance was estimated at−3.542% of GDP in 2021 (IMF, 2022), maintaining the traditional deficit throughout the years. North Macedonia is a moderately indebted country, maintaining the general government debt at 53.202% of GDP in 2021, almost doubling its debt since the estimated 27.728% of GDP in 2011 (IMF, 2022). In 2021 a total of 72,922 business entities operate in the country with 30% being in the trade (wholesale and retail) sector, 10.9% in the manufacturing sector, 10.7% being in the professional, scientific, and technical activities, and 7.4% in the real estate business (State Statistical Office, 2022d). North Macedonia is a country of SMEs, making up 99.7% of total firms—of those 99.7%, the portion of micro and small business entities together is 89.5% of total Macedonian firms (an additional 8.2% are firms with no data attainable for their number of employees), while 2% are medium enterprises, leaving out only 0.3% of large companies (State Statistical Office, 2022d).

As a small and open economy, North Macedonia is highly dependent on its trade openness—toward its European partners. In the context of the business activity and trade of the hidden champions in the Macedonian economy, it is necessary to focus on foreign trade to contextualize their business environment. The foreign trade coverage ratio is estimated at 71.9% for 2021, increasing 8.2% points in the last decade due to higher growth rates of exports (State Statistical Office, 2022b). North Macedonia's major trade partners are mainly from Europe—first, the countries in its closest proximity, and then other EU countries and China from the Asian continent. Namely, when it comes to exporting, they include Germany (46.73%), Bulgaria (4.85%), Kosovo (4.37%), Serbia (4.22%), Hungary (3.07%), Italy (3%), Greece (2.98%), the United Kingdom (2.57%), China (2.25%), and the Slovak Republic (1.92%) (State Statistical Office, 2022b). Importing in North Macedonia is also more or less done with these countries as well as with other countries from the central and southern parts of Europe. More precisely, the top 10 importing partners of North Macedonia are the United Kingdom (17.65%), Germany (10.17%), Greece (7.65%), Serbia (6.84%), China (6.68%), Türkiye (5.5%), Italy (4.33%), Bulgaria (4.27%), Poland (2.98%), and Romania (2.61%) (State Statistical Office, 2022b).

With that in mind, North Macedonia mainly exports machinery and transport equipment, taking up the largest portion among the industries (30.44%) and chemicals, while food and live animals is less prevalent (State Statistical Office, 2022c). In comparison, the export outlook a decade ago was different. Then, the country's chief objects of export were manufactured goods from iron and steel, while chemicals, fuels, lubricants, and related materials remained steady over time (State Statistical Office, 2022c). On the other hand, manufactured goods from non-ferrous metals and other material took the number one spot when it comes to most common imported goods. These are followed by machinery and transport equipment, chemicals, and fuels, and lubricants to a lesser degree. In this sense, North Macedonia's importing practices have remained consistent over time—in 2011, the most imported goods were still manufactured goods from metals, mineral fuels, lubricants, and machinery (State Statistical Office, 2022c). The exporting and importing activities of the country are also reflected in the highlighted hidden champions from the country, which mostly cover the aforementioned industries. Considering this, it is expected these trends to continue in the future.

According to the 2021 competitiveness report of the OECD (2021), North Macedonia's highest average scores are in the dimensions of trade, energy, tax, employment, and anti-corruption policy, outperforming the Western Balkan average. However, strong ties between the export-oriented FDI sector and local SMEs have limited the influence of diversification and the expansion of the trade sector on total GDP growth (OECD, 2021). Contextual data on the most important variables depicting the country's economic activity, conditions, and dynamics are depicted in Exhibit 1.

In such an economic environment, the Macedonian hidden champions (HC) integrate into the domestic economy and global niche markets based on innovation, refinement, and product differentiation.

2 Characteristics of Hidden Champions from North Macedonia

This book chapter provides an in-depth overview of four hidden champions that primarily operate from the territory of North Macedonia. Interestingly, two of them (Mikrosam and Ading have been analyzed before (Santa & Kekenovski, 2013), while two are under the hidden champions microscope for the first time—Mermer Imperijal and Korab Trnica.

These companies were selected because of their dominance in their respective market shares, their size, which was usually small or medium, low visibility, and sales revenues which have not exceeded a billion dollars as some formal criteria for hidden champions worldwide (Simon, 2021). Besides these, the identified companies exemplify leadership, the spirit of family-driven businesses, export and niche market orientation, innovation, and uniqueness, which makes them more captivating for further research.

While the market leadership characteristics have stayed the same for Mikrosam and Ading, there have been notable changes since the last analysis of these hidden champions. In this regard, the companies' business operations have been affected by the recent disruptions of the pandemic, the geopolitical tensions, and the energy and economic crises. Despite these occurrences, the companies were prompted to up their game and heavily invest in digitalization and new equipment to streamline the production processes and make them more efficient. Considering this, all analyzed companies are diverse as they represent different industries and subindustries—from the production and sales of marble and heavy machinery to processing food and selling dairy products.

Exhibit 1 Core economic indicators for North Macedonia

	2017	2018	2019	2020	2021	2022	2023	2024
GDP per capita (current US$)	5450.49	6108.74	6718.86	6659.60	7620.80	7606.24	8624.29	..
GDP per capita growth (annual %)	0.98	2.80	4.62	−3.65	5.59	3.06	2.29	..
Unemployment, total (% of total labor force) (modeled ILO estimate)	22.4	20.7	17.41	16.58	15.8	14.48	13.17	13.42
Foreign direct investment, net inflows (% of GDP)	3.4	5.1	4.36	0.06	4.97	6.13	4.07	..
GDP (current US$, mio)	11307.06	12683.07	12606.34	12361.04	14000.28	13932.44	15763.62	..
Exports of goods and services (current US$, mio)	6235.36	7657.42	7867.37	7141.15	9162.33	10140.78	10690.52	..
Exports of goods and services (% of GDP)	55.15	60.38	62.41	57.77	65.44	72.79	67.82	..
Merchandise exports (current US$, mio)	5668	6911	7189	6638	8186	8727	8999	..
Merchandise exports to high-income economies (% of total merchandise exports)	77.71	79.28	82.34	82.48	81.52	81.93	81.52	..

(continued)

Exhibit 1 (continued)

	2017	2018	2019	2020	2021	2022	2023	2024
Merchandise exports to low-and middle-income economies in Europe & Central Asia (% of total merchandise exports)	20.48	18.37	13.05	12.77	14.24	15.14	15.2	..
Ores and metals exports (% of merchandise exports)	5.32	5.11	4.8	4.46	5.16	4.62	3.99	4.69
Agricultural raw materials exports (% of merchandise exports)	0.53	0.44	0.42	0.43	0.45	0.46	0.43	0.49
Food exports (% of merchandise exports)	10.29	8.94	9.36	9.83	8.7	8.21	8.95	10.64
Fuel exports (% of merchandise exports)	1.50	1.70	2.04	1.41	1.83	4.39	4.12	3.46
Manufactures exports (% of merchandise exports)	82.29	83.74	83.3	83.79	83.78	82.23	82.41	80.6
High-technology exports (% of manufactured exports)	3.98	4.05	4.22	4.18	4.03	4.01	5.23	6.36

Source: World Bank, 2025

The nature of the industry notwithstanding, to stay relevant and to grow, these companies opted to come up with innovations and new products that meet the rapidly changing demands of the clients. In the case of Ading, this meant creating a product that was the first of its kind on the market. All these conditions tested these companies' flexibility and willingness to change and learn, demonstrating that even market leaders should continuously invest in human capital and life-long learning. What is common about Mermer Imperijal and Korab Trnica is that they try to embed the tradition of their companies and families as well as the local raw materials and resources into their respective product lines, while blending that with new packaging and innovative production processes to offer fresh products that are exported to other countries, too. Remarkably, all of this is done in a corporate culture like a family business.

These companies emphasize that some of the vital lessons they learned along the way are related to the vigilance of new opportunities, staying close to the clients and the utmost quality in everything the companies do, investing in people, and being brave to try new things with the products, among other things. Common for all of them, too, is the acknowledgment that there is still room for improvement by identifying some development needs. These refer to the need for new competitive skills, especially for salespeople and engineers, a growing marketing presence and effort, the need for additional financing for larger teams and research and development as well as better cooperation with key decision-makers on national and regional levels.

3 Case Studies of Selected Hidden Champions

3.1 Korab Trnica

Overview
Address: S. Trnica 1, Mavrovo, Republic of North Macedonia
Tel: +38922034800
Email: b.dabevski@korabtrnica.mk
Web: https://korabtrnica.mk

Company Information
Industry: Manufacturing
Year of Establishment: 2014
Sales Revenues in 2021: 7,470,806 euros
Average number of employees in 2023: 111
Brainer(s) behind the company: The company's partners

3.1.1 Nature of Market Leadership

Korab Trnica has focused exclusively on the primary industry, being production of dairy products including cheeses, milk, yogurts, and more. This has led to extensive focus on the key performance indicators and parameters, as well as ensuring product quality and customer relationship management. Considering that the company operates in a fragmented market, it is still considered a regional market leader, operating in a business environment with multiple competitors, with estimates suggesting that it holds up to around 15% of different niche market categories like cheese.

3.1.2 Nature of Competitive Advantage

The company takes pride in being a market leader in dairy production, originating from North Macedonia. Through strong leadership in the previous years during the pandemic, Korab Trnica has managed to maintain its leadership position. By offering unique products on the market, with continuous investment in the production equipment and bringing innovations to various product lines. Specific focus has also been placed on maintaining existing customer relationships.

3.1.3 Core Lessons Learned on the Path to Success

1. Focusing on the primary industry.
2. Market research and planning, through a well-designed feedback loop and monitoring of market indicators with a proactive approach.
3. Maintaining the high quality of production facilities and final products being delivered to consumers, as this entails success in the long run.

3.1.4 Management and Leadership Development Needs

The company highlights the need for improvement of technological knowledge, techniques for recognition of possibilities, skills for working in teams, enhancing both internal and external communication, decision-making, motivation, and similar. In this sense, the organization considers the competencies related to information and communication technologies (ICT) as the most underdeveloped ones because of some traditional views of segments of the workforce that are resistant to change and strive to exist in the comfort zone. Thus, they highlight the need for education as necessary in all segments of the work, believing that only through a continuous process of learning can the internal infrastructure of the company and its resistance to external influences be strengthened. Another important set of skills which was identified was related to marketing. The company has recognized the value of a continuous marketing approach—primarily in the digital channels, due to the characteristics of other markets, but also in combination with TV and radio.

3.1.5 Financing and Regulatory Environment Development Needs

Korab Trnica focuses on the financing and regulatory environment development needs from their own perspective as potential agents of change instead of just passively waiting for external stakeholders to do something about these challenges. Hence, the company considers it should invest more in modernizing the production process and improving energy efficiency in their processes, which climbs up on the agenda of many companies following the energy crises and the recent sustainability trends. The common ground is that the need for using modern ICT tools and applications is vital on the path to complete digitalization of the business sector.

3.1.6 Pandemic's Impact on "Hidden Champions" Business Approach

Considering the company focuses on the production and sales of dairy products, the consensus is that they did not feel the pandemic strongly reshaped their business operations. Some of the challenges the company dealt with during this period were a lack of raw materials in quantity and quality as well as the movement restrictions and economic measures imposed by the regulators. To tackle this, Korab Trnica implemented practices of quick decision-making and realized larger investments in equipment. Organization-wise, the company did an internal restructuring to maintain flexibility and agility.

3.1.7 Effects of the Ukraine War on "Hidden Champions" Business Operations

The war in Ukraine has resulted in consequences for the supply chain and energy infrastructure of Korab Trnica, too. Since the start of the war, the company has experienced rising energy prices, increased prices of raw materials, as well as risks related to unfair competition and untimely payments from clients. This provoked the company to come up with mitigation strategies that included the utilization of cost optimization models, continuous communication with strategic suppliers and buyers, more careful selection of buyers, and changes in production management.

3.1.8 Cheese to Please: Unveiling the Story of a Hidden Dairy Champion

The origins of the brand Korab Trnica can be traced even to 1945 when the first business activity was sheep farming and with producing and independent sales of meat and dairy products through a network of shops. This was the point when the original dairy products were starting to be produced. Today, Korab Trnica is known for its renowned traditional products and some flagstone ones like the Korab yellow cheese, Trnica's sour milk, Trnica cheese, and more. Besides its primary activity of producing dairy products, Korab Trnica expanded into the hospitality industry in the

1970s, opening its own restaurant, which was afterward complemented by an accommodation facility. Still, the signature cheeses and milk products remained a significant part of the Korab Trnica story and are ubiquitous on the restaurant's menu.

Yet, 2014 saw the company's most significant moment when a decision was made to modernize Korab Trnica, in parallel with a comprehensive process of large investments and developing a new company-wide strategy. The following year was pivotal for bringing the former glory to the brand "Korab Trnica," too, when the modern company started getting more of the market share and a large investment cycle commenced. This meant that the organization had to keep the good practices of the past while introducing new aspects. Thus, the company realized that modernization and development of the business process is equally important as nurturing the traditional spirit.

This resulted in the wide promotion of Korab Trnica's concept, whose foundation is "from the nature to the table," meaning that the company strives to produce natural products and is completely in charge of their sale. Furthermore, the company considers this both as its biggest competitive advantage as well as a challenge to maintain. This means that their cows, sheep, goats, and bees consume food and nutrients from untouched nature on the Korab mountain, which is rich with herbs, flowers, teas, and clean mountain water, which reflects in the final products on the consumers' tables, too.

Namely, the product palette mainly consists of white and yellow cheeses, cottage cheese, yogurt, whey, sour cream, and milk. Connected to this, besides dairy, the product lines also include chicken pâté, natural honey, and more. So, besides the Macedonian market, the citizens in Serbia, Montenegro, and Kosovo can enjoy the company's fresh cheeses and milk products thanks to the wide regional export network. This led to increases in sales revenues from 3,221,057 euros in 2019 to 7,470,806 euros in less than four years besides the destructive effects of the pandemic and the following crises.

Korab Trnica is recognized as a market leader due to its commitment to excellence, high brand awareness, and consistent product quality. While the company's position as one of the market leaders has remained over the years, it still believes that its market leadership has changed due to its strong focus on the primary subindustry, which is the production of dairy products. Moreover, an attempt to cover the entire spectrum of work, from cattle breeding, fodder production, milk production, milk processing, and cheese production was unsuccessful, which is why the company stayed faithful to only the latter, specializing in this market niche.

Related to the main strengths of the company, the company exhibits the strong personality of a market leader, while nurturing the long history of customer relationships. Additionally, the company takes pride in investing in the workforce and their engagement, motivation, and knowledge of the market. The challenges imposed by the pandemic and the war in Ukraine have demonstrated to the company that their flexibility is also a plus when dealing with products that rely on strong and healthy supply chains.

This adaptability and willingness to try something new can be seen in the new packages of the Korab Trnica products, which maintain the authentic and traditional look, while still being modern. In this regard, the company's key messages visible on the dairy products are "From Trnica, with love since 1945" and "Natural, with a taste," alluding to the organic segment of the products straight from nature's resources at Korab mountain. Speaking of marketing practices, the company acknowledges the need for increased digital marketing efforts, especially when entering other markets. Besides that, the company strongly relies on a word-of-mouth strategy with the customers being the ones who will advertise the products to their friends, families, and colleagues.

Despite this, the company has faced an onset of barriers brought mainly by recent geopolitical events and the pandemic crises. Hence, the energy, resources, and health crises, combined with the economic policies of the country have been at the top of the management agenda. But what lies ahead? Korab Trnica plans to focus more on innovation and look further into introducing new products. Its sales strategy remains deeply embedded in the principles of direct sales through company stores instead of using the well-established networks of large retail stores and supermarkets. The management and the Korab Trnica team see their original products as promoters of the Macedonian natural beauty and tradition, which can result in a more equitable socio-economic development of all areas of the country—both urban and rural.

3.2 *Mermer Imperijal DOO Prilep*

Overview
Address: Aleksandar Makedonski BB, Prilep, Republic of North Macedonia
Tel: +38948416040
Email: info@mermerimperijal.mk
Web: https://mermerimperijal.mk

Company Information
Industry: Construction
Year of Establishment: 2010
Sales Revenues in 2021: 766,051 euros
Average number of employees in 2023: 15
Brainer(s) behind the company: Management team

3.2.1 Nature of Market Leadership

The company has large and modern production facilities and equipment, which allows it to fulfill the needs of complex projects, placing it as one of the top Bianco Sivec marble suppliers in the region and beyond. The proximity to the port of Thessaloniki, Greece, which is used as a main logistics hub, enables the distribution of their materials to various destinations throughout several continents. Hence, the company estimates that it is regional market leader, having a market share of up to 50%.

3.2.2 Nature of Competitive Advantage

Mermer Imperijal is a small family-run business, placing the key to its success in its highly skilled employees' motivation and the atmosphere in the company to pursue business opportunities. Beyond that, it enables flexibility in their approach to potential clients in their offerings and moving to new markets quickly. Additionally, the company prides itself on its financial stability, undertaking several large and complex projects at once and delivering in full.

3.2.3 Core Lessons Learned on the Path to Success

1. The market landscape requires patience and persistence in all strategic and operational activities to endure various phases of growth.
2. Continuing the flow of logistics and transportation of materials is essential, especially in times of crisis.
3. The input of each member is incredibly important in maintaining successful customer relationships in the long term, especially for small teams.

3.2.4 Management and Leadership Development Needs

The company has identified marketing skills and competencies as crucial for maintaining and advancing the leadership position. The small number of employees does not have the opportunity to focus solely on updating the website, social media channels, and making advertisements, which could be solved by having a larger marketing team. Additionally, the management believes that investing in building the know-how of the sales managers and team is vital as these people oversee the entire sales process and the so-called *blood flow* of the company.

3.2.5 Financing and Regulatory Environment Development Needs

While the company does not note major regulatory environment development needs and constraints, it believes it would benefit more from having more loan opportunities and better credit lines from financial institutions. These available funds would be used for investing in state-of-the-art equipment and increasing production capacities.

3.2.6 Pandemic's Impact on "Hidden Champions" Business Approach

The pandemic had severe negative impacts on the business operations of the company. Consequently, the work stagnated because of the closed borders and the stillness of the markets. This was also negatively reflected in the exports. Moreover, the rising positive cases of the COVID-19 virus among employees additionally overburdened the production process, which was stopped a few times during the crisis.

3.2.7 Effects of the Ukraine War on "Hidden Champions" Business Operations

The main effects of the war in Ukraine mostly refer to the subsequent rising inflation and energy prices. Namely, the company experiences minor challenges with electricity supply as well as some countries opting out of buying marble. Connected to this, production costs, especially those of electricity as a main input and production resource, increased dramatically. So, the company was prompted to find new ways to acquire new customers to increase exports.

3.2.8 Success Set in Stone: From a Family Business to a Hidden Champion

One of the first characteristics of Mermer Imperijal is that it was established as a family business in Prilep, North Macedonia and it stayed that way from its humble beginnings in 2010. Its workforce is slowly growing, too, from just including the family members to nine employees in 2019 and 15 in 2021. More than 10 years forward, the company is still working in the construction industry as one of the market leaders in the region when it comes to processing and sales of marble.

The company first started with a small capacity in charge of processing travertine and Bianco Sivec marble, supplying quality products to local partners. The marble and other raw materials needed for creating stone and marble products were local and directly obtained from the quarries, which are situated around 10 kilometers from the production facility. This has had multiple effects on the company's business operations. Getting necessary resources nearby meant higher cost-efficiency, promotion of local products, and advancement of the local economy through opening new local jobs.

Moreover, as a younger member of the family of well-established companies, Mermer Imperijal credits the hard work, work philosophy, and increasing investments as crucial predictors of its growth and expansion. Today, Mermer Imperijal has large and contemporary production facilities and equipment, which allows it to carry out big and complex projects—from grandiose homes and mansions to hospitality businesses such as one of the country's most popular wineries, winery Sopot.

Going beyond the country's borders, Mermer Imperijal is a supplier and contractor for travertine projects throughout the Balkans. To achieve this, the company counts on the proximity to the port of Thessaloniki, Greece, which is around 200 kilometers away from the production plant. As one of the region's main logistics hubs, this port allows direct distribution of materials and products to other countries and continents.

In the years Mermer Imperijal has existed on the market, it has seen major changes in the factors affecting the market leadership. Hence, the company recognized there are greater opportunities to acquire new customers on a global level, which has been made even more possible with exceedingly rapid digitalization, social media, and the internet evolution where it is possible for a client from a different continent to order marble from a distant corner of the world. Related to this, the company reported an increase in exports due to higher production and finding new customers via the Internet. Additionally, to accommodate these market conditions, the company's capital has increased as have the production possibilities.

The last few years have not brought straightforward growth for the company, especially considering the destructive effects of the pandemic, the energy crisis, and the war in Ukraine on the global both value and supply chains. Namely, its sales were slightly lowered from 2019 when they were 993,739 euros to 763,818 euros in 2021. Yet, the company is getting back on track as it aims to focus on international markets in the next period. In this sense, the company views the size of the production as one of the prevalent current challenges, while its ambitions to increase its participation in the global market is a future challenge to be worked on.

To address these barriers, the company relies on the customers' loyalty to the brand, its flexibility, and the total quality philosophy it has from its roots. As a smaller and agile company, Mermer Imperijal has felt the negative effects of putting more effort into gaining a bigger market share to the positive effects of being more able to successfully introduce and scale up innovations in the production and logistics processes.

3.3 Ading

Overview
Address: Novoselski pat (St. 1409) 11, 1060 Skopje, Republic of North Macedonia
Tel: +38922034800
Email: ading@ading.com.mk
Web: https://www.ading.com.mk/

Company Information
Industry: Manufacturing
Year of Establishment: 1969 (privatized in 1996)
Sales Revenues in 2021: 7,316,074 euros
Average number of employees in 2023: 150
Brainer(s) behind the company: The employees

3.3.1 Nature of Market Leadership

The driving force of its market leadership is the regional uniqueness of the company's products which are additives, admixtures, coatings, mortars, adhesives and supporting construction chemicals for the construction industry. These additives are used for mending, waterproofing, maintaining, protecting, and reconstructing concrete constructions to enhance durability. Hence, Ading dominates the market of South-East Europe (SEE). The nature of the market leadership changed due to the rising need to reduce the emission of harmful gases during production and participation in the mission to achieve net zero. Hence, the aggressive effects of the atmosphere on existing or new reinforced concrete structures have increased the need for protective coatings and specific materials for their repair and maintenance. Considering all of this, the concrete manufacturers' impact on the environment has been heavily under public scrutiny.

To deal with this and maintain the leader position, Ading's focal points were adaptability, flexibility, and knowledge of the markets in the SEE region. With this in mind, they promote a tailor-made approach with continuous support for the client even after the purchase has been made, which is rare in the industry.

3.3.2 Nature of Competitive Advantage

The company's nature of competitive advantage has drastically changed since 2018, partly because more than 10 large competitors from different regions of the world appeared in similar fields and disciplines. The company underwent some internal changes, too. They changed their focus on profitability to also include sustainability and their own contribution to building a better tomorrow. In recent years Ading became a purpose-driven company, reshaping its core values. Yet, Ading's competitive advantage is the people, that is, the engineering teams, the support teams from other services, and the new generations who joined the workforce in the meantime. This means that the company builds a long history of relationships with stakeholders and customers while relying on its strength of innovation, knowledge of the market, loyalty, and qualifications of the employees.

3.3.3 Core Lessons Learned on the Path to Success

1. Investing in human resources and the care of the people.
2. Establishing a system for a rapid internal transfer of accumulated knowledge.
3. Having a vision and leadership, and making sure the employees have mutual objectives.
4. Diversifying the product portfolio and covering more areas to be more flexible and disperse risks.

3.3.4 Management and Leadership Development Needs

Ading acknowledges that progress in its industry occurs almost daily, and the needs of the construction industry are consistently changing. They believe that skills for encouraging further innovation, intrapreneurship, and supporting proactivity among employees, allowing them more space and freedom to create and come up with proposals for the realization of their ideas are crucial for advancing the management and leadership capacities. Connected to the dynamic nature of the industry, skills for research and development (R&D), technical application, and sales are needed, too. Lastly, competencies related to marketing for the part of the production program, which is intended for retail sales, are needed as well. Considering this, Ading highlights the need to attract new human potential as a precursor to business success.

3.3.5 Financing and Regulatory Environment Development Needs

Ensuring equal market conditions for the industry through regulators and decision-makers is crucial and needed according to Ading's point of view. The company believes that certifications and compliance with all regulations and rules should be equally important for domestic and foreign brands. In this sense, there should be greater engagement and support between policymakers and the industry members in the aspects of demonstration and promotion of the expertise, know-how, and experiences these companies have. This increased collaboration can result in leveraging the insights into sustainable solutions for the socio-economic development of the industry and the country.

3.3.6 Pandemic's Impact on "Hidden Champions" Business Approach

The pandemic has impacted Ading's work on multiple levels, beginning with the internal processes and the growth of the responsibility of the teams, their independence and agility, and the ability for rapid mutual coordination. Moreover, the company experienced difficulties in operation, unpredictability, rising costs of employee health and security, and disruptions of the production processes. To mitigate this, they turned toward developing new, unknown operations, and introducing remote work paired with constant adaptation and increased vigilance across all sectors and activities internally as well as careful consideration of the external environment.

3.3.7 Effects of the Ukraine War on "Hidden Champions" Business Operations

Some of the main obstacles Ading faced due to the Ukraine war were the additional disruptions of global supply chains and the unpredictability of raw materials prices. Still, the company was quick to implement solutions and strategies such as thorough procurement and logistics planning and financial management, cutting unnecessary costs, making adaptations to the production processes, and investing in renewable energy sources. The latter was prompted by the widespread energy crisis, which ensued shortly after the start of the war. As a result, sustainability has become the new credo of the company as its management is on the lookout for new ways of optimizing and improving their and their partners' processes. Additionally, this situation has made them more aware, responsible, and willing to prioritize the company's contribution to the environment.

3.3.8 Cementing Excellence: The Hidden Champion Revolutionizing Cement and Admixture Innovations

As a joint-stock company, Ading focuses on producing and selling admixtures and other supporting chemicals for the construction industry. It is also known for repairing, reconstructing, and protecting reinforced concrete constructions. Since its establishment in 1969, the company grew and reformed, becoming a joint-stock company in 1996, almost 30 years after the start of the business operations.

Ading's story began with just five people, embarking on a vision and mission to manufacture specific products, which had been unheard of at that time. Now, Ading Group employs more than 150 employees of which around 40% are architects, engineers, and experienced professionals. In Skopje, the company has its headquarters, where it offers additional services like wholesale and retail sales of construction and chemical materials, finish and rehabilitation of construction works, design, marketing, soft landscaping, and property valuation through its three daughter companies and a joint venture. This enables Ading to offer a comprehensive solution from design and manufacturing to implementation and maintenance.

After securing its position in the domestic market, Ading set its aspirations internationally and has reached South-Eastern Europe, the rest of the European countries, the Middle East, Asia, and Africa. To meet the needs of the diverse and geographically dispersed customers, Ading Group has international members in Serbia, Bulgaria, Greece, and Kazakhstan while maintaining a wide range of international distributors in Libya, Montenegro, Croatia, Albania, Kosovo, Bosnia and Herzegovina, Hungary, Romania, Ukraine, Russia, Iran, and more.

On the domestic market, Ading leads in concrete additives, waterproofing, and materials for repair and protection. Even though the company managed to maintain its position in the market, that does not mean that the market conditions, per se, remained the same. Subsequently, the industry has seen more pronounced and aggressive competition, disruptions in supply chains, and even a serious brain drain when it comes to a qualified and professional workforce, which is characteristic of the country and the region at large. Additionally, several consolidations, mergers, and acquisitions occurred in and around the industry, impacting the business existence of many companies.

Connected to this, some of the prevalent business challenges the company faced related to the creation of added value for Ading's partners, and through them to contribute to the sustainability of the community. With the rising awareness of environmental protection and care for the well-being of communities and the planet, the company embarked on a complete transformation of its operations and vision toward achieving a sustainable way of working.

On this strategic journey, Ading has relied on the customers and employees as the crucial company beneficiary. On the one hand, the company utilized its long history of customer relationships and its direct, personal approach to customers. To include the customer in the production process, the company is acknowledged for its early-detection system for client needs (Berberović et al., 2019). Thanks to this system and the services offered in the area, the customers can see the big picture from the beginning and get involved in putting the right product in the right hands, which often means that the company detects the clients' need before the competition, giving it an advantage over the rest.

On the other hand, the company depends on the workforce's knowledge of the market, loyalty, qualifications, teamwork, and innovation capacities, which the company has built with continuous education of its human resources. This combined two-fold effect led to the rise of one of Ading's biggest strengths, which is the development of products and technologies that help optimize production as well as products and technologies that protect new reinforced concrete structures or extend the life of existing buildings of this type.

Recognized as "construction pharmacists," the experienced and skilled people of Ading have positioned themselves as go-to producers for innovative products and technologies that can solve both general and specific construction issues. Ading's products are based on concrete and cement admixtures, which add value and support the construction processes afterward. The company has diversified and reinvented what it does by introducing new products. More precisely, its product portfolio includes more than 100 products, including admixtures, floor-finishing products, joint sealants, protective coatings, adhesives, decorative coatings, leveling compounds, and even products for grouting and sealing, concrete repair, waterproofing, fire protection, and more. Considering this, in the last 10 years, the company has introduced radical changes in the range of products. It developed a series of products for the needs of the cement industry, "grinding agents" that help reduce CO_2 emissions.

With its pioneering technologies and products, Ading has played a key role in some of the vital infrastructure projects in the Balkans. Its strategy focuses on improving its product lines and selling in domestic and international markets. All these efforts almost doubled the sales revenues from 2019 until 2021; the sales revenues in the former year being 4,876,901 euros and 7,316,074 euros two years later. These effects spilled over into the company's return on assets (ROA) and return on equity (ROE). The ROA in 2019 was 3.47, while in 2021 it equaled 4.09. A similar situation is evident with the ROE indicator which jumped from 4.94 in 2019 to 5.99 in 2021.

The company uses its competitive advantage to intensively collaborate with universities and scientific institutions in civil engineering to exchange know-how and support the academic community. This is one of the strategic directions of the current management. It also believes in the constant development of the key resource of Ading—its people.

3.4 Mikrosam

Overview
Address: Krusevski pat b.b., 7500 Prilep, Republic of North Macedonia
Tel: +389(0)48400100
Email: info@mikrosam.com
Web: https://www.mikrosam.com/

Company Information
Industry: Manufacturing
Year of Establishment: 1990
Sales Revenues in 2021: 13,018,843 euros
Average number of employees in 2023: 179
Brainer(s) behind the company: Professor Blagoja Samakoski, Liljana Samakoska, Vele Samak, Samoil Samak, and Fanija Samak

3.4.1 Nature of Market Leadership

In the past 10 years, Mikrosam's market leadership nature changed as it increased market share in more than 43 countries and entered the US market. Mikrosam became known for the world's most extensive product line for CNG and hydrogen tanks, while extensively partnering and including the customers in terms of development and improvement projects. By not having a preferential domestic market, the company is pushed to compete globally. This creates the need for a broad technology portfolio and taking on new challenges.

Since university degrees in composites are not available, the company takes upon upskilling and reskilling its workforce, driving further its human capital, innovation capabilities, and thus market position. The nature of the market leadership also stems from the brand value and recognizability in this area as well as the engineered-to-order machines, which positively contributed to the market influence.

3.4.2 Nature of Competitive Advantage

Mikrosam's competitive advantage is rooted in its innovation, engineered-to-order machines, knowledge of key composite production, automation, and software development competencies, strong international sales and marketing presence, and willingness to support customer development and training projects. There are around three relevant competitors in Europe and around five relevant competitors in the United States. Based on the company's competitive advantage analysis, there are others in local markets, but most are not present globally.

3.4.3 Core Lessons Learned on the Path to Success

1. People should not sell themselves short and learn when to say no.
2. Being brave and taking on the things and challenges that other suppliers simply reject leads to success.
3. Creating opportunities even if there are none and finding ways to get the job done keeps the organization afloat.
4. Relying on innovation and using best practices.

3.4.4 Management and Leadership Development Needs

Most of the management and leadership development needs the company has identified are related to human resource management with a special focus on hiring and retaining employees. This includes skills for onboarding and paying special attention to new hires that can ensure they are willing to take part in improving the workplace culture, skills for knowledge training and transfer, skills for attracting and retaining employees, and similar. This gap in organizational knowledge is likely due to several reasons such as broader educational failures, the location of the company, and new recruitment methods.

When it comes to marketing, the company would benefit from new events to generate more leads and sales, larger investments in email and digital marketing, employee branding, and building a bigger marketing team.

3.4.5 Financing and Regulatory Environment Development Needs

In this area, Mikrosam strives to create a financial structure where sufficient liquidity can cover operating expenses without tapping into external resources. Related to that, the company believes that more prudent financial decisions and a re-focus on capital expenditure to be more competitive are needed. Establishing a system of tracking and analyzing variances in delivery schedules and supplier cost inflations would be a nice addition to the company's financial approach, too.

3.4.6 Pandemic's Impact on "Hidden Champions" Business Approach

Due to the movement restrictions, the company introduced online meetings, and changing work schedules, which considered the maintenance of machine delivery timelines and solving supply-chain issues. All this was done to make the organization more flexible and adaptable to the daily changes. The contemporary working arrangements in the new normal resulted in work from home and in shifts, which significantly impacted the communication with the existing customers and the project deadlines that frequently had to be extended. Mikrosam managed to stay true to its engineered-to-order philosophy, so it started providing remote installations of the machines at the premises of the customers. This meant that the company often sent small teams to install a machine; hence factories received the equipment remotely and the Mikrosam remotely installed it. The company also included virtual assistance for remote installations, hence only a few onsite workers were required to be present while they received virtual instructions and manuals from Mikrosam.

3.4.7 Effects of the Ukraine War on "Hidden Champions" Business Operations

As the company also exported to Russia, the Russian market became closed to Mikrosam's machines since they are dual-use equipment. Prior to the conflict, the company started seeing major challenges from its electronic component suppliers regarding the delivery schedules. So, the unresolved issues with electronic component delays from European suppliers made the company assess alternatives. Mikrosam found that they were not alone in these issues in the industry. By relying on its analytical capability, the company grew to better understand and manage its supply chain. To tackle the supply chain disruptions, they integrated internal material resource planning with purchasing, project management, and sales teams to proactively manage timelines and schedules for current and new projects. Further, the war in Ukraine impacted the energy resources, so the company had to invest in meeting its energy needs using solar power to soften the massive inflation in electricity costs. On the market, the demand for hydrogen tanks continued to grow, making Mikrosam re-focus on being more innovative and competitive with customers for such machines.

3.4.8 Composite Innovators: The Hidden Champion Pioneering Integrated Solutions

Mikrosam is the first company globally to offer integrated solutions for manufacturing products from composite materials, making it a renowned composites manufacturing and development equipment producer. Since it started doing business internationally, it has successfully installed more than 300 production lines in around 43 countries.

Mikrosam's story began in April 1990 with five employees whose first big successes included the successful installation of one of the first computer networks for a Macedonian corporation and the design and testing of the first digital units for measuring electricity consumption in the Macedonian economy. Until the end of that century, Mikrosam focused on design consulting and setting the groundwork for their massive operations of manufacturing products from composite materials by building and designing the first machines and integral electronic components for making this type of manufacturing possible. The company celebrated the start of the new millennium with an entry into the Chinese market in 2000. Quickly after that, the management team realized the company's need for expansion and replaced the design office with a large, brand-new manufacturing factory for developing state-of-the-art, specialized machinery in 2003. With this, Mikrosam achieved full control of the entire machine manufacturing, from its design to its buy-out and installation at the customers' premises.

The company focuses on factory automation, composite production, motion control, and process automation, integrated with its custom-made software for simulating and automating composite manufacturing processes. In Mikrosam's research and development center, the team works on tests, prototypes, technology advancement, and product design. Its products involve sophisticated filament winding and fiber placement machinery, pre-preg making machines, integrated manufacturing lines, and tailor-made composite machining centers, using automated fiber placement, automated tape laying technology, thermos-set, and thermoplastics.

One of Mikrosam's biggest achievements is the automated fiber placement machine. This type of machine has a part in manufacturing vital parts, using composites for aviation and space industries. This was an important step forward for the company's future ground-breaking innovations. Another important milestone is Mikrosam's production of the first fully automated line of tanks that work on compressed natural gas for the automotive industry. A string of firsts followed that and in 2017, the company delivered the first hybrid fiber winding and automated fiber placement machine for space applications, followed by the delivery of the largest completely automated line for tanks that work on compressed natural and hydrogen gas on the planet in 2019.

Mikrosam's facilities are situated on the outskirts of the city of Prilep. Today, the Mikrosam campus is a hub for engineering and design, as well as complete manufacturing and assembling of products. The campus consists of parks and green spaces for relaxation and inspiration and warehouses with high ceilings, secure flooring, heavy-lifting machinery and equipment, workstations for mechanics and electronics, presses, multi-axis CNC machines, and other equipment. This helps the company perform simultaneous acceptance tests of various machinery lines and prepare customer buy-offs.

Due to a strong organizational learning process, the company builds from previously proven solutions and upgrades them to meet current demands through innovative designs and know-how. As a result, all the machinery is built as engineered-to-order. As a result, the sales revenues in the past 10 years have grown more than fivefold; in 2011 they were 2,370,874 euros while in 2021 they equaled 13,018,843 euros.

Every project is spearheaded by a designated project team of mechanical and electrical design engineers. Additionally, lead and senior engineers joined by production supervisors and software and control programmers supervise the entire process. Most of the employees at Mikrosam have lengthy career paths in the company with more than 60% of them being engineers, as well as doctors and masters of science, and university professors, and more than 30% of them being experienced assembly and CNC technicians and operators. The company believes that production workers and engineers are the business professions and profiles that are in most need of education due to constant changes, new technologies, and fresh ways of learning, and working, prompted by the recent revolutions in the workplace. Mikrosam considers this an asset that ensures stability, a growth mindset, a constantly upgrading skills base, and continuity and maintenance of strong relationships with the customers. The project teams have direct and continuous communication with clients through all phases of designing, building out, buying out, installing, and support.

Thanks to its specialized and unusual work and strategic focus on research and development, Mikrosam constantly invests in training, developing, and shaping the new engineer minds of tomorrow, who will one day break new manufacturing grounds and trailblaze innovation. The company opened its own Mikrosam Academy, offering free and personal education for a few passionate adult community members. Also, Mikrosam founded the Institute for Advanced Composites and Robotics (IACR), which represents the first private institute of this kind with the ambition to grow into a hub for fostering practical research for social good. 2015 saw the graduation of the first class of post-graduate students with Master of Science degrees in composites and robotics. This, together with investments in research and development has resulted in a plethora of patents, awards, and recognitions in Europe and abroad. These recognitions include the Eureka award in Brussels in 2001, Patent of the Year awards, and ACE Award Finalist for the first multi-robot, toolless, automated fiber placement cell.

Still, the company is not immune to the business challenges of the dynamic market conditions. The ability to answer global market needs in a competitive way, address new opportunities that require deeper and longer engineering commitment, manage cash flow, and maintain a hungry attitude are something that the company will tackle to achieve even bigger accomplishments.

In market conditions with growing global competitors, Mikrosam managed to use improved visibility, innovation, presence at industry events, engineering leadership, and manufacturing skills to tackle difficult projects and provide automated production equipment. Its identified key strengths are the vision and mission to design and build the future of advanced materials, a strategy toward strong engineering input and detailed customer understanding and maintaining clear responsibility and accountability across all teams. In this sense, the management commitment to innovation and customer success, the strategic orientation on technologies and cross-pollination of ideas, and the organization-wide innovation culture and engineering input are the main driving factors that influence this innovativeness.

4 Conclusions and Recommendations

This book chapter aimed to present and analyze four hidden champions from North Macedonia, their market leadership, development needs, challenges, and opportunities. So, as a result, some common areas emerge for the landscape and business operations of these companies in terms of the product-and production-related competitive advantages and market orientation. Further, the production processes strive to maintain sustainability and flexibility, while making efforts to significantly invest in human resources. Considering this, the product lines of these hidden champions focus on quality, new, custom-tailored solutions, and diversified product portfolios. In turn, these products are often exported internationally—first in the region, while major steps are made toward a comprehensive global increase in the market size. The companies' response to the COVID-19 pandemic and the war in Ukraine can be characterized as fast, finding alternative ways to lower prices, reinventing supply chains, reallocating funds, and introducing remote work processes as most of the companies note short-term influence.

However, there are some common challenges, too, that these companies collectively face. These include maintaining competitiveness in dynamic market conditions with a growing number of competitors, penetrating global markets, and transitioning to full environmental sustainability besides implementing short-term, ad hoc initiatives. Additionally, organization-and management-wise, the Macedonian hidden champions plan to focus on boosting employee motivation and engagement, which would result in higher retention rates in the workforce. Challenges related to increasing organization capacities are also present as companies are required to decide where to allocate the investments they have at their disposal.

Even though North Macedonia is a small country, these hidden champions are examples of how one can succeed internationally with quality products and services. So, some of the recommendations from the analysis can be summed up:

1. Governments and decision-makers should recognize hidden champions as strategic partners in the country's sustainable socio-economic growth, providing policy support and incentives aimed at building an ecosystem and fostering public–private partnerships and innovation.
2. Financial institutions can aid the development of hidden champions by offering customized financial products in the form of supportive credit lines, long-term loans for sustainable innovation and investing in human capital, export credit guarantees, and similar. Additionally, through risk mitigation and advisory services, financial institutions can help build meaningful relationships with this separate type of emerging companies in North Macedonia.
3. Higher education institutions can adapt the curriculum for future business students who can learn from these companies as successful case studies as role models. At the same time, they can offer specialized programs and courses focused on developing the capacities of hidden champions with a multidisciplinary approach encompassing international business, product innovation, export management, strategic management, and similar. Business schools can

act as hubs of knowledge transfer and innovation with incubation and acceleration services custom-tailored to the needs of hidden champions. These institutions can also get involved in talent development and job placement for hidden champions through internships, executive education, and being a bridge between the future workforce and hidden champions as employers.

Through the work of the hidden champions, it is evident that a focus on building leadership qualities and employee engagement, relying on national resources and the best practices, offering complete products that bring value to a regional supply chain, competing in niche markets at first and exporting, following principles from hidden champions in developed countries, innovating, and adapting can yield positive results in the long run for hidden champions.

References

Berberović, D., Činjarević, M., & Kožo, A. (2019). Success despite lack of support: lessons learned from hidden champions doing business in fragile business environments. *Sarajevo Business and Economics Review, 37*, 192–204.

IMF. (2022). *World economic outlook database*, Retrieved December 11, 2022, from https://www.imf.org/en/Publications/WEO/weo-database/2022/October/weo-report?c=962,&s=NGDP_R,NGDP_RPCH,NGDP,NGDPD,PPPGDP,NGDP_D,NGDPRPC,NGDPRPPPPC,NGDPPC,NGDPDPC,PPPPC,PPPSH,PPPEX,NGSD_NGDP,PCPI,PCPIPCH,PCPIE,PCPIEPCH,TM_RPCH,TMG_RPCH,TX_RPCH,TXG_RPCH,LUR,LP,GGR,GGR_NGDP,GGX,GGX_NGDP,GGXCNL,GGXCNL_NGDP,GGXONLB,GGXONLB_NGDP,GGXWDN,GGXWDN_NGDP,GGXWDG,GGXWDG_NGDP,NGDP_FY,BCA,BCA_NGDPD,&sy=1991&ey=2021&ssm=0&scsm=1&scc=0&ssd=1&ssc=0&sic=0&sort=country&ds=.&br=1

OECD. (2021). *Competitiveness in South East Europe 2021: A policy outlook, competitiveness and private sector development*, OECD Publishing, Paris, https://doi.org/10.1787/dcbc2ea9-en

Santa, M., & Kekenovski, L. (2013). Hidden champions of the republic of Macedonia. In P. McKiernan & D. Purg (Eds.), *Hidden champions in CEE and Turkey*. Springer. https://doi.org/10.1007/978-3-642-40504-4_16

Simon, H. (2021). The secrets of the hidden champions. In *Many worlds, one life*. Copernicus, Cham. https://doi.org/10.1007/978-3-030-60758-6_10

State Statistical Office. (2022a). *Labor market–active population in the republic of North macedonia results from the labour force survey, I, II and III quarter 2022 1*, Retrieved December 10, 2022, from https://www.stat.gov.mk/PrikaziSoopstenie_en.aspx?rbrtxt=98

State Statistical Office. (2022b). *Foreign trade—import coverage by export*, Retrieved December 11, 2022, from https://www.stat.gov.mk/OblastOpsto_en.aspx?id=23

State Statistical Office. (2022c). *Foreign trade—external trade grouped according to categories of goods as defined by SITC, cumulative data*, Retrieved December 12, 2022, from http://makstat.stat.gov.mk/PXWeb/pxweb/en/MakStat/MakStat__NadvoresnaTrgovija__KumulativniPod/160_SMTK_godisni_ml.px/table/tableViewLayout2/?rxid=3855a4d2-3257-4393-8149-b7ac30b5f4bc

State Statistical Office. (2022d). *MAKStat database, Number of active business entities by sectors of activity according to NKD Rev. 2 and by number of persons employed, by years*, Retrieved December 17, 2022, from http://makstat.stat.gov.mk/PXWeb/pxweb/en/MakStat/MakStat__DelovniSubj__AktDelovniSubjekti/225_DelSub_Mk_02DeSSeV_ang.px/?rxid=102a5c42-9619-4e58-893b-9ad2b2ee7ec9

The World Bank. (2022). *Data, countries and economies*. http://data.worldbank.org/country
The World Bank. (2025). *World development indicators—North Macedonia*, Retrieved July 07, 2025, from https://databank.worldbank.org/reports.aspx?source=2&country=MKD#
UNDP. (2022). *Uncertain times, unsettled lives: Shaping our future in a transforming world*, Human Development Report 2021/2022 Overview, p. 25. https://hdr.undp.org/system/files/documents/global-report-document/hdr2021-22overviewenpdf.pdf

Violeta Cvetkoska is a Professor of Operational Research and Machine Learning for Management, Coordinator of the Fundamentals of Business Analytics course, and Head of the EUi at Ss. Cyril and Methodius University in Skopje, Faculty of Economics—Skopje. She holds a master's degree in Operational Research and Quantitative Methods from the University of Belgrade, alongside a PhD in Economics from Ss. Cyril and Methodius University in Skopje. A passionate educator and mentor, Prof. Cvetkoska translates her extensive knowledge into real-world impact, empowering students and managers to become data-driven professionals. Her work in operational research, business analytics, and AI strategically supports companies in gaining a competitive edge. Prof. Cvetkoska's international perspective is shaped by academic visits and active participation in conferences, symposia, and workshops across Europe, the Americas, and Asia. An advocate of experiential learning, she is a certified MonsoonSIM trainer, leveraging its AI-driven platform to equip future leaders with analytical skills. She has published numerous scientific papers in respected international journals and conference proceedings. Beyond her research, Prof. Cvetkoska contributes to the scholarly community by serving on editorial boards of international journals, on scientific boards of major conferences, and as an active member of professional societies like the Croatian Operational Research Society (CRORR), the Society for Economic Measurement (SEM), the EURO Working Groups on Multicriteria Decision Aiding and Behavioural Operational Research (BOR). Her current research interests span digital transformation, performance measurement, labor market, education, banking, and finance, driving innovation and excellence in the dynamic field of business analytics.

Martin Kiselicki is a researcher and academic with over a decade of experience in e-business, organizational sciences, and gamification. Holding a PhD in Organizational Sciences and Management and a master's degree in E-Business Management from Ss. Cyril and Methodius University in Skopje, he has been at the forefront of integrating digital technologies into business and learning environments. He is currently serving as a Teaching and Research Assistant at the Ss. Cyril and Methodius University in Skopje, Faculty of Economics—Skopje. His early contribution to the field includes the publication of the book "Social Media Marketing" in 2012, recognized as one of the foundational works in the regional digital marketing space. He has also contributed to several EU-funded Erasmus+ and Central European Program (CEP) projects, focusing on youth empowerment, gamification, and digital skills training. He has published numerous academic papers and has participated in international scientific conferences all over the world.

Filip Peovski was born in 1996 in the Republic of North Macedonia. He is a Teaching and Research Assistant at the Department of Mathematics and Statistics at the Faculty of Economics—Skopje, Ss. Cyril and Methodius University in Skopje. Holding a master's degree in Monetary Economics, Finance and Banking and a doctoral degree in Economic Sciences, his primary teaching activities involve the courses Mathematics for Economists and Fundamentals of Business Analytics, alongside others. Peovski's primary research combines quantitative methods to address macroeconomic forecasting, financial-market behavior, insurance efficiency, and labor-market dynamics. He has published multiple journal articles, co-authored a university monograph, took part in several international scientific conferences presenting his research, and co-authored the Business Analytics, Second Edition textbook alongside Prof. Violeta Cvetkoska, PhD. His extensive international collaboration within Horizon, Erasmus+, and CEEMAN projects involves solving wicked problems, promoting inclusive education, pinpointing core economic agents, and studying labor market phenomena. Beyond research, Peovski serves on academic committees for teaching quality and student support.

Bojan Kitanovikj is a Teaching and Research Assistant at the Faculty of Economics—Skopje, Ss. Cyril and Methodius University in Skopje, where he is also currently pursuing his PhD in Organizational Sciences and Management. He earned a BSc in Economics in 2021, magna cum laude, receiving scholarships and the best bachelor thesis award, after which he earned his master's degree in Organizational Sciences. Beyond academia, he has experience in civil society and the entrepreneurial ecosystem. He contributes to the Yunus Social Business Centre and the EUi Centre at the Faculty of Economics—Skopje. He is an active member of the Academy of Management, the #Humanizing Digital Work network, and several other international research networks. Kitanovikj is author or co-author of multiple international publications, including scientific journal articles, Springer book chapters, articles in conference proceedings, guides, and blogs in the fields of digital work, job design, artificial intelligence, operational research applications, neuromanagement, entrepreneurial role models, and similar. He has participated in EU-funded and national projects (Erasmus+, Horizon), acting as a researcher and deputy co-leader of a work package, and has completed numerous academic visits in triple-accredited business schools. Additionally, he serves on organizing committees for international conferences.

Hidden Champions of Poland

Magdalena M. Popowska and Julita E. Wasilczuk

Abstract Poland's entrepreneurial culture, vibrant and dynamic, has seen the rise of its Hidden Champions (HC) that have become an integral part of the country's business landscape. The transition from communism to a market economy in 1989 was pivotal, sparking the emergence of private small businesses focused on the domestic market. These Hidden Champions, a product of this transition, have played a significant role in shaping the business landscape in Poland. The country's accession to the European Union in 2004 was another game-changer, opening doors to international markets, financial support, educational advancements, and regulatory reforms. This influx of foreign direct investment and cutting-edge technologies has further shaped the landscape for Polish businesses. The advent of liberal democracy in Poland catalyzed the growth of Hidden Champions across various industries. This political shift created a favorable environment for small businesses to thrive, leading to a surge in their numbers. Large multinational corporations later acquired many of these, enhancing their scalability and performance. Despite the challenges posed by Poland's comparatively lower business culture and regulatory complexities, which elevate transaction costs and business risks, Polish Hidden Champions have shown remarkable resilience, solidifying their market position through robust partnerships with suppliers and customers.

This resilience is particularly critical in the current period of crisis. The COVID-19 pandemic and geopolitical conflicts are expected to reshape the competitive landscape for the coming years. Economies with solid Indigenous energy production supplies, supply chains, and favorable trade balances have been able to cope with and even benefit from these macroeconomic shifts. For Poland, with its Hidden Champions and vibrant entrepreneurial culture, the need for an agile government and access to vital markets and trading partners is not just important, but it is urgent and potentially beneficial. These factors are not only crucial for Poland's

M. M. Popowska (✉) · J. E. Wasilczuk
Faculty of Management and Economics, Gdańsk University of Technology, Gdansk, Poland
e-mail: mpop@pg.edu.pl; jwas@pg.edu.pl

D. Berberović, D. Purg (eds.), *Hidden Champions in Rising Economies*, Contributions to Management Science,
https://doi.org/10.1007/978-3-032-08263-3_32

green transition and possibly strengthening its currency by entering the Eurozone, but they also hold the promise of a brighter economic future for the country.

Policymakers must create an environment enabling businesses to thrive and contribute to Poland's long-term prosperity by prioritizing judicial independence, access to EU funds, economic stability, workforce development, innovation, environmental sustainability, and regulatory reform.

Overview

Official name: Republic of Poland (POL)
Type of government: democratic, with the Prime Minister as the head of government
The President is the head of state
Population in 2022: 36,82 million
Land area: 312.7 thousand sq. km

History

1569–1795	Polish-Lithuanian Commonwealth: At the beginning of the period of prosperity, the seventeenth and eighteenth century, the state was weakened by internal problems with the law and external threats, such as wars with Sweden, Russia, and the Ottoman Empire.
1795	The third partition of Poland led to the country's dissolution. It was preceded by two earlier partitions, in 1772 and 1793. The Commonwealth was gradually divided by its powerful neighbors, Russia, Prussia, and Austria.
Nineteenth century	Numerous attempts were made to regain independence, especially during the November Uprising (1830–1831) and January Uprising (1863–1864).
1918	Poland regained its independence after 123 years of partitions.
1918–1939	New institutions were created, building the foundations of a modern state. Despite facing economic and political challenges, the country experienced economic and social development.
1939	The German invasion of Poland marked the beginning of World War II. At the same time, Poland is attacked by the Soviet Union. This is the result of the Ribbentrop-Molotov Agreement, under which Poland was divided between Nazi Germany and the Soviet Union.
1939–1945	Poles did not give up. They created the most robust resistance movement in Europe, culminating in the Warsaw Uprising at the end of 1944.
1945	Poland came under Russian influence and was subordinated in terms of its economy, politics, and military. The borders were shifted, incorporating a large part of Poland's territory into the Soviet Union while simultaneously annexing the eastern territories of Germany to the country.

1945–1946	Reactivation of plants by pre-war owners.
1946	Nationalization of industry and small craft, suppression of entrepreneurship, and repression of pre-war entrepreneurs.
1949–1955	Poland adopted a centrally planned economy, modeled after the Soviet system. Farmers' resistance prevented the complete collectivization of agriculture, a unique phenomenon among Eastern Bloc countries.
1956–1970	Economic stagnation and crises, combined with supply shortages.
1970–1980	An attempt to fix the economy improved the situation and increased the standard of living, but at the cost of high debts that the country could not repay.
1980–1989	A deep crisis and market shortages led to the creation of Solidarity (1980), a workers' movement that initiated political changes in Central and Eastern Europe. However, the final political and economic changes were delayed by the introduction of martial law for two and a half years at the end of 1981.
1989	The collapse of the communist system in Poland and the beginning of social, political, and economic transformation from a centrally planned economy to a market economy.
1989–1995	The recovery period, shock therapy, and market reforms.
1999	Access to the North Atlantic Treaty Organization.
2004	Access to the European Union opened up new possibilities for financing economic development. Poland is the largest net payer in Europe. By 2022, 157 billion euros had been invested in the country.
2021	During the initial period of the COVID-19 pandemic, the Polish economy came to a standstill due to the lockdown. The government implemented several measures to help businesses.
2022	Russia's full-scale invasion of Ukraine affected the Polish economy, mainly through the increase in electricity prices, which contributed to the increase in inflation. At the same time, as a result of humanitarian aid, people from Ukraine flooded into Poland, strengthening the labor market.

1 Introduction: Context and History

For many years, Poland operated under a centrally planned economy, heavily dependent on the satellite countries of Eastern and Central Europe, with a particular emphasis on the former Soviet Union (USSR). Political changes, initiated by workers' protests in Poland in 1980 and subsequently in other countries, ultimately led to the collapse of the USSR and the political and economic system it imposed on the

Eastern and Central European bloc. Actual economic transformations began in 1989, with the definitive fall of the socialist regime, and were rapid and tumultuous from an economic perspective. These transformations led to high inflation and unemployment, resulting from the restructuring of large state-owned enterprises and the emergence of spontaneous, grassroots entrepreneurship. The developing entrepreneurial ecosystem, supported by numerous aid institutions and attracting substantial financial resources, strengthened existing businesses. Another milestone toward the democratization and marketization of the Polish economy was its accession to the European Union in 2004. This brought another wave of support funds and also organized the system of supporting entrepreneurship, which had been built since 1996 by the Polish Agency for Enterprise Development (PARP).

1.1 Political Context in Poland

In 2015, the populist Law and Justice party (Prawo i Sprawiedliwość, PiS) came to power, and its representative also became the country's President. The president's role is to sign bills passed by the Sejm (the lower house of parliament), and he is supposed to maintain complete political neutrality. However, in this case, the President signs all bills directed to him despite opposition from constitutional experts who argue that some of these bills are unconstitutional. In the name of reforming the judiciary system, which is crucial for resolving disputes, including economic ones, PiS began implementing significant changes that led to constitutional tensions (Kawczyńska, 2020; Żurek, 2019). The ruling party's judicial reforms have sparked controversy and threaten the rule of law, including forced retirements, disciplinary proceedings, and political appointments of judges, exposing the judiciary to legislative and governmental control (Winczorek & Muszyński, 2022). This, in turn, prompted the European Commission to suspend payments from the Recovery and Resilience Facility (RRF), justifying it with the conditionality mechanism, which operates on the principle of "money for the rule of law." According to the Polish Supreme Audit Office (Najwyższa Izba Kontroli), irregularities also appeared in the allocation of funds for development projects intended for entrepreneurs.[1]

After the election at the end of 2023, the Civic Coalition (Koalicja Obywatelska), a center-to-center-right liberal, in alliance with left and conservative wings, took power. Thanks to the efforts of the new government aimed at restoring the rule of law, the European Commission has unlocked access to the Next Generation EU funds and the Cohesion Funds.[2] This delay in future access to up to €137 billion in

[1] https://www.money.pl/gospodarka/afera-w-ncbr-jest-sledztwo-po-zgloszeniu-nik-7013003739863648a.html

[2] https://ec.europa.eu/commission/presscorner/detail/en/ip_24_1222

EU funds was unfavorable for entrepreneurs seeking to develop their activities after the COVID-19-induced stagnation.

1.2 Economic Context in Poland

After the perturbations of the transition period, Poland's economy grew at an average annual rate of nearly 6% between 2017 and 2022, with a 0.2% decline in 2020 during the COVID-19 pandemic. As of 2024, Poland's GDP growth rate is projected to be moderate, recovering from the pandemic-induced slowdown, at 2.4%.[3]

The country has recently experienced higher inflation rates, driven by global supply chain disruptions, rising energy prices, and increased domestic demand pressures. However, its level has recently started to fall slightly; in April 2023, it was 14.7%, and in April 2024, it was only 2.4%.[4] Poland's fiscal policy has focused on supporting economic recovery following the pandemic, with significant public spending on health, social welfare, and economic stimulus measures. This has resulted in an increased budget deficit and public debt levels. Although public debt has increased, it remains manageable compared to that of many other EU countries. The government is currently working on fiscal consolidation strategies to ensure long-term sustainability.

The manufacturing sector, particularly automotive, machinery, and electronics, is vital to the Polish economy. However, the service sector, including finance, IT, and professional services, continues to proliferate and contributes significantly to GDP. On the other hand, agriculture's share in GDP is declining but remains essential, with Poland being a significant producer of food products in Europe.

One of the increasing challenges, but also an opportunity, is the need to transition to greener energy sources. Poland relies heavily on coal, and shifting to renewable energy sources requires significant investment.

1.3 Social Situation in Poland

Poland faces a severe demographic challenge due to low birth rates and emigration. The latest data from the Central Statistical Office (GUS), covering the period from April 2023 to March 2024, show the lowest birth rate in history, at 265.4 thousand. Only the decrease in the death rate has mitigated the deepening negative natural increase. In addition to the low fertility rate, there is also a decline in the number of women of reproductive age. As a result of the declining birth rate, Poland is facing rapid population aging, leading to a significant increase in the proportion of people

[3] https://pie.net.pl/26-proc-wyniesie-wzrost-pkb-polski-w-2024-r-wynika-z-prognozy-pie/

[4] https://stat.gov.pl/wykres/1.html

aged 65 and above (Perek-Białas et al., 2017). Demographic forecasts indicate that by 2050, 57% of the population will be of working age, 32% will be post-working age, and 11% will be pre-working age.[5] These demographic changes, particularly in an aging society, have severe implications for the country's economy, healthcare, and retirement systems (Sobczak et al., 2020). Moreover, Poland is one of the few European countries where the retirement age for women and men differs: 60 years for women and 65 years for men.

The decreasing number of working-age employees and the migration of Poles abroad have forced employers to seek workers among immigrants, including those from Ukraine, who make up 83% of employed foreigners in Poland.[6] More than 18% of companies operating in Poland employ foreigners. However, this is still insufficient, and there is a shortage of workers for both physical and specialized jobs. Employment shortages lead to pressure to increase wages, which, combined with inflation, poses a significant problem.

In summary, Poland's demographic situation is characterized by rapid population aging, diverse migration patterns, and challenges related to fertility rates and gender differences in retirement age. These trends have a significant impact on the country's economy, social policies, and regional disparities. While attempts have been made to address these challenges through family policies and territorial approaches, the complexity of the demographic situation requires a multifaceted and coordinated response.

1.4 Technology Context in Poland

The technological context of Polish enterprises primarily revolves around developing the Information and Communication Technologies (ICT) sector and access to energy. The expansion of ICT stimulates innovation growth and increases economic competitiveness. The government has implemented various policies to support the growth of the ICT sector, including tax incentives and grants for research and development. Poland complies with EU data protection and cybersecurity regulations, including the GDPR. Broad access to ICT is crucial for contemporary societal development in Poland and Europe (Misztal & Kupis-Fijałkowska, 2020).

The digitization of Polish industry is part of the global Industry 4.0 trend, which involves using technologies such as artificial intelligence, the Internet of Things, and cloud computing to create smart factories and production networks. Poland is one of the leaders in industrial digitization in Central and Eastern Europe. It ranks seventh in the world in terms of the number of industrial robots per thousand employees. In recent years, the Polish industry has undergone significant changes,

[5] https://stat.gov.pl/obszary-tematyczne/ludnosc/prognoza-ludnosci/prognoza-ludnosci-rezydujacej-dla-polski-na-lata-2015-2050,8,1.html

[6] Labour Market Barometer 2024. https://pl.gigroup.com/wp-content/uploads/2024/04/Gi-Group-Holding-Labour-market-barometer_18th_edition_compressed.pdf

resulting in a higher level of adoption of digital technologies by manufacturing companies in Poland. This trend is driving improvements in efficiency, quality, and innovation. According to the Siemens Digi Index 2022 report, the digitization index rose from 1.8 points in 2021 to 2.4 points in 2022 on a scale of 0 to 4. The automotive industry recorded the highest index at 2.6.[7] This indicates changes in companies' strategic planning, organization, administration, systems integration, production and operational activities, data management, and the application of digital processes. This, in turn, means an increase in the speed of information flow, which is crucial for operating today. The acceleration at the national level results from the activities of companies in this sector. Following the stagnation caused by COVID-19, companies recognized that investments in digitization were becoming increasingly essential. Therefore, declarations in 2022 indicate that 70% of manufacturing companies will invest in digitization, and 40% will increase their budgets by the end of 2023.[8] E-government services are also crucial for entrepreneurs as they facilitate operations. Although Poland is not among the leading European countries in developing these services, their quality is improving.

Poland relies on coal for energy security and is increasingly emphasizing renewable energy sources, such as biomass. To modernize the energy sector, discussions are ongoing about increasing the role of natural gas and constructing the country's first nuclear power plant (Dzikuć et al., 2022).

1.5 *Environmental Issues in Poland*

Poland heavily relies on coal as its primary energy resource, resulting in some of Europe's highest air pollution levels (Dmuchowski et al., 2021). The country faces substantial environmental protection problems. Local governments require sustainable investments to address climate change adaptation and mitigation, primarily related to transitioning from coal to more environmentally friendly energy sources.

Poland's slow changes in energy balance and its reliance on non-renewable resources pose challenges to meeting EU environmental requirements, particularly in the slow development of renewable energy sources (Jonek-Kowalska, 2017). Ecological problems are linked to political, economic, and psychological factors, with the post-communist transformation affecting the environmental situation (Pawlowska & Pawlowski, 2017). Poland's accession to the EU has led to the introduction of EU environmental law and the availability of funds for environmental protection activities, which have had a significant impact on the ecological situation in the region (Bień, 2016).

[7] https://www.siemens.com/pl/pl/o-firmie/raporty-siemens/digi-index-2022.html

[8] Cyfryzacja polskiego przemysłu wskoczyła na wyższy poziom. https://crn.pl/aktualnosci/cyfryzacja-polskiego-przemyslu-wskoczyla-na-wyzszy-poziom/used in: 17.03.2023

In summary, Poland's environmental situation is shaped by its significant reliance on coal, the effects of climate change, political and economic transformations, challenges in renewable energy development, and the impact of EU policies and financial support.

1.6 Institutional Situation in Poland

The institutional environment, including the quality of institutions, plays a significant role in the functioning of businesses. However, the quality of institutions can lead to unproductive behaviors, including seeking solutions on the fringes of the law, abusing the legal path by suing competitors and prolonging resolutions (Baumol, 1995; Dominiak et al., 2016).

Poland initiated its institutional transformation in parallel with the political and economic changes of the 1990s. Building a new institutional order accelerated with its accession to the European Union in 2004. Poland adopted many institutional solutions inspired by EU countries, both when required for accession and voluntarily. However, entrepreneurs criticize the quality of Polish institutions, and frequent changes in the law hinder business operations and increase transaction costs (Dominiak et al., 2016).

Frequent changes in legal regulations in Poland often coincide with changes in the ruling party. After the Law and Justice party came to power in 2015, the new government introduced reforms in various areas, including education and science, which directly affected business operations and the legal system. In the name of improving the judicial system, it implemented many changes criticized by specialists (Kawczyńska, 2020), which attracted international interest due to a constitutional crisis and changes in the legislative process (Jankovic, 2016). Moreover, changes in the media, civil service, police, and prosecution laws have not improved the functioning of these areas, mainly due to the quality of both the enactment process and their effects. Entrepreneurs complain about unclear legal regulations and frequent changes (Serowaniec, 2023). The country's economic situation is illustrated in detail in the table below (Exhibit 1).

2 Case Studies of Selected Hidden Champions

2.1 MB Pneumatyka Sp. z o.o.

Overview

Address: ul. Rozwojowa 5, 66–100 Sulechów
Tel: +48 68 419 02 99
Email: mb-pneumatyka@mb-pneumatyka.pl
Web: https://mbp.mbgroup.com.pl/en

Exhibit 1 Core economic indicators for Poland

	2019	2020	2021	2022	2023	2024
GDP per capita (current US$)	15,700	15,816	18,050	18,688	22,056.67	..
GDP per capita growth (annual %)	4,40	−2,00	6,90	5,30	0.51	..
Unemployment, total (% of total labor force) (modeled ILO estimate)	3,3	3,2	3,4	2,9	2.74	2.47
Foreign direct investment, net inflows (% of GDP)	3,0	3,2	5,3	5,4	4.24	..
GDP (current US$, mio)	596,06	599,44	681,35	688,13	809200.70	..
Exports of goods and services (current US$, mio)	317,08	317,65	393,13	431,35	470255.65	..
Exports of goods and services (% of GDP)	53,2	53,0	57,7	62,7	58.11	..
Merchandise exports (current US$)	266,6	273,83	340,63	360,54	381,517	..
Merchandise exports to high-income economies (% of total merchandise exports)	87,5	87,0	nd	nd	88.85	..
Merchandise exports to developing economies in Europe and Central Asia (% of total merchandise exports)	8,50	nd	nd	nd	6.87	..
Ores and metals exports (% of merchandise exports)	3,23	3,22	3,97	3,71	3.05	3.2
Agricultural raw materials exports (% of merchandise exports)	1	1	1	1	0.92	0.98
Food exports (% of merchandise exports)	13	14	13	14	14.42	14.92
Fuel exports (% of merchandise exports)	2	2	2	4	3.05	2.58
Manufactures exports (% of merchandise exports)	79,91	79,64	79,40	76,59	78.31	78.06
High-technology exports (% of manufactured exports)	10	10	9	11	9.89	..

Source: World Bank, 2025, https://data.worldbank.org/

Company Information

Industry[9]: Designer and manufacturer of air brake systems for the automotive industry
Year of Establishment: 2002
Sales Revenues in 2017: 5 005 608,16 EUR
Sales Revenues in 2023: 5 730 983,99 EUR
Average number of employees in 2023: 100
Brainer(s) behind the company: Małgorzata Bieniaszewska, Andrzej Bieniaszewski (father)

[9] *According to NACE Rev. 2–please check the technical instructions included in this document (pg. 9).*

2.1.1 Nature of Market Leadership

MB Pneumatyka's market leadership is characterized by a blend of innovation, strong market presence, customer-centric solutions, sustainable values, and strategic adaptability. MB Pneumatyka holds an impressive market share of around 80% in Poland and is one of the top four manufacturers in Europe for connectors for pneumatic systems in commercial vehicles. Despite intense competition from the market leader Raufoss, MB Pneumatyka maintains a significant presence.

Market leadership is also innovation-driven. The company places a high emphasis on innovation, regularly applying for new patents and striving to introduce globally innovative products. This continuous innovation is part of its competitive strategy. Moreover, MB Pneumatyka differentiates itself through exceptional customer service. Instead of just selling products, the company provides tailored solutions by reviewing and optimizing customers' vehicle technology. This long-term, relationship-focused approach fosters customer loyalty.

The company's leadership, under Małgorzata Bieniaszewska, embodies sustainable practices and values, including respect for people, reputation, and ethical behavior. This includes refraining from bribery and maintaining transparency in business operations, even during a crisis. The company benefits from a solid family-owned heritage, which instills a sense of continuity and long-term vision in its operations and strategic decisions. Thanks to this heritage and strong values, MB Pneumatyka has shown resilience in times of crisis, such as during the COVID-19 pandemic and the war in Ukraine, by maintaining employment, adapting business strategies, and making ethically driven decisions even at the cost of short-term financial losses. Two years ago, the company strategically expanded its international operations, including the opening of a production facility in India to tap into a rapidly growing market.

2.1.2 Nature of Competitive Advantage

MB Pneumatyka's competitive advantage stems from a multifaceted strategy that emphasizes customer-centric solutions, innovation, long-term relationships, and ethical business practices.

Firstly, the company's primary edge lies in its customer-centric approach. MB Pneumatyka goes beyond merely selling products by providing comprehensive solutions tailored to each customer's needs. This involves sending engineers to work directly with customers to optimize their vehicle technology using MB Pneumatyka's fittings, ensuring a bespoke solution that enhances efficiency and effectiveness.

Innovation is another critical component of MB Pneumatyka's competitive advantage. The company consistently develops and introduces new products, applying for patents annually to maintain a cutting-edge position in the market. Although innovation alone does not fully differentiate the company due to the industry's high patent activity, it remains a crucial aspect of its competitive strategy.

The company's focus on building long-term customer relationships is a significant differentiator. MB Pneumatyka prioritizes long-term partnerships over one-off sales, resulting in lower margins but fostering customer loyalty and sustained business relationships. This commitment to customer service includes addressing and resolving complaints promptly and effectively, which builds trust and reliability.

As a family-owned business, MB Pneumatyka upholds values of people, respect, and reputation. These values are deeply embedded in the company's operations, translating into ethical business practices such as avoiding bribes and maintaining transparency. This moral stance enhances the company's reputation and trustworthiness.

The company also places significant emphasis on its workforce. By hiring individuals with potential and providing extensive training, MB Pneumatyka ensures its employees are well-equipped to meet the company's standards and contribute to its innovative and customer-focused strategies.

Under the leadership of Małgorzata Bieniaszewska, the company exemplifies sustainable and ethical business practices. This leadership style is crucial in maintaining the company's values and driving its competitive advantage in a global market. The strategic international expansion further bolsters MB Pneumatyka's competitive position. Establishing a production facility in India demonstrates the company's approach to tapping into high-growth markets, enhancing its global footprint.

Lastly, MB Pneumatyka's ability to adapt during crises showcases its resilience and commitment to its values. The company retained employees during the COVID-19 pandemic and made principled decisions during the Ukraine conflict, underscoring its adaptability and ethical commitment.

2.1.3 Core Lessons Learned on the Path to Success

MB Pneumatyka's journey to success has imparted several valuable lessons integral to its growth and resilience. These core lessons offer a blueprint for building a thriving and sustainable business. The four main lessons are as follows:

- Commitment to innovation as a critical driver. Continuously developing new products and applying for patents annually have kept the company at the forefront of the industry. Innovation is not just about staying relevant; it drives competitiveness and helps maintain a cutting-edge position in the market. In this respect, having one's R&D team is a crucial commitment.
- Building long-term relationships instead of focusing on short-term sales fosters customer loyalty, ensuring a stable and growing customer base, even if it sometimes results in lower margins. High customer service standards are integral to maintaining a positive reputation and ensuring customer satisfaction. Promptly and effectively resolving customer complaints fosters trust and reliability, which are essential for long-term success.

- Ethical business practices, such as upholding respect and transparency, have been crucial. Avoiding unethical practices enhances the company's reputation and trustworthiness, which are invaluable assets in the business world.
- Investing in the workforce by hiring individuals with potential and providing comprehensive training ensures that employees are well-equipped to contribute to the company's success. A skilled and dedicated workforce is one of the company's most significant assets.

2.1.4 COVID-19 Pandemic Experience

The COVID-19 pandemic was a challenging experience. MB Pneumatics, recalling the difficult time of the 2008–2009 crisis when it laid off many employees, which, in retrospect, the owner now views as short-sighted and painful, has decided to retain all employees. The mode and rules of work were adapted to the new conditions and sanitary requirements. However, the production was conducted on-site, while the administration was remote. The stoppage of the automotive market, however, resulted in a lack of orders, at which point the team spirit developed over the years by the owner kicked in. The entire staff team took it upon themselves to look for customers outside the existing industry. Employees also recorded themselves on FB and talked about the personal challenges of changing living conditions. Over time, orders came in for various products that proved to be needed. Although the pandemic period was professionally very challenging, it showed the owner that she had a very close-knit team who knew and understood the business's purpose and saw a place for themselves in achieving it. It also showed certain, sometimes value-free, attitudes of the company's competitors.

2.1.5 War in Ukraine Experience

During the war crisis in Ukraine, particularly at the outset of the conflict, tough decisions had to be made, often resulting in significant financial losses. MB Pneumatics' managers decided not to send an order that had been completed for a customer from Russia. The company lost two customers from this country during this time. Forbes magazine reports Bieniaszewska's testimony: *"On the day the war broke out, we were just packing a shipment to a customer from Russia. I met with the employees because we also employ Ukrainians, and said: "Listen, we are supporting you, we are sending money, we are bringing people, families." Later, the sales manager asked: "Margaret, what are we doing about the shipping to Russia?" The board recommended that we not send it, but I took it upon myself, and we sent it. I figured the losses would be huge. I was up all night. The next day, I convened the board again, and we informed the Russian customers that we would no longer continue to do business with them. Depending on the month, it meant a loss of between 5 and 10 percent of revenue. At first, I wanted to look at it purely in business terms, but I could not. Consequently, I am proud of it, even more so of my team. I was the one who was breaking even. They had no doubts.*"[10]

2.1.6 Management and Leadership Development Needs

MB Pneumatyka faces several critical challenges in management and leadership development, primarily focused on enhancing project management competencies and improving organizational communication.

One of the foremost challenges identified by the company is the development of project management skills. The increasing number of projects has highlighted a significant gap in time management and project oversight. Despite frequent suggestions to hire additional staff, the core issue appears to be a deficiency in effective project management practices. This necessitates targeted training and development programs to equip the current workforce with the necessary skills to manage projects more efficiently and effectively.

Another critical area for development is communication. MB Pneumatyka acknowledges the importance of understanding diverse communication styles and personalities, which is essential for fostering individual motivation and team cohesion. The company employs neurodiverse individuals, and initial experiences have revealed gaps in handling such diversity. Addressing these shortcomings through comprehensive communication training ensures that all employees feel understood and valued.

As observed in the company's international experiences, there is a recognized need to separate marketing from sales more distinctly in the marketing domain. Unlike in Poland, where marketing and sales are often intertwined, countries like India treat them as distinct functions. Developing a nuanced and effective marketing strategy, particularly for social media, remains a significant challenge. Despite the challenges of promoting industrial products, such as automotive fittings, on platforms like Facebook and LinkedIn, the company's leadership actively shares managerial and leadership insights to establish a solid online presence.

The company's response to crises, such as the COVID-19 pandemic and the war in Ukraine, highlighted the need for robust crisis management skills. Retaining all employees during the pandemic and making ethical decisions during the Ukraine conflict demonstrated the importance of maintaining team spirit and ethical leadership even in financially challenging situations.

---

[10] https://www.forbes.pl/forbeswomen/polski-biznes-w-indiach-malgorzata-bieniaszewska-z-mb-pneumatyka/h2h9zs1

2.1.7 Financing and Regulatory Environment Development Needs

Navigating financial and regulatory landscapes presents another significant development need. The company's financial transparency is an asset, but Poland's complex and often ambiguous regulatory environment poses challenges. Securing adequate funding for expansion and innovation is crucial. The company must continuously explore and apply for grants, loans, and other financial support mechanisms, which can be cumbersome and time-consuming. Economic instability, whether due to global market fluctuations or local economic conditions, adds complexity to financial planning and risk management. Ensuring compliance while leveraging available financial opportunities requires meticulous understanding and strategic planning.

Another significant challenge is staying up-to-date with and adapting to rapidly changing laws and regulations. Businesses must remain informed and agile to ensure ongoing compliance and capitalize on regulatory changes that may benefit them. Participating in industry associations and advocacy groups can help influence regulatory changes and provide a platform for voicing concerns and suggestions to policymakers.

The cooperation between science and business in Poland is still evolving, and the mutual lack of understanding between academic institutions and the business community has decreased. MB Pneumatyka has taken steps to bridge this gap by introducing professional onboarding programs and detailed deployment schedules for interns from local technical schools. This initiative helps new employees gain a comprehensive understanding of the company's operations and fosters a sense of belonging and teamwork.

2.1.8 MB Pneumatyka: Innovating Tradition and Female Leadership in the Automotive Industry

Established in 2002 as a family endeavor, MB Pneumatyka traces its origins to visionary initiatives in the engineering landscape dating back to 1984. Specializing in manufacturing couplings for pneumatic systems in heavy commercial vehicles, the company has consistently epitomized manufacturing excellence from its inception. With a strong focus on innovation and customer-centricity, MB Pneumatyka has secured a dominant position in the industry, commanding an impressive 80% market share in Poland and ranking among Europe's top four manufacturers.

A pivotal moment in the company's trajectory came with a change in leadership, ushering in Małgorzata Bieniaszewska as a prominent figure in the traditionally male-dominated manufacturing sector. Her journey underscores the challenges and opportunities women leaders face in such environments, breaking stereotypes and paving the way for greater diversity. Bieniaszewska's leadership style, marked by empathy, collaboration, and strong communication skills, has fostered a positive work environment and strengthened team dynamics, emphasizing respect and ethical practices. Under Bieniaszewska's leadership, the company successfully navigated development obstacles, recently establishing a respected presence in the Indian automotive sector. This expansion showcased MB Pneumatyka's adaptability and resilience, reinforcing its global reputation as a formidable industry leader.

The female leader's professional success raises interest in the company's ecosystem. In 2019, Małgorzata Bieniaszewska was appointed to the Presidential Council for Entrepreneurship. In 2020, Forbes magazine named her Forbes Women, BrandMe CEO 2020. Recently, together with Katarzyna Olszyńska, the owner has also published the book "*Leader not Ideal*," a collection of 14 lessons in effective leadership based on authentic stories from the life of the founder of MB Pneumatyka.

Committed to driving innovation, excellence, and sustainability, MB Pneumatyka adopts a leadership model that prioritizes employee well-being, community engagement, and environmental stewardship. Through initiatives ranging from volunteer programs to investments in renewable energy, the company remains committed to its mission of positively impacting society and the environment. Nowadays, the company is positioned at the forefront of pneumatic systems technology and is poised to shape the future while upholding a legacy of integrity and excellence.

3 Conclusions and Recommendations

Hidden Champions are a distinct category of companies prioritizing achieving and maintaining a top-ranking position while operating discreetly in the public eye. These companies dedicate significant efforts to fostering close and robust relationships within their business ecosystems, including customers, partners, employees, competitors, regulators, and media outlets. The external environment, which varies based on the company's scale of operations and market reach (local, European, Central and Eastern European, or global), presents diverse expectations, opportunities, and threats, necessitating tailored adjustments.

In sectors characterized by intense competition and rapid growth, innovation emerges as a critical determinant of success for Hidden Champions. Staying ahead of competitors is imperative, prompting these companies to vigilantly monitor market dynamics, such as growth potential, innovation pace, profitability, market structure vis-a-vis major competitors, M&A activities, and positioning. By assuming leadership roles, Hidden Champions dictate the trajectory and nature of innovation, reshaping the competitive landscape and stimulating new demand trends.

Even for large global manufacturers, customization is pivotal alongside mass production and value/quality considerations. Adapting products, services, and solutions to the specific needs of major clients requires flexible and efficient manufacturing systems. Hidden Champions proactively scan for early signals regarding technological advancements, new materials, machinery, distribution channels, promotional strategies, transaction costs, and evolving consumer preferences to anticipate forthcoming changes. Rather than relying on external scientific research and analyses, they prefer to spearhead their research initiatives to drive innovation.

Staff development is paramount for Hidden Champions, encompassing professional skills and proficiency in foreign languages to facilitate expansion and foster enduring relationships with strategic partners. Polish Hidden Champions often operate within narrow, highly specialized market niches, constantly updating their offerings to remain competitive. Their size varies based on industry specifics, with companies engaged in mass production typically boasting higher employment rates than those specializing in niche markets. Emphasizing cost efficiency and leveraging modern technology and skilled labor in Poland, these companies prioritize design excellence and meticulous craftsmanship to outshine competitors and expand their operations.

The main conclusions and recommendations to support Polish Hidden Champions can be summarized as follows:

- Strengthening judicial independence: Recent political changes in Poland, particularly under the Law and Justice party (PiS), have raised concerns about the rule of law and judicial independence. The government must ensure a transparent and impartial judiciary system that upholds constitutional principles. By restoring confidence in the legal system, businesses can operate in a stable environment conducive to growth and investment.
- Enhancing access to EU funds: Poland's integration into the European Union has brought significant financial support for entrepreneurship and economic development. However, political tensions and concerns over the rule of law have sometimes hindered access to these funds. The government must prioritize alignment with EU standards and regulations to ensure continued access to vital resources for business expansion and innovation.
- Promoting economic stability and fiscal discipline: Despite Poland's impressive economic growth, inflation, budget deficits, and public debt remain. The government should implement prudent fiscal policies to maintain macroeconomic stability and sustainable growth. By managing inflationary pressures and fiscal imbalances effectively, businesses can operate in a more predictable and favorable economic environment.
- Investing in human capital and workforce development: Poland's demographic challenges, including the aging population and emigration, pose risks to the labor market and economic productivity. To address these issues, policymakers should prioritize investments in education, skills training, and workforce development initiatives. By nurturing a skilled and adaptable workforce, businesses can mitigate labor shortages and drive productivity gains. A wise migration policy can also support labor shortages.
- Fostering innovation and digital transformation: Poland's transition to a knowledge-based economy requires a concerted effort to promote innovation and technological advancement. Government support for research and development, digital infrastructure, and entrepreneurship ecosystems is essential for fostering innovation-driven growth. By embracing digital transformation and leveraging emerging technologies, businesses can enhance their competitiveness and resilience in a rapidly evolving global marketplace.

- Addressing environmental challenges: Poland's heavy reliance on coal and environmental pollution pose significant challenges to sustainable development. Policymakers should prioritize investments in clean energy technologies, environmental conservation, and climate change mitigation measures. By transitioning to greener energy sources and adopting sustainable practices, businesses can contribute to environmental protection while ensuring long-term viability and competitiveness.
- Improving regulatory stability and business environment: Frequent changes in legal regulations and institutional uncertainties have created challenges for businesses operating in Poland. The government should improve regulatory stability, reduce bureaucratic hurdles, and enhance business efficiency. Policymakers can foster investor confidence and stimulate entrepreneurial activity by providing a transparent and predictable regulatory environment.

In conclusion, addressing the challenges mentioned above and implementing the recommended strategies will be crucial for supporting the growth and competitiveness of Polish companies in an increasingly complex and dynamic global economy. By prioritizing judicial independence, access to EU funds, economic stability, workforce development, innovation, environmental sustainability, and regulatory reform, policymakers can create an environment that enables businesses to thrive and contribute to Poland's long-term prosperity.

References

Baumol, W. J. (1995). Entrepreneurship: Productive, unproductive, and destructive. *Journal of Business Venturing, 11*(1), 3–22. https://doi.org/10.1016/0883-9026(94)00014-X

Bień, E. (2016). EU funds and adaptation of enterprises to the requirements of environmental protection. *Desalination and Water Treatment, 57*(3), 951–963. https://doi.org/10.1080/19443994.2014.988410

Dmuchowski, P., Dmuchowski, W., Baczewska-Dąbrowska, A. H., & Gworek, B. (2021). Green economy—growth and maintenance of the conditions of green growth at the level of polish local authorities. *Journal of Cleaner Production, 301*, 126975. https://doi.org/10.1016/j.jclepro.2021.126975

Dominiak, P., Wasilczuk, J. E., & Starnawska, M. (2016). *Przedsiębiorczość nieproduktywna w świetle ekonomii instytucjonalnej: Analiza zjawiska w Polsce*. PWN Warszawa.

Dzikuć, M., Piwowar, A., & Dzikuć, M. (2022). The importance and potential of photovoltaics in the context of low-carbon development in Poland. *Energy Storage and Saving, 1*(3), 162–165. https://doi.org/10.1016/j.enss.2022.07.001

Jankovic, S. (2016). Polish democracy under threat? An issue of mere politics or a real danger? *Baltic Journal of Law and Politics, 9*(1). https://doi.org/10.1515/bjlp-2016-0003

Jonek-Kowalska, I. (2017). The impact of renewables on polish energy balance–opportunities and threats for green energy development. *International Multidisciplinary Scientific GeoConference: SGEM, 17*, 797–804. https://doi.org/10.5593/sgem2017H/43

Kawczyńska, M. (2020). Combating the constitutional crisis in Poland–can the European Union provide an effective remedy? *Hungarian Journal of Legal Studies, 61*, 2. https://doi.org/10.1556/2052.2020.00269

Misztal, M., & Kupis-Fijałkowska, A. (2020). Development of ICT in Poland in comparison with the European Union countries—Multivariate statistical analysis. In K. Jajuga, J. Batóg, & M. Walesiak (Eds.), *Classification and data analysis. SKAD 2019. Studies in classification, data analysis, and knowledge organization*. Springer. https://doi.org/10.1007/978-3-030-52348-0_13

Pawlowska, M., & Pawlowski, L. (Eds.). (2017). *Environmental engineering V* (1st ed.). CRC Press. https://doi.org/10.1201/9781315281971

Perek-Białas, J., Sagan, I., Stronkowski, P., & Szukalski, P. (2017). Regional approaches to demographic change in Poland. In *Demographic transition, labour markets and regional resilience* (pp. 29–72). Springer.

Serowaniec, M. (2023). A few reflections on the current standards of law making in Poland. *Pravny Obzor, 3*, 202–214. https://doi.org/10.31577/pravnyobzor.2023.3.03

Sobczak, E., Bartniczak, B., & Raszkowski, A. (2020). Aging society and the selected aspects of environmental threats: Evidence from Poland. *Sustainability, 12*(11). https://doi.org/10.3390/su12114648

Winczorek, J., & Muszyński, K. (2022). The access to justice gap and the rule of law crisis in Poland. *Zeitschrift für Rechtssoziologie, 42*(1), 5–42. https://doi.org/10.1515/zfrs-2022-0002

Żurek, J. (2019). Polish constitution after 20 years. *International Comparative Jurisprudence, 5*(1). https://doi.org/10.13165/j.icj.2019.05.002

Magdalena Maria Popowska is a researcher and lecturer in Organization Science and Entrepreneurship at the Faculty of Management and Economics of Gdańsk University of Technology. For many years, she was responsible for internationalization processes, serving as Vice-Dean for International and Public Affairs from 2008 to 2016, and later as a Dean's Proxy for International Cooperation. Visiting scholar at European and Chinese universities. Today, her research mainly focuses on corporate social responsibility, sustainability, and entrepreneurship education.

Julita E. Wasilczuk is a Professor of Gdańsk University of Technology at the Faculty of Management and Economics. She has been affiliated with Gdańsk University of Technology since 1993. From 2012 to 2020, she served as Dean of the Faculty of Management and Economics, and she previously held the position of Head of the Department of Entrepreneurship and Business Law.

Her research focuses on entrepreneurship, with particular emphasis on small and medium-sized enterprises (SMEs), women's entrepreneurship, and the concept of unproductive entrepreneurship. Her academic interests also include non-technological innovation, entrepreneurship education, and the institutional conditions supporting entrepreneurial activity. Her postdoctoral dissertation addressed the challenges of small business growth.

She has initiated and coordinated numerous national and international research projects, including the SEAS (Survey on Entrepreneurial Attitudes of Students), an international study conducted since 2008. She has served as an expert in projects funded by the European Union and the Polish National Science Centre (NCN). She is an active member European Council of Small Business, and since 2018, she has served as the Vice President for Poland. Between 2019 and 2023, she was a member of the Presidential Council for Entrepreneurship in Poland.

She is a co-founder of the Education for Entrepreneurship Association, where she served on the governing council for many years, as well as a co-founder of the Women of the Fahrenheit Universities Association.

Hidden Champions of Romania

Bogdan Rusu

Abstract Romania offers a unique combination of promising opportunities and challenging risks. The National Recovery and Resilience Plan (NRRP) budget is €28 billion, structured on seven pillars. The national GDP per capita has reached 80% of the EU average. Additionally, the country faces a series of vulnerabilities and emerging risks related to large government deficits, as highlighted by the European Commission in its in-depth review. Data from the three hidden champions was collected through direct interviews with the key decision-makers behind the companies during on-site visits to manufacturing firms.

Cătalin and Oana love wool. They make high-quality duvets in different sizes and thicknesses to provide comfort and a good night's sleep. Sanodor gets about 40% of its revenue from exports.

Electra has 35 years of experience in designing and making access control systems. It has expanded internationally thanks to its R&D and integrated manufacturing system, which can produce in-house 90% of its products, enhance quality, and reduce costs using industrial robots.

Romsoft is integrated into its clients' software solutions. It operates in the medical industry, blockchain technology, artificial intelligence, and desktop and mobile add-ons for PowerPoint. Its positive working environment and high-quality workforce make it a reliable software solution provider.

Success depends on a good company culture, talented staff, R&D based on customer needs, and modern equipment. The core lessons learned on the path to success, pandemic's impact, and effects of Ukraine War are analyzed for each hidden champion.

B. Rusu (✉)
Engineering and Management Department, "Gheorghe Asachi" Technical University of Iaşi, Iaşi, Romania
e-mail: bogdan.rusu@academic.tuiasi.ro

D. Berberović, D. Purg (eds.), *Hidden Champions in Rising Economies*, Contributions to Management Science,
https://doi.org/10.1007/978-3-032-08263-3_33

Overview
Official name: Romania.
Type of government: semi-presidential republic.
Population in 2023: 19.1 million.
Land area: 238,397 km2 (92,046 miles2).

History

1940	Romania allies with Nazi Germany after general Ion Antonescu seizes power.
1944	Romania switches sides and joins the Allies. In 1945 a Soviet-backed government is installed.
1965	Nicolae Ceasuşescu becomes the Communist leader. Its foreign policy frequently diverged from Moscow's guidance while increasing repressive rule and personality cult in Romania.
1989	Romanian "revolution" started the transition from communism to democracy.
1993	Romania applies for membership of the European Union.
2004	Romania joins NATO.
2007	Romania becomes a European Union Member state.
2024	Romania joins Schengen Area for air and sea travel.

1 Introduction: Context and History

Since its accession to the European Union, Romania has been demonstrating a notable advancement in terms of GDP per capita and productivity, aligning itself with the rest of the member states. Nevertheless, despite notable advancements, with GDP per capita increasing from 59% of the EU average in 2016 to 80% in 2023 (Eurostat, 2024, June 19). In 2021, Romania continued to demonstrate a considerable prevalence of individuals residing below the poverty line, with a proportion of 21.2%. Additionally, the country is distinguished by an unequal distribution of economic opportunity and poverty across regions and between urban and rural areas. Additionally, Romania is among the most rural countries in the EU (De Rosa et al., 2018). Nevertheless, the Romanian capital, Bucharest, has surpassed the EU average income per capita, thereby exacerbating the already considerable disparity between regions.

On May 31, 2021, Romania submitted its National Recovery and Resilience Plan (NRRP), valued at €29.2 billion, to the European Commission. On September 8, 2023, Romania submitted an amended NRRP containing a REPowerEU chapter. While no existing measures were removed, the amendment introduced changes to 56 measures, including a reduction in investment and the transfer of certain investments to the REPowerEU chapter (Mileusnic and Killmayer, EPRS, March, 2024). The NRRP, in conjunction with foreign direct investment, constituted the primary sources of external funding for the Romanian economy. There are seven pillars of the Romanian NRRP.

1. “Green transition” aims to decarbonize energy and transport through renewable energy, efficiency, water and waste management, biodiversity, and sustainable mobility. The latter represents half the cost of the pillar, due to investments in railways and the Trans-European Transport Network (TEN-T). This pillar will support the green transition across all sectors and is funded by 13.1 billion Euros of RRF funding which represents nearly half of the Romanian RRF. (European Commission, SWD (27.09.2021) 276) and (European Commission SWD (21.11.2023) 382).
2. “Digital transformation” aims to develop digital public services for citizens and businesses. Planned reforms and investments address connectivity, cybersecurity, and digital skills.
3. “Smart, sustainable, and inclusive growth” covers tax administration, the tax system, the budget, and the sustainability of the pension system. It also aims to improve the business environment, especially in R&D&I.
4. “Social and territorial cohesion” aims to implement green and digital policies in urban mobility, tourism, culture, and other areas, enhancing territorial cohesion.
5. “Health and economic and social resilience” entails measures to enhance healthcare quality and accessibility, modernize health infrastructure, reform public administration, and enhance governance of state-owned enterprises.
6. “Next generation” proposes reforms in education and training sector. It aims to enhance quality and align with labor market requirements.
7. “REPowerEU” initiative advances Romania’s green energy economy through renewable energy, diversified supplies, efficiency, and green energy training, while eliminating fossil fuel reliance.

The Romanian economy experienced a period of considerable stability between 2023 and 2024, characterized by a remarkably stable exchange rate and political stability despite the energy price shock and turbulence caused by Russia’s war of aggression against Ukraine (European Commission, Institutional Paper 275, March, 2024). The report also exhibited a series of macroeconomic vulnerabilities. The Romanian economy slowed in 2023 but should grow again in 2024. However, downside risks remain. Real GDP grew 2% in 2023, below 2022’s 4.1% and 2021’s 5.7%. Inflation, tighter financial conditions, and lower global demand slowed growth.

In 2023, gross fixed capital formation drove economic growth, benefiting from EU-funded public infrastructure. The rate of inflation fell to 7% in December 2023, down from a peak of over 14% in November 2022. Core inflation declined less than expected, due to rapid wage increases, particularly in the private sector. By the end of 2023, the rate remained just above 10%. Real wage increases remain in excess of productivity growth, posing a risk to external competitiveness.

The current account deficit is projected to decline from 9.3% to 7.0% of GDP. The general government deficit remained high in 2023, contributing to the current account deficit. The Commission forecasts 3% growth in 2024 and 2025. Households’ real disposable incomes are set to grow thanks to lower inflation and improved financial conditions. However, the economic outlook is currently characterized by a greater degree of uncertainty. This is due to a number of potential factors, including lower-than-expected growth in Romania's trading partners and slower disinflation. These factors could have a negative impact on growth (European Commission, Institutional Paper 275, March, 2024). Comparing inflation across EU member states, in August 2023 Romania had 9.5% (Eurostat, Euro Indicators, 18 September 2024).

Human Development Index (HDI) assesses average achievement in three dimensions of human development: life expectancy, access to knowledge, and standard of living. In 2022, Romania's HDI value was 0.827, placing it in the Very High category and 53rd out of 193 countries (HDI, 13.03.2024).

The main indicators of the Romanian economy are presented in Exhibit 1.

Among the most successful companies are those that have prioritized research and development (R&D) and have developed innovative products and services based on customer needs. Similarly, companies that have invested in software development and the use of artificial intelligence (AI) have also demonstrated remarkable growth and resilience. These companies are all led by individuals with a strong background in manufacturing or software, who possess the passion and commitment necessary to drive success in their respective fields. As they all engage in competition within the EU and international markets, they have come to recognize the value of their human resources and have focused on reducing costs while improving the quality of their goods and associated services. This study examines a number of exemplary cases of hidden champions that display these characteristics.

2 Case Study 1

2.1 Sanodor

Overview

Address: Dumbravei 5, Piatra Neamţ, Neamţ, 610,202 România
Tel: +40744-650.096
Fax: +40744-650.096
Email: contact@sanodor.ro
Web: https://sanodor.ro/, https://www.confortmerino.ro, https://www.valeria-home.com/ro/

Company Information

Industry: Manufacture of made-up textile articles (except apparel and underwear)
Year of Establishment2014
Sales Revenues in 2017: 140,000 Euro
Sales Revenues in 2023: 1,3 million Euro
Average number of employees in 2023: 16
Brainer(s) behind the company: Oana and Cătălin Tatu

Exhibit 1 Core economic indicators for Romania

	2017	2018	2019	2020	2021	2022	2023
GDP per capita (current US$)	10.728	12.494	12.958	13.047	14.947	15.692	18.419
GDP per capita growth (annual %)	8.82	6.65	4.40	−3.15	6.50	4.52	2.10
Long-term unemployment rate (% of total unemployment) [a]	2.4	2.2	2.0	1.8	2.0	2.2	2.2
Foreign direct investment, net inflows (% of GDP)	2.83	3.02	2.93	1.43	4.11	3.84	..
GDP (current US$, mio)	210,147	243,316	251,018	251,363	285,810	298,892	351,003
Exports of goods and services (current US$, mio)	88,964	101,078	100,910	92,694	116,013	129,342	137,336
Exports of goods and services (% of GDP)	42.33	41.54	40.20	36.88	40.59	43.27	39.13
Merchandise exports (current US$)	70,761	79,660	76,871	70,718	87,388	96,699	100,612
Merchandise exports to high-income economies (% of total merchandise exports)	78.51	80.25	79.66	80.98	..	..	..
Merchandise exports to developing economies in Europe & Central Asia (% of total merchandise exports)	13.07	12.50	13.35	13.06	..	..	..
Ores and metals exports (% of merchandise exports)	2.11	2.23	2.19	2.30	2.80	2.79	2.48
Agricultural raw materials exports (% of merchandise exports)	1.17	1.11	1.07	1.20	1.32	1.16	0.83
Food exports (% of merchandise exports)	10.13	9.46	10.34	11.14	12.71	12.92	13.04
Fuel exports (% of merchandise exports)	3.77	4.10	3.78	2.42	3.52	7.63	5.31
Manufactures exports (% of merchandise exports)	80.48	82.25	81.72	82.36	79.05	74.31	76.23
High-technology exports (% of manufactured exports)	9.78	10.08	11.07	11.94	11.49	11.61	..

Source: World Bank, (09, 2024), [a] Trading Economics, (09, 2024 computed as average from quarter values

2.1.1 Nature of Market Leadership

Sanodor's expertise in wool allows the production of high-quality wool duvets that provide optimal comfort and quality sleep through effective thermoregulation, draping, and sustainable practices. The product filling is light, warm, and odorless. The products are meticulously crafted to precise technical specifications to facilitate the transfer of moisture outside the bed, thereby regulating body temperature. While they cannot compete with the larger duvet manufacturers, they have identified and filled a niche market that is underserved by other manufacturers. They offer the highest quality wool duvets that are 100% natural, comfortable, durable, and sustainable.

2.1.2 Nature of Competitive Advantage

Sanodor designs and manufactures high-quality wool duvets that provide comfort and quality sleep through excellent thermoregulation, drapability, and sustainability.

The main factors contributing to the company's success can be attributed to three key areas: innovation, responsiveness to customer needs, and fostering collaboration with small, family-owned businesses in Germany for both wool processing and linen. In addition, the company has developed customized equipment for removing odors from wool and offers a comprehensive range of duvets and bed linen in various sizes and thicknesses, tailored to the typical sleeping habits observed in the European Union.

2.1.3 Core Lessons Learned on the Path to Success

There are four key lessons:

1. Long-term success comes from serving the customer.
2. Develop a reliable system to collect feedback and involve your partners in the process (Sanodor use it every six months and randomly survey minimum 100 customers every year about their experiences).
3. Analyze your feedback and survey data. Sanodor reduced return and replacement rates.
4. Develop and adapt your products and services after listening to your customers (whether they buy directly or virtually, including social-media).

2.1.4 Management and Leadership Development Needs

As Sanodor grows, the extended product lines, customized sizes, and number of export countries, it needs to implement adequate systems to deal with high diversity/number of products and dimension range, according to country and sleeping habits. Now the number of customers and product portfolio is very large compared to a decade ago. As a result, it has become almost impossible to manage them using Excel files, purchase orders, and email. This increased complexity has also made financial and performance analysis more difficult, and Sanodor will invest in an ERP system to improve its operations. Both employees and managers will learn, adapt, and make a successful transition that will increase the efficiency and effectiveness of daily operations.

Piatra Neamţ is a county capital, but relatively small. The city lacks professionals in finance, sales and marketing. There are few young, educated graduates. It's hard to find locals with expertise in digital design, image editing, and online marketing for sustainable products. These people should have the knowledge and expertise to manage relationships with international brands that work with Sanodor.

2.1.5 Financing and Regulatory Environment Development Needs

One of the main challenges for Sanodor is to adapt its business model and operations to price increases. Due to the very high inflation rate in Romania (9.7% in 2023 and projected to reach 5.9% in 2024 (European Commission, 2024, May 15), banks charged high interest rates for investment loans, and investment tax credits are disadvantageous compared to those from Germany. This made it difficult for Sanodor to compete in exports.

Romania had the highest annual inflation rate in August 2024 (5.3%), along with Belgium (4.3%) and Poland (4.0%). The countries with the lowest annual inflation rates were Lithuania (0.8%), Latvia (0.9%) and Ireland, Slovenia, and Finland, which all registered 1.1% (Eurostat—Euro Indicators, 2024 September 18).

Over the past decade, the price of online advertising has increased tenfold. As more and more customers are now buying online, companies are allocating higher budgets for marketing and advertising. If in the first years of its existence Sanodor had a budget of 5% of its turnover for marketing; in 2024 it uses about 200,000 Euros, representing about 15% of its turnover. The company estimates that it would need 25% of its revenue for online promotion and marketing, but such an amount is not accessible. Sanodor would also benefit if universities became bridges between academic learning and the needs of the private sector for practical application of knowledge, needs that include the Small and Medium Enterprises (SMEs) sector.

2.1.6 Pandemic's Impact on "Hidden Champions" Business Approach

The first two weeks of the closure were very difficult as people stopped buying and Sanodor went into "survival mode." However, Sanodor saw an opportunity in the closure of brick-and-mortar stores such as Ikea, JISK, and City Mall, as there were significant transportation difficulties. Many companies tried to cut costs and stopped online advertising, which was a great opportunity for Sanodor. They started online advertising with simple messages such as "Comfort from your home" and "A good night's sleep." But they were able to support local efforts to supply hospitals with masks, medical protective suits for surgeons, and surgical suits for hospitals; using raw materials from the Piatra Neamţ community. It was all quiet online. But even without export, by producing face masks and medical garments used during the SARS-CoV-2 pandemic, Sanodor had a higher turnover in 2020 than in 2019.

2.1.7 Effects of the Ukraine War on "Hidden Champions" Business Operations

Just after Sanodor invested in the new premises located in an industrial park on the outskirts of Piatra Neamţ, the war in Ukraine started. The world stopped. Their foreign partners were frightened by the lack of information and uncertainty. They were kind and supportive, inviting Oana and Cătălin to come over as refugees. It was not necessary because everyday life in Romania was not affected by the war. There was a lot of stress, but not because of the conflict, which took place outside the country's borders. Probably the main causes were ambiguity, lack of clear and trustworthy information, which in turn fueled possible alarming and intimidating scenarios regarding fighting so close to the Romanian borders. It took some time to convince export partners to continue placing orders and that life in Romania was normal. Export kept them busy, especially from Canada and the UK. Soon online orders recovered and the company could function normally.

2.1.8 "We Love Wool"

Founded in 2014 by Oana and Cătălin Tatu as a family business, the company produces duvets, pillows, mattress protectors, and bed linen using natural, high-quality raw materials, unbleached and undyed. After 1990, everything that was imported was considered better by most Romanians. Thus, the 5-cm thick woolen blankets used by our grandparents disappeared. But Oana and Cătălin saw that wool was used in USA, France, Australia, UK, Spain, Denmark, and all over Europe. They decided that through education, it should become popular also among Romanians living in houses and apartments. But wool was associated with bad smell (like naphthalene used to protect it from clothes moths) and prickling. So, they started their journey to improve wool duvets, benefiting from Cătălin's knowledge and expertise as a textile engineer.

Their first customers were people over 60-years old who could no longer buy from the old village workshop that used to make thick wool duvets, as they all closed down for lack of customers. This market segment was happy to find a high-quality equivalent wool product that was 100% natural, lighter, odorless, beautifully designed, and incredibly comfortable. Based on their experience, they repeated the purchase and sent the product to their children abroad in Italy, Spain, and the UK; to name just a few EU countries. And the kids loved it, so Sanodor decided to open its online stores.

They started working with a Romanian wool specialist and together they developed the first wool filling for duvets according to Sanodor's technical specifications.

The result had a spectacular effect on the quality of the product, which has since been continuously improved.

Many customers who ordered a duvet found it to be far beyond their expectations. They did not believe that it could provide so much comfort, as their reaction was "I have not slept so well since I was a child." Such sincere and emotional feedback on the websites gave Oana and Cătălin a positive, vibrant energy that made them eager to come to work every day.

A decade ago, the investment was small and the price of the product was high compared to salaries, rent, and taxes, allowing the company to be self-financing.

Their love for wool and successive improvements based on research and innovation allowed them to develop a duvet that is light, warm, and odorless. It wicks moisture out of the bed and regulates body temperature. In order to design and manufacture the highest quality duvet, they compared competitive products in terms of comfort, durability, sustainability, and health hazards.

To continue to grow in international markets, Sanodor needed a larger volume of high-quality wool filling. It had to be produced according to their technical specifications and certified in the EU and worldwide. The challenge they faced was to find a strategic partner who could reliably supply high-quality wool according to Sanodor's design requirements. They identified and developed a strategic partnership with a small German family business with a long tradition in wool processing. There were several iterations from the first sample of filling provided to the German partner until, based on Sanodor's feedback, they produced an excellent wool filling that met all the technical criteria. Sanodor uses only natural, high-quality materials for the linen.

It has a very specific density/m^2, physical structure, and composition. This gives the filling a high thermoregulatory capacity, which is the main function of the duvets. This combination also enables excellent draping as the ability to stay in contact with the human body. The only duvets that have a higher draping capacity are those with silk fillings, but silk has a lower thermoregulatory capacity compared to Sanodor's wool. Goose down fillings have excellent thermoregulatory capacity, but poor draping.

Comfort includes both thermoregulation and drapability. Innovation has allowed them to design specific densities/m^2 for thin and thick duvets adapted to specific temperature ranges (i.e., 18^0–22 °C, 23^0–26 °C, or four seasons sets) with excellent thermoregulating and draping capacity. They are superior to quilts made of goose down, cotton, silk, polyester, or microfiber.

Wool also has a natural fire resistance and low price for the technical proprieties that it provides.

Conventional sewing machines used in the manufacturing process were a technical limitation to increase sales and growth of the company. Therefore, in 2018, the company purchased a CNC quilting machine with EU funding, which improved quality, productivity, and product variety.

Although it is a significant cost for the company, attending important trade fairs such as Heimtextil in Frankfurt every year has given Sanodor the opportunity to see and be seen, to learn about the latest trends in colors and materials, and to attract export customers. Today, about 40% of the company's turnover comes from exports to the UK, the USA, and EU countries.

The key factors for success are innovation to solve customer needs, cooperation with small family businesses in Germany for both wool processing and linen, custom-made equipment to remove odor from wool, and a large range of duvet and linen sizes and thicknesses based on EU sleeping habits.

There are over 30 duvet sizes in Europe, with significant differences from northern to southern countries. Analyzing different cultures shows that people sleep in different bed sizes, some use a single large bed mattress while others use two single mattresses to allow for different softness and duvet. Some like their house to be very warm in winter, while others keep it cold. Sanodor has seen this range of behavior as an opportunity to adapt to customer needs and increase its product diversity to respond to market diversity. Unable to compete with the large duvet manufacturers, they focused on niches that were not well served. They concentrated on high-quality duvets with wool filling.

Finding and educating customers about comfort and a good night's sleep is one of the company's future challenges, as sometimes people decide to buy based on price alone.

The company encourages employee involvement and responsibility for quality. They will report any problems on the production line that may affect the quality of the duvet. If they can, they will be adequately addressed and resolved or will ask for help and technical support.

The company now serves a large customer base and offers a wide range of products. As a result, it has become increasingly difficult to manage these processes using Excel files, purchase orders, and email. The increased complexity has also made financial and performance analysis more difficult. In response, Sanodor is ready to invest in an ERP system to improve operational efficiency.

Piatra Neamţ, where Sanodor is located, is a county capital, but is relatively small compared to larger cities. As a result, the city fails to attract a significant number of highly qualified professionals in finance, sales, and marketing. There is a lack of young, well-educated graduates choosing to work and live in the city. It is difficult to find locals with expertise in digital design and image editing, content creation, and online marketing for sustainable products. These individuals should be able to manage the interface and relationships with international brands and online stores where the company operates online. Sanodor has developed a system to collect customer feedback through a variety of channels, including social media, online stores, and direct requests for feedback at specific intervals, namely sixty days, one year, three years, and five years from the date of purchase. On an annual basis, they and their international partners conduct surveys of 100 new and existing customers. Using a random sample, they ask for feedback and satisfaction using standardized questions. The data is then analyzed with the goal of improving the quality of their products. This includes reducing the number of returns or product replacements.

3 Case Study 2

3.1 Electra Group

Overview

Address: Parc Industrial Miroslava, Str. Principală nr. 33, Corp A, Bratuleni-Miroslava, 707307, Jud. IASI, ROMANIA
Tel: +40 232 214.370
Fax: +40 232 232.830
Email: office@electra.ro
Web: https://www.electra.ro, http://electra-grup.electra.ro, https://www.ems-electra.ro, https://www.pcb-electra.ro, https://www.electra-automation.at, https://www.bellcome.com/en

Company Information

Industry: Manufacture of loaded electronic boards (loaded printed circuit boards), manufacture of communication equipment (door phones)
Year of Establishment: 1991
Sales Revenues in 2017: 7.31 million euros
Sales Revenues in 2023: 8.44 million euros
Average number of employees in 2023: 126
Brainer behind the company: Marian Berdan, CEO

3.1.1 Nature of Market Leadership

As it enters its 35th year of operations, Electra Group maintains its position as the dominant player in the Romanian access control market. The company's product range includes access control, interphone systems, and door phones, which it designs, manufactures, and provides services for. With an 80% market share in Romania, the company has expanded its operations internationally, with exports accounting for approximately 30% of its total revenue. The company has established an office in Vienna, Austria (ELEKTRA Building Communications GmbH), through which it oversees the international distribution of BELLCOME products. The company's products are available for purchase via the online platform Conrad. The group is currently active in Austria, Germany, Switzerland, Belgium, Northern Africa, Great Britain, Poland, and the Republic of Moldova.

3.1.2 Nature of Competitive Advantage

The competitive advantage of the Electra Group is shaped by a combination of technological and cultural factors.

Technological drivers include research and development (R&D) and in-house manufacturing capabilities.

The company's expertise and experience in R&D are crucial factors that contribute to its competitive advantage and enable it to maintain a strong presence in the market, particularly in the context of a shrinking product lifecycle. The Electra Group allocates approximately half a million euros annually to its research and development team. The products were designed with aesthetic appeal and user-friendly features and interfaces. Over the years, the company has been awarded several patents and certificates of industrial design by the State Office for Inventions and Trademarks (OSIM Bucharest).

It is a daunting task to manufacture products to the requisite specifications, and the challenges faced by engineering companies in integrating their production systems are often undervalued by the general public. For Electra, the context is even more challenging due to the lack of alternative small suppliers in its geographical vicinity that could provide parts and sub-assemblies, thereby supporting horizontal integration.

Prior to the advent of the pandemic, Electra made a substantial investment and relocated to its new 11,000-square meter, state-of-the-art facilities. The modern design facilitated the integration of workflows within the company's specialized compartments, with each compartment benefiting from new and highly efficient machinery and industrial robots. These endeavors enhanced operational efficacy and enabled the company to effectively compete against East Asian rivals.

From a cultural standpoint, the company benefits from Mr. Berdan's personality and leadership style. The company's success can be attributed to its vision and perseverance in achieving its goals. He recognized the necessity of a competent human resources (HR) workforce and implemented effective policies to recruit and retain individuals with a proclivity for technical pursuits. There is no other engineering company in Iași that offers its employees the opportunity to express their creativity, flourish, and take pride in their achievements.

The company's business model enabled it to design and manufacture high-quality products and to install and service its systems through key partners in various locations throughout Romania. Electra has established robust internal mechanisms for monitoring customer needs and complaints. In the event that such monitoring identifies the need for assistance, the company is equipped to provide customers with fast and reliable customer service. A comparable operational model is employed in the company's international markets.

For 35 years, Electra has served as a trusted access point for Romanian customers "in Romanian pockets—as access key," as evidenced by the company's reputation for reliability and trustworthiness. Its interphones and control access systems have been instrumental in fostering this perception, establishing the brand as a reliable and dependable partner in the Romanian market.

3.1.3 Core Lessons Learned on the Path to Success

The company's culture is guided by six core values:

1. Passion—The company's dedication to the design and manufacture of video and audio door phones and access control systems is a reflection of its substantial experience and the multitude of potential avenues for growth. The company is thus prepared for new opportunities and growth, ensuring that the Electra Group will be ready to capitalize on these developments when they arise.
2. Innovation is a prerequisite for progress. In order to maintain a competitive advantage, it is essential to continuously monitor customer needs, emerging technologies, and design trends.
3. Quality—The path to achieving it is not one that can be bypassed. Such a strategy necessitates a long-term commitment and investments in order to ensure survival and success in the marketplace.
4. Simplicity and elegance—the products were designed by professionals to be aesthetically pleasing, elegant, and modern, while also being technically sophisticated, Electra's products are "complex but not complicated."
5. Authenticity is another key aspect of our design philosophy. We endeavor to create a 100% Romanian product that reflects pride and quality, and is worthy of the Romanian reputation for excellence.
6. Respect for people—Electra places a premium on the value of its human capital and is committed to ongoing HR investment, ensuring that employees are a primary asset for the company. These factors enable the company to provide customers with superior products across the R&D, manufacturing, and support phases. The use of state-of-the-art technology allows for the reduction of costs while simultaneously minimizing the number of defects.

3.1.4 Management and Leadership Development Needs

Although there are no apparent deficiencies in terms of knowledge, competencies, or skills, CEO Marian Berdan is preoccupied with the company's succession, which is a family business (as he owns 80% of the company). One potential avenue for consideration is the listing of the company on the Bucharest Stock Exchange.

3.1.5 Financing and Regulatory Environment Development Needs

Electra is currently pursuing further development based on an analysis of market knowledge and growth potential. The company has access to modern manufacturing equipment, a highly qualified workforce, and optimized production flows.

While robust domestic demand is fueling growth, ongoing wage increases and a projected high government deficit, according to EU forecasts (European Commission, 2024, May 15), are posing challenges. In light of the aforementioned economic projections, which indicate a lack of legislative and fiscal predictability, Mr. Berdan has chosen to refrain from pursuing any further investment opportunities or projects funded by the European Union.

In its ongoing pursuit of growth, Electra is seeking to extend its product range to encompass small buildings. This strategic decision is based on the company's substantial expertise in the domain of large-scale residential complexes. In the context of the ongoing conflict in Ukraine, the company has become increasingly aware of the necessity for enhanced data protection and digitalization for video interphones, which now encompass data transmission, sound, and video stream. In order to address these needs, it is imperative that more robust security protocols and protection against cyber-attacks be implemented. In addition to the imperative of incorporating novel and enhanced functionality into its product range, Electra must persist in its endeavors to further reduce production costs through the implementation of design principles aimed at facilitating automated assembly and automation.

3.1.6 Pandemic's Impact on "Hidden Champions" Business Approach

The company demonstrated resilience and adaptability during the SARS-CoV-2 pandemic by maintaining continuous operations. All recommended measures for preventing virus transmission were implemented, and the company became compliant with medical protocols. Furthermore, the company was fortunate to have a sufficient supply of raw materials, which allowed it to focus on manufacturing.

Conrad Electronic offered the company the opportunity to expand its reach into the European market, where at that time its larger Chinese rivals such as Hikvision and Huawei were not present. Throughout the majority of the pandemic, Electra was the sole Eastern European supplier. Consequently, individuals with access to the Conrad distribution system procured and installed Electra systems in their residences. Detailed instructions were developed to facilitate customer-driven installation of the systems, eliminating the necessity for external technical assistance. The equipment was aesthetically pleasing and dependable, performing admirably in the domestic settings in which it was installed.

3.1.7 Effects of the Ukraine War on "Hidden Champions" Business Operations

The conflict in Ukraine had no discernible impact on the Electra Group, either in terms of its operations in Romania or its global customer base. As a consequence of the company's policy of self-reliance in terms of in-house manufacturing, the potential impact of any disruption in the supply chain is minimal.

3.1.8 Tenacity and Determination in Pursuing a Dream

As it enters its 35th year of operations, Electra Group remains the dominant player in the access control market. The company has maintained its market share of over 80% in Romania based on the superior quality of its products, which have over time been perceived as reliable and trustworthy by end users. In order to adequately manage and coordinate the complexity of the R&D and manufacturing system, the Electra Group was formed in 2008 through the division of the production facilities into three specialized firms. The Electra Group comprises three distinct entities:

1. ELECTRA, a producer of video door phones and access control systems,
2. PCB-ELECTRA, a producer of printed circuit boards, and.
3. EMS-ELECTRA, a supplier of SMD & THT electronic assembly services.

The group has since expanded and now operates an office in Vienna, Austria (ELECTRA Building Communications GmbH), as well as a BELLCOME international products brand, which has enabled the creation of an international distribution network. The company operates in Austria, Germany, Switzerland, Belgium, Great Britain, Poland, and the Republic of Moldova.

The company's product range has evolved from the PASS Analog to the PASS Digital and, most recently, the Touch Line (comprising the Smart+, Extra and Security models) and Access Line ranges. This evolution is the result of the company's innovative design capabilities.

The latest developments incorporate more complex functions, such as access control (including video interphone) to a specific apartment from a large residential compound using any of multiple entrances/access points. The Touch Line—4 Wires system may be installed in residential buildings with one to eight families and apartment buildings with up to 40 apartments. The Touch Line—Residential system may be installed in buildings with up to 255 apartments and provides solutions for residential centers. The product range is designed to appeal to both Romanian and international customers, offering a sophisticated yet accessible selection of items characterized by a natural and enduring elegance. The product is manufactured from chemically toughened glass, which ensures that it is resistant to scratching and shocks, impermeable, easy to maintain, and retains its polished appearance over time. Its minimalist design combines intuitive functionality with advanced technical specifications. The slim design, premium appearance, and accessible prices of these products provide appropriate solutions for houses, apartment buildings, and residential centers.

The company's success can be attributed to two key factors: innovation and passion. Marian Berdan, the company's founder and CEO, is an advocate of resilience. In order to achieve one's aspirations, it is imperative to persevere in the pursuit of one's goals.

Romanian customers are aware that, over time, should their existing Interphone system require servicing, they can rely on Electra to dispatch a team to address the issue. Moreover, customers have the option to upgrade their access control system with a new, state-of-the-art Electra model.

Operating from a new, modern, aesthetically pleasing, and functionally efficient 11,000-square meter facility, Electra allocates a significant portion of its resources toward innovation, with approximately half a million euros dedicated to research and development salaries. Additionally, the company manufactures over 90% of its products internally across all three specialized entities that comprise the group. The facility contains a number of specialized compartments, some of which serve the entire Electra Group. The most significant of these is the research and development (R&D) department, which comprises mechanical engineers specializing in die design and manufacture, electrical and electronics engineers responsible for circuit board design, and technicians.

PCB-Electra is responsible for circuit design, while the shop floor is equipped with machinery that manufactures and tests circuits prior to and following the assembly of electronic components. This process significantly reduces the incidence of defects. EMS-Electra has access to specialized equipment and robotic systems for electronic and mechanical assembly.

A dedicated area on the production floor is allocated to injection molding, while another is designated for mechanical operations involving presses and dies, which are used to manufacture mechanical parts and various types of cases or enclosures for electronic devices.

The integration of production facilities has enabled Electra to become self-reliant, reduce product manufacturing time, defect rates, and costs. It is regrettable that other smaller Romanian producers of interphones and access control systems were unable to withstand the competition from eastern Asian manufacturers and subsequently ceased operations.

A portion of the research and development team is dedicated to the advancement of robotized assembly design. Such endeavors are oriented toward reducing costs and enhancing quality, necessitating that Electra invest in cutting-edge equipment and technology. The products are now designed with the objective of facilitating automatic assembly, and the plant has six operational robots. Plans have been made to introduce another six robots over the next couple of years, including robots for plastic molding. In order to maintain its competitive advantage, the Electra Group must enhance functionality with new features while simultaneously reducing costs and improving quality through automation and robotization.

Furthermore, Electra regularly exhibits at international trade fairs, including Light + Building in Frankfurt and Expo Seguridat in Mexico. Such attendance offers the opportunity to gain insight into the latest products on the market, to learn from the experience of exposure to these products, and to gain an understanding of the needs and desires of potential customers. Such interactions provide a robust foundation upon which to base future product redesigns and improvements.

One of the challenges currently facing the Electra Group is the introduction of a product range for houses and small buildings, based on the company's considerable expertise in the field of large residential complexes. Another challenge that has emerged since the onset of the Ukraine war is the protection of data and the digitalization of video interphones, which now include data transmission, sound, and video streams. These systems require enhanced security protocols and protection from cyber-attacks. One of the future challenges for Electra is identifying an appropriate successor who will continue and build upon Mr. Berdan's values and results, as he owns 80% of the business. One potential outcome is listing the company on the Bucharest Stock Exchange (BSE).

4 Case Study 3

4.1 Romsoft

Overview
Address: Chimiei 2 bis, Excel Business Center, 700391 Iasi, Romania
Tel: +40 332 800002
Fax: +40 232 266831
Email: office@rms.ro
Web: http://www.rms.ro

Company Information
Industry: Computer programming activities
Year of Establishment2001
Sales Revenues in 2017: 2.63 million euros
Sales Revenues in 2023: 5.66 million euros
Average number of employees in 2023: 117
Brainer behind the company: Dorin Cristea, CEO and founder

4.1.1 Nature of Market Leadership

Romsoft is a provider of unique, customized software development solutions for its clients. As the software packages are integrated into their clients' applications, he can be considered a "hidden" champion. Approximately 40% of the company's sales turnover is derived from the medical industry. Its scope encompasses applications tailored to specific laboratories, automated robots deployed within medical laboratory settings, and blockchain technology in the medical industry. Additionally, the company produces specific software programs for the management of medical data for a big medical company in Germany, a branch of a Japanese corporation. Such collaboration necessitated adherence to all pertinent quality standards for software in the medical industry. Additionally, the applications developed for desktop, software as a service (SaaS), mobile, and add-ons to PowerPoint for Office Timeline, which accounts for approximately half of its revenue, are also classified as "hidden." The remaining 10% is derived from their participation as partners or beneficiaries in international and national research grants.

4.1.2 Nature of Competitive Advantage

The company demonstrates considerable expertise in the application of artificial intelligence (AI) and machine learning (ML) for image recognition. Such examples include quality control in the automotive industry for sub-assemblies that require visual inspection and medical Imagistics that may support physicians' diagnoses and decision-making processes. Moreover, the company possesses expertise in blockchain technology, which facilitates information sharing within a business network. This sophisticated database mechanism stores data blocks that are linked together in a chain.

The medical laboratory industry provides a reliable source of revenue, exhibiting minimal fluctuations in sales during periods of economic downturn or expansion.

With over two decades of experience, competitive pricing, a highly skilled workforce, reliable software solutions and maintenance, and a commitment to long-term customer relationships, Romsoft has established itself as a reliable partner in the industry.

4.1.3 Core Lessons Learned on the Path to Success

The companies for which the software is being developed tend to be discreet regarding their suppliers, particularly if the supplier provides excellent value for money and maintains a competitive edge. Consequently, Romsoft proceeded to further develop its ecosystem in collaboration with its major customers, with a view to grasping and anticipating the needs and requirements of the end user. The value created is contingent upon a company culture that is predicated on a positive work environment, wherein human resources (HR) are duly compensated in terms of personal development, flexibility, and performance-related pay. A system of compensated time off is made available to employees who require time to acquire new knowledge and skills.

Engaging Romsoft as a partner in international research programs in collaboration with foreign universities and research entities not only generates revenue for the company but also has a beneficial impact on its human resources. Such involvement offers opportunities for professional growth, learning, and new challenges that would make the participating employees proud of their achievements, enhance their esteem, and facilitate their self-actualization.

4.1.4 Management and Leadership Development Needs

Romsoft maintains a competitive position by remaining well integrated within the ecosystems of its key clients. However, considering the particularities of their services and the company's integration within their ecosystems, Romsoft does not have a sales department. Just a business development unit, with an underdeveloped sales subdivision that needs further development based on enhanced cooperation with Romsoft key customers.

4.1.5 Financing and Regulatory Environment Development Needs

While the Romanian government implemented a substantial increase in taxation for the Information and Communication Technology (ICT) sector in 2018, the primary challenge confronting the company is the imperative to enhance remuneration for HR, which elevates operational expenses. This phenomenon persists even when all HR personnel originate from Romania, as stipulated by major clients for personnel engaged in their projects. While inflation does not represent a concern for the company, the lack of legislative stability, predictability, and the extremely high deficit based on borrowing must be addressed for the benefit of a healthier Romanian economy.

Although the company recruits some graduates who are pursuing doctoral studies or have already obtained a doctoral degree, it would be advantageous if the legislative framework were less conservative and permitted universities to update their curricula more rapidly, thereby aligning them with the frequent changes occurring across industries. In the field of information and communication technology (ICT), it would be advantageous for curricula to encompass the most recent software (such as Java) and technologies, as some of the taught material is three to five years old.

4.1.6 Pandemic's Impact on "Hidden Champions" Business Approach

For a considerable proportion of employees in the ICT sector, the option of working from home has become a standard expectation. However, over time, there has been a notable shift in staff behavior, with only 10% of them currently reporting to the physical office. This transformation has been propelled by a desire for enhanced autonomy over both personal and professional domains. Notwithstanding the apparent reduction in physical contact, work performance has remained consistent. One challenge associated with remote work is the potential for employees to feel less connected and engaged with the company, given the lack of regular physical interaction. Such circumstances could conceivably result in feelings of alienation.

4.1.7 Effects of the Ukraine War on "Hidden Champions" Business Operations

The conflict in Ukraine had no discernible impact on the company's operations. Neither their established and loyal customer base nor their research partners in international projects exerted any influence on business activities. However, in the ICT market, a prospective major client from the US tourism industry, who had previously engaged in discussions and appeared to be prepared to enter into a contractual agreement, likely became deterred by the proximity of the conflict to the Romanian border and ceased negotiations.

4.1.8 "Hidden" in Key Customers' Ecosystem, Swelling in International Research Projects

Founded by Dorin Cristea and Nicu Popescu in 2001, Romsoft benefited from their expertise, enthusiasm, and professionalism. The software company has a unique blend of stability and engagement in challenging projects by providing custom-made software and applications for its clients. Their major areas of expertise include the medical industry, office applications for desktop, mobile, add-in and participation in international research projects whereas a partner Romsoft holds specific knowledge and expertise.

The custom-made software for medical analysis focuses on automatization in laboratory work, blockchain, and health data collection and analysis integrated in various medical data management applications. Romsoft is responsible for developing software solutions and it is recognized as a stable and reliable provider. Being "Hidden" with SYSMEX Europe' ecosystem. Therefore, any of the classical marketing mechanisms cannot be applied because are not relevant. Due to its cooperation within SYSMEX Europe, its quality management system is compliant with specific standards required by software for medical devices such as IEC 62304 and ISO 13485 and was successfully audited, as part of Sysmex Integrated Quality Management System.

Romsoft success bases on competitive prices for software solutions in Eastern Europe, long-term cooperation with key customers, know-how and integration in software development processes, and excellence in software quality. The company does not make specific efforts to maintain its major clients. It just focuses on doing a job well done day after day.

There are mechanisms to identify and understand customer and end user's needs, which are transformed into specific features and included in the software, so the computer program does what the customer expects it to do. These continuous improvement steps provide stability, trust and reliability built in its 24 years of existence leading to confidence in future symbiosis and cooperation.

Software quality would not be possible without excellent HR. They are creative, satisfied with their flat and flexible culture and benefits. There are opportunities for personal development, growth, and performance-based promotions; employees being proud of the results of their work.

Partnership in many projects since 2008 (see Fig. 1), the company provided expertise in three categories of research: eHealth, data privacy and blockchain, and others.

EMIM is a free online management platform developed by Romsoft for doctors, patients, and pharmacists. It is designed to simplify data administration and management, providing quick access to patient medical information and improving collaboration between healthcare professionals.

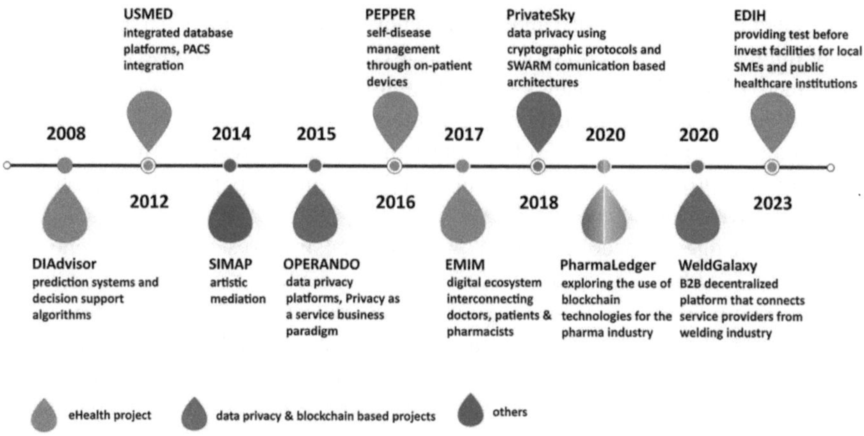

Fig. 1 International projects where Romsoft was involved since 2008 classified on their specific expertise. (Source–Rom soft internal document)

The platform primarily serves doctors who want to manage their practices in a virtual, integrated environment. EMIM allows the creation of a virtual practice from scratch and offers features such as appointment scheduling, service management, payment tracking, inventory control, and online communication with laboratories. Both doctors and patients can access the platform directly from a browser, without the need to install any software. With patient consent, doctors can securely share medical records with other practices. Moreover, EMIM supports telemedicine for remote consultations.

Coordinated by Alexandru Ioan Cuza University from Iaşi, Romania, the PrivateSky project aims to develop an open-source, decentralized platform for secure data sharing and privacy management.

It seeks to enable individuals and organizations to maintain control over their data while sharing it in a secure, trusted environment. By leveraging advanced cryptographic techniques and blockchain technology, PrivateSky facilitates privacy-preserving decentralized applications (dApps), addressing the needs of privacy-sensitive sectors such as healthcare, finance, and supply chain management. Romsoft provided essential technical support in designing the platform's architecture and implementing various decentralized applications. Their expertise ensured the platform's scalability, security, and user-friendliness, allowing it to serve real-world use cases. Romsoft's contributions helped bridge the gap between the theoretical framework and practical solutions, bringing blockchain-enabled privacy tools to a wide range of industries.

WeldGalaxy is a European initiative designed to create a digital marketplace that connects manufacturers, suppliers, and end users in the welding industry. The platform facilitates the exchange of welding equipment, consumables, and services while fostering collaboration and innovation. Leveraging PrivateSky technologies, WeldGalaxy ensures secure and decentralized data sharing, allowing stakeholders to conduct business with trust and transparency. Romsoft developed a decentralized tendering/bidding application for materials used in the welding industry. This dApp, powered by blockchain, enables suppliers and buyers to securely submit and manage bids, ensuring the confidentiality and integrity of sensitive business information throughout the process. Romsoft's contributions provided a robust solution for streamlining procurement and bidding while maintaining privacy and security within the WeldGalaxy ecosystem.

PharmaLedger is a collaborative initiative that involves various stakeholders across the healthcare industry, including pharmaceutical companies, regulators, healthcare providers, and technology firms. The project's primary focus is on using blockchain technology to improve transparency, security, and efficiency within the healthcare ecosystem. It aims to create a blockchain-based platform that addresses key challenges like counterfeit drugs, supply chain inefficiencies, patient data security, and clinical trial management. By leveraging blockchain's decentralized and immutable nature, it seeks to build trust among all participants while promoting innovation in healthcare solutions. As a key technology partner, Romsoft brings in its expertise in software development and healthcare technology and supports the design and implementation of blockchain-based solutions within the project's framework. Its primary focus is to create the technical architecture that supports various healthcare applications using blockchain technology.

The DiZ-EDIH (Digital Innovation Zone—European Digital Innovation Hub) project is part of the European Commission's initiative to establish a network of hubs that drive digital transformation across Europe. These hubs provide small and medium-sized enterprises (SMEs) and public organizations with access to cutting-edge digital technologies, expertise, and support. The goal of DiZ-EDIH is to foster the adoption of advanced digital solutions such as artificial intelligence, cybersecurity, and big data, helping businesses improve efficiency, innovation, and competitiveness. The project is particularly focused on underdeveloped regions, aiming to bridge the digital divide and promote innovation in key sectors like healthcare, manufacturing, and agriculture.

RomSoft plays a key role in the DiZ-EDIH project, bringing its extensive expertise in software development and healthcare technology to support the digital transformation of the healthcare sector. RomSoft collaborates with healthcare providers such as clinics to create innovative digital solutions that improve patient care and streamline administrative processes. These solutions include systems that enable personalized medicine, allowing healthcare providers to offer more targeted treatments based on individual patient data. RomSoft also focuses on enhancing communication between doctors and patients through digital platforms that simplify appointment scheduling, facilitate real-time consultations, and provide easy access to medical records.

As part of DiZ-EDIH, RomSoft is also involved in helping healthcare providers integrate emerging technologies into their practices. By leveraging artificial intelligence and big data analytics, RomSoft enables clinics to gain deeper insights into patient health trends, optimize treatment plans, and improve overall patient outcomes. Through its involvement in DiZ-EDIH, RomSoft is helping to drive the

Table 1 Detailed budgets for projects where Romsoft was partner since 2027

No.	Project Name	Business description	Grand Amount	RMS contribution	Total budget
1	EMIM	eHEALTH	€ 535,337	€ 392,173	€ 927,510
2	PrivateSky	blockchain and data privacy	€ 139,862	€ 47,933	€ 187,795
3	WeldGalaxy	blockchain	€ 347,375	€ 132,192	€ 479,567
4	PharmaLedger	blockchain	€ 1,058,561	€ 0	€ 1,058,561
5	DiZ-eDIH	eHEALTH	€ 240,750	€ 0	€ 240,750
TOTAL BUDGET			€ 2,321,885	€ 572,298	€ 2,894,183

digital revolution in healthcare, ensuring that both public and private healthcare organizations can harness the full potential of digital innovation to provide better, more personalized care to patients. Since 2017, Romsoft was a partner in five projects with a company's budget of 2.89 million euros and a total contribution of 0.57 million euros (see Table 1).

In Romsoft, there are no periodic re-qualifications as all staff engage learning whenever new customer requirements, technologies, and software requires it. Many have experience in working in international projects with distributed teams and all have and European Engineering Mindset. While the pressure on higher salaries affected Romsoft, the ICT industry is now affected by the economic crisis from other industries. Massive layoffs from large software companies including the giants from United States had reduced the pressure on salary in Romania. Now the company can recruit highly skilled personnel much more easily. The company has excellent collaboration with universities from Iaşi for recruiting graduates, PhD students, providing internships placements, and benefiting from specific development programs. Some of the HR come from Faculty of Automatic Control and Computer Engineering part of "Gheorghe Asachi" Technical University and Faculty of Computer Science at "Alexandru Ioan Cuza" University.

5 Conclusions and Recommendations

Sanodor's possesses considerable expertise in the design and manufacture of wool filings that adhere to exacting technical specifications, including density per square meter, physical structure, and composition. The entrepreneurial spirit of Cătalin and Oana has fostered a company culture that prioritizes innovation, sensitivity to customer needs, and robust manufacturing capabilities, including the use of CNC quilting equipment. Their strategic alliance with a small German enterprise that specializes in wool products has provided them with a competitive advantage in the niche market for high-quality duvets that promote a good night's sleep. The product range encompasses a multitude of sizes and thicknesses, catering to diverse sleeping habits within and beyond the European Union. Approximately 40% of Sanodor's revenue is derived from exports. The company's products are distinguished by thermoregulation, drapability, and proprietary technology for odor removal; rendering them challenging to replicate. Sanodor engages in ongoing customer feedback collection through standardized questionnaires, enabling them to refine their products in accordance with customer preferences. The necessity for a new ERP system arises from Sanodor's expansion of product lines, introduction of customized sizes, and increase in export countries. Beyond the financial implications, the implementation of this system will necessitate proficiency in its use among both management and staff. The company's operating environment is becoming increasingly challenging, with Romania experiencing a significant inflationary pressure compared to the EU average and the cost of online advertising rising exponentially over the past decade, reaching approximately 200,000 Euros in 2024.

For the past 35 years, Electra has been engaged in the design and manufacture of access control systems, interphone systems, and door phones. The products are designed with an elegant minimalist aesthetic and are intuitive to operate, offering a balance between sophistication and simplicity. The company has expanded its operations internationally, with approximately 30% of its revenue generated outside of Romania, where it currently holds an 80% market share. The company's competitive advantage is largely attributable to its robust research and development (R&D) operations, which are allocated a budget of approximately half a million euros annually. The company's new, state-of-the-art facilities, spanning 11,000 square meters, facilitate the integration of advanced manufacturing capabilities, including the use of robots. The company is capable of manufacturing approximately 90% of its products internally, integrating research and development, design, manufacturing, and testing and assembly of printed circuit boards, injection molding, and case manufacturing. Another crucial factor contributing to its success is Mr. Berdan's personality and leadership style, which fostered a sense of pride among employees while simultaneously enhancing quality and reducing costs.

Romsoft is not readily identified as a software solutions provider due to its practice of integrating its offerings into the applications and ecosystems of its clients. The company provides bespoke software development solutions for the medical industry, including tailored applications for specific laboratories, automated robots within laboratory settings, blockchain technology and the management of medical data. Additionally, the company offers a range of applications for desktop, software as a service (SaaS), mobile and add-ons for PowerPoint. Additionally, the company has demonstrated expertise in the application of artificial intelligence (AI) and machine learning (ML) for image recognition in the context of quality control for visual inspection in both automotive and medical imaging, with the potential to support diagnostic and decision-making processes. The company's expertise has been utilized in international research projects, contributing approximately €three million to its budget since 2017. Of this amount, Romsoft's total contribution exceeded €500,000. The company's human resources are a significant contributing factor to its success, fostering a culture of excellence and innovation in new technologies. Based on a positive working environment, Romsoft promotes personal and professional development, flexibility, and adequate rewards that instill a sense of pride in employees. Over two decades in business, the company has established itself as a reliable and stable provider, offering excellent value for money to its customers.

By addressing the financial deficit and adjusting spending, the Romanian government will foster a more favorable business environment, thereby reducing inflation and other identified vulnerabilities (European Commission, Institutional Paper 275, 2024, March).

It is evident that all manufacturing firms would benefit from specific measures aimed at increasing their export competitiveness. Such measures could include the provision of appropriate legislation and financial support for investment tax credits, which in Romania are currently disadvantageous compared to those available in Germany. Hidden Champions encounter challenges in recruiting highly qualified human resources. The recruitment of graduates who have undergone training and gained practical experience through internships would enhance the competitiveness of all companies. Universities should serve as interconnecting entities, facilitating the application of practical knowledge between the private sector (including SMEs) and academic learning. The legislative framework for higher education should be more flexible to allow for a more rapid alignment of curricula with changes in all business sectors.

References

De Rosa, D., Kim, Y. S., Chatzinikolaou, A., Bulman, D. J., Hopkins, J., Dospinescu, A. S., Karver, J. G., Meisner, C. M., Murisic, M., Pauna, C., & Tsoungui Belinga, V. P. (2018). *From uneven growth to inclusive development: Romania's path to shared prosperity—systematic country diagnostic*. World Bank Group.

European Commission, Economy and Finance Romania. (2024, May 15), *Economic forecast for Romania; The latest macroeconomic forecast for Romania*, European Commission, Retrieved September 15, 2024, from https://economy-finance.ec.europa.eu/economic-surveillance-eu-economies/romania/economic-forecast-romania_en

European Commission, Institutional Paper 275. (2024, March), *In Depth Review 2024, Romania*, Retrieved September 12, 2024, from https://economy-finance.ec.europa.eu/document/download/c5b5a8cb-6114-46e6-b7be-e47c689022c4_en?filename=ip275_en.pdf. European Economy Institutional Papers, ISBN 978-92-68-13776-5 ISSN 2443-8014 https://doi.org/10.2765/897378. KC-BC-24-002-EN-N.

European Commission, Staff Working Document (SWD 276). (2021, September 09), *COMMISSION STAFF WORKING DOCUMENT Analysis of the recovery and resilience plan of Romania Accompanying the document Proposal for a COUNCIL IMPLEMENTING DECISION on the approval of the assessment of the recovery and resilience plan for Romania, SWD/2021/276 final,* Retrieved October 09, 2024, from https://eur-lex.europa.eu/legal-content/EN/TXT/?uri=CELEX:52021SC0276

European Commission, Staff Working Document (SWD 382). (2023, November 21), *COMMISSION STAFF WORKING DOCUMENT Analysis of the recovery and resilience plan of Romania Accompanying the document Proposal for a COUNCIL IMPLEMENTING DECISION amending Implementing Decision (EU) (ST 12319/2021, ST 12319/2021 ADD 1) of 29 October 2021 on the approval of the assessment of the recovery and resilience plan for Romania,* SWD/2023/382, Retrieved October 09, 2024, from *https://eur-lex.europa.eu/legal-content/EN/TXT/?uri=SWD:2023:382:FIN*

Eurostat—Euro Indicators. (2024, September 18), *Annual inflation down to 2,2% in the euro area*, Retrieved September 25, 2024, from https://ec.europa.eu/eurostat/web/products-euro-indicators/w/2-18092024-ap#:~:text=European%20Union%20annual%20inflation%20was,and%20Finland%20(all%201.1%25)

Eurostat—Statisticsexplained.(2024,June19),*GDPpercapita,consumptionpercapitaandpricelevel indices*, Retrieved September 15, 2024, from https://ec.europa.eu/eurostat/statistics-explained/index.php?title=GDP_per_capita,_consumption_per_capita_and_price_level_indices

Human Development Index (HDI). (2024, March, 13), *Romania*, Retrieved September 09, 2024, from https://hdr.undp.org/data-center/specific-country-data#/countries/ROU

Mileusnic Marin, Killmayer Lucille, EPRS (European Parliamentary Research Service). (2024, March), *BRIEFING Next Generation EU (NGEU) delivery—how are the member states doing? next generation EU monitoring service, members' research service PE 733.641, Romania's national recovery and resilience plan—latest state of play,* Retrieved September 30, 2024, from https://www.europarl.europa.eu/RegData/etudes/BRIE/2022/733641/EPRS_BRI(2022)733641_EN.pdf

Trading Economics. (2024), *Romania long term unemployment rate,* Retrieved September 25, 2024, from https://tradingeconomics.com/romania/long-term-unemployment-rate-eurostat-data.html

Bogdan Rusu is an associate professor in the School of Industrial Design and Business Management (IDBM), Engineering and Management Department of "Gheorghe Asachi" Technical University of Iasi (TUIASI), Romania.

He received a Bachelor in Mechanical Engineering from TUIASI, an MBA from Derby University UK and his Ph.D. in Management from "Alexandru Ioan Cuza" University of Iasi. He was an associate professor for Romanian-Canadian MBA in Bucharest teaching Consumer Behavior, Director of the Center for Continuing Education (CETEX) Iaşi and vice-dean of IDBM. He is teaching Quality Management and Management of SMEs subjects to undergraduate and master students. His research interests include Consumer Behavior, Entrepreneurship and Innovation, Quality Management, and Design Thinking.

Hidden Champions of Serbia

Goran Pitić, Jelisaveta Lazarević, Kori Udovički, Miloš Erić, Nebojša Savić, Ema Marinković, and Zoja Kukić

Abstract Micro, small, and medium-sized enterprises (MSMEs) play a crucial role in Serbia's economy, driving employment, value addition, and innovation. Serbia's "hidden champions" are standout enterprises originating from traditional, highly competitive sectors of the economy. These companies excel by leveraging new technologies in product and service development, demonstrating a strong commitment to employee satisfaction, which positively impacts employee retention. A key trait of these champions is their continuous investment in research and development, driving ongoing improvements in products, processes, and services to maintain their competitive edge. Their close relationships with customers enable them to create tailored solutions that meet specific needs. Predominantly exporting their products, these Serbian hidden champions cater to a discerning, highly regulated international clientele and often emerge as world leaders in specialized niches. This chapter illustrates how these firms' strategic focus on innovation, employee well-being, and customer-centric approaches contributes significantly to their success and positions them as key players in the global market.

Overview[1]

Official name: Republic of Serbia
Type of government: Republic

[1] *Please provide World Bank data and a history overview of your country.*

G. Pitić · J. Lazarević (✉) · M. Erić · N. Savić · E. Marinković
FEFA Faculty, Metropolitan University, Belgrade, Serbia
e-mail: gpitic@fefa.edu.rs; jlazarevic@fefa.edu.rs; meric@fefa.edu.rs; nsavic@fefa.edu.rs; emarinkovic@fefa.edu.rs

K. Udovički
Center for Advanced Economic Studies (CEVES), Belgrade, Serbia
e-mail: kori.udovicki@ceves.org.rs

Z. Kukić
SEE ICT, Belgrade, Serbia

D. Berberović, D. Purg (eds.), *Hidden Champions in Rising Economies*, Contributions to Management Science,
https://doi.org/10.1007/978-3-032-08263-3_34

Population in 2023: 6.6 million
Land area: 88.499 km^2

History

Twelfth and thirteenth century	First Serbian state and constitution recorded, the formation of the Kingdom of Serbia.
Fourteenth century	Ottoman conquest of the Balkans. By 1521, Serbia is completely occupied.
Nineteenth century	Serbia is, following two uprisings, once again an independent nation. The New Kingdom's first constitution was adopted in 1835.
1912–1918	After the two Balkan wars and the First World War, Serbia becomes a part of the Kingdom of Serbs, Croats and Slovenes, later renamed the Kingdom of Yugoslavia.
1941–1945	Breaking up Yugoslavia, Nazi Germany occupies Serbia.
1945	Under Josip Broz Tito, the new Socialist Federal Republic of Yugoslavia was formed together with the other five constituent republics.
1948	Tito-Stalin split, Yugoslavia disassociates itself from the communist bloc.
1980	Josip Broz Tito dies, the onset of the political crisis that led to the breakup of the country.
1991–1992	Slovenia, Croatia, Macedonia, and Bosnia and Herzegovina declare their independence.
1992	The remaining two constituent republics, Serbia and Montenegro, form the new Federal Republic of Yugoslavia.
1992–1994	UN embargo, hyperinflation, one of the biggest in the history of the world's economy.
1995	The Dayton Agreement brought an end to UN sanctions and civil war.
1999	NATO bombing of Yugoslavia, de facto ending Serbian sovereignty over its southern province of Kosovo.
2000	Milošević was ousted from power in mass peaceful demonstrations.
2001	The first democratic government in the Republic of Serbia led by Prime Minister Zoran Djindjic.
2003	Serbia and Montenegro decided to abolish the name Yugoslavia and form a loose confederation. Serbian Prime Minister Zoran Djindjić was assassinated.
2006	Serbia becomes independent, as Montenegro secedes from the confederation.
2012	Serbia becomes an EU candidate country.
2014	EU opens accession negotiations with Serbia.
2021	Serbia, along with Albania and North Macedonia, launched the Open Balkan initiative aimed at creating a free economic zone to enhance regional cooperation and economic integration in the Western Balkans.

1 Introduction: Context and History

Serbia, situated in Southeastern Europe, is a landlocked nation home to 6.6 million residents. Its capital, Belgrade, with a population of 1.7 million, serves as the country's administrative, economic, transportation, and cultural center. The nation boasts abundant natural resources and fertile land, along with ample fresh water sources, including the major navigable rivers, the Danube and the Sava. Serbia generates sufficient electricity for domestic consumption and exports the excess. However, it depends on imported crude oil and natural gas due to its limited internal reserves.

Serbia is currently a candidate country in the process of accession to the European Union. The country was identified as a potential candidate in 2003 and officially applied for membership in 2009. Serbia became an EU candidate in March 2012 and started the formal negotiations in January 2014. So far, Serbia has opened 22 out of 35 negotiation chapters, which are important steps in aligning its laws with EU standards. Notably, it has provisionally closed two chapters.

Serbia, an upper-middle-income country, witnessed a significant rise in GDP per capita since 2000, with peak growth of 9% in 2004 and sustained high rates until 2008 (5.3% annually on average). Growth was disrupted during the global crisis (2009–2012) and by the 2014 floods. Recovery began in 2017, supported by structural reforms, increased infrastructure investment, and growing exports, especially to EU markets. Despite the COVID-19 pandemic's impact in 2020, swift policy responses helped mitigate the downturn. Robust fiscal stimulus programs in 2020 and 2021 limited the recession and facilitated a swift recovery in 2021, resulting in a higher fiscal deficit (World Bank Strategy, 2022; Exhibit 1).

GDP grew 3.8% in 2023 (real growth), with an acceleration in the second half of the year, primarily driven by recoveries in the agriculture and construction sectors. Mining, energy, and ICT sectors continued to positively influence the economy, while manufacturing and government spending had a neutral impact. In 2023, Serbia's ICT service exports surged to 3.4 billion EUR. The country is emerging as a burgeoning tech hub, boasting robust tech faculties and a pool of talented individuals creating products and services that compete on a global scale. According to Startup Genome, the combined value of Belgrade and Novi Sad's ecosystems stands at 910 million $ (Startup Genome). Serbia has formulated a Strategy for Artificial Intelligence Development and is actively establishing tech parks across various regions. It has strong ecosystems in Gaming, Blockchain, and Life Sciences. The construction of the BIO4 Campus, the first Life Sciences campus in the region to gather the scientific community and private sector, is currently underway and expected to be completed by 2026.

Serbia has embarked on its green transition, with significant potential still to be realized. According to research by the International Renewable Energy Agency (IRENA), Serbia's wind energy potential stands at 1.8 GW, three times the 500 MW capacity available at the end of 2023. The country's solar energy potential is estimated at 3.6 GW, yet the current capacity is only 137 MW, or about 4% of this potential (Bloomberg Adria Analytics, 2024). The scale of solar projects is

Exhibit 1 Core economic indicators for (insert the country)

	2018	2019	2020	2021	2022	2023	2024
GDP per capita (current US$)	7559	7755	8098	9,680	10,023	12,281.51	13,523
GDP per capita growth (annual %)	5.2	5.3	−0.3	9	5.2	4.5	4.4
Unemployment (% of total labour force, modeled ILO estimate)	12.7	10.4	9.0	9.8	8.4	8.3	7.4
Foreign direct investment, net inflows (% of GDP)	7.7	7.9	6.2	7.0	6.9	6.1	6.3
GDP (current US$, billion)	52.79	53.86	55.87	66.16	66.8	81.34	89.08
Exports of goods and services (current US$, billion)	25.69	26.37	25.76	34.63	40.58	44.8	46.94
Exports of goods and services (% of GDP)	48.7	49	46.1	52.3	60.7	55.1	52.7
Merchandise exports (current US$, billion)	19.23	19.63	19.5	25.56	29.06	30,93	31.59
Merchandise exports to high-income economies (% of total merchandise exports)	81.2	79.9	76.2	75.3	75	74.2	..
Merchandise exports to low and middle-income economies in Europe & Central Asia (% of total merchandise exports)	16.3	16.1	19	18.5	18.8	18.9	..
Ores and metals exports (% of merchandise exports)	4.5	4.7	4.2	4.8	5.1		
Agricultural raw materials exports (% of merchandise exports)	2.6	2.4	2.3	2.2	2.1		
Food exports (% of merchandise exports)	21.3	21.1	21	21.7	21.9		
Fuel exports (% of merchandise exports)	3.4	3.3	3.1	3.6	3.8		
Manufactures exports (% of merchandise exports)	68.4	69.5	69.2	68.9	68.1		
High-technology exports (% of manufactured exports)	4.3	4.5	4.6	4.8	5.0		

Source: World Bank, 2025

gradually increasing. Notably, Serbia has signed a contract with Hyundai to construct a 1 GW self-balancing solar power plant for EPS, which will be built on a turnkey basis.

In 2023, Serbia achieved a record inflow of foreign direct investment (FDI), with FDI inflows totaling 4.5 billion euros. When considering the proportion of FDI relative to GDP, Serbia outpaces other countries in the Adriatic region and the CEE4 group. While investments from China constituted approximately 30% of total investments in both 2022 and 2023, the primary source of investment remains the European Union, which channels investments into the Adriatic region (Bloomberg Adria Analytics, 2024). The sectoral structure of FDI inflows has also changed recently, to emphasize services (especially real estate and construction) and mining on account of manufacturing.

Serbia has a well-developed highway network, linking vital cities and regions. The focal point of this network is the E-75 corridor, stretching from the northern border with Hungary through the capital city, Belgrade, and extending southward to the border with North Macedonia. Another significant artery is the E-70 highway, which links Belgrade to Croatia in the west and Romania in the east. Additionally, Serbia operates two airports catering to scheduled international passenger traffic. Its national carrier, Air Serbia, serves approximately 70 international destinations, primarily from its hub in Belgrade.

Since 2012, there has been a consistent decline in the unemployment rate, hitting a low point of 9.4% in 2023. The heightened need for workers has led to tangible growth in private sector wages by 2.8% in real terms, while wages in the public sector have stagnated. Over several years, Serbia's labor market has witnessed rising activity rates, diminishing unemployment figures, a shift of workers from informal to formal employment sectors, and notably swifter wage increases in the private sector compared to the public sector, largely due to shortages in labor (CEVES, 2023).

Micro, small, and medium-sized enterprises (MSMEs) are pivotal in driving the Serbian economy, particularly in terms of employment generation, value addition, and fostering innovation. With over 400,000 MSMEs, accounting for 99.9% of all enterprises, they contribute significantly, providing 64.4% of employment and 59.2% of Gross Value Added (CEVES, 2023). Although the average productivity of MSMEs, measured by GVA per employee, is slightly lower compared to large enterprises, as is their export orientation, these differences stem from the unique characteristics of MSMEs. The most competitive sectors within Serbia's MSME landscape encompass agrifood, light machinery and equipment, wood and furniture, rubber and plastics, and ICT industries. Historically, the Yugoslav economy was diversified, emphasizing industrialization and manufacturing, initially aligning with Western European counterparts through reparations and subsequent partnerships. However, significant capacity was lost in the 1990s due to war, sanctions, and prolonged privatization processes, leading to the survival of sectors with inherent competitive advantages, such as access to natural resources, skilled labor, and established foreign connections. Notably competitive MSME industries in Serbia include agrifood, light machinery and equipment encompassing various sectors like lighting and food packaging; wood and furniture production ranging from interior solutions to panel furniture; and the rubber and plastics sector serving automotive, food, and pharmaceutical industries. These industries offered Serbia's SMEs the opportunity to reconfigure productive capabilities developed in socialist times, primarily relying on the plentifully available engineering and technical skills rather than substantial investments of capital. Typically, if not related to natural resources (access to wood and favorable farmland) the companies positioned themselves in technical skill-or innovation-intensive industries. Nevertheless, agrifood is still the largest single SME export sector (accounting for some 20% of the total), catering principally to consumers in the broader Western Balkans region. The adaptability of these industries to produce diverse and often sophisticated products is a key factor in their success, recognized in Serbia's Smart Specialization Strategy for 2020–2027, as well as possibly in MSME and Industrial Strategies and research conducted by CEVES (CEVES 2017, 2021, and 2022).

Identified hidden champions of Serbia come from both IT (and more recently embedded IT), but more dominantly, traditional sectors of the economy, which proved to be the most competitive in the overall Serbian economy.

The shared traits of Serbian hidden champions primarily revolve around their adept utilization of new technologies in product and service development. This chapter demonstrates that hidden champions prioritize investment in their employees' satisfaction, leading to positive spillover effects in terms of employee retention within the company. Moreover, these Serbian hidden champions are committed to continuous development and investment in research and development, facilitating ongoing enhancements to products, processes, and services, thereby maintaining and establishing a competitive edge. Another prevalent characteristic among these companies is their close rapport with customers, allowing for the creation of products and services tailored to their specific needs. Most notably, these companies predominantly sell their products in foreign markets, catering to a discerning clientele predominantly operating in highly regulated and competitive industries, often serving as world leaders in specific niches.

2 Characteristics of Hidden Champions from Serbia

Serbian Hidden Champions are companies from the new (IT) and traditional sectors of the economy. Technology in general, particularly IT, is the common denominator of their success, together with strong customer relations and a human-centric approach that places employees' knowledge and satisfaction at the core of business success.

HCs of Serbia are developing market leadership in the specific niche by constantly innovating in products and services while meeting specific customer needs. Strong and long-term developed cooperation with customers is also one important determinant of both market leadership and competitive advantage. The strength of Serbian HC lies in cost-efficient, complex, and very practical experiential knowledge that is constantly being improved through meeting market needs and investing in innovation.

Companies adopt the latest industry standards and constantly track market trends. HCs of Serbia are building their leadership positions not only by working with cutting-edge technologies but also by embracing sustainability and green economy principles.

Employee development is one of the key priorities, together with investments in the human and capital most intensive process of R&D.

Core lessons learned are aligned with the overall characteristics of HC companies. Therefore, they are related to the importance of the defined end goal, strongly nurtured by developing both employee and customer satisfaction.

When it comes to development needs in terms of financing or the regulatory environment, most of them stated the importance of the Serbian EU accession process as a significant factor not only for the business environment in general but also for their businesses. The complexity of the local regulatory environment, together with an underdeveloped capital market, is another challenge for some companies.

For this book, we have chosen to feature two companies highlighted in the previous edition of the Book of Hidden Champions from 2021. The primary rationale behind this selection is their successful adaptation during the COVID-19 crisis, which involved the development of entirely new processes or products/services. Additionally, we have introduced two new hidden champions from different regions of Serbia. These companies have emerged as European and global market leaders in specific niches.

3 Case Study 1

3.1 BG Reklam

Overview
Address: 29. NOVEMBRA 1 M, Barajevo, Serbia
Tel: + 381 11 785 64 64
Fax: N/A
Email: info@bgreklam.rs
Web: www.bgreklam.rs

Company Information
Industry: Printing.
Year of establishment: 2001.
Sales Revenues in 2017: 4.7 Mil. EUR
Sales Revenues in 2023: 19.5 Mil. EUR
Average number of employees in 2023: 157
Brainer(s) behind the company: Luka Stanić, General Manager

3.1.1 Nature of Market Leadership

The company produces premium, permanent POS materials (POSM) that enable intensive lighting and a high level of interaction between customers and point of sales (POS). The company is a leader in Southeast Europe in the niche of premium, permanent POS materials.

3.1.2 Nature of Competitive Advantage

The entire production process takes place in a single location, and clients who cooperate with BG Reklam have their needs met in one place, enabling them to be focused on their core business instead of this part of the process, since they get a turnkey.

Besides strong customer relations, the company also developed strong relationships with retailers.

Another important factor is related to sustainability; they have invested a lot in the past few years in this field. The company procures in a responsible way and designs the products to be recyclable after their lifetime. The sustainability of products and business distinguishes the company from competitors.

3.1.3 Core Lessons Learned on the Path to Success

- When conquering developed markets, it is crucial to have an educated and experienced team that can gain the trust of clients in different developed markets.
- Not only the sales team but also the whole company team needs to have clients' confidence.
- To achieve outstanding success, the team must constantly develop.

3.1.4 Company's Development Needs in Terms of Management and Leadership

There are needs that change constantly as the company grows.

(a) There are some positions that did not exist earlier, such as video production (for presenting products and how they look in the shop) and positions related to ecology.
(b) When it comes to general, most underdeveloped skills are related to certain back-office positions—supportive functions because they follow the company's growth not going ahead of the company's growth. On the other hand, production and sales are one step ahead of the company's growth.

3.1.5 Company's Development Needs in Terms of Financing or the Regulatory Environment in Order to Keep or Advance Business Results

The fact that Serbia is not in the EU created different challenges in terms of administration and export. In 2018, the company opened an office in Hamburg and thus solved its export problem.

3.1.6 BG Reklam, the Hidden Champion

Established in 2001, BG Reklam emerged from an entrepreneurial vision that began in a humble garage setting. Identified as a hidden champion in a 2018 study (Pitić et al., 2021), the company produces premium, durable POS materials designed for enhanced visibility and customer engagement, thereby elevating overall customer experience. By prioritizing innovation, BG Reklam has maintained its leadership position in Southeast Europe within the niche market of premium, permanent POS materials.

BG Reklam has sustained its market leadership through its steadfast commitment to innovation, consistently integrated into its POSM offerings. One key factor contributing to its success lies in its dedication to ongoing innovation driven by the specific requirements of global leaders like Google. By collaborating with a diverse range of industries—including cosmetics, consumer electronics, and tobacco—and operating across multiple markets, such as German-speaking regions, the UK, and BENELUX, BG Reklam leverages this cross-sector synergy to fortify and maintain its leadership position.

Since 2018, the company has faced increased competition, witnessed market consolidation, and observed a shift toward the premium segment within the industry. Besides consolidation, the COVID-19 pandemic has triggered significant market changes. Lockdown measures in Western Europe have led to a dramatic transformation in consumer behavior, with a notable decrease in investments in FMCG POS materials as online took the stand. Despite challenges, from 2018 to 2022, BG Reklam experienced substantial growth, with revenues doubling and exports rising to 96% of total revenues. In 2016, exports comprised over 50% of the company's revenue, a figure that increased to 70% by 2018, and in the subsequent 2 years, exports surpassed 90% of total revenues.

Every crisis harbors an opportunity for those capable of adapting to market shifts and emerging trends. The company's adaptability, often characterized by its ability to navigate ambiguity, was evident during the recent crisis. Despite the closure of traditional retail outlets, a substantial portion of retail activity shifted to gas stations. In response, the company demonstrated flexibility by swiftly adjusting to the regulations governing POSM at gas stations.

The COVID-19 pandemic highlighted that certain industries, such as cosmetics and consumer electronics, are less impacted by online sales, as consumers prefer to physically try products before purchasing. BG Reklam took a stand in this field. In addition to acknowledging market trends, the company attributes its success to continuous innovation and ongoing investment in its two core pillars: its workforce and technology. Leveraging insights gained from previous collaborations with global industry leaders, BG Reklam consistently applies its expertise and experience to each new project, even across different sectors.

In 2021, we detailed the expansion of the company's production process and highlighted the critical role of quality control in maintaining a leadership position. BG Reklam's primary competitive edge stems from its vertically integrated production process, which allows clients to fulfill all their needs under one roof. Years of collaboration with installation companies have equipped BG Reklam to take care of the installation as well. Clients can track this process through proprietary software developed in-house after 2018.

The COVID-19 crisis and the war in Ukraine affected the company similarly to other businesses, reflected in rising raw material prices and supply chain disruptions due to lockdowns. BG Reklam adapts to challenges and exhibits flexibility by continually evolving and upgrading its operations to meet customer demands. With the onset of COVID-19, clients' decision-making processes changed, prompting the company's initial investment in professional video recording equipment. Upon completing product samples, BG Reklam's skilled production team creates short videos showcasing the products, which are then sent to clients for approval. Once approved, production proceeds.

BG Reklam is not a supplier, but a strategic partner to its clients, underscoring its status as a hidden champion. The company excels in understanding and empathizing with its clients' needs, fostering enduring relationships built on trust and collaboration. In addition to client partnerships, BG Reklam has cultivated strong ties with other stakeholders in the value chain, including retailers.

BG Reklam is an innovative company built on a foundation of knowledge. The company prioritizes investment in its people, followed by substantial investments in research and development. BG Reklam excels in fostering a multifunctional team dynamic and placing employees at the forefront of digital transformation and innovation initiatives. Emphasizing a hands-off management approach, the company empowers employees as project owners, granting them autonomy—a crucial factor in fostering proactive behavior and facilitating the generation and implementation of innovative ideas. This leadership philosophy minimizes employee resistance to change, fostering a culture of adaptability and openness to new ideas and processes.

Sustainability can be regarded as the upcoming pivotal factor for hidden champions. Just as clients exert positive pressure for continuous innovation, there is a parallel trend toward global consensus on sustainability and renewable energy. This trend is clearly evident in the case of BG Reklam, as the company's clients are setting targets related to CO2 reduction. BG Reklam is deeply committed to sustainability and holds a 20,400 ISO certificate, which underscores its dedication to responsible procurement practices. Moreover, in product design, BG Reklam prioritizes creating products that are recyclable at the end of their lifespan, further demonstrating its commitment to environmental sustainability.

4 Case Study 2

4.1 DMV

Overview

Address: Kraljevića Marka bb, Niš, Serbia
Tel: +381 184,591 552

Fax: N/A
Email: info@dmv.rs
Web: https://www.dmv.rs/

Company Information

Industry: Manufacturing industry
Production of measuring, research, and navigation instruments and devices
Year of establishment: 1991
Sales Revenues in 2017: 3.5 Mil. EUR
Sales Revenues in 2023: 9.3 Mil. EUR
Average number of employees in 2023: 227
Brainer(s) behind the company: Dušan Šarković, Founder

4.1.1 Nature of Market Leadership

DMV produces LED displays for a broad array of products, and particularly for traffic signalization and sports scoreboards. Three companies from China dominate the market where very large series with full color displays are involved. In the case of customized products, however, the series produced is substantially smaller and this allows for a much greater diversification of suppliers. DMV's position is the strongest in the market for adapted traffic signalization where standards are highest. In this market, they are positioned among the ten leading suppliers globally (three are Chinese, the rest European) and under certain specific circumstances they are among the top three.

4.1.2 Nature of Competitive Advantage

The company's key advantage is the capacity to maintain and develop a very broad spectrum of different products, owing to extreme cost-effectiveness in product development. The latter is particularly high in the little standardized pictorial (rather than matrix) displays. The key to DMV's success has been the possession of a software that helps it reduce the number of engineers needed to develop (not just reconfigure) a product's software to approximately a fifth of the number normally required. They were among the first to see the possibility of applying and combining different existing functions from different products, so they aimed to organize different technological characteristics in their software packages in such a way as to leave them accessible for new configurations. For example, a traffic statistics function embedded in the product developed for one company now can be used in some ten different types of products. The compactness of the software development team builds more well-rounded and versatile engineers and allows for not only constant technology innovation but also the transfer of innovation across different product types. That said, they do not need the highest levels of software creativity, but rather quality engineers willing to fit within a disciplined system of "standardized change" which allows them to stay both flexible and cost effective.

4.1.3 Core Lessons Learned on the Path to Success

It is important to care for and believe in the product the company is creating. The whole team needs to be interested and genuinely motivated by what they are doing. Problems will happen, but a belief in solutions is needed. It is also important to constantly plan, think about the future, keep abreast of, be on the lookout for, where technology and demand—product requirements—are going. This ensures the ability to meet the market.

4.1.4 Company's Development Needs in Terms of Management and Leadership

The company is working on professionalizing its management team. An executive board has been created with eight managers from the company. They are all motivated, among other things by the prospect of 20% ownership in the company. But, this is only the beginning. The owner is only beginning to talk with corporatization advisors.

4.1.5 Company's Development Needs in Terms of Financing or the Regulatory Environment in Order to Keep or Advance Business Results

A substantial disadvantage for Serbia is that EU funding is limited. While companies in EU member states ultimately benefit from structural funds, in Serbia, all assistance is subject to the de minimis limit. It is not clear if this is up to EU regulation or Serbia's interpretation of the assistance that it does give to its SMEs. Also, the company has been fighting an unbelievably long and senseless battle regarding administrative barriers to the completion of ownership conversion on a brownfield.

4.1.6 DMV, Hidden Champion

DMV has been producing professional LED electronics for over 30 years. The company was established in 1991 by Dušan Šarković, following his 2-year tenure at Elektronska Industrija Niš, which went bankrupt in the 1990s. While many of his contemporaries chose to leave Serbia, Dušan embarked on developing a company that manufactures devices for traffic (ranging from speed signs to weather stations), sports (from football to cricket), and industry (including clocks and injury countdown displays for workplaces). DMV's customers are primarily system integrators who collaborate with government entities, concessionaires, and other stakeholders in the value chain.

When founding the company, its creator envisioned producing a product that could be maintained and would generate consistent growth. It appears he succeeded, as the company has been growing for 32 years. Throughout this period of expansion and development, the founder primarily worked with partners. Four years ago, the company underwent a division, leaving Dušan Šarković as the sole owner. He then made a strategic decision to establish a professional management team, further professionalizing the company. This move provided employees with clearer responsibilities and tasks. The newly formed executive board also received a stake in the company, with Mr. Šarković remaining the majority owner. A 20% division of the company will be completed over the next 5 years.

Friends and acquaintances who left the country during the 1990s provided an excellent connection to foreign markets, allowing Mr. Šarković to focus his sales efforts internationally. Today, the company exports 80% of its production to over 90 countries worldwide, including New Zealand, Russia, the Middle East, the USA, Mexico, and as far south as Chile. They also export to closer markets, primarily the UK, the Nordic countries, Poland, the Czech Republic, Spain, Austria, and Serbia neighboring countries. Interestingly, the company is involved in regional infrastructure and road construction projects. Regarding revenue distribution by product, 80% of the company's revenue comes from traffic products, 10% from sports products, and 10% from other categories. This ratio has remained stable over the past 7–8 years. These proportions have evolved; the company expanded into the traffic sector once it had grown sufficiently in 2007.

In the 1990s, they defined their market orientation to focus on large mechanical systems, specifically large displays for sports and traffic. Their products are now sold on all continents. One anecdote that Mr. Šarković often shares is related to Cape Town. When his daughter, Anđela Šarković, won a medal at the Mathematical Olympiad in Cape Town, friends, family, and colleagues called to congratulate him on this extraordinary achievement. On these occasions, he would humorously remark that the real congratulations should be for the fact that the traffic light in the hall where Anđela took her tests was produced by DMV from Niš.

The hardware platform they have been working on has been in use since the company's founding. The company is highly self-sufficient in its production process: it designs its mechanics and hardware, owns 6000 printed circuit boards, and develops both the software and the supporting cloud software in-house.

However, constant technological changes also impact this company, necessitating multiple updates to its hardware platform. As industry standards evolve, DMV must continuously adapt and adopt these standards, often taking on the role of educating its customers in the process. The company also aims to participate in standardization bodies to influence industry standards. Long-term employees are particularly adept at anticipating technological changes, tracking developments, and initiating internal adjustments. DMV faces unique challenges in applying tech solutions. For instance, they developed their own ERP software because the available market options were too rigid and could not meet their needs. This custom ERP system has proven to be highly effective for them.

One of the company's new products is meteorological stations that monitor road conditions, wind speed and direction, visibility, road surface conditions, and ice risk. These meteorological stations can connect this data with traffic signs. DMV uses its existing hardware to provide an integrated solution. With this product, they aim to expand their presence on regional roads.

The company strives to be data-driven and aims to integrate production data into its systems to enhance operations. This data include information collected from production robots, CNC machines, and air quality sensors within the company. Utilizing this data will enable the company to improve its business processes. Interestingly, the products sold by the company already collect similar data. Air quality measurement sensors are integrated into their standard hardware platform, which is part of their building management and smart city platform. This allows their products to connect seamlessly with smart city systems. Uređaji koje kompanije proizvodi radi na solarne panele.

As technological and sustainable trends shape the industry, this company is getting to grips with these transformative forces. Their devices, including traffic signs, are increasingly powered by solar panels, currently comprising 5% of their products, with this percentage steadily growing. Additionally, the company owns a solar power plant on its roof and sells the electricity it generates.

The COVID crisis, as such, did not have much direct impact on the company, with little effect on the way the business is conducted. However, they did lose several younger, promising IT engineers at the height of the crisis to higher-paying jobs. As to the war in Ukraine, it initially affected the company by raising the prices of steel, and not much since. The company is concerned about collaborating with Russian partners but has not had the opportunity to work with them since the start of the war.

5 Case Study 3

5.1 Uniplast

Overview

Address: Stara Pruga, Preljina, Serbia
Tel: + 381 32 22 50 54
Fax: 381 32 380 286
Email: office@uniplast.rs
Web: http: //www.uniplast.rs/

Company Information

Industry: Manufacture of plastic packing goods
Year of Establishment: 1991
Sales Revenues in 2017: 0.7 Mil. EUR
Sales Revenues in 2023:2.4 Mil. EUR
Average number of employees in 2023: 40
Brainer(s) behind the company: Djordje Jovanović, General Manager

5.1.1 Nature of Market Leadership

The company is still No. 2 in the Western Balkans in the manufacture and distribution of pharmaceutical (galenic laboratories and pharmaceutical manufacturers), medical, and cosmetic packaging.

From 2018, the company positioned itself to be the number 1 in Southeast Europe in the production of active packaging with silver ions for cosmetic and pharmaceutical products in Southeast Europe, which extends the shelf life of preparations with fewer preservatives and destroys the transfer of microorganisms from hands-on the bottle.

5.1.2 Nature of Competitive Advantage

Uniplast focuses on the production of value-added products that comply with the latest industry standards. The company actively monitors market trends and remains flexible to adapt to changing conditions. As a family business, Uniplast places a strong emphasis on the continuous improvement of its professional management.

While many companies across Europe have extended their delivery times from 1 month to 6 months due to the ongoing energy crisis, Uniplast has demonstrated resilience. By installing solar panels, the company sources approximately 45% of its energy needs from solar power, allowing it to maintain efficient operations despite external challenges.

5.1.3 Core Lessons Learned on the Path to Success

The crisis presented an opportunity for growth, allowing the company to achieve full production capacity during the COVID-19 pandemic. Through this experience, the company recognized that even in the most difficult times, solutions are always possible, and the motivation of its people is crucial to overcoming challenges. Prioritizing short-term profit gains during a crisis is not sustainable; instead, long-term strategic thinking is key. Above all, maintaining the trust of existing clients remains a priority, even amid uncertainty and crisis.

5.1.4 Company's Development Needs in Terms of Management and Leadership

First, there is a need to strengthen the marketing team by introducing new tools. Second, improving technical expertise is important for better management of personnel in the production department. Lastly, optimizing internal processes is vital for boosting operational efficiency across the company.

5.1.5 Company's Development Needs in Terms of Financing or the Regulatory Environment to Keep or Advance Business Results

The company secures project funding from various sources, ranging from banks to grant funds. Bank resources are allocated toward renovating machinery and upgrading technological processes, while grants are utilized for research and development (R&D). Uniplast is actively reinvesting in process digitization.

5.1.6 Uniplast, the Hidden Champion

The company is No. 2 in the Western Balkans in the manufacture and distribution of pharmaceutical (galenic laboratories and pharmaceutical manufacturers), medical, and cosmetic packaging. Since 2018, the company has aimed to become the leading producer of active packaging with silver ions for cosmetic and pharmaceutical products in Southeast Europe. This innovative packaging extends the shelf life of preparations with less need for preservatives and prevents the transfer of microorganisms from the hands to the bottle.

Uniplast is a family-owned company with robust corporate governance and 33 years of industry experience. By developing innovative products and adhering to global production standards essential in this sector, the company effectively addresses the challenges encountered by its customers. Its unwavering commitment to value addition and innovative design has allowed it to maintain a prominent market leadership position. Moreover, the company's ambiguity enables it to swiftly respond to market changes. Uniplast approaches challenges from the perspective of the user, remaining focused on enhancing its products while constantly considering the "job to be done"—identifying the specific problems or challenges that their products solve for their customers.

In the realm of active packaging with silver, Uniplast diligently monitors market trends. Recognizing the growing demand for reduced preservatives in products, the company's technology team developed a solution to address this need. Additionally, Mr. Jovanović highlighted the scarcity of certified packaging manufacturers in the market. With safety-conscious clients seeking certified packaging options, Uniplast stands out in its niche, boasting five operational standards and the strongest position in the field.

Export accounts for 30% of total sales, and they are covering imports with current exports. The company targets exports to account for 50%. Since 2018, Uniplast has expanded its market presence in Serbia by strengthening collaborations with healthcare institutions and pharmacies. Furthermore, clients with long-term strategies opt to partner with Uniplast, partly due to the successful transition of the family-owned company to the second generation. Internally, the company is committed to developing management capabilities to ensure its readiness for future leadership.

Amid the COVID-19 pandemic and the surge in demand for their products, the company discovered its true production capabilities as it operated round the clock,

24/7. In 2020, Uniplast achieved a remarkable 82% increase in revenue, fuelled by heightened demand for the company's products during the COVID-19 pandemic. In 2021, revenue rose by 56% compared to 2019; however, it experienced a modest decline of 15–20% from the exceptional performance of 2020. Nevertheless, the company attained another record-breaking year in 2022, surpassing the growth of 2020. This success was attributed to vigilant monitoring of market trends. Uniplast identified a shift in demand from Chinese to European suppliers in Europe and effectively capitalized on the ensuing opportunities in the market. Mr. Jovanović explains that new opportunities are emerging in the Russian market. Previously, producers who sourced from Germany encountered challenges due to sanctions. As Serbia maintains no sanctions against Russia, it facilitates exports to this market. Additionally, owing to disrupted supply chains, numerous European companies have shortened delivery deadlines from one year to six months. Uniplast's competitive edge lies in its ability to meet these altered demand conditions.

Uniplast is committed to sustainability, driven by its philosophy of fostering meaningful business practices that benefit both the company and society. For instance, the company has installed solar panels, providing about 45% of its electricity needs from solar energy. The company is deeply committed to cultivating and retaining talent by fostering teamwork, ensuring individuals recognize their value and the impact of their work on satisfying clients' needs. Nevertheless, Uniplast still faces challenges in recruiting quality personnel, as there is limited willingness among the workforce to relocate from Belgrade to smaller cities across Serbia. In terms of process and management development, the company successfully transitioned to the second generation and established a corporate governance framework with professional management. Moving forward, Uniplast is striving to evolve into a fully professional management structure, independent of family involvement.

6 Case Study 4

6.1 Dmiteh

Overview

Address: Gruzanska 1, Gornji Milanovac, Serbia
Tel: +381 32 512 0772
Fax: +381 32 710 759
Email: n.dmitrovic@dmiteh.rs
Web: https://www.dmiteh.rs/

Company Information

Industry: Machinery
Year of establishment: 2008
Sales Revenues in 2017: 0.9 Mil. EUR

Sales Revenues in 2023: 1.1 Mil. EUR
Average number of employees in 2023: 10
Brainer(s) behind the company: Nenad Dmitrović, CEO, and Owner

6.1.1 Nature of Market Leadership

Dmiteh is the global leader (outside the USA) in the production of premium flexo printing presses for sausage casings. Dmiteh produces flexo printing machines for sausage casings, it holds about 1/3 of the global market of premium machines (of which only about four are produced annually), and it is the single global producer of top-of-the-line premium machines that cost about 3x more than standard ones [premium or others]. They were the first to produce a gearless (harmonic transmission) machine in this market globally, and they keep meeting ever more demanding customer requirements. Each costs about Eur one million.

6.1.2 Nature of Competitive Advantage

The ability to continuously innovate at a relatively low cost has been key.

Printing machines for sausage cases are large and costly to make relative to the size of the company (initially seven and today 12 employees) itself that mainly adds the value of engineering design and assembly. Developing prototypes to showcase innovation would be forbiddingly expensive. Instead, the company's practice from the outset has been to innovate on the machine currently being made, over and above the contracted features. Then, the most recently sold piece of equipment also serves as a showcase of the latest innovation.

6.1.3 Core Lessons Learned on the Path to Success

Need to have a vision and build partner trust on the way to realizing it. The founder was set on producing this kind of machine.

6.1.4 Company's Development Needs in Terms of Management and Leadership

The company's philosophy is not to grow beyond the low teen employee numbers, exactly so that there is no need to invest in developing a complex management structure.

6.1.5 Company's Development Needs in Terms of Financing or the Regulatory Environment in Order to Keep or Advance Business Results

The key obstacle in obtaining financing is that banks treat the company as an SME because that makes Dmiteh unbankable. Dmiteh's product cycle characteristics require high debt/revenue ratios throughout a specific project cycle. "Corporate" treatment allows for project financing and hence much higher debt ratios. In Serbia, the requirement for corporate status ranges from Eur one million of turnover for smaller to Eur 1,five million in larger banks. Dmiteh generally does not meet EUR 1,five million, and can at times fall below the EUR one million one. When it does, it becomes unbankable.

As to regulation, the government has a number of instruments of assistance that are very fragmented, and it is hard to learn and find more information about them. A small company does not have the research resources needed to find out about what is on offer. Dmiteh did recently receive a grant from the innovation fund. It helped the company accelerate innovation work that would otherwise have taken longer. Now they regularly receive information from the Fund.

6.1.6 Dmiteh, the Hidden Champion

Founded in 2008 by seasoned experts in the printing industry and machine production sector, Dmiteh immediately positioned itself at the top of the market, competing with a Japanese and a German producer that it squeezed out in the subsequent years, to conquer about 75–80% of the market for top-of-the-line machines. Through insightful market analysis, including evaluating capacity and competitiveness, but above all offering innovative solutions, Dmiteh has developed into a company offering original machine design, complete machine assembly, and has the ability to produce some parts as well.

Dmiteh's main product is a flexo printing machine for printing wrappers (casings) for salami and sausages. Ninety percent of their machines are sold internationally to customers ranging from small family businesses to large multinational companies. The company holds about one-third, 30–40% of the global market for flexo printing machines for sausage casings. This is a small, niche market in which Dmiteh produces only about four machines annually. Within the Premium segment, Dmiteh is one of two global producers of top-of-the-line premium machines, at a cost of approximately three times more than standard models. These larger machines are only made about once a year. Serial production is not possible in this niche market; each machine is unique, and this allows the company to continually innovate.

From the beginning, the company's strategy has been to produce high-performing, high-end, rather than cheap, machines. They were the first in the world to produce a gearless (harmonic transmission) machine in this market and continue to meet increasingly demanding customer requirements. Each machine costs about EUR one million. In this market, few companies buy new machines, preferring instead to purchase used ones to upgrade their technology. There used to be Japanese and German competitors in the top-of-the-line segment, but Dmiteh has outperformed them in terms of cost-effectiveness, driving them out of the market. Recently, a Hungarian company has entered the market, but it has not yet threatened Dmiteh's position.

Dmiteh has always upheld the belief that innovation is crucial for its survival, growth, and development. Consequently, the ability to continuously innovate at a relatively low cost has been key to its global success. From the very beginning, engineers have been the backbone of the company, with around 40% of the total workforce (four out of 10 employees) being engineers. The engineering team designs products tailored to customer needs, utilizing insights from the experienced sales team, which carefully monitors the market and consistently prioritizes customer satisfaction.

This market is challenging for small startups to break into due to the significant costs and time required to develop cutting-edge technology. Machinery manufacturing is capital-intensive, with machines taking a full year to build, tying up substantial operating capital. From this perspective, it was critical for Dmiteh to obtain the first bank loan, to fund the production of the first premium machine (which was accomplished thanks to guarantors collateral, based on personal relations). However, demonstrating innovation and proving its effectiveness has been essential for further sales success. Dmiteh's method has been to innovate on machines they are currently manufacturing, even if the innovation is not a part of the product's specification. By doing so, if successful, they not only exceed the customer's expectations but also showcase a tangible example of the innovation in action for other potential customers. Those approaches enable Dmitech's machines to be distributed across a wide array of global markets, spanning Serbia, North Macedonia, Poland, Bulgaria, Algeria, Morocco, Mexico, Latvia, and the Netherlands. Within these diverse regions, the company is dedicated to offering dependable and top-quality machinery that caters to the dynamic requirements of businesses and industries worldwide.

Because of the war in Ukraine, the largest producer of sausage casings, which is a Russian company, has been shut out from the market. This has increased the demand for the machines Dmiteh makes, but the company cannot take advantage of this higher demand because of a shortage of electronic parts on the market. This, a continued reverberation of the COVID crisis, has extended its production cycle from 9 to over 12 months. It also spurred the company to keep higher stocks of spare parts—presenting a significant financial burden.

As is often observed among Hidden Champions, Dmiteh also maintains a robust association with the R&D Institute. The Research and Development Institute Lola stands out as a key partner in the ecosystem, playing a pivotal role in contributing to the company's success. Dmiteh received the Serbian Innovation Fund Collaborative Grant Scheme award, which aims to encourage collaboration between private sector companies and public sector R&D organizations to undertake joint R&D projects to develop new products and services. Dmiteh partnered with the Lola Institute on a project related to technology for automating the packaging process of sausages, designed to increase packaging capacity by 30% compared to the industry standard (Serbian Innovation Fund).[2]

One other common characteristic of Serbian HC champions is a strong position in retaining talent in the company. Dmiteh is also successful in this field, and the company has never reduced the number of staff. The company's unwavering commitment to investing in knowledge and fostering employee development continues to rank among its highest priorities and critical factors driving its success. To attract talent, the company offers a positive and stimulating environment that nurtures employee development. In retaining talent, it utilizes competitive compensation packages, flexible working hours, and opportunities for employees to unleash their creativity in the workplace. Dmiteh has a practice of hiring young individuals straight out of school, actively supporting their development and advancement toward higher, more responsible positions within the company.

Throughout its developmental journey, Dmiteh has gleaned valuable lessons, particularly emphasizing the importance of having a clear vision and cultivating trust with partners to realize it. The founder of Dmiteh was steadfast in his determination to produce this specialized type of machine. Overcoming the significant obstacle of establishing trust with customers and securing funding for the initial press was crucial for success in this niche industry. Fortunately, the founder was able to demonstrate his proficiency in manufacturing similar sophisticated machines while working in a socialist-owned company. Additionally, he leveraged strong business connections to secure the necessary funding through loans or guarantees. Once customers witnessed the company's ability to consistently deliver reliable products, the inherent value of the product—a combination of quality and cost-effectiveness—spoke for itself.

7 Conclusions and Recommendations

Micro, small, and medium-sized enterprises (MSMEs) are critical to Serbia's economic landscape, contributing significantly to employment and innovation. Serbia's example shows that in times when the inflow of FDI has lagged, or where foreign companies offer limited opportunities for local supplier development, SMEs have served as a way to preserve capabilities and develop them through, most often, step-by-step and cumulative innovation. Such MSMEs have tended to develop through exports, either from the outset or increasingly over time, as Serbia's very small but highly diversified manufacturing market could not offer the variety of potential customers needed to acquire the necessary economy of scope, as well as scale. As Serbia's economy opened to trade and investment at the turn of 2001, SME merchandise exports grew steadily and fast. From 2005 to 2022, the number of SMEs

[2] https://www.inovacionifond.rs/en/programs/collaborative-grant-scheme-program/funded

with ten or more employees exporting more than 100 thousand euros increased over fivefold, and the value of their exports tenfold.[3]

In the areas where SMEs could establish a niche by relying on skilled labor and access to foreign markets, the key to preserving a competitive advantage has been adaptability, i.e., responsiveness and flexibility. It is this flexibility, a matter of spirit, ingenuity, and size, that has allowed some exporting SMEs to adapt to client demands swiftly, respond to market needs, and deliver tailored products and services efficiently on the global (or at least European). These are Serbia's "hidden champions," companies excelling in niche markets through technological innovation, customer focus, and continuous development.

The median age of Serbia's exporter SMEs is 22 years—these companies have typically emerged from traditional sectors, evolving from small shop suppliers, large state-owned enterprises, or from their parts, to become market leaders in specialized niches. Serving large global companies has continuously put pressure on these companies to improve and perform, resulting in the creation of high-value, competitive offerings. They have accomplished this through incremental innovation, fostering deep and long-term relationships with their customers, investing in research and development (R&D), and maintaining strong ties to global value chains and academic institutions.

To scale the hidden champions model to a broader range of SMEs and further support the development of existing hidden champions, the following recommendations are prioritized. The first and by far most important factor is the business environment. Presently, a disturbing number of Serbia's successful exporter SMEs in traditional sectors express a lack of interest in scaling. The main reason is a reluctance to face the additional risks that need to be confronted to accomplish this. And while a part of these risks is inherent to the growth/scaling process, much depends on the predictability of the business environment. Throughout the years, these companies' fortunes have been buffeted not only by Serbia's recent history, global economic developments, and policy shifts but also by political factors. Many explicitly state that they chose to focus on exports amid the Global financial crisis and its aftermath, as for half a decade, payments collection on the domestic market was a matter of substantial uncertainty. Leveling the playing field in line with the EU's principle of "think small first," and strengthening the rule of law, especially in establishing clear and transparent rules framing access to developed land, would greatly increase the rate at which SMEs in Serbia scale.

Another challenge comes from the fact that hidden champions tend to be family-owned businesses, often relying on a key person for innovation and vision. Professional management is quite often a key differentiator, and increasingly so as the generation of transitional business leaders is reaching retirement age. While assistance is on offer by development partners such as EBRD, a policy is not in place to support these companies in their corporatization and succession efforts.

[3] This tenfold increase is in fact understated, as the early year figures include also the exports of some large legacy companies that eventually shrank to small size.

Finally, the green transition and seizing the opportunities that new technologies offer is a final challenge that also requires a far more forceful policy response than is currently on offer. Serbia's champions' orientation is predominantly to the EU market, and they are aware of the existence of EU green regulation promoting circular economy as well as decarbonization, especially the Carbon Border Adjustment Mechanism (CBAM) that they will need to align with. Yet, at present, there is no systematic effort to provide clear guidance on the rules and procedures that need to be implemented, nor has a dedicated implementing authority been identified. Ideally, a strategy should be adopted that would clearly lay out the path of regulatory change and its implementation, as well as allocate accountabilities.

Greening generally requires advanced digitalization, but the rise of new technologies offers opportunities (as well as the threat of disrupted markets) on their own. Of particular interest is artificial intelligence (AI), which is significantly reshaping businesses. Serbian SMEs would benefit from enhanced advisory support to adopt these technologies in ways that boost efficiency and foster development beyond incremental innovations.

References

Doprinos nedržavnog sektora zvaničnom izveštaju o napretku implementacije COR-a. 2022. *Center for advanced economic studies—Ceves*. https://ceves.org.rs/wp-content/uploads/2022/12/Doprinos-nedrzavnog-sektora-zvanicnom-izvestaju-o-napretku-implementacije-COR-a.pdf

Foreign Direct Investments Adria region: FDI to rebound in 2024. 2024. *Bloomberg Adria analytics*.

Performance and Value Chain Analysis of Selected Sectors. 2017. *Consortium CEVES and chamber of commerce Serbia*. https://ceves.org.rs/wp-content/uploads/2019/04/Integrated-Report-on-Performance-and-Value-Chain-Analysis-of-Selected-Sectors.pdf

Pitić, G., Savić, N., Erić, M., Lazarević, J., Kukić, Z., & Marinković, E. (2021). Hidden champions of Serbia. In *Hidden champions in dynamically changing societies: Critical success factors for market leadership* (pp. 387–405). Springer International Publishing.

Serbia 2030: It is a time for SMEs. 2023. *Center for advanced economic studies—Ceves*. https://ceves.org.rs/wp-content/uploads/2023/10/Inicijative_MSP100_web-2.pdf

The analysis of the labour market and labour force needs in the context of migration governance. 2023. The analysis was undertaken under Activity 2.2.2 of the Action Plan (2021–2023) implementing the Economic Migration Strategy of the Republic of Serbia (2021–2027). *Center for advanced economic studies—Ceves*. https://ceves.org.rs/wp-content/uploads/2023/06/Analiza-potreba-trzista-rada-i-radne-snage-u-kontekstu-upravljanja-migracijama_ENG.pdf

Wind and solar industry report: Unlocking the Adria potential—harnessing untapped wind and solar energy. 2024. *Bloomberg Adria analytics*.

Goran Pitić is Professor of Digital Economy at FEFA Faculty and president of the FEFA Council. With over 30 years of experience, he has played key roles in planning and implementing financial and private sector development policies, with a track record spanning academic, governmental, and corporate sectors. Prof. Pitić holds a Ph.D. and Master's degree from the University of Belgrade, a Master's degree from the University of Toronto, and a specialization in Quantitative Development Economics from the University of Warwick. He further enhanced his expertise at the London School of Economics, Harvard Business School, and several prestigious institutions across

Europe and North America. From 2000 to 2004, Prof. Pitić served as Minister for Economic Relations of the Republic of Serbia, where he was instrumental in shaping post-transition economic reforms and fostering international economic relations. As a Chairman of BoD of Societe Generale Serbia (for 15 years), a Board member of Credit Agricole Serbia (for 3 years), and a Board member of AIK bank since 2023, he has gained significant experience in banking and assessing the investment potential of companies in various industries and various sizes, from SMEs to large. Since 2008 he has been a board member at Metalac Holding, one of the leading companies in the market. Professor Pitic played pivotal roles in numerous prestigious organizations, such as president of the Board of Directors of the Association of Serbian Banks and the Alliance for Fair Competition. He was/is a member of several Boards (Foreign Investors Council, NALED, Innovation Fund, Palace of Science, etc.). He has also led or participated in numerous international conferences on financial investment, collaborating with international financial institutions (IFIs) and private equity investors.

Jelisaveta Lazarevic is an assistant professor and Vice Dean at the FEFA Faculty. She is also the Chief Content Officer at Bloomberg Adria.She started her career at the Center for Advanced Economic Studies, where she had the opportunity to work on a World Bank project for the Ministry of Economy: Employment and Competitiveness, where she specifically focused on the analysis of value chains in the sectors of the economy with the greatest development potential. She is a strong believer in inclusive innovation-driven development and for 2 years she was Head of corporate partnerships at All for All organization, where she is a board member. Jelisaveta completed her undergraduate and master's studies at the FEFA Faculty as a student of the generation. During her undergraduate studies, she was named one of the best economics students in Serbia by the Serbian Association of Economists. She defended her Ph.D. dissertation at the FEFA Faculty in the field of business economics on the topic: Essays on strategy and innovation. During her career so far, she has received several awards, such as being selected as a future leader of Europe by the French Ministry of Europe and Foreign Affairs. She participated in the Open World Leadership Program funded by the U.S. Congress. Jelisaveta has been awarded two Campus France scholarships for research in the field of scientific research commercialization and science-industry collaboration, which she carried out at Lille University, the FEMTO-St Institute, and INRIA.

Kori Udovički —President of the Governing Board and Chief Economist, Center for Advanced Economic Studies (CEVES). She is the founder and head of the independent Center for Advanced Economic Studies (CEVES) in Belgrade. CEVES is Serbia's leading economic think-and-do tank, founded in 2004 and dedicated to the country's sustainable development, with a particular focus on SME competitiveness and stakeholder mobilization across Serbia and the Western Balkans. She is also a current member of the United Nations High-Level Advisory Board on Economic and Social Affairs, and of the UN Committee for Development Policy. Previously she was Deputy Prime Minister and Minister of Public Administration and Local Self-Government (2014–2016) and Minister of Energy and Mines (2002–2003) in the Government of Serbia. She also served as the first woman Governor of the National Bank of Serbia (2003–2004). In 2007–2012, Kori served as Assistant Secretary General of the UN, Assistant Administrator and Director of the Bureau for Europe and CIS of UNDP. Prior to joining UNDP, in addition to CEVES she founded the Foundation for the Advancement of Economics (FREN) in Serbia and established and edited its flagship publication, the Quarterly Monitor of Economic Trends and Policies in Serbia. From 1993 to 2001, Kori worked as an Economist at the International Monetary Fund.

Miloš Erić is an Associate Professor at FEFA—Belgrade Metropolitan University, where he engages in research on green economy, EU integration, decarbonization, and socioeconomic development. He has published several papers in top-tier journals focusing on energy efficiency, the same area where he earned his Ph.D. investigating energy-development nexus. In addition, he secured substantial EU and national support for multi-institutional projects.

In addition to his 17 years of experience in academia, Miloš is also working as Senior Manager at PwC, where he leads digital transformation and strategic consulting projects across the SEE region and the firm's public-sector practice in Serbia, working with public-sector clients, financial institutions, and startups to develop innovative solutions that enhance digital capabilities and foster economic development. His expertise includes leading high-impact projects for organizations like the World Bank, European Commission, UNDP and others, focusing on areas such as eGovernment, digital finance, and energy.

Nebojša Savić is professor emeritus at FEFA Faculty. He was a dean of FEFA from 2003 to 2009. Between 2007 and 2024, he was an affiliated professor of microeconomics at the Institute for Strategy and Competitiveness, Harvard Business School, Harvard University.

He participated in specialized programs at the US National Bureau of Economic Research (NBER) and Harvard Business School, Harvard University.

His experience in economic policy management, macroeconomic and stabilization policies, transition to the market economy, structural adjustment, enterprise restructuring and building institutions of the market economy spans several decades.

Prof. Savić was a member of the Board of Directors of Alfa Banka Serbia (2006–2012), member and president of the Board of Directors of Komercijalna Banka (2003–2005), and member and president of the Supervisory Board of Komercijalna Banka (1998–2003).

He served as director of economic research at the Economics Institute in Belgrade and editor-in-chief of the Economic Barometer. As a member of the economic team led by governor Dr. Dragoslav Avramović, he took part in the monetary reform and introduction of the new dinar (1993–1995).

He was a member of the Serbian Government's National Competitiveness Council from 2008 to 2012. Prof. Savic was President of the Council of the Gouverner of National Bank of Serbia (2012-2024). He has authored a number of books and over 50 papers in domestic and foreign publications. He was president of the Yugoslav Economic Association and is now a member of the Presidency of the Serbian Economists Association. He has also participated at World Congresses of the International Economic Association with his scientific papers.

Ema Marinković is an economist and international development professional with a strong academic foundation and wide-ranging experience in research, teaching, and donor-funded project development. She is a Teaching Assistant at the FEFA Faculty, University Metropolitan in Belgrade, where she teaches Microeconomics, Monetary Economics, and International Economics. She holds a bachelor's degree in Economics from the FEFA Faculty, a master's degree in Finance and Banking from the University of Sheffield, and is currently pursuing a PhD, with her research focusing on the macroeconomic effects of decarbonization in Serbia and the Western Balkans.

Ema currently works within Tetra Tech's International Energy Services division, where she supports the development of technical assistance projects for major international donors. Her work includes coordinating multidisciplinary teams, drafting technical content, and contributing to proposal strategies in areas such as sustainable energy, energy efficiency, and infrastructure development. She combines economic analysis with practical implementation insight to help shape evidence-based and context-driven development solutions.

In addition to her consulting work, Ema has an active academic profile, contributing to research publications and participating in international conferences.

Zoja Kukić has been part of the startup ecosystem for over a decade. She was part of the founding teams of Startit/SEE ICT and the "Digital Serbia" Initiative, spearheading startup ecosystem in Serbia and the region. From 2020, she's working with her team with startups and innovators launching and growing new products. So far, she worked across five continents.

She is a part of the Google for startups mentoring network. Zoja actively supports women in the tech industry and entrepreneurship and looks for ways to bring technology closer to girls.

Hidden Champions of Slovakia

Lenka Theodoulides and Janka Táborecká

Abstract This chapter presents a continuation of research, which began in 2011, investigating hidden champions (HCs) in Slovakia(Táborecká-Petrovičová, et al., 2013, Táborecká-Petrovičová, et al., 2021). Over 12 years, the research was carried out in three phases. The chapter aims to reflect on the essential findings and changes in the business environment in the context of previous research and key parameters originated by Hermann Simon (1992). Central to HCs' success is their commitment to innovation, with significant investments in digitalization that maintain their growth and foreign expansion. Their intense focus on innovation ensures that HCs remain competitive and meet specific customer needs. Two case studies are presented in this chapter, i.e., Gevorkyan j.s.c. as an identified HC and FOSALI Ltd. as a potential HC. Both are family-run companies, focusing on the niche markets of powder metallurgy and led customized lighting systems, respectively. These companies enabled a deeper analysis of their market leadership, competitive advantage, and management and leadership development needs. Their innovative products, customer-centered approach, and their founders' visionary leadership have been identified in their business stories. Despite being traditionally conservative in finance and operations, there is a growing need for these companies to embrace sustainable growth and integrate social values and non-profit activities into their business practices, such as collaboration with educational institutions and communities. Hidden champions of Slovakia serve as best practice examples for stamina and dedication in entrepreneurship.

Overview[1]
Official name: Slovak Republic (Slovakia)
Type of government: parliamentary democratic republic

[1] Please, provide World Bank data and a history overview of your country.

L. Theodoulides · J. Táborecká (✉)
Faculty of Economics, University of Matej Bel, Banska Bystrica, Slovakia
e-mail: lena.theodoulides@umb.sk; janka.taborecka@umb.sk

D. Berberović, D. Purg (eds.), *Hidden Champions in Rising Economies*, Contributions to Management Science,
https://doi.org/10.1007/978-3-032-08263-3_35

Population in 2023: 5,428,792 (Statistical Office of the Slovak Republic)
Land area: 48,080.0 km2

History

November 17, 1989	The Velvet Revolution brings democracy. The downfall of Communist Party rule in Czechoslovakia. The first free elections in Czechoslovakia since 1948 took place in June 1990.
January 1, 1993	Declaration of the independence of the Slovak Republic simultaneously and peacefully with the Czech Republic. Both states attained immediate recognition from the USA and their European neighbors.
January 1, 1993	In connection with the split of Czechoslovakia, both countries acquired membership in the IMF on January 1, 1993. (The former Czechoslovak Republic was one of the founding members of the IMF.)
2000	Slovakia is invited to join the OECD and is invited by the European Union to begin the accession process.
March 29, 2004	Slovakia admitted to NATO.
May 1, 2004	Slovakia joins the EU.
December 21, 2007	Slovakia becomes a member of the Schengen Area.
January 1, 2009	Slovakia adopts the single European currency, the euro.

1 Introduction: Context and History

The external environment encompasses exogenous factors that influence organizational efficiency (Njoroge et al., 2016) and the conditions faced by entrepreneurs (Alkali, 2012). Across all industries, these factors affect firms striving for strategic competitiveness (Hitt et al., 2011). This environment is dynamically complex, including social, technological, economic, political, and legal factors beyond their control, imposing limitations on organizational activities. Organizational survival and success hinge on management's ability to interact skilfully with the external environment and respond timely to changes, accounting for its impact on the business (Kuznetsova & Alekseeva, 2016). Lazauskas et al. (2012) emphasize that enterprises' adaptability to a changing environment and ability to maintain stability is crucial for competitiveness. The external environment includes shifts in international and national economies, technology, national culture, industry characteristics, legislation, and competitor and trade union activities (Genş, 2014). Studying these elements enhances organizational competitiveness by identifying potential opportunities and threats, which is necessary for strategic development (Kuznetsova, 2015). Effective management must predict threats and opportunities, develop plans and strategies to achieve goals, and turn potential threats into opportunities. PESTEL analysis (political, economic, social, technological, and ecological factors) is a valuable framework for analyzing macro-environmental factors and identifying trends, helping organizations anticipate change proactively. According to Rakesh (2014), PESTEL analysis aids environmental analysis by identifying key influences, long-term change drivers, and the varying impacts of external influences historically or in the future. While endogenous factors are the primary causes of business failure, exogenous factors significantly influence around one-third of small business failures (Everett & Watson, 1998).

The turbulent socio-economic, political, and historical background of Slovakia, which, among other things, formed the conditions for the development of HCs in Slovakia, can be dated back to the start of market liberalization in 1989, which continues up to the present. A global data report (Slovakia PESTLE Insights—A Macroeconomic Outlook Report, 2024) states that according to the World Bank, Slovakia has a strong percentile score of 63.7 in terms of government effectiveness, which measures the quality of public services as one of the political factors. It also measures the quality of the civil service and its independence from political pressures, the quality of policy formulation and implementation, and the credibility of the government's commitment to its stated policies. Furthermore, Slovakia's newly formed government, in a program endorsed on November 13, 2023, plans to increase various taxes, including those on banks, to finance higher pensions and overall spending while gradually reducing the eurozone's highest budget deficit. Regarding economic factors, Slovakia boasts a robust heritage in the automotive industry, making it the preeminent economic sector and the primary catalyst for the nation's economic growth. Presently, it stands as the most influential sector, contributing significantly to the Slovak GDP, export figures, and employment opportunities. Slovakia stands to benefit economically as modern trends in the automotive industry, featuring alternative powertrains and autonomous control, pose both a challenge and a significant opportunity. The country has the potential to attract new investment projects associated with this transformative shift, enhancing its economic strength. GDP growth was 1.6% in 2023 before picking up to 2.2% in 2024. High inflation was weighing on private consumption growth, although the impact has been mitigated by substantial government support measures. Investment growth was supported by the absorption of substantial EU funds in 2023. The recovery of global demand and continued easing of supply chain disruptions will boost export growth in 2024. The main risks to the projections are related to the possible escalation of Russia's war of aggression against Ukraine, which would curtail foreign demand and could lead to a resurgence of global energy prices, increased inflation, and lower growth. Fiscal support to households and firms to mitigate the rise in energy prices should be better targeted to limit additional demand pressures at a time of high inflation. Specific consolidation measures should be spelled out to ensure fiscal sustainability. Accelerating investment in the green transition, including improvements to the energy efficiency of buildings, will help enhance energy security and mitigate climate change (OECD Economic Outlook, 2023, Economic forecast for Slovakia, 2024). Slovakia is not found to experience imbalances. Vulnerabilities relating to competitiveness, housing, household debt, and external balance have been increasing, but overall seem contained in the near future and are expected to ease as economic conditions normalize. The economy was strongly hit by the energy price shock and the rapid rise of inflation. Core inflation and unit labor costs growth are well above the euro area average. While they are forecast to normalize, there is the risk that pressure on cost competitiveness could take time to unwind, and that strong domestic demand will continue to put pressure on external accounts. The current account deteriorated markedly in 2022 owing to higher energy import prices as well as marked falls in net exports of non-energy goods. The current account deficit is forecast to improve mildly but to remain large in 2023 and 2024, despite the falling energy prices. Nonetheless, external sustainability risks are assessed to be limited in the near term. Government deficits are forecast to be significant for this year and the next, and to correct from 2024. House prices appear to be mildly overvalued after several years of marked growth. That occurred alongside high borrowing, which is now cooling, and a strong increase in household debt, which altogether present some risk for financial stability. However, the banking sector remains well capitalized and highly profitable, and is recording low nonperforming loans. Continued efforts are needed to tackle Slovakia's economic vulnerabilities. In particular, excess demand should be reined in to support the correction of the current account deficit and the core inflation differential vis-à-vis the rest of the euro area. That can be achieved by ensuring adequate fiscal consolidation and measures to address household debt, while retaining housing affordability through property taxation and measures supporting housing supply (In-Depth Review 2023 Slovakia, 2023). According to a Euromonitor report (PEST analysis Slovakia, 2023), socio-demographic trends show that although unemployment is relatively low, wages are increasing, also adding to very high inflation (11% in 2023, but growth has slowed amid high inflation in 2024 to 4.1% (OECD Economic Surveys: Slovak Republic 2024). A shrinking and elderly population is not a barrier for the consumer market, given a strong trend in rising incomes. According to the ManpowerGroup Employment Outlook Survey for Q3 2023 (https://go.manpowergroup.com/meos), 31% of Slovak employers expected an increase in the number of employees, while 19% anticipated a decrease. Despite this, Slovakia faced significant challenges in recruitment, particularly due to geopolitical uncertainties. Slovakia experienced notable labor shortages, especially in sectors like automotive and agriculture (Slovakia: Continued growth in the employment and economic activity of migrants, European Website on Integration, europa.eu). There were nearly 100,000 job vacancies that companies struggled to fill. In response to these shortages, Slovakia expanded its national visa program to facilitate the entry of third-country nationals. However, the effectiveness of these measures was still under evaluation (Slovakia: Expansion of national visa program in response to labor shortage, European Website on Integration, europa.eu). In the case of technological factors, Internet and mobile use continue to expand, but innovation is stymied by limited investment.

After a deep recession in 2020, the Slovak Republic was affected by 3 years of global pandemic. These negative effects of external threats were followed by the ongoing conflict in Ukraine. At the same time, the new Slovak government (from the parliamentary elections in September 2023) needs to deal with many challenges in the medium term, including rapid population aging, which is expected to exacerbate fiscal challenges. To prepare for an aging population, many immediate reforms are needed in health and long-term care to extend working lives, improve the health of the aging population, and increase the efficiency of public spending. In addition, the EU funds and the drawdown of the Recovery and Resilience Plan, which raised funds to support reforms and investment in response to the pandemic, may also help to boost the investment (Exhibit 1).

2 Characteristics of Hidden Champions from Slovakia

For the purpose of this research, around 150 companies were studied for further analysis according to the HC criteria. From this database, around 40 potential HC companies were analyzed in depth and presented in the Slovak country report for 2022. Some key findings and trends can be formulated by synthesizing the findings from previous HC research activities and comparing them with this third cycle of research. The majority of analyzed HC companies are located in different regions (including the companies from our case studies), not predominantly in the capital city as was the case in the past. They operate mostly in business-to-business (B2B) and IT sectors and in niche markets as identified by Hermann Simon. We have identified an exciting pool of other actual or potential HC companies in various industries and market segments. Those featured, for instance: a leader in the sports video game industry, open-source IT technology, a manufacturer of high-tech kiteboards, a family-owned company manufacturing tailor-made kayaks and canoes (including for the Olympic games), a manufacturer of conveyors and collaborative robots, IT data processing, the world's leading CX platform, one of the fastest-growing e-commerce platforms for fitness supplements in Europe, multiplex and quantitative diagnostic technologies, and tests for oncology patients, an IT outsourcing/freelancers concept, research, and experimental development in the field of natural and technical sciences, noncontact plasma drilling and milling, the world's leading manufacturers and brokers of graphite and graphite materials, and one of the market leaders in the carbon slide bearings market. Since the analysis remained based on rather limited secondary data (not all of which were approved by the companies through interviews), we could not confirm it to the full extent. Two companies were interviewed and presented in the case studies section. The first one, Gevorkyan (leader in powder metallurgy), can be confirmed as a real HC and FOSALI (tailor-made LED lighting solutions) as a potential HC.

In the third wave of research conducted in 2022, we can confirm the positions of two real hidden champions and one potential hidden champion. Examining HC companies in Slovakia from research conducted for the first time in 2011 to the third phase of research in 2023 offers a fascinating glimpse into the dynamics of market leadership, innovation, competitive advantage, and the nuances of management and leadership development. Some companies that meet HC criteria have been recently acquired (this is happening to Slovak potential or real HCs quite often) by other bigger players; therefore, they have been excluded from the evaluation in 2022. Other potential HCs failed on their journey to success, e.g., the flying car producer,

Exhibit 1 Core economic indicators for Slovakia

Series name	2017	2018	2019	2020	2021	2022	2023
GDP per capita (current US$)	17585,197	19486,39368	19381,89055	19552,09111	21768,14867	21256,80843	24,491.38
GDP per capita growth (annual %)	2,778454293	3,886398879	2,372623516	−3,418371978	5,011911889	2,040708666	1.47
Long-term unemployment (% of total unemployment)	8,14	6,54	5,76	6,72	6,89	6,14	5.84
Foreign direct investment, net inflows (% of GDP)	4,417755844	212068481	2,156631368	−1,069696973	2,293601976	3,507030085	−0.25
GDP (current US$)	95649966261	106138E+11	105712E+11	106731E+11	118576E+11	115462E+11	132908.34
Exports of goods and services (BoP, current US$)	90,274774490	100763E+11	96858697753	90545983831	109565E+11	114678E+11	122207.17
Merchandise exports (current US$)	83414000000	93425000000	89509000000	86640000000	103891E+11	107771E+11	91.95
Merchandise exports to high-income economies (% of total merchandise exports)	91,43405062	91,71297009	91,12227274	90,60967177	..	..	117293
Merchandise exports to low-and middle-income economies in Europe & Central Asia (% of total merchandise exports)	5,521759204	4,886309806	49278232	5,017941575	..	..	91.26
Ores and metals exports (% of merchandise exports)	2,094775221	2,05889199	2,025625227	1,825303374	2,335377495	2,142285902	4.01
Agricultural raw materials exports (% of merchandise exports)	0,839803259	0,872419986	0,814354959	0,828066261	0,986199761	0,934840296	1.47
Food exports (% of merchandise exports)	3,717795118	3,466495046	3,563516287	4,015226012	3,965156662	4,532908774	0.66
Fuel exports (% of merchandise exports)	3,340039056	3,017545825	2,912371139	2,400489741	320008878	5,171280701	4.53
Manufactured exports (% of merchandise exports)	89,73347202	90,26287942	90,30544388	90,67438496	89,33379449	86,94244768	3.49
High-technology exports (% of manufactured exports)	11,7654026	10,6363646	9,9122358	9 99731572	9 00129797	8,39213075	89.6
							9.65

Source: World Bank, 2024, Statistical office SR, 2023

attributing its failure in acquiring new investments to the negative mood in the venture capital market. Its availability has fallen by more than 80% since April 2023, in part due to the market's distrust of different concepts, such as electric flying devices with vertical takeoff and landing. We discovered that some HCs from research conducted in 2011 and 2019 are no longer HCs. One of them can be considered a corporation that does not entirely fit HC criteria. The founders are considering the company's entry to the stock exchange, and their initial public offering (IPO) would be comparable to that of some US giants. As of 2022, they had 1521 employees, 564 million euros in sales, and 85 million euros of profit. They are continuing in their successful journey, considered a global cybersecurity leader and recognized as a Top Player in Radicati's 2021 Endpoint Security Market Quadrant. Another HC was strongly affected by the coronavirus pandemic situation and the war in Ukraine. Their sales dropped almost in half, profit to zero, and they had to release a significant number of employees. This situation resulted in their acquisition by another global industrial leader. Another HC was also acquired within 2 years by a global player. They still keep a headquarters in Bratislava, Slovakia, but since 2024, after a complete acquisition, we probably can no longer consider them as a hidden champion. We can summarize that Slovak hidden champions are rather vulnerable and they are frequently acquired by other global players in the industry. This was the case for both potential and also real hidden champions. Through comprehensive analysis, we have uncovered the principles that drive HCs' success and learned how these principles can be applied across various business contexts.

Hidden champions are companies that excel in dominating specific, often narrowly defined, global market niches. HCs typically remain under the radar, unlike more prominent corporate giants, yet they lead their respective fields through highly specialized products or services. For instance, Innovatrics and Microstep have established themselves as leaders in biometric technology and precision measurement systems, respectively. These companies showcase remarkable sustained revenue and market share growth, often surpassing larger competitors within their specialized niches. Some other HCs' further growth and successful operations are linked to specific global and societal challenges; for instance, the war in Ukraine has enhanced the investments into military and IT/security segments, impacting a company called Grand Power, which produces light/personal weapons. HCs' dominant presence in niche markets underscores their strategic focus and ability to leverage market specifics.

The commitment to technological innovation is at the heart of hidden champions' success. These companies invest heavily in research and development (R&D), maintaining a competitive technological edge. Innovatrics, for example, continually refines its biometric solutions to stay ahead in a rapidly evolving field. Similarly, Microstep's precision measurement technology advancements illustrate the importance of continuous innovation. HCs typically create high-quality, unique products that meet specific customer needs. Spinea, specializing in high-precision machinery, and CrazyFly, known for its state-of-the-art kiteboards, exemplify how specialization in product offerings can lead to market dominance.

This targeted innovation sets them apart from competitors and solidifies their leadership within their niches.

A profound understanding of their markets grants hidden champions a significant competitive advantage. This deep market insight allows them to respond to changes and capitalize on emerging opportunities swiftly. Furthermore, a customer-centric approach is central to their strategy. By prioritizing the needs of their customers, HCs cultivate strong loyalty and long-term relationships. The merger of Exponea with Bloomreach highlights this strategy; the integration aimed to leverage Exponea's deep customer understanding to enhance marketing efficiency, thus driving business growth. This customer-centric strategy is a cornerstone for many HCs, ensuring they remain relevant and responsive to market demands.

Several key lessons emerge from studying the trajectories of hidden champion companies:

1. Focus on Core Strengths: Companies like ESET and Sygic, which eventually lost their HC status, highlight the critical importance of focusing on core competencies and continuous innovation within those areas.
2. Adaptability: Adapting to evolving market conditions and technological advancements is vital. This adaptability is crucial for maintaining a competitive edge over time.
3. Sustainable Growth Strategies: Financial stability and strategic investments are essential for sustained growth. Grand Power's significant growth trajectory exemplifies the importance of strategic planning and investment.
4. Impact of Acquisitions: Acquisitions can significantly influence a company's trajectory, sometimes leading to losing HC status. Exponea's acquisition by Bloomreach altered its strategic focus and market position, demonstrating how external changes can impact internal dynamics.

The effective management of hidden champion companies requires leaders with a clear, long-term vision. The leaders focus on sustaining market leadership through ongoing innovation and technological investments to maintain the company's growth. An agile and resilient organizational culture is crucial, enabling the company to adapt quickly to market changes and overcome challenges. This strategic vision is foundational for maintaining the company's trajectory and ensuring long-term success.

Investing in continuous professional development is essential for maintaining a skilled workforce. Hidden champions employ diverse, experienced professionals and experts who keep them abreast of the latest technologies and market trends. Additionally, HCs' leadership is predominantly focused on technological development and innovation.

Operational efficiency is another crucial factor in maintaining a competitive edge. Hidden champions streamline their operations to reduce costs and improve efficiency, adopting best practices in investing in the latest technologies, continuous growth, and good customer service in the B2B segment. Maintaining high technological standards in products and services helps build and sustain a strong reputation in their niche market, further solidifying their competitive advantage.

3 Case Study 1

3.1 Gevorkyan J.s.c

Overview

An Armenian citizen, Artur Gevorkyan established the company in 1997 in Slovakia. It produces products for all industries related to powder metallurgy, more specifically, powder metallurgy, metal injection molding, hot isostatic pressing, and additive manufacturing. It combines the most modern technologies under one roof, where it develops a vast range of new products each year. It has a top-class laboratory and a modern tool shop with three-shift operations. It is a reliable global supplier for large multinational companies operating their plants worldwide. The Gevorkyan company has become one of the most stable suppliers of the SKF engineering firm and one of the largest manufacturers of bearings in the world. The management decision in 2022 to enter the stock exchange brought the necessary capital for further growth, and the company became a joint stock company (Table 1).

Address: Továrenská 504, 976 31 Vlkanová, Slovakia
Tel.: +421,910,376,112
Email: gevorkyan@gevorkyan.sk
Web: https://www.gevorkyan.sk/

3.1.1 Nature of Market Leadership

The company has been operating for 27 years and still produces the parts for its very first customer. The products are made using specific technology in the metallurgy industry, i.e., metal injection molding, hot isostatic pressing, and additive manufacturing, which are widely used in several sectors and segments such as engineering, oil, guns, new cars, the most modern pumps, air conditioners, hand tools and robots, weapons, and even in cosmetics and medicine. Since the world's largest powder metallurgy (PM) companies are mainly located in the USA, the biggest competitors in Europe are Eurobalt (Estonia) and Temsa (Spain). Gevorkyan is considered a leader in the European market and one of the most

Table 1 Company information

Industry	Powder metallurgy/pressing of metal parts from special powder mixtures at high pressures.
Year of establishment	1997
Sales revenues in 2021	€470 mil.
EBITDA	€19 mil.
Average number of employees	150–199
Brain(s) behind the company	CEO: Dipl. Ing. Artur Gevorkyan, owner 73%

Source: FinStat, 2022

innovative companies in this industry segment worldwide. It designs and develops over 150 brand-new products per year in one place using cutting-edge technology, and produces over 5 million parts per month of over 2000 different types. It ships worldwide, including to Europe, the USA, Latin America, Canada, Asia, and Australia.

3.1.2 Nature of Competitive Advantage

The company's competitive advantage lies in its proprietary expertise in powder mixing, custom product development, and an in-house tool shop. Products made by powder metallurgy technology have many uses, including in the engineering, oil, weapons, and healthcare industries, as well as in costume jewelery and cosmetics/packaging. Two technologies are used: sintering and metal injection molding. This technology is cheaper (no-waste technology), but it is a large-scale production; it is more economical only for a large quantity of products. This ability to rapidly design and develop tailored solutions, coupled with high levels of automation and robotization, allows Gevorkyan to achieve financial results comparable to larger competitors while employing fewer people. The customer-centered focus is unique, and no other company within this segment can offer this with such an approach. Gevorkyan has built its own laboratory research and development center.

3.1.3 Core Lessons Learned on the Path to Success

The company's path to success is associated with the life story of the founder. He had a strong determination and tenacity to establish his company. In 2008, it started production on its own land in the small village of Vlkanova in Central Slovakia. The company was slowly growing, accepting "crazy projects" those big players refused to do. The owner's motto is "Use the crisis and adapt to the situation." Each crisis strengthened the company's business. During the financial crisis in 2008, struggling companies were offering some premises and machines for sale. Gevorkyan acquired some machines on lease at a better price. With this strategy, the company was able to show customers its distinguishing competencies, gaining Gevorkyan the reputation of a small company able to satisfy their requirements. Within the organizational culture, there is a continuous focus on the latest technologies and innovations.

3.1.4 Management and Leadership Development Needs

The roots of leadership success reflect the aims of the founder. He merged the family tradition in powder metallurgy with his vision of running his own business. The business goal focuses on the continuous growth of sales while maintaining the number of employees, which is fulfilled by the extensive automation of the main operation processes. Presently, around 70 robots are used in production. The company's main challenge is expanding production while keeping up with the trend in robotization; at present, it can't even keep up with all the current orders and projects. The company has strengthened its energy independence by purchasing additional plots of land adjacent to the company's premises for further expansion. The management continuously investigates and analyzes potential entry into new industries such as the production of arms, the oil industry, the automotive segment related to electric cars, bicycles, and even the jewellery market.

3.1.5 Financing and Regulatory Environment Development Needs

The company has struggled to satisfy the enormous demand (because of insufficient capacity). Therefore, management entered the Czech stock exchange (27% shareholders, two funds, and many small retail investors) to raise additional capital for expected growth. The new financial capital of 29 million euros (keeping 73% ownership) ensures the expansion of the company's operations and innovations. Last year, the largest Swedish producer outsourced its powder metallurgy production to the Gevorkyan company. At the beginning of 2024, the company completed the acquisition of the competing company Atha Powder Metallurgy in Poland. This company has a 20-year history as a daughter subsidiary of its parent company in Germany. It employs 80 people, and its sales are around 5 million euros annually. It produces products mainly for the automotive industry. Due to these successful business expansions, there is a financial estimate for Gevorkyan to achieve sales of 90 million euros in the year 2024. Last year, sales reached 75 million euros, a yearly increase of around 30%.

Since one-third of Gevorkyan's staff is composed of foreign workers from Ukraine, Armenia, and Belarus, he needs to deal with the associated legal conditions. The company is faced with very strict legislation, representing the main obstacle preventing, for instance, establishing childcare premises for their female employees.

3.1.6 The Pandemic's Impact on Gevorkyan's Business Approach

The COVID-19 pandemic did not have an impact on their business, neither from an operational nor a financial point of view. In fact, the company invented and produced its own masks/respirators with a special filter, which were supplied at cost to hospitals. This action can be seen as an example of corporate citizenship and Gevorkyan's social responsibility during unprecedented times.

The company negatively perceived the government's double standards regarding masks and the additional approval requirements placed on Slovak producers, although they met EU certification standards.

3.1.7 Effects of the War in Ukraine on Gevorkyan's Business Operations

The company does not conduct business with Russia or Ukraine. On the other hand, it shows solid social involvement, with one-third of its employees being foreigners (mainly from Ukraine, Armenia, and Belarus), especially in production operations, but also among administrative staff. Regarding the reliance on energy resources, the company is building its own solar sources. This strategic plan aims to provide energy independence that corresponds with the latest EU legislation and strategies for green economies.

3.1.8 From Scrap to Innovation: A Journey to Market Leadership in Powder Metallurgy

In the heart of Slovakia, the year was 1997 when Artur Gevorkyan, a determined and visionary Armenian, embarked on a journey that would forever change the face of the powder metallurgy business segment. Born in Armenia and armed with a rich background as a military aviation engineer, Artur brought a wealth of managerial experience from his time in Ukraine. The bureaucratic challenges he faced in Ukraine pushed him to pursue his dream of starting a business in Slovakia, which offered more entrepreneurial opportunities. At that time, Slovakia's landscape was nearly devoid of powder metallurgy; only traditional milling technology had existed until 1996. Undeterred by the nascent state of the industry, Artur Gevorkyan saw an opportunity to innovate and excel. With determination and a few scrap materials collected from junkyards, he began crafting his first product—a hairdryer. This modest start laid the foundation for Gevorkyan Ltd., a powerhouse in the powder metallurgy industry. From the outset, Gevorkyan's approach was unconventional. The Gevorkyan company took on projects that larger companies deemed too risky or unfeasible. These "crazy projects," as Artur called them, allowed him to demonstrate his company's capability to deliver innovative and reliable solutions. Slowly but surely, Gevorkyan built a reputation as a company that could meet the most demanding customer requirements with precision and creativity.

A visionary and strategic thinker, CEO Artur Gevorkyan emphasized technological innovation. He strategically invested in automation to replace human labor in production, continuously purchasing pressing machines. His latest investment of about 1 million euros for an Italian pressing machine highlights his commitment to efficiency and innovation, enabling the production of thousands of components per working shift. Refusing numerous acquisition offers from international companies, the company remains focused on maintaining its spirit as a successful SME and family-owned business. Negative experiences with local banks led him to make a bold decision: to enter the Czech stock market. In July 2022, amidst geopolitical risks, this unique move for a local Slovak company ensured continued growth and retained the decision-making power. Gevorkyan's first significant breakthrough came with developing specialized parts using advanced powder metallurgy techniques. These parts found applications across various industries, including engineering, automotive, medical, and weaponry. The company's ability to innovate and adapt quickly sets it apart from competitors. Gevorkyan develops a huge range of new products and small parts, serving a global customer base. The company's technological methods, faster and cheaper than traditional techniques, have provided a significant edge. Some parts produced by Gevorkyan's methods couldn't be manufactured through any other means, highlighting the uniqueness of their capabilities. The company was awarded for the fourth time in the "Diamonds of Slovak Business" competition in 2021, a testament to its excellence and innovation. Artur's leadership earned him the Slovak Crystal Wing award for 2023 in the business and entrepreneurship category. His vision extends beyond immediate business goals, focusing on long-term strategies like energy independence and extensive automation. Despite preferring direct interaction with employees over digital communication, Artur's strategic foresight has kept Gevorkyan at the industry's forefront.

Innovation at Gevorkyan is not just about keeping up with trends—it is about necessity and survival. Collaborations with institutions like the Slovak Academy of Sciences and the University of Cambridge ensure that the company remains on the cutting edge of technological advancements. "Innovating for the sake of innovation or feeling good makes no sense. At Gevorkyan, we innovate for money. Innovations must be born from necessity, need and pain. The greatest innovations come precisely in times of crisis when suddenly everyone has problems. Innovation forces us to invent ways to survive. Innovation generates demand for further innovation and thus supports continuous improvement" (Inovato press release, Artur Gevorkyan, workshop and presentation at the roadshow on February 15, 2023, Vlkanová). During the COVID-19 pandemic, Gevorkyan showcased its innovative spirit by developing respirators for hospitals, highlighting its ability to respond to urgent needs with creative solutions. Automation plays a crucial role in Gevorkyan's strategy. The company continually invests in new technologies and machines to enhance production efficiency. Recent investments also include a high-capacity pressing machine from Italy, significantly boosting production capabilities. The company's strong emphasis on modernization in technologies is expressed by the CEO's vision: "I dream of a factory without people. Our goal is to introduce hybrid jobs. The robot does not go on sick leave; it is more efficient."

Gevorkyan's strategic planning is focused on growth and efficiency. Over the past decade, the company saw continuous sales growth while maintaining a stable workforce of about 190 employees. With 70 robots currently in production, Gevorkyan exemplifies Artur's vision of a highly automated factory. Despite nonstop production, the company has to refuse some projects as production has already been contracted for the next 7–8 years. Energy self-sufficiency is another pillar of Gevorkyan's strategy. The company is building its own nitrogen generators, solar panels, and transformer stations, ensuring independence from the energy crisis. By exploring new industries such as arms manufacturing, oil, electric vehicles, and jewellery, Gevorkyan aims to leverage its technological expertise and capture new market opportunities.

Managing rapid growth while maintaining a commitment to innovation and automation has posed challenges. To keep up with increasing demand, the company has expanded its production capacity with the recent cooperation with Swedish SVK and the latest acquisition of the Polish subsidiary of Atha Powder Metallurgy of the German international company. The energy crisis has not affected them; they have contracted prices for a longer period of time. The company is responding to the energy crisis by enhancing its energy independence through several decisions, for instance, having its own nitrogen generator and installing solar panels. They are completing a hydrogen generator and their own transformer stations. The energy is needed mainly in sintering, which is a key process for production. In the context of all environmental activities, the company created the position of environmental manager. Continuous technological innovation and environmental sustainability are critical issues, supported by professional training programs and dedicated environmental continuous improvements.

The CEO's leadership style, though directive and hands-on, is deeply rooted in a commitment to employee welfare. The company provides generous benefits, such as company cars for personal use, accommodation and support for foreign workers (mainly from Ukraine, Belarus, and Armenia), and career development opportunities for the young generation from the region. The company helps various communities through various foundations and donations. Despite the "old school" approach of the CEO, who does not fancy using ICT in his work, and his use of the open-space office with other managers, Artur's leadership fosters a supportive and innovative work environment. As Gevorkyan looks to the future, the leadership transition is already in motion. Artur's son, Róbert Gevorkyan, is preparing to take over, ensuring the company's innovative spirit and strategic vision continue. With a strong foundation built on innovation, strategic planning, and a commitment to quality, Gevorkyan can maintain its market leadership and achieve sustained growth. From scrap to innovation, Artur Gevorkyan's journey has been a testament to the power of vision, determination, and strategic foresight. His legacy of innovation and leadership will continue to shape the future of powder metallurgy, ensuring that Gevorkyan remains a beacon of excellence and ingenuity in the industry.

4 Case Study 2

4.1 FOSALI j.s.c

Overview

The name FOSALI stands for the words "fiber optic solutions and lighting." It manufactures designer chandeliers based on optical fiber LED technologies and handblown glass (niche market). Production started in 2015 with the establishment of a company called LEDeco Solution, which is now the parent company. The business is technically focused on producing its own strips, designing various lighting, projection, installation, powder coating, and assembly. The foreign expansion into new markets was strategically overtaken by the new company FOSALI j.s.c. (Table 2).

Table 2 Company information

Industry	Production installation of electric lights and other electric devices
Year of establishment	2015
Sales revenues in 2021	€ 245 millions
Revenues in 2015	€ 13 millions
Average number of employees	11
Brainer(s) behind the company	Co-founders Jozef Slivka, Marianna Slivková, and Tomas Fiser

Source: FinStat, 2022

Address: Sládkovičova 37/A, 974 05 Banská Bystrica, Slovakia
Tel.: +421,948,559,790.
Email: fosali@fosali.com
Web: www.FOSALI.com

4.1.1 Nature of Market Leadership

FOSALI is a family-owned company offering lighting design and manufacturing in the B2B segment. The company strongly focuses on technological quality based on its R&D (Jozef Slivka, one of the co-founders, is responsible for the technological area). Another co-founder, Jozef's sister, who left the UK with her family to help the business grow and establish the FOSALI brand, is responsible for marketing and sales. The complex know–how for LED technology was invented in-house. The chandeliers and lighting designs are manufactured to get the best out of optical fiber technology. Their production is unique, and they believe they are number one within the Central Eastern Europe region of this market. The company receives most of its orders from the Middle East and the EU, with total exports accounting for around 80% of total sales.

4.1.2 Nature of Competitive Advantage

Their complex lighting solutions (LED and fiber optic), which implement the latest technologies, differentiate them from their competitors. It means one's design, hand-made lights (of different sizes) and simple installation. FOSALI developed product solutions with their know–how, and thus, the company managed to create an entire portfolio of chandeliers with innovative and timeless designs, with the utmost luxury, excellent functionality, and long life. The strategy is to create lights that are simple and customer-friendly, enabling customers to perform the installation themselves. In-depth knowledge enables them to manufacture luminaires with all the benefits of LEDs, i.e., low energy consumption, maximum lighting output, efficiency, and great flexibility in color choices to match materials or other luminaires in the room. The company is famous for its tailored solutions. FOSALI's competitive advantage lies in its ability to blend cutting-edge technology with handcrafted artistry. Their products, often available in fiber optic and pure LED module versions, are designed to be visually stunning, energy-efficient, and easy to install. This focus on innovation, versatility, and customer-centric design has placed FOSALI ahead of its competitors, who often rely on more traditional crystal lighting designs.

4.1.3 Core Lessons Learned on the Path to Success

Initially, the company placed a strong emphasis on quality, innovation, and added value, rather than competing on price. This innovation-focused approach led them to adopt LED technology, which has been available since 2007. FOSALI prioritizes high-quality LED technology producers known for their excellent light features and commitment to continuous innovation. The company's success is strengthened by the family's core competencies—with the brother bringing deep technical expertise and the sister, Marianna, returning from the UK to focus on customer engagement and sales. While not every tailored project has yielded immediate profits, the company has recognized other benefits such as promoting the brand and exploring exciting technological solutions. Despite its focus on innovative solutions, FOSALI remains committed to a customer-centric approach by ensuring that the installation of its products is simple for the end user. The ongoing challenge of balancing innovation and creativity with standardization, simplification, cost reduction, and scaling has been central to FOSALI's success. Over time, the company has continued its journey of technological innovation, beginning production of in-house LED lighting and establishing its own SMT (Surface-Mount Technology) line.

4.1.4 Management and Leadership Development Needs

The company's strategic approach has been to grow its business with the same number of employees and to be innovation-driven. They constantly improve and standardize processes, thereby scaling and thus ensuring growth expansion into new markets. They have plans to become a world leader in high-design lighting while innovating simultaneously—that's a big dilemma for management. It plans to protect its products with trademarks on its designs. Moreover, the company has a strong focus on marketing, people, and ongoing improvements. An expansion into new markets highlights the need to hire new employees. The critical leadership challenges include maintaining their strong identification with the products and ensuring their perfect fit into the dynamic organizational culture.

4.1.5 Financing and Regulatory Environment Development Needs

The company was approached by an investor (venture capital) who made an offer to finance the company's growth. They rejected this offer because they felt they had already created a strong potential and had done a lot of work at the beginning in implementing all the technological innovation and their aim to create a solid company name. The family owners felt they might have lost all that effort and personal involvement. They preferred to use their resources to continue on their current path, even if the growth was slow. Global trends and the EU's strong emphasis on a green economy and environmental behavior, aiming to replace traditional energy sources, are with the more extensive use of LED technology.

4.1.6 The Pandemic's Impact on FOSALI'S Business Approach

Since its business operates in the B2B market, the pandemic lockdowns and other regulations did not affect FOSALI's operations. In the distant future, due to some adverse global and social developments that emerged during the pandemic, the middle-income target group of customers could be reduced. The company strengthened its presence in the online space during the pandemic period.

4.1.7 Effects of the War in Ukraine on FOSALI'S Business Operations

The global crisis, connected with the war in Ukraine or rising energy prices, does not impact the company's performance. They operate in various markets, enabling them to diversify the risks.

4.1.8 Triggering Emotions Through Lighting

The family-owned company, as well as the mother company LEDeco solution Ltd., which specializes in lighting design, manufacturing optic fibers, and LED technology, operates mainly in the Slovak market. The original founder, Jozef was always very passionate about technology, and he has always sought out novel opportunities. His critical leadership approach reflects his strong conviction that technological quality, continuous production improvement, and research and development should reflect on customer requirements—individual solutions. The success of both LEDeco and FOSALI was driven by the passionate leadership of all three co-founders. Jozef is deeply committed to technological excellence and continuous improvement. His sister, Marianna Slivkova, an award-winning entrepreneur in 2014, has brought a strong focus on marketing and sales, helping to expand FOSALI's reach into new markets. Together with her partner Tomas, they have cultivated a culture of innovation and high standards, ensuring that FOSALI remains at the forefront of the lighting industry.

They all work to manage FOSALI's path to becoming a leader in unique LED lighting solutions. From its humble beginnings, FOSALI embarked on a mission to illuminate the world with unparalleled elegance and innovation. FOSALI quickly distinguished itself in the niche fiber optic and LED technology market, offering product solutions that went beyond mere illumination to create breathtaking visual experiences. The fiber optic technology market has been developing for years. The company positions itself as a producer of fiber optic lighting products and as a solution provider. The company has designers and technicians who deliver the products, installation, and related services to its customers. The products are intended for places where it is necessary to ensure sufficient lighting for the movement of people, to create a festive atmosphere, or where there are hard-to-reach and non-serviceable areas. FOSALI does not offer a classic chandelier. The technology is based on optical fibers and LED illuminators merged into creative designs. They developed them with their know–how, and thus, the company has managed to create an entire portfolio of chandeliers, the design of which is innovative, timeless, luxurious, and, of course, offers fantastic functionality and long life. Custom-designed chandeliers represent a narrower product segment than ordinary chandeliers. With this strategic approach, they are ahead of their competitors. Estimating their market share is difficult as they are active in multiple segments. Still, they operate in a particular niche segment and consider themselves to be number one in this niche. The most significant competitors are companies focused on designing, crystal, and lighting, e.g., the following Czech companies: Preciosa (with 150 years of experience, a global company), Lasvit, and Sans Souci Lighting.

The appreciation of hand-made craft techniques and local production is reflected by the high demand in its sector. The company features these attributes, and being located in Central Europe, it seems to be a perfect match. Some of their designs feature a fiber optic version or a new option based purely on LED modules. The lighting market is mature, and while the clients seek innovations, they also wish to own an eye-pleasing piece of light in their interiors. "We offer beautiful products which trigger emotion" became FOSALI's mantra. This philosophy has permeated every aspect of their business, from the initial design phase to the final installation directly at the customer's location. FOSALI's designers and technicians have worked meticulously to ensure each piece is a work of art. Their deep understanding of LED technology has allowed them to create lighting solutions that offer low energy consumption, high efficiency, and an impressive range of color options to suit any interior.

From the beginning, the company has built its name on technological innovations. FOSALI offers serious lighting solutions that focus on innovation, versatile designs, and spectacular lighting elements with a great touch of originality. Not every innovation or tailor-made project has brought profit, but there have been benefits in other areas—an exciting order, building a name on the market, and presentation in the media. Expansion into new markets seems to be the key management focus for the near future. The management has realized they have great business potential that they are not yet using. Commenting on their market and what makes them competitive, "The lighting industry is now focused on innovations in

LED-based products, and the clients expect high quality, durability, and service-free products; this has become a standard." As a market leader, FOSALI's reputation has been solidified by its consistent presence at two of the world's most prestigious international fairs in Frankfurt and Milan. These events showcase their complex LED technology know–how and fiber optic mastery. Their chandeliers and lighting designs, revered for their spectacular aesthetics and functional brilliance, cater to an elite clientele. Most customers (involving members of the royal families in foreign countries) are from the Middle East (FOSALI participated in Expo Dubai 2020), and it is present in many European markets, including the USA and Sri Lanka. FOSALI's focus on foreign markets has paid off, with 80% of its sales coming from exports. They have developed a robust network of international partners, allowing them to tap into new opportunities and mitigate risks associated with market fluctuations.

The company has acknowledged the necessity of simplifying processes and scalability, thus simplifying installation work at the customer's location. It faces the constant dilemma between technological innovation and creativity versus standard processes (standardization), as well as questions of simplification, scaling, and cost reduction. There are a few key strategies to maintain success, such as a strong orientation on foreign markets and developing a network of partners abroad. As its market is still significant, FOSALI must reflect on more opportunities. Despite reducing its workforce from 30 to 12 employees, FOSALI has managed to streamline its processes and maintain high standards of quality and innovation. That can be fulfilled by streamlining the entire process through standardization and sustaining the scaling strategy. Innovation starts with the courage to try new things, learning to learn, independence, tackling new challenges, and making decisions, often leaving one's comfort zone and not giving up quickly. Since the company's primary goal is to expand abroad, the company places a strong emphasis on the ability to communicate in foreign languages while actively participating in international exhibitions. There is a high demand for understanding social media and networks and doing marketing activities in a virtual environment.

The primary challenge for FOSALI was balancing the need for constant innovation with the demands of standardization and scalability. They recognized the importance of simplifying processes to support growth and expansion while continuing to push the boundaries of lighting technology. FOSALI needs to continue evolving with the same number of employees to sustain its growth. Such an aim requires focusing on innovation-driven strategies and a commitment to ongoing improvement. The company also saw the need for closer cooperation with educational institutions to attract talented graduates with the necessary skills and mindset to drive FOSALI's vision forward. FOSALI's decision to reject an offer from a venture capital investor highlights their confidence in their potential and the desire to maintain control over their growth trajectory. Using their own resources ensured that their values and vision remained intact, even if it meant a slower pace of expansion. FOSALI's journey from a small family business to a global leader in high-design lighting is a testament to its unwavering commitment to quality, innovation, and customer satisfaction. By blending cutting-edge technology with handcrafted artistry, they have created lighting solutions that illuminate spaces and inspire emotions. As they continue to expand and innovate, FOSALI remains a shining example of how passion, dedication, and strategic vision can light the path to success.

5 Conclusions and Recommendations

The criteria to identify HCs as defined by German author Herman Simon (McKierman & Purg, 2013, p. 3) provide a foundation for general conclusions on current HCs. It also fosters some reflection on the global and societal challenges, for instance, the COVID pandemic, war conflicts in Ukraine and the Middle East, climate crises, and social sustainability, which might cause some modifications to the original concept of HCs launched in 1996. The criteria defining an HC as a small or medium-sized company, usually with sales revenue not exceeding 1 billion US dollars, have been confirmed in the examined companies. In the original concept, the organizational form of family-run entities was mentioned. Such a form appears in researched and described case studies, but has not been observed to a larger extent. Other criteria and specific characteristics also help us identify HCs, such as market leadership in niche and B2B markets.

Another criterion, stating that an HC should occupy the number one or two position in the world market and the number one position in the European market or a closer regional market, e.g., CEE, Visegrad 4, as measured by market share, has also been followed. This criterion had already been modified to HCs for the CEE region in the previous research from 2011, which compared HCs originating from old Europe, e.g., Germany. However, since SMEs have relatively limited resources and capabilities concerning their international market research, concept of the HCs can be difficult to provide evidence in the environment of the SMEs to be gathered by quantitative data; therefore, the concept of HCs can be difficult to justify. Simon's criterion that HCs typically maintain a low public profile contrasts with increasing recognition through media and awards, highlighting their innovations and contributions, especially during crises. HCs have become more visible by integrating social values and nonprofit activities into their business practices, as exemplified by companies like the studied company, Gevorkyan, during the COVID-19 pandemic. Together with HCs' activities related to both social and environmental sustainability, it establishes the grounds for the concept of corporate global citizenship. HCs' strategies to build alternative energy sources and employ diverse labor, including foreigners, marginalized groups, and the young generation, correspond with the EU's emphasis, highlighted by the ESG legislation.

Despite being traditionally conservative in finance and operations, focusing on single products and markets, there is a growing need for these companies to embrace sustainable growth. Gevorkyan sustained its growth and further development by successfully entering the Prague stock exchange and acquiring a Polish competitor. Gevorkyan's story contradicts another criterion from Simon (1992): HCs are more conservative and not very open to modern concepts concerning financing and organizational forms. The vast majority of businesses in Slovakia focus purely on expanding into new markets and on continuous innovation, which helps the company reduce costs. Concerning global crises, e.g., climate, energy, migration, and war, the focus on traditional economic growth does not reflect these challenges. In 2017, Kate Raworth from Oxford University published the book *Doughnut Economics: Seven Ways to Think Like a twenty-first-Century Economist*, where she developed the concept of "Doughnut Economics" in more detail. It seemed to be a counterproposal to mainstream economic thinking, focusing predominantly on economic growth and profit. According to Raworth (2017), sustainable growth defends the conditions for creating a sustainable economy while reflecting on the social sustainability presented by the UN's agenda of Sustainable Development Goals for 2030.

In the business environment, this can be manifested through global corporate citizenship, in which SMEs function as responsible citizens in their regions and communities. In the original characteristics, hidden champions are expected to maintain their economic growth and expansion in a traditional way, operating efficiently, innovating, and maximizing results to sustain their leading positions in their respective market segments. However, we argue that a modified business approach is expected from hidden champions, in which they present their understanding of current environmental and social sustainability challenges. It will integrate their global leadership with a range of social values and nonprofit activities that increase their diversity and equality awareness (Theodoulides, 2024). This approach has already been identified in several HCs in Slovakia, e.g., ESET, Gevorkyan, and MultiplexDX, who recognize the mutuality of interests and practices between society and business, as well as between the community and various stakeholders. Some of the examined HCs played a crucial role in helping civil society solve the unprecedented pandemic crisis with their R&D activities and production of medical devices.

According to the OECD Economic Surveys: Slovak Republic (2022), the share of firms receiving government support for innovation is low. In the new "Resilience and Recovery Plan," Slovakia will invest 0.7 billion EUR in science, research, and innovation (among other priorities) to improve the coordination of innovation policy and support research collaboration between companies, academia, and research organizations. Slovak HCs have never had the ambition to compete with giant multinational corporations with their products and services. They rather opt to focus on unique, innovative products, often operating without state subsidies. On the contrary, they develop specific, unique, innovative products/services using their know–how, inventions, or patents. The Slovak government supports innovation through initiatives such as various European programs for a green economy, with a structural emphasis on science, research, and innovation. The collaboration with educational institutions is crucial for addressing skill and labor shortages in the professional world. Developing transversal skills is increasingly essential in adapting to rapid technological, environmental, and societal changes. Addressing skill imbalances and "brain drain" is vital for the economic competitiveness of Slovak companies. In 2020, after the outbreak of the COVID-19 pandemic, the European Union reacted to the newly increased need for specific work and life competencies. In the document European Skills Agenda (July 2020), the EU proposed twelve actions for Europe to be able to recover from the losses due to the pandemic, among them the development of skills for life ("digital, information and media literacy, civic competences, and financial, environmental and health literacy") and transversal skills ("complex and systemic thinking, collaborative problem—solving and abilities in critical thinking"). Transversal skills and competencies are yet another relatively new synonym for soft skills, key competencies, twenty-first-century skills, and global competencies. The transversality of competencies emphasizes cross-sectionality in terms of the content, not a specific task/role/discipline, but usability in various contexts. They may include an emphasis on humanity and the holistic development of learners' personalities based on collaboration, self-discipline, resourcefulness, and environmental respect. These are skills that all types of education, work and careers have in common and can serve as a bridge between education and work and between different jobs and personal lives (Hanesova & Theodoulides, 2022). Moreover, the quality of education of the labor force as an obstacle to business development is increasingly cited in Slovak business surveys. It was also confirmed in the report "Employ Slovakia," published in June 2021 (www.espon.eu). The urgent need to focus on transversal competencies is vividly apparent in a world where organizations, workforces, and individuals are continuously subject to unprecedented complex change: rapid and radical technological advancements, the transformational forces and challenges of globalization, environmental sustainability, demographic shifts and migration, and political uncertainty (Whittemore, 2018).

The emigration of young and well-educated Slovaks further exacerbates skills imbalances in Slovakia. The negative impact of "brain drain" on the economic competitiveness of companies in Slovakia is among the highest in Europe (OECD Skills Strategy Slovak Republic Report, 2020). This is one of the lingering problems provoked by the current state of Slovak higher education. Most companies in Slovakia (including HCs) have tried to stabilize this situation by helping the universities (mainly in regions where they operate) with qualified speakers, financial support, or student internship offers. Some HCs realize the importance of collaborating with educational institutions as they prepare a potential human resource for them as crucial employers in regions and segments. Slovak HCs repeatedly mentioned the shortage of technically qualified potential employees, more specifically, those with a good level of digital skills. At present, the education system in Slovakia is challenged by reform, which is in the process of being prepared. The enhancement of soft skills is necessary among companies' personnel to develop the complex skills needed for the era of AI, information, and innovations. Those skills will equip the graduates with a positive approach to continuous learning and change, braveness to try new things, and more extensive resilience and responsibility.

References

Alkali, M. (2012). Assessing the influence of external environmental factors on the performance of small business manufacturing enterprises in Bauchi state, Nigeria. *Interdisciplinary Journal of Contemporary Research in Business, 4*(7), 621–628.

Espon, Employ Slovakia, Final report published. (2021 June). [Data file]. www.espon.eu/sites/default/files/attachments/EMPLOY-Slovakia.pdf

European Commission, Economic Forecast for Slovakia. (2024). Retrieved August 2024, from https://economy-finance.ec.europa.eu/economic-surveillance-eu-economies/slovakia/economic-forecast-slovakia_en

European Commission, Macroeconomic Forecast of Slovakia. (2023). *[Data file]*. Retrieved January 2024, from https://economy-finance.ec.europa.eu/economic-surveillance-eueconomies/slovakia/economic-forecast-slovakia_en

European union, Country profile Slovakia. (2020). *[Data file]*. https://european-union.europa.eu/principles-countries-history/country-profiles/slovakia_en

Everett, J., & Watson, J. (1998). Small business failure and external risk factors. *Small Business Economics, 11*, 371–390.

Genş, K. Y. (2014). Environmental factors affecting human resources management activities of Turkish large firms. *International Journal of Business and Management, 9*(11), 102–122.

Globsec report. (2021). Slovakia: An automotive industry perspective. *[Data file]*. https://www.globsec.org/what-we-do/publications/slovakia-automotive-industry-perspective

Hanesova, D., & Theodoulides, L. (2022). *Mastering transversal competences in a higher education environment. Through processes of critical thinking and reflection*. UMB, Belianum. https://doi.org/10.24040/2022.9788055720159

Hitt, M. A., Ireland, R. D., Sirmo, D. G., & Trahms, C. A. (2011). Strategic entrepreneurship: creating value for individuals, organizations, and society. *The Academy of Management Perspectives, 25*(2), 57–76.

In-Depth Review. (2023). *Slovakia: Institutional paper 223*. https://economy-finance.ec.europa.eu/document/download/e7d31b6d-0cdb-4413-8b22-8ec2236ddd3c_en?filename=ip223_en.pdf. ISSN: 2443-8014.

Kuznetsova, N. V. (2015). Tools for assessing the external environment of public catering enterprises: PEST analysis. *Socio-sphere, 3*, 25–31.

Kuznetsova, N.V., & Alekseeva, E.A. (2016). *The role of the external environment in increasing the competitiveness of the organization*. In the collection: Achievements of modern science: a materials collection of the XIII International Scientific and Practical Conference, 417–423.

Lazauskas, J., Gintautas, B., Valiūnas, V., Pečeliūnas, R., Matijošius, J., & Saulius, N. (2012). The research on competitiveness of road transport enterprises: Lithuanian case. *Transport and Telecommunication, 13*(2), 138–147.

ManpowerGroup Employment Outlook Survey. (2023). https://go.manpowergroup.com/meos

McKiernan, P., & Purg, D. (2013). *Hidden champions in CEE and Turkey: carving out a global niche* (pp. 1–437). Springer. https://doi.org/10.1007/978-3-642-40504-4. www.scopus.com

Njoroge, J. K., Ongeti, W. J., Kinuu, D., & Kasomi, F. M. (2016). Does external environment influence organizational performance? The case of Kenyan state corporations. *Management and Organizational Studies, 3*(3), 41–51.

OECD. (2020). *OECD skills strategy slovak republic: Assessment and recommendations, OECD skills studies*, OECD Publishing, Paris, https://doi.org/10.1787/bb688e68-en

OECD. (2023). *OECD economic outlook, volume 2023 issue 1,* OECD Publishing, Paris, https://doi.org/10.1787/ce188438-en

OECD. (2024). *OECD economic surveys: Slovak republic 2024*, OECD Publishing, Paris, https://doi.org/10.1787/397ca086-en

OECD Economics surveys Slovak Republic. (2022). https://www.oecd.org/economy/surveys/Slovak-Republic-2022-OECD-economic-survey-overview.pdf

PEST analysis: Slovakia. (2023). *Euromonitor international*. Retrieved June 2024, from https://www.euromonitor.com/pest-analysis-slovakia/report

Rakesh, C. (2014). PEST analysis for micro small medium enterprises sustainability. *Journal of Management & Commerce, 1*(1), 18–22.

Raworth, K. (2017). *The doughnut economy: Seven ways to think like 21st century economist*. Chelsea Green Publishing.

Simon, H. (1992). Lessons from Germany's midsize giants. *Harvard Business Review, 70*(2), 115–123. https://hbr.org/1992/03/lessons-from-germanys-midsize-giants

Slovakia PESTLE Insights—A Macroeconomic Outlook Report. (2024). *GlobalData*. Retrieved May 2024, from https://www.globaldata.com/store/report/slovakia-pestle-macroeconomic-analysis/

Statistical Office SR. (2023). https://slovak.statistics.sk/

Táborecká-Petrovičová, J., Ďaďo, J., & Bobáková, T. (2013). Hidden champions of Slovakia. In P. McKiernan & D. Purg (Eds.), *Hidden champions in CEE and Turkey*. Springer. https://doi.org/10.1007/978-3-642-40504-4_20

Táborecká-Petrovičová, J., Ďaďo, J., & Budinský, M. (2021). Hidden champions in dynamically changing societies: The case of Slovakia. In A. Braček Lalić & D. Purg (Eds.), *Hidden champions in dynamically changing societies*. Springer. https://doi.org/10.1007/978-3-030-65451-1_25

Theodoulides, L. (2024). Critical reflection analysis: A method for developing diversity awareness among (future) business leaders. In A. Šilenskytė, M. Cordova, M. A. Schmitz, & S. M. Toh (Eds.), *The Palgrave handbook of social sustainability in business education*. Palgrave Macmillan. https://doi.org/10.1007/978-3-031-50168-5_1

Whittemore, S. (2018). Transversal competencies essential for future proofing the workforce. Retrieved May 23, 2024, from https://www.researchgate.net/publication/328318972

World bank, 2024: https://data.worldbank.org/topic/economy-and-growth

Internet Sources and Other Databases

Európsky patentový úrad EPO https://register.epo.org/regviewer
Úrad priemyselného vlastníctva SR https://wbr.indprop.gov.sk/WebRegistre
Svetový úrad duševného vlatníctva WIPO https://www3.wipo.int/madrid/monitor/en
Úrad EÚ pre duševné vlastníctvo https://euipo.europa.eu/ohimportal/cs/web/guest/home
Finstat www.finstat.sk
Obchodný register www.orsr.sk

Lenka Theodoulides is Assistant Professor at Matej Bel University (UMB), Faculty of Economics in Slovakia. She is teaching subjects related to management, i.e. international management, management of innovations, and case studies in management. Her research interests focus on socioeconomic perspectives of the organizational theory such as leadership, diversity management, processes of assessment and evaluation based on the critical thinking, coaching, feedback, and reflection. She is the co-author of an innovative research method called Critical Reflection Analysis. She focuses on the qualitative research methods, such as case studies, grounded theory, and situational analysis. Lenka is author and co-author of several monographs and articles focusing on transversal competences, leadership, and social sustainability. In her academic career, Lenka cooperates with a number of local and international companies with the aim to develop networks and collaboration between academia and practice. She is a certified trainer in leadership awarded by Achieve Global Inc. and a member of Critical Thinking Foundation, US.

Janka Táborecká works at the Faculty of Economics, Matej Bel University in Banská Bystrica, Slovakia, where she serves as the guarantor of the Bachelor's program and co-guarantor of the Master's and PhD programs in Business Economics and Management. She is also a member of the coordination team of the European University Alliance EMERGE, where she leads the work package focused on community engagement. In addition, she serves as Head of the Marketing Research Centre at the European Marketing and Management Association (EUMMAS) and holds the position of Vice President of the Honorary Board of the association. She is also an assessor for the Slovak Accreditation Agency for Higher Education. Her long-term pedagogical, project-based, and research focus lies in the fields of marketing and consumer behavior, currently with an emphasis on sustainability and digital transformation. Over the years, she has demonstrated extensive experience in the coordination and implementation of 20 scientific and applied research projects, including national grants (VEGA), practice-oriented collaborations (NFP—Operational Programme Integrated Infrastructure), and international initiatives (CEEMAN & EBRD). Dr. Táborecká has authored or co-authored over 100 scholarly publications, including 27 indexed in Web of Science (WoS) and Scopus, with over 300 citations.

Hidden Champions of Slovenia

Elnura Irmatova and Arnold Walravens

Abstract From former studies on Hidden Champions, Slovenia is recognized as a cradle for small and medium-sized companies that gain substantial market positions locally, regionally, and often globally. In an ongoing effort to explain this phenomenon, the high quality of university studies emerges as a key element, particularly in technological programs such as electronics and computer science. The second crucial element is the excellence of the Jožef Stefan Institute, which covers a broad spectrum of basic and applied sciences. This institute provides students with the space and guidance to explore and apply their knowledge, resulting in many Slovenian hidden champions being startups founded by former trainees or employees of the institute's technological faculties. The third element is the entrepreneurial courage of individuals who take the initiative and risks to transform their dreams, ideas, and research findings into products that significantly contribute to the success of Slovenian industries and services. The three companies of this research—Qlector, Arctur, and Dewesoft—are exemplary cases that reflect the aforementioned points. These companies not only excel in various technological fields but also inspire with their leadership and entrepreneurship. They offer valuable lessons on the impact of cooperation in creating purposeful knowledge, the power of vision and intuition, the importance of agility, and customer-centric innovation.

Overview
Official name: Republic of Slovenia
Type of government: Parliamentary Democratic Republic
Population in 2022: 2,108,732 (Portal GOV.SI, 2022)
Land area: 20,271 km^2

E. Irmatova (✉) · A. Walravens
IEDC-Bled School of Management, Bled, Slovenia
e-mail: elnura.irmatova@iedc.si; Arnold.Walravens@iedc.si

D. Berberović, D. Purg (eds.), *Hidden Champions in Rising Economies*, Contributions to Management Science,
https://doi.org/10.1007/978-3-032-08263-3_36

History

1945 At the end of World War II, Slovenia becomes a constituent republic of the Socialist Federative Republic of Yugoslavia.
1991 Slovenia, along with Croatia, declares its independence. The Yugoslav federal army intervenes. Slovene forces defend the country. After the Ten-Day War, the Yugoslav army withdraws.
1992 The EU recognizes Slovenia's independence, followed by the USA and many other countries around the world. Slovenia joins the United Nations. First, parliamentary and presidential elections in the newly independent country.
1993 Slovenia joins the International Monetary Fund.
1998 Slovenia officials started the accession process to join the European Union.
2004 Slovenia was admitted to NATO.
2004 Slovenia is one of ten new states to join the EU.
2007 Slovenia adopts the single European currency, the euro.
2008 Slovenia takes over the EU presidency.
2008 Slovenia was hit by a major economic crisis, and later on successfully resolved it.
2009 Slovenia starts the presidency of the Council of Europe.
2010 Slovenia becomes a member of the OECD.
2016 Ljubljana was named as a European Green Capital.
2017 The United Nations declared Slovenia as the world's most sustainable country (Braček Lalić & Purg, 2021). Also, Slovenia introduced the action plan "Slovenia—The Land of Innovative Start-Up Companies" to support the startup environment.
2018 Slovenia became the first country in the EU that embrace the Blockchain Technology Action Plan.
2021 Slovenia adopted a national program to promote the development and use of artificial intelligence.
2022 Slovenia ranked 22nd in the UN's Human Development Index and ranked first in Eastern Europe in the Environmental Performance Index 2022.
2023 Slovenia adopted the "Digital Slovenia 2030" strategy, aiming to become the leading hub of advanced digital technologies.

1 Introduction: Context and History

Slovenia has been a part of Yugoslavia since 1918, and it became a part of the Socialist Federal Republic of Yugoslavia in 1945.

After claiming independence on June 25, 1991, Slovenia started changing its political and economic systems. Slovenia became a republic with a parliamentary democracy. The Program for economic restructuring included extensive measures related to macroeconomic and monetary policies, actions related to enterprises in a loss, and commercial banks and privatization (Pleskovic & Sachs, 1994). Enterprises were no longer "self-managed" and could become shareholder companies. In the economy, the legal principles, regulations, and structures of self-management have been replaced by the act representing a Slovene variant of the legal principles and structures of other Western Europeans.

Such a transformation required a drastic change in the mindset of companies' operations, as before, "the word "management" was viewed as a "technocratic" tool for manipulating workers" (Purg & Bracek Lalic, 2017, p. 2). The new management required obtaining the necessary skills and competencies for strategizing, internationalization, and decision-making in the new system. The beginning of professionalization of a management function was initiated by the establishment in 1986 "The Center for Educating Leading Workers in the Economy" which nowadays is known as the IEDC-Bled School of Management. Throughout the years, IEDC prepared Slovenian managers and leaders for thriving in the new environment. The aim was not just to develop leadership as a craft with excellent functional knowledge and skills, but also leadership as an art promoting the use of senses, intuition, creativity, and empathy through business ethics, sustainability, and arts for nurturing responsible and future-oriented leadership in Slovenia and the CEE region. Nowadays, Slovenia has fully transitioned into a competitive market economy integrated into the global trade networks.

Slovenia has a favorable investment climate with a stable economy, developed infrastructure, and high-skilled professionals (Exhibit 1). The Slovenian economy can be characterized as open, innovative, and resilient. The Slovenian economy rapidly recovered after COVID, and the annual GDP growth rate in 2022 accounted for 2.46%, almost reaching the levels of 2019. The share of FDI inflows in GDP increased by 2.7% in 2022 compared to 2020. Despite the challenges faced in 2020, the proportion of high-technology exports within the category of manufactured exports continued to exhibit a positive growth trend, reaching 8.5%. Similarly, this trend extends to employment within high-technology sectors. Slovenia has been actively recruiting highly skilled professionals, with the share of such employment reaching 6.4% of the total employment in 2022.

Furthermore, Slovenia was ranked 23rd among 146 world economies in the Global Attractiveness Index 2023 (The European House—Ambrosetti, 2023) and it was 28th among 134 countries in the Global Talent Competitiveness Index 2023 (INSEAD; Descartes Institute for the Future; Human Capital Leadership Institute, 2023). Moreover, Slovenia is classified within the category of very high human development, and in 2022, it secured 22nd place in the UN's Human Development Index (United Nations Development Programme, 2022). The indices show that the country has high levels of sustainable development and future attractiveness prospects of the economy, and Slovenia is successfully attracting, growing, and retaining talented people, especially those having global knowledge skills, including creativity and decision-making for managerial and leadership positions. It comes as no surprise that the unique context of Slovenia attracts international students, and in the period 2017–2020, international student mobility almost doubled. Slovenia's progressive views on gender equality, diversity, and inclusion are additional factors enhancing its appeal to talented individuals. According to the UN Gender Inequality

Exhibit 1 Core economic indicators for Slovenia

	2018	2019	2020	2021	2022	2023
GDP per capita (current US$)	26124	26042	25558	29331	28439	32,610.11
GDP per capita growth (annual %)	4.08	2.80	−4.88	7.94	2.27	1.71
Long-term unemployment (% of total unemployment)	42.92	42.96	38.79	39.13	41.74	3.65
Foreign direct investment, net inflows (% of GDP)	2.84	3.96	0.94	3.59	3.63	2.09
GDP (current US$, mio)	54178	54387	53735	61832	60063	69148.47
Exports of goods and services (current US$, mio)	45939	45475	41784	51669	56547	57566.83
Exports of goods and services (% of GDP)	84.79	83.61	77.76	83.56	94.15	83.25
Merchandise exports (current US$, mio)	44200	44943	44832	57352	69701	73,200
Merchandise exports to high-income economies (% of total merchandise exports)	82.53	82.86	82.95	n/a	n/a	87.81
Merchandise exports to developing economies in Europe and Central Asia (% of total merchandise exports)	12.58	12.89	12.95	n/a	n/a	8.9
Ores and metals exports (% of merchandise exports)	4.28	4.03	3.64	4.34	3.90	3.14
Agricultural raw materials exports (% of merchandise exports)	1.93	1.59	1.42	1.51	1.41	1.15
Food exports (% of merchandise exports)	4.47	4.40	4.62	4.40	3.76	3.8
Fuel exports (% of merchandise exports)	5.21	5.30	3.06	4.11	7.90	5.56
Manufactures exports (% of merchandise exports)	83.94	84.44	87.01	85.41	82.81	86.18
High-technology exports (% of manufactured exports)	6.83	7.35	7.80	6.21	8.47	8.2

Source: World Bank, March, 2024; OECD, 2024

Index, Slovenia ranked 13th in 2022 with an indicator value of 0.049. It reflects that men and women have equal opportunities when it comes to reproductive health, empowerment, and the labor market. Overall, Slovenian companies recognize the importance of investing in human capital, which is why they support the ongoing development of employees' skills and competencies (Domadenik et al., 2019).

When it comes to innovations, Slovenia is named a moderate innovator (Hollanders et al., 2023) by the latest data of the European Innovation Scorecard. The report showed that Slovenia is strong in product innovators, lifelong learning, and providing ICT training, and since 2022, the country has increased venture capital expenditures.

Slovenia fosters a startup-friendly environment. In 2017 Slovenia introduced the action plan "Slovenia—The Land of Innovative Start-Up Companies" (Republika Slovenija, Ministrstvo za gospodarski razvoj in tehnologijo, 2018) intended to support entrepreneurship and nurture the startup environment by tackling the existing obstacles in creating and operating startups.

Slovenia actively promotes the development and implementation of advanced digital technologies to become the "leading hub of advanced digital technologies in Europe and in the wider region of Central and Eastern Europe" (Republic of Slovenia. Ministry of Economic Development and Technology, 2022, p. 14). That is why, in March 2023, the country adopted the "Digital Slovenia 2030" (Vlade Republike Slovenije, 2023) strategy setting digital transformation as one of the national priorities.

Before, in 2018, Slovenia became the first country in the EU that embrace the Blockchain Technology Action Plan and later in 2021 introduced a national program focusing on enhancing and developing activities related to artificial intelligence (European Commission AI Watch, 2021), including research in the AI field and establishing a National AI Observatory, integrating AI solutions in industry, public sector and society and creating an AI-supportive environment overall.

In 2021, Slovenia ranked 13th in the Digital Economy and Society Index (DESI) (European Commission, 2021) highlighting the national orientation on becoming strong in high-performance computing, robust cyber security, and the widespread availability of user-friendly digital public services.

In addition to the aforementioned initiatives, the future endeavors outlined in the 2030 strategy are directed at building digital competencies and social inclusion, supporting the gigabit infrastructure, and transitioning toward a smart society 5.0.

Shifting toward a low-carbon circular economy is among Slovenia's strategic priorities (Ministry of Economic Development and Technology, 2023). Slovenian cities, municipalities, and businesses are taking a proactive position in supporting this transition. For instance, in 2016, Ljubljana was recognized as a European Green Capital, and in 2018, Bled joined the Smart Villages Declaration, while municipality associations adopted a circularity agenda for touristic experiences (Ministry of Environment and Spatial Planning, Republic of Slovenia, & Circular Change Platform, 2018). Principles of circularity are integrated in many Slovenian sectors, spanning the food system, forest-based value chains, manufacturing industry, and mobility, e.g., Paradajz, Slovenian Steel Group, Avant2GO, etc. Companies create state-of-the-art solutions to ensure minimal influence on the environment.

Furthermore, Slovenia secured the seventh position globally out of 180 countries and ranked first in Eastern Europe in the Environmental Performance Index 2022 (Wolf et al., 2022), which shows the proximity to achieving the UN sustainable development goals and other initiatives directed at environmental and ecosystem vitality. Over the period 2017 to 2022, Slovenia decreased in CO2 emissions per capita (Our World in Data, 2023) by 13.89% reflecting the effectiveness of the actions toward becoming a circular economy.

Nowadays, Slovenia is well-known for green tourism, and people come to enjoy the clean water and air along with picturesque views of various landscapes—from the alpine mountains to the Adriatic Sea.

To conclude, Slovenia has a highly favorable economic, political, and business environment for establishing and developing companies. Small and medium-sized companies can benefit from Slovenia's openness to innovations, attracting qualified human capital and progressive approaches to the digitalization of society and advancements of the circular economy. Thus, it is not surprizing that many Hidden Champions found their place in Slovenia (Braček Lalić & Purg, 2021; McKiernan & Purg, 2013). Slovenian Hidden Champions have an entrepreneurial spirit and risk-taking nature as founders and employees dare to turn their ideas, dreams, and research into tangible unique products. They are prioritizing visionary thinking, innovativeness, customer-centricity, and acting out of the box. These companies succeed in establishing and nurturing a caring culture that creates a family-like feeling in the workplace. For Slovenian Hidden Champions, it is not just about making a profit; they strive to offer products and solutions that would make the lives of their clients easier and better.

In the next section, we present three more Hidden Champions: Qlector, Arctur, and Dewesoft. These companies not only excel in various technological fields but also inspire with their leadership and entrepreneurship. They offer valuable lessons on the impact of cooperation in creating purposeful knowledge, the power of vision and intuition, the importance of agility, and customer-centric innovation.

2 Case Studies of Selected Hidden Champions

2.1 Case Study 1

2.1.1 Qlector

Overview
Address: Tržaška cesta 68A, 1000 Ljubljana—Slovenia
Tel: +386 40 644 535
Fax: N/A
Email: info@qlector.com
Web: https://qlector.com/

Company Information
Industry: Professional, Scientific and Technical Activities (*NACE Rev. 2)*
Year of Establishment: 2018
Sales Revenues in 2017: N/A
Sales Revenues in 2023: 0,8 mio EUR
Average number of employees in 2023: 16
Brainer(s) behind the company: Mateja Lavrič, Matjaž Grosek, Maja Škrjanc, Gregor Sablič, Mario Karlovčec.

Nature of Market Leadership

Qlector is an established market leader in artificial intelligence (AI) solutions applicable to discrete and process manufacturing in production companies. The company successfully combines scientific knowledge and sound business practices through the joint venture of the renowned Jožef Stefan Institute and the Kolektor Group. Such a unique knowledge base allows Qlector to adopt an innovative approach to manufacturing digitalization and, thus, maintain a focused niche market with unique positioning. Moreover, Qlector prioritizes building a diverse and highly competent team.

Therefore, the main points of Qlector's market leadership are:

Innovative approach and capabilities. The innovative approach is based on developing and implementing cutting-edge technology and software solutions, including AI and machine learning, into manufacturing for predicting anomalies in the production process and throughout the entire supply chain and further directing production, so that the optimal goal for the company is achieved.

A strong network of scientific and research communities. Qlector is well-connected to the Artificial Intelligence Laboratory at Jožef Stefan Institute.

Focused niche market with unique positioning. Qlector is positioned between manufacturing execution systems, MESs, ERPs, and APS systems. The company doesn't have direct competitors as other companies address similar challenges traditionally. Qlector offers not just a tool for optimizing production planning, but a tool that directs production, allowing the company to target a focused niche market.

Nature of Competitive Advantage

The nature of Qlector's competitive advantage is based on several points:

Unique Product Offering. Qlector developed an innovative AI solution for manufacturing companies named the QLECTOR LEAP AI platform. This tool offers a novel, user-friendly approach to addressing existing production challenges. Thus, using Qlector Leap goes beyond optimizations and allows for developing achievable production plans, tracking and forecasting plan realization, and timely anticipation of downtimes and alerting of employees.

Comprehensive Solutions Offering. Qlector has a diverse and comprehensive solutions portfolio that targets both discrete and process manufacturing. Moreover, diversification is also related to various industries Qlector is working with, including automotive, electronics, home appliances, pharmaceutical, chemical, and food & beverage.

Technology Leadership. Qlector's competitive advantage is also based on technology leadership, as the company is driven by a vision and strong motivation to adopt advanced technology in manufacturing to bring quality and process optimization to manufacturing companies.

Core Lessons Learned on the Path to Success

Being an innovative company, Qlector has many lessons to share with us, and there are two of them that particularly stand out.

Building Purposeful Knowledge. Qlector explained that it seized the opportunity to make something new in the Slovenian environment and combine high-tech knowledge with purposeful knowledge.

Build a team of competent motivated people from the very beginning to develop and live the purpose-driven culture. Qlector hired people because of their competencies and their loyalty, and "blind faith in vision" helped to drive ideas forward. The vision connected people and it supported the fast development of the company.

Management and Leadership Development Needs

Qlector shared a couple of points on their development and business needs.

There is a challenge and a need to find local senior representatives for selling the complex product. Qlector explained that the success of finding new customers is based on generating qualified leads. Thus, they need to find competent local senior sales representatives, which is a hard task as there are few of them. Such a senior representative should have experience in large corporations or consulting companies, have a wide network, and have a very good understanding of the customers themselves and production processes, including the technical side. Although Qlector has access to universities, they cannot find those people there, as such a representative should already have a network.

There is a need to strengthen the team for customer satisfaction and/or for customer success. Qlector believes that customer satisfaction is the primary goal; thus, it is important to develop the team to achieve, maintain, and nurture excellent customer satisfaction.

These two business challenges indirectly lead to the management and leadership development needs. To address the first challenge, Qlector might focus on the internal development of senior sales representatives. Strengthening customer excellence practices can also be achieved through building internal development programs and/or outsourcing development efforts to business schools and other experts.

Financing and Regulatory Environment Development Needs

When it comes to financing needs, Qlector explained that they have a natural need to find more financing sources. They pointed out that additional financing can be streamed into team development to ensure that the product is developed to the end and sales growth. As the business model is based on monthly subscription sales, Qlector is still on the way to gaining the critical mass of customers to climb upward on the profit curve. Until that moment, they need to operate on investment support.

Regarding the regulatory environment, Qlector noted that the startup ecosystem in Slovenia is well-developed for the initial stages of establishing a startup. It is especially related to investment support which can be in the forms of grants or convertible loans. However, in the later stages of startup growth, there are yet no mechanisms of direct support. Thus, the regulatory environment needs to develop such instruments and procedures for addressing the expansion stage of startups.

The Impact of Cooperation to Create Purposeful Knowledge

Knowing what you learn and why you learn it, and the ability to apply the knowledge you have to create value, is an art. It is also called "purposeful knowledge", and Qlector successfully applied this principle through synergetic cooperation to build an innovative, purpose-driven company.

In the very beginning, the management of Kolektor and the leadership of Quintelligence, who knew each other from collaboration on other European projects, got together. Quintelligence comes from the Department of Artificial Intelligence at the Jožef Štefan Institute and has competencies in the field of AI, and Kolektor is a player with purposeful knowledge. That was a match made in heaven, as a synergy of domain knowledge and practice between these two companies could open the door to developing customer solutions that could be immediately tested in the real environment. That was 2018 when Qlector was established, and the idea was to help manufacturing companies elevate efficiency through advanced high-tech solutions. Since then, the company has developed a successful product (Qlector LEAP), built a team of highly motivated and engaged professionals with diverse expertise who believe in the company's vision, and managed to build a pool of customer success stories based on the applications of Qlector LEAP into practice.

The company's flagship product Qlector LEAP is based on methodology resulting from an intelligent cooperation of the Josef Stefan Institute and Bloomberg. Qlector LEAP's innovativeness is one of the reasons why Qlector became a market leader in their niche and has a strong competitive advantage. Moreover, corporate culture supporting innovations and proactiveness allowed Qlector to create a large portfolio of customized offerings for digitalization in discrete manufacturing (automotive, electronics, and home appliances industries) and process manufacturing (pharmaceutical, chemical, and food & beverage sectors). Being a supporter of Industry 4.0 ideas, Qlector offers solutions based on predictive intelligence for directed decision-making that supports boosting planning effectiveness, reducing error count, inventory level, work-in-progress and organizational downtime, and increasing on-time delivery.

Qlector believes in the importance of integrating holistic expertise into business practices. That is why the company built a diverse team of highly competent professionals. They come from various fields, including data science and machine learning, manufacturing planning, engineering, and marketing, and they work side by side to ensure the relevance and quality of product offerings. Having a team of passionate like-minded people drives the innovations and creativity of Qlector.

Interestingly, Qlector's real business challenges are not that much internal but are conditioned by the external environment in which it operates. Despite the excitement created around the concepts of digital transformation, smart factories, and Industry 4.0, in practice, many companies have made little progress with digitalization and still rely on traditional manual entry methods. For Qlector, this means their products and solutions primarily appeal to "early adopters," who represent a smaller segment of the market. Potential customers do not yet possess a digitally mature mindset. That is why, Qlector's sales and marketing strategies heavily focus on generating new leads and acquiring new customers. Qlector, being well-connected with universities, has no trouble hiring competent IT professionals. However, when it comes to sales, they face the challenge of finding individuals who can become expert-level sales representatives. What is more, being a relatively young company, Qlector is also focusing on building stronger brand recognition. Besides, as a startup, Qlector recognizes the necessity of building trust to ensure that client companies feel confident in establishing a stable, long-term partnership with them. Qlector noted that having an industrial company and a client as their founders helps build the company's reputable image.

Notwithstanding the existing business challenges, Qlector remains resilient in the face of crises occurring worldwide. For instance, the COVID situation did not create issues for Qlector. Instead, Qlector's mindset is not fixated on problems, but rather on the opportunities and solutions that the external environment can present. They believe understanding the pain of their customers allows them to optimize clients' costs and offer solutions for production optimization.

To conclude, Qlector is an innovative company offering creative approaches to solving existing challenges of manufacturing companies. Qlector's courage and progressive vision to digitalize manufacturing inspire and motivate their team, leading to numerous success stories for their clients.

2.2 Case Study 2

2.2.1 Arctur

Overview

Address: Industrijska cesta 1 a, 5000 Nova Gorica
Tel: +386 5 3029070
Fax: N/A
Email: info@arctur.si
Web: https://www.arctur.si/

Company Information

Industry[1]: Professional, Scientific and Technical Activities (NACE Rev. 2)

[1] *According to NACE Rev. 2—please check the technical instructions included in this document (pg. 9).*

Year of establishment: 1992
Sales Revenues in 2017: 2.446.860,90€
Sales Revenues in 2023: 3.500 000€
Average number of employees in 2023: 46
Brainer(s) behind the company: Tomi Ilijaš, Martina Murovec, Darja Podgornik, Urska Starc Peceny

Nature of Market Leadership

Arctur is a respected market leader, providing innovative IT and R&D solutions on the edge of science, research, art, and business for more than 30 years. The nature of Arctur's market leadership is based on market dominance, implementation of cutting-edge technologies, and knowledge-intensive capabilities.

Arctur was the first private company in Europe to acquire a supercomputer to rent it out and offer services under innovative business models elsewhere. Today, they remain the largest private provider of such services in this region of Europe. Besides that, they practically do not have large competitors in Slovenia regarding the project management direction. In the supercomputers segment, their main competitors are national centers across Europe. However, Arctur still holds market dominance in Central Europe.

Arctur embraces the values and principles of Industry 5.0, and that is why they develop products and solutions that can nudge digitalization and integration of advanced IT technologies.

Although Arctur operates as a company, the foundation of its work resembles that of a private research institution. Their team is knowledgeable, creative, and highly proactive so they produce many more innovations and patents that they are capable of bringing to the market.

Nature of Competitive Advantage

Wide Portfolio of Solutions and Quality Product Offerings. Arctur's portfolio includes numerous projects helping companies to implement big data processing, machine learning and AI, 3D solutions, high-performance computing and cloud services, assessment tools, project management tools, and many more. Customers benefit from high-quality solutions, resulting in successfully completed projects.

Innovation Ecosystem. As Arctur targets various sectors, including eHealth, tourism, heritage, industry, government, and NGOs, they have built a portfolio of ideas and products that can transfer across sectors. This approach leads to continuous improvement and differentiation. Such an ecosystem enables the company to keep up with and adapt to the changing demands of its clients, offering personalized solutions to tackle their challenges.

Reputable customer network. Over the years, Arctur built a reputable customer network through numerous successful projects. Their ability to combine creativity, research capabilities, and scientific knowledge made their brand image strong, trusted, and distinctive.

Core Lessons Learned on the Path to Success

Arctur shared with us the experiences that helped to develop a thriving organization:

Invest in and raise the people. When Arctur began its journey, it could only employ failed students and individuals who had been overlooked for other jobs—"uneducated geniuses that no one noticed", as they described them. They were not a perfect match with the job requirements, but rather young and confident, fresh out of school. These people were like rough diamonds in the rough, so Arctur recognized their talents and decided to raise the people and nurture their careers. That is why the company never experienced issues with people turnover.

Create a caring corporate culture. Arctur has a caring corporate culture based on appreciation, which directly influences people's motivation and engagement, allowing them to fully express their creative abilities. At Arctur, they prioritize not only career development but also the holistic well-being of individuals.

Invest in the education of employees. Arctur also believes in the importance of investing in the education of employees, which is instrumental to their approach to raising the people and fostering a caring corporate culture.

Management and Leadership Development Needs

Develop people for a creative environment. Contrary to the widespread idea that being in a creative environment is an ideal workplace, in practice, it often proves to be challenging as many people enjoy following concrete work instructions and certainty about the expected actions and tasks. A creative environment, on the other hand, implies a certain degree of chaos and unpredictability. As Arctur nurtures such a creative atmosphere, it's crucial for them to ensure that people not only appreciate the possibilities it offers but also minimize the stress and fear it can occasionally evoke.

Build a psychologically safe environment with a matrix organization. Psychological safety is crucial for Arctur to thrive in a highly competitive IT environment. As a result, Arctur nurtures this aspect through a matrix organization. This structure allows for a high level of involvement in decision-making and execution, not only by managers but also by experts and relevant team members. Such an organization demands a high level of responsibility while providing significant autonomy.

Develop public speaking skills for engineers. As is common among individuals in engineering professions, public speaking may not be their strongest skill. Thus, Arctur recognizes it as an essential area for development.

Financing and Regulatory Environment Development Needs

In general, Arctur believes that there should be fewer legal obligations. They have observed that the number of formal bureaucratic procedures they must comply with is increasing, and they are beginning to perceive them as increasingly unnecessary.

The Impact of Vision and Intuition

Envisioning the future is and always has been one of the most challenging (if not impossible) tasks for a human. But if humans are not obliged to think about it, creating a vision is essential for a company to survive and thrive. It is, however, still puzzling how to balance rational thinking and intuition when shaping the vision. Is it really possible to have the courage to trust intuition? Arctur is an exemplary company that, for more than 30 years proved with many successful projects that relying on intuition can and should be an immanent element of shaping the future of an organization.

Arctur is an established market leader operating at the cutting edge of business, research, and science, and offering innovative products and services for HPC & DC management, project management, and software design and development. Their vision and change-oriented mindset to create a "more sustainable and equitable future" and "inspire and empower organizations to reinvent themselves" has transformed the business practices of many companies in the industry, eHealth, and tourism sectors. It has also supported governments and NGOs and reinvented methods for preserving cultural heritage.

In the early days, Arctur faced competition from at least 20 companies in Gorizia that they believed were stronger and could have become Internet providers. However, Arctur took the initiative. Despite uncertainty about the exact direction, they had an intuition that Internet services would become popular shortly. While Telekom initially ignored this sector for 3 years, Arctur seized the opportunity to develop web portals. Once Telekom entered and monopolized the market, Arctur had already shifted ahead, once again trusting their intuition.

However, it is not just about trusting intuition, but also the ability to envision an unimaginable future. Arctur recalls a time at a conference in Portorož where they shared their vision with the audience: "There will come a time when we will buy shoes and cars on the Internet." The audience simply laughed. Nowadays, we cannot believe how we lived without the things that back in the 90 s could be seen as an unfeasible fantasy. So, trusting their hunches, possessing a strong motivation to create positive change, and believing that the unimaginable can come true have made Arctur the prosperous company it is today.

Although vision and intuition are major factors in Arctur's success, they are certainly not the only ones. Arctur believes in raising people and finding, tracking, and nurturing talents starting from their school years onward. Hence, 46% of our employees are young talents under 35. Also, to support the ongoing talent hunting, the company has established two laboratories at the University of Ljubljana's

Faculty of Computer Science. They also regularly provide scholarship opportunities, internships, and coaching programs.

What is more, Arctur established a caring, supportive atmosphere in the company. They believe that there is more to life than only work, so they encourage people to invest time in interests, hobbies, and social activities. For them, success is about owning your time and your life, which goes beyond living an illusionary life with goals to possess things. Individuals should invest time in their wholesome development; thus, Arctur nudges people to have a healthy work-life balance. It is vital to feel the drive, joy, energy, and fullness of life with work, serving an exciting place where people can realize their potential and ideas, leading to positive change for a better life. Arctur is committed to creating and maintaining a safe and supportive environment where people can feel like "one family", knowing that they can solve problems together.

Building a caring corporate culture also supports Arctur's drive for creativity and innovation. People merge their diverse experiences and perspectives from business, art, and science to collaborate and co-create meaningful win-win solutions for a better future for companies and communities. Arctur embraces diversity and inclusion and removes gender inequality cliches so that 43% of employees are women and 67% of women are in top management positions.

To uphold the highest management standards and excellence of their work, Arctur aligned their operations with the comprehensive ISO quality certification requirements. Since 2014, they obtained ISO in quality management systems, information security, cybersecurity and privacy protection, and environmental management systems, reaffirming their commitment to delivering excellent quality and results.

Having a strong knowledge base, high-quality offerings of products and services, and a supportive corporate culture ensured Arctur's resilience to crises. Nevertheless, COVID-19 was challenging for them in terms of socializing, Arctur's team grabbed the opportunity to create a new platform and even received an award for the best solution in the field of tourism using artificial intelligence. Overall, they don't believe in crises as they refer to them as "inconveniences", and the way to tackle them is to "tighten a little belt, put costs to zero, and survive".

In conclusion, throughout many years, Arctur showcases how a transformative vision with strong intuition and a people-caring approach could lead them to gain market dominance and an undeniable competitive advantage. Maintaining a change-oriented mindset that prioritizes honesty, ethics, and collaboration has been crucial in building sustainable, long-term success.

2.3 *Case Study 3*

2.3.1 Dewesoft

Overview
Address: Gabrsko 11a, 1420 Trbovlje, Slovenia
Tel: +386 3 562 53 00

Fax: N/A
Email: dewesoft@dewesoft.com
Web: https://dewesoft.com/

Company Information
Industry: Professional, Scientific and Technical Activities (NACE Rev. 2)
Year of Establishment: 2000
Sales Revenues in 2017: 17.977.790 EUR
Sales Revenues in 2023: 61.351.269 EUR
Average number of employees in 2023: 179
Brainer(s) behind the company: Dr. Jure Knez, Tilen Sotler, Dr. Tomaž Kos

Nature of Market Leadership

Dewesoft has been a game-changer in the area of test and measurement solutions for test engineers for almost 25 years. Their undeniable market leadership is based on:

Clear Vision Based on Market Needs. The company began its way with a clear understanding of market needs and a vision to develop the "dream" test and measurement instruments for engineers that would solve the existing challenges. The synergy of knowledge and understanding of varied market needs has been crucial in the development of instruments that continue to prove successful to this day.

Open Innovation. Dewesoft develops its state-of-the-art products and solutions by incorporating the principle of open innovation. In addition to their internal knowledge base, they continuously gather ideas from engineers and technicians working in the testing and measurement field, ensuring a deep understanding of existing relevant challenges.

Customer-Centric Approach. A customer-centric approach is ingrained in Dewesoft's DNA. They firmly believe, and show through their hard work, that their instruments should be designed for the customer and based on their demands. Dewesoft strives for customer satisfaction which is further supported by their cooperation with customers through the open innovation approach.

Nature of Competitive Advantage

Innovative and differentiated product offering. Dewesoft offers a versatile set of innovative tools for test and measurement engineers. They designed them to be easy to use, customizable, and able to handle huge data sets in the blink of an eye. The innovativeness of Dewesoft's instruments lies in a pioneering approach to solving challenges.

Ecosystem Creation and Development. To provide customers with excellent, intuitive user experiences, Dewesoft created and built an ecosystem in which their products can be connected to multiple devices so that people can have seamlessly integrated solutions. Although the concept of ecosystem is not a novel one as a whole, for Dewesoft's niche market, they are pioneers.

High Core Technical Knowledge and Experienced Professionals. The company was founded by highly competent and creative test engineers who shared similar experiences in their work. Their passion for making change, combined with advanced competencies and high core technical knowledge, ensures ongoing development and learning.

Financial Stability Based on Self-Financing. Dewesoft has a special financing structure. Unlike many companies, they don't rely on external debt funding and the company is completely owned by the employees. Such a structure ensures their financial stability and creditworthiness proved by the AAA Bisnode credit rating.

Core Lessons Learned on the Path to Success

Stay agile because this gives you direction. The rapid growth of Dewesoft nudged them into a paradigm of continuous change to maintain their high level of innovation capabilities. What puzzled them was that, based on the experiences of large companies, they questioned why many corporations act slowly when it comes to innovation. After some observations, they discovered that large companies have to handle piles of bureaucracy so that the focus gets shifted from thinking about development to solving these formal issues. Another point is that having complex hierarchical structures also implies having distributed pieces of knowledge, and for creating something new knowledge should be concentrated in the process. Only in this way, there is a possibility to go through the steps of ideation, implementation, and value creation for making something truly innovative. Although there are some successful examples of large corporations that can be seen as exemplary cases of innovation, this is more of an exception than the rule. Dewesoft quickly realized that simple truth and decided to build an agile organization to be flexible and not fall into the traps of bureaucracy.

Management and Leadership Development Needs

Knowledge and values succession for maintaining a sustainable model throughout the years. Dewesoft understands the importance of building a sustainable organization in which knowledge and values can be smoothly transferred to the next generations. Now the knowledge passes over and integration of corporate culture values goes intuitively, through various messages and internal networking; however, with some time Dewesoft thinks the process should take a more structured form.

Developing a holistic perspective on modern issues for maintaining agility. Around half of the Dewesoft managers were developed internally, and others were hired from the market. On the one hand, it allows them to have a synergy and balance of perspectives. Thus, internal ones bring core values, mission, and ways of work to the table, whereas external ones contribute through their diverse experiences. To maintain the agile organization, ideally, managers who were hired from outside should adapt to how things are done in Dewesoft and live their values, and internal ones should be open-minded to having a holistic perspective on business matters. Nevertheless, in Dewesoft, they balance perspectives effectively; still, the latter leaves some room for improvement.

Financing and Regulatory Environment Development Needs

To ensure innovation, relevance, and the high quality of its product offerings, Dewesoft streams nearly all of its annual gross profit toward R&D activities and the enhancement or establishment of novel infrastructural capabilities. For example, one of such financing articles is their novel project named Katapult, which is a startup accelerator.

Regarding the regulatory environment, Dewesoft believes that, from the legislative point of view, there should be easier conditions for establishing and developing small and medium-sized companies. With more regulations coming into place, implying paperwork, organizing special processes and departments in the companies, hiring specialists for compliance, and many more, the new companies would have very high barriers to entering the market. In the long run, that can lead to the inability to establish new SMEs and the disappearance of many existing SMEs. That can also negatively affect the level of innovation.

The Impact of Agility and Customer-Centric Innovation

How can an organization keep up with the fast-changing times and demands of its customers? Well, they say becoming agile can provide the answer, as agile ways of working involve fast responses to changes, and building organizational flexibility and adaptability. Dewesoft is a vivid example of how becoming agile can ensure market leadership and fulfill its belief in continuous learning to achieve its high mission of advancing humanity.

To begin with, Dewesoft, founded in the year 2000, provides the world's leading companies with high-quality, customer-oriented data acquisition instruments. Since then, their market share has been rapidly growing every year thanks to their constant development of new, diversified solutions. The portfolio of Dewesoft's data acquisition products includes numerous offers such as Data Acquisition systems, Data Acquisition Software, Sensors, Transducers and Actuators, Monitoring and IoT Devices, and many more. Creating unique offerings from the very beginning is one of Dewesoft's major success factors, as they could provide the market with something that had never been done before.

It all started with the founders of Dewesoft having a clear vision of what the "dream instrument" should be like drawing from years of experience in the field and facing testing and measurement challenges on a daily basis. But challenges always evolve, so how can an organization keep up with them on time?

To address this, Dewesoft ingrained a highly customer-centric mindset in their innovation processes, probing, and operations. They adopt a philosophy of releasing early, finding early adopters, collecting feedback, and then adjusting the product to meet customer needs. It's not about being perfect from the first launch, but about ultimately providing their users with relevant solutions. Moreover, Dewesoft has sales companies in 19 countries because they believe they need to be present where they aim to be successful and where they want to offer and implement their solutions.

Additionally, to support Dewesoft's strive for customer excellence, they operationalized the concept of agility to nurture innovative capacities and ensure fast decision-making. They built a special business structure with a main company focusing on core technologies and so-called "bubbles"—small companies of 10–20 people under Dewesoft's umbrella that have full autonomy to develop products and solutions independently. This structure allows room for creating new ideas, as the "bubbles" are not burdened by internal processes, regulations, and compliance procedures. The main part of the company supports the "bubbles" and vouches for them when needed. Dewesoft believes that building this structure is one of its crucial success factors and that being agile can provide a company with direction and a vision for the future.

Dewesoft believes in continuous change as a way of living, focusing on comparing its progress with its past achievements. They want to be a part of something big and meaningful, whether it's about going to space or creating a breakthrough medical device. They work because they love what they do, and they have a dream they are not afraid to follow. So it comes as no surprise that they invest around 90% of the profit in R&D. That is why they could also become pioneers in integrating an ecosystem approach in their market segment. What it means is that the measurement system would have to have one platform where users can connect different devices and use them as one system. Through the development of this ecosystem solution, Dewesoft wishes to bring the user community to an entirely new level. They want to create win-win solutions based on high interconnectivity, enabling customers to use old systems alongside new ones from Dewesoft or other companies.

Pursuing unimaginable dreams is supported by Dewesoft's international creative speak-up environment, where engineering, marketing, sales, and applications teams can brainstorm and co-create together with their leaders. Active listening is what they preach in Dewesoft, both for internal cooperation and when working with customers. Having such a friendly, family-like atmosphere, they managed to set a collaborative, purpose-driven culture. Dewesoft values transparency, commitment, accountability, caring, and an innovative mindset. These corporate values are ingrained in the company's DNA, and people commit to them through their daily actions. Moreover, employees have many opportunities for development through trainings, mentorships, and attending unique events like SpaceX. Working for Dewesoft is more than just a job; it is a way of living with passion and motivation to make a difference.

In fact, the company is 100% owned by employees, so they understand that only their actions, engagement, and ability to work together and co-create can lead to overall success. Such a structure was one of the factors that ensured the company's resilience during the COVID-19 pandemic. Additionally, since Dewesoft has branches in China, they could gather information about the seriousness of the COVID situation early on, allowing them time to prepare for it. Overall, they believe that being an employee-owned company can ensure robustness in crises, alongside established communication in the organization.

Notwithstanding Dewesoft's flexible approach to doing business, like any other company, it experiences some business challenges. One of the biggest ones that they shared is the instability of the geopolitical situation, especially related to trade tensions. As Dewesoft's business is international, they can constantly adapt to new situations to ensure smooth operations serving their customers without delays and other disruptions.

One can say Dewesoft is already so progressive, but how can they further develop? Well, their mission to advance humanity is a never-ending journey. They shared that in the next 10 years; they wish to support a community of like-minded people and help young individuals build their businesses. How would they do that? Dewesoft is already working on two projects, one is called Katapult, which is a business accelerator, and another one is called "The City of Acrobats". Katapult is intended to support a startup community to build more innovative ways of work, also through continuous guidance and mentorship support of Dewesoft. The City of Acrobats is planned to become the largest technological campus in Europe, spanning 40,000 square meters with the capacity to accommodate around 2000 people. It would be the place where companies, startups, entrepreneurs, and educational institutions can collaborate, learn, grow, and even live together.

One who wants to make a difference will always find a way to do so, and Dewesoft's success story shows how to envision and transform reality through agility, innovation, and a customer-centric approach.

3 Conclusions and Recommendations

Slovenia has a competitive market economy, a favorable investment climate, developed infrastructure, highly competent professionals, and a progressive vision for the future. Slovenia's high positions in numerous global rankings demonstrate its support for human development, an entrepreneurial startup environment, the implementation of advanced digital technologies, and the development of a circular economy. Therefore, it comes as no surprise that Hidden Champions choose to develop their innovative products and solutions in this country.

Although hidden champions enjoy numerous benefits of the Slovenian environment, they have also noted some areas for improvement. Despite significant investments in promoting digitalization, digital transformation remains largely a modern myth, with only a small percentage of the market open to this disruptive change. For companies that support the ideas of Industry 4.0 and 5.0 and envision building smart cities and factories through innovative high-tech products and solutions, the market's lack of readiness becomes a substantial obstacle.

Another challenge noted by one of the hidden champions relates to the overly bureaucratic processes that small and medium enterprises have to comply with. Such an environment has the potential to suffocate the creativity and innovation that hidden champions bring to the table. Additionally, many hidden champions begin as startups, and the Slovenian ecosystem offers only initial support for their efforts. The latter stages of their growth are not yet addressed, potentially leading to the loss of truly innovative ideas due to startups' inability to establish rigorous business processes.

Therefore, to address existing challenges and make Slovenia's business environment more progressive, the national government can consider the following actions:

1. Developing an action plan for stimulating companies to digitalize their processes and implement advanced technologies in the companies' interests.
2. Expanding the functions of business and startup accelerators by creating programs supporting startups in their expansion phases. Programs can include mentorships, networking events, lectures and seminars on demanded topics, support with creating strategic partnerships, etc.
3. Developing easier regulatory procedures for small and medium-sized enterprises.

Financial institutions can actively support the government's efforts to encourage companies to digitalize by offering special financing schemes and better loan conditions for enterprises considering digital transformation. At the same time, startup incubators can establish strategic partnerships with business schools to offer numerous interactive sessions, workshops, and events for creating a knowledge-sharing environment. Governments can also collaborate with business schools to promote digitalization by offering grants for company management to attend programs focused on AI, technology leadership, and digital transformation. Such collaboration can also involve creating tailored programs to support the digitalization of company processes.

Despite these minor challenges, hidden champions benefit from many favorable factors that the Slovenian environment offers for building prosperous, innovative businesses. Their unique success stories speak for themselves, and with Slovenia's vision of becoming a "leading hub of advanced digital technologies," we believe many more hidden champions can establish themselves in this country.

References

Braček Lalić, A., & Purg, D. (2021). *Hidden champions in dynamically changing societies*. Springer.

Domadenik, P., Koman, M., & Redek, T. (2019). *Innovation governance: Leading the winners*. Časnik Finance, d. o. o.

European Commission. (2021). *Digital economy and society index (DESI). Slovenia.*

European Commission AI Watch. (2021). *Slovenia AI strategy report*. https://ai-watch.ec.europa.eu/countries/slovenia/slovenia-ai-strategy-report_en#:~:text=In%20August%202020%2C%20the%20Slovenian,2021%20(Slovenia%2C%202020)

Hollanders, H., Es-Sadki, N., & Khalilova, A. (2023). *European innovation scoreboard 2023. Country profile Slovenia.* European Commission.
INSEAD; Descartes Institute for the Future; Human Capital Leadership Institute. (2023). *The global talent competitiveness index.*
McKiernan, P., & Purg, D. (2013). *Hidden champions in CEE and Turkey. Carving out a global niche*. Springer.
Ministry of Economic Development and Technology. (2023). *Circular economy—resource efficiency*. Retrieved from Republic of Slovenia, GOV.SI: https://www.gov.si/en/registries/projects/the-recovery-and-resilience-plan/about-the-recovery-and-resilience-plan/green-transition/circular-economy-resource-efficiency/
Ministry of Environment and Spatial Planning, Republic of Slovenia & Circular Change Platform. (2018). *Roadmap towards the circular economy in Slovenia.*
Our World in Data. (2023). *Per capita CO_2 emissions*. https://ourworldindata.org/grapher/co-emissions-per-capita?tab=table
Pleskovic, B., & Sachs, J. D. (1994). Political independence and economic reform in Slovenia. In I. K. A. Olivier & J. Blanchard (Eds.), *The transition in Eastern Europe, volume 1* (pp. 191–220). University of Chicago Press.
Portal GOV.SI. (2022). *About Slovenia*. Retrieved from Republic of Slovenia, GOV.SI: https://www.gov.si/en/policies/state-and-society/about-slovenia/
Purg, D., & Bracek Lalic, A. (2017). *Development of management education in central and Eastern Europe (1985–2016).* William Davidson Institute at the University of Michigan.
Republic of Slovenia. Ministry of Economic Development and Technology. (2022). *Strategy of digital transformation of the economy.*
Republika Slovenija, Ministrstvo za gospodarski razvoj in tehnologijo. (2018). *Akcijski načrt. Slovenija—dežela inovativnih zagonskih (startup) podjetij.* Retrieved from Start-up Slovenia.
The European House—Ambrosetti. (2023). *Global attractiveness index. The thermometer of a country's attractiveness.*
United Nations Development Programme. (2022). *Human development reports*. https://hdr.undp.org/data-center/documentation-and-downloads
Vlade Republike Slovenije. (2023). *Digitalna Slovenija 2030.*
Wolf, M. J., Emerson, J. W., Esty, D. C., de Sherbinin, A., Wendling, Z. A., et al. (2022). *2022 environmental performance index*. Yale Center for Environmental Law & Policy.

Elnura Irmatova is a researcher at the NLB Chair in Leadership Development and a DBA candidate at the IEDC-Bled School of Management. Within the NLB Chair, she conducts research at the intersection of academia and practice, offering NLB solutions for a Holistic Framework of Leadership Development and an Authentic Leader Development Framework.

She co-authored a publication with Prof. Danica Purg in the Academy of International Business and, together with Prof. Purg and Mrs. Edina Selesković, co-presented at the ILA Conference 2020 on the topic Learning Leadership from the Art Metaphor. She has also shared her research on the humanization of leadership education at the Developing Leadership Capacity Conference in the UK.

In collaboration with Prof. Pierre Casse, Ms. Irmatova contributed a leadership column to The Slovenia Times and published two series of articles on Leadership of Tomorrow in the Ambition journal (Association of MBAs). Together with her doctoral supervisor, Prof. Arnold Walravens, she conducts research in the fields of arts and leadership, specifically exploring arts-based leadership exercises for fostering leadership self-awareness.

Elnura Irmatova holds two MSc degrees: one in finance and economics from the Russian Presidential Academy, and another in management from the Silk Road Leaders program at Zhejiang University, China. Her current research interests include arts & leadership, leadership development, leader identity, and complexity leadership.

Arnold Walravens is a Professor of Arts & Leadership and Corporate Governance, Chair of the Postgraduate Studies and Quality Commission at IEDC-Bled School of Management. He teaches the courses on Corporate Governance and Arts and Leadership in Executive MBA and General Management Programs at IEDC-Bled School of Management.

He is Professor Emeritus of Economic Sociology at the University of Technology, Delft, The Netherlands, where he also served as the dean of the Faculty of Philosophy and Social Sciences. He received his Ph.D. from the University of Technology, Twente, the Netherlands and served as faculty member at the Free University of Amsterdam.

His academic research focuses on various topics, such as participation and human resources, corporate governance, arts and leadership, executive development, and artificial intelligence. As UNDP/ILO consultant, he was active in Zambia, dealing with workers' participation, privatization issues, and corporate governance. For fifteen years he served as the chairman of the Commission for Entrepreneurship of the Dutch Economic Institute for Small and Medium-sized Companies.

Professor Walravens served as Chairman of the Supervisory Board Achmea Insurances, Connexxion, Tauw Infra Consult, and Sneep bv, and as a member of the board of multinational companies as Bull Netherlands, CSM, Rabobank, and Wolters-Kluwer. He is director-owner of "Aan de Oude Delft," Art and Auction Services.

Hidden Champions of Türkiye

Mehmet Yeşilyaprak, Hasan Yazar, and M. Mustafa Erdoğdu

Abstract This study examines Türkiye's Hidden Champions, namely Smart Güneş Enerjisi Teknolojileri Araştırma Geliştirme Üretim Sanayi ve Ticaret Anonim Şirketi and Berkosan Yalıtım ve Tecrit Maddeleri Üretim ve Ticaret A.Ş. The reasons these companies are leaders or potential leaders in their sectors in Türkiye are discussed. Furthermore, several aspects of Hidden Champions were identified, including the quality of their products and the satisfaction of employees and customers. Additionally, the financial and managerial challenges faced by these prominent companies in their sectors were identified, along with the responsibilities of governments and other stakeholders.

Overview

Official name: Republic of Türkiye
Type of government: Presidential Republic
Population in 2023: 85.8 million (World Bank, 2024)
Land area: 769.630 km^2

History

1923 The Republic of Türkiye was established.
1929 The Great Depression.
1948 Marshall Aid was granted to Türkiye.
1950 Anti-statist Democratic Party took over power.
1952 Türkiye joined the North Atlantic Treaty Organization.
1960 Military coup.
1961 The State Planning Organization (SPO) was established and made responsible for the implementation of the five-year development plans.
1971 Military memorandum.

M. Yeşilyaprak (✉) · M. M. Erdoğdu
Beykoz University, Istanbul, Türkiye
e-mail: mehmetyesilyaprak@beykoz.edu.tr; mustafaerdogdu@beykoz.edu.tr

H. Yazar
Manisa Celal Bayar University, Manisa, Türkiye

D. Berberović, D. Purg (eds.), *Hidden Champions in Rising Economies*, Contributions to Management Science,
https://doi.org/10.1007/978-3-032-08263-3_37

1980 A stabilization and structural adjustment program is announced with a radical transformation of economic policies.
1980 Military coup.
1989 The Turkish money became convertible and international capital movements were liberalized.
1991 Economic crisis in Türkiye.
1994 Economic crisis in Türkiye.
1996 A Customs Union agreement with the European Union (EU) was signed.
1997 Post-modern coup.
1999 Economic crisis in Türkiye.
2001 Economic crisis in Türkiye.
2008 The global financial crisis.
2016 July 15 coup attempt.
2017 Türkiye's new presidential system.
2020 COVID-19 Pandemic.

1 Introduction: Context and History

On October 29, 1923, under the leadership of Mustafa Kemal Atatürk, the Republic of Türkiye was proclaimed, marking the official end of the Ottoman Empire and the abolition of the sultanate (Zürcher, 2017). Atatürk's main task was to establish a modern, Western-oriented community on the ruins of the Ottoman Empire. A few years after founding the Republic, serious efforts were made to minimize the influence of religion in all areas of social and political life and impose a positivistic and materialistic worldview. Radical changes were also made in the legal system, education, the form of writing, as well as in headgear and clothing. All of these reforms were sought to enforce a separation of state and religion, with religion being subordinated to the authority of the secular state (Özdalga, 1998).

In the early years of the Republic, a national economic perspective was adopted. Nevertheless, the Lausanne Treaty imposed inherited debts from the Ottoman Empire and trade restrictions, which constrained the economy (Boratav, 2019). Moreover, during this period, there was minimal industrial development in Türkiye and a dearth of a substantial working class (Ahmad, 1993). The İzmir Economic Congress, held shortly after the establishment of the Republic, was a significant event in terms of economic policy. The congress aimed to recover from the dire economic conditions left by the Ottoman Empire and to establish a new economic structure. Among the decisions made at this congress were the provision of credit support to farmers through the Agricultural Bank, the abolition of excessive taxes, and the promotion of agriculture and livestock. During this period, policies that encouraged industrialization and economic growth both internally and externally were pursued (Boratav, 2019; Eğilmez, 2018).

When the Great Depression of 1929 affected Türkiye, the country moved away from liberal policies toward a more statist economic model. The establishment of

Sümerbank in 1933 marked the state's active role in the economy, and the first 5-year industrial plans were implemented. The establishment of the Central Bank and the enactment of the Law for the Protection of the Turkish Currency were part of the state's economic interventions during this period (Durmuş & Aydemír, 2016). Between 1927 and 1935, the national income grew at an average rate of 3.3%, while between 1935 and 1938, it achieved an average growth rate of 6% (Okyar, 1979).

The onset of World War II marked a period of heightened focus on defense expenditures. The economy, which contracted during the war, entered a phase of rapid development following its conclusion. During these years, significant attention was given to infrastructure and transportation alongside agriculture, adopting a relatively free-market economy (Ahmad, 1993). By 1947, Türkiye had become a member of the IMF and the World Bank (Eğilmez, 2018). Two major events occurred immediately after World War II. On the economic front, Türkiye received Marshall Aid in 1948. This increased the availability of economic resources and exposed the country to more liberal ideas. On the political front, with the introduction of democracy and the dissolution of the one-party system, the new anti-state Democratic Party emerged, which ultimately took power from the Republican People's Party in 1950 (Hershlag, 1988). Domestic changes were followed by international developments, and Türkiye joined NATO in 1952 (Okyar, 1979).

From 1960 to 1980, Turkish democracy experienced crises marked by military interventions every 10 years. The military coup against the Menderes regime in May 1960 military coup highlighted the special role of the military as a carrier of the Kemalist principle of "guided democracy." Planning was reintroduced as a guiding principle of economic policy, and the State Planning Organization (SPO) was established and tasked with implementing the five-year development plans. In the meantime, the implementation of import substitution industrialization (ISI) began. The main weakness of the economy during the ISI period was its inability to increase export earnings to cover necessary import bills and its over-reliance on capital goods imports (Kirkpatrick & Öniş, 1991.). However, measured in terms of the growth rate of industrial and total production, the period 1963–1977 was impressive. The average annual growth rate of GNP was 7.0% and the average growth rate of industrial production was 9.0% (Erdoğdu, 2023).

By the 1970s, Türkiye's economy had diverged significantly from the 1930s and 1950s, achieving considerable industrial progress, economic diversification, a decrease in agriculture's share of national income, and substantial urbanization (Kazgan, 2021). However, the oil crises of the 1970s and economic crises in the balance of payments hurt the Turkish economy.

Türkiye began 1980 with triple-digit inflation and a severe balance-of-payments crisis, as well as great political instability (Erdoğdu, 2023). After the failure of two IMF programs, the government announced a stabilization and structural adjustment program on January 24, 1980. This program represented a radical change in economic policy with profound implications for the entire economy. Although the original aim of the program was to solve the twin problems of inflation and balance-of-payments deficit, policymakers also decided to reorient the country's development strategy from a national development strategy to an export-oriented strategy (Aşıkoğlu & Uçtum, 1992).

From 1980 onward, a new period focused on export-oriented economic growth began (Çeçen et al., 1994; Gormez & Yiğit, 2009). The architect of this radical transformation of economic policy, Turgut Özal, opened Turkish markets to foreign competition. Protectionist policies supporting the ISI were gradually abandoned, and government intervention was redirected to help entrepreneurs take risks aimed at exporting their products. During this period, the Turkish economy opened up to global markets, rapidly increasing foreign capital. Following structural changes and reforms, Türkiye experienced relatively high growth rates in GDP. However, by the late 1980s, the performance of private investments did not meet expectations, and the debt burden continuously increased. Similarly, inflation gradually rose, and economic growth performance declined (Kıray, 1990; Selçuk & Ertuğrul, 2001).

The opening of the capital account and the full convertibility of international capital movements in August 1989 had very important consequences. This made interest rates less the subject of direct government policy measures and more the whims of international capital movements (Şenses, 1996). Another important development was that Türkiye signed a Customs Union agreement with the European Union (EU) on January 1, 1996. As a result, tariffs for EU countries were abolished, and all subsidies the state previously provided were gradually eliminated. The 1990s witnessed considerable fluctuations in the Turkish economy. International crises significantly impacted national economies, and the capacity of nation-states to formulate policy was constrained (Yentürk, 2003). The end result was a lost decade for the Turkish economy (Gormez & Yiğit, 2009).

Türkiye entered the twenty-first century with the crises of November 2000 and February 2001 and found itself obliged to implement a new structural reform program, known as the "Transition to a Strong Economy." This program was designed to facilitate the transition from a state of economic fragility to a more resilient economy and received political stability and support from the IMF and the World Bank. In the 2002 elections, the Justice and Development Party (AKP) emerged victorious and proceeded to implement the program.

The AKP adopted a series of reforms aimed at restructuring state-market relations according to the new logic of the post-Washington Consensus. Reforms included large-scale privatizations aimed at reducing the role of the state in the economy, the creation of independent regulatory institutions to consolidate the rule-based market economy, and the independence of the central bank to maintain price stability. Overly generous international liquidity provided funds for a rapid economic recovery in the early 2000s. Together with the EU anchor, the IMF and the World Bank shaped the crisis management process and the post-crisis reform agenda. The AKP government fully embraced the prescriptions of regulatory neoliberalism until 2008–2009 (Öniş & Kutlay, 2021). Until the global financial crisis of 2008, there was continuous growth in GDP and a significant increase in per capita income. Although not as severely affected as the United States and European countries, Türkiye experienced an economic contraction of 4.7% in 2009 (Eğilmez, 2018; Sungur, 2016).

Subsequently, the Turkish political economy gradually shifted away from regulatory neoliberalism to top–down state capitalism, which was based on active participation in the economy through formal and informal mechanisms, such as public–private partnerships and personalized capital accumulation networks through public procurement. The new model of state capitalism is based on widespread privileges granted to powerful business interests closely linked to the hegemonic political party. As a highly opaque mechanism for capital accumulation and wealth creation, public-private partnerships became popular toward the end of the AKP era, totalling US$114 billion between 2009 and 2019 (Öniş & Kutlay, 2021).

In 2010 and 2011, Türkiye's economic growth resumed a significant upward trend, mainly due to expansionary monetary and fiscal policies in the global economy (Susam, 2022). Since 2015, Türkiye's internal and external relations have put significant strain on its economy. In 2015, after a Russian aircraft was shot down for violating Turkish airspace, economic sanctions imposed by Russia resulted in a loss of approximately $12 billion in trade between the two countries. On July 15, 2016, an attempted coup in Türkiye led to a reclassification by credit rating agencies and a decline in foreign direct investment. In 2018, the United States suspended export permits and licenses for Türkiye's Defense Industries Directorate, and the threat of economic sanctions negatively impacted the Turkish economy. Türkiye's GDP in USD terms, which was $864.3 billion in 2015, fell to $761.4 billion in 2019 (Al-Shaghel & Al-Wahaib, 2022).

In 2020, the global outbreak of COVID-19 resulted in millions of deaths and severely disrupted individual well-being and macroeconomic indicators of countries. During the pandemic, Türkiye experienced increased budget deficits, rising public debt, depleted reserves, and spikes in the current account deficit, exchange rates, inflation, and unemployment (Demir & Esen, 2021). Toward the end of 2021, the central bank's policy rate cuts led to the implementation of the so-called "Türkiye Economy Model." This decision was unexpected as inflation was on the rise. When this policy started on September 21, 2021, the USD/TRY exchange rate was 8.75, which rose to 18 TRY by December 20, 2021. The Currency Protected Deposit scheme was introduced to curb the rise in the exchange rate at a high cost. Inflation, on the other hand, continued to rise, reaching 85% by October 2022 (Gerek, 2024). After the parliamentary elections in 2023, the economic administration changed, and the central bank's policy rates increased again.

2 Characteristics of Hidden Champions from Türkiye

Türkiye's Hidden Champions, such as Smart Güneş Enerjisi Teknolojileri Araştırma Geliştirme Üretim Sanayi ve Ticaret A.Ş. and Berkosan Yalıtım ve Tecrit Maddeleri Üretim ve Ticaret A.Ş., exemplify a unique blend of innovation, niche market dominance, and resilience in a dynamic economic environment. Often, small and medium-sized enterprises (SMEs), these companies cater to both domestic and international markets. By focusing on high-quality, eco-friendly products, they lead their respective sectors. They sustain competitive advantages through strategic investments in research and development (R&D). A defining feature of these firms is their ability to build a broad customer base and foster employee loyalty. They expand their market share by adhering to global standards, such as those of the European Union. They also significantly contribute to Turkey's economic diversity and export growth.

A key characteristic of Türkiye's Hidden Champions is their ability to navigate economic and geopolitical challenges, such as currency fluctuations and global supply chain disruptions. These companies anticipate market trends and adapt swiftly to changing conditions. They prioritize technological advancements and green energy solutions, aligning with global sustainability goals and positioning themselves as industry leaders. Often characterized by a family-oriented corporate structure, they are strengthened by the involvement of professional managers. With these qualities, they serve as a model for both national and international SMEs (Exhibit 1).

3 Case Studies of Selected Hidden Champions

3.1 Case Study 1

3.1.1 Smart Güneş Enerjisi Teknolojileri Araştırma Geliştirme Üretim Sanayi ve Ticaret Anonim Şirketi

Overview

Address: Energy Plaza Rüzgarlıbahçe Mah. Feragat Sok. No:2 Kat:6 Beykoz/İstanbul
Tel: +90 (216) 225 72 00
Fax: 0850 225 7209
Email: info@smartsolar.com.tr
Web: www.smartsolar.com.tr

Company Information

Industry: Electricity, gas, steam and air-conditioning supply
Year of Establishment: 2014
Sales Revenues in 2017: N/A
Sales Revenues in 2023: $275 million US
Average number of employees in 2023: +1000
Brainer(s) behind the company: Founder: Halil Demirdağ

Exhibit 1 Core economic indicators for Türkiye

	2019	2020	2021	2022	2023	2024
GDP per capita (current US$)	9215.4	8638.7	9743.2	10,674.5	13,105.66	..
GDP per capita growth (annual %)	–0.6	0.9	10.4	4.5	4.68	..
Long-term unemployment (% of total unemployment)	23.5	25.1	31.2	24.0	9.39	8.45
Foreign direct investment, net inflows (% of GDP)	1.3	1.1	1.6	1.4	0.98	..
GDP (current US$, mio)	761,005,946,788.2	720,338,498,174.7	819,865,253,669.7	907,118,435,952.7	1118252.96	..
Exports of goods and services (current US$, mio)	251,696,740,784.3	209,768,260,359.9	293,050,134,140.7	350,004,410,847.6	356899.78	..
Exports of goods and services (% of GDP)	33.1	29.1	35.7	38.6	31.92	..
Merchandise exports (current US$)	180,833,000,000.0	169,638,000,000.0	225,214,000,000.0	254,192,000,000.0	255,438	..
Merchandise exports to high-income economies (% of total merchandise exports)	64.3	64.0	n/a	n/a	68.6	..
Merchandise exports to developing economies in Europe and Central Asia (% of total merchandise exports)	10.8	11.8	n/a	n/a	9.26	..
Ores and metals exports (% of merchandise exports)	3.7	4.0	5.0	5.2	4.37	4.3
Agricultural raw materials exports (% of merchandise exports)	2.6	2.3	2.6	2.6	0.7	0.64
Food exports (% of merchandise exports)	10.7	12.0	10.9	11.6	11.96	12.28
Fuel exports (% of merchandise exports)	4.5	2.7	3.7	6.3	6.36	6.16
Manufactures exports (% of merchandise exports)	78.2	78.0	77.3	74.2	73.26	73.64
High-technology exports (% of manufactured exports)	3.0	3.2	3.3	3.6	4.52	5.14

Source: (World Bank, 2024)

Nature of Market Leadership

Founded in Istanbul in 2014, Smart Solar Technologies is one of the world's most innovative solar energy technology companies. Smart Solar Technologies operates three manufacturing facilities in Türkiye—Gebze, Dilovası, and Aliağa—and serves hundreds of customers in 20 countries and regions worldwide. By the fourth quarter of 2024, the company expects an annual production capacity of 2.9 GW of solar modules and 2 GW of solar cells. Smart Solar Technologies is certified as a responsible company in the area of human rights in the workplace and employs more than 1000 people. The company has recently entered the solar energy sector with the production of solar cells. While around 20 solar panel manufacturers in Türkiye, none are involved in cell production. China is the world leader in cell production and holds approximately 70% of the global market share in total solar energy system production. Smart Solar Technologies is the second-largest company in this sector in Türkiye. With a corporate structure, the company cooperates with various sectors. The company has established subsidiaries in Ukraine, Germany, Spain, the Netherlands, and Bulgaria to expand its impact through international sales and marketing investment strategies. In 2023, a new company, Smart Solar Technologies AD, was established in Bulgaria. In addition, during the period, Smart Solar Technologies entered into a long-term cooperation agreement with Sumec Energy Holdings Co., Ltd., a state-owned enterprise of the People's Republic of China, to create a joint sales and marketing channel targeting the Balkan countries.

Nature of Competitive Advantage

Founded in 2014, the company completed the installation of Türkiye's first photovoltaic (PV) power plant. In 2016, Smart Solar Technologies entered into a strategic partnership with SUMEC Group, one of the world's leading companies in the solar energy sector, for the production of PV cells. In 2017, the company completed the installation of the world's second-largest CAM–CAM panel PV project. With the investment in its cell manufacturing facility, Smart Solar Technologies has also intensified its research and development (R&D) efforts. It has launched the clean energy transition partnership (CETP) project in collaboration with several major European laboratories and companies, including Fraunhofer and Nines PV.

Core Lessons Learned on the Path to Success

- In the solar energy sector, the technical knowledge and expertise of the human resources in the management of a company are crucial to anticipating future needs.
- The presence of professional teams with expertise in the field, rather than family members, in the management of companies is a fundamental condition for progress in the sector.

- Keeping a close eye on industry developments and making early investment decisions in needed areas is crucial.
- Keeping abreast of technical and financial developments, particularly government incentives, is essential to guide investment and gain a competitive advantage.
- The durability and quality of the products produced in the sector are key factors in maintaining market share.
- Low-quality cheap products can have negative consequences for the company's future.
- The company's main objectives are an innovative outlook and adherence to quality standards at every stage of production.

Management and Leadership Development Needs

The Chairman of the Board, Halil Demirdağ, is a graduate of the Industrial Engineering Department of Boğaziçi University. In April 2009, he invested in solar energy technologies and founded Smart Solar Technologies Renewable Energy Investment Company. As the company's innovative international investments and strategic partnerships gained attention, Demirdağ led the establishment of the group's offices in Türkiye, Bulgaria, Romania, Greece, Germany, Switzerland, and Ukraine. The company aims to become a future leader by creating value through its innovative renewable energy and technology solutions. However, due to the relatively new nature of the sector, there is a significant need for training personnel, particularly technical staff.

Financing and Regulatory Environment Development Needs

Smart Solar Technologies faces several key challenges. The first is financial difficulties, and the second is a shortage of skilled personnel. Prices in the solar energy sector are highly volatile, causing some financial problems. For example, global prices for solar panels have fallen by 40% in the last six months. The company's other financial challenges are specific to Türkiye. Significant collateral is required to secure investment loans in Türkiye. Although Smart Solar Technologies would like to purchase new equipment and expand its investments through loans, the lack of collateral prevents it from taking advantage of financial opportunities. In addition, Türkiye's low credit rating from international rating agencies makes it costly to obtain foreign loans. Finding long-term and relatively inexpensive funding is a challenge.

Furthermore, as the solar energy sector has developed rapidly in recent years, it is difficult to find qualified personnel in this field. The demand for workers in the sector is increasing as the market grows. When new companies enter the sector, they can attract the necessary workers by offering high salaries. However, the relative newness of the solar energy sector means that the production equipment is also new, so workers need to learn how to operate it. In this respect, the support of vocational and technical schools is crucial. These institutions can help fill the gap by training the necessary workforce.

Pandemic's Impact on "Hidden Champions" Business Approach

The COVID-19 pandemic was accompanied by raw material supply difficulties and price increases. Despite all the negative effects of the pandemic, the company achieved growth of around 20% compared to the previous year. In 2020, the company launched the Smart Academy, an educational platform that began development in 2019. However, due to the pandemic, which affected 2020–2021, the company had to suspend the training sessions shortly after the establishment of the Smart Academy.

Meetings with employees were held online, which saved the company time and money. However, as the company continued production, workers had to be physically present in the factories. This situation led to fewer workers being employed and a reduction in production. Throughout the pandemic, production continued due to government regulations.

Effects of the Ukraine War on "Hidden Champions" Business Operations

Smart Solar Technologies had established a solar panel farm in Ukraine in partnership with another company. However, this investment was disrupted by the war. Otherwise, the company was not significantly affected by the war in Ukraine, as most of the equipment and machinery in the sector is generally manufactured in China.

A Nature-Friendly Company Powered by the Sun

Founded in 2014, the company adopted its current trade name, Smart Güneş Enerjisi Teknolojileri Araştırma Geliştirme Üretim Sanayi ve Ticaret Anonim Şirketi, in 2016 and decided to invest in the production of photovoltaic solar panels and started the investment process for a production facility in Gebze. Over the years, the company has strengthened its capital and continued to invest in production lines. At its state-of-the-art automated production lines in Gebze, with an annual capacity of 1200 MW and a closed area of 23,500 m^2, the company produces high-efficiency, high-quality solar panels using multi-busbar, PERC, half-cut cell, and bifacial technologies. In July 2022, the company increased its production capacity with the commissioning of the Dilovası plant, which has an area of 10,000 m^2 and a production capacity of 500 MW. In 2023, the panel production lines of the Aliağa panel and cell production plant were commissioned, bringing the total production capacity to 2900 MW. Smart Solar Technologies, one of Europe's leading integrated solar energy companies in turnkey installation services and PV module production, offers a wide range of solar energy solutions for commercial and residential users. Headquartered in Istanbul, the company has offices and dealerships in Türkiye, the Netherlands, Spain, Germany, and Ukraine, as well as manufacturing facilities in Gebze, Dilovası, and Aliağa.

The Chairman of the Board, Halil Demirdağ, founded Smart Solar Technologies Renewable Energy Investment Company by investing in solar energy technologies. The company's international investments and strategic partnerships have been carried out under the leadership of Halil Demirdağ. Halil Demirdağ's educational background has been particularly effective in tracking industry developments and forecasting future trends. This underlines the importance of having knowledgeable and skilled human resources in the management of a company to be a leader in its sector. As a result of the company's activities and successful operations, its growth and development have been reflected in positive financial results, with turnover and profitability increasing over the years. By the end of 2023, the company's turnover had increased by 104% compared to the previous year, reaching TL 8.1 billion (equivalent to $250 million today).

3.2 Case Study 2

3.2.1 (Berkosan Yalıtım ve Tecrit Maddeleri Üretim ve Ticaret A.Ş.)

Overview
Address: Seba Office Boulevard Ayazaga Mh. Mimarsinan Sk. No:21 K:6 D:41
34485 Sariyer / Istanbul—Türkiye
Tel: +90 212 830 44 55 (Pbx)
Fax: +90 212 830 50 61
Email: www.berkosan.com
Web: https://www.berkosan.com/tr

Company Information
Industry: Construction, Automotive, Fitting, Shoes & Bags, Packaging, Lifestyle
Year of Establishment: 1993
Sales Revenues in 2017: N/A
Sales Revenues in 2023: $19 million USD
Average number of employees in 2023: +250
Brainer(s) behind the company: Founder: Memet Aldıkaçtı

Nature of Market Leadership

Berkosan Yalıtım ve Tecrit Maddeleri Üretim ve Ticaret A.Ş., which was established in Istanbul in 1993, is currently the inaugural company to have its shares offered for sale on the Emerging Companies Market under the Istanbul Stock Exchange, with approximately 300 employees. Following the Emerging Companies Market, Berkosan A.Ş. commenced trading on the Second National Market in 2012. Berkosan develops products in the categories of non-crosslinked polyethylene, polypropylene, and cross-linked polyethylene foam for leading companies in sectors such as automotive, plumbing, construction, packaging, footwear, and bags. It is the first company in Türkiye to start production in these three product lines, which indicates its early steps toward becoming a hidden champion. The company's founder and manager, who has served in public institutions for a considerable time, has established two factories in Tekirdağ Saray and Bilecik.

Berkosan continues to operate its Tekirdağ, Saray factory, which is constructed on 30,000 m^2 of open area and has 7850 m^2 of covered area. The Bilecik, Bozüyük factory, which is situated on 45,000 m^2 of land and has 6500 m^2 of covered area, commenced operations in 2014. Furthermore, in Europe, the company has production facilities in Valencia, Spain, with 2000 m^2 of covered area, and in Nova Pazova, Serbia, with 3500 m^2 of covered area. Additionally, Berkosan has two subsidiaries in Serbia and Italy. Berkosan Yalıtım has a corporate structure and is produced by European Union standards. It is one of the rare companies that predominantly manufactures for the construction sector.

All products manufactured by the company are designed to facilitate the use of green energy. They are not produced outside of European Union standards. The company's main sector is construction, where it produces interior and exterior insulation materials, as well as sound and heat insulation materials for buildings. One notable product, which can be considered a hidden champion product, is a protective material used during the transportation of delicate items to prevent breakage. This product is called Foamex. Foamex is a cross-linked polyethylene foam material with a closed-cell structure, resistant to moisture, odorless, elastic, and free from any harmful chemicals or heavy metals. It does not contain mold, fungi, or bacteria and does not wear or deform over time. Additionally, it offers flexible production options for providing sound and heat insulation comfort in building insulation. The company's production of specialized products has resulted in a high customer base, including corporate firms in Türkiye such as Arçelik, Vestel, and Koleksiyon Mobilya.

A significant proportion of the company's total turnover is derived from exports, with sales to numerous countries worldwide. The business is a family-run enterprise, with family members assuming managerial roles. In addition to the family members, there is a retired judge responsible for legal matters and a board member who has held senior management positions in banks, responsible for financial matters. Approximately 70% of the total loans used by the company are for construction activities. They primarily use loans from Eximbank and do not use foreign currency loans to avoid exchange rate risk. They meticulously record all their activities, paying attention to avoid any off-the-books transactions. The company adheres to the highest standards of financial responsibility, paying its debts to both the public and private sectors on time. Despite its status as an SME, it manufactures according to European Union standards, a rarity in the construction sector.

Nature of Competitive Advantage

Berkosan is one of the rare companies primarily focused on production for the construction sector. It specializes in high-quality thin products for sound and heat insulation rather than thick products, making its offerings highly sought after in the industry. Its products are generally designed to prevent damage to other products and align with the green economy. By strictly adhering to European Union standards, Berkosan ensures high-quality production, giving it a competitive edge over other firms. Additionally, the company finances its operations primarily through Eximbank-backed loans and avoids foreign currency-based loans to shield itself from the volatility of Turkey's economy. This approach reduces financial vulnerability and ensures business continuity.

Core Lessons Learned on the Path to Success

- Ensuring customer satisfaction is of paramount importance for the long-term viability and growth of the company.
- Increasing investments in R&D to develop new products plays a pivotal role in leading the industry.
- A highly educated, conscious, motivated, and dynamic workforce enables the company to meet customer demands most quickly and accurately.
- The company's small and medium-sized enterprise (SME) status fosters a more intimate working environment and increases employee loyalty.
- The selection of senior managers and managerial candidates inside the company serves to maintain the loyalty of employees to the company.

Management and Leadership Development Needs

Berkosan's objective is to enhance the quality of life in the sector it leads. To this end, the company is focused on customer satisfaction, the production of import-substitute products through R&D efforts, the retention of national resources within the country, and the achievement of maximum competitive power in both domestic and international markets. This is to be achieved through the utilization of the most advanced technologies and a robust financial structure. However, as is the case with many sectors of this kind, one of Berkosan's significant needs is skilled technical personnel. The demand for such employees in a company oriented toward innovation and the use of technological equipment and products can be met by emphasizing technical and vocational high schools.

Additionally, the company's biggest challenge is public sourcing. There are some infrastructure issues in the factory buildings located in Tekirdağ Saray and Bilecik. Local administrations present a significant challenge in the areas where the factories are situated. A significant portion of these issues is related to energy and wastewater. Another challenge is the difficulty in recruiting personnel to work in the factories because the cities where the factories are located are small and not densely populated. Moreover, it is very difficult to access a qualified workforce.

Financing and Regulatory Environment Development Needs

The thermal and acoustic insulation sector in which Berkosan operates is open to innovation, and products are generally manufactured for industries such as construction, home appliances, furniture, and electronics. Therefore, new products must be of higher quality and produced according to European standards. It is important to note that environmentally friendly production is a necessity, requiring investments in technology and machinery. However, such investments cannot be made in a short time. Like many production sectors in Türkiye, there is a need for financial resources for investment expenditures. It is unfortunate that, in recent years, financing sources in Türkiye have become very limited and expensive. This is due to the low credit rating of Türkiye, which results in high credit interest rates. To mitigate liquidity risk, the group management maintains sufficient cash and similar resources to meet current and potential obligations, as well as distribute fund sources. When necessary, factoring services are utilized. The group is exposed to interest rate risk due to changes in interest rates from Libor-indexed bank loans. While fixed-rate bank loans do not carry any risk, future bank loans are affected by interest rates. Berkosan Yalıtım's investments progress slowly due to its reluctance to take on exchange rate risk and its desire to avoid high-cost borrowing.

Another pressing need in Berkosan is education, particularly for blue-collar workers. Blue-collar workers are vital for production and are required to operate newly acquired machinery. Without them, it is not possible to transition to sustainable production without the use of technological products, and carbon footprint targets cannot be met. Therefore, blue-collar workers must be trained with new products and devices. Türkiye's fundamental problem in education is the low demand for vocational high schools and technical schools. Technical schools are of great importance in the training of mid-level skilled workers. These employees are of great value to companies, as they are the driving force behind the production process. Without the input of technical workers, many companies would be unable to carry out production.

Pandemic's Impact on "Hidden Champions" Business Approach

It is beyond dispute that the global pandemic, which began in 2020 and continued into 2021, had a profound impact on Türkiye. As with the rest of the world, the pandemic placed significant demands on the logistics sector, resulting in challenges in the timely supply of raw materials. Furthermore, there were upward trends in production and labor costs. White-collar workers were able to work remotely, without having to attend the office, which provided both time and cost advantages to the company. The pandemic also accelerated the transition to a digital signature system within the company, facilitating the movement of documents in electronic format and minimizing time loss. Blue-collar workers were physically present in the factory to ensure that production continued. However, production was carried out with an eye to social distancing.

Effects of the Ukraine War on "Hidden Champions" Business Operations

Berkosan Yalıtım does not export to Ukraine. In general, exports are made to European Union countries such as Sweden, Finland, Germany, and the United Kingdom. The conflict in Ukraine has hardly hurt the company.

Center for Sustainable Insulation and Packaging Solutions for Human Life

Berkosan Insulation and Isolation Materials Production and Trading Inc. is the first company to offer shares on the Emerging Enterprises Market (EEM) of the Istanbul Stock Exchange (ISE) and currently employs around 300 people. The company's product range encompasses six distinct brands, with products developed in the categories of straight-linked polyethylene, polypropylene, and cross-linked polyethylene foam for leading organizations in sectors including automotive, plumbing, construction, packaging, footwear, and bags. Berkosan is the first Turkish company to commence production in these three product categories. Berkosan continues its production with its Tekirdağ, Saray factory, which is built on 30,000 m^2 of open space with 7850 m^2 of closed area.

Additionally, the company has established a second factory in Bilecik, Bozüyük, which commenced operations in 2014. This factory is built on 45,000 m^2 of land with 6500 m^2 of closed area. Furthermore, production occurs in Valencia, Spain, with 2000 m^2 of closed area, and Nova Pazova, Serbia, with 3500 m^2 of closed area in Europe. As of the end of 2023, Berkosan Yalıtım's total equity amounts to 383,848,060 TL (approximately 12 million $ at today's value).

The products of Berkosan are in high demand in infrastructure projects abroad. Furthermore, Berkosan is typically selected for the protective materials utilized during the transportation of products. The products are preferred due to their high performance in terms of material quality and insulation. Berkosan Insulation places a premium on quality production, eschewing marketing policies in favor of a focus on the production of quality, green, and sustainable products. As the company achieves these goals, it increases its customer potential abroad and is rewarded domestically for its economic contributions. In the 2014 SME and Entrepreneurship Awards Ceremony, which was held on a national scale and organized by the Small and Medium Enterprises Development and Support Administration of the Republic of Türkiye (KOSGEB), Berkosan Insulation and Isolation Materials Production and Trading Inc. was presented with a Success Certificate in recognition of its success in reaching the final in the category of "SUCCESSFUL SME OF THE YEAR AWARD." In the 2015 fourth SME and Entrepreneurship Awards Ceremony, the company once again received the "SUCCESSFUL SME OF THE YEAR AWARD."

4 Conclusions and Recommendations

Upon closer examination, it becomes evident that Hidden Champions possess a set of distinctive characteristics that set them apart from other companies in their respective industries. The technical knowledge and expertise of the human resources involved in the management of a company are of paramount importance to Hidden Champions when predicting future needs in their sector. It is of critical value for Hidden Champions to maintain a close watch on industry developments and to make early investment decisions in areas where there is a need. It is of critical importance to monitor technical and financial developments in the sector, especially government incentives, to determine the direction of investments and ensure a competitive advantage. The durability and quality of products produced in the sector are of paramount importance for improving market share. Low-quality cheap products can create adversity for the company in the future. Ensuring customer satisfaction is essential for the company's continuity and growth. Increasing investments in R&D plays a critical role in product development and leading the industry. The selection of top executives and managerial candidates from within the company helps to maintain employee loyalty. The company's main objectives include maintaining an innovative perspective and working according to high-quality standards at every stage of production.

Hidden Champions have identifiable development needs. One such company, especially if it operates in a relatively new sector, may encounter difficulties in training personnel. There is a high demand for technical expertise, and companies that closely monitor technological advancements require qualified personnel. Therefore, certain responsibilities fall upon educational institutions in Türkiye. In particular, the activation of technical and vocational high schools, the provision of incentives to encourage their activity, and the enhancement of the quality of education will contribute to the satisfaction of the sector's needs while effectively managing employment in the country's economy. Reforms in these high schools and universities will facilitate early employment. Furthermore, the establishment of a continuous interaction between Hidden Champions and researchers in higher education institutions will enhance the company's competitiveness and help resolve existing issues.

After the global financial crisis of 2008, Türkiye was one of the countries that experienced relatively positive economic progress. However, the country has experienced a continued increase in economic difficulties from 2016 onward, which can be attributed to several factors. One of the main reasons for this is the evaluations made by credit rating agencies regarding Türkiye. These events made it difficult for Hidden Champions to find long-term and relatively cheap credit. At the same time, they damaged the country's economic stability. The financial difficulties experienced by these companies, which make significant contributions to national economies, have a detrimental impact on their competitiveness in the sector and hinder their investments. Consequently, governments can implement policies to support these companies. In particular, those that export a certain percentage and have a domestic production rate above a certain level can be financially relieved through tax incentive systems. Furthermore, their development can be supported by providing project-based cheap loans through public banks. Nevertheless, it is of paramount importance to ensure that the process of loan provision is as expedient as possible. Otherwise, if financing cannot be accessed promptly, the intended investment may not materialize. Consequently, even if Hidden Champions are unable to obtain the foreign loans they require, their tax costs will decrease, and they will be able to expand their investments by accessing domestic loans.

Another challenge faced by Hidden Champions is the insufficient infrastructure support from local governments and the lack of an adequate workforce in the region. In this regard, local governments have significant responsibilities. These factories can make the local municipalities attractive and draw people to the region. The infrastructure support provided by local governments to Hidden Champions is critical for long-term success.

References

Ahmad, F. (1993). *The Making of Modern Turkey*. Routledge.

Al-Shaghel, H., & Al-Wahaib, M. (2022, August 3). *Türkiye'de Son 5 Yılda Yaşanan Gelişmeler | EKONOMİ 2015–2020*. Anadolu Yakın Doğu Araştırmaları Merkezi. https://ayam.com.tr/arastirma/turkiyede-son-5-yilda-yasanan-gelismeler-ekonomi-2015-2020/

Aşıkoğlu, Y., & Uçtum, M. (1992). A critical evaluation of exchange rate policy in Turkey. *World Development, 20*(10), 1501–1514.

Boratav, K. (2019). *Türkiye İktisat Tarihi 1908–2015*. İmge Kitabevi Yayınları.

Çeçen, A. A., Doğruel, A. S., & Doğruel, F. (1994). Economic growth and structural change in Turkey 1960–88. *International Journal of Middle East Studies, 26*(1), 37–56. https://doi.org/10.1017/S0020743800059754

Demir, O., & Esen, A. (2021). Covid 19'un Yıkıcı Ekonomik Etkileri ve Türkiye Ekonomisinde Dönüşüm İhtiyacı. *JOEEP: Journal of Emerging Economies and Policy, 6*(1), 88.

Durmuş, S., & Aydemir, N. K. (2016). Atatürk Dönemi Türkiye Ekonomisi (1923—1938). *Kafkas University, Journal of Economics & Administrative Sciences Faculty / Kafkas Üniversitesi Iktisadi ve Idari Bilimler Fakültesi Dergisi, 7*(12), 155–167. https://doi.org/10.9775/kauiibfd.2016.008

Eğilmez, M. (2018). *Değişim Sürecinde Türkiye Osmanlı'dan Cumhuriyet'e Sosyo-Ekonomik Bir Değerlendirme*. Remzi Kitabevi.

Erdoğdu, M. M. (2023). Divergent developmental performance of Turkey and South Korea: An appraisal from political economy perspective. *Turkish Studies, 24*, 1. https://doi.org/10.1080/14683849.2023.2210765

Gerek, Ö. A. (2024, April 22). *Türkiye Ekonomi Modeli ve Enflasyon Sorunu*. Özgürlük Araştırmaları Derneği. https://oad.org.tr/yayinlar/analiz/turkiye-ekonomi-modeli-ve-enflasyon-sorunu/

Gormez, Y., & Yiğit, S. (2009, March 1). *The economic and financial stability in Turkey: A historical perspective*. https://www.semanticscholar.org/paper/The-economic-and-financial-stability-in-Turkey%3A-a-Gormez-Yi%CC%87%C4%9Fi%CC%87t/d18cfdcf08d7869fb1a3eb2186c9b91de82ba854

Hershlag, Z. Y. (1988). *The contemporary Turkish economy*. Routledge.

Kazgan, G. (2021). *Türkiye Ekonomisinde Krizler (1929–2009) Ekonomi Politik Açısından Bir İrdeleme*. İstanbul Bilgi Üniversitesi.

Kıray, E. (1990). Turkish debt and conditionality. In T. Aricanli & D. Rodrik (Eds.), *Historical perspective: A comparison of the 1980s with the 1860s* (pp. 254–268). Palgrave Macmillan. https://doi.org/10.1007/978-1-349-11274-6_12

Kirkpatrick, C., & Öniş, Z. (1991). Turkey. In P. Mosley, J. Harrigan, & J. Toye (Eds.), *Aid and power: The world bank & policy-based lending* (Vol. 2, pp. 1–29). Routledge.

Okyar, O. (1979). Development background of the Turkish economy, 1923–1973. *International Journal of Middle East Studies, 10*(3), 325–344.

Öniş, Z., & Kutlay, M. (2021). The anatomy of Turkey's new heterodox crisis: The interplay of domestic politics and global dynamics. *Turkish Studies, 22*(4), 499–529.

Özdalga, E. (1998). *The veiling issue, official secularism and popular Islam in modern Turkey*. Curzon Press.

Selçuk, F., & Ertuğrul, A. (2001). A brief account of the Turkish economy: 1980–2000. *Macroeconomics eJournal, 37*, 6. https://www.semanticscholar.org/paper/A-Brief-Account-of-the-Turkish-Economy%3A-1980-2000-Sel%C3%A7uk-Ertu%C4%9Frul/f0218e8142c9286dd529ff47872d09f83e87dd4a

Şenses, F. (1996). *Structural adjustment policies and employment in Turkey*. ERC Working Paper, No. 96/01, METU Economic Research Center (Ankara).

Sungur, O. (2016). 2000 Sonrası Türkiye Ekonomisi: Büyüme, Enflasyon, İşsizlik, Borçlanma ve Dış Ticarette Gelişmeler. *Toplum ve Demokrasi Dergisi, 9*(19), 243.

Susam, N. (2022). *Türkiye Ekonomisi ve Maliyesi (1923–2023)*. Beta Basım Yayım.

World Bank. (2024). *The world bank in Türkiye*. World Bank. https://www.worldbank.org/en/country/turkey/overview

Yentürk, N. (2003). *Körlerin yürüyüşü: Türkiye ekonomisi ve 1990 sonrası krizler* (Vol. 1). İstanbul Bilgi Üniversitesi Yayınları. https://www.academia.edu/download/92719126/ECOBARCE244.pdf

Zürcher, E. J. (2017). *Turkey: A modern history*. I. B. Tauris.

Mehmet Yeşilyaprak was born in Manisa, Turkey in 1967. He graduated from the Finance Department of Dokuz Eylül University in 1988. He completed his Master's degree at the Banking Department of Marmara University Banking and Insurance Institute in 1999 and his PhD in the same institute in 2011. He started his professional career at Faisal Finance Institution in 1991 and worked at Ihlas Finance Institution between 1995 and 2001. He served as the finance and accounting manager in the real sector in 2001. Starting from 2002, he worked as a Manager in General Management units and branches at Family Finance and Türkiye Finans Participation Bank. In 2013, he received foreign language education at Indiana University in the USA. Upon his return, he started working as the Head of Insurance and Guarantee Transactions Department at Turkish Eximbank at the end of the same year. He held various positions in this bank between 2013 and 2020. In addition to these positions, he has been working as a part-time Lecturer at Marmara University since 2016. He received the title of Associate Professor in 2020. Since 2021, he has been working as an Associate Professor in the Department of Business Administration at Beykoz University Faculty of Business and Management Sciences. He is a Certified Public Accountant and Independent Auditor, a member of Istanbul Chamber of Certified Public Accountants, and speaks English. He is married and has two children, a son and a daughter.

Hasan Yazar was born in Istanbul in 1993 and completed his pre-university education in the same city. In 2015, he graduated from the Department of Public Finance at Marmara University's Faculty of Economics. In 2020, he completed his master's degree in the Public Finance Theory program at Marmara University's Institute of Social Sciences. His master's thesis examined the impact of the public sector's economic size on rent-seeking behavior. He is currently pursuing a PhD in the same program at Marmara University's Institute of Social Sciences. His doctoral dissertation focuses on the role and importance of public financial instruments in the green economy. Additionally, he has studies in the fields of sustainable development, green economy, and public finance. Since 2018, he has been working as a Research Assistant in the Department of Public Finance at the Faculty of Economics and Administrative Sciences, Salihli, Manisa Celal Bayar University.

M. Mustafa Erdoğdu is a Professor of International Trade and Finance at the Faculty of Business and Administrative Sciences, Beykoz University in Istanbul, Turkey. He earned his PhD in Development Economics and MA in Development Studies from the University of Manchester, following earlier degrees in Economics and Public Finance from Marmara University. With over three decades of academic experience, Erdoğdu has held professorial and leadership roles at Marmara University before joining Beykoz University, where he also served as Dean between 2023 and 2024. His scholarly contributions include one authored book, the editorship of 14 volumes, and over 50 articles and book chapters in national and international publications. He is the Co-Chair of the International Conference of Political Economy (ICOPEC), Associate Editor of the International Journal of Applied Behavioral Economics. He serves on the editorial and advisory boards of several journals, including the Turkish Studies Journal. Erdoğdu's research interests span a wide range, including economic development, sustainable industrial policy, technological change, renewable energy, behavioral public finance, financial crises, and refugee integration. His recent work explores dual-use defense investments, the developmental role of the state, and the transition toward green and circular economies. He has supervised multiple doctoral and master's theses and regularly speaks at international conferences. His interdisciplinary approach combines critical political economy with policy-relevant analysis, aiming to bridge academic rigor and real-world impact. ORCID ID: 0000-0003-4541-6686

Hidden Champions of Ukraine

Olexandr Kalinin, Oksana Sedashova, Tetyana Kravchenko, and Lyudmila Kosovych

Abstract This study investigates the emergence and characteristics of "hidden champions" in Ukraine amidst a complex socio-economic landscape. The research uses a comprehensive PESTEL analysis to explore the political, economic, social, technological, environmental, and legal factors influencing the Ukrainian business environment. Historical context reveals a nation grappling with ongoing conflict, political instability, and economic challenges, yet demonstrating resilience and adaptability through significant reforms and European integration efforts.

The focal point of this study is the Building Guild of Ukraine LLC, a leading supplier of construction materials that exemplifies the attributes of a hidden champion. Critical criteria for evaluating such companies include resilience, adaptability, market leadership, innovation, competitive advantage, and sustainability. Building Guild of Ukraine LLC has achieved notable success by closely monitoring market trends, emphasizing customer orientation, and maintaining high service standards.

Their strategic approach involves diversifying product offerings, enhancing logistics efficiency, and leveraging a robust network of partners. The company's commitment to continuous improvement through education and training in new building materials and technologies further cements its market position. Despite the challenges posed by the ongoing Russian aggression and economic instability, Ukraine's skilled workforce and rich natural resources present significant potential for economic growth.

The findings underscore the importance of sustained investment in innovation, digital transformation, and legal reforms to foster an environment conducive to the growth of hidden champions. This study contributes to the understanding of how businesses in volatile environments can achieve competitive success and provides a framework for identifying and nurturing potential hidden champions in Ukraine and similar contexts.

O. Kalinin
Management and Innovation Development of KROK Business School, Kyiv, Ukraine
e-mail: AlexKV@krok.edu.ua

O. Sedashova (✉) · T. Kravchenko · L. Kosovych
KROK Business School, Kyiv, Ukraine
e-mail: SedashovaOA@krok.edu.ua; tetyanakt@krok.edu.ua; kosovychl@krok.edu.ua

D. Berberović, D. Purg (eds.), *Hidden Champions in Rising Economies*, Contributions to Management Science,
https://doi.org/10.1007/978-3-032-08263-3_38

Overview

Official name: Ukraine
Type of government: Unitary parliamentary–presidential republic
Population in 2023: 36,700,000
Land area (in sq. km): 603,628

History

Ninth century	The formation of Kyivan Rus', a federation of Slavic tribes under the rule of the Varangians, marks the beginning of Ukrainian history. Kyiv has become the center of this powerful state.
988	Grand Prince Vladimir (Volodymyr) of Kyiv converts to Christianity and baptizes the Kyivan Rus, aligning it with the Byzantine Orthodox tradition.
1240	The Mongol invasion destroyed Kyiv, and Kyivan Rus fragmented into smaller states.
Fourteenth century	Much of Ukraine comes under the control of the Grand Duchy of Lithuania and later the Polish–Lithuanian Commonwealth.
1648–1657	The Khmelnytsky uprising, led by Bohdan Khmelnytsky, establishes a Cossack Hetmanate in central Ukraine and fights for autonomy from Polish rule.
1654	The treaty of Pereyaslav brings the Cossack Hetmanate under the suzerainty of the Russian Tsar, though with considerable autonomy.
1772–1795	Partitions of Poland brought western Ukrainian lands under Habsburg rule (Austrian Empire), while central and eastern Ukraine came fully under Russian control.
1840s	The rise of a Ukrainian national movement, with the publication of works by national poet Taras Shevchenko.
1917–1921	Ukraine briefly declared independence after the Russian Revolution, leading to the Ukrainian War of Independence. However, by 1921, the Ukrainian Soviet Socialist Republic was established and became part of the Soviet Union.
1932–1933	The Holodomor, a man-made famine, causes the deaths of millions of Ukrainians due to policies implemented by Joseph Stalin's regime.
1941–1944	Ukraine is occupied by Nazi Germany during World War II, suffering significant devastation and loss of life.
1945	Postwar borders are established, with Ukraine being a founding member of the United Nations as part of the USSR.
1991	Ukraine declared independence from the Soviet Union on August 24, following a failed coup in Moscow. A national referendum on December 1 confirmed this.
2004	The orange revolution, a series of protests and political events, led to the annulment of a rigged presidential election and the eventual election of Viktor Yushchenko.

2014	The Euromaidan protests led to the ousting of President Viktor Yanukovych. Russia annexes Crimea, and conflict erupts in Eastern Ukraine, leading to the ongoing war in the Donbas region.
2019	Volodymyr Zelenskyy is elected president in a landslide victory.
2022	Russia launches a full-scale invasion of Ukraine on February 24, leading to widespread international condemnation and significant military and civilian casualties. The war results in severe humanitarian crises and impacts global geopolitics.

1 Introduction: Context and History

During its 30 years of independence, Ukraine has faced numerous economic challenges, exacerbated by political instability and social upheaval. The Revolution of Dignity in 2013 and the subsequent conflict in eastern Ukraine significantly impacted the nation's economy. Ukraine has shown resilience and adaptability despite these challenges, implementing several crucial reforms since 2014. These reforms include energy tariff adjustments, social service improvements, business deregulation, fiscal consolidation, and banking sector stabilization. The Deep and Comprehensive Free Trade Area (DCFTA) with the European Union, effective since January 1, 2016, has also provided a framework for integrating Ukraine's economy with European markets.

The country boasts a skilled workforce, a growing IT sector, and rich natural resources. However, its path to economic prosperity could be more straightforward. This chapter explores the key PESTEL (political, economic, social, technological, environmental, and legal) factors shaping the Ukrainian business environment and their potential impact on the emergence of Hidden Champions.

The ongoing conflict in eastern Ukraine casts a long shadow over the nation's economic prospects. Infrastructure damage, population displacement, and political instability disrupt business activity and deter foreign investment. The World Bank estimates that the war has caused $70 billion in infrastructure losses alone (The World Bank, 2023). Transparency International ranks Ukraine 122nd out of 180 on its Corruption Perception Index, highlighting ongoing challenges in this area (Transparency International, 2022).

The country's association agreement with the European Union offers a path toward closer economic integration and access to new markets. This agreement has led to a 23% increase in trade between Ukraine and the EU since 2016 (Food and Agriculture Organization of the United Nations, 2022). Efforts to combat corruption, though slow, indicate a commitment to reform.

The World Bank estimates that Ukraine's GDP shrunk 30% in 2022 (Food and Agriculture Organization of the United Nations, 2022). The country's heavy reliance on commodity exports like steel and agriculture makes it vulnerable to price fluctuations. For instance, the war has disrupted global food supply chains, pushing wheat prices up by 20% in 2022 (DOU, 2023).

Despite these challenges, Ukraine possesses significant economic potential. The country boasts a large and skilled workforce, particularly in the IT and technology sectors. A report by DOU, a leading Ukrainian IT recruitment platform, found that Ukraine has over 200,000 IT professionals (United Nations Office for the Coordination of Humanitarian Affairs, 2023). However, the conflict has led to brain drain, with skilled workers seeking opportunities abroad.

The social fabric of the nation has been strained by the conflict, with displacement and poverty becoming stark realities for many. The UN estimates that over 14 million Ukrainians require humanitarian assistance (DOU, 2023).

However, this crisis has also fostered a strong sense of national unity and a determination to rebuild. The country has a growing middle class with a rising demand for skilled labor. This is particularly evident in the IT sector, where wages have grown by 15% annually in recent years (Organization for Economic Co-operation and Development (OECD), 2022).

An aging population presents a long-term challenge. Ukraine's birth rate is well below replacement levels, and the conflict has exacerbated this trend. This could lead to labor shortages in the future, making it crucial to invest in education and training programs to equip the workforce with the skills needed for a knowledge-based economy.

Technologically, Ukraine strives to modernize its industrial base and embrace digital transformation. The country's technology sector, particularly IT and software development, has shown robust growth and international competitiveness. However, widespread technological advancements across other industries still need to be improved, hindered by outdated infrastructure and limited investment. Efforts to modernize Ukraine's technological landscape include fostering innovation hubs, improving digital literacy, and attracting foreign tech investments. Ukraine has a flourishing IT sector with a growing pool of IT talent. This sector has the potential to be a significant driver of economic growth. Lviv, a major IT hub in western Ukraine, is home to numerous startups and IT outsourcing companies.

However, investment in research and development (R&D) still needs to be improved. Ukraine spends only 1.2% of its GDP on R&D, compared to an average of 3.2% among OECD countries (The Ministry of Energy of Ukraine, 2020). This lack of investment can hinder technological innovation and make it difficult for Ukrainian companies to compete globally.

Digitalization offers a significant opportunity for Ukraine. The government has launched initiatives to promote e-governance and digital literacy. Increasing Internet penetration rates and broader adoption of digital technologies can improve efficiency across various sectors, from agriculture to healthcare.

Environmental considerations are becoming increasingly important in Ukraine's business and economic strategies. The country faces significant environmental challenges, including pollution and inefficient energy use. Reforms in energy tariffs and moves toward renewable energy sources are part of the broader strategy to improve environmental sustainability. Additionally, aligning with EU environmental standards as part of the DCFTA has prompted Ukraine to adopt more rigorous environmental regulations and practices. Ukraine has rich natural resources, including fertile land and abundant mineral deposits. However, environmental pollution remains a serious concern. Heavy industry and outdated infrastructure contribute to air and water pollution. The war has also caused environmental damage, with shelling and bomb blasts contaminating soil and water resources.

There is a growing awareness of the need for sustainable development. The Ukrainian government has set a target of generating 25% of its electricity from renewable sources by 2035 (The World Bank, 2019). Investment in clean technologies and green infrastructure can help Ukraine address its environmental challenges and create new economic opportunities.

The Ukrainian legal system is currently undergoing reform, focusing on improving transparency and attracting investment. The country has made progress in streamlining business registration processes and strengthening protection for intellectual property rights. However, these reforms are ongoing, and the legal system remains complex. The ongoing conflict further complicates the legal landscape. Businesses operating in Ukraine face uncertainties due to the war and its impact on regulations and enforcement mechanisms.

Ukraine's path toward economic prosperity is fraught with challenges. The ongoing conflict casts a long shadow, but the country also possesses significant potential. A skilled workforce, a growing IT sector, and rich natural resources provide a solid foundation for growth. Navigating the complex PESTEL landscape will be crucial for Ukraine's success. By addressing political instability, fostering economic diversification, investing in its people and technology, and embracing sustainable practices, Ukraine can create an environment where Hidden Champions can emerge and thrive.

2 Characteristics of Hidden Champions from Ukraine

Evaluating hidden champions among Ukrainian companies involves several critical criteria, each reflecting business strength and potential. Here's a detailed description of each criterion:

2.1 Resilience

Resilience refers to the ability of a company to endure and recover from challenges such as economic downturns, political instability, and other disruptions. Resilient companies often demonstrate the following:

Financial Stability: Maintaining solid financial health through prudent management of resources, diversification of income streams, and effective cost control.

2.2 *Crisis Management*

Crisis management is the implementation of robust risk management strategies and contingency plans to navigate crises efficiently.

Operational Continuity: Ensuring operations can continue without significant interruptions through flexible supply chains and robust IT infrastructure.

2.3 *Adaptability*

Adaptability is the ability to adjust quickly to changing market conditions, customer preferences, and technological advancements. This involves:

Agility: The ability to swiftly pivot or shift business models, product lines, or strategies in response to market changes.

Learning Culture: Promoting continuous employee learning and development to stay updated with industry trends and skills.

Innovative Practices: Adopting new technologies and processes to stay competitive and meet evolving market demands.

2.4 *Market Leadership*

Market leadership signifies a company's dominant position within its niche or industry. Key aspects include:

Market Share: Holding a significant portion of the market compared to competitors.

Brand Recognition: Achieving high levels of recognition and reputation among consumers and industry peers.

Influence: Setting industry standards, influencing market trends, and having a solid voice in industry-related discussions.

2.5 *Innovation*

Innovation involves developing and implementing new ideas, products, or processes that provide a competitive edge. It is characterized by:

R&D Investment: Committing resources to research and development to foster innovation.

New Products/Services: Continuously launching new or improved products and services that meet customer needs better than existing options.
Technological Advancement: Leveraging cutting-edge technologies to enhance product offerings and operational efficiencies.

2.6 Competitive Advantage

Competitive Advantage is the unique advantage that allows a company to outperform its competitors. This includes:

Unique Selling Proposition (USP): Offering distinctive features or benefits that are not available from competitors.
Cost Leadership: Achieving lower operational costs, enabling competitive pricing while maintaining profitability.

2.7 Sustainability

Sustainability is the company's commitment to environmental, social, and governance (ESG) principles. This involves:

Environmental Impact: Implementing practices that reduce the company's carbon footprint, such as using renewable energy sources and reducing waste.
Social Responsibility: Social responsibility is engaging in activities that benefit society, such as community development programs, fair labor practices, and employee welfare initiatives.
Good governance: Good governance ensures transparency, ethical practices, and accountability in business operations.

These criteria together provide a comprehensive framework to identify hidden champions — companies that excel not only in their financial performance but also in their contributions to innovation, market leadership, and sustainable practices (Exhibit 1).

Ukrainian Hidden Champion is reviewed in this chapter.

Building Guild of Ukraine LLC is a leading comprehensive supplier of goods for housing construction, repair, and furnishing. The company provides various building materials, such as insulation, facade plaster, dry mixes, plasterboard systems, suspended ceilings, paint for interior and exterior work, waterproofing, and additional finishing materials. The company is known for helping with selecting, purchasing, and supplying building materials for construction sites.

Exhibit 1 Core Economic Indicators for Ukraine

Indicators	2017	2018	2019	2020	2021	2022	2023
GDP per capita (current US$)	2638.2	3096.5	3661.4	3751.6	4827.7	4534.1	3820.8
GDP per capita growth (annual %)	2.4	3.5	3.2	−3.8	3.4	−29.1	
Long-term unemployment (% of total unemployment)	9.5	8.8	8.2	9.5	9.8		
Foreign direct investment, net inflows (% of GDP)	3.3	3.8	3.8	0.2	4	0.2	
GDP (current US$, mio)	112.09	130.89	153.88	156.62	199.77	160.5	150.6
Exports of goods and services (current US$, mio)	53.94	59.21	63.45	60.8	81.28	56.91	
Exports of goods and services (% of GDP)	48.1	45.2	41.2	38.8	40.7	35.5	
Merchandise exports (current US$)	43.27	47.34	50.05	49.19	68.07	44.38	
Merchandise exports to high-income economies (% of total merchandise exports)	47.9	50.1	49.2	45.1			
Merchandise exports to developing economies in Europe and Central Asia (% of total merchandise exports)	24.5	22.7	21.3	19.4			
Ores and metals exports (% of merchandise exports)	9.4	9.4	9.6	11.1	13.3	8.1	
Agricultural raw materials exports (% of merchandise exports)	2	2	2	2	2	2	
Food exports (% of merchandise exports)	41	39	44	45	40	53	
Fuel exports (% of merchandise exports)	2	2	2	1	1	2	
Manufactures exports (% of merchandise exports)	45	47	43	43	41	35	
High-technology exports (% of manufactured exports)	6	5	5	6	5	6	

Source: World Bank, May 2024

3 Case Study of Selected Hidden Champion

3.1 *Case Study*

3.1.1 Building Guild of Ukraine LLC

Overview

Address: Kyiv, str. Saperno-Slobidska 57
Tel: +38 (044) 494 22 68
+38 (067) 408 51 55
Email: office@budgild.com.ua
Web: https://budgild.com.ua/

Company Information
Industry: Trade in construction materials
Year of establishment: 2007
Sales Revenues in 2017: EUR 8 205 228,61
Sales Revenue in 2023: EUR 20 293 557,75
Average number of employees in 2017: 67
Brainer(s) behind the company: CEO Polina Ovcharova

Nature of Market Leadership

To gain and maintain a leading position in the building materials market, Building Guild of Ukraine LLC constantly monitors market trends and quickly responds to trends, adapting to changes in consumer preferences. For this, a project team was created that regularly researched trends and demand in the building materials market and construction methods, architecture, renovation, and design methods. The management team analyzes customer requests and suggests changes in product range and customer service. This customer orientation allows us to provide the highest-class service and to distinguish the company in the construction materials supply market. Building Guild of Ukraine makes every effort to ensure the highest level of quality customer service because all managers undergo regular training, as well as due to the introduction of innovative electronic technologies for processing orders and their payment. The transition to electronic document management not only contributes to the achievement of the SDGs and the development of the "green economy" but also significantly speeds up the processing of orders, providing customers with an unparalleled experience of interaction with the company, which promotes loyalty and returning customers to create new orders.

Building Guild of Ukraine LLC has created a reliable network of partners who produce and supply high-quality construction products and are, in turn, market leaders. This allows us to provide customers with the best quality. For this purpose, quality managers check the availability of quality certificates and monitor the quality of products entering the warehouse. The company's employees know exactly how this or that product is produced because visiting the manufacturers' factories is a good tradition when creating partnerships and organizing business interactions.

Warehouse logistics of Building Guild of Ukraine LLC is organized at the highest level, which ensures the quality of storage of products in warehouses from the moment they enter the warehouse and are shipped to the end consumer.

Nature of the Competitive Advantage

1. Customer orientation. The main goal and main principle in work is customer satisfaction. Customer care is the main competitive advantage that ensures impeccable service. The company knows how to get discounts from manufacturers and suppliers and offers customers the best prices for the highest quality

products. The company's management is characterized by empathy, which is aimed at understanding the needs of each client. Clients have a personal manager who always reminds them about related products and offers more profitable analogs. There is a system of discounts for regular customers.
2. Trend Watching. Building Guild of Ukraine LLC regularly researches market trends and keeps its finger on the pulse, monitoring changes in production and supply of goods. Regular competitive analysis allows you to control the cost of the order.
3. Transportation Swiftness. Thanks to its fleet, Building Guild of Ukraine LLC offers additional savings on transport in Kyiv and the Kyiv region. They also have agreements with various market-leading logistics companies for fast and safe delivery of orders across Ukraine.

Core Lessons Learned on the Path to Success

Building Guild of Ukraine LLC has achieved considerable success in the building materials market in Ukraine for 16 years. Thanks to an extensive range of products, an established supply system, and a high level of service, the company has become a reliable partner for many construction projects. Many life lessons have been learned on the path to success; here are the main ones.

1. A wide range of products is critical to meeting the needs of various customers and increasing market share.
2. Coverage of a broad geographic market ensures stable risk and allows the reduction of the risks associated with economic fluctuations in individual regions.
3. Well-established supply processes and efficient logistics are critical to meeting customer needs promptly and building long-term relationships.
4. A high level of service, including the availability of goods in warehouses and fast delivery, is a place to retain customers and increase their loyalty.
5. Continuous development and expansion are necessary to maintain the competitiveness and growth of the company.

The key to the success of the Building Guild of Ukraine LLC is a steady effort to adapt to market conditions.

Management and Leadership Development Needs

The company must regularly update its knowledge about building materials to develop management and leadership. Therefore, together with partners, the Building Guild of Ukraine constantly conducts education and training at enterprises with visits to production. The need for such measures increases yearly because new materials, production, and construction technologies are available.

Beyond technical knowledge, education should focus on fostering strategic foresight, agile decision-making, and the ability to lead change, allowing these companies to thrive in a constantly evolving industry.

Education initiatives should move beyond general management principles and focus on areas like technology integration leadership, sustainable innovation management, and supply chain resilience. Leaders need to be empowered to navigate the complexities of adopting new materials and technologies, driving efficiency, and fostering a culture of continuous improvement within their organizations.

The future of the Hidden Champions program requires a dynamic approach to management and leadership education, built on collaborative learning and strong industry partnerships. Educational programs should facilitate knowledge sharing, mentorship, and practical experience through initiatives like industry visits and collaborative projects. This will enable leaders to stay abreast of the latest advancements, build strong networks, and develop the strategic vision necessary to lead their companies into the future. The program must leverage partnerships, like those with the Building Guild of Ukraine, to ensure that the educational content remains relevant and cutting-edge.

For the Hidden Champions program to remain effective, future management and leadership education must emphasize strategic foresight and technological agility. Leaders need to be equipped to anticipate and adapt to the rapid influx of new building materials and production methods. This requires a focus on developing skills in innovation management, changing leadership, and the ability to translate technological advancements into competitive advantage.

Financing and Regulatory Environment Development Needs

To develop the regulatory environment, the company invests in its product range and improves warehouse capabilities to ensure a wide selection, availability, and quality of construction materials for customers. It is appropriate to finance marketing and advertising activities that help increase the company's reputation among potential partners and customers. Participation in construction forums, conferences, and other events to improve stability and transparency in the entire industry is essential for development.

Building materials wholesaling companies face significant financial and regulatory challenges. Navigating complex and evolving building codes and environmental regulations demands substantial investment in compliance measures. Maintaining a diverse and compliant product range requires continuous capital expenditure for inventory and warehouse upgrades. Furthermore, fluctuating market conditions and increasing competition necessitate strategic financial planning to manage cash flow and ensure profitability, especially when faced with the costs of regulatory adjustments and potential penalties.

The building materials wholesaling sector is characterized by tight margins and significant financial risks. Companies must contend with volatile material prices, fluctuating demand, and the substantial capital tied up in inventory. Regulatory changes, such as new environmental standards or import/export restrictions, can further exacerbate these financial pressures. Securing adequate financing, managing credit risk, and implementing robust financial controls are essential for survival and growth in this challenging environment.

Wholesaling building materials presents a unique set of regulatory and financial hurdles. Companies must invest heavily in ensuring their product lines meet stringent safety and environmental standards, often requiring extensive testing and certification. This regulatory burden, combined with intense competition, necessitates careful financial management. Balancing the need for competitive pricing with the costs of compliance and operational efficiency is a constant challenge, demanding strategic investment decisions and proactive risk management.

Building materials wholesalers grapple with significant financial and regulatory pressures. Capital-intensive inventory management, fluctuating material costs, and strict compliance requirements create a complex financial landscape. Navigating evolving regulations and maintaining competitive pricing while ensuring profitability demands astute financial planning and risk mitigation strategies.

Pandemic's Impact on "Hidden Champions" Business Approach

Expectations at the beginning of the lockdown were not encouraging, but the recovery in demand and sales were relatively fast. The company quickly adapted to safety and hygiene protocols—most of the sales managers and other employees (supply managers, accountants) of the company worked remotely, all payments were accepted electronically as much as possible, customers were accepted in the office only for the shipment of goods or payment (if it was not possible to pay otherwise).

Effects of the Ukraine War on "Hidden Champions" Business Operations

The war in Ukraine had a significant impact on business. After the full-scale invasion, some companies ceased to exist, resulting in not only good customers and suppliers being lost but also money because they worked with some of them on postpaid contracts. New customers must be more carefully checked for solvency and honesty in business. Since the beginning of the war, it has been necessary to calculate risks for the company more often and consider more risk factors. Some business partners had to move their production abroad, and the company began to experience significant shortages and disruptions in specific categories of goods. On the other hand, due to this shortage, the company started to look for other manufacturers of these types of goods and thus expanded its range.

Building Guild of Ukraine LLC is the market leader in the supply of construction materials in Ukraine, and builders throughout the country trust it. This is a professional company with 16 years of experience selling building materials and solutions in the construction field. The company offers high-quality materials and effective solutions for any construction project. Its services include consulting, sales, and delivery of construction materials. The company works with all types of customers, guarantees access to the best materials and innovative technologies, and knows how to help customers make high-quality solutions that meet their needs.

Contributing to its role as the market leader, Building Guild of Ukraine LLC specializes in a complex supply of goods for housing construction, repair, and furnishing. The company offers various building materials, such as insulation, facade plaster, dry mixes, plasterboard systems, suspended ceilings, paint for interior and exterior work, waterproofing, and additional finishing materials. The company works with proven manufacturers, such as BAUMIT, Ceresit, Sika, Siltek, Izovat, Isover, Rockwool, Sweetondale, Caparol, Botament, Polimin, Dufa, Siniat, Bostik, Botament, Kompozit, Spectrum, Wellton, Armstrong, and others.

Building Guild of Ukraine LLC is focused on the following strategic activities:

- Leading positions and building long-term partnerships with clients in the construction market.
- Benchmark for sales conversion.
- Increasing basic knowledge of materials and solutions through training.
- Increasing the sales competencies of the managerial staff.
- Increasing the number of active managers.
- Opening of new company branches.

The company needs to adhere not only to its goals but also to SDGs:

- Education — The company encourages employees to receive high-quality education and improve their qualifications, and organizes seminars and trainings in its own offices with its partners. (SDG No. 4). Provide training to construction professionals on the use of new, sustainable building materials. Offer educational workshops for local communities on energy-efficient building practices.
- Building Guild of Ukraine LLC supports gender equality (SDG No. 5).
- The company supports energy saving and participates in programs to improve energy efficiency (SDG No. 7). Prioritize the wholesale of energy-efficient insulation, windows, and solar panel components.

Partner with manufacturers of sustainable building technologies.

- Building Guild of Ukraine LLC ensures that each employee receives a decent salary and comfortable and safe working conditions; the company provides everything necessary for work (SDG No. 8). Ensure fair wages and safe working conditions for all employees.
- Support local manufacturers, contributing to regional economic growth.
- By focusing on local producers, they are helping to ensure continued jobs within the country.
- The company advocates a healthy lifestyle and encourages the company's employees and partners to do so (SDG No. 3). Promoting health and well-being enhances employee productivity and creates a positive work environment, contributing to a healthier society. This shows a holistic approach to employee care.

- Building Guild of Ukraine LLC is a transparent company which do not support corruption (SDG No. 17).
- Support Ukraine! Building Guild of Ukraine LLC is a Ukrainian company that works with local manufacturers as much as possible and supports the Armed Forces (SDG No. 17).

In May 2023, the Building Guild of Ukraine LLC became a partner of "eRecovery" — a state assistance program for homeowners affected by hostilities in the East of Ukraine. This program allows you to get financing for repairing and reconstructing broken homes. As part of this program, Building Guild of Ukraine LLC offers a wide range of building materials: dry building mixes, insulation, paint and varnish materials, roofing materials, plasterboard systems, floor coverings, etc. Each participant of the "eRecovery" program receives a 15% discount on any product category from the Building Guild of Ukraine LLC. In this way, the company helps Ukrainians to restore their housing as quickly, qualitatively, and economically as possible.

In May 2024, the Building Guild of Ukraine LLC became a member of the Board of Directors of the "Conference of Builders of Ukraine." This is an essential step towards the reconstruction of Ukraine and the development of the construction industry. Building Guild of Ukraine LLC is a powerful player and part of the construction community to join forces to discuss the industry's current challenges and for the future reconstruction of Ukraine.

The company believes that by communicating and establishing partnership relations with other construction companies, the Building Guild of Ukraine LLC will reach new heights and provide a stable future for Ukraine's construction industry.

4 Conclusions and Recommendations

The Ukrainian business landscape presents a fascinating paradox. While the ongoing conflict casts a long shadow, creating political instability and economic uncertainty, the country possesses remarkable potential. A skilled workforce, a flourishing IT sector, and rich natural resources form a solid foundation for growth. Unraveling the complexities of this environment and identifying potential Hidden Champions is crucial for fostering a sustainable and thriving Ukrainian economy.

Hidden Champions, often overlooked but undeniably successful, are companies exhibiting strong financial performance, resilience, and innovation. They are frequently leaders in niche markets, driving local and regional economic development. A deeper analysis of the political, economic, social, technological, environmental, and legal (PESTEL) factors in Ukraine sheds light on the characteristics that Hidden Champions companies might possess.

Operating within a complex political and economic landscape demands exceptional resilience. Hidden Champions in Ukraine likely excel in navigating these uncertainties, adapting their strategies and operations to overcome obstacles. These companies may specialize in specific sectors or cater to unique customer segments. This focused approach allows them to avoid direct competition with more prominent players and carve out a sustainable market position. Continuous improvement and a commitment to innovation are vital for Hidden Champions to stay ahead of the curve. This might involve developing cutting-edge products and services, optimizing internal processes, or adopting novel technologies. As environmental awareness grows, Hidden Champions will likely embrace sustainable practices. This could involve implementing green technologies, reducing environmental footprints, or promoting responsible resource management.

Several key actions can be taken to nurture Hidden Champions and unlock Ukraine's economic potential:

The government can play a crucial role by providing tax breaks, streamlining regulations, and investing in infrastructure development.

Universities and research institutions can also offer targeted programs on innovation, entrepreneurship, and international business. These elements will create a supportive environment conducive to the growth of Hidden Champions.

This organization would act as a catalyst, identifying promising companies with the potential to become future Hidden Champions. It would offer these companies invaluable resources, including mentorship, training programs, networking opportunities, and access to funding. Furthermore, the guild could foster collaboration and knowledge sharing among companies, creating a vibrant learning environment.

It is vital to conduct in-depth research to identify established companies that embody the core characteristics of Hidden Champions. Once identified, targeted support can enhance their growth and global competitiveness. This can involve facilitating access to international markets, assisting with technology adoption, or providing expertise in specific areas.

Encouraging Hidden Champions to embrace environmentally responsible practices is critical to long-term success. This can involve promoting the adoption of renewable energy sources, implementing resource-efficient manufacturing processes, and fostering a culture of sustainability within these companies.

By implementing these recommendations, Ukraine can cultivate a thriving ecosystem that fosters the emergence and development of Hidden Champions. This will drive economic growth and job creation and solidify Ukraine's position as a global financial player built on resilience, innovation, and a commitment to a sustainable future.

References

DOU. (2023, January 10). *IT industry report 2022*. https://dou.ua/

Food and Agriculture Organization of the United Nations. (2022, March 15). *Food price monitoring and analysis*. https://www.fao.org/giews/food-prices/home/en/

Organization for Economic Co-operation and Development (OECD). (2022). *Research and development expenditure (indicator)*.

The Ministry of Energy of Ukraine. (2020, July 14). *Strategy for the development of the renewable energy sector of Ukraine for the period up to 2035.*
The World Bank. (2019). *GDP (current US$).* Accessed May 25, 2025, from https://data.worldbank.org/indicator/NY.GDP.MKTP.CD?most_recent_value_desc¼true&year_high_desctrue
The World Bank. (2023, April 10). *The war in Ukraine: Economic impact assessment.* https://www.worldbank.org/en/events/2022/12/06/local-and-global-economic-impacts-of-the-war-in-ukraine
Transparency International. (2022). *Corruption perception index 2022.* https://www.transparency.org/en/cpi/2022
United Nations Office for the Coordination of Humanitarian Affairs. (2023, May 25). *Ukraine humanitarian situation report no. 33.* https://reports.unocha.org/en/country/ukraine/

Olexandr Kalinin, PhD in Economics, is Professor and Head of the Department of Management and Innovative Development at KROK Business School in Kyiv. He specializes in marketing management, investment marketing, risk management, and business administration, with a strong academic and consulting background.

Dr. Kalinin holds two master's degrees — in Economics (2009) and Philology (2021) — and defended his PhD in 2013. In 2020, he earned his Doctor of Economic Sciences, focusing on "Formation and Management of the Investment Marketing System of Diversified Enterprises." He received the title of Associate Professor in 2018 and Professor in 2022.

His professional experience includes over a decade of teaching and research in economics, marketing, and business management, as well as practical work in entrepreneurship, logistics, and digitalization projects. He has supervised PhD students and participated in numerous Erasmus+ initiatives, such as Crisis and Risks Engineering for Transport Services (CRENG) and Digitalization of Economy for Sustainable Development (DigEco).

Dr. Kalinin is the author of a research monograph, and numerous articles indexed in Scopus and Web of Science, covering investment marketing, mergers and acquisitions, risk management, and sustainable business strategies. He also serves on editorial boards and is a Corresponding Member of the Academy of Economic Sciences of Ukraine.

His teaching portfolio includes Marketing Management, Advertising Management, Digital Marketing, Risk Management, and Investment Marketing. He actively engages in international cooperation and capacity-building projects.

Oksana Sedashova is an Associate Professor at KROK Business School, an organizational psychologist, business trainer, and PhD in Pedagogy. With over 20 years of experience in adult education and leadership development, she specializes in creativity, innovation, and business psychology.

She leads programs in management, leadership, and design thinking at KROK Business School, where she also heads the Creativity Research Center. Oksana is the founder of the World Creativity and Innovation Week in Ukraine and a certified mediator, and International Creativity Ambassador in Ukraine.

Her expertise spans organizational psychology, facilitation, conflict resolution, emotional intelligence, and creative problem-solving. She has delivered more than 18,000 hours of training for executives, entrepreneurs, and professionals in both the corporate and public sectors, including certified programs such as Certified Creativity Professional.

Oksana has represented Ukraine at international conferences all over the world and completed professional internships in Latvia, Netherlands, and Spain. She is among the Top 10 Women Innovators in Ukraine, actively promoting creative leadership and innovation culture.

Author of numerous articles and educational programs, Oksana designs courses on creative and design thinking, communication, mediation, and innovative management. Her mission is to empower leaders and teams to see new opportunities and build resilience through creativity and collaboration.

Key focus areas: creative thinking, design thinking, innovation strategies, leadership, emotional intelligence, and communication.

Tetyana Kravchenko is a PhD in Economics, Head of Venture Investor Relations, Toloca.vc, Business Instructor, Innovative Products Promotion Expert. She brings over 17 years of experience supporting innovation-driven startups and guiding teams in business development and investment readiness

As Deputy Director for Financial Affairs at the business accelerator Business Sharks, Tetiana plays a key role in financial mentoring and strategic growth for early-stage ventures. She has served as a mentor for CRDF GLOBAL in Ukraine, aiding startups in scaling and accessing new markets

Her contributions extend to high-impact innovation events — she co-organized the Ukrainian Innovation Expo 2016 together with Ukraine's Ministry of Foreign Affairs, showcasing cutting-edge Ukrainian startups and technologies.

Tetyana has mentored several successful innovation-driven projects, including Hideez, WoodRover, Demut, IntRobots, Luciding, and Talk With Me!, helping them refine business models, increase sales, and attract investment.

With a deep focus on innovation strategy, investment readiness, and sales growth, Tetyana equips entrepreneurs and corporate leaders with practical tools and structured frameworks to navigate the startup ecosystem.

Core strengths include: financial strategy, accelerator mentorship, innovation ecosystem development, startup scaling, and investment facilitation.

Lyudmila Kosovych is an invited lecturer at KROK Business School and a recognized expert in marketing, communications, and employer branding. With over 20 years of experience in communications and 10 years in consulting and research, she brings deep practical expertise across multiple industries as a consultant, mentor, auditor, and outsourced communications specialist.

Her core competencies include business development and market segmentation, brand creation and communication (including private labels), employer branding strategies, marketing communications, research and audits, and naming.

Lyudmila holds a Master's degree in International Economics, and has completed advanced programs with Ernst & Young, Internews, SIT, and Ericsson Coaching Institute. Her work has been recognized with multiple Effie Awards Ukraine and advertising festival honors.

At KROK Business School, she teaches Marketing Communications in MBA programs and leads initiatives such as the Center for Sustainable Development Goals. She is also actively engaged in the Central and Eastern Europe (CEE) Chapter community as Vice-President, promoting knowledge exchange and professional growth in the region.

Hidden Champions of Uzbekistan ERMAK Uzbekistan: Innovating Tradition in Central Asia's Snack Industry

Hikmat Abdurahmanov, Akmal Khudaykulov, and Zukhra Abdurakhmanova

Abstract This case study explores the development and success of ERMAK, a prominent food products company in Uzbekistan, founded by Valijon Solixov in 1992. The study provides a comprehensive overview of the socio-economic transitions in post-Soviet Uzbekistan, illustrating the entrepreneurial challenges and opportunities during the shift from a centrally planned to a market-oriented economy. It highlights ERMAK's strategic focus on identifying market gaps, product innovation, and vertical integration, which have been crucial in overcoming market scepticism and operational hurdles. The company's commitment to quality, customer-centric approaches, and ethical practices has been pivotal in building strong customer relationships and ensuring sustainable growth. ERMAK's human resources strategy emphasizes continuous improvement and employee well-being, increasing employee satisfaction and retention rates.

Additionally, the study details ERMAK's successful expansion into international markets and diversification of its product line, reflecting its strategic agility and market responsiveness. ERMAK's corporate social responsibility initiatives and environmental sustainability efforts are also examined. The case provides valuable insights for entrepreneurs and managers in emerging markets, emphasizing the importance of understanding market needs, maintaining high-quality standards, fostering strong relationships, and adhering to ethical business practices for achieving sustainable success.

H. Abdurahmanov · A. Khudaykulov (✉)
TEAM University, Tashkent, Uzbekistan
e-mail: hikmat@teamuni.uz; akmal.khudaykulov@teamuni.uz

Z. Abdurakhmanova
Representative Office, AVDO, London, UK

Central Asia and the Representative Office in Tashkent, Tashkent, Uzbekistan
e-mail: zukhra.a@avdo.uk

D. Berberović, D. Purg (eds.), *Hidden Champions in Rising Economies*, Contributions to Management Science,
https://doi.org/10.1007/978-3-032-08263-3_39

Overview[1]

Official name: Republic of Uzbekistan
Type of government: Authoritarian state
Population in 2023: 35,163,944
Land area: 448,900 km^2

History

1991 Uzbekistan announces its independence from the Soviet Union following its disintegration in a peaceful manner. The republic is in a transition phase towards a market economy and democracy.

1992 Islam Karimov is elected the first President of independent Uzbekistan in elections throughout the country.

1990s Uzbekistan concentrates on reconstruction of the economy and infrastructure in the face of difficulties of the post-Soviet transition. Considerable progress has been made in developing the natural resource sectors of the country such as gas, cotton and gold.

2000s The economic growth continues with an increasing level of natural resource and agricultural exports. There is a movement towards modernising industries and attracting foreign direct investment.

2005 Uzbekistan marks the 14th anniversary of its independence with celebrations and cultural events throughout the country celebrating the heritage of the country.

2016 Shavkat Mirziyoyev becomes the new President and lays stress on continuing the development of Uzbekistan through economic reform and the introduction of widespread reforms to improve the welfare of the population and also to increase international co-operation.

2017 The government launches new initiatives in support of entrepreneurship, foreign direct investment and diversification of the economy away from natural resources.

2019 Uzbekistan hosts the Asian Youth Games, a major international sporting occasion, demonstrating to an international audience the hospitality and technical infrastructure of the country.

2021 Major investments are made in the tourism sector trying to attract visits and investment to its historic cities, Such as Samakand, Bukhara and Khiva which presents any opportunity of cultural tourism.

2023 Uzbekistan celebrates 32 years of independence from the Soviet Union and can be proud of progress in its economic development, social reforms and indeed increasing awareness of the rich cultural heritage of the republic.

2024 The country develops its strategy of "Uzbekistan - 2030" whose role is that to continue its strategy of digital transformation, green energy and educational reform. The opening of solar and wind farms at Samarkand and Navoi and major contracts are developed and agreed with major interna-

[1] Please provide World Bank data and a history overview of your country.

tional partners in the role of innovative sustainability through the reduction of pollution, environmental difficulties and sustainability of growth and development of a greater regional connectivity.

2025 Uzbekistan celebrates its 34th year of independence. Achievements in the diversification of the economy, technological development and the growth and modernisation of infrastructure can be confidently celebrated by the country which follows up with proposals in artificial intelligence, smart agriculture and the development of systems of innovation. With the introduction of major scientific and cultural forums within the area of Samarkand international consideration and discussion is now peculiarly healthy and development can take place so that Uzbekistan can become a centre of development, dialogue and co-operation in Central Asia.

1 Introduction: Context and History

Uzbekistan's transition from a centrally planned to a market economy followed patterns seen across post-Soviet states (Åslund, 2007; Kornai, 1992; Pomfret, 2000; Smith, 1996).Uzbekistan continues to refine its governance and economy, while gradually achieving steady progress in transparency and efficiency of the public sector. The government's strong fiscal position, increasingly large remittances, buoyant exports and large internal consumption are all contributory features of a booming economy. Inflation remains aloof, but with continuing reforms and efficient fiscal management, the elimination of inflationary pressure becomes easier. Important recognition has been given to Uzbekistan's excellent work in the field of existence of forced labour, as also to the general improvement of labour rights. With a youthful and enterprising population, the fertility rate is still high, creating a future demographic potential. Although gender inequality remains a socio-economic problem, the opening up of new educational and professional opportunities for women, is gradually increasing the social mobility of the population. Although the level of innovation is still low, increased state-financed investment in science, technology, R&D, and digitalisation, is yielding a fruitful harvest in new modernisation and creativity in the country.

2 Pest Analysis

2.1 Main Pest Points in Uzbekistan

2.1.1 Political Environment

Opportunities

Very Low Tax Burden: With a top individual income tax rate of only 12.0% and a corporate tax rate that is also low at 15.0%, Uzbekistan has a very low tax burden, and this pillar is the country's best-performing in the Index of Economic Freedom 2023. Low taxation is beneficial for both consumers and businesses. For the former, it increases purchasing power that can drive consumer expenditure, while for the latter, they can reinvest in their operations and distribute profits more generously.

Improving Corruption Ranking: Over 2014–2022, Uzbekistan's ranking in the Corruption Perceptions Index improved steadily to reach 126th globally. Prevention of corruption has been a key target for the government in recent years, which has put in place an anti-corruption agency and created a more transparent public procurement procedure that has lessened incidences of graft. Small-scale corruption affecting the traffic police has also been reduced through cameras, which has led to fewer bribes being paid. Security services that were in place under the Karimov presidency have largely been disbanded owing to accusations of corrupt practices. Still, these are being replaced by President Shavkat Mirziyoyev's security detail. Provincial governments are facing greater scrutiny, resulting in the removal of governors and mayors in several regions, in a bid to stamp out misappropriation of state funds at a regional level. Despite these efforts to reduce graft, Uzbekistan's unfavourable ranking in the index demonstrates that corruption remains a problem for the country and is an impediment to the development of democracy.

Better State Finances: The budget deficit narrowed from 4.6% of GDP in 2021 to 3.9% in 2022, owing to fiscal prudence and higher government revenues. Consequently, public debt also fell from 35.4% of GDP in 2021 to 34.3% in 2022. Implementing planned reforms to energy tariffs is expected to lead to lower public debt and reduce the risks of balance sheet liabilities accrued by utility companies in the medium term. Uzbekistan's government finances remain sustainable and are not a threat to stability. Its public-debt-to-GDP ratio was significantly below the Asia Pacific average of 95.3% in 2022.

2.1.2 Economic Environment

Opportunities

Robust Economic Performance: Due to the strength in remittance inflows, solid consumer expenditure, and higher exports, Uzbekistan's economic momentum remained favourable in 2022, with annual real GDP growth of 5.7%. Non-gold exports were also resilient and increased meaningfully, particularly textiles, fertilizers, and food exports, while exports to Russia were also higher. Although output development is expected to slightly moderate in the short term, it is set to remain robust. Still, the war in Ukraine will somewhat affect it, leading to elevated food and energy prices. Nevertheless, annual real GDP growth is expected to be 5.1% in 2023. The average annual real GDP growth is forecast at 5.4% over 2023–2027, higher than the Asia Pacific average of 4.4% in that timeframe.

Considerably higher remittances: In 2022, remittance inflows increased markedly by 80.4% year-on-year in USD terms. Remittance inflows were particularly strong, owing to an appreciation in the Russian ruble and greater Russian immigration to the country, which led to higher money transfers from this group. Higher remittance inflows also led to a marked decline in the poverty rate in Uzbekistan in 2022. According to the World Bank, the percentage of the population living below the national poverty line fell from 17.0% in 2021 to 14.0% in 2022, a significant reduction in just 1 year. Although remittance inflows are anticipated to moderate somewhat in the short term, they will remain a major contributor to consumer incomes, which will help consumption in the medium term.

Greater FDI Intensity Than Peers: Foreign direct investment (FDI) inflows equated to 3.1% of GDP in 2022 and were higher than 2.0% for the Asia Pacific average. This demonstrates that FDI is a relatively important driver of economic development in Uzbekistan. As part of the country's modernization strategy, the president has been actively courting foreign investment through reforms such as greater transactions in foreign currency and the creation of seven special economic zones (SEZs) that afford tax incentives to foreign investors. ERMAK's rapid internationalization aligns with born-global characteristics identified by Cavusgil and Knight (2015). Legislation relating to SEZs adopted in 2020 has increased foreign investment in the energy and communications sectors. Germany's Volkswagen Group, Saudi Arabia's ACWA Power, and Russia's telecoms provider MegaFon have been recent investors in the country since 2020. Privatization of sectors like financial services, hydrocarbons, manufacturing, transport, agriculture, and telecommunications is expected to be a source of FDI. Additionally, the country's strategic location giving access to China and Europe, is appealing to investors, as is its abundant natural resources.

Challenges

Significant reliance on commodities and Russia: In 2022, commodity exports, including gold, cotton, and natural gas, accounted for nearly half of all goods exports. This raises the vulnerability of the external sector to global commodity price fluctuations and makes the export base undiversified and overly dependent on commodities. Uzbekistan is also exposed to demand shocks from its trading partners that consume its commodities. Given that Russia is the country's single most significant trading partner, Russia's economic challenges in the face of sanctions imposed by the West and its ongoing commitment to its invasion of Ukraine could result in such shocks for Uzbekistan. Furthermore, Uzbekistan could be the victim of secondary sanctions because of its significant economic links with Russia. Exports destined for Russia accounted for 12.8% of total goods exports in 2022.

Elevated Inflation: Uzbekistan's inflation rate of 10.9% in 2022 was considerably above the Asia Pacific average of 4.3% that year. Higher inflation has been caused by the war in Ukraine, which has led to rising food and energy prices in Uzbekistan. Transportation costs have also increased in the country, negatively impacting logistics. Although inflation fell to 9.0% in August 2023 from a short-term high of 12.3% in December 2022, it remains high. Increases in energy tariffs are expected to keep inflation elevated in 2024.

2.1.3 Social Environment

Opportunities

Progress Made on Forced Labour: For years, Uzbekistan's cotton sector, an essential component of the economy and a key employer, has been accused of using forced labour. However, since the mid-2010s, the Uzbek authorities have been implementing reforms to the cotton sector that have significantly reduced forced and child labour. The International Labour Organization (ILO) conducted extensive research involving thousands of interviews with the country's cotton pickers in 2021, which revealed that all regions in Uzbekistan were free from forced labour or had a minimal number of cases reported. The Cotton Campaign, a key industry observer, also reported in March 2022 that it had not witnessed any incidence of forced labour. Compliance with international agri-food standards further strengthens market competitiveness (Henson & Reardon, 2005; Kramer, 2017). Consequently, it terminated its campaign to dissuade more than 330 international companies from boycotting the Uzbek cotton sector. The removal of the stigma attached to Uzbekistan's cotton sector is expected to benefit incomes in the country, as work on cotton fields is more formalized and regulated, particularly as around 12.5% of working-age people are involved in the cotton harvest, according to trade sources.

Fertility Rate to Remain Relatively High: Although falling, the fertility rate in Uzbekistan is expected to be relatively high over 2023–2040, at 2.2 children born per female, and will remain above the replacement rate of 2.1 at the end of this period. While children (those aged 0–14) are expected to decline by 5.0% in the forecast timeframe compared with total population growth of 19.6%, the portion is anticipated to stand at 24.0% in 2040, a share that is relatively large and should help to sustain demand in child-related segments in the consumer market.

Challenges

Tertiary Education Quality is Questionable: Although Uzbekistan's higher educational attainment rate is exceptionally high, at 46.0% in 2022 and significantly above the Asia Pacific average of 13.2%, the quality of its undergraduate education has been called into question. The high rate of tertiary education is attributable to policies enacted by the president since taking office in 2016, which have reduced the costs of studying at university. Indeed, the number of admissions for undergraduate courses will rise from nearly 63,000 in 2016 to a massive 381,000 for the 2023–2024 academic year, according to trade sources. A presidential decree 2019 set a target of achieving a higher educational attainment rate of over 50.0% by 2030, which is partly responsible for the elevated rate in 2022. Admission to higher educational institutions has become easier, owing to the lowering of the qualifying threshold for applicants. Corruption at universities is also rife, allowing undergraduates to gain a degree through bribery, while there has been a proliferation of private higher educational institutions, which is also diluting the quality of degrees earned.

Large Gender Gap: The gender gap remains a key issue in Uzbekistan. In 2022, the female employment rate stood at 50.8%, while the male equivalent was 72.1%, and men had 56.1% greater disposable income than women that year. Women are more likely to stay at home and care for the family, while they are less likely to secure such economic and social opportunities as attaining higher education and access to healthcare, owing to paternalistic customs. Reducing the gender income gap is essential for businesses in the country, as women often tend to be the decision-makers for household purchases and are usually more lavish with their spending on family needs than men. The widespread gender gap will hinder female consumer influence over the direction of the total consumer market in the forecast period and inhibit women's social mobility.

Mixed Health Picture: Improvements in the standard of living, including widening access to drinking water, as well as investment in healthcare and education, should boost life expectancy up to 2040. However, it remains lower than the regional average, as poverty remains elevated in some, particularly rural, areas. Additionally, increasingly sedentary lifestyles with more convenience food will lead to rising rates of obesity and diabetes up to 2040. Deaths from circulatory diseases will remain the leading cause of death over this timeframe.

2.1.4 Technological Environment

Opportunities

Greater State Focus on ICT: The Uzbek government has been placing increasing importance on developing the information and communications technology (ICT) sector. Consequently, ICT skills have improved, e-governance has expanded meaningfully, and digital infrastructure has also been boosted. The IT park has been a key contributor to ICT growth, with additional branches opening in provincial locations. This has increased the number of foreign companies from four to 200 between 2016 and 2023. The state also places increasing importance on ICT skills for young people and has reimbursed the costs of attaining an internationally recognized IT certificate by 50.0%. From October 2023, any young person receiving such certificates will have their costs fully reimbursed. Additionally, e-government services have expanded from 197 in 2016 to more than 430 in July 2023, with 6.3 million users. Fibre-optic cable rollout increased exponentially from 20,000 km in 2016 to 170,000 in 2023, helping connect more remote locations.

5G Rollout Gaining Momentum: In 2023, Uzbekistan has been making strides in the rollout of 5G networks across the country. Uzbektelecom, the state-owned telecoms operator, started to upgrade base stations in March 2023 in preparation for the launch of 5G services. In April 2023, Uzbektelecom switched on its 5G signal in a limited number of base stations in Tashkent, the capital, whilst the signal was switched on in Samarkand, the country's second biggest city, in July 2023. Given the hiatus in the rollout of 5G since 2021, these developments are encouraging for the country. They will help Uzbekistan become more competitive in a regional context.

Challenges

Low Potential for e-Commerce Development: Uzbekistan's Internet penetration was above the Asia Pacific average, with 76.6% of the population using the Internet in 2022, versus 57.8% for the regional average. However, the relatively low penetration rate compared to more advanced peers is mainly due to a substantial proportion of the population residing in rural areas with less access to connectivity infrastructure. Consequently, the development of e-commerce in Uzbekistan is hampered, as is evident from the low figure of 5.3% of the population selling goods and services online in 2022. Progress in e-banking is also likely slower than peers, as only 4.4% of the population used Internet banking in 2022, nearly half the penetration rate of the Asia Pacific average at 10.0%.

R&D Intensity Below Peers: In 2022, research and development (R&D) expenditure equated to only 0.1% of GDP, considerably lower than the Asia Pacific average of 2.2% that year. This points to low innovation capacity, with greater weight given to primary sector activities such as cotton production and mining for gold. Consequently, Uzbekistan could be at a competitive disadvantage to its more advanced regional peers. Without a solid innovation ecosystem, the country is also likely to make less headway in the digital age. It must import innovation to modernize key sectors like agriculture.

Start-ups Face Challenges: Although the number of ICT start-ups in Uzbekistan has expanded strongly over the review period, the sector is only in the embryonic stage of development and encounters significant challenges. One of the main barriers for start-ups is access to finance, with founders of start-up firms often providing funding from their savings or help from friends and family. Greater access to finance is crucial for start-ups to expand their offering meaningfully. To this end, the state has created the National Venture Fund, but it is too early to say whether this will generate funding.

3 Characteristics of Hidden Champions from Uzbekistan

Exhibit 1 Core economic indicators for Uzbekistan

	2018	2019	2020	2021	2022	2023	2024
GDP per capita (current US$)	1604.3	1795.2	1759.3	1993.4	2252.2.	2496.1	3161.7
GDP per capita growth (annual %)	4.1	4.0	0.1	5.3	3.5	4.7	4.4
Long-term unemployment (% of total unemployment)	5.4	4.9	5.3	5.4	4.5	4.3	4.49
Foreign direct investment, net inflows (% of GDP)	1.2	3.8	2.9	3.3	3.1	3.1	2.5
GDP (current US$, billions)	52.87	60.28	60.22	69.22	69.60	80.39	114.9
Exports of goods and services (current US$, billions)	14.19	17.06	14.56	16.48	21.92	24.4	26.9
Exports of goods and services (% of GDP)	26.8	28.3	24.2	23.7	27.3	26.5	22.8

(continued)

(continued)

	2018	2019	2020	2021	2022	2023	2024
Merchandise exports (current US$, billions)	10.92	14.93	13.28	14.09	15.29	24.4	26.9
Merchandise exports to high-income economies (% of total merchandise exports)			32.9			37	..
Merchandise exports to developing economies in Europe and Central Asia (% of total merchandise exports)	41.5	38.2	32.5		36.4	36.8	..
Ores and metals exports (% of merchandise exports)	7.6	8.4	8.3	14	11.3		7.7
Agricultural raw materials exports (% of merchandise exports)	3	3	3	3	2	1.4	1.2
Food exports (% of merchandise exports)	9	10	10	9	10	7.6	7.5
Fuel exports (% of merchandise exports)	25	17	6	7	7	3.9	5.3
Manufactures exports (% of merchandise exports)	23	23.7	17.2	22.6	22.2	16.6	28
High-technology exports (% of manufactured exports)	0.5	0.7	1.3	0.31	1.4	3.0	

Source: World Bank, 2025 https://databank.worldbank.org/source/world-development-indicators

4 Case Studies of Selected Hidden Champions

4.1 Case Study 1

4.1.1 ERMAK

Overview
Address: Tashkent, 100057, Akhmad Donish Street 110
Tel: +998 78 148 03 03, +998 95 170 23 33
Fax:
Email: ermak.uzb@gmail.com
Web: https://ermak.uz

Company Information
Industry[2]: Manufacturing
Year of Establishment: 1992
Sales Revenues in 2017:
Sales Revenues in 2023:
Average number of employees in 2023: 200
Brainer(s) behind the company: Valijon Solixov

[2]According to NACE Rev. 2—please check the technical instructions included in this document (pg. 9).

4.1.2 Nature of Market Leadership

ERMAK's competitive advantage is rooted in several key strategic elements that have enabled the company to distinguish itself in the food products market in Uzbekistan and internationally.

Establishing Leadership in a Dynamic Market
The process of its growth to a dominant market position started in 1992 as the company saw a new, unexplored area in the Uzbek food market. During that period, ordinary local snack foods, such as sunflower seeds and kurt, were often sold in a raw and/or unpackaged state. Being able to realize the opportunity of updating these products, ERMAK, owing to the new packets—pure and hygienic snacks—changed consumers' perceptions and created postindustrial standards. By 1996, the prepared food product manufacturing company had proved viable, with only one drying chamber for its 10 tons daily output.

This has enabled ERMAK to gain market leadership through offering consumers what they desire in their respective areas. At the beginning of the 2000s, consumer consciousness regarding the usage of healthier, natural food products increased worldwide. In this context, ERMAK established strategic emphasis on organic food products as well as minimally processed products. By 2023, ERMAK had expanded its portfolio to other products such as ayran, made from nut paste, and marmalades. This strategic diversification exposed ERMAK as a reliable local and international brand exporter to countries such as the USA, Israel, and the Persian Gulf.

Dominance through Innovation and Scale
It involved innovative specialization, production, and marketing techniques as a key to the leadership of ERMAK. From $5000 in 1993, they introduced a roasting machine to process and pack sunflower seeds under the brand name, ERMAK. But the company did not give up and slowly and steadily succeeded in developing a good market with the help of consumers through convincing the market regarding the nutritional values of Sunflower seeds, which are enriched with Vitamin E and antioxidants. In the same year 2024, the company has a product portfolio that includes not only traditional snack products but also new generation solutions like kurtaba, launched in 2020, and dessert pastes launched this year; all of which fit the needs of the consumers as described by Radjou and Prabhu (2015).

Another aspect that puts ERMAK in a leadership position is the production scale. What began as one bag of sunflower seeds has grown into a company that produces over 10 tons of products daily and has over 400 workers in its production outlets. Its investment in superior packaging technologies, including vacuum packing, has seen the products retain their freshness; this is translated into more shelf life, a key aspect that has enabled it to build trust with consumers and open up for a larger market share.

Market Recognition and Export Success
ERMAK's leadership is not limited to domestic markets only. The organization exported its products to the USA, Kazakhstan, Israel, and the Persian Gulf countries

by 2023, earning more than one million US dollars in export revenue in 2022. It is highly accredited through various international quality certifications, such as the Halal certificate in Gulf markets. It is necessary to note that ERMAK plans to enter the European market deeply; moreover, it has already started trial shipments to Lithuania and Latvia; the company also participates in events like the International Green Week in Berlin.

Another value of leadership within this company concerns its attempts to meet unsatisfied needs. ERMAK has been able to increase its production by 1.5 times within the last 6 months and still has more trade demand for its products, proving its market demand. Subsequently, by 2024, the company aims to add energy bars and grape seed oils to the food list and remain a market leader in the Uzbek food business and internationally.

Commitment to Quality and Hygiene

Since the beginning of the operation, ERMAK has been pursuing quality and hygiene as a guiding principle. Unlike some conventional merchandise found in bazaar-like outlets, snacks produced by ERMAK bear high sanitary standards, and each procedure is controlled and scrutinized. Such commitment has given the company the recognition of the consumers, business partners, and positioned it as the market leader in the Uzbekistan packaged food market (Juran, 1992).

4.1.3 Nature of Competitive Advantage

ERMAK's competitive advantage is built on several strategic pillars that distinguish the company in the competitive landscape of Uzbekistan and beyond. ERMAK's internal resources and capabilities function as key sources of sustained competitive advantage (Barney, 1991; Porter, 1985). These pillars include a steadfast commitment to quality, continuous innovation, strategic diversification, effective vertical integration, strong customer relationships, and a dedication to ethical practices and sustainability.

Commitment to Quality

One factor that has helped ERMAK stay ahead of its rivals is its cardinal policy, which has emphasized quality and hygiene since its formation in 1992. In contrast with many similar companies, there are no instances of artificial additives and fillers being used. For example, its kurt consists of no raw flour used in the market but has used pure natural elements for its production, for a reasonable price of nearly $25 per kg, equivalent to a quality Parmesan cheese. Such attention to product excellence echoes Juran's (1992) total quality design principles and Drucker's (1954) emphasis on effective management practices. This has built consumer confidence since products undergo quality checks from time to time across all outlets to meet the set standards of ERMAK (Juran, 1992).

Continuous Innovation

Strategic management has pointed out that innovation has been the key strength that has supported ERMAK's success. Alcoholic lemonades known as kurtaba were launched in 2020 to develop kurt and target younger and healthier consumers. Until 2022, to meet the global tendencies towards natural plant-based pastes, ERMAK introduced dessert pastes made of peanuts, sesame, and cashews. Regional innovation ecosystems often amplify such firm-level creativity (Saxenian, 2006). These products have obtained a lot of market acceptance, especially in the Baltic and Gulf regions, where customers prefer organic and natural products.

From its prospective visions of various products, we can see that ERMAK already has a greater vision for the company. The Company's plans for a significant new product launch in 2024 include energy bars made predominantly from nuts, honey, and fruits, geared at the expanded consumer trend towards "snacking". Further, ERMAK's extraction of oil from grape and pomegranate seeds, started in 2023, proves a steady focus on waste elimination as well as value addition.

Strategic Diversification

For several years, various risks have been counterbalanced, and new opportunities have been captured thanks to the flexibility and variety of services provided by ERMAK. Originally, the company only offered packaged sunflower seeds, but in the following years it widened its range of products to ayran, nut pastes, marmalades and organic juices. Using this diversification strategy, ERMAK has benefited from the opportunities to cover all its target consumers, including the conventional snack lovers and people who care about the quality of their food and snacks. In 2023, ERMAK began exporting its products to over five countries, namely the USA, Israel, and Kazakhstan, with over $ 1 million export revenue in 2022 (Ansoff, 1957). ERMAK's entrepreneurial expansion reflects the opportunity-recognition logic central to entrepreneurship research (Shane & Venkataraman, 2000; Hisrich et al., 2017).

Effective Vertical Integration

Vertical integration has been ERMAK's key growth strategy to maintain the quality of the supply chain. This ensures the company meets the local and international demand for sunflower seeds while using quality seeds from China. ERMAK has total control over the manufacturing process from the purchase of raw materials to the packaging, which has ensured and implemented strict quality control measures while ensuring efficient cost control. With the help of this approach, it became possible to make more than 10 tons of snacks per day to satisfy people's increased need and, at the same time, maintain affordable prices for products (Williamson, 1975).

Strong Customer Relationships

ERMAK's capability to sustain a good relationship with its clients enhances and outlines a good strategy for this company. The company is also consumer-friendly mainly due to its frequent market research and feedback taking. For instance, the initial export of kurt to the USA was aimed at the Russian immigrants, but has since adapted to other Americans as more people increase their knowledge of what it contains. Besides targeting the consumers' needs and wants, this has created sales and helped build ERMAK as a reputable brand (Kotler & Keller, 2016). Active customer engagement and relationship-marketing strategies enhance brand loyalty and long-term equity (Brodie et al., 2011; Gummesson, 2002; Homburg et al., 2017; Ries & Trout, 2001).

Dedication to Ethical Practices and Sustainability
This is an innovation to the competitors since ERMAK tends to adopt ethical practices and sustainability. By 2023, the company had managed to make the production line free from waste by extracting oil from the residue materials, such as grape and pomegranate seeds. At some extent, ERMAK does not use any nonrecyclable packaging material or packaging materials that pose a threat to the environment. This commitment to sustainability is in tune with other consumers worldwide; it has influenced ERMAK to acquire different forms of certifications, like the Halal certification of its products in the countries in the Gulf that have certified its products, enhancing customer demand.

At ERMAK, the company's key strengths are the combination of tradition and innovation, high quality and environmental responsibility, domestic talent, and international best practices. These factors that always adjust to the market demands, take steps toward vertical integration, and ensure a high level of customer satisfaction make ERMAK have a very strong and unique niche. They keep checking ERMAK's strategic preview and maintain its sustainable advancement for further development within the food industry that will never stand still.

4.1.4 Core Lessons Learned on the Path to Success

ERMAK's journey from a small start-up to a leading food products company in Uzbekistan offers several core lessons that are instrumental for understanding its path to success. These lessons revolve around market understanding, continuous quality improvement, innovation, employee development, and strategic adaptability.

Importance of Market Understanding
One of the most critical lessons learned by ERMAK is the importance of deeply understanding market needs and consumer preferences. Initially, the company faced significant market scepticism, particularly concerning the hygienically packaged versions of traditional snacks like sunflower seeds, kurt, and kurtoba. ERMAK overcame this challenge by conducting thorough market research to identify gaps and consumer demands. ERMAK successfully transformed market perceptions and built a loyal customer base by tailoring its products to meet these specific needs. This lesson underscores the value of consumer-centric strategies in driving business success (Kotler & Keller, 2016).

Continuous Quality Improvement
Maintaining high-quality standards has been a cornerstone of ERMAK's success. The company has learned that continuous quality improvement is essential for satisfying current customers and attracting new ones. ERMAK's commitment to

rigorous quality control and hygienic packaging has set it apart from competitors and established it as a trusted brand. This approach aligns with Total Quality Management (TQM) principles, emphasizing ongoing efforts to improve products, services, and processes (Juran, 1992). ERMAK's experience demonstrates that a relentless focus on quality can lead to sustained competitive advantage and market leadership.

Embracing Innovation

Innovation has played a pivotal role in ERMAK's growth and success. The company has learned that adopting low-cost innovation techniques and continuously improving its processes are vital for staying competitive. ERMAK's ability to innovate within budget constraints, such as through lean manufacturing principles, has enabled it to enhance product quality and operational efficiency. Additionally, the company's diversification into new product lines, like organic juices and nut butters, reflects its commitment to innovation in meeting evolving consumer preferences (Radjou & Prabhu, 2015). This lesson highlights the importance of fostering a culture of innovation to drive business growth.

Employee Development and Well-being

ERMAK has also recognized the critical role of employee development and well-being in achieving business success. The company has learned that investing in employees' professional growth and creating a supportive work environment leads to higher job satisfaction, retention rates, and overall productivity. Valijon's emphasis on on-the-job training, continuous improvement, and providing a safe and inclusive workplace has been instrumental in building a committed and capable workforce (Freeman, 1984). This lesson underscores the value of prioritizing employee welfare as a strategic asset for the company. Supportive HR practices enhance employee retention (Allen et al., 2003), while job design that fosters autonomy improves motivation (Hackman & Oldham, 1976). Investment in human capital further increases productivity and long-term growth (Becker, 1964).

Strategic Adaptability

Finally, ERMAK's journey has highlighted the importance of strategic adaptability. The company has demonstrated an ability to navigate various challenges, including market scepticism, operational hurdles, and regulatory complexities, by being flexible and responsive to changing market conditions. ERMAK's strategic moves, such as vertical integration to control supply chain quality and costs, and expanding into international markets, reflect its adaptive approach to growth (Ansoff, 1957). This lesson emphasizes the necessity of strategic agility in sustaining long-term business success in a dynamic environment.

4.1.5 Management and Leadership Development Needs

ERMAK's impressive growth and success have underscored the importance of robust management and leadership development to sustain its competitive edge and drive future expansion. The company's journey highlights specific knowledge, competencies, and skills essential for current and future leaders within the organization.

Knowledge Development
To navigate the complexities of both domestic and international markets, ERMAK's management needs a deep understanding of market dynamics, consumer behaviour, and global business practices. Knowledge in market research, competitive analysis, and international trade regulations is crucial. For instance, ERMAK's triumphant entry into markets like the USA, Germany, and Japan necessitates comprehensive knowledge of these markets' regulatory landscapes and consumer preferences. Leaders must stay informed about global trends in the food industry, particularly the growing demand for organic and minimally processed products, to align the company's strategies with market opportunities (Porter & Kramer, 2006).

Competence in Strategic Planning and Innovation
ERMAK's management must continue to enhance its strategic planning capabilities to adapt to changing market conditions and sustain growth. This includes competencies in strategic diversification, as demonstrated by ERMAK's expansion into new product lines such as organic juices and nut butters. Effective strategic planning requires anticipating market trends, identifying growth opportunities, and developing actionable plans to capitalize on them (Ansoff, 1957). Additionally, fostering a culture of innovation is critical. Managers should be competent in encouraging and managing innovation, ensuring that the company remains at the forefront of industry developments and can continuously improve its products and processes (Radjou & Prabhu, 2015).

Leadership Skills in Employee Development and Engagement
ERMAK's leadership development must emphasize skills in employee development and engagement. Given the company's focus on creating a supportive and inclusive work environment, leaders must be adept at fostering a culture of continuous improvement and professional growth. Skills in coaching, mentoring, and providing constructive feedback are essential to help employees achieve their full potential. Valijon's emphasis on employee well-being, such as providing meals and ensuring a psychologically safe workplace, highlights the need for empathetic and supportive leadership (Freeman, 1984). Leaders must build strong teams, enhance employee satisfaction, and reduce turnover through effective people management practices.

Financial Acumen and Operational Efficiency
As ERMAK continues to scale its operations, financial acumen, and operational efficiency become increasingly important. Leaders must be proficient in financial management, including budgeting, economic analysis, and cost control.

Understanding the economic implications of strategic decisions and ensuring the company's financial health are critical for sustaining growth. Additionally, skills in operational management, such as optimizing supply chain processes and implementing lean manufacturing principles, are essential for maintaining cost-effectiveness and high product quality (Juran, 1992).

Adaptability and Risk Management
The dynamic nature of the food industry and the global market necessitates adaptability and strong risk management skills. ERMAK's leaders must be able to respond swiftly to changes in the market environment, such as new regulatory requirements or shifts in consumer preferences. This requires a proactive approach to risk identification, assessment, and mitigation. Effective risk management ensures the company can navigate uncertainties and maintain its competitive advantage (Hubbard, 2009). Leaders should also be skilled in change management, guiding the organization through transition periods and ensuring that employees are aligned with new strategic directions.

4.1.6 Financing and Regulatory Environment Development Needs

For ERMAK to sustain its growth and expand, addressing the development needs related to financing and the regulatory environment is crucial. The company must navigate these areas effectively to secure the necessary resources and maintain compliance with evolving regulations.

Financing Development Needs
As ERMAK continues to scale its operations and diversify its product line, securing adequate financing becomes increasingly essential. The company needs capital to invest in new technologies, expand production capacity, and enter new markets. Initially, ERMAK managed to grow with limited resources, such as the $300 investment in equipment and purchasing a production facility for 30,000 Uzbek som coupons. However, future growth will require more substantial and sustained financial support.

One of the primary development needs is accessing diverse sources of financing, including bank loans, venture capital, and government grants. ERMAK could benefit from building relationships with financial institutions that understand the unique challenges and opportunities in the food industry. Additionally, exploring partnerships with international investors can provide not only capital but also valuable insights and connections to global markets. Developing a robust financial strategy with a mix of debt and equity financing will be critical for supporting ERMAK's expansion plans.

Moreover, ERMAK needs to enhance its financial management capabilities to allocate resources and manage risks associated with financial investments efficiently. This includes developing expertise in financial planning, budgeting, and analysis to ensure the company can sustain its growth trajectory while maintaining financial health. Implementing advanced financial management systems can help track performance and make informed decisions.

Regulatory Environment Development Needs
Navigating the regulatory environment is another critical aspect of ERMAK's development needs. The regulatory landscape in Uzbekistan has been evolving, with the government introducing reforms to improve the business climate and attract foreign investment. While these reforms have created a more favourable environment for businesses, ERMAK must remain vigilant in ensuring compliance with local and international regulations.

ERMAK's expansion into international markets, such as the USA, Germany, and Japan, requires strict adherence to diverse regulatory standards. This includes obtaining necessary certifications for food safety, organic production, and environmental sustainability. The company has already committed to these standards by securing certifications from laboratories in Latvia, Turkey, and Germany. However, maintaining and updating these certifications will require ongoing attention and resources.

The company must also stay abreast of changes in local regulations that may impact its operations. This includes food safety, labour, environmental protection, and trade laws. Engaging with regulatory bodies and participating in industry associations can provide ERMAK with valuable insights and a voice in shaping regulations that affect the food industry. Building a dedicated regulatory compliance team within the company can ensure that ERMAK remains proactive in managing regulatory risks and can respond quickly to any changes.

Furthermore, ERMAK could benefit from leveraging government programmes and incentives to support business growth and innovation. This includes grants, tax incentives, and other forms of support for companies that prioritize quality, sustainability, and social responsibility. By aligning its strategic goals with these programmes, ERMAK can enhance its competitive advantage and secure additional resources for development.

4.1.7 Pandemic's Impact on "Hidden Champions" Business Approach

The pandemic reached every corner of the world, it was a painful ordeal for people and families, and required people to stay isolated with limited ability to be entertained. For ERMAK, such an environment was quite favourable for focus on consumers' needs and wants, primarily pointed to the easily accessible, healthy and enjoyable products that can bring people some relief. Entrepreneurial agility during crises illustrates the importance of adaptive leadership and opportunity recognition (Hisrich et al., 2017). The company's name in Uzbek, which translates as "pleasant pastime" was a reminder of temporary relief during the lockdowns. Sunflower seed is a snack that has vitamins E and B-complex; it grows well with families who need snacks, most of which are healthy, therefore, buying snacks like the sunflower seeds from ERMAK.

To meet this unprecedented demand, ERMAK experienced a growth in production rates in 2019, from 8 tons to over 10 tons a day by mid-year 2020. At the same time, it provided its consumers with what can now be regarded as a trend of choosing products preserved from chemical goods. This trend suited perfectly the environmental corporate image of ERMAK, which led to reconsideration of the firm's packaging, design, and products. By the end of 2021, ERMAK had pioneered biodegradable packaging and redesigned its visual identity to attract the consumer's concern with their health.

The pandemic also impeded ERMAK's diversification into related product types. It entered the natural fruit juices and dessert pastes market in 2021, with natural products having health benefits highlighted. In response to this growth and to maintain quality, ERMAK acquired new technologies, including Automated vacuum packing machines, and recruited more than 50 employees. The company also used digital solutions in its accounting and data processing within its profitable operations. In addition, ERMAK finally selected and cultivated young and outstanding employees in IT and then sent them to specialized training to apply new technologies in the production process.

Therefore, it is quite evident that COVID-19 posed a threat to companies all over the globe, but it was beneficial to ERMAK due to its versatility and focus on the customer. The campaign meant that while helping families get through these challenging periods through enjoyable and nutritious snacks, it also helped build ERMAK's competitive advantage as a natural and healthy snack market leader.

4.1.8 Effects of the Ukraine War on "Hidden Champions" Business Operations

The emergence of the Ukraine war in 2022 affected supply chains and caused problems for businesses. Although ERMAK was not directly involved with Ukraine or Russia, this conflict also bombarded the international trade sphere. Exports from Ukraine declined significantly, and the sanctions imposed on Russia limited supply even more. For ERMAK, these disruptions entailed several risks that were optimistically balanced with potential benefits.

On the opportunity side, the void seen in the international snack niche contributed to a spike in ERMAK's demand for the products in novel regions, such as the European Union, Korea, Japan, and the Persian Gulf. Thus, by the end of 2022, the overall export volume in ERMAK has risen by 40%, and ERMAK's key markets are asking for additional volumes of sunflower seeds and kurt. This growth required immediate changes to product form and cover to cater to all customer tastes, especially the European market, which prefers simple and recycled materials.

In response to this growing demand, ERMAK began making preparations to increase manufacturing capability. Since the beginning of the new year 2023, the company has started purchasing new plants in other zones of Uzbekistan, in Fergana valley regions and Angren economic zone. These are expected to come on stream by 2024, and export production will be the main thrust area. With this expansion,

ERMAK should be able to double production and output more than 20 tonnes per day by 2025.

But the war also introduced some major problems, especially in sourcing raw materials and swelling logistics expenses. With the foregoing in mind, ERMAK worked at enhancing supplier relations and considering options of sourcing materials from outside the locality. The company also saw the need to invest in technologies that would help deal with increasing transport costs.

4.1.9 ERMAK'S Journey: Leveraging Quality and Innovation for Market Leadership

ERMAK was established in 1992 by Valijon Kuchkarovich, who was 41 years old. Before founding ERMAK, he had spent two decades working in the construction industry, specifically in the Mechanization Department, where he managed the preparation of construction sites throughout Tashkent. His extensive experience included overseeing the excavation of approximately 500 pits, and he advanced from a foreman to the position of chief engineer.

With the dissolution of the Soviet Union and the emergence of an independent Uzbekistan in 1991, there was a pressing need to create a new economy and infrastructure. This period was marked by significant shortages of various products, including food. The government allowed private property and private enterprises, prompting individuals like Kuchkarovich to take the initiative. In 1992, he and his partners established a small enterprise named "Zafar", later renamed "Zafarkhon".

ERMAK's initial years were focused on drying fruits and vegetables such as grapes, melons, and onions. However, it soon became apparent that the volumes produced by their dryer were insufficient for a sustainable business. In 1993–1994, FoodMash introduced food equipment to Uzbekistan, including a small coffee roasting machine costing $5000. Encouraged by the potential profitability of the snack business, ERMAK purchased the machine and entered the sunflower seed market.

At that time, sunflower seeds were not popular and were often considered an uncultured snack, sold in paper bags with the shells discarded carelessly. ERMAK aimed to change this perception by offering healthy, enjoyable, and hygienically packaged sunflower seeds. This innovation led to the successful introduction of a new product category in the republic. Initially, the company produced one or two bags of seeds, using a drying chamber with only one cubic metre capacity. Today, ERMAK produces over 10 tons of products daily, using equipment 500 times more capable than the original.

ERMAK sourced its first sunflower seeds from Kazakhstan and later incorporated local Uzbek and Chinese seeds into its production. The company also ventured into producing Kurt, a traditional and nutritious product typically sold without proper packaging. ERMAK was the first to package Kurt and later introduced Kurtoba, a liquid version of Kurt. Recently, they started producing Shinny, a juice concentrate known worldwide, and are preparing to launch energy bars.

The company's approach to product development emphasizes natural, healthy ingredients without the use of sugar or additives, which has become increasingly appealing to health-conscious consumers, especially following the COVID-19 pandemic. ERMAK's commitment to quality and natural products has helped them establish a strong domestic and international market presence. The company exports to several countries, including the USA, Russia, Kazakhstan, Israel, and is expanding to the Gulf countries with products certified by international safety standards, including Halal certification.

Valijon Kuchkarovich attributes ERMAK's success to its focus on natural, high-quality products and a deep understanding of market needs. Despite initial challenges and competition from traditional sellers, ERMAK has maintained a commitment to innovation and quality, which has allowed it to grow significantly. The company now employs about 400 people and continues to pursue new opportunities for expansion and product development, with a vision of growing to employ thousands in the future.

5 Conclusions and Recommendations

The scope of Hidden Champions, such as company ERMAK, is to reach a world market leadership through extended innovative capabilities, strategic diversification, and a strongly emphasized local orientation to quality and sustainability. These companies firmly rely on strengths, customer loyalty, and market adaptability. But, they must keep sustaining this kind of success; they need an enabling environment from the government, financial institutions, and business schools.

Recommendations

1. Recommendations for Government.
   - Create a Level Playing Field: Governments need to establish policies that will allow big and small firms to operate effectively. This comprises reducing the environmental factors and administrative red tape, bringing down the cost of doing business, and encouraging economic forecasting for the future. For instance, WTO membership, particularly the recent accession of Uzbekistan, can greatly decrease bureaucratic encumbrances and the cost of transactions and consequently offer new markets for Hidden Champions in international markets.
   - Support Economic Growth: Encourage "vertical integration" through which companies seek to increase the volume of the product produced to take advantage of the cost benefits associated with scale. These are tax credits for research and development, and funds for funding companies that are interested in long-term business as opposed to situational business.
   - Develop a Robust Financial Sector: A strong, independent financial sector is essential for developing the private sector. Governments should apply pressure for competition in banks to reduce interest rates while increasing lending.

This is a necessity for a firm like ERMAK that relies on cheap funds to increase operations and fuel innovation.
- Legislation for Emerging Trends: Encourage the proper legislation and the enhancement of the forms of financing, such as Islamic financing. This will give companies opportunities to diversify, and offer better financing options for those who have been excluded from the traditional forms of funding.

2. Recommendations for Financial Institutions.

   - Active Participation in Private Sector Development: International development banks and local portfolios of the financial sector should work together to design and offer financial solutions for development programmes. Such programmes may include capacity-building programmes with lending activities so that companies can develop the capability and other necessities for steady growth.
   - Focus on Sector-Specific Needs: To begin with, institutions can offer specific financing based on Hidden Champions' peculiarities. For example, ERMAK's diversification into organic and sustainable products can add value to green financing programmes.
   - Promote Competitive Interest Rates: Increased competition from within the banking industry, therefore, sees institutions offering more reasonable interest rates on the funds they provide to Hidden Champions, which in turn can be reinvested in expansion and growth.
   - Leverage Islamic Finance: As the demand for Islamic financial products increases, it is the responsibility of the bank to provide and market the Islamic-compliant financing products. This will attract more people to Nigeria as more business people feel the need to deal with developing countries, especially those with a larger Muslim population.

3. Recommendations for Business Schools and Higher Education Institutions.

   - Develop Relevant Case Studies: Business schools can contribute to developing case studies around Hidden Champions like ERMAK. Such acknowledgment should involve prescriptive, workable information that can help firms cope with threats and capitalize on opportunities.
   - Engage Hidden Champions in Academic Activities: Companies must participate in career fairs, management development courses, and research projects of institutions. For instance, to become competitive and develop efficient strategies, it is possible to invite ERMAK to join research and development projects.
   - Promote Awareness Among Youth: Business schools, for instance, can arrange to visit Hidden Champions and present success stories about them in a bid to popularize them among young people. They need to show that the future can and will be better to encourage up-and-coming businesspeople and create a stable base of talent for their businesses.
   - Executive Training Programmes: It is important that management trainers offer programmes that deal with strategic management, leadership training,

and management across borders. This will help Hidden Champions create better management teams that can competently manage the environment within the market.

In conclusion, therefore it can be asserted that the continued growth and success of Hidden Champions depend on productive cooperation with governments, required financial institutions, and educational organizations. Through providing such a readiness environment, offering specific financial incentives, as well as participating in collaboration with academic institutions, these stakeholders can guarantee further development and the existence of firms such as ERMAK, and thus contribute to economic development domestically, as well as internationally.

References

Allen, D. G., Shore, L. M., & Griffeth, R. W. (2003). The role of perceived organizational support and supportive human resource practices in the turnover process. *Journal of Management, 29*(1), 99–118.

Ansoff, H. I. (1957). Strategies for diversification. *Harvard Business Review, 35*(5), 113–124.

Åslund, A. (2007). *How capitalism was built: The transformation of central and Eastern Europe, Russia, and Central Asia*. Cambridge University Press.

Barney, J. (1991). Firm resources and sustained competitive advantage. *Journal of Management, 17*(1), 99–120.

Becker, G. S. (1964). *Human capital: A theoretical and empirical analysis, with special reference to education*. University of Chicago Press.

Brodie, R. J., Hollebeek, L. D., Juric, B., & Ilic, A. (2011). Customer engagement: Conceptual domain, fundamental propositions, and implications for research. *Journal of Service Research, 14*(3), 252–271.

Cavusgil, S. T., & Knight, G. (2015). The born global firm: An entrepreneurial and capabilities perspective on early and rapid internationalization. *Journal of International Business Studies, 46*(1), 3–16.

Drucker, P. F. (1954). *The practice of management*. Harper & Row.

Freeman, R. E. (1984). Strategic management: A stakeholder approach..

Gummesson, E. (2002). *Total relationship marketing: Marketing management, relationship strategy, and CRM approaches for the network economy*. Butterworth-Heinemann.

Hackman, J. R., & Oldham, G. R. (1976). Motivation through the design of work: Test of a theory. *Organizational Behavior and Human Performance, 16*(2), 250–279.

Henson, S., & Reardon, T. (2005). Private agri-food standards: Implications for food policy and the agri-food system. *Food Policy, 30*(3), 241–253.

Hisrich, R. D., Peters, M. P., & Shepherd, D. A. (2017). *Entrepreneurship*. McGraw-Hill Education.

Homburg, C., Jozić, D., & Kuehnl, C. (2017). Customer experience management: Toward implementing an evolving marketing concept. *Journal of the Academy of Marketing Science, 45*(3), 377–401.

Hubbard, D. W. (2009). *The failure of risk management: Why it's broken and how to fix it*. Wiley.

Juran, J. M. (1992). *Juran on quality by design: The new steps for planning quality into goods and services*. Free Press.

Kornai, J. (1992). *The socialist system: The political economy of communism*. Princeton University Press.

Kotler, P., & Keller, K. L. (2016). *Marketing management* (15th ed.). Pearson Education.

Kramer, A. (2017). Food safety and quality management in developing countries. *European Journal of Nutrition & Food Safety, 7*(3), 151–168.
Pomfret, R. (2000). The Uzbek model of economic development, 1991–1999. *The Economics of Transition, 8*(3), 733–748.
Porter, M. E. (1985). *Competitive advantage: Creating and sustaining superior performance*. Free Press.
Porter, M. E., & Kramer, M. R. (2006). Strategy and society: The link between competitive advantage and corporate social responsibility. *Harvard Business Review, 84*(12), 78–92.
Radjou, N., & Prabhu, J. (2015). *Frugal innovation: How to do more with less*. The Economist.
Ries, A., & Trout, J. (2001). *Positioning: The battle for your mind*. McGraw-Hill.
Saxenian, A. (2006). *The new argonauts: Regional advantage in a global economy*. Harvard University Press.
Shane, S., & Venkataraman, S. (2000). The promise of entrepreneurship as a field of research. *Academy of Management Review, 25*(1), 217–226.
Smith, A. (1996). *Transition economies: An IMF perspective on progress and prospects*. International Monetary Fund.
The World Bank. 2024. World Bank open data. Accessed June 1, 2024, from https://data.worldbank.org/country/uzbekistan
Williamson, O. E. (1975). *Markets and hierarchies: Analysis and antitrust implications*. Free Press.
World Bank. (2019). *Uzbekistan economic update: Growth amid uncertainty*. World Bank Group.

Hikmat Abdurahmanov is the co-founder and CEO of TEAM University and Chairman of the Association of International Business and Technologies (AMBiT) in Uzbekistan. He also serves as Chair of the Public Council of Tashkent City and co-founded HUMO Partners, a diversified group operating in international trade, finance, logistics, business education, and advisory services. With over 100 employees, the group connects Uzbek SMEs to global markets across China, Turkey, the EU, the USA, and Southeast Asia. A serial entrepreneur and civic leader, Hikmat is the driving force behind initiatives such as Business Lab, a media project that promotes entrepreneurship, and a network of co-working spaces in Tashkent serving as startup hubs. He leads the organization of Uzbekistan's annual Global Entrepreneurship Week campaign, engaging public and private stakeholders. Hikmat actively shapes public policy, contributes to the Tashkent 2025 strategic vision, advocates for civil society and a business-friendly environment, and serves as an independent director on several corporate boards. Educated in Uzbekistan and the UK, Hikmat holds a BA and MA in International Economic Relations from the University of World Economy and Diplomacy, and an MA in International Business from the University of St. Andrews. He is an alumnus of executive programs at Skolkovo and fellowships, including the Rumsfeld Fellowship, Mashav, IVLP, and British Foreign Office Leadership Program. Hikmat is a seasoned speaker and mentor committed to fostering entrepreneurship and innovation in Central Asia.

Akmal Khudaykulov is an innovative and results-driven professional with over a decade of experience in the fields of marketing management, organizational behavior, economics, and entrepreneurship. With his extended international education and business management exposure, Akmal is the perfect person to translate theoretical insights into applied strategies. Currently an Assistant Professor of Marketing at TEAM University, Akmal formerly served as a Visiting Scholar at the University of Michigan, Trinity College Dublin and University of Leicester where he worked on research related to social commerce, psychological well-being, and managerial effectiveness. In addition to his appointments at ISMA University of Applied Sciences and Central Asian University, and he holds a PhD in Management Science from Wuhan University of Science and Technology, he has served as Head of Research and Innovation and Academic Manager for several significant projects, showcasing skills in project management and leadership areas. Akmal integrates case learning, digital tools, and data-driven insights into his teaching while mentoring both graduate and undergraduate students. Akmal is widely published with over 20 research publications focusing on economic uncertainty, the impact of social media, and organizational readiness.

Zukhra Abdurakhmanova is the Managing Partner for Central Asia at AVDO Consulting, UK, and has been the Head of AVDO's Uzbekistan office since 2019. With over two decades of experience in strategic and operational consulting, she specializes in transformation strategy based on the Adizes methodology. Zukhra has a strong background in business development, startup ecosystem building, and international project management. She serves as Deputy Director of the Public Council under the Tashkent City Municipality and is the Program Designer and Project Leader of the Business Accelerator at GroundZero. She has held leadership roles such as Executive Director of the Association of International Business and Technology (AMBiT) and has co-organized numerous international initiatives with the embassies of the United States, India, the UK, China, and Israel. Zukhra is also a key partner of Global Entrepreneurship Week in Uzbekistan. Her expertise includes innovation and startup policy, mentoring, and judging tech competitions. She is a member of the Scientific and Technical Council on Startup Initiatives under the Ministry of Innovation of Uzbekistan. She has collaborated on projects like Startup Haifa, CIS GEN Startup, StudentHack, Falling Walls, UNICORNS SCO, and USAID-supported women's competitions. She also contributes as a speaker and expert for UNDP, IT Park, and Techstars programs. Zukhra began her career in 2001 as a coordinator of U.S.-funded higher education projects and has co-founded agencies in sociological research and IT recruitment. Her core strengths lie in strategy development, innovation consulting, and launching international projects with high social and economic impact.

Hidden Champions of Zambia

Bryson Mumba and Macmillan Handema

Abstract This study sought to profile the characteristics of hidden champions in emerging economies using SARO Agro Industrial Ltd. as a case in point in Zambia. The company was selected by the attributes of hidden champions defined by Simon (1996). The exploratory design and abduction logic was adopted to understand the study from the perspective of the company's Managing Director. A semi-structured interview was used to collect the data, and discourse analysis was used to analyze the data. The study established that the key success factors of hidden champions in emerging economies were not significantly different from other economies, as shown in the literature. The study found that the success of hidden champions was influenced by closeness to customers, dynamic ability to cope with the changes in the business environmental conditions, product quality, investment in highly skilled manpower and modern technology, and ability to control the growth of the business to continue influencing business activities. The study also established that hidden champions suffered from the lack of readily available manpower with perfectly required skills and knowledge, and non-supportive regulation in some cases. The study recommends that training institutions should collaborate with the industry to synchronize the knowledge and skills required by the industry and the training of academic institutions. It is also recommended that the government and its regulatory agencies engage the SMEs from time to time to understand the main regulatory challenges inhibiting growth to hidden champions and beyond.

Overview
Official name: The Republic of Zambia
Type of government: Democracy
Population in 2022: 20,017,675
Land area: 752,614 km^2

B. Mumba (✉) · M. Handema
School of Business, Economics and Management, University of Lusaka, Lusaka, Zambia

D. Berberović, D. Purg (eds.), *Hidden Champions in Rising Economies*, Contributions to Management Science,
https://doi.org/10.1007/978-3-032-08263-3_40

History

1964	Zambia gains independence from Britain on 24 October.
1968	First postindependence general elections held.
1972	One-party state declared as UNIP becomes the sole legal political party.
1973	New constitution adopted to legalize one-party rule and strengthen presidential powers.
1980	Economic decline begins due to falling copper prices, leading to debt, inflation, and civil unrest.
1990	Attempted coup and mass riots force President Kaunda to begin democratic reforms.
1991	Multiparty democracy restored; MMD takes over power from UNIP.
1993	Corruption scandals surface during MMD rule, sparking early public criticism.
2001	Levy Mwanawasa elected as president and launches anti-corruption campaign.
2006	Mwanawasa re-elected amid praise for stabilizing economy and fighting corruption.
2008	President Mwanawasa dies in office; Vice President Rupiah Banda wins the subsequent election.
2011	Michael Sata (PF) wins presidency, ending MMD's 20-year rule with promises of pro-poor policies.
2014	President Sata dies in office; Guy Scott becomes interim President, the first white head of state in Africa in modern times.
2015	Edgar Lungu wins special election to complete Sata's term.
2016	Lungu re-elected amid rising political tension and accusations of authoritarianism.
2017–2020	Zambia faces a worsening economic crisis with growing debt, inflation, and public dissatisfaction.
2021	Hakainde Hichilema (UPND) defeats Lungu in peaceful democratic elections.
2022	Zambia enters debt restructuring talks with the IMF and global creditors.
2023	Government implements economic recovery and reform strategies, focusing on mining, agriculture, and education.
2024	Reforms continue as Zambia strengthens governance, democracy, and fiscal discipline.
2025	Zambia prepares for general elections with political realignments and economic recovery as top issues.

1 Introduction: Context and History

Zambia is considered a stable country with successful democratic elections held every 5 years. After many years of a one-party state, Zambia became a multiparty state in 1991. Zambia's democracy is evident in the nine presidential elections and four different political parties that have so far ruled the country. Among them are the United National Independence Party (UNIP 1964–1991), Movement for Multiparty Democracy (MMD 1996–2011), Patriotic Front (PF2011–2021), and currently the United Party for National Development (UPND).

Various institutions and statutes exist to support and regulate business activities. It is expected that all business activities will be done within the confines of the labor, consumer protection, environmental protection, marketing, and finance laws.

Zambia gained independence from British colonial rule on 24 October 1964 and held its first postindependence general elections in 1968. In 1972, the country was declared a one-party state under the United National Independence Party (UNIP), and a new constitution in 1973 further entrenched presidential powers. This political centralization coincided with increasing economic challenges in the 1980s, largely driven by falling copper prices, rising debt, inflation, and growing social unrest.

By 1990, mounting dissatisfaction led to mass riots and an attempted coup, forcing President Kenneth Kaunda to initiate democratic reforms. Multiparty democracy was restored in 1991, and the Movement for Multi-Party Democracy (MMD) took power. However, the MMD era was soon marred by corruption scandals, particularly from 1993 onward, prompting calls for greater accountability. In 2001, Levy Mwanawasa became president and launched a notable anti-corruption campaign, winning re-election in 2006 with widespread support for his reformist stance. His death in 2008 brought Rupiah Banda to power, who was later defeated by Michael Sata of the Patriotic Front (PF) in 2011.

Sata's presidency emphasized pro-poor policies, but his death in 2014 led to a transitional period with Guy Scott serving briefly as interim president, making him the first white head of state in modern Africa. Edgar Lungu won the 2015 special election and was re-elected in 2016 amid rising concerns about authoritarianism and political repression. From 2017 to 2020, Zambia faced a severe economic downturn, characterized by ballooning debt, inflation, and widespread public dissatisfaction.

In 2021, opposition leader Hakainde Hichilema of the United Party for National Development (UPND) won a landmark election, signaling a return to democratic consolidation. The new government entered into debt restructuring talks with international creditors and the IMF in 2022. By 2023, economic recovery strategies were underway, focusing on key sectors such as mining, agriculture, and education. Reforms aimed at improving governance, fiscal discipline, and institutional capacity continued through 2024. As Zambia heads toward general elections in 2025, political realignments and economic recovery remain the central issues shaping the national agenda.

The economic environment has been volatile for some time. Despite protracted debt restructuring, Zambia's economy is recovering from the multiple and compounding crises. Real GDP grew at an average rate of 5.7% in 2021–23, primarily driven by growth in transport, information and communications, finance and insurance, and a rebound in hospitality and education. However, the current account narrowed and slipped into deficit in 2023 due to a contraction in copper production and exports for three consecutive years, significantly reducing foreign currency earnings. Combined with the uncertainties around the debt restructuring process, the exchange rate was put under pressure, leading to a 41.8% depreciation in 2023. The depreciation also fuelled inflation to rise way above the Bank of Zambia's 6–8% target range, despite monetary restraint and fiscal prudence. The cholera epidemic and severe drought in 2024 have adversely impacted agriculture and food production, electricity availability, and water supply will dampen growth even further. An expected upturn in mining driven by foreign direct investment inflows in green energy transition minerals, if realized, may offset some of the losses.

Zambia ranks among the countries with the highest levels of poverty and inequality globally. Poverty reached 60% of the population in 2022, up from 54.4% in 2015, worsened by limited job creation and declining labor earnings. The urban population recorded the highest reversal, with an 8.5% point increase in poverty incidence reaching 31.9% in 2022. The spike is undoubtedly linked to the COVID-19 pandemic and the ensuing debt crisis. However, the growth deceleration that preceded the crises was already manifesting in weakening labor market indicators such as formal employment and earnings. Meanwhile, rural poverty remained widespread and stagnant, surpassing 75% since 2010. Rural/urban disparities in access to essential services remain stark, hindering human capital development and labor productivity.

With a population of 20,017,675 (2022), Zambia is one of the world's youngest countries by median age. The population has a rapid growth rate of 2.7% per year, reflecting the relatively high fertility rate. Much of Zambia's population is youthful and biased to urban areas. As the large youth population attains reproductive age, the population is anticipated to double in the next 25 years, resulting in additional pressure on the demand for jobs, health care, and other social services.

2 Characteristics of Hidden Champions from Zambia

Three hidden champions were identified in Zambia using the attributes of hidden champions defined by Simon (1996). The attributes considered included the level of global orientation, evidence of innovativeness, market focus, closeness to customers, and source of competitiveness in the market. These attributes are also supported by findings from other researchers (Fryges, 2006; Byungun, 2013). The firms considered included SARO Agro Industrial Ltd., Trade Kings Limited and Zambeef Products Plc. This report only details SARO Agro Industrial Ltd., as the other two firms did not respond to the interview requests to participate in the study. The study on SARO Agro Industrial Ltd. established that the key success factors of hidden champions in emerging economies were not significantly different from other economies, as shown in the literature (Irini et al., 2000; Fryges, 2006; Johann et al., 2021). The study found that the success of hidden champions was influenced by closeness to customers, dynamic ability to cope with the changes in the business environmental conditions, product quality, investment in highly skilled manpower and modern technology, and ability to control the growth of the business to continue influencing business activities. The study also established that hidden champions suffered from the lack of readily available manpower with perfectly required skills and knowledge, and non-supportive regulation in some cases. The study recommends that training institutions should collaborate with the industry to synchronize the knowledge and skills required by the industry and training of academic institutions. It is also recommended that the government and its regulatory agencies engage the SMEs from time to time to understand the main regulatory challenges inhibiting growth to hidden champions and beyond. Exhibit 1 presents the core economic indicators of the operating environment for hidden champions in Zambia.

Exhibit 1 Core economic indicators for Zambia

	2018	2019	2020	2021	2022	2023
GDP per capita (current US$)	1475	1268	957	1135	1457	1330.73
GDP per capita growth (annual %)	–1.37%	–14.04%	–24.55%	18.59%	28.39%	2.46
Long-term unemployment (% of total unemployment)	5.03%	5.54%	6.03%	5.20%	4.37%	5.91
Foreign direct investment, net inflows (% of GDP)	1.55%	2.35%	1.35%	1.78%	–0.22%	0.31
GDP (current US$, mio)	26,310	23,310	18,110	22,100	29,160	27577.96
Exports of goods and services (current US$, mio)	0 9987	0 8073	0 8473	0 11,537	0 11,722	11264.53
Exports of goods and services (% of GDP)	37.96	34.64	46.79	52.22	40.19	40.85
Merchandise exports (current US$, mio)	9034	7039	7924	10,101	11,651	10,431
Merchandise exports to high-income economies (% of total merchandise exports)	59.85	55.62	59.55	73.89	75.69	50.96
Merchandise exports to developing economies in Europe and Central Asia (% of total merchandise exports)	0.009	0.010	0.024	n/a	n/a	0.05
Ores and metals exports (% of merchandise exports)	77.43	74.58	78.80	79.50	74.51	71.36
Agricultural raw materials exports (% of merchandise exports)	0.94	1.33	0.86	0.70	0.41	0.58
Food exports (% of merchandise exports)	6.21	7.31	7.49	7.67	9.20	10.61
Fuel exports (% of merchandise exports)	1.02	1.37	1.74	1.46	2.72	4.1
Manufactures exports (% of merchandise exports)	13.29	14.29	10.17	9.99	12.64	12.85
High-technology exports (% of manufactured exports)	2.14	2.20	1.36	0.93	0.76	1.16

Source: World Bank, 2025

3 Case Studies of Selected Hidden Champions

3.1 SARO Agro Industrial Ltd

Overview
Address: Plot No.5284 Buyantashi Road Lusaka, off Lumumba Road, Heavy Industrial Area Lusaka ZM, 10101
Tel: (+260) (211) 241477/387001/9
Email: saro@saroagri.co.zm
Web: https://www.sarozambia.com

Company Information
Industry: Agro Machine Production
Year of Establishment: 1984
Average number of employees in 2023: 320
Brainer(s) behind the company: Mr Ashok Oza

3.1.1 Nature of Market Leadership

SARO Engineering demonstrates a grounded and organic form of market leadership, built over decades through steady expansion and reputation rather than through formal recognition or aggressive branding. Although industry data is limited, the MD estimates that "our market position is 30 to 40 percent" in key segments such as tractors, with dominance rising to 60% in some procurement cycles. Despite these strong figures, they maintain a cautious stance, stating, "We don't know. In Zambia, information is very limited…half of it is guesswork." Rather than chasing recognition, the company focuses on quality and customer satisfaction: "We must do what we do to be the best," he explained. This philosophy has earned SARO a reputation that customers acknowledge: "People will say they would pay a higher price to SARO rather than buying from other competitors, because they know ours is a quality product."

The analysis shows that SARO never worries so much about the leadership position in the marketplace but seeks to thrive on quality, as every other customer eventually is concerned about the quality of agricultural equipment. The following statements by the MD explained the importance of quality regardless of the market position: "…we would compete with everyone on quality, and that takes time to build up particularly because when you're dealing with emerging and small scale farming community, to whom prices is more important than the quality of the product, especially when they have not been using machinery in the past, it's only when they start using machinery that they realize the importance of the quality and reliability of the machine that you are using. To ensure quality market offerings, the company has invested in highly skilled manpower in its workshops."

3.1.2 Nature of Competitive Advantage

SARO's competitive edge stems from three interlinked elements: locally adapted products, technical know–how, and dependable after-sales service. Unlike competitors who import foreign machinery unsuited for Zambian conditions, the MD emphasized, "Whatever product we manufacture, we make it for local conditions." Even for imported products, SARO modifies and upgrades machinery before it reaches customers: "We know what the faults in that machine are, so we import it, but we make changes before we put it in the market." This technical adaptability is coupled with strong in-house expertise: "We've built up a very good manpower base…technical resources within SARO are unmatched in any other company of our type in Zambia." Perhaps most crucially, SARO has refused to compete solely on price. As he noted, "We tried to compete with the Chinese to a limited extent, but not on prices. We would compete with them on quality." To remain afloat, the company has also continued to invest in modern technology to increase productivity, efficiency and product quality. Apart from the local market, the company is also exporting its products within the southern African region.

3.1.3 Core Lessons Learned on the Path to Success

SARO's long-term success reveals critical insights about surviving and thriving in a challenging economic environment. One major lesson is the value of organic, reinvestment-driven growth. "Just reinvest your profits. To hell with returns on investment… just go ahead and reinvest," the interviewee asserted, pointing out that the company never declared dividends but chose to reinvest all earnings to build a resilient operation. This strategy allowed them to remain largely debt-free and survive volatile interest rates and economic downturns. Another key insight is a people-first approach to business development: "We were not driven entirely by the profit motive… as long as we were living comfortably, educating our children, paying our staff." This mindset extended to their customer relationships: "Small and medium-scale farmers are critical to our growth…they need product knowledge and support, not just equipment." Lastly, the company recognizes the need to evolve its governance: "We have now outgrown that family ownership level, but have not adapted to that change…and we need to adapt." This admission underscores SARO's awareness that long-term success demands both operational and structural transformation.

3.1.4 Management and Leadership Development Needs

To continue on the growth trajectory, the management is aware of the need to professionalize the operation by engaging external professionals to enhance decision-making and make them more objective. As SARO continues to expand beyond the founding family's direct oversight, the company faces a clear need to build a more structured, professional management system. While the technical and operational capacities of the company are strong, much of the management culture still reflects informal, founder-led decision-making. As the interviewee noted, "We have now outgrown that family ownership level, but have not adapted to that change." This signals a need for formalized systems in areas like succession planning, performance management, and strategic coordination. Middle management, in particular, requires investment in supervisory training and exposure to broader business practices beyond technical knowledge. The company would benefit from structured mentorship programs, internal promotion pathways, and managerial training tailored to the local context. This will bridge the gap between technical expertise and leadership capability. The MD is also concerned about business control and states, "The biggest thing is control. Once we've spread out, control must not go; that is critical, without that, the company is going to fail." This means that at the center of a successful firm is the need for effective control and corporate governance systems to provide the much-needed confidence to all the stakeholders of the business. The ability for managers to plan and prepare budgets is another important management capability for managing uncertainty.

The evolution of SARO from a founder-led enterprise to a professionally managed company also requires a deliberate focus on leadership development. The interviewee candidly acknowledged the challenge; "We are not grooming the next generation of leadership fast enough." While the current leadership has deep institutional knowledge and strong relationships with clients and suppliers, the next generation must be equipped to handle increasing complexity, competition, and cross-border opportunities. Leadership development at SARO must go beyond technical skill to include strategic thinking, change management, and stakeholder engagement. Embedding leadership pathways within the company, through structured rotations, external exposure, and leadership coaching will be essential to ensure continuity and adaptability. Importantly, this development must include not only family members but also high-potential staff from outside the founding circle, ensuring a more inclusive and resilient leadership bench for the future.

3.1.5 Financing and Regulatory Environment Development Needs

Although SARO has historically taken a conservative approach to financing, reinvesting profits and avoiding debt, this model is becoming increasingly limiting as the company seeks to scale and modernize. As the interviewee explained, "We never declared dividends… we just reinvested everything we earned." While this strategy has provided stability and resilience, it also constrains the company's ability to seize new opportunities that require larger capital outlays, such as regional expansion, technology upgrades, or supply chain integration. To support its next phase of growth, SARO needs to explore diversified financing instruments beyond internal cash flow, including development finance, blended capital, and partnerships with local or international institutions that understand long-term industrial investment. Additionally, building internal capacity in financial planning and investment readiness will be crucial to engage confidently with lenders or equity partners without compromising the company's values and control. The company has collaborated and partnered with its leasing partners to finance the acquisition of its assets on a lease basis. In addition to other financing alternatives available to the customers, such as CDF and the Citizens Economic Empowerment Commission (CEEC), the arrangement by SARO provides another alternative that small-scale farmers with limited financial resources can take advantage of.

The regulatory environment in Zambia presents both challenges and opportunities for companies like SARO that operate in agriculture and manufacturing. The interviewee noted several constraints related to policy inconsistency and limited government support for local manufacturing. For instance, the lack of reliable data on market sizes and imports makes it difficult to plan or advocate effectively: "We don't know. In Zambia, information is very limited… half of it is guesswork." Regulatory processes, such as standards certification, import licensing, and access to industrial land, are often slow or opaque, which discourages innovation and expansion. To create a more enabling environment for companies like SARO, there is a need for regulatory reform that supports local value addition, improves transparency, and facilitates easier access to infrastructure and incentives. SARO would also benefit from stronger industry associations or platforms that can engage with the government on policy dialogue, allowing private-sector voices to shape the development of a more supportive regulatory ecosystem. The analysis shows that the tax regulatory environment is not so friendly to support business growth and sustainability. A case in point is the value-added tax (VAT) refund system that does not allow companies to offset VAT refunds owed to them against the periodical tax obligations. It also takes very long for the tax authorities to meet their obligation without interest on the funds owed.

One of the cited challenges being faced by the company is the non-availability of ready-to-use skills in the labor market from Universities and Colleges. The MD recounted that "There's no ready-made skills available in Zambia, quite frankly, whatever skills they have acquired in the institutions are enhanced to our requirement here, on the job." This brings in the need for colleges and universities to be closer to industry and provide the needed skills according to industry needs and expectations. The company is also proposing that universities and Colleges may use memoranda of understanding (MoUs) with the industry to bridge the gap between the education sector and the industry requirements. The MD provided that: "…the apprenticeship system definitely needs to be reintroduced as soon as possible because that will be direct connection between the institutions and the manufacturer, along with the industry." The MD argued that a deliberate government policy to fund apprenticeship programs will empower the graduate beyond the classroom knowledge, and that will exist as the ready-to-use to use labor force at all times.

3.1.6 The Effect of Current Trends

When asked about the impact of current trends and issues around the globe, such as COVID-19 and the war in Ukraine, on the business activities of SARO, the MD gave the following explanation:

"That problem in Ukraine has affected the supply of grain, especially to Africa and that in itself just exposes our weaknesses but in the case of SARO it is an opportunity because the government will realize that …we don't need to depend on the outside environment so that's why even currently I think the government is doing as much as possible, …to promote agriculture. So for us it's an opportunity, we stand ready today to meet every challenge. Mechanization is the talk everywhere now …I think we have invested quite some money in mechanization. …There's also a program, it's a funded project by SHA (Self Help Africa). Self Help Africa is trying to promote mechanization, so we've partnered with them, they have given us a small grant to promote mechanization so we have an outreach team that goes out, meet farmers, do the demos, encourage them, brings them on board."

This means that the war in Ukraine brings more opportunities to SARO than adverse effects. The main problem of food insecurity in Africa is an opportunity for more business growth for SARO through the supply and provision of more agricultural equipment. With more mechanization, it is expected that economic productivity will increase. With regards to COVID-19, the MD stated that it had affected the supply chain of the business and inflated the cost of doing business as it was difficult to procure some of the equipment needed for business activities and directly affected the profit margins. The analysis shows that the company managed the electricity energy crisis by adjusting the working schedule to be in line with the rationing of electricity. The company also saw it as an opportunity to supply electricity energy alternatives to hydropower, such as solar pumps.

The analysis shows that the company has development needs in corporate governance and effective systems for accountability and reporting in light of company's expansion into various parts of the country and beyond. Other required areas of development needs include finance to support business expansion and employees' capacity building in planning and budgeting. The MD stated that SARO has operated and developed as a family-owned business that needs to develop appropriate systems to support business expansion. He also emphasized the need for a system that will enable senior management to retain control of business activities in the light of expanded business activities. He stated that the company needs assistance in developing corporate governance systems for the business to remain afloat. The MD stated, "…we are a family owned company that has grown from that point of view, and has now outgrown that family ownership level, but has not adapted to that change, and we need to adapt. So we need to further professionalize both our board of directors and other operations…" In relation to the challenges coming with company growth.

3.1.7 From Workshop to Market Leader: The Enduring Development of SARO in Zambia's Agricultural Sector

SARO's transformation from a small workshop into a leading player in Zambia's agricultural sector exemplifies a story of resilience, strategic vision, and adaptive innovation. Initially established to provide basic engineering services, the company gradually evolved by responding directly to the specific needs of Zambian farmers. This locally grounded approach allowed SARO to differentiate itself through products that are both relevant and reliable. The company's growth has been underpinned by a consistent commitment to quality and technical excellence. Unlike many competitors who import low-cost machinery, SARO has focused on robust, locally adapted solutions that offer long-term value. Customers appreciate the durability of SARO equipment and the technical support provided, which has contributed significantly to brand loyalty and sustained demand.

A key element of SARO's development has been its conservative and disciplined approach to financing. The company has avoided external debt, opting instead to reinvest profits into its operations to support gradual and sustainable expansion. While this strategy has provided financial stability, it also limits the company's ability to rapidly scale up and modernize in response to emerging opportunities and technological changes. Management and leadership development has become increasingly important as SARO transitions into a more complex organization. Historically reliant on founder-led decision-making, the company now recognizes the need for formalized governance structures and succession planning. Developing a strong cadre of middle managers and future leaders is essential to ensure continuity, operational efficiency, and strategic growth.

The regulatory environment in Zambia presents both challenges and opportunities for industrial firms like SARO. Inconsistent policies, limited access to affordable financing, and delays in public procurement processes hinder innovation and long term planning. Addressing these regulatory constraints would not only benefit SARO but also enhance the broader industrial ecosystem necessary for sustainable agricultural development. Despite these challenges, SARO's journey reflects a strong foundation built on integrity, local relevance, and long-term thinking. The company's ability to withstand economic fluctuations, retain customer trust, and steadily expand its operations speaks to the strength of its model. As it looks to the future, SARO offers a compelling example of how local firms can lead industrial transformation in emerging markets through strategic investment, institutional growth, and customer-centered innovation.

4 Conclusions and Recommendations

With regard to the success factors of SARO, the factors explaining sustainability are similar to the findings of other studies. The in-depth interviews revealed that SARO has survived through a number of attributes that include dynamic ability to fit into the dictates of the business environment, having a clearly defined market, closeness to the customers and ensuring product quality, investment in the skilled labor force and management control of business activities.

Closeness to the customers enabled the company to identify what the customers needed and wanted. This understanding facilitated the growth of the company and the definition of the valued product range. The importance of closeness to the customer was also echoed in previous studies as being important in the growth and survival of HCs (Melita & Simona, 2017; Eva et al., 2017; Rammer & Spielkamp, 2019). A product is only quality if it is able to meet or exceed the expectations of the customer. Closeness to the customer enables the firm to clearly understand what they need and want (Muñoz et al., 2017). This study established that product quality is everything that every other customer values, and the more a firm understands this, the more likely that the firm will succeed.

Understanding the business environmental conditions and being able to make appropriate adjustments is an important feature of firm survival. The natural environment, economic environment and the agricultural policies of the government highly influenced the performance of SARO. The company demonstrated dynamism to business environmental changes by identifying and managing threats and taking advantage of the opportunities coming with the same. This finding is consistent with the assertion by Lalić and Purg (2021) that dynamic capability to environmental changes is a critical feature of HCs. However, this study established that the response to the dictates of the external environment should be controlled for management to retain its influence on business activities.

This study established that investment in highly skilled manpower enables the provision of quality products and the success of the company. Audretsch et al. (2018) established that when the highly skilled workforce is coupled with modern technology, customers are locked in through product quality. Thus, the more a firm continues to innovate and invest in highly skilled workforce, the customer base is expected to be growing. A Study by Rammer and Spielkamp (2019) also concluded that investment in superior technology leads to superior performance and competitive advantage. This is also consistent with the postulation of the resource-based theory that the performance of the business depends on the resources and competencies that a business has (Johnson et al., 2008; Purg et al., 2016).

To ensure a sustainable and growing SMEs sector in Zambia that graduates into HCs, the following recommendations have been made:

1. Universities and colleges should collaborate with the industry through MoUs and synchronize the knowledge and skills requirements of the industry and that which is taught by the education sector. This will ensure that a graduate is ready and available for work as they graduate from college or university without the need for further retraining.
2. The government and its agencies should be able to promote the growth of SMEs beyond just being SMEs, to HCs by having supportive policies and a regulatory environment. Engagement of SMEs from time to time will help the government to understand the challenges the SMEs are facing and develop policies that are

friendly and attend to challenges faced by this important sector to economic well-beings.
3. SMEs should engage Universities and other training institutions from time to time to have customized trainings and solutions related to business-specific identified gaps or challenges. This will ensure that businesses always remain competitive by appropriately positioning themselves in accordance with the dictates of the dynamic business environment.

References

Audretsch, D. B., Lehmann, E. E., & Schenkenhofer, J. (2018). Internationalization strategies of hidden champions: Lessons from Germany. *Multinational Business Review, 26*(1), 2–24.

Byungun, Y. (2013). How do hidden champions differ from normal small and medium enterprises (SMEs) in innovation activities. *Journal of Applied Sciences Research, 9*(13), 6257–6263.

Eva, P., Ripoll-i-Alcon, J., & Silvente, V. B. (2017). Hidden champions in Spain: The path to successful business decisions, Revista de Métodos. *Universidad Pablo de Olavide Sevilla, 24*, 190–208.

Fryges, H. (2006). Hidden champions-how young and small technology-oriented firms can attain high export-sales ratios. *ZEW-Centre for European Economic Research Discussion Paper, 06*(045), 1.

Irini, V., Spyros, L., Spyros, M., & Yiannis, S. (2000). Greek hidden champions: Lessons from small, little-known firms in Greece. *European Management Journal, 18*(6), 663–674.

Johann, M. S., Block, J. H., & Benz, L. (2021). Financial performance of hidden champions: Evidence from German manufacturing firms. *Small Business Economics, 59*, 1–20.

Johnson, G., Scholes, K., & Whittington, R. (2008). *Exploring corporate strategy* (8th ed.). Pearson Education Limited.

Lalić, B., & Purg, D. (2021). *Hidden champions in dynamically changing societies*. Springer International Publishing.

Melita, B. R., & Simona, K. C. (2017). Becoming a hidden champion: From selective use of customer intimacy and product leadership to business attractiveness. *South East European Journal of Economics and Business, 12*(1), 89–103.

Muñoz, E. P., Ripoll-i-Alcon, J., & Silvente, V. B. (2017). Hidden champions in Spain: The path to successful business decisions. *Revista de Métodos Cuantitativos para la Economía y la Empresa, 24*, 190–208.

Purg, D., Saginova, O., Skorobogatykh, I., & Musatova, Z. (2016). Family owned hidden champions in Russia: Innovations, human capital and internationalization. *Indian Journal of Science and Technology, 9*(12), 1–10.

Rammer, C., & Spielkamp, A. (2019). The distinct features of hidden champions in Germany: A dynamic capabilities view. *ZEW-Centre for European Economic Research Discussion Paper, 19*(012), 1.

Simon, H., 1996, *Hidden Champions: Lessons from 500 of the World's Best Unknown Companies*, Boston, Harvard Business School Press.

Bryson Mumba holds a PhD in Accounting and Finance from the University of Lusaka, Zambia, a Master of Business Administration Degree from Edinburgh Business School, Heriot Watt University Scotland, a Master's in Accountancy Degree from Dundee University, Scotland and a Bachelor of Science (Honours) Degree in Computer Science from Loughborough University of Science and Technology, England. He is a Chartered Accountant and a Fellow of the Association of Chartered Certified Accountants (ACCA) and a Fellow of the Zambia Institute of Chartered Accountants (ZICA). He is also a Fellow and accredited trainer of the Institute of Directors of Zambia.

He has been involved with accounting education in higher education institutions over many years holding lecturing positions at the University of Dundee, Scotland, Institute of Development Management (IDM) in Botswana and the University of Lusaka. He is currently Associate Professor in Accounting and Finance and the Deputy Vice Chancellor—Academic at the University of Lusaka having previously served as Executive Dean of the School of Business, Economics and Management. He possesses vast industrial experience in financial and management accounting, auditing, ICT, and corporate governance. He has served on various Boards of Directors as Board and Committee member including Bank of Zambia, Micro Finance Zambia Limited, Institute of Directors Zambia, Lusaka South Multi-Facility Economic Zone Limited, ZAMREN, and the Zambia Seed Company Limited. He served in several senior management positions including being Managing Director, Director Finance, Fund Manager, Manager Finance & Administration, and Financial Controller.

Macmillan Handema is an expert in Business and Financial Management. He holds a PhD in Business Management, a Master of Business Administration, and a Master of Arts in Economic Policy Management. He also holds a Postgraduate Diploma in Lecturing Methodology and a Bachelor's degree in Business Administration. His research interests include entrepreneurship and wealth creation, business sustainability strategies, investment and portfolio management, financial management, and financial economics. With over 15 years of experience in both the public and private sectors, Dr. Handema currently serves as a Lecturer, Researcher, and Head of Department in the School of Business at the University of Lusaka. He is a team player with strong analytical and communication skills, and is known for being self-motivated, innovative, results-oriented, and committed to professional excellence.